Facilitation of Therapeutic Recreation Services:

An Evidence-Based and Best Practice Approach to Techniques and Processes

Facilitation of Therapeutic Recreation Services:

An Evidence-Based and Best Practice Approach to Techniques and Processes

Edited by

Norma J. Stumbo and Brad Wardlaw

Library of Congress Catalogue Card Number: 2011937242
ISBN-10: 1-892132-94-X
ISBN-13: 978-1-892132-94-9

This book has been adventure almost ten years in the making. My strong belief in the power of evidence-based practice started with an interest in systematic program design, outcomes, and field-based research. Many colleagues across the globe have fanned the embers of this passion—so many that it would be impossible to acknowledge them all. I hope that each of you know that our many conversations and interactions as well as your own work have allowed me to learn more quickly and think more deeply. Thanks to each of you for working so hard to create a better future for therapeutic recreation professionals.

Thanks also to my personal cheering section of Randy, Barb, and Nancy. Love you all.

—*Norma Stumbo*

To my parents and Cortney, thank you for all your support through this process.

—*Brad Wardlaw*

Table of Contents

Chapter 9: Problem-Solving Therapy
Norma J. Stumbo 155

Chapter 10: Anger Management
Norma J. Stumbo 173

Chapter 11: Social Skills Training
Norma J. Stumbo and Brad Wardlaw 189

Chapter 12: Assertiveness Training
Deborah Hutchins.. 237

Chapter 21: Virtual Reality Technologies
Norma J. Stumbo and Shane Pegg

List of Tables and Insets

List of Figures

» CHAPTER 1 »

The Need for Evidence-Based Practice in Therapeutic Recreation Services

Norma J. Stumbo, Ph.D., CTRS

West, Kinney, and Witman (2008), in the second edition of the *Guidelines for Competency Assessment and Curriculum Planning for Recreation Therapy Practice*, delineated a comprehensive list of modalities and facilitation techniques that can be applied to therapeutic recreation practice. They listed modalities such as anger management, community reintegration, coping skills training, horticulture, journal/writing, meditation, reality orientation, values clarification, and the like. They also listed a number of facilitation techniques such as behavioral theory/therapy/modification, counseling theories, learned optimism/positive psychology, and resiliency/hardiness theories. In general, it is difficult to separate modalities from facilitation techniques. However, by definition, modalities are methods of therapy or treatment and often have "content" associated with them, such as the step-by-step method used in problem-solving therapy; facilitation techniques are the processes used to allow clients to reach their outcomes more efficiently and effectively. For example, knowing the underlying principles of cognitive behavioral therapy (a facilitation technique) is important to helping people make desired changes by focusing on their thoughts and behaviors.

West et al. (2008) made a very strong case for the wise selection and use of therapeutic modalities and techniques:

> Selection of modalities and techniques to be used in treatment should be based on the *evidence that exists specific to their utility to address specific needs to improve patient functioning*. Practitioners need to access available evidence that explains the effectiveness of particular interventions. (emphasis added) (p. 15)

Purpose of This Book

The intent of this book is to improve the systematic application of various techniques and modalities to the practice of therapeutic recreation. Improving and standardizing practice is fundamental to increasing our ability to select interventions based on their potential to impact client outcomes. When we fully realize the potential of specific interventions to help clients arrive at certain outcomes, then we can choose these interventions and techniques with greater skill and confidence.

"Systematic application," however, depends on a number of key factors to succeed. These include: (a) evidence-based and theory-based programming, (b) systematic program design, and (c) well-targeted client outcomes. First, every profession benefits from the application of evidence and theory to their practice. Evidence-based practice (i.e., the application of research evidence to intervention design) and theory-based practice (i.e., the application of relevant theory to intervention design) are both equally important to ensure that programs, interventions, or treatments are built on "best practices." Conversely, programs that are designed haphazardly or lackadaisically, say from tradition, therapist interest, or sheer inertia, are unlikely to help clients achieve their goals and fulfill their full potential. Second, program design and planning need to be done with care and through a systematic process using established procedures. Comprehensive program design, activity analysis, protocol development, and program evaluation are a few of the steps of systematic program design used by therapeutic recreation specialists. Third, targeting important and valued client outcomes is extremely important. Clients and their families need to be assured that professionals are providing the best possible care, in the most efficient and effective manner possible, to arrive at the most vital and significant outcomes.

The aim of this book is to vastly improve our frameworks for interventions by extracting and synthesizing the best possible evidence and theory, so that therapists can then apply systematic program design and build effective and meaningful programs aimed at specific and known outcomes. To do this, we started with the question: "What interventions and programs are therapeutic recreation specialists, regardless of specific settings or client groups or geographic regions, most likely to design, based on our scope of practice?" The answer to that question then became the topical outline for this book. We start out with eight introductory chapters:

1: Need for Evidence-Based Practice
2: Overview of Leisure Education
3: Selecting Programs and Activities Based on Goals and Outcomes
4: Planning and Leading Group Activities/Group Interventions
5: Communication Techniques
6: Instructional Techniques
7: Counseling Techniques
8: Behavior Change Strategies

These chapters are intended to provide the backdrop for selecting, planning, and implementing therapeutic recreation interventions using the most promising and noteworthy practices. Each chapter has considerable research and literature support to ensure readers and therapists that the ideas and guidelines provided therein are grounded in substantial theory, evidence, and, whenever possible, research data.

The remaining chapters address some of the most popular and specific interventions and techniques within therapeutic recreation practice. Topics and evidence were selected by the following criteria:

- Only interventions and practices common to and most often used in therapeutic recreation were included.
- The research and evidence provided was representative of the recent published literature in these areas. The cited studies generally reflect the whole of the available literature, however, only a percentage of all available literature is included.
- Only that research evidence applicable to the provision of therapeutic recreation services was included.
- The sole purpose of inclusion of any data or evidence was the improvement of therapeutic recreation practice and client outcomes.
- When and where possible, information directly applicable to certain client groups was provided.

These criteria resulted in the following 13 chapters on facilitation techniques or modalities.

9: Problem-Solving Therapy
10: Anger Management
11: Social Skills Training
12: Assertiveness Training
13: Physical Activity
14: Pain Management
15: Cognitive Behavioral Approaches
16: Intergenerational Programming
17: Stress Management
18: Sensory Stimulation and Sensory Integration
19: Reality Orientation, Validation, and Reminiscence
20: Community Integration
21: Virtual Reality

In each of these 13 chapters, authors were challenged —and rose to the task with diligence and fortitude!— to present the most recent, compelling, and applicable research concerning their topics. Each chapter contains introductory information, followed by research evidence to support the technique, and related studies in the therapeutic recreation literature. A sampling of resources and illustrative activities are included in most chapters as well.

The intent of this book is to provide students and practitioners with solid information that will improve their practice; that is, improve the likelihood that the interventions they provide are the most powerful and most effective. In order for interventions to be powerful and effective, a number of conditions must be must. Among these are: (a) the use of evidence, (b) the use of theory, (c) systematic program design, and (d) a continuous focus on client outcomes. The remainder of this chapter will review these stipulations.

Intervention as a Means for Creating and Measuring Client Change

A program that is designed and implemented to be *intervention* has, as its outcome, some degree of client behavioral change (that is, behavioral change is the purpose of the program) (Shank & Kinney, 1991; Stumbo, 2000, 2003a, 2003b; Stumbo & Hess, 2001). This may mean an increase in knowledge, an increase in skill, a decrease in some behavior, an increase in functional ability, and so forth.

The targeted outcomes must be applicable to the client upon discharge or exit from the program. It is part of the specialist's responsibility to identify relevant, meaningful, and timely outcomes that will affect the individual's future leisure lifestyle. To be accountable for producing client change, a program has to be well-designed and implemented according to a plan that uses best practices to address the desired, specific participant change. On the other hand, programs that are not accountable often lack forethought into the content and process of delivery or the intended outcomes.

Intervention services are those that are: (a) based on client needs or deficits, (b) designed and implemented to improve, reduce, or eliminate those needs or deficits, and (c) targeted toward specific client outcomes as the result of participation in those programs. This implies that functional intervention programs, leisure education programs, and, sometimes, recreation participation programs are "intervention" or "treatment" in that they are goal-oriented and implemented for the specific purpose of producing client outcomes. Each specific program, intervention, or treatment can be evaluated independently from other specific programs, interventions, or treatments. In addition, specific programs or interventions have very distinct characteristics.

According to Connolly (1984):

the bottom line of designing a program is to put together a strategy, intervention, or approach that will aid those who participate in the program to accomplish behavioral change in the form of improved functional abilities and/or acquisition of new knowledge and skills. One measure of the effectiveness of a program, therefore, is documenting the outcomes clients attain as a consequence of participating in the program. (p. 159)

Riley (1991a) draws attention to the concepts of "measurable change" and "relationship" (p. 59). "The causal relationship between the process of care (intervention) and the outcomes of care (change in patient behavior) is critical" (Riley, 1991a, p. 59). Several authors advocate that there must be a direct and proven link between the goals of the program, the type of program being delivered, and the client outcomes expected from participation in the program. It is this link that is central to the concept of intervention and accountability for services (Carruthers, 2003; Ross & Ashton-Shaeffer, 2003).

Intervention- or outcome-oriented programs have unique characteristics that are distinguishable from nonintervention programs. In order for therapeutic recreation programs to be considered intervention, the delivery of the intervention or treatment must be:

- focused on a systematic assessment of client characteristics, needs, and/or deficits

- designed in advance to be efficient and effective in its delivery
- able to produce targeted, meaningful, timely, and desired client outcomes
- able to produce evaluation data indicating achievement (or non-achievement) of client outcomes
- part of a larger systematic, comprehensive set of quality programs (Stumbo & Peterson, 2009)

These characteristics imply that the designer must specify the intended outcomes as well as the process to accomplish the outcomes *prior* to the implementation of the program. Intervention assumes a well-defined, goal-oriented *purpose* to the activity or program being provided. There is a well-thought-out plan for getting the participant from point A to point B, through his or her participation in a program or programs that are specifically designed for that purpose (Carruthers, 2003; Ross & Ashton-Shaeffer, 2003). These well-thought-out plans often require the underpinnings of research evidence and theory in order to best target client outcomes.

Clinical Decisions Using Evidence, Theory, and Systematic Design

Decisions about which interventions are most effective and efficient for a particular client or group of clients are often difficult to make with confidence, for both new and experienced clinicians alike. Most often, these decisions can be improved by searching for related research and theories and by applying them to develop best practice; that is, making sure the interventions we provide are the most likely of all possible options to produce the desired outcomes in the most systematic, efficient, and effective manner (Stumbo & Peterson, 2009).

Research evidence and theories of intervention are important to program development, not only at the comprehensive design level but also at the specific program level (Caldwell, 2001, 2003; Stumbo, 2003c; Widmer, Zabriskie, & Wells, 2003). Using research evidence and theories of intervention can aid the therapeutic recreation specialist in many ways, including:

- reducing the amount of time and effort in creating "from-scratch" program designs by providing an overall framework and implementation strategies

- improving the connection between clients' needs, program design and implementation, and client outcomes
- improving standardization of and consensus about programs for specific client groups
- improving the ability to evaluate program effectiveness for individual clients, for groups of clients, and for therapeutic recreation as a service

There are many ways in which the therapeutic recreation specialist can improve the likelihood that interventions can address client needs and be delivered efficiently and effectively. Two recent trends in health and human services are affecting therapeutic recreation program design: (a) evidence-based practice and (b) theory-based programming.

Evidence-Based Practice

The first trend is evidence-based practice. The overall aim of evidence-based practice is to reduce wide (and unintended) variations in practice, and instead use the best, accumulated evidence possible to inform, enlighten, and direct practice. "Evidence-based practice can be described as the selection of treatments for which there is some evidence of efficacy" (Denton, Walsh, & Daniel, 2002, p. 40). Evidence-based practice improves the predictability and causality of service outcomes and provides regulators, payers, and consumers increased assurance of quality care. Through the use of evidence-based practice, each professional should increase his/her confidence that the services being provided are the most meaningful, most targeted, and most successful approaches possible (Stumbo, 2003d). Evidence-based practice means conducting or using research results to inform the design and delivery of therapeutic recreation practice (McCormick & Lee, 2001).

This research provides a foundation for evidence-based practice of therapeutic recreation services by bringing forth the best possible information that is available on some of our most used techniques and interventions. Evidence-based practice in therapeutic recreation services has been advocated strongly to ensure that clients receive the best treatments possible (Lee & McCormick, 2002; Stumbo, 2003a, 2003b, 2003c; Stumbo & Pegg, 2010; Stumbo & Peterson, 2009; West et al., 2008). Through diligently using the best possible evidence of effectiveness (often through research results), we are more likely to provide those interventions and programs that move clients most steadfastly to the targeted end. In that way, evidence-based practice allows us to be much more confident that our intervention choices are based on a solid foundation,

instead of programs being offered because of tradition, ease of implementation, or therapists' interests and skills. "The foundation of evidence-based practice de-emphasizes decision making based on opinion, custom, or ritual. . . . Rather, emphasis is placed on applying the best available research findings to specific clinical situations" (King & Teo, 2000, p. 597).

For example, if research shows that meditation practices are more effective than aerobic exercise at inducing relaxation for older individuals, then therapeutic recreation program designs and their delivery should reflect the evidence from these research studies. In a second example, Stumbo (Chapter 10 of this text) cites a number of research studies that demonstrate that relaxation training, social skills instruction, and cognitive behavioral training are highly effective in significantly improving youths' ability to manage anger. Therapeutic recreation specialists who use this research in their program development will (a) shorten the time it takes to conceptualize, design, deliver, and evaluate their anger management program; (b) be more assured of producing desirable client outcomes; (c) be able to judge whether the same outcomes result from their programs; and (d) show proof that services are up-to-date, accountable, and based both on best practices and evidence.

However, searching for and obtaining such reports—and actually practicing evidence-based health care—is often beyond the capabilities and resources (time, effort, cost, and administrative disincentives) of the professional (Glanville, Haines, & Auston, 1998). One of the possible solutions to this dilemma is for the profession (likely, researchers) to conduct systematic reviews of the research literature and make these syntheses available to working professionals and students. Elsewhere, Stumbo (2003c, 2003d, 2003e) has written on the importance of conducting and understanding systematic reviews for improving therapeutic recreation practice. Each chapter of this book has been written with extreme care and diligence, although not each has used a systematic review protocol per se. Instead of a posing a "clinical question" that would be applicable to one setting or one group of clients (Stumbo, 2003d, 2003e), we posed a much larger set of "professional questions." That is, we first asked, "What interventions and programs are therapeutic recreation specialists, regardless of specific settings or client groups or geographic regions, most likely to design, based on our scope of practice? What are the best available theories and research investigations that support these interventions? What are the implications of these theories and investigations for therapeutic recreation practice?"

So perhaps instead of applying the term "systematic review" for the process used throughout this book, the better term might be "clinical review," as suggested by Clegg and colleagues (2000) and Siwek and colleagues (2002). According to Bhandari et al. (2002), clinical reviews answer "background questions" such as overall effectiveness of a technique or intervention, while systematic reviews ask "foreground questions" pertaining to a more specific aspect of client care, perhaps about a specific diagnosis.

Regardless, supporting programming decisions with research evidence and applicable theories is appropriate, necessary, and beneficial in both cases. First, the use of research and theory ensures that practitioners are more able to predict a precise estimate of the treatment effect of specific interventions for a specific group of clients (Bhandari et al., 2002). Second, the value or the outcome of the intervention is more easily communicated to treatment team members and clients and their families. And third, when quality systematic reviews are available, the professional can choose from recommendations and tailor them to the clients' needs, spending more time with clients and less time struggling for ideas (Myers, Pritchett, & Johnson, 2001).

It is clear that evidence-based practice, because it improves the likelihood of clients achieving the desired outcomes in the most direct and potent manner, is here to stay. Therapeutic recreation specialists who use evidence-based practice will shorten their overall preparation time and heighten their ability to reach meaningful client outcomes. Evidence-based practice, like theory-based programming, will enhance the effectiveness and efficiency of therapeutic recreation programs.

Theory-Based Programming

Led by several scholars in the field, theory-based programming is an idea whose time has come. Caldwell (2001, 2003) and Widmer, Zabriskie, and Wells (2003) provided numerous examples of theories that might be used in therapeutic recreation programming. Some of these examples are: (a) self-efficacy, (b) perceived freedom, and (c) stress-coping.

Becoming skilled in using theories to develop therapeutic recreation (TR) assessments, programs, and evaluations can lead to many important outcomes, such as increased programmatic efficacy and ability to better communicate with colleagues. . . . Theories provide the foundation for understanding TR programming, and as a result, can become one of the most important

tools a TRS can use. . . . All competent TRSs provide some reasoning behind what they do. Answers such as "I want to improve self-efficacy" or "The patient needs to increase anger-management skills" explain in general what the TRS's treatment goals might be. A good theory, however, will provide the tool to specify beforehand what might happen, and even more important, why it might happen. (Caldwell, 2001, p. 349)

An example of the extensive use of theory in program development is work done by Hood and Carruthers (Carruthers & Hood, 2002; Hood & Carruthers, 2002). Believing that "[t]heory is an extremely useful tool for understanding, predicting, and/or changing human behavior" (Hood & Carruthers, 2002, p. 138), these researchers studied stress-coping theory and applied it to individuals with alcoholism. Two major intervention strategies emerged: (a) decreasing negative demands and (b) increasing positive resources. Each of these strategies included a number of substrategies, such as using social networks for support.

After this thorough review of the literature, they designed and tested a seven-session coping skills program, with goals, implementation details, and an evaluation strategy (Carruthers & Hood, 2002). After implementing the stress-coping program at three different hospitals, they reported that clients perceived the goals of the coping skills intervention program as very important, clients believed their own improvement on the goals as a result of the program was approximately 75 percent, and clients actually achieved the behavioral goals approximately 80 to 95 percent of the time. The specialists who implemented the program at the three different hospitals felt the intervention was brief but more effective than previous attempts in this area. Compared the effectiveness of most of therapeutic recreation programs, these results are phenomenal, both from a client-change perspective and from a therapist-utility standpoint.

These are but a few examples of the growing base of evidence-based practice and theory-based programming in the therapeutic recreation literature. It is anticipated that this text will be a major step forward in identifying applicable theories that are suitable for therapeutic recreation services.

Why do evidence-based practice and theory-based programming matter to therapeutic recreation? The answers are many. First, they improve the chances of getting to client outcomes more quickly by focusing programming efforts on sound and proven information. Second, they improve the justification or rationale for services that are based on specific evidence and theory, rather than on happenstance or whim. Third, both efforts becoming more accepted and universally applied will improve the standardization of practice and create common ground among therapeutic recreation professionals and with their colleagues from other disciplines. Clearly, evidence-based practice and theory-based programming can greatly aid comprehensive and specific program designs' rationale and effectiveness.

Tied in with the notion of evidence-based practice and theory-based programming is a parallel concept of systems design; that is, knowing that the whole of the program is far greater than each of its parts individually. For that to occur, several systems or procedures must be in place before accountable services can be delivered to clients dependably.

Systems Design and Therapeutic Recreation Intervention

The beauty of using a systems approach for designing therapeutic recreation programs is that the designer must specify the intended outcome as well as the process to get there *prior* to the implementation of the program. That is, systems design assumes that there is a well-defined, goal-oriented *purpose* to the activity or program being provided. Objectives, goals, and outcome measures help define where the program is going and how it is going to get there. There is a well-defined plan for getting the participant from point A to point B, through his or her participation in a program that has been specifically designed for that purpose. This is a major factor that helps system-designed programs to become intervention.

The general theory of systems is based on two concepts. The first is the concept of "wholeness." This implies that any entity can be viewed as a system and can be studied for its dynamics as a complete entity. Readers are familiar with the use of "systems"—for example, stereo systems, the solar system, the criminal justice system, the public school system, the welfare system, a weather system, a car's cooling system, a body's circulatory system, the ecosystem, etc. Although the parts can be identified, broken down, analyzed, and studied, the total entity has characteristics and dimensions that are greater than the sum of its parts. Thus, viewing just the parts or components does not give a realistic picture of the total entity.

The second concept of general systems theory is that of "interrelatedness." This concept attempts to explain that parts or components of a system interrelate with one another. These interrelationships between parts are as important as the individual parts.

Systems theory, including the concepts of "wholeness" and "interrelatedness," have brought a new perspective to the study of many entities—natural phenomena, man-made entities, organizations, and human delivery systems, as the examples above illustrate. The systems concept has facilitated the understanding of complex human, social, and natural entities.

Systems theory, however, is more than a method of analysis and description. It has been translated into many practical applications. One of the most common applications is to the process of program planning. Systems planning models provide developed steps or procedures for program design, implementation, and evaluation. The models are not designed for any one discipline but rather are procedures that can be used in any field of service.

The flexibility of the systems approach enables diverse program content and structure to exist. The planning, implementation, and evaluation procedures guide the planner systematically through program development without dictating actual content or implementation strategies. However, the method facilitates logical design in interrelated stages, providing continuity and accountability to the program plan.

Simply stated, a systems approach to program planning focuses on three basic concerns:

1. Determining what the program is to accomplish (where you're going)
2. Designing a set of procedures to get to those goals (how you're going to get there)
3. Developing criteria to determine if the program did what it was designed to do (how do you know if you got there?)

Many systems planning models have been developed and implemented for various planning needs. Some are very complex and rely on computer technology; others are quite simple and basically outline the major stages of program development. Regardless of the level of sophistication, seven basic components are built into any systems planning model:

1. Determining the purpose, goals, and objectives
2. Designing a specific set of procedures and content to accomplish the purpose, goals, and objectives
3. Specifying implementation of delivery strategies
4. Designating an evaluation procedure
5. Implementing the program
6. Evaluating the program
7. Revising the program based on evaluation data

It is easy to see that these seven steps are clearly related to therapeutic recreation intervention or treatment programming. A program that is designed and implemented to be intervention has as its outcome some degree of client behavioral change (that is, behavioral change is the purpose of the program). This may mean an increase in knowledge, an increase in skill, a decrease in some behavior, and so on. To be considered intervention, a program has to be well-designed and implemented according to a plan—a *system*—that specifically addresses participant change. A systems approach is a useful tool for intervention designers to ensure that clients attain the desired and intended outcomes.

Client Outcomes

Focusing on client outcomes in the development, delivery, and evaluation of therapeutic recreation interventions is more important than ever. A number of authors have emphasized that outcomes are the documentable changes in client behavior, skills, and/or attitudes that can be attributed to active participation in the therapeutic recreation intervention program (Dunn, Sneegas, & Carruthers, 1991; Shank & Kinney, 1991; Stumbo, 1996, 2002; Stumbo & Peterson, 2009). "Outcomes are the observed changes in a client's status as a result of our interventions and interactions. Outcomes can be attributed to the process of providing care, and this should enable us to determine if we are doing for our clients that which we purport to do" (Shank & Kinney,

1991, p. 76). Some of the definitions of outcomes that appear in the literature are listed in Table 1.1.

The majority of these definitions concur that outcomes represent the differences in the client from the beginning compared to end of treatment (and perhaps beyond). Of course, most clinicians are hopeful that client changes or outcomes are positive (in the desired direction of treatment) and result directly from active participation within treatment services. In all cases, outcomes must be targeted prior to the intervention and must be measurable.

Client outcomes are the results or changes in the client that result from participation and involvement in services, and therefore, need to be clarified and targeted before any intervention or service is conceptualized or designed. Navar (1991) explained this as "providing the right patient with the right service [at] the right time in the right setting at the right intensity and for the right duration" (p. 5). Client outcomes can be categorized in many ways; a useful schema was suggested by Gorski (1995):

- changes in clinical status (effect of treatment on patient's symptoms)
- changes in functionality (effect of treatment on client's lifestyle)
- change in utilization of medical resources (effect of treatment on using additional health-care services)
- recidivism (examining patterns of relapse or re-entry into the medical system)

Table 1.1. Definitions of Client Outcomes

- The [change in a] state or situation that arises as a result of some process of intervention (Wade, 1999, p. 93)
- Refers to change in a client's status over time (McCormick & Funderburk, 2000, p. 10)
- Outcomes are reported as changes in the score between two points of time on individual level standardized instruments (Blankertz & Cook, 1998, p. 170)
- The results of performance (or non-performance) of a function or process(es) (JCAHO, 1995, p. 717)
- Outcomes are the observed changes in a client's status as a result of our interventions and interactions, whether intended or not. Outcomes are the complications, adverse events, or short- or long-term changes experienced by our clients, and represent the efforts of our care. Outcomes can be attributed to the process of providing care, and this should enable us to determine if we are doing for our clients that which we purport to do (Shank & Kinney, 1991, p. 76)
- The direct effects of service upon the well being of both the individual and specified populations; the end result of medical care; what happened to the patient in terms of palliation, control of illness, cure, or rehabilitation (Riley, 1991a, p. 58)
- Clinical results (Scalenghe, 1991, p. 30)

Therapeutic recreation may target and contribute to the achievement of any and all of these broad client outcomes. Because client outcomes represent the differences in the client from the beginning compared to the end of services (and likely beyond), they are crucial to many services and efforts. Being accountable means being able to design and deliver programs that will bring about some predetermined outcome or behavioral change in the client. In essence, targets for behavioral change must be identified *before* programs can be designed and delivered to create that change. This implies that each service, such as nursing, social work, or therapeutic recreation, must be able to target specific behavioral change in the client that will occur as a result of the client's participation in that discipline's service. There must be a direct link between the process or delivery of care, and the outcomes expected from it (Riley, 1987, 1991a).

The ability to produce client outcomes is contingent on well-designed and systematic programs into which clients are placed based on the needs shown from assessment results. The relationship or causal link is a strong one (Riley, 1987, 1991a; Stumbo, 2000, 2003b, 2003c, 2003d; Stumbo & Hess, 2001).

Important Characteristics of Outcomes

Dunn, Sneegas, and Carruthers (1991) noted that within the profession of therapeutic recreation a variety of terms (e.g., "objectives," "behavioral objectives," "performance measures") have been used to define what is currently termed 'outcome measures.' What outcomes are relevant? What outcomes carry the greatest importance to clients, given their demographic, ethnic, and cultural characteristics? What outcomes are attainable during (especially brief) intervention? The answers to these questions may be unique for each individual agency.

Stumbo (2000) documented six characteristics of outcomes that are valued and have utility for measurement purposes. These six characteristics are as follows (see also Table 1.2).

Table 1.2. Characteristics of Client Outcomes

Client outcomes must be:

- Identifiable
- Measurable
- Achievable
- Demonstrable or Documented
- Predictable or Causal
- Meaningful

- Outcomes must be *identifiable*. This task is of primary importance and must be done before other measurement tasks are undertaken (Johnson & Ashton-Shaeffer, 2000; Stumbo, 2000; Stumbo & Hess, 2001). What outcomes from the therapeutic recreation service are important to the clients seen at this facility? What target outcomes fit within the scope of therapeutic recreation practice that will benefit these clients and fall within the intent of this facility and its other health care disciplines?
- Outcomes must be *measurable* (Buettner, 2000; Hodges & Luken, 2000; Stumbo, 2000). While most health-care providers believe their services contribute to the overall, global health and well-being of their clients, these "measures" often are deemed too broad and lack meaning in today's health-care environment. There is greater interest in defining outcomes more specifically and in smaller terms. Therapeutic recreation specialists need to locate and document outcomes in five areas: clinical status, functional status, well-being or quality of life, satisfaction with care, and cost/resource utilization (see Stumbo, 2003c). What categories of outcomes or outcome indicators are produced by therapeutic recreation services? What important outcomes of therapeutic recreation services are measurable, and how and when will they be measured? Will these measurements be sensitive to change within a short time period?
- Outcomes must be *achievable* (Hodges & Luken, 2000; Johnson & Ashton-Shaeffer, 2000). Shortened lengths of stay have complicated the accomplishments of most health-care professionals. With fewer days of inpatient or even outpatient care, it is difficult and sometimes impossible to achieve the outcomes that may have been identified five or ten years ago. What can be accomplished within a patient's two-day or five-day stay? What is important in this person's treatment, and how can it be achieved? It has been a difficult task for most therapeutic recreation professionals to narrow their scope of measurement (and programming) to fit the patient's length of stay.
- Outcomes must be *demonstrable* or *documented* (Buettner, 2000; Stumbo, 2000). For example, if a stress-management program is to produce measurable changes in the clients' behavior, attitude, or level of stress, the therapeutic recreation specialist must be able to document that change.

Often, this means having valid and reliable instruments or tools that measure the level of behavior, attitude, or knowledge that is targeted, and how that changed as the result of care. It also means having a body of research that supports these outcomes (Seibert, 1991).

- Outcomes must be *predictable* or *causal* (Riley, 1991b). That is, there must be a direct relationship between the intervention and the outcome. Using the example of a stress-management program, it would be unwise to measure differences in leisure attitudes as an outcome, since a change in leisure attitudes is unlikely to be directly attributable to a stress management program.

- Outcomes must be *meaningful* (Buettner, 2000; Devine & Wilhite, 1999; Johnson & Ashton-Shaeffer, 2000; Lee & Yang, 2000; McCormick & Funderburk, 2000; Shank, Coyle, Kinney, & Lay, 1994/1995; Stumbo, 2000). With all the constraints above, client outcomes must still be meaningful to the client and his or her recovery or health status, as well as valuable to third-party payers. What important contribution does therapeutic recreation make to the client's success? What unique contribution does therapeutic recreation make to other services provided by the health-care team? What outcome changes in the client would make the most difference in his or her life?

A great deal of effort on the part of the specialist should be spent considering which client behaviors, skills, or attitudes can be changed, given the goals and design of the program. For example, if clients' average length of stay is seven days, it would seem difficult to change attitudes that took a lifetime to develop. Instead, the specialist might choose to help the client increase his or her knowledge of community leisure resources, an outcome that typically can be expected within seven days of intervention. The outcome has relevance, importance, and is attainable. Smaller, more measurable client outcomes may be preferable to larger, less measurable outcomes.

Several authors have provided guidelines for selecting and developing client outcome statements (Anderson, Ball, Murphy, & associates, 1975, as cited in Dunn, Sneegas, & Carruthers, 1991; Shank & Kinney, 1991). These authors suggested that the specialist create and implement client outcome statements that consider:

- the efficiency and effectiveness of demonstrating client change

- a reasonable relationship between the services provided and the expected outcome
- the connection between occurrence of the outcome and the timing of data collection
- the relevance to the client, his or her culture, and society
- the goals and intent of the program
- an appropriate level of specification, but not reduced to trivial detail
- individual client variation within any given program
- both long-term and short-term goals and objectives
- the social, home, and community environment to which the client will return
- behaviors that are generalizable and transferable to a variety of settings and situations

It is clear that client outcomes and the specific programs or interventions that are designed to attain them are intricately related; interventions must be created and delivered in a way that client outcomes will result.

Benefits of Evidence-Based, Theory-Based, and Systems-Inspired Outcomes

The benefits of evidence-based, theory-based, and systems-inspired intervention programming are wide ranging. Below are some of the professional benefits of these best practices in therapeutic recreation services:

- provides reasonable guarantee to client and others that programs are designed and delivered for a specific purpose
- helps specialist focus on meeting client needs rather than providing programs without purpose
- ensures relative consistency of treatment from client to client, day to day, specialist to specialist
- places clients into programs based on need rather than convenience
- helps determine content of client assessments
- provides direction for content of client documentation
- aids in producing predictable client results from programs
- allows better data collection about program efficacy in meeting the needs of clients
- increases communication between therapeutic recreation specialists throughout the country, as well as with other disciplines

- provides explanation of therapeutic recreation services to auditing groups such as third-party payers, accrediting bodies, and administrative policy makers (Stumbo & Peterson, 2009)

These benefits can be divided into areas regarding the program, the clients, therapeutic recreation specialists, and external (to therapeutic recreation) audiences. Benefits to the overall therapeutic recreation program result as close attention is paid to the planning, selecting, and designing of programs to meet a specific purpose or area of client need. This requires systematic forethought and diligence on the part of the therapeutic recreation specialist as well as a reasonable knowledge of research evidence and theories related to intervention.

Benefits to clients stem from the systematic and purposeful planning that must take place with evidence-based practice and protocols. Clients can be reasonably assured that there is a specific purpose, implementation plan, and predicted outcomes that remain the focus of the program. Clients are more guaranteed that there is a desirable end result of participation in the program. For many clients this assurance results in increased motivation to participate actively in the programs described in the protocol.

Benefits to therapeutic recreation specialists are many. Knowing that programs have a defined purpose, solid foundation, and targeted outcomes helps the specialist implement and evaluate them with more confidence and uniformity. Program delivery becomes standardized rather than haphazard, as does professional terminology.

Another benefit then becomes the ability to better communicate and market therapeutic recreation services to outside constituents. This may include other disciplines, health-care administrators, external accrediting bodies, insurance companies, and clients themselves. The ability to provide consistent, high-quality, and predictable client care is essential in this era of accountability. Shorter lengths of client stay support more predictable timelines for intervention and both evidence-based practice and use of clinical guidelines allow therapeutic recreation specialists to be more responsive in this area. These efforts form the foundation of common practices that move the profession toward greater accountability.

Summary

- The purpose of this book is to improve therapeutic recreation specialists' systematic application of various techniques and modalities.
- Evidence-based practice, theory-based practice, systems-designed practice, and the continual focus of client outcomes are important to the improvement of therapeutic recreation services.
- Interventions are those services which have as their outcome some degree of client behavioral change (behavior, knowledge, attitudes, skills).
- Evidence-based practice uses research and evaluation results as the basis for the design and implementation of services.
- Theory-based practice uses sound theories, such as self-efficacy, perceived freedom, and stress-coping, as the foundation to design and implement services.
- Systems-designed programs are based on three broad questions: Where are you going? How are you going to get there? How do you know if you got there?
- Focusing on client outcomes; that is, the change in clients based on our services helps therapeutic recreation specialists to design streamlined and purposeful programs.
- There are numerous benefits to embracing evidence-based, theory-based, systems-inspired programs within therapeutic recreation services.

References

Anderson, S. B., Ball, S., Murphy, R. T., & Associates. (1975). *Encyclopedia of educational evaluation.* San Francisco, CA: Jossey-Bass.

Bhandari, M., Guyatt, G. H., Montori, V., Devereaux, P. J., & Swiontkowski, M. F. (2002). User's guide to the orthopaedic literature: How to use a systematic literature review. *Journal of Bone & Joint Surgery, American Volume, 84*(9), 1672–1682.

Blankertz, L., & Cook, J. A. (1998). Choosing and using outcome measures. *Psychiatric Rehabilitation Journal, 22*(2), 167–174.

Buettner, L. L. (2000). Gerontological recreation therapy: Examining the trends and making a forecast. *Annual in Therapeutic Recreation, 9,* 35–46.

Caldwell, L. L. (2001). The role of theory in therapeutic recreation: A practical approach. In N. J. Stumbo (Ed.), *Professional issues in therapeutic recreation: On competence and outcomes* (pp. 349–364). Champaign, IL: Sagamore.

Caldwell, L. L. (2003). Basing outcomes on theory: Theories of intervention and explanation. In N. J. Stumbo (Ed.), *Client outcomes in therapeutic recreation services* (pp. 67–86). State College, PA: Venture Publishing, Inc.

Carruthers, C. (2003). Objectives-based approach to evaluating the effectiveness of therapeutic recreation services. In N. J. Stumbo (Ed.), *Client outcomes in therapeutic recreation services* (pp. 187–202). State College, PA: Venture Publishing, Inc.

Carruthers, C. P., & Hood, C. D. (2002). Coping skills program for individuals with alcoholism. *Therapeutic Recreation Journal, 36*(2), 154–171.

Clegg, A., Hewitson, P., & Milne, R. (2000). Explicit and reproducible: How to assess the quality of the evidence in a systematic review. *Student British Medical Journal, 8*, 1–44.

Connolly, P. (1984). Program evaluation. In C. A. Peterson & S. L. Gunn, *Therapeutic recreation program design: Principles and procedures* (2nd ed.) (pp. 136–179). Englewood Cliffs, NJ: Prentice-Hall.

Denton, W. H., Walsh, S. R., & Daniel, S. S. (2002). Evidence-based practice in family therapy: Adolescent depression as an example. *Journal of Marital and Family Therapy, 28*(1), 39–45.

Devine, M. A., & Wilhite, B. (1999). Theory application in therapeutic recreation practice and research. *Therapeutic Recreation Journal, 33*(1), 29–45.

Dunn, J. K., Sneegas, J. J., & Carruthers, C. A. (1991). Outcome measures: Monitoring patient progress. In B. Riley (Ed.), *Quality management: Applications for therapeutic recreation* (pp. 107–115). State College, PA: Venture Publishing, Inc.

Glanville, J., Haines, M., & Auston, I. (1998). Finding information on clinical effectiveness. *British Medical Journal, 317*, 200–203.

Gorski, T. T. (1995). The strategic advantage perspective on outcomes. *Behavioral Health Management, 15*(3), 33–36.

Hodges, J. S., & Luken, K. (2000). Services and support as a means to meaningful outcomes for persons with developmental disabilities. *Annual in Therapeutic Recreation, 9*, 47–56.

Hood, C. D., & Carruthers, C. P. (2002). Coping skills theory as an underlying framework for therapeutic recreation services. *Therapeutic Recreation Journal, 36*(2), 137–153.

Johnson, D. E., & Ashton-Shaeffer, C. (2000). A framework for therapeutic recreation outcomes in school-based settings. *Annual in Therapeutic Recreation, 9*, 57–70.

Joint Commission on Accreditation of Healthcare Organizations (1995). *1996 Comprehensive Accreditation Manual for Hospitals*. Oakbrook Terrace, IL: Author.

King, K. M., & Teo, K. K. (2000). Integrating clinical quality improvement strategies with nursing research. *Western Journal of Nursing Research, 22*(5), 596–608.

Lee, Y. & McCormick, B. P. (2002). Toward evidence-based therapeutic recreation practice. In D. R. Austin, J. Dattilo, & B. P. McCormick (Eds.), *Conceptual foundations for therapeutic recreation* (pp. 165–183). State College, PA: Venture Publishing, Inc.

Lee, Y., & Yang, H. (2000). A review of therapeutic recreation outcomes in physical medicine and rehabilitation between 1991–2000. *Annual in Therapeutic Recreation, 9*, 21–34.

McCormick, B. P., & Funderburk, J. (2000). Therapeutic recreation outcomes in mental health practice. *Annual in Therapeutic Recreation, 9*, 9–19.

McCormick, B. P., & Lee, Y. (2001). Research into practice: Building knowledge through empirical practice. In N. J. Stumbo (Ed.), *Professional issues in therapeutic recreation: On competence and outcomes* (pp. 383–400). Champaign, IL: Sagamore.

Myers, E. F., Pritchett, E., & Johnson, E. Q. (2001). Evidence-based practice guidelines vs. protocols: What's the difference? *Journal of the American Dietetic Association, 101*(9), 1085–1090.

Navar, N. (1991). Advancing therapeutic recreation through quality assurance: A perspective on the changing nature of quality in therapeutic recreation. In B. Riley (Ed.), *Quality management: Applications for therapeutic recreation* (pp. 3–20). State College, PA: Venture Publishing, Inc.

Riley, B. (1987). Conceptual basis of quality assurance: Application to therapeutic recreation service. In B. Riley (Ed.), *Evaluation of therapeutic recreation through quality assurance* (pp. 7–24). State College, PA: Venture Publishing, Inc.

Riley, B. (1991a). Quality assessment: The use of outcome indicators. In B. Riley (Ed.), *Quality management: Applications for therapeutic recreation* (pp. 53–67). State College, PA: Venture Publishing, Inc.

Riley, B. (1991b). *Quality management: Applications for therapeutic recreation*. State College, PA: Venture Publishing, Inc.

Ross, J. E., & Ashton-Shaeffer, C. (2003). Selecting and designing intervention programs for outcomes. In N. J. Stumbo (Ed.), *Client outcomes in therapeutic recreation services* (pp. 129–150). State College, PA: Venture Publishing, Inc.

Scalenghe, R. (1991). The Joint Commission's "Agenda for change" as related to the provision of therapeutic recreation services. In B. Riley (Ed.), *Quality management: Applications for therapeutic recreation* (pp. 29–42). State College, PA: Venture Publishing, Inc.

Seibert, M. L. (1991). Keynote. In C. P. Coyle, W. B. Kinney, B. Riley, & J. W. Shank (Eds.), *Benefits of therapeutic recreation: A consensus view* (pp. 5–15). Philadelphia, PA: Temple University.

Shank, J. W., & Kinney, W. B. (1991). Monitoring and measuring outcomes in therapeutic recreation. In B. Riley (Ed.), *Quality management: Applications for therapeutic recreation* (pp. 69–82). State College, PA: Venture Publishing, Inc.

Shank, J. W., Coyle, C. P., Kinney, W. B., & Lay, C. (1994/95). Using existing data to examine therapeutic recreation services. *Annual in Therapeutic Recreation, 5*, 5–12.

Siwek, J., Gourlay, M. L., Slawson, D. C., & Shaughnessy, A. F. (2002). How to write an evidence-based clinical review article. *American Family Physician, 65*(2), 251–258.

Stumbo, N. J. (1996). A proposed accountability model for therapeutic recreation services. *Therapeutic Recreation Journal, 30*(4), 246–259.

Stumbo, N. J. (2000). Outcome measurement in health care: Implications for therapeutic recreation. *Annual in Therapeutic Recreation, 9*, 1–8.

Stumbo, N. J. (2002). *Client assessment in therapeutic recreation*. State College, PA: Venture Publishing, Inc.

Stumbo, N. J. (2003a). Assessment: The key to outcomes and evidence-based practice. In N. J. Stumbo (Ed.), *Client outcomes in therapeutic recreation services* (pp. 167–186). State College, PA: Venture Publishing, Inc.

Stumbo, N. J. (2003b). The importance of evidence-based practice in therapeutic recreation. In N. J. Stumbo (Ed.), *Client outcomes in therapeutic recreation services* (pp. 25–48). State College, PA: Venture Publishing, Inc.

Stumbo, N. J. (2003c). Outcomes, accountability, and therapeutic recreation. In N. J. Stumbo (Ed.), *Client outcomes in therapeutic recreation services* (pp. 1–24). State College, PA: Venture Publishing, Inc.

Stumbo, N. J. (2003d). Systematic reviews part I: How to conduct systematic reviews for evidence-based practice. *Annual in Therapeutic Recreation, 12*, 29–44.

Stumbo, N. J. (2003e). Systematic reviews part II: How to appraise systematic reviews for evidence-based practice. *Annual in Therapeutic Recreation, 12*, 45–56.

Stumbo, N. J., & Hess, M. E. (2001). On competencies and outcomes in therapeutic recreation. In N. J. Stumbo (Ed.), *Professional issues in therapeutic recreation: On competence and outcomes* (pp. 3–20). Champaign, IL: Sagamore.

Stumbo, N. J., & Pegg, S. (2010). Outcomes and evidence-based practice: Moving forward. *Annual in Therapeutic Recreation, 18*, 12–23.

Stumbo, N. J., & Peterson, C. A. (2009). *Therapeutic recreation program design: Principles and procedures* (5th ed.). San Francisco, CA: Benjamin Cummings.

Wade, D. T. (1999). Editorial: Outcome measurement and rehabilitation. *Clinical Rehabilitation, 13*, 93–95.

Widmer, M. A., Zabriskie, R., & Wells, M. A. (2003). Program evaluation: Collecting data to measure outcomes. In N. J. Stumbo (Ed.), *Client outcomes in therapeutic recreation services* (pp. 203–220). State College, PA: Venture Publishing, Inc.

West, R. E., Kinney, T. & Witman, J. (Eds.) (2008). *Guidelines for competency assessment and curriculum planning for recreational therapy practice*. Hattiesburg, MS: American Therapeutic Recreation Association.

» CHAPTER 2 »

Leisure Education

Norma J. Stumbo, Ph.D., CTRS, Jin Kim, M.S., and Young-Gyoung Kim, Ed.D.

Leisure education is an important area of service within therapeutic recreation. It provides a backdrop for much of the interventions therapeutic recreation specialists offer to clients. The purpose of this chapter is to provide a brief overview of the importance of leisure and the history of leisure education models, and to describe the Leisure Education Content Model (Stumbo & Peterson, 2009) in more depth. It is often within the context of leisure education that the modalities and facilitation techniques described in this book are designed and implemented.

The Importance of Leisure

Mannell (2006) reviewed the literature related to health, well-being, and leisure and came to several important conclusions. Among these are the following:

- Healthy and satisfying leisure participation contributes to the health and well-being, and subsequently, the quality of life of individuals.
- Leisure is one life domain in which individuals have the greatest control (versus work) to make choices about their own behaviors. For example, many individuals choose to be sedentary and watch television rather than be physically active.
- Those who choose physically active or socially active leisure tend to experience better well-being and quality of life.
- Leisure experiences provide a platform for identify formation and affirmation, stress coping, relaxation, fun, well-being, relationship formation and enhancement, and life satisfaction.

Mannell also talks about the need for continuing research on the relationships between health and leisure, including cross-cultural comparisons.

It is clear that leisure has the *potential* to be a monumental force in individuals' lives. However, participation in leisure is dependent on a number of factors. These include:

- a valuing of the leisure experience and of health and well-being
- the ability to socially interact in appropriate ways with others in various settings
- the ability to locate and utilize leisure resources in the home, neighborhood, community, and perhaps beyond
- skills and abilities to participate, at least to a minimal degree, in leisure and recreation activities

It is also believed that many individuals with disabilities and/or illnesses lack these knowledges, skills, and attitudes, as well as other factors, such as basic functional abilities (Stumbo & Peterson, 2009). It is important, then, that therapeutic recreation specialists provide intervention that improves these conditions, places the person in a better position to enjoy leisure and recreation, and, hopefully, enables a better sense of health, well-being, and quality of life.

This section is provided to briefly acquaint the user with the history, concepts, and uses of leisure education. Throughout this overview, the reader will note that several terms—leisure counseling, avocational counseling, recreation counseling and leisure education—sometimes are used synonymously. Although these terms are used as the original authors have used them, the overview is intended to guide the reader to a fuller understanding and more appropriate use of the term "leisure education."

A Brief History of Leisure Education within Therapeutic Recreation Services

Olson and McCormack were the first to use the term "recreation counseling" as early as 1957. During the 15-year span from 1957 to 1972, only a handful of articles on the subject (approximately 15) appeared in the professional literature. In 1972, however, the literature began to contain increasing numbers of articles and soon became inundated with articles and books. During the next thirteen years, from 1972 to 1984, well over 200 articles were published in the leisure and recreation and therapeutic recreation literature.

Throughout the 1970s, several conferences were convened specifically to address the topic of leisure education and leisure counseling. In 1974, the Society of Park and Recreation Educators (SPRE), a former branch of the National Recreation and Park Association (NRPA), formed a National Leisure Education Committee. This group sponsored a Leisure Education Conference in Florida in January of 1975. In November of 1975, the Milwaukee Leisure Counseling Project held a special workshop. And in 1976, NRPA sponsored a "mini conference" on leisure counseling in conjunction with its annual congress in Boston. Similarly, the professional institute of the 1978 Midwest Symposium on Therapeutic Recreation focused on leisure education (Szymanski & Hitzhusen, 1979).

Numerous articles were written and some were collected into edited works. Six of these collections that may be of particular interest to readers are Compton and Goldstein (1977); Dowd (1984); Epperson, Witt, and Hitzhusen (1977); Humphrey, Kelley, and Hamilton (1980); *Leisure Today/JOPER* (1977, April); and the *Therapeutic Recreation Journal* (1981; 15, 4).

Conceptual Definitions

Several terms, often used synonymously, have surfaced since the early 1970s. Several of these definitions will be presented so that the reader may become familiar with the history of the leisure education movement.

Avocational Counseling

Overs and other individuals who worked on the Milwaukee project have coined, almost singularly, the term *avocational counseling*. The choice of this term was explained by Overs, Taylor, and Adkins (1977b) in describing their activity classification system:

> The authors have included a major category code 800, Volunteer Activities, which partly explains why they prefer, for their purposes, the broader term of "avocational counseling" to "recreational counseling" . . . In addition, using the term "avocational" as a parallel construct to vocational enables the authors to define with a minimal degree of precision the area of human behavior which they wish to examine and classify. A final argument is that life is only tolerable when it holds meaning. The authors believe that meaningful activity is essential for long-term satisfaction with it. To attain

meaningful involvement for a sustained period of time usually requires commitment. In the authors' opinion, the construct of commitment fits better under the term "avocational" than under either the term "leisure" or "recreation." (pp. 106–107)

The Milwaukee project staff quite consciously chose the term avocational for its comparability to vocational counseling, a popular term in the 1970s. In addition they felt the term avocational held more substance and meaning than alternative terms, such as leisure and recreation, and could be more broadly applied to a wider range of life activities. As the Milwaukee Project grew and expanded its services, the focus seemed to expand as well and to reflect a change in terms. Another group of researchers on the Milwaukee Project noted that:

> The Milwaukee Model, as applied to special populations such as the disabled and the elderly, continues to be referred to as "avocational counseling" by Overs, but the term "leisure counseling" was applied by Wilson in reference to the model's use with mainstream populations. (Wilson, Mirenda, & Rutkowski, 1977, p. 272)

Recreation Counseling

Recreation counseling generally emphasizes activity skills and available resources for involvement. O'Morrow (1977) defined recreation counseling as:

> A technique in the rehabilitation process whereby a professional person uses all the information gathered about a person prior to release or discharge to further explore interest and attitudes, with respect to leisure, recreation, and social relationships, in order to enable a patient to identify, locate, and use recreation resources in the community and thereby become an active community participant. (p. 15)

Stracke (1977) defined recreation counseling in similar terms: "The third type of counseling is called recreation counseling because it is designed to provide groups with information concerning locating community resources based upon an understanding of why recreation is necessary. Sessions are usually activity or facility-oriented" (p. 37). Recreation counseling was seen generally as teaching individuals new activity skills or helping them identify existing activity skills for participation in community activities. A direct connection was made between skill development and community involvement, focusing on teaching skills that could be utilized immediately within a community setting.

Hayes (1977a, 1977b, 1977c) did not separate the terms leisure education and recreation counseling. In discussing his conceptual model, Hayes (1977b) stated:

> Leisure education and recreation counseling is a developmental, remedial, preventive, and/or therapeutic process, whereby a professional person with specialized skill in and knowledge of leisure and recreation, developmental, cognitive, and affective domains of individual growth and development, individual and group facilitation techniques, helps the individual (the client) through establishment of a framework for communication, facilitation of individual decision and action through discussions, personal encounter and activity involvement, observation in activities and discussions, identification of community leisure resources, follow-up assistance through transitional phase into the community to acquire personal values and attitudes, individual goals and objectives, self-confidence and self-esteem, skills, knowledges, competencies and successful experiences. (pp. 77–78)

While Hayes provided a broader definition, most authors viewed recreation counseling in similar terms as avocational counseling. Recreation counseling, as with avocational counseling, seemed to focus heavily on matching client interests and skills with specific activities provided in community settings. Some individuals went beyond a simpler activity-inventory and resource-file approach to group process and personal decision making. The terms "recreation counseling" and "avocational counseling" are not in widespread use today.

Leisure Counseling

In addition to activity skills and resources, leisure counseling focuses on leisure attitudes and awareness and generally requires a degree of expertise in counseling techniques. McDowell (1976b) defined leisure counseling as "a helping process which facilitates interpretive, affective, and/or behavioral changes in others toward the attainment of their leisure well-being" (p. 9). Edwards (1977) offered the following: "Leisure counseling is a method of (1) helping individuals, alone or in groups, to go through the process of selecting satisfying and practical leisure activities, and (2) assisting them to find the time and place to enjoy these activities" (p. 38).

A more descriptive definition was offered by Gunn (1977a) who stated that "leisure counseling can therefore be defined as a process utilizing verbal facilitation techniques to promote self-awareness, awareness of leisure attitudes, values and feelings, and the development of decision-making and problem-solving skills related to leisure participation" (p. 35). In this sense, leisure counseling utilizes a "process" approach to assist participants in gaining insights into their own behaviors and choices, examining those choices in light of a leisure lifestyle, and making conscious decisions about their patterns of involvement.

Leisure Education

Leisure education is the broadest of the interpretations presented thus far. While it generally emphasizes leisure attitudes, awareness, social skills, decision-making, activities, and resources, it takes on an educational focus using instructional techniques. Mundy and Odum (1979, p. 2) defined leisure education as "a total developmental process through which individuals develop an understanding of self, leisure, and the relationship of leisure to their own lifestyles and the fabric of society." Further, they stated:

> As a result of leisure education, an individual will be able to (1) enhance the quality of his or her life in leisure, (2) understand the opportunities, potential, and challenges in leisure, (3) understand the impact of leisure on the quality of his or her life individually and the fabric of society, and (4) have the knowledge, skills and appreciations that enable broad leisure choices. (1979, p. 51; 1998, p. 50)

Peterson and Gunn (1984), in the second edition of their text, provided this definition that becomes highlighted within their model:

> Leisure education is a broad category of services that focuses on the development and acquisition of various leisure-related skills, attitudes, and knowledge. The establishment and expression of an appropriate leisure lifestyle appears to be dependent on the acquisition of diverse knowledge and skills. A repertoire of activity skills is not the only requirement. A cognitive understanding of leisure, a positive attitude toward leisure experiences, and various participatory and decision-making skills, as well as knowledge of and ability to utilize resources, appear to be significant aspects of satisfying leisure involvement. (p. 22)

As Chinn and Joswiak (1981, p. 5) have noted, both the Mundy and Odum and the original Peterson and Gunn models and definitions are similar in that the major focus of both is on the development and acquisition of:

- leisure attitudes and awareness
- social interaction skills
- leisure activity skills
- self-awareness
- knowledge of leisure resources
- decision-making skills

Leisure Counseling or Leisure Education?

From the definitions documented above, one can see that there are distinct similarities between leisure counseling and leisure education. The similarities are evident in the intent or goals of these efforts; that is, to help the individual in identifying and understanding a variety of values, attitudes, skills, and knowledges that will enable him or her to enjoy and benefit from leisure involvement. "However, it is the process and techniques employed which are instrumental in determining the appropriate term" (Chinn & Joswiak, 1981, p. 5). Further, these authors stated:

Leisure education focuses on the acquisition of leisure knowledge and skills. Educational techniques employed could be behavior management, task analysis, a learning center approach, or individualized prescriptions. Leisure counseling is viewed as being problem centered. The techniques used are counseling in nature, such as problem solving, conflict management, and values clarification. Many practitioners stating that they are doing leisure counseling may actually be doing leisure education. (pp. 5–6)

Stumbo and Peterson (2009) expanded on the distinction between leisure counseling and leisure education:

There is a legitimate service area that can be called leisure counseling. It is, however, quite different and distinct from the leisure education programs. . . . Leisure education has a specific and predetermined content, which is operationalized into programs. . . . Leisure counseling, as well as other forms of counseling, does not start usually with predetermined content. Rather, the problem or focus of counseling originates from the individual client. This major distinction between counseling and education is an important one. It is, however, common for counselors to use educational techniques

within the counseling process. Likewise educators often use counseling techniques with the educational process. Leisure counseling also has some significant differences when it comes to the issue of qualifications and credentials. In general, it is reasonable to assume that most therapeutic recreation specialists are qualified to use some basic counseling techniques. It is not appropriate to assume they have sufficient training to use the term 'counselor.' (p. 49)

Conceptual Models

Conceptual models, which were largely introduced in the late 1970s and refined in the early 1980s, are widely divergent. First, some models may be viewed as "process" models while others may be seen as "content" models. The process models usually describe "how to," or give directives about the implementation of a program. Content models usually describe the "what," or the subject matter on which the program should center.

Second, models also differ on their original conceptualization as avocational counseling, recreation counseling, leisure counseling, or leisure education models. These terms were discussed in the previous section, and again it will be noted here that the models that use the word "counseling" generally require a different, more in-depth strategy for implementation. It may also be pointed out here that usually "process" models have been associated with counseling and the "content" models have been utilized for leisure education.

Third, the models differ in their theoretical bases. While some have argued that models cannot be constructed without a solid foundation or established theory, others have stated that theories cannot be built or tested until working models are provided. Each model differs on the extent to which a theoretical support is implied or stated.

In an effort to clarify the above discussion using concrete examples and to give the user a broader familiarity with the underlying concepts, six representative models are reviewed below. These reviews are not intended to yield an in-depth analysis but are, in part, intended to show the reader how leisure education was originally conceptualized and developed throughout the years.

Overs' Avocational Counseling Model

One of the earliest models was Overs' Avocational Counseling Model (Overs, 1971, 1976; Overs & Page, 1974; Overs & Taylor, 1977; Overs, Taylor, & Adkins, 1974, 1977a, 1977b, 1977c). Funded in part by a federal grant and the Milwaukee, Wisconsin Public School system, the project was based on a classification system of over 800 specific activities. These activities were grouped under nine headings (e.g., Games, Volunteer Activities) that in turn were subdivided into two more levels. Following is an example:

100 Games

110 Active Games

111 Running Games

112 Throwing Games, etc.

120 Target and Skill Games, etc.

In addition to the classification system, a large file was created to store information about the activities, including local resources. The purpose of this approach was to match the clients' interests and abilities with available and accessible resources. To assist in this process of "matching," either previously published avocational interest inventories or "picture" inventories were utilized. Because the Overs' project served individuals with severe disabilities or literacy problems, six instruments were developed based on visual or audio information (i.e., Avocational Title Card Sort, Avocational Picture Card Sort, Slide Projected Picture Sort, Avocational Magazine Picture Card Sort, Avocational Plaque Card Sort, and Cassette Audio Recordings or Avocational Activities Interviews).

Once the client and counselor had determined an interest and a choice was made, the next step was to search the Avocational Activities File (the classification system of activities mentioned previously) to locate activity opportunities and learn how to enroll or otherwise begin pursuing them. Another instrument, the Milwaukee Avocational Satisfaction Questionnaire, was developed and used by the Overs' project staff for evaluation purposes in a follow-up interview.

Following this initial development, the project, renamed the Milwaukee Leisure Counseling Model, changed in three significant aspects. First, the population was expanded to include all adults within the Milwaukee area. Second, the Mirenda Leisure Interest Finder was developed and introduced as an assessment tool to determine interest levels in a wide variety of leisure pursuits. Third, the information/resource retrieval system was computerized.

Hayes' Leisure Education and Recreation Counseling Model

By the previous definitions, Hayes' Leisure Education and Recreation Counseling Model (Hayes, 1974, 1977a, 1977b, 1977c) would be classified as a "process" model, describing the implementation strategies of a leisure education/recreation counseling program. This model, created in 1974, was based upon the following concepts:

> Because complete fulfillment in our leisure and recreation cannot be experienced without adequate life skills, leisure education and recreation counseling represent the model in which the individual's deficient life, leisure, and recreation skills are strengthened through a developmental, remedial, or therapeutic process. This enables (or facilitates) the individual in the process of achieving his own individualized goals and objectives as they relate directly to the involvement in recreation and leisure experiences.

Hayes developed this model based upon experience with individuals with intellectual disabilities, though he contended the model could be operationalized with a variety of populations. Hayes' model consists of nine interrelated steps of implementation. These nine phases, though depicted slightly differently by Hayes, are as follows:

1. Entry in program facility or institution;
2. Initial contact; establish rapport, initial interview, give interest inventory;
3. Consultation with rehabilitation team or its equivalent;
4. Develop individualized program to enhance individual and group skills;
5. Leisure education and recreation counseling service;
6. Obtain consensus of discharge data and discharge location; pre-discharge sessions;
7. Discharge; follow-up assistance; visitations;
8. Evaluation and assessment of community involvement; and
9. Termination or suggested remedial or alternative plan of action.

For each of these nine steps, specific goals and objectives that further describe the process were given.

McDowell's Leisure Counseling Model

One of the most well-documented and theoretically based models is McDowell's Leisure Counseling Model (McDowell, 1973, 1974, 1975, 1976a, 1976b, 1977a, 1977b, 1977c, 1979, 1980a, 1980b, 1984).

Since its early beginnings, the model has undergone several revisions, based upon increasing sophistication in this area. As such, only the most recent edition of McDowell's model will be discussed.

The basic model presents a typology or hierarchy of four leisure counseling orientations. These orientations are:

- leisure-related (interruptive) behavior concerns
- leisure lifestyle awareness
- leisure resource guidance
- leisure-related skills and concerns

Briefly, leisure-related behavior concerns are based on learning theory which states that one can cognitively resolve leisure problems by developing appropriate strategies. Leisure lifestyle awareness centers on the individual's continuous seeking of self and his or her responsibility for controlling and changing behavior and destiny. Leisure resource guidance involves matching leisure interests and needs with leisure resources. Leisure-related skills and concerns focuses on the acquisition and development of skills for leisure and life development.

Throughout the refinement of the model, McDowell has compared these four leisure counseling orientations with levels of counseling theories in order to bring a theoretical perspective to the model. In addition, his latest available work combines the above model with lifestyle issues, wellness, and client concerns. In this complex synopsis of literature, McDowell continually revised his model to more comprehensively address the current issues of the time and to make the model more applicable to implementation and practice.

Mundy's Leisure Education Model

Mundy (1976, 1981, 1984; Mundy & Odum, 1979, 1998) introduced two models for leisure education that were conceptually rearranged and organized into one working model. The first model introduced was the Scope and Sequence Model. This model was conceptualized using the following six categories:

- self-awareness
- leisure awareness
- attitudes
- decision making
- social interaction
- leisure activity skills

All of these categories are depicted along a developmental lifespan continuum. At each life stage,

progressive levels of objectives to be achieved are documented. This model takes a very developmental approach to each of the stated goals of the model. Goals state that the individual should be able to:

- enhance the quality of his or her life in leisure
- understand the opportunities, potentials, and challenges in leisure
- understand the impact of leisure on the quality of his or her life individually and within the fabric of society
- have the knowledge, skills, and appreciations that enable broad leisure choices

Due to difficulty in operationalizing the Scope and Sequence Model, a second model was developed. The Systems Approach Model was rooted in system design and analysis. The model was depicted through a graphic network of interdependent program components, making it one of the first "content" models. The five program components that comprise the model are:

- leisure awareness
- self-awareness
- decision making
- leisure skills
- social interaction

Further, these components are broken down in several sub-components. For example, the sub-components of leisure awareness are:

- leisure
- leisure experiences
- relationship to one's life
- relationship to quality of life
- relationship to one's lifestyle
- relationship to society

Also utilizing systems design, Mundy has outlined an Input–Process–Output graphic that is most useful for determining client outcomes or goals for all five components of the Systems Approach Model.

In accordance with the previous two models, Mundy has also introduced "clusters of leisure education objectives," that can be broken down and used as a basis for program development. In the Mundy and Odum (1979) book, *Leisure Education: Theory and Practice*, and in its second reprinting in 1998, approximately 100 pages are devoted to the explanation and provision of objectives and activities that are appropriate to each cluster of objectives.

However, even though the "clusters of objectives" work is a more recent development, the Systems Approach Model is the best known and most widely used of Mundy's models. It should be noted that Mundy's works broadly interpret the appropriateness of leisure education for individuals with and without disabilities alike and was the first to propose a developmental, lifespan approach.

Peterson and Gunn's Leisure Education Content Model

Peterson and Gunn's Model was first documented in 1977 and has since undergone several revisions (Gunn, 1977a, 1977b; Gunn & Peterson, 1977; Peterson, 1977; Peterson & Gunn, 1977, 1984; Peterson & Stumbo, 2000; Stumbo & Peterson, 1998, 2004, 2009). The Leisure Education Content Model is one component of a larger conceptualization of therapeutic recreation services, namely the Therapeutic Recreation Service Model or the Leisure Ability Model. Briefly, the other two categories of the Leisure Ability Model are functional intervention and recreation participation. Services within the functional intervention category address functional behavioral areas that are prerequisites to, or a necessary part of, leisure involvement and lifestyle. Recreation participation services strive to provide individuals with opportunities for self-expression, enjoyment, and satisfaction within an organized delivery system. All three components are conceptualized to facilitate the development, maintenance and expression of a satisfying leisure lifestyle.

The leisure education component has been developed into the Leisure Education Content Model. This model has four components:

- leisure awareness
- leisure resources
- social interaction skills
- leisure activity skills

Dattilo's Model of Leisure Education

Dattilo, in the third edition of his text *Leisure Education Program Planning: A Systematic Approach* (2008), lists seven areas important to leisure behavior. Under each of the seven areas, content that therapeutic recreation specialists should facilitate with clients is listed. See Table 2.1.

The next section discusses in more detail the current Stumbo and Peterson (2009) Leisure Education Content Model. Although the four original components have not changed, the content specified under some of the components has.

Table 2.1. Dattilo's Model of Leisure Education (2008)

To appreciate leisure
- Understand leisure
- Consider leisure benefits
- Realize flexibility of leisure
- Identify contexts for leisure

To be aware of self in leisure
- Identify preferences
- Reflect on past participation
- Consider current involvement
- Project future leisure
- Understand skills
- Examine values and attitudes
- Determine satisfaction

To be self-determined in leisure
- Take responsibility
- Make choices
- Terminate involvement
- Become assertive

To interact socially during leisure
- Communicate nonverbally
- Communicate verbally
- Understand social rules
- Acquire social competence
- Develop friendships

To use resources facilitating leisure
- Identify people
- Locate facilities
- Understand participation requirements
- Match skills to activity requirements
- Obtain answers

To make decisions about leisure
- Awareness of self
- Appreciation of leisure
- Development of self-determination
- Ability to identify goals
- Ability to solve problems

To acquire recreation activity skills

The Stumbo and Peterson (2009) Leisure Education Content Model

Although the Leisure Education Content Model has the same limitations as any two-dimensional model trying to depict a complex, multi-dimensional concept, it also presents many advantages to beginners as well as to seasoned professionals. Among these advantages are:

- Leisure education (and all of therapeutic recreation services) views the individual holistically, recognizing that an individual is more than just the sum of his or her parts or pathology. This presents a tremendous opportunity for therapeutic recreation specialists to impact participants in different ways than most health care professionals.

- Leisure education services utilize an educational model, as opposed to the medical model. This implies that individuals are willing and capable of learning and changing former patterns. The educational model operates on the assumption that behavior can change and improve as the individual acquires new knowledge, skills, attitudes, and abilities. These changes occur through a learning process. The client is an active participant in the process, sharing responsibility for the change or growth that is targeted. Although illness or disability must be considered both in the content to be learned and the process through which learning takes place, the illness or disability is not the primary concern at this point. Behavioral growth and change are targeted independently of the person's condition.

- Leisure education services are based on the characteristics and behaviors of non-disabled adult leisure behavior. That is, leisure education is based on normalized, not marginalized, leisure behavior. In this way, participants are much more likely to be learn the skills necessary to be accepted fully into inclusionary or "normal" leisure services and facilities. This allows the individual a more complete range of services from which to choose, rather than being forced into segregated services due to lack of normalized skills and abilities.

- The Leisure Education Content Model is not designed to address the needs of only one specific illness or disability group. The Model crosses disability lines to identify aspects of leisure involvement and lifestyle development. Likewise, it is not specific for any given agency, whether they be clinical, community, or residential settings. The Model has been used to design programs for individuals without disabilities as well as individuals with disabilities. Selection of content and the design of specific intervention techniques obviously will vary depending on the population and setting.

- Categories of leisure education services are interrelated yet flexible. Although the model presents the four components individually, each category of service is related to and dependent on successful learning and behaviors in the other

three categories. This may mean that activities or programs might need to be sequential in their presentation, building on one another, or might be presented simultaneously, depending on the targeted outcomes. The model then becomes flexible to meet the demands of a variety of client groups in a diversity of settings.

Leisure education, then, is the variety of services, activities, and programs used by therapeutic recreation specialists to aid individuals in learning the skills, attitudes, and knowledge necessary for healthy and meaningful leisure involvement. The Model provides both students and practitioners with identified areas of possible client need (and therefore program content) related to the development of various leisure-related skills, knowledge, attitudes, and abilities. According to the Leisure Education Content Model (Stumbo & Peterson, 2009) these areas of program content include: (a) leisure awareness, (b) social and interaction skills, (c) leisure activity skills, and (d) leisure resources. A more detailed description of the content and purpose of each of these categories follows. Figure 2.1 presents this expanded Leisure Education Content Model.

The Four Components of Leisure Education Services

Four components have been conceptualized to identify the major aspects of leisure education content. Each of the four components will be described separately on the following pages.

Leisure Awareness

An important aspect of leisure lifestyle and involvement appears to be a cognitive or intellectual awareness of leisure and its benefits, a valuing of the leisure experience, and a thoughtful decision-making process to activate involvement. These cognitive aspects seem to be what was missing in so much of traditional recreation and therapeutic recreation programming. The erroneous assumption seems to be that individuals only needed to acquire recreation activity skills, and from there, they would apply those skills in some meaningful pattern of leisure involvement. That approach does not seem to influence positively the leisure involvement of most clients beyond the passive participation in the segmented agency-sponsored programs. The more contemporary approach, which focuses on some understanding of leisure, appears to have a better chance of facilitating the development and display of a successful leisure lifestyle. Regardless of whether

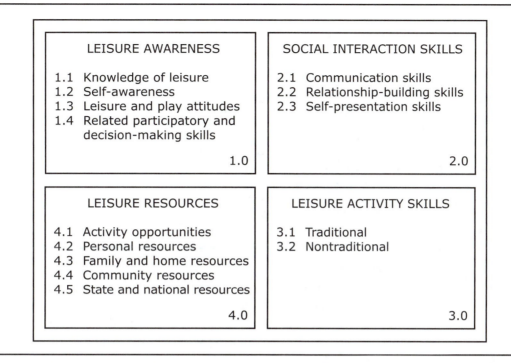

Figure 2.1. Leisure Education Content Model (Stumbo & Peterson, 2009)

individuals immediately respond to leisure education programs offered, they are still exposed to knowledge and information that may be useful to them at some later point.

Within the component of leisure awareness, at least four content areas can be identified that appear essential in facilitating the development and expression of an appropriate leisure lifestyle. The first of these is *knowledge of leisure*. See Table 2.2.

The second area is that of *self-awareness*. This area focuses on a more personal understanding of leisure and the individual. This revolves around what the individual brings to his or her leisure experiences, how he or she shapes them and is shaped by them. This area focuses on the individuality of the leisure experience. Table 2.3 (p. 22) includes some possible content for self-awareness activities.

Because attitudes and values are so important to the acceptance, development, and expression of a leisure lifestyle, this content area is separated from the previous two. *Leisure and play attitudes* is the third content area of the first leisure education component. Within this area, existing attitudes about play and leisure can be explored. This is often a critical point in terms of redirecting, or moving toward change in, leisure lifestyle development. See Table 2.4 (p. 22) for suggestions of content pertaining to leisure and play attitudes.

The fourth content area of the first component is related *leisure participatory and decision-making skills*. This area concentrates on the individual's responsibility for his or her own leisure satisfaction, through planning for, making decisions about, and following through with leisure participation. The combination of these factors may have a great influence

Table 2.2. Possible Content for Leisure Awareness: Knowledge of Leisure

- The concept of leisure and its relation to quality of life
- The difference between leisure behaviors and other behaviors
- Benefits and possible outcomes of leisure involvement
- Necessity or importance of leisure within one's life
- Barriers to leisure involvement
- Forms of leisure involvement
- Finding personal meaning in leisure
- Leisure as a context to learn new skills, meet new people, experience new events
- The concept of leisure lifestyle or pattern of leisure
- The balance between leisure, work, and other obligations
- The concept of personal responsibility for leisure lifestyle

Table 2.3. Possible Content for Leisure Awareness: Self-Awareness

- Actual and perceived abilities and skills that impact leisure involvement
- Actual and perceived limitations that impact leisure involvement
- Effects of a disability or illness on leisure behavior
- Actual versus desired levels of leisure participation
- Influences on the development of a leisure lifestyle
- Past leisure and play patterns and activities
- Effects of the family unit on attitudes toward leisure
- Current leisure involvement and satisfaction
- Areas for future discovery and involvement
- Personal preferences for leisure participation
- Personal resources for leisure involvement
- Goal areas for development through leisure
- Effects of family and friends on personal leisure development

on the individual's perceived leisure satisfaction and enjoyment, and they are quite teachable and learnable. Again, a variety of topics and processes can be identified or content inclusion in this area, as can be seen on Table 2.5.

Many of the above topics are "generic," in that there are several decision-making and problem-solving models that emphasize a general step-by-step approach. These models can be presented with a focus on application to leisure participation. All of these areas are processes that may require substantial time for learning. However, these skills appear essential if meaningful changes are to take place in the individual's leisure lifestyle and involvement.

This fourth area of *related participatory and decision-making skills* also includes topics that may vary considerably, depending on the specific population being served by the program. Examples of topics specific to groups of people with disabilities are outlined on Table 2.6.

These examples are for illustration only. Obviously, none of the lists of possible related participatory skills or topics is complete. In addition, many other populations and settings are not included at all. The reader, however, can develop such topic areas as needed.

This section has identified content related to the first component of the presented leisure education model. The identified content areas need to be conceptualized and developed into appropriate program structures prior to implementation.

Social Interaction Skills

The second component presented here focuses on social interaction skills. Refer back to Figure 2.1 (p. 21) to view the three sub-areas within social interaction skills.

The acquisition of social interaction skills, like any other skill acquisition, requires the planning of specific programs designed to facilitate the learning of the designated behavior. If social interaction skills are identified as a major area of need, then specific programs addressing these skills need to be developed. Depending on the population and setting, social interaction skill development may be a significant aspect of the comprehensive leisure education and therapeutic recreation mission. It is only after some basic skills are mastered that the skills may be practiced in leisure activities. Examples of social interaction skills within various participant groups are included on Table 2.7 (p. 24).

There are many ways to conceptualize social interaction skills. As will be seen in Chapter 11, many

Table 2.4. Possible Content for Leisure Awareness: Leisure and Play Attitudes

- Past, current, and future societal attitudes related to leisure
- Origin of one's personal beliefs and values about leisure
- Relationship between attitudes and behavior
- Appropriateness of former leisure attitudes with regard to current life situation
- How leisure attitudes are developed and modified
- Relationship between leisure attitudes/values and life satisfaction
- How leisure attitudes and values affect leisure involvement
- Prioritizing leisure within one's total lifestyle
- Impact of leisure attitudes on current and future leisure lifestyle
- Evolution of attitudes about leisure throughout the lifespan

models of social skills have been developed over the last four decades. Social development schemes have been provided by various disciplines and some are very extensive. A brief conceptual scheme is presented as part of the social interaction skills component. These three categories are general and are intended to cut across all disability categories. These categories may be very limited, however, when applied to a specific disability group or to a given individual. The scheme is described here to provide just one brief view of some considerations within the social interaction area.

Table 2.5. Possible Content for Leisure Awareness: Leisure Participatory and Decision-Making Skills

- Decision-making skills with regard to leisure involvement
- Leisure planning skills
- Problem-solving techniques for daily use
- Long-term coping and adaptation strategies
- Creating and evaluating options for leisure participation
- Taking responsibility for leisure decisions
- Managing and prioritizing time for leisure
- Allocating personal resources for leisure involvement
- Reducing and managing stress through conscious planning and decision-making

---

Table 2.6. Possible Content for Leisure Awareness: Leisure Participatory and Decision-Making Skills Specific to Groups of Individuals with Disabilities

Substance Abuse Center for Addicts
- Selecting sober activities for involvement
- Developing a positive attitude toward leisure
- Making choices about how time is managed/used
- Making sober leisure a lifestyle priority
- Identifying barriers to sober leisure involvement
- Using a structured system for making healthy, sobriety-enhancing choices
- Selecting health-promoting activities of interest

Group Home for Individuals with Intellectual Disabilities
- Reviewing options for leisure involvement
- Planning for involvement in leisure events
- Planning for holidays and special events
- Making choices about segregated or inclusionary participation
- Examining consequences of participation or non-participation
- Making choices about leisure involvement and participation
- Deciding which leisure activities are most enjoyable
- Reducing problems or barriers to leisure involvement

Rehabilitation Center for Individuals with Spinal Cord Injuries
- Asking appropriate questions about physical accessibility of transportation
- Asking for assistance when necessary
- Deciding how to spend personal energy throughout the day
- Locating information about resources available to individuals with spinal cord injuries
- Learning to problem-solve how to remain safe during involvement
- Interacting with nondisabled people in leisure participation (friends, staff, strangers)
- Deciding in which activity opportunities to participate
- Making long-term adjustments to a personal leisure lifestyle

Psychiatric Inpatient Unit for Individuals with Mental Health Difficulties
- Planning for leisure involvement post-discharge
- Using leisure to counter the effects of living with stressful situations
- Making appropriate decisions with regard to leisure involvement
- Making daily choices for leisure on the unit
- Deciding which leisure skills the individual would like to learn
- Planning for leisure participation, considering fatigue levels, interest, availability, etc.
- Problem-solving difficult social situations

Table 2.7. Possible Content for Social Interaction Skills Specific to Groups of Individuals with Disabilities

Individuals with Intellectual Disabilities
- Appropriate conversation openings and closings
- Maintaining eye contact during conversation
- Listening attentively to the speaker
- Physical proximity to others while talking
- Taking turns at the appropriate time
- Setting boundaries for self-disclosure
- Good oral hygiene

Individuals with Spinal Cord Injury
- Building trust in relationships
- Responsibility for dressing and attire
- Being able to ask for assistance as necessary
- Locating and using social supports
- Appropriately expressing emotions

Individuals with Substance Addictions
- Controlling and expressing anger
- Negotiating conflicts assertively
- Being social while being sober
- Being able to take another's perspective
- Respecting the rights of others
- Problem-solving in socially challenging situations

Communication Skills. This set of skills enables an individual to communicate with others. It is felt that clear and honest communication is a necessity in everyday life, and since so much of leisure is social by nature, communication becomes important in this area as well. Many client groups have needs in this area, and an improvement in skills would enable them to participate more appropriately with others in a variety of leisure pursuits. A host of skills may be taught in this area, but some typical topics are included on Table 2.8.

Relationship-Building Skills. Relationship-building skills address those areas that assist an individual in locating, maintaining, and developing friendships and other relationships. Significant others play important roles in most people's lives and many skills are needed to maintain and sustain healthy relationships.

Social networks and social support are important aspects to most individuals, and leisure pursuits provide many opportunities to develop these. Some client groups will need more work on social skills than others. Most individuals, however, find that relationships are an important contributor to their quality of life. Some typical skills that might be taught in this area are included in Table 2.9.

Self-Presentation Skills. In order for communication skills and relationship building skills to be utilized, the individual also must maintain some basic social etiquette. Some clients groups will need more training in this area than others, but all will need to exhibit fundamental baseline skills. Often, the lack of these skills prevents an individual from being accepted and becoming friends with or meeting other individuals. Examples of these skills are included on Table 2.10.

Social interaction ability is an essential aspect of successful leisure involvement and lifestyle. Since the behaviors and skills involved can be learned and are, for the most part, independent of illness or disability itself, it is included as a component of leisure education. If the development of interaction skills is a need of clients, then appropriate programs need to be conceptualized and implemented that focus on this area. The absence of adequate interaction ability can be as much a barrier to leisure involvement as the absence of activity skills or knowledge of leisure and its significance.

This section does not intend to discount or ignore those leisure activities and experiences that the individual engages in and enjoys while alone. Indeed, there is a great need to assist individuals in developing a repertoire of activities and interests that can be done alone. Likewise, helping them to understand the need for and develop a positive attitude toward solitary leisure appears to be a significant aspect of an overall leisure lifestyle. This section, however, focuses on interaction skills that are not utilized within solitary leisure experiences.

Table 2.8. Possible Content for Communication Skills

- Assertiveness skills
- Communicating needs, wants, and desires effectively
- Skills involving negotiation, disagreement, conflict, and compromise
- Conversational skills
- Active listening skills and responsive behavior
- Expressing feelings and thoughts
- Social proximity and distance; body language; gestures; eye contact; touching
- Information-seeking and information-giving skills
- Empathy and perspective-taking skills

Table 2.9. Possible Content for Relationship Building Skills

- Greeting and initiation skills, such as locating leisure partners
- Forming appropriate attachments to and connections with people
- Friendship development skills
- Self-disclosure and privacy issues
- Cooperation and competitive skills
- Developing and maintaining social networks
- Helping others in time of need
- Reciprocal social support (expressing care and concern for others and vice versa)

Table 2.10. Possible Content for Self-Presentation Skills

- Skills involving politeness, etiquette, and manners, such as taking turns, sharing, etc.
- Body image and body awareness
- Hygiene, health, and grooming skills
- Appropriate attire and dressing for height, weight, weather, and activity
- Responsibility for self-care

Leisure Skills Development

Expressing a satisfying leisure lifestyle implies that the individual has a sense of freedom and choice in leisure involvement. Choice involves having options and alternatives. Consequently, it appears logical that a repertoire of leisure activities and related interests is necessary for meaningful experiences. The issue is not simply one of acquiring as many leisure skills as possible. It seems more important to assist the individual in selecting and developing adequate skills in a number of activities that potentially could be sources of enjoyment and personal satisfaction for the individual across his or her lifespan.

In the past, most activity-skill-development programs have focused on traditional recreation activities. These activities are ones commonly identified as recreational and sanctioned by the society. They have been promoted and programmed by the leisure and recreation profession. Countless classification and categorical systems have been developed to identify them. Table 2.11 presents an example of the types of activities frequently referred to within the traditional recreation category.

There is nothing inherently wrong or inappropriate with activities that fall under the label of traditional recreation. Indeed, individuals with disabling conditions may need and want activity skills from the traditional categories. The problem, however, is the assumption that only these activities are important or appropriate. Observing what adults actually do with their leisure results in very different list of activities and events. Table 2.12 attempts to identify by category the types of adult leisure pursuits and involvements that are common. These are in addition to the traditional activities previously identified.

Involvement in nontraditional leisure activities more adequately represents the content and nature of adult leisure lifestyles. Many of the actions are engaged in alone or with significant others, as opposed to organized activity-centered groups. Many of the activities are less structured, with fewer exact procedures or rules. Most often the environment for participation is

---

Table 2.11. Possible Content for "Traditional" Leisure Activities

---

- Team and Individual Sports
- Dance
- Aquatics and Water-Related Activities
- Drama
- Outdoor Activities
- Music
- Arts and Crafts
- Other Expressive Arts
- Mental Games and Activities
- Hobbies

---

the home or some general environment, as opposed to a specific recreation facility. The dimension of time is also different for many of the activities. Nontraditional activities are less likely to require a specific amount of time or time scheduled by someone else. An immediately obvious difference between these activities and traditional recreation activities is the absence of a program structure by a leisure service delivery agency.

Table 2.12. Possible Content for "Nontraditional" Leisure Activities

---

- Social Interaction
- Spectating and Appreciating
- Leadership and Community Service
- Fitness and Exercise
- Relaxation and Meditation
- Cognitive and Mental Activities
- Eating
- Food Preparation
- Shopping
- Home Improvement
- Maintenance of Living Things—Pets and Plants
- Self-Development
- Education
- Computer and Internet Activities; Social Media
- Travel
- Fantasy and Daydreaming
- Intimacy and Sexually Related Activity
- Substance Use—Alcohol, Drugs, Tobacco
- Volunteering and Community Service
- Meditative Practices, such as Tai Chi Chuan, Yoga, Prayer, Walking
- Nothing
- Home Maintenance
- Going to Auctions and Sales
- Interaction with Family and Friends
- Telephone/E-mail Conversations
- Online Social Networking
- Spa Experiences or Grooming, such as Manicures, Facials, Pedicures
- Virtual Reality
- Geocaching

Assisting the client in the development of appropriate leisure skills takes on new dimensions when using this leisure lifestyle approach. The concern shifts from focus on the skills of a specific traditional activity to broader participatory abilities that include knowledge of leisure possibilities, selecting and learning appropriate leisure activities, and integrating leisure involvement within the total life situation. This does not mean that specific leisure skills are not part of the total programming focus. It merely means that specific activity skills must be viewed and selected within a broader context.

In clinical and community settings, there is a need for leisure skills development programs for individuals with disabling conditions. Indeed, many clients lack specific and general leisure activity skills appropriate for a meaningful, ongoing leisure lifestyle. The task of the therapeutic recreation specialist is the selection of appropriate content for these leisure skill development programs. The concept of leisure lifestyle and the previously identified lists of activity categories may be useful in the selection process. Table 2.13 presents some of the criteria for selecting leisure skills to be taught to clients.

It is obviously difficult to determine how many and what kinds of leisure activity skills an individual needs. There are no absolutes or established standards that can be applied. Indeed, the absence of such global absolutes should be respected. The concept of an individualized and unique leisure lifestyle and activity repertoire deserves to be protected. Professional knowledge and judgment of the therapeutic recreation specialist, with input from the client, becomes the basis for decision making related to the development of a leisure-skill repertoire of a given client. A well-developed, comprehensive scheme or model of leisure lifestyle that includes leisure skills can be very useful in the assessment and programming efforts related to this component of leisure education.

Leisure Resources

Leisure Resources is the fourth component of the Leisure Education Content Model. The establishment and expression of an appropriate leisure lifestyle appears to be dependent on knowledge of leisure resources and the ability to utilize these resources. It should not be assumed that clients have a basic knowledge of information acquisition and utilization. Sometimes, therapeutic recreation specialists have not identified the importance of locating resources and assisting the client in acquiring the ability to be independent through the use of such resources. The concept of an independent leisure lifestyle requires that the client be able to seek out information and use it appropriately.

The Leisure Resources component highlights five areas: (a) activity opportunities, (b) personal resources, (c) family and home resources, (d), community resources, and (e) state and national resources. The following section provide more specific details for each of these areas.

Activity Opportunities. Many clients may need information regarding the vast number of different leisure activities available. Thus, identifying possible leisure activities could be a valuable area of program content. Helping clients understand the wide range of activities available to them is important to allowing them choice and freedom in decision making. Increased knowledge of the potential of diverse activities translates into increased opportunities for selecting options that are intrinsically motivating, interesting, and challenging to the individual. Not to be confused with the actual development of activity skills, knowledge of activity opportunities means that the individual understands that the list of possible activities for participation may be limitless. The individual cannot be responsible for choice and self-selection of activities that he/she knows nothing about. The intent here is both to expand the clients' awareness of leisure opportunities as well as to assist them in identifying preferences for possible inclusion in their personal repertoire. This goes beyond

---

Table 2.13. Additional Criteria for Selecting Leisure Skills for Client Instruction

- Choice by the individual (selected from a range of options)
- Within functional ability and interests of the clients (evaluated through activity analysis)
- Feasible for clients' resources (money, equipment, access to facilities, etc.)
- Compatible with the overall life situation of the individual
- Compatible with leisure interests of those with whom the individual may live
- Age-appropriate but also provide opportunity for continued development and involvement at later life stages
- Other considerations (e.g., place of residence, socioeconomic status, educational level, ethnicity, and religion)
- Opportunity for continuing leisure involvement rather than on a short-term focus
- Transfer of responsibility for leisure involvement to clients and helping them define and prepare for a leisure lifestyle independent of the current agency program structure
- Nature and mandate of the agency delivering the services

the more generic "knowledge of leisure" content covered in Leisure Awareness (p. 20). Many clients simply do not know the varied options available for leisure, and they need to be made aware of the specific, available choices that may become alternatives for their later participation.

Personal Resources. Because leisure is not well-understood, many individuals may have limited awareness of possible leisure involvement that is already within their ability and experience. Identifying these resources can expand individuals' leisure repertoire considerably by merely bringing attention to the opportunity. Examples of this might be verbal and interaction ability that can be used for leisure enjoyment. For some individuals, walking and jogging are possible leisure activities. This category also can be expanded to identify functional abilities and limitations that influence leisure. Other characteristics, such as finances, educational level, athleticism, creativity, and past leisure experiences, can be explored for possible present day and future leisure involvement.

Family and Home Resources. The people with whom one lives (family members, partners, friends, or individuals in the facility) can be considered leisure resources. Thus, the identification of leisure interests of others can expand the repertoire of leisure possibilities for a given client. The "home," whether it is the client's own house or a facility in which he or she lives, is another source of potential leisure involvement. Since most people spend a considerable amount of time in their places of residence, the home becomes an important leisure resource. Frequently, assistance is needed to help the client identify various aspects of the home that are possible leisure resources. Obvious ones, such as television, books, magazines, and games, are easily identified. However, general objects and places often are more abstract. Newspapers, the kitchen, a garage, plants, and pets often are overlooked as leisure resources. When engaged in such discussion, identifying "what is" can be supplemented with "what could be." How objects or places could be used for leisure involvement is an interesting and expanding experience, especially for those individuals for whom the home may be the primary environment for leisure involvement.

Community Resources. Most communities have a variety of agencies, commercial enterprises, places, and facilities that are leisure resources. It cannot be assumed that a given client is aware of these opportunities. Thus, some aspect of programming needs to focus on the identification of these leisure resources, as well as on a consideration of the participatory requirements. Most commonly recognized recreation resources would include the public recreation programs, services, and facilities, such as a city's recreation department or park district; programs offered through the school district, often listed as adult education or community education; and the voluntary, nonprofit agency programs and facilities, such as the YMCA, YWCA, Scouting, Campfire, and Boys' and Girls' Clubs.

Within the leisure lifestyle philosophy, many other leisure resources would be identified. Commercial recreation plays a major role in the leisure involvement of most people; therefore, these resources also need to be identified and understood. Bowling alleys, movie theaters, billiards centers, dance studios, golf courses, game arcades, and roller- and ice-skating rinks are a few examples of commercial recreation activity establishments. Swim clubs, racquet clubs, health spas, and fitness centers are examples of another type of commercial leisure involvement. Commercial transportation options may be another area of concern for clients. The commercial category can be extended to a wide variety of other establishments. For example, arts and crafts, fabric and yarn, in-line skate rental facilities, and photography stores often sponsor classes and other group participation opportunities. Within most communities, a large number of non-agency-sponsored clubs exist. Examples would be square dance, bridge, motorcycle, or model airplane clubs.

Youth, social, and service organizations and clubs also are considered part of the leisure resource network. Thus, groups like Soroptomists, Lions, and Rotary International need to be identified for possible leisure resources. In addition, the multiple opportunities for volunteer work or service can be viewed as a leisure opportunity. Newer additions to the list may include Internet sites, chat rooms, electronic bulletin boards, web television, and the like. Obviously, a complete list of possible leisure resources in a community cannot be identified here. The issue remains: a broad conceptualization of community resources is needed, and an appropriate method of introducing this information to clients is important.

State and National Resources. In addition to the personal, immediate home environment and community resources, there are leisure opportunities on a state and national level that may be appropriate to introduce to clients. This area can be conceptualized many ways, since there are multiple public and commercial resources and opportunities. By definition, information about travel is imperative within this category.

The knowledge and awareness of leisure resources is only one aspect of this component of leisure education. Equally important is the area of utilization skills related to resources. Of primary significance is assisting clients in being able to identify and locate leisure re-sources on their own. This information, along with the knowledge of various participatory and utilization aspects, is vital in the process of facilitating an inde-pendent leisure lifestyle. For most individuals, obtain-ing and being able to utilize these skills require the opportunity to practice them in natural settings. Uti-lizing skills in naturalized situations parallel to future independent involvement typically increases the trans-ferability and generalizability of the skills learned. Clients are most successful later in the community when they have had ample opportunity to practice and use a set of skills under the guidance of a specialist. Professionals should consider allowing clients adequate experiences to gain mastery of skills necessary for pro-jected involvement.

Leisure Education Efficacy Research

Research on leisure education as an intervention is a reasonably recent phenomena, with most research be-ing published since 1990. Prior to that, most leisure education literature was descriptive in nature and de-scribed leisure education models and/or program con-tent. However, at least two intervention studies were published as early as 1982.

While leisure education research has covered near-ly all client groups of therapeutic recreation services, the majority of published studies have involved (a) older adults, (b) at-risk or emotionally disturbed youth, (c) individuals who have experienced strokes, and (d) individuals with intellectual disabilities.

Due to space limitations, only a handful of studies from each area will be reviewed here. The reviewed studies were selected based on the following criteria: (a) the study contained a leisure education intervention program, (b) the intervention program contained ele-ments of leisure education found in the Leisure Educa-tion Content Model (Stumbo & Peterson, 2009); (c) the study evaluated the effects of the leisure education program on clients/participants, (c) the publication was available in full text. While this is not a systematic review of the leisure education literature, the studies selected are representative of those in print.

At-Risk Youth

Reynolds and Arthur (1982) studied the efficacy of a peer-modeling and cognitive self-guidance program on the social play of eight 7- to 11-year-olds diagnosed with behavior disorders. The eight children were ran-domly assigned into a treatment and a control group,

with treatment reversal. The intervention involved vid-eotaped models and then an in-person instructor who demonstrated cooperative play using a block picture toy. The researchers looked at whether these two types of training would impact the cooperative play skills of the children over time and with other toys. Their results indicated that the training resulted in a short-term increase in cooperative play for the individuals in each group after they had experienced the training. However, the effects did not carry over to additional toys. They noted this strategy has promise for children with behavior disorders but needs more time. They felt the intervention was practical, economical, and easily taught to various staff.

Aguilar (1987) conducted a study on a leisure education program that was held for two hours per day, one day per week, for five weeks. The five top-ics included: (a) leisure awareness, (b) self-awareness, (c) leisure skills, (d) decision-making skills, and (e) social interaction. The sample included 60 youth, age 12 to 18, living in a juvenile correctional institution in north-central Texas. The 60 youth were randomly assigned to either the treatment or control group, and due to retention problems, only 38 completed the study (20 in treatment, 18 in control). The investigator de-veloped and tested the Adolescent Attitudes Scale, which had three major factors: (a) recreation (e.g., music, television), (b) delinquency (e.g., fist fights, shoplifting), and (c) delinquency-related (e.g., drugs, alcohol). The results were mixed: (a) the control group reported more positive attitudes toward recreation activities; (b) the control group reported more positive attitudes toward delinquent activities; and (c) there was no difference between the two groups with regard to delinquency-related attitudes. Aguilar suggested the leisure education program be expanded, that this study be replicated, and that additional outcomes besides at-titudes be studied.

Long (2001) studied the infusion of leisure edu-cation in a transition-planning program for students with emotional disturbances as they moved from high school to adult life in the community. The intent of the program was to determine if participation would (a) affect their knowledge of leisure and transition plan-ning, (b) impact their participation at transition plan-ning meetings, and (c) result in inclusion of student leisure preferences in the student's IEP. Fifteen students (7 in treatment and 8 in control group) took part in the study. The intervention lasted four weeks, meet-ing three times per week: twice in a leisure education/ transition planning program, and once per week with a teacher and a therapeutic recreation specialist focus-ing on lifelong physical activities in the community. The program was effective in improving student knowledge and involvement in the transition planning process. Both students and teachers reported positive effects.

Older Adults

Mahon and Searle have been involved in a number of leisure education intervention studies. Three of those studies, all focusing on older adults, will be reviewed here. Mahon and Searle (1994) studied 44 older adults who attended a municipal day hospital in Canada. The subjects were divided into treatment (22 subjects) and control groups (22 subjects). The leisure education intervention was implemented for eight weeks for one hour per week. The content included improvement of knowledge of leisure resources and leisure-related skills and the role of leisure within a lifestyle. The outcomes measured included leisure participation, life satisfaction, and leisure satisfaction. The results show that the intervention had positive, significant effects for the treatment group on measures of leisure participation and life satisfaction, but not on leisure satisfaction. However, the gains were not sustained at the three-month follow-up.

Searle, Mahon, and colleagues (1995) studied older Canadians who had reported that their leisure participation had been recently restricted. Thirteen individuals were in the treatment group and 15 were in the control group. The intervention consisted of 12 units that employed techniques such as discussion exercises, paper-and-pencil exercises, role playing, and recreation activity participation accompanied by a self-directed, self-paced learning manual. Individuals within the group took 14 to 25 weeks to finish the manual, with the average number of weeks being 17. The treatment group had significant positive increases in leisure control, leisure competence, and life satisfaction, as well as significant decreases in leisure boredom.

In a follow-up study published in 1998, Searle, Mahon, and colleagues re-tested 22 of the original sample of 28 older Canadians (10 in the treatment and 10 in the control group). Improvements in leisure control and leisure competence, as well as decreases in leisure boredom, were found at the follow-up. Positive increases in life satisfaction were not maintained; however, positive increases in generalized locus of control were seen (although increased locus of control was not found in the original post-test). They concluded that leisure education can foster feelings of competence, control, and a sense of independence in older adults.

Janssen (2004) focused on quality of life for older adults after receiving a leisure education intervention. The sample consisted of 47 residents, ranging in age from 62 to 99, from three residential retirement facili-

ties in the midwestern United States. The subjects were randomly assigned to either the treatment or control. The treatment group received a six-week leisure education intervention that focused on leisure appreciation, awareness of self in leisure, self-determination in leisure, making decisions, knowledge and utilization of resources facilitating leisure, and leisure and quality of life. The results showed that the leisure education intervention positively influenced scores on getting out with others, having hobbies, indoor and outdoor activities, and socializing with family and friends. Janssen noted:

> Having a greater understanding of the role that leisure has in the perceptions of quality of life allowed the participants an opportunity to relate leisure to other aspects of their lives, learning that through an active and healthy leisure lifestyle, individuals may take control of the possibilities that enhance their independence and freedom to choose. (Janssen, 2004, p. 284)

Older Adults with Strokes

Drummond and Walker (1995) conducted a randomized control trial of 65 older individuals from the United Kingdom. They randomized individuals into three groups: (a) "leisure rehabilitation," (b) occupational therapy, and (c) control group with no intervention. The Nottingham Leisure Questionnaire was used as a pre- and post-test measure. The content of the home-visit-based leisure rehabilitation program included ADLs, equipment, adaptations, advice on funding and transportation, and liaison with community resources. They found that the leisure rehabilitation group received significantly higher scores than individuals from the other two groups, for their frequency of participating in leisure activities. They concluded: "leisure rehabilitation is an effective way of maintaining and increasing leisure participation after stroke" (p. 289). They added: "There is a possibility that providing a counseling service on leisure could be as valuable as providing an actual treatment package [of occupational therapy]" (p. 289).

Nour, Desrosiers, Guathier, and Carbonneau (2002) used a treatment/control group design with 13 individuals from Quebec who had experienced a stroke. The leisure education program focused on self-awareness, leisure awareness, and competency development over 10 sessions and was individualized to each client. The control group was given a "social" program as a placebo. The leisure education group scored significantly better on the psychological, physical, and total scales measuring quality of life. No significant changes were found in levels of depression. The field notes from the researcher also revealed that (a) participants were more interested in resuming former activities than learning new ones, (b) home-based activities were preferred over community-based, (c) home activities were more frequent with the presence of a in-home caregiver, (d) barriers included lack of ability, anxiety about stigma, apprehension about community accessibility, and fatigue. The investigators reported that the leisure education program was successful in raising at least some aspects of quality of life for older adults with stroke.

Desrosiers and colleagues (2007) conducted a treatment/control group study with pre- and post-tests of elderly Canadians who had experienced stroke. Thirty-three individuals were in the treatment group and 29 were in the control group. The leisure education intervention consisted of a home-based program delivered once a week for 8 to 12 weeks. The leisure education program was the same as described above in Nour et al. (2002). They used a range of data collection instruments and concluded that the experimental/ treatment group (a) participated in more active than passive leisure activities, (b) had longer duration of activities, (c) participated in a greater number of activities, and (d) felt higher satisfaction and lower depression. They found no statistical significance on general well-being and overall health-related quality of life. On distinguishing reasons why this study produced significant results when other comparable studies did not, the authors highlighted the importance of the *content* and *process* of leisure education:

> The program is mainly based on an educational process that aims to enhance the empowerment of participants in optimizing their leisure. By recognizing the importance of leisure in their lives, by having a better perception of their value and residual abilities, and by developing competency in using and integrating resources related to leisure, participants might achieve a higher level of engagement in leisure. (p. 1099)

Individuals with Intellectual Disabilities

Bedini, Bullock, and Driscoll (1993) examined whether leisure education taught within a public school system had a significant effect on students' transition from secondary school to adult life. A total of 38 individuals with intellectual disabilities completed both pre- and post-test measures. The 10-unit curriculum focused on: (a) leisure awareness, (b) self-awareness in leisure, (c) leisure opportunities, (d) community resource awareness, (e) barriers, (f) personal resources and responsibility, (g) planning, (h) planning an outing, (i) the outing, and (j) outing evaluation and future plans. The leisure

education program was delivered both in small group and one-to-one session formats and was held twice a week for 26 weeks. The treatment group did not differ from the control on measures of competence, perceived control, communication, social skills, self-esteem, and satisfaction. Identifying and participating in leisure activities did improve for the leisure education group. Both teachers and parents of individuals in the leisure education group reported positive outcomes in terms of social skills, leisure skills, and assertiveness.

Dattilo and Hoge (1999) tested the Transition through Recreation and Integration for Life (TRAIL) leisure education program, a program similar to the one used above by Bedini et al. (1993). It included leisure education instruction of five units (leisure appreciation, social interaction and friendship, leisure resources, self-determination, and decision making), fortnightly meetings with family members, and leisure coaches to accompany participants into the community and to advocate to community providers. They found that participants showed higher positive affect (smiles, etc.) during community leisure participation than in the classroom and after the intervention had ended. The participants also demonstrated acquisition of knowledge related to leisure participation. Participants, teachers, and parents all felt the TRAIL program was important and supported its continued use.

Lanagan and Dattilo (1989) used a single subject ABAB design, such that the 40 participants with intellectual disabilities were involved in a recreation participation program (A), then a leisure education (B), and then both were repeated. Two types of leadership styles, democratic and authoritarian, were employed during the two phases of leisure education. The four-week leisure education program included (a) benefits and rationale for leisure, (b) barriers to leisure participation, (c) sources of information, and (d) hobbies and other recreation activities. They found that the behavior increased from baseline to recreation participation but went even higher during leisure education. They also found no difference between the sessions led with democratic or authoritarian styles. The investigators noted that participants were most involved during leisure education sessions, regardless of leadership style, and the leisure education program improved knowledge retention. They encouraged therapeutic recreation specialists to include leisure education in their services.

Mahon and Goatcher (1999) used a quasi-experimental study on 10 older adults with intellectual disabilities to assess the effectiveness of a leisure education intervention to improve life and leisure satisfaction and reduce leisure constraints. The leisure education program focused on later-life planning and was divided into three phases: (a) retirement, leisure awareness, and decision making, (b) planning for a hopeful future, and (c) leisure initiation. The treatment group did experience a significant increase in leisure and life satisfaction, and although they had a reduction in leisure constraints, it was not significant. They concluded that the intervention could be more targeted to address constraints, but was effective in contributing to later-life planning for older adults with intellectual disabilities.

These are but a few of scores of studies of the effectiveness of leisure education interventions. Although they are varied in the groups under study, their variables of interest, their leisure education content, and their methods of investigation, in general we can conclude:

- Leisure education is a viable and valuable service to individuals who are older and/or have disabilities/illnesses; and, in fact, it may in some cases be more efficacious than other therapies.
- Leisure education is applicable to a wide range of client conditions.
- Although there are variations, leisure education program content tends to focus on (a) leisure awareness, (b) social and interaction skills, (c) leisure activity skills, and (d) leisure resource knowledge and utilization.
- Leisure education research has enjoyed more stringent methodologies in recent years.
- Leisure education research has enjoyed a growing interest in theory-based and model-based interventions.
- Leisure education research continues to be of interest to leisure investigators worldwide, with no hint of decline.

Summary

- Leisure education is a broad category of services that helps individuals with disabilities and/or illnesses to acquire and utilize leisure-related attitudes, knowledges, and skills.
- Facilitation techniques and treatment modalities need to be evidence-based in order to provide the most benefit to clients.
- Leisure is important to health and well-being.
- Leisure education, or its predecessors recreation counseling or avocational counseling, had its beginnings in the late 1950s, and through the years many leisure education models and literature have been produced.

- The model chosen for this book is the Leisure Education Content Model (Stumbo & Peterson, 2009) that contains: (a) leisure awareness, (b) social and interaction skills, (c) leisure activity skills, and (d) leisure resources.
- Leisure education intervention research on a number of groups who receive therapeutic recreation services is growing in popularity. Methods are becoming more stringent, more theory- and model-based, and diverse.
- Most leisure education research shows promising results in achieving participant outcomes. More research is always needed.

References

Aguilar, T. E. (1987). Effects of a leisure education program on expressed attitudes of delinquent adolescents. *Therapeutic Recreation Journal, 21*(4), 43–51.

Bedini, L. A., Bullock, C. C., & Driscoll, L. B. (1993). The effects of leisure education on factors contributing to the successful transition of students with mental retardation from school to adult life. *Therapeutic Recreation Journal, 27*(2), 70–82.

Caldwell, L. L., Baldwin, C. K., Walls, T., & Smith, E. A. (2004). Preliminary effects of a leisure education program to promote healthy use of free time among middle school adolescents. *Journal of Leisure Research, 36*(3), 310–335.

Chinn, K. A., & Joswiak, K. F. (1981). Leisure education and leisure counseling. *Therapeutic Recreation Journal, 15*(4), 4–7.

Compton, D. W., & Goldstein, J. E. (Eds.). (1977). *Perspectives of leisure counseling*. Alexandria, VA: National Recreation and Park Association.

Dattilo, J. (2008). *Leisure education program planning: A systematic approach* (3rd ed.). State College, PA: Venture Publishing, Inc.

Dattilo, J., & Hoge, G. (1999). Effects of a leisure education program on youth with mental retardation. *Education and Training in Mental Retardation and Developmental Disabilities, 34*(1), 20–34.

Desrosiers, J., Noreau, L., Rochette, A., Carbonneau, H., Fontaine, L., Viscogliosi, C., et al. (2007). Effect of a home leisure education program after stroke: A randomized controlled trial. *Archives of Physical Medicine and Rehabilitation, 88*, 1095–1100.

Drummond, A. E., & Walker, M. F. (1995). A randomized controlled trial of leisure rehabilitation after stroke. *Clinical Rehabilitation, 9*, 283–290.

Dowd, E. T. (Ed.). (1984). *Leisure counseling: Concepts and applications*. Springfield, IL: Charles C. Thomas.

Edwards, P. B. (1977). The bridges of leisure counseling. In D. M. Compton & J. E. Goldstein (Eds.), *Perspectives of leisure counseling* (pp. 37–57). Alexandria, VA: National Recreation and Park Association.

Epperson, A., Witt, P. A., & Hitzhusen, G. (Eds.). (1977). *Leisure counseling: An aspect of leisure education*. Springfield, IL: Charles C. Thomas.

Gunn, S. L. (1977a). Leisure counseling using techniques of assertiveness training and values clarification. In G. Hitzhusen, G. O'Morrow, & J. Oliver (Eds.), *Expanding horizons in therapeutic recreation IV* (pp. 35–41). Columbia, MO: Curators University of Missouri.

Gunn, S. L. (1977b). A systems approach to leisure counseling. *Leisure Today/JOPER,* (April), 8–11.

Gunn, S. L., & Peterson, C. A. (1977). Therapy and leisure education. *Parks and Recreation, 12*(11), 22–25, 51–52.

Hayes, G. (1974). *Model of leisure education and counseling in therapeutic recreation*. Unpublished paper, Ontario, Canada: University of Waterloo.

Hayes, G. A. (1977a). Leisure education and recreation counseling. In A. Epperson, P. A. Witt, & G. Hitzhusen (Eds.), *Leisure counseling: An aspect of leisure education* (pp. 208–218). Springfield, IL: Charles C. Thomas.

Hayes, G. (1977b). Leisure education and recreation counseling. In D. M. Compton & J. E. Goldstein (Eds.), *Perspectives of leisure counseling* (pp. 77–87). Alexandria, VA: National Recreation and Park Association.

Hayes, G. (1977c). Professional preparation and leisure counseling. *Leisure Today/ JOPER,* (April), 12–14.

Humphrey, F., Kelley, J. D., & Hamilton, E. J. (Eds.). (1980). *Facilitating leisure development for the disabled: A status report on leisure counseling*. College Park, MD: The University of Maryland.

Janssen, M. A. (2004). The effects of leisure education on quality of life in older adults. *Therapeutic Recreation Journal, 38*(3), 275–288.

Lanagan, D. Y., & Dattilo, J. (1989). Effects of leisure education using different leadership styles on adults with mental retardation. *Therapeutic Recreation Journal, 23*(4), 62–72.

Lee, Y., & McCormick, B. P. (2002). Toward evidence-based therapeutic recreation practice. In D. R. Austin, J. Dattilo, & B. P. McCormick (Eds.), *Conceptual*

foundations for therapeutic recreation. (pp. 165–184). State College, PA: Venture Publishing, Inc.

Leisure Today/Journal of Physical Education and Recreation. (1977). Volume 48.

Long, T. D. (2001). *Constructivist and didactic leisure education programs for at-risk youth: Enhancing knowledge, meaning, and behavioral intentions*. Dissertation, University of Utah.

Mahon, M. J., & Goatcher, S. (1999). Later-life planning for older adults with mental retardation: A field experiment. *Mental Retardation, 37*(5), 371–382.

Mahon, M. J., & Searle, M. S. (1994). Leisure education: Its effect on older adults. *JOPERD: The Journal of Physical Education, Recreation, & Dance, 64*(4), 36–41.

Mannell, R. C. (2006). Health, well-being, and leisure. In E. L. Jackson (ed.), *Leisure and the quality of life: Impacts on social, economic and cultural development, Hangzhou Consensus* (pp. 65–74). Zhejiang University Press.

McDowell, C. F. (1973). *Approaching leisure counseling with a Self-Leisure Interest Profile (SLIP)*. Unpublished Master's thesis, California State University-Los Angeles.

McDowell, C. F. (1974). Leisure counseling: Review of emerging concepts and orientations. *Journal of Leisurability, 2*(4), 1–26.

McDowell, C. F. (1975). *Suggested leisure counseling model: Its use and effectiveness in a therapeutic community*. Unpublished doctoral dissertation, University of Utah, Salt Lake City, UT.

McDowell, C. F. (1976a). Leisure counseling: Professional considerations for therapeutic recreation. *Journal of Physical Education and Recreation, 47*(1), 26–27.

McDowell, C. F. (1976b). *Leisure counseling: Selected lifestyle processes*. Eugene, OR: Center for Leisure Studies, University of Oregon.

McDowell, C. F. (1977a). An analysis of leisure counseling orientations and models and their integrative possibilities. In D. M. Compton & J. E. Goldstein (Eds.), *Perspectives of leisure counseling* (pp. 59–75). Alexandria, VA: National Recreation and Park Association.

McDowell, C. F. (1977b). Integrating theory and practice in leisure counseling. *Leisure Today/JOPER,* (April), 27–30.

McDowell, C. F. (1977c). Leisure counseling: A review of emerging concepts and orientations. In A. Epperson, P. A. Witt, & G. Hitzhusen (Eds.), *Leisure counseling: An aspect of leisure education* (pp. 137–148). Springfield, IL: Charles C. Thomas.

McDowell, C. F. (1979). Leisure well-being: A counseling mandate? *Leisure Information Newsletter, 6*(1), 6–8.

McDowell, C. F. (1980a). *Counseling for leisure.* Englewood Cliffs, NJ: Prentice-Hall, Inc.

McDowell, C. F. (1980b). Leisure counseling issues: Reviews, overviews and previews. In F. Humphrey, J. D. Kelley, & E. Hamilton (Eds.), *Facilitating leisure development for the disabled: A status report on leisure counseling.* College Park, MD: University of Maryland.

McDowell, C. F. (1984). Leisure: Consciousness, well-being, and counseling. In E. T. Dowd (Ed.), *Leisure counseling: Concepts and applications* (pp. 5–51). Springfield, IL: Charles C. Thomas.

Mundy, J. (1976). A conceptualization and program design. *Leisure Today/JOPER,* (March), 17–19.

Mundy, J. (1981). Whose role leisure education? (Editorial) *Parks and Recreation, 16*(3), 22.

Mundy, J. (1984). What prevents people from enjoying leisure? *Parks and Recreation, 19*(9), 64.

Mundy, J., & Odum, L. (1979). *Leisure education: Theory and practice.* New York, NY: John Wiley and Sons.

Mundy, J., & Odum, L. (1998). *Leisure education: Theory and practice* (2nd ed.). Champaign, IL: Sagamore.

Nour, K., Desrosiers, J., Gauthier, P., & Carbonneau, H. (2002). Impact of a home leisure educational program for older adults who have had a stroke (home leisure education program). *Therapeutic Recreation Journal, 36*(1), 48–64.

Olson, W. E., & McCormack, J. B. (1957). Recreational counseling in the psychiatric service of a general hospital. *Journal of Nervous and Mental Disease, 25*(2), 237–239.

O'Morrow, G. S. (1977). Recreation counseling: A challenge to rehabilitation. In A. Epperson, P. A. Witt, & G. Hitzhusen (Eds.), *Leisure counseling: An aspect of leisure education* (pp. 7–30). Springfield, IL: Charles C. Thomas.

Overs, R. P. (1971). Avocational counseling inventory (Revised). *Milwaukee Media for Rehabilitation Research Report, No. 5A.* Milwaukee, WI: Recreation and Adult Education Division, Milwaukee Public Schools.

Overs, R. P. (1976). Unpublished research note. Milwaukee, WI: Avocational Counseling Research, Inc.

Overs, R. P., & Page, C. M. (1974). Avocational title card sort. *Milwaukee Media for Rehabilitation Research Reports, No. 5F.* Grand Forks, ND: Medical Center Rehabilitation Hospital.

Overs, R. P., & Taylor, S. (1977). Avocational counseling instrumentation. In D. M. Compton & J. E. Goldstein (Eds.), *Perspectives of leisure counseling* (pp. 89–105). Alexandria, VA: National Recreation and Park Association.

Overs, R. P., Taylor, S., & Adkins, C. (1974). Avocational counseling in Milwaukee. Final report on project H-2334366. *Milwaukee Media for Rehabilitation Research Reports, No. 5D.* Milwaukee, WI: DePaul Rehabilitation, Inc.

Overs, R. P., Taylor, S., & Adkins, C. (1977a). Avocational counseling for the elderly. *Leisure Today/JOPER,* (April), 20–21.

Overs, R. P., Taylor, S., & Adkins, C. (1977b). Avocational counseling: A field trial. In A. Epperson, P. A. Witt, & G. Hitzhusen (Eds.), *Leisure counseling: An aspect of leisure education* (pp. 106–136). Springfield, IL: Charles C. Thomas.

Overs, R. P., Taylor, S., & Adkins, C. (1977c). *Avocational counseling manual: A complete guide to leisure guidance.* Washington, DC: Hawkins and Associates, Inc.

Peterson, C. A. (1977). Leisure counseling: Concepts and contexts. In D. M. Compton & J. E. Goldstein (Eds.), *Perspectives of leisure counseling* (pp. 9–17). Alexandria, VA: National Recreation and Park Association.

Peterson, C. A., & Gunn, S. L. (1977). Leisure counseling: An aspect of leisure education. *Leisure Today/JOPER,* (April), 5–6.

Peterson, C. A., & Gunn, S. L. (1984). *Therapeutic recreation program design: Principles and procedures* (2nd ed.). Englewood Cliffs, NJ: Prentice-Hall, Inc.

Peterson, C. A., & Stumbo, N. J. (2000). *Therapeutic recreation program design: Principles and procedures* (3rd ed.). San Francisco, CA: Pearson Benjamin Cummings.

Reynolds, R. P., & Arthur, M. H. (1982). Effects of peer modeling and cognitive self guidance on the social play of emotionally disturbed children. *Therapeutic Recreation Journal, 16*(1), 33–40.

Searle, M. A., Mahon, M. J., Iso-Ahola, S. E., Sdrolias, H. A., & van Dyck, J. (1995). Enhancing a sense of independence and psychological well-being among the elderly: A field experiment. *Journal of Leisure Research, 27*(2), 107–124.

Searle, M. S., Mahon, M. J., Iso-Ahola, S. E., Sdrolias, H. A., & van Dyck, J. (1998). Examining the long-term effects of leisure education on a sense of independence and psychological well-being among the elderly. *Journal of Leisure Research, 30*(3), 331–340.

Stracke, R. (1977). An overview of leisure counseling. In A. Epperson, P. A. Witt, & G. Hitzhusen (Eds.), *Leisure counseling: An aspect of leisure education* (pp. 31–40). Springfield, IL: Charles C. Thomas.

Stumbo, N. J. (2003a). Systematic reviews part I: How to conduct systematic reviews for evidence-based practice. *Annual in Therapeutic Recreation, 12*, 29–44.

Stumbo, N. J. (2003b). Systematic reviews part II: How to appraise systematic reviews for evidence-based practice. *Annual in Therapeutic Recreation, 12*, 45–56.

Stumbo, N. J. (2003c). The language of quality healthcare. *American Journal of Recreational Therapy, 2*(3), 33–40.

Stumbo, N. J., & Pegg, S. (2010). Outcomes and evidence-based practice: Moving forward. *Annual in Therapeutic Recreation, 18*, 12–24.

Stumbo, N. J., & Peterson, C. A. (1998). The leisure ability model. *Therapeutic Recreation Journal, 32*(2), 82–96.

Stumbo, N. J., & Peterson, C. A. (2004). *Therapeutic recreation program design: Principles and procedures* (4th ed.). San Francisco, CA: Pearson Benjamin Cummings.

Stumbo, N. J., & Peterson, C. A. (2009). *Therapeutic recreation program design: Principles and procedures* (5th ed.). San Francisco, CA: Pearson Benjamin Cummings.

Szymanski, D. J., & Hitzhusen, G. L. (Eds.). (1979). *Expanding horizons in therapeutic recreation VI.* Columbia, MO: University of Missouri Press.

Therapeutic Recreation Journal. (1981). Volume 15, 4th quarter.

Wegner, L., Flisher, A. J., Muller, M., & Lombard, C. (2006). Leisure boredom and substance use among high school students in South Africa. *Journal of Leisure Research, 38*(2), 249–266.

West, R. E. (2009). Integrating evidence into recreational therapy practice: An important focus for the profession. In N. J. Stumbo (Ed.), *Professional issues in therapeutic recreation services: On outcomes and competence* (2nd ed.) (pp. 249–268). Champaign, IL: Sagamore.

West, R. E., Kinney, T., & Witman, J. (2008). *Guidelines for competency assessment and curriculum planning for recreational therapy practice* (2nd ed.). Hattiesburg, MS: American Therapeutic Recreation Association.

Wilson, G. T., Mirenda, J. J., & Rutkowski, B. A. (1977). Milwaukee leisure counseling model. In A. Epperson, P. A. Witt, & G. Hitzhusen (Eds.), *Leisure counseling: An aspect of leisure education* (pp. 271–282). Springfield, IL: Charles C. Thomas.

» CHAPTER 3 »

Selecting Programs and Activities Based on Goals and Outcomes

Norma J. Stumbo, Ph.D., CTRS

One of the most important tasks for a therapeutic recreation specialist is to select the right programs and activities for client participation in order that the intended outcomes—changes in behaviors, skills, attitudes, and knowledges—are achieved. Since the ultimate mission of therapeutic recreation intervention is to change some aspects of client behavior, and this is done through the client's participation in specific, selected activities, it becomes quickly apparent how important the process of activity selection is. However, this selection process can be challenging and requires a tremendous amount of skill, flexibility, and creativity on the part of the therapeutic recreation specialist. One method of ensuring higher-quality, more outcome-oriented interventions is evidence-based practice; that is, using only those interventions or procedures that are found, through research, to be effective and efficient in helping the client reach his or her goals. Helping therapeutic recreation specialists progress toward greater use of evidence in selecting and designing programs and activities is the intent of this book.

Proper selection of activities and programs is more than just planning games and exercises. It involves understanding the needs and goals of the clients, the characteristics and possibilities of activities, and how to facilitate involvement within activities so the goals and outcomes are achieved. The purpose of this chapter is to address some of the broader issues of activity and program selection as well as more specific design considerations involved with leisure education games and exercises.

Before a discussion about factors and principles affecting activity selection begins, it is useful to review some of the basic assumptions about producing client outcomes and therapeutic recreation specialist competencies. The focus on outcomes presents several challenges to therapeutic recreation specialists in particular. First, it means that simple activity provision (often called cafeteria-style programming) is no longer viable. Therapeutic recreation specialists either will adapt to this call for accountability and complement other professions in the production of client outcomes, or they will be viewed as peripheral to the health and human service arena. Only those professions that move clients toward essential outcomes will remain viable.

Second, therapeutic recreation specialists will need to continue to learn new skills and face new directions. Not only does this include new activities and modalities, it means keeping abreast of new processes of accountability, such as critical pathways, protocols, clinical competencies, and performance measures. Part of being a professional means being responsible for keeping current with the latest professional developments.

Making Activities Count

Therapeutic recreation requires more than simply providing enjoyable recreation and leisure activities to persons with disabilities and/or illnesses. Therapeutic recreation involves selecting experiences and activities in which the clients can learn and practice new skills, attitudes, behaviors, and knowledges that will eventually lead to independent community engagement of their choice and, hopefully, a high quality of life. In order to make this happen, therapeutic recreation specialists need to possess several sets of knowledge and skill competencies. These include: (a) the purpose of therapeutic recreation, (b) client needs, (c) client outcomes, (d) a variety and requirements of activities, and (e) facilitation techniques.

Purpose of Therapeutic Recreation

How the therapeutic recreation specialist interprets therapeutic recreation impacts greatly the types of services he or she will deliver to clients. For example, if Leisure Ability (Stumbo & Peterson, 2009) is the preferred therapeutic recreation service model, the therapeutic recreation specialist will focus on the leisure-related attitudes, knowledge, and skills necessary for a healthy, satisfying, and meaningful leisure lifestyle. The Leisure Ability Model provides content for programs (functional intervention, leisure education, and recreation participation), as well as direction for future client outcomes, through the concept of leisure lifestyle. Chapter 2 of this text speaks specifically to the content of the leisure education portion of this model.

Client Needs

Because client needs drive all program development and implementation, the therapeutic recreation specialist must be aware of the characteristics of disabilities and illnesses, including the impact of secondary conditions. Client "needs clusters" are important to consider as the therapeutic recreation specialist begins the program design process, and they continue to be important as program implementation and evaluation occur. Each specialist must be knowledgeable about the implications of a range of diagnoses, prognoses, medical procedures and treatments, and medications. This often includes a working knowledge of medical terminology, anatomy, and pharmacology.

Client Outcomes

Client outcomes are also an important consideration. See Figure 3.1 for a graphic display of the measuring points of assessment and reassessment (evaluation), with intervention occurring in-between these points. The outcomes are the results of the intervention that appear at reassessment, including the amount and degree of information the client has gained (or lost).

Why should a client participate in therapeutic recreation programs and activities? What changes will be evident from the person's participation in these activities? Selecting or designing programs and activities that produce client change implies a relationship between where the client enters the service at

Point A, takes part in Program B, and comes out with changed behavior at Point C. This means there must be a strong, logical, and systematic *relationship* between each of the three points. For example, if a client enters a facility with a lack of social skills (Point A) and participates actively in a well-designed social skills program (Point B), it is logical that the client will exit with increased social skills (Point C). Point A, Point B, and Point C all have a direct relationship.

On the other hand, if a different client has the same need—lack of social skills—(Point A) and participates in painting (Point D) instead of a social skills program (Point B), the client in this scenario is likely to exit at Point E, with painting skills, rather than improved social skills. Point A, Point D, and Point E do not have a direct relationship. The client is ending up with skills other than those that he or she needed at Point A. Figure 3.2 demonstrates the two paths ending in different outcomes.

The client in the first scenario is likely to exit with the targeted outcomes (improved social skills) while the client in the second scenario is likely to exit with a second, different set of outcomes (painting skills). In other words, in order for the client to reach his or her targeted outcome, the need or goal, program, and outcome must have a strong, logical, and systematic relationship. These scenarios also address *causality* (participation in Program B is likely to cause outcome C), *predictability* (outcome C can be reasonably predicted from participation in Program B), and *replicability* (outcome C is likely to occur for all or nearly all clients in Program B).

This logical approach is the focus of selecting and designing programs that enable a client to change his or her behavior, knowledge, or skills. In addition,

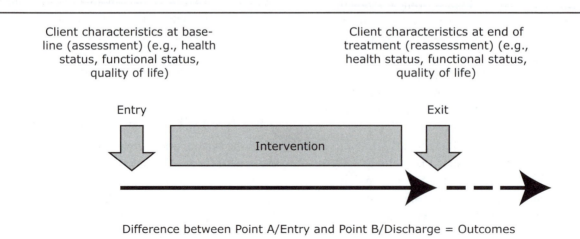

Client characteristics at baseline (assessment) (e.g., health status, functional status, quality of life)

Client characteristics at end of treatment (reassessment) (e.g., health status, functional status, quality of life)

Entry

Exit

Intervention

Difference between Point A/Entry and Point B/Discharge = Outcomes

Figure 3.1. Outcomes Equal the Difference between Point A (Entry) and Point B (Exit)

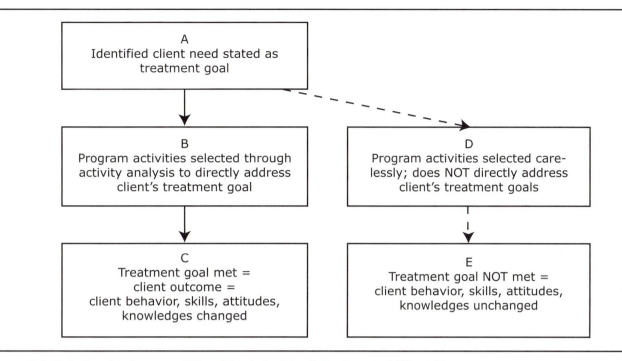

Figure 3.2. Relationship between Client Need, Activity Selection, and Client Outcomes

it needs to be stated that each intervention program focuses on this A-B-C sequence. In most clinical facilities, activities or programs must be geared toward intervention; that is, changing some aspect of client behavior, knowledge, or skills. In most facilities and for most clients, activities that are provided for pure enjoyment or entertainment are not seen as part of the treatment package, and are typically not funded by third-party payers. When offered, diversional programs often are implemented by paraprofessionals or volunteers.

Nonintervention activities, however, may be worthwhile in some settings and with some clients, but even then must have a clear-cut purpose and reason for implementation. For example, one legitimate purpose may be to observe clients when they have the opportunity for independent choices. The therapeutic recreation specialist might observe during recreational activities if clients have competence in decision making, problem solving, planning, social interaction skills, and so on. If the clients show difficulty in areas being targeted through treatment goals, this observational assessment opportunity leads to a prescription of new or revised intervention programs.

Variety and Requirements of Activities

It is a given that the therapeutic recreation specialist must be knowledgeable about a wide variety of activities, programs, and services in order to deliver the same to clients. This means knowing the rules to a variety of games, activities, and sports; understanding the requirements of nontraditional activities; and comprehending the reasons and motivations behind people's participation in activities. This also implies that the specialist be very familiar with different programming formats, from one-on-one sessions to small-group discussions to round-robin tournaments, in order to select the most appropriate format for client participation. All of the above implies a very strong understanding of the principles and uses of activity analysis and activity modification. The therapeutic recreation specialist must be able to design, deliver, and evaluate diverse programs, taking all these factors into consideration.

Facilitation Techniques

The content of activities is important, but so too is the process by which the therapeutic recreation specialist delivers the activity. Facilitation techniques often are needed in order to deliver the program or activity in the most effective and efficient manner possible. The competent therapeutic recreation specialist is well versed in a variety of facilitation techniques. The intent of this book is to increase competence in various facilitation techniques and modalities. Much like activity skills, the more competent the therapeutic recreation specialist is with a variety of facilitation techniques, the more likely the specialist will be able to rapidly and meaningfully facilitate change in client behavior, and produce client outcomes.

Each of these five factors—philosophy, client needs, client outcomes, activities, and facilitation techniques—

impacts which activities the specialist selects and how they are implemented for individuals or groups of clients. It is imperative that the therapeutic recreation specialist has a clear and thorough understanding and working knowledge of each of these five areas.

Factors Influencing Selection of Activities

Stumbo and Peterson (2009) discussed at length three factors that influence the selection and implementation of intervention. These factors include: (a) activity content and process; (b) client characteristics, and (c) resource factors. They will be briefly discussed here.

Activity Content and Process

Activities are the method by which therapeutic recreation specialists help clients change their abilities, knowledge, and attitudes. Therefore, a clear understanding of their usefulness and purpose is needed. Nine factors concerning activity characteristics are presented.

1: *Activities must have a direct relationship to the client goal.*

That is, activities must be able to contribute to the achievement of the goal. As mentioned early in this chapter, the A-B-C relationship must be logical, systematic, and reproducible. Specialists should select and implement only those activities that a thorough activity analysis demonstrates are useful in helping the client achieve his or her goals. Selecting an activity for client participation simply because it is known to the specialist, easy to implement, or currently popular is inadequate when the intention is to produce client outcomes. Each activity in which a client participates must be able to move the client in the desired direction.

2: *Functional intervention activities should focus on the ability of the activity to help the client reach his or her goals, rather than on the activity for activity's sake.*

In other words, select activities with which the client is familiar or that are easily learned, so that the focus is on the attainment of outcomes rather than the participation requirements of the activity per se. At times, clients may benefit from participating in known activities so that they do not have to learn new rules and strategies when that is not the designated purpose of their participation. For example, if clients are unfamiliar with computers, it may be detrimental to use logging on to the Internet as an activity to teach

sequential skills. Too much time may be spent becoming familiar with the hardware and software, with little attention paid to learning and practicing sequencing skills. Similarly, the finished product of a birdhouse may not be as important as other functional intervention client outcomes such as the ability to follow sequential directions, improve fine motor control, or increase concentration. The role of the specialist is to help clients focus on the goals or purpose of the activities. At the same time, the specialist should consider the carryover value of the activity for the client's future lifestyle.

3: *Functional intervention and leisure education activities should have very predominant characteristics that are related to the problem, skill, or knowledge being addressed.*

This speaks to the importance and power of activity analysis. Activities that have the strongest capability of producing outcomes are those that need to be selected for client participation. For example, if a client needs assistance with improving social skills, activities such as bingo, softball, and in-line skating are not likely to help this occur. A thorough activity analysis would find that interactional skills are not required to a great degree in these activities and that other activities that do have social skills as a primary component would serve as better selections for teaching clients social skills. Choosing activities that teach social skills directly (as with any other skill-improvement program) is the most direct and productive way to ensure skill attainment. Selecting activities that have a primary, rather than byproduct, relationship will help ensure goal attainment. The therapeutic recreation specialist has a primary responsibility to conduct an activity analysis of several activities and select the one(s) that *best* address the client need. Activity analysis is covered thoroughly in Stumbo and Peterson (2009), as well as in other therapeutic recreation textbooks.

4: *Activity characteristics are important considerations for the successful implementation of a program.*

Several considerations must be reviewed carefully before final selection of an activity. Some important characteristics, such as social interaction patterns, are discovered through a complete and thorough activity analysis. Others, such as whether to provide an activity in a group or individual format, are less obvious but still important. The format of a program will depend on the staff/client ratio, available resources, intended outcomes, and so on. Often, however, it is easy to use one primary format to the exclusion of others, even when other formats may be more appropriate. Likewise, the content of the program is also crucial. The specialist's decision whether to choose traditional versus nontraditional leisure activities is an important one. The specialist always must consider the factors that will help make the program the most successful and the most relevant to the client group to be served. For example, not every activity should be delivered in a small-group discussion, paper-and-pencil exercise format. Most individuals process information at a higher level by being actively involved, rather than by simply listening (see Chapter 6). Children, especially those with behavior disorders, may benefit more from activities that actively engage them (e.g., scavenger hunts, board games, role-playing) rather than those that constrain them to sit quietly and complete a worksheet.

5: *Clients should be able to place an activity in some context in order for them to see it as useful and applicable to their overall rehabilitation or treatment outcomes.*

While creativity and innovation are to be encouraged, the value of participating in activities may be diminished when the activities are extremely unfamiliar to the clients or are seen as outrageous by them. When clients see no purpose, meaning, or relevant outcome to an activity, their participation is hindered and their outcomes less likely. For example, teaching clients a rare Argentinean dance in order to promote flexibility and movement might be unique, intriguing, and fun. It is likely to be less successful in producing desired outcomes than other dances such as ballroom and line dancing, which are more familiar to more clients. Too often clients would focus on the uniqueness, intrigue, and fun, and not get to the real purpose of increasing flexibility and movement. This is not saying that Argentinean dance is unimportant. However, for most people, relevance is important to the learning process, a context in which to place the activity for future participation is necessary (see Chapter 6).

6: *A single activity or session is not likely to produce a desired behavioral change.*

Many of the skills, knowledge, and attitudes addressed by therapeutic recreation services are complex and are designed to replace deeply embedded notions held by the client. Many long-held skill and knowledge deficits cannot be changed quickly. Thus, when selecting or designing activities, the therapeutic recreation specialist needs to think about a sequence of activities within a session and over a series of sessions. Skill building may need to occur over time, to be addressed

through a variety of program formats, to use activities of progressing complexity and challenge, and to use a variety of media. Learning research shows that multimedia methods work best for most people. Seeing, hearing, touching, doing—all present different avenues that help clients learn more efficiently and effectively.

Most people learn better through discovery and actual hands-on practice, including clients. For example, a client is more likely to become aware of his or her own leisure attitudes if a program series uses visual cues, written or creative exercises, verbal discussion, and in-depth exploration, than if any of these methods are used singularly in one individual activity. Likewise, a client is more likely to learn a new leisure skill when he or she can view a videotape of the skill, see and hear a personal demonstration by the instructor, and practice with the necessary equipment. Skill building, attitude change, and knowledge acquisition take time, practice, and mastery. The therapeutic recreation specialist needs to be familiar with teaching–learning concepts, such as learner readiness and repetition of content, and the principles outlined in Chapter 6.

7: *Consider the types of activities in which people will engage when they have the choice.*

Therapeutic recreation specialists should attempt to provide activities that are of interest and benefit to clients (rather than of interest to the therapeutic recreation specialist). This is especially true when working with leisure-activity-skills-acquisition programs. Again, creativity in programming is prized, but the end result must be a skill in which the client can gain proficiency and can engage in, in his or her own leisure time. Often this means looking to nontraditional leisure skill areas. In the past there was an overly heavy emphasis on sports skills, especially those for large competitive groups (using intergroup participation patterns). However, it is recognized that most clients, especially older adults, do not have opportunities or the desire to participate in large-group competitive sports. Whenever possible, client choice of activity should be taken into consideration, even in those activities in which functional intervention is the predominant goal. A primary consideration is a projection of the client's future lifestyle—in what activities will the person be involved in the future? The therapeutic recreation specialist should be familiar with nontraditional activities as well as more traditional activities.

8: *Program to the client's outcomes and priorities.*

In recent years, clients' length of stay in most healthcare and human service facilities has been shortened.

In many agencies, this may mean that clients spend less than one week in treatment. This puts the emphasis of programs squarely on the outcomes and treatment priorities of the client, with little time to squander or waste in misdirected programs. Like all other disciplines, this means that therapeutic recreation specialists must focus very specifically on the targeted outcomes and maintain that focus throughout service provision. This, in turn, may mean some shifting in terms of the core priorities of the program. It may mean teaching clients about "processes" instead of specific content. As one example, the specialist may teach a client about a decision-making process of reviewing alternatives, weighing benefits and consequences, and selecting the option that has fewest costs and most benefits, rather than teaching the clients specifically how to make a leisure decision for next weekend. The former teaches a generic process that can be used for any decision; the latter focuses on one decision.

In another example, the therapeutic recreation specialist may function as a resource person and be the bridge to community programs that teach necessary skills. Instead of teaching leisure skills within the facility, the specialist may help clients develop a cognitive understanding of the value of leisure participation and teach clients once they are discharged how to access community resources that teach leisure skills. The specialist's time is spent on teaching the client the *process* of finding community resources rather than teaching the *content* of finding one specific resource. Both of these examples show that the specialist must continue to focus on the actual needs of the clients, while considering all the constraints under which programs are implemented. With the reduction of staff-client contact hours comes the clear need to rethink and prioritize program direction.

9: *Client involvement in activities should be enjoyable (or at least not drudgery).*

It is not possible or desirable for clients to be entertained, laughing, and frolicking every moment within therapeutic recreation programs. That is not the point. However, learning or behavior change best takes place under generally enjoyable conditions. The specialist has everything to gain if he or she can design programs that focus on outcomes while making the experience enjoyable for clients. This includes the environment in which activities take place, materials used for activities, and the general attitude of the staff. It also includes selecting activities that have the potential to be enjoyable. When rooms are dreary, materials old or worn, and staff sour or uninviting, the clients' motivation to participate fully will be decreased. Clients often reflect back what they see in staff and the surroundings. It is the responsibility of the therapeutic recreation specialist to ensure a proper environment for clients to participate fully in intervention activities. Figure 3.3 provides a summary of the nine factors of Activity Content and Process.

Client Characteristics

Client characteristics are important in the selection of activities. Programs are designed or selected based on the unique mix of the community, agency, and client characteristics. Clients bring with them to the agency a background and history that is important to acknowledge, because it both affects them as individuals and affects the implementation of programs. Two factors apply.

1: *Clients' demographic characteristics, such as gender, age, socioeconomic status, family composition, ethnicity, education level, religious orientation, and financial condition, need to be considered while selecting or designing programs.*

1: Activities must have a direct relationship to the client goal.
2: Functional intervention activities should focus on the ability of the activity to help the client reach his or her goals, rather than on the activity for activity's sake.
3: Functional intervention and leisure education activities should have very predominant characteristics that are related to the problem, skill, or knowledge being addressed.
4: Activity characteristics are important considerations for the successful implementation of a program.
5: Clients should be able to place an activity in some context in order for them to see it as useful and applicable to their overall rehabilitation or treatment outcomes.
6: A single activity or session is not likely to produce a desired behavioral change.
7: Consider the types of activities in which people will engage when they have choice.
8: Program to the client's outcomes and priorities.
9: Client involvement in activities should be enjoyable (or at least not drudgery).

Figure 3.3. Nine Factors of Activity Content and Process

Consideration of these characteristics is important for several reasons. First, these characteristics will affect the background, history, and experiences of the clients. These in turn affect their preferences and future orientations, and of course, their leisure preferences and leisure orientations. As mentioned before, clients are more likely to participate willingly when they see relevance, importance, and timeliness in the services offered. Resistance to involvement or lack of motivation become less of a problem when services and programs are of interest and immediate value to the clients. The specialist who understands the demographic and cultural characteristics of clients entering the agency's services will be better prepared to design and implement more meaningful and targeted programs.

2: Clients should see obvious carryover value in activity participation.

Similar to the above, clients should be able to detect immediate relevance to their future in the programs that are offered. The therapeutic recreation specialist must be aware of future goals of the clients and focus on skills and knowledges that are both transferable and generalizable to the clients' future lifestyle. Skills that have limited applicability or limited use are of little value to most clients. This means that the specialist needs to know to what environment the client will be returning when he or she leaves the facility (if ever), and what that environment holds in terms of the individual's leisure lifestyle.

Since the specialist would be hard pressed to be familiar with every community to which clients might return, one alternative is to teach clients about "processes," such as decision making, leisure planning, relaxation, stress management, and locating community leisure resources. This is more likely to help the client develop a satisfying leisure lifestyle than teaching isolated, individual skills, such as locating the zoo, planning for one weekend event, or making one leisure decision. If clients learn basic processes, then they are able to apply these processes in the future to any individual situation that they may encounter.

1: Clients' demographic characteristics such as gender, age, socioeconomic status, family composition, ethnicity, education level, religious orientation, and financial condition need to be considered while selecting or designing programs.
2: Clients should see obvious carryover value in activity participation.

Figure 3.4. Two Factors of Client Characteristics

Figure 3.4 provides a summary of the two factors of client characteristics.

Resource Factors

Resources are also important considerations when selecting activities. Adequate staff and resources help keep the focus on productive, worthwhile programs. Three considerations for program selection center on resource factors.

1: The number of clients to be included in the activity and the number of staff conducting the session have implications for the degree of difficulty of the activity selected and the safety concerns.

This notion has immediate recognition for many "risk" activities, such as ropes courses, snowboarding, and kayaking. However, the principle is applicable to all activities regardless of "risk." Inadequate resources and staff result in several consequences: (a) degree of activity difficulty needs to be reduced, (b) less content will be covered or learned in the same amount of time, (c) more time is needed to reach the targeted goal(s), and (d) clients may be put at higher risk.

The converse of each of these statements is true when adequate resources and staff are present. This means that the specialist has to take into account available resources before determining activities so that the program goes as planned, and the client reaches the intended destination safely. Inattention to these details will result in frustration for both the client and the staff. For example, the specialist cannot teach twenty clients to use a telephone book for locating community resources in a half hour when only one telephone book and one staff member is available. This is too much to ask from limited resources (telephone books and half-hour time limit) and staff (one specialist). If there were fewer clients, more telephone books, more staff, or more time, the targeted goal would likely be more easily reached.

In planning the activity or program, the specialist must make an honest assessment of available resources and limitations. Often this is one of the reasons why selecting smaller goals that can be accomplished, given the client load and available resources, is a better choice than ambitious goals that are unattainable. The therapeutic recreation specialist is accountable for client outcomes, but usually has considerable latitude in selecting which goals to target.

2: For all programs, but especially for leisure education skill development programs, consider adequate time to learn, practice, and enjoy parts of the skill.

As mentioned earlier, most new learning, whether it is new knowledge, a new attitude, or a new skill, takes time. Clients who lack certain knowledge, have negative or unfocused attitudes, or lack specific skills will not master these skills quickly. This may depend to some degree on the clients' status. That is, if the client has little experience in learning new things, then the client will need more time, especially to learn the unfamiliar. Clients who have been active learners are more likely to pick up new knowledge, skills, and attitudes more quickly. In both cases though, the specialist needs to allow adequate time for learning, practice, and mastery. Clients who do not have some sense of mastery or competence will be less likely to follow up with the skill postdischarge. A client who is taught how to use a VCR, but who is not allowed to practice the skill until mastery, is less likely to be able to initiate this skill when in his or her home. If the goal is to change some aspect of the client's behavior, then therapeutic recreation specialists have to be able to teach them the skills to do so.

3: *Too much equipment or lots of highly specialized equipment detracts from the focus on the treatment goal.*

There is much to be said for adaptive equipment when it suits a purpose and fills a need. However, overuse of equipment can detract from the client's involvement and may not be available to the client in the future. A corollary is not overmodifying the rules of an activity. The further the activity or its equipment appears from the original, the less "normalized" the activity becomes. In some cases, such weight is given to the use of equipment for equipment's sake that the meaning and context of the activity are lost. In addition, equipment often needs repair, often has only a single purpose, gets lost or damaged, and is sometimes expensive.

Bowling ramps, used by individuals with physical limitations to head the bowling ball down the lane with momentum, can provide an example. First of all, not all bowling alleys have bowling ramps, which means the individual who was taught bowling only using the ramps would need to supply his or her own or not go bowling. To bowl, the individual then becomes responsible for purchasing the ramp and transporting the ramp to the alley. Second, there is no other logical purpose for a bowling ramp, so that while it can be used for bowling, it has no use for other leisure activities. For an individual to buy adaptive equipment for every leisure activity in which he or she participates, both money and storage space would be needed. Third, while the use of a bowling ramp may be essential for some, for others it may signal a certain degree of segregation and dependence. Reliance on adaptive aids

when the person has the potential to develop the skill means unnecessary dependence on devices rather than skill development. While some adaptive equipment is required, it is in the best interest of most clients to develop skills as close as possible to those of their counterparts without disabilities. Full inclusion is more likely to occur when individuals with disabilities develop prerequisite skills. Figure 3.5 provides a summary of the three factors of resources.

The skilled therapeutic recreation specialist will have a comprehensive understanding of these factors that affect the selection of programs and activities for client participation. Another related skill is the actual designing of leisure education games and activities. The next section will address some of the considerations for developing interventions through a game format, as well as address specific steps in developing games and activities. This section ends with some forms that have been found helpful to game designers and game evaluators.

Designing Games and Activities for Leisure Education

The four areas or components of leisure-education content often are introduced to participants through a "game" or "activity" format. In this way, the participant can gain knowledge, insights, and comprehension of rather complex subject matter in a fun and challenging manner. Leisure education often uses this "learning while playing" approach. This section provides a framework for specialists to create their own activities, through a systematic design process.

Why a Gaming Format?

Games and activities can provide a stimulating and novel situation in which participants may learn specified knowledges and/or skills in a non-threatening environment. They can provide an opportunity for people

---

1: The number of clients to be included in the activity and the number of staff conducting the session have implications for the degree of difficulty of the activity selected and the safety concerns.
2: For all programs, but especially for leisure education skill development programs, consider adequate time to learn, practice, and enjoy parts of the skill.
3: Too much equipment or lots of highly specialized equipment detracts from the focus on the treatment goal.

Figure 3.5. Three Factors of Resources

to gain new ideas, see other people's reactions, understand their own values, or experience both winning and losing without directly threatening who they are or what they know. This situation allows the participants to interact freely within a controlled environment, without the hazards of rejection or embarrassment through a situation that might arise in reality. The gaming format is protective, yet it allows the participant to become knowledgeable of how situations might occur, to develop and explore alternatives, and choose a course of action without dire consequences.

Advantages to Using Games and Activities

There are eight major advantages to using a game or activity format for leisure education programs. These advantages are: (a) ability to induce changes in the participant; (b) flexibility and relevance of the game/activity to real-life situations; (c) promotion of group cohesiveness; (d) depth of involvement; (e) level of motivation; (f) receptiveness of participants; (g) promotion of individual and group responsibility; and (h) a safe, non-threatening environment. These eight advantages will be discussed in more detail below and highlighted in Figure 3.6.

Ability to Induce Changes in the Participant

Games and activities can be powerful tools for changing participant behavior. They can allow participants to view various alternatives for behavior, distinguish between socially appropriate and inappropriate behaviors, and see logical consequences for behavioral actions. A participant may be more likely to accept suggestions to change his/her behavior during a game, rather than through a direct confrontation. Since most activities require that the participant explore alternatives, the natural course would be for the participant to examine and practice options that are more suitable during the game, and then apply these alternatives during "real-life" interactions.

---

1. Ability to induce changes in the participant
2. Flexibility and relevance to real-life situations
3. Group cohesiveness
4. Depth of involvement
5. Level of motivation
6. Receptiveness
7. Responsibility
8. Safe environment

Figure 3.6. Eight Advantages to Using Games

Flexibility and Relevance to Real-Life Situations

One of the best features of leisure education games and activities is that they can be designed to correspond with whatever leisure education content is being introduced and can be customized to a specific group of participants and their needs. Leisure education games and activities can be modified according to participant skill level, needs, disability, home or community situation, etc. The possibilities for adapting activities are limitless and allow the specialist to create the perfect activity for a specific group of clients. Not only can this flexibility and relevance help the specialist target directed participant outcomes, it allows for several basic activities to be repeated within a program cycle without being repetitious for participants.

Group Cohesiveness

Most games or activities require participation by a small group of people. Often, cooperation, rather than competition, is stressed to get to the final outcome of the game and each player must make some kind of contribution to the larger whole to ensure success. These cooperation requirements can inspire a sense of camaraderie, cohesiveness, and equality among participants. Since these skills are usually necessary in the community, a game format seems a natural way to reinforce these concepts.

Depth of Involvement

Most people easily can become engaged in an activity, when it has a clear purpose and an interesting format. Rather than simply lecture, counsel, or provide written materials, the specialist can often get the message across more quickly and deeply when games and activities are used. There is something about being involved in a situation that parallels reality but lacks its immediate consequences that helps get clients entrenched in its play. This notion is explored in Chapter 6, during the discussion of principles of learning.

Level of Motivation

Related to depth of involvement, motivation is another asset to leisure education games and activities. Because they are conducted usually within a short time span and involve several players, each participant can maintain a relatively high level of motivation and enthusiasm. Some activities may examine attitudes, others may teach new knowledge, while others allow the participant to practice new skills. Whatever direction they take, well-designed activities tend to hold the participant's attention and allow for high motivation. We have grown up with all types of games (e.g., Candyland,

Monopoly, Battleship, Dodgeball) and are accustomed to general rules of play. Most people want to continue to play until the end of the activity to see what the outcome will be.

Receptiveness

Games and activities provide an environment for the participant to be less defensive about certain situations versus how he/she may react in normal life situations. The specialist can help the participant examine certain behaviors or attitudes that may be blocking fuller participation in a game situation in a much less threatening way than in real life. This advantage may help the participant voice real opinions or concerns that otherwise could not be spoken. Participants also seem more willing to accept constructive criticism and look for alternatives during activities than in real-life situations.

Responsibility

Most leisure education activities require that the participants take responsibility for their actions. Unlike the more staff-controlled treatment type of programs, leisure education activities attempt to shift the responsibility from the specialist to the participant. This includes showing responsibility to other group members, taking responsibility for making personal decisions, and learning the consequences of making those decisions. Through leisure education games and activities, the participant can learn what the probable and potential consequences of his/her decisions will be. Many leisure education activities can help the participant learn planning and decision-making skills in relation to his/her leisure lifestyle, enabling the participant to become solely responsible for his/her own level of comfort and satisfaction.

Safe Environment

Since many leisure education activities are at least partial simulations of real life, they can provide a meaningful, but sheltered environment to learn and experiment with new behaviors and choices. Games can provide a controlled and "safe" environment in which skills can be practiced before they are used in real life. Participants often find it useful to practice new knowledge or skills in a less threatening setting before actually being called upon to do so in front of people with whom they are not familiar. Because of the sheltered setting, participants may feel freer to experiment with new choices and behaviors that they can use later in life.

All eight of these factors point to the usefulness of leisure education games and activities when working with participants. Together, they provide distinct advantages that are not found in other program formats.

General Rules and Considerations for Constructing Games

The following are general rules for creating and designing new leisure education games and activities (see Figure 3.7). The Leisure Education Activity Planning Worksheet (adapted from J. Levy, 1989) that is located in Appendix A will also help guide in the creation of new activities and games.

1. *Decide the overall purpose and goal of the game or activity.*

Most creators design activities because they have a specific purpose in mind and have not yet found another activity that meets this purpose. The purpose of the game must be fairly clear-cut and usually is rather narrow. The selection of the overall goal depends on what area of leisure education is to be the focus, the general abilities of the participant group, how much time can be spent on the activity, etc. For example, a social skills activity for a half-hour session with people who have traumatic brain injury may be more narrow in focus than a social skills activity for an hour session for people with substance abuse problems. The specialist may find that throughout the creation process, the overall goals may need to be revised as the activity is developed.

Some sample overall purposes for leisure education activities are:

- to teach participants how to locate and use leisure resources in the community
- to improve participants' ability to apply a problem-solving process to leisure situations
- to teach clients how to find and approach leisure partners
- to improve participants' ability to select appropriate attire for various leisure activities
- to increase participants' understanding of the importance of leisure in a balanced lifestyle

---

1. Decide the overall purpose and goal of the game or activity.
2. Write specific intended participant objectives for outcomes related to participation in the activity.
3. Select the general format of the game or activity.
4. Develop the rules of the game.
5. Gather or create the necessary materials to play.
6. Play the game with other people.
7. Revise the game, if necessary.

Figure 3.7. General Rules for Creating and Designing Games and Activities

- to increase participants' awareness of appropriate self-disclosure in social situations
- to improve participants' ability to examine options and select the best alternative
- to improve participants' ability to access state leisure resources
- to increase participants' understanding of the need for leisure planning
- to teach participants a process for examining choices/options and making decisions
- to teach participants how to locate low-cost activities and events in the community

Each activity or program has a fairly focused purpose that relates to a specific area of leisure education content.

2. *Write specific participant objectives for outcomes related to participation in the activity.*

The participant objectives help guide the development of the activity and keep the designer focused on what the activity is meant to do. These should include measurable objectives aimed at specific behaviors or knowledges when possible. The development of three to five measurable objectives aids the specialist in later evaluating the effects of the activity on the participants and helps in documenting client outcomes (e.g., treatment plans, progress notes, participation records, etc.). Participant outcome objectives are important to the activity development process and should not be overlooked. The reader is encouraged to review the section on taxonomies in Chapter 6 to understand the "levels" of learning that are applicable to objectives. Figure 3.8 illustrates sample objectives for an overall goal focused on leisure resources.

From the objectives in Figure 3.8, it becomes clear that the leisure education activity itself should target the participant behaviors of identifying and using leisure resource information, selecting activities of interest to the participant, contacting agencies for additional information when needed, making transportation arrangements, and following through with the leisure plan.

The level of specificity of the participant objectives depends to a great extent on the abilities of the participants. How much do they know before the activity begins (e.g., about bus schedules, city maps, making change)? How quickly can they be expected to learn new information within the activity? How will this activity relate to other leisure education activities and other therapies? The nature and pace of the activity should match the participants' abilities. Once the specialist has identified general participant abilities and measurable participant objectives, an activity or game can be developed further.

3. *Select the general format of the game or activity.*

The general structure of the activity is the next step in further defining how it will be created. Will the activity consist of a board game, a paper-and-pencil exercise, a discussion group, an initiative game, a community out trip, a one-to-one session, a "take-home" exercise? Selecting the format depends on what kind of environment or setting is required to learn the content of the participant objectives. For example, a board game can teach both cooperative and competitive skills and may allow for individual input from all participants; a paper-and-pencil exercise can be used to have individuals think about their responses before sharing with the group or coming to a consensus; a discussion group allows for all individuals to communicate and have input and may be used to brainstorm to select the best ideas. Each activity format has advantages and disadvantages that have to be considered.

Selecting the activity structure depends on the abilities of the participants, what they are supposed to gain from the activity (the goals and objectives), and the content they are intended to learn. Also included at the end of this chapter, in Appendix A, is a planning worksheet that may be helpful in deciding the details of the activity.

Overall goal: "To teach participants how to locate and use leisure resources in the community"
Sample objectives:
1. At the conclusion of the activity, the participant will verbally name three sources of community leisure information (newspaper, program brochures, telephone directory, etc.) with 66% accuracy.
2. At the conclusion of the activity and using the information sources provided, the participant will verbally name two community leisure resources in which he/she is interested in participating in the next month, with 100% accuracy.
3. At the conclusion of the activity, the participant will register for one leisure program in the community.
4. Within the next 7 days, the participant will arrange the transportation to participate in the identified community leisure activities.
5. Within the next 30 days, the participant will participate in the identified community leisure activity.

Figure 3.8. Leisure Resource Client Goal and Sample Objectives

4. *Develop the rules of the game.*

The rules should be detailed enough for participation but should not overly confine the participants. Complex games that present complicated rules are often not as fun or as easy to learn quickly as those that can be played almost immediately without a lot of prior knowledge. In most instances, the creator should attempt to develop a game that another person could lead easily without the creator having to be there. Two suggestions may be helpful. One is to look at the rules included in other published games (such as Yahtzee, Uno, Scattergories, Scruples, Monopoly) to see how play is described. The second is to adapt commonly played, familiar games, such as the above, so that most participants are already familiar with how the activity is played. In that way, start-up time is reduced and the content becomes the focus of play.

5. *Gather or create the necessary materials to play.*

This step includes gathering the materials needed for the game, developing the activity sheets or game board and playing pieces. Activity sheets, game boards, playing pieces, and the like can either be made by the creator or taken from existing games. The activity may require spinners (for taking turns), dice, game cards, players' pieces, tokens, etc. (And don't forget that many "miniatures" shops carry small replicas of busses, trees, buildings, houses, food items, tennis racquets, and the like that make great game pieces or prompts!) Whenever possible, the game materials should be durable, visually appealing, relate well to the intent of the game, and reflect real life as much as possible.

6. *Play the game with other people.*

After the game is finished, playing it with other people who are unfamiliar with it will help to uncover problem areas. This will help determine how others react to the game board and rules, and to see what kinds of questions they have. There may be a question or situation where the participants are expected to respond or act one way, but when others play the game, they interpret the question or situation in a different way so that the meaning is unclear. Every rule or situation within the game should be aimed at participants achieving the objectives and being able to translate the information for use in real life.

A Leisure Education Activity Evaluation Sheet (adapted from P. Malik, 1991) is located in Appendix B to help in the assessment of newly created games or activities. It may be advisable that each player complete this form after finishing the activity or game, so the designer gets an outside perspective on how others view it. The Evaluation Sheet contains 12 areas,

and those that receive a rating of 3 (Fair) or 4 (Poor) should be redesigned.

7. *Revise the game, if necessary.*

Based on the previous "test" of playing the game and the results of the Evaluation Sheet, the creator may have to revise the intent of the game or some aspect of the game itself. This final step is necessary to assure that the outcomes of the game match the intended goals and objectives.

Selecting Activities

This chapter has looked at factors affecting the selection of games and activities, as well as at a systematic method to designing and evaluating these experiences. A review of the relationship between client goals and activities is in order. There are two ways to look at this relationship. One is to start with a client goal (outcome) and work toward the activity. The other is to look at an activity for the potential outcomes it may help produce. Both of these are highly dependent upon the specialist's ability to conduct a thorough activity analysis (see Chapter 7 of Stumbo and Peterson, 2009, for a discussion of, as well as forms to use in, an activity analysis).

Selecting Activities Based on Client Goals

First, start with a client goal (outcome) of "improve conversational abilities." The therapeutic recreation specialist determines there are three activity options that may be available for this purpose: (1) a small group discussion, with a one-to-one role play practicing telephone skills with the therapeutic recreation specialist; (2) an arts and crafts project in which clients are required to share supplies; and (3) a group trip to the mall to purchase personal toiletries that requires interaction between clients and salesclerks.

These activities likely will have varying degrees of success in helping clients "to improve conversational skills." An activity analysis conducted on each of the three activities would help the therapeutic recreation specialist determine that the role play is the most likely to address the client goal. This activity directly *teaches* the individuals in the small group the skills necessary to improve their conversational abilities using the telephone. During the role play, the specialist may use a variety of facilitation techniques, especially instructional techniques such as demonstration, repetition, and practice, to teach conversational skills.

The arts and crafts project was designed to force sharing by having a limited amount of supplies on hand, but this does not necessarily translate into improved conversational abilities of the clients. This may be a situation where clients can *practice* conversational skills, but only if they have been taught these skills prior to the arts and crafts activity. The activity itself probably will not *teach* them the necessary conversational skills. The role play is a better choice for teaching conversational abilities.

The value of the mall trip depends on how the leader designs the activity. If there is a large number of clients per an individual or few staff members, then likely these staff are more concerned about overall client safety than actual skill improvement. The smaller the number of clients per staff member, the more likely that instruction in conversational skills can take place, although to do this in public may not be in the best interests of the clients. A ratio of one client to one staff member may make the teaching-learning situation more appropriate but will still require the staff member to be unobtrusive in the teaching of conversational skills. Therefore, the role play is the most natural choice, given the three choices, to *teach* conversational skills, although the design and delivery of an activity greatly affects its ability to address the client goal.

Selecting Client Goals Based on Activities

A second way to view activity selection is by looking directly at the actual activity first (versus the client goal). Let's look at three activities: volleyball, handheld computer games, and hiking alone. A quick activity analysis of volleyball reveals that it is an intergroup activity that requires coordinated gross motor movements such as jumping and knowledge of rules and strategy. A quick analysis of handheld computer games reveals that they are an extra-individual activity that requires fine motor control, vision, and quick hand-eye coordination. Hiking alone requires gross motor movements such as walking and minimal social, emotional, or intellectual skills.

Given the diversity and similarities, which of these activities might the specialist choose for the client goal of "to improve cooperation skills"? "To improve fine motor hand-eye coordination"? "To improve emotional control"? "To improve long-term memory"? "To improve physical endurance"?

Volleyball is the only one of the three activities mentioned that requires cooperation, with one team cooperating to compete against another team. Handheld computer games is the activity most likely to improve fine motor hand-eye coordination. Hiking is probably the one to choose for endurance, in that it usually requires more continual physical activity from the participant than team sports like volleyball, in which the action is shared among team members. Probably

none of the above three activities should be chosen for goals of long-term memory or emotional control, as these are not basic elements of these activities. (An astute therapeutic recreation specialist skilled in activity modification could change these activities to meet other goals, but he or she would need to be cautious that the original intent of the program and the client goal are both considered simultaneously.)

The point to be made is that *nearly every activity can be designed and implemented to meet a client goal, but not every activity can meet every client goal.* Specialists, through a thorough activity analysis and selection process, choose the best activity (usually in its most natural state) to meet the intended goal. All aspects of the activity as well as typical client characteristics must be examined.

For example, far too often clients have difficulty with an activity (or refuse to play) because the interactional skills required are too demanding or just not part of their current functional ability. For example, a client may know the activity skills necessary to play volleyball but avoids the game because he or she cannot handle the verbal interactions needed to be a team member. Another example might be expecting a child with behavioral disorders to bowl on a team, an activity that, in addition to complex physical skills, requires a delicate balance of cooperative and competitive skills, skills that he or she may not yet possess. A third example might be adolescents with developmental disability who have the physical and cognitive skills to eat at a restaurant but lack the social interaction skills expected in public places. The analysis of interactional requirements is, thus, critical for total comprehension of participation demands.

One of the most prominent skills of the therapeutic recreation specialist not held by individuals in other human service or healthcare disciplines is that of being able to analyze, select, and modify activities to meet specific client goals. Activity leadership can be learned by many. Selecting the right activity, based on a thorough analysis of the activity requirements and its potential to address client needs, is indeed an extraordinary skill. Providing intervention programs that bring about a desired change in client behavior is a skill unique to the therapeutic recreation professional.

Activity Resources

The therapeutic recreation specialist must be familiar with a wide range of activities, both nontraditional and traditional. There are literally thousands of books containing activity ideas. Some are specific to therapeutic recreation intervention activities, such as those focused on leisure education activities, and some are more generalized materials, such as those on tennis or card games. University and public libraries have dozens of these resources. In addition, some publishing companies specifically focus on recreation, parks, and leisure literature, and often carry books on therapeutic recreation activities. Appendix C of this chapter mentions some of the most prominent book companies in this area.

Summary

- The intent of this chapter is to help specialists develop competence in selecting, designing, and evaluating activities and programs for client participation.
- Each program or activity needs to "count" and be planned with interventions and outcomes in mind.
- Important consideration include: (a) purpose, (b) client needs, (c) client outcomes, (d) variety and requirements of activities, and (e) facilitation techniques.
- The factors that influence activity selection include: (a) activity content and process, (b) client characteristics, and (c) resource factors.
- Games and activities have many advantages for client involvement and for reaching client outcomes.
- There are seven rules or steps to designing intervention games and activities.
- A number of resources are available to help provide intervention activities and games to clients of therapeutic recreation services.

References

Levy, J. (1989). Leisure education activity planning worksheet. Unpublished document, University of Illinois, Champaign, IL.

Malik, P. B. (1991). Leisure education evaluation sheet. Unpublished document, Illinois State University, Normal, IL.

Stumbo, N. J., & Peterson, C. A. (2009). *Therapeutic recreation program design principles & procedures* (5th ed.). San Francisco, CA: Pearson Benjamin Cummings.

Appendix A

Leisure Education Activity Planning Worksheet (adapted from J. Levy, 1989)

1. What is the overall goal of the activity? What area of leisure education content is to be addressed? What is the object of the game?

2. What are the participant objectives for the activity? At the end of the activity or game, what should they have gained?

3. What format will be used to play or participate in the activity?

4. What are the rules of the activity? For example:
   - How will play start? (Roll of the dice? Specific person in the group?)
   - Are the players in teams or as individuals? (If teams, how selected?)
   - How do players move around the gameboard? (Moves correspond to dice numbers or a spinner? Each person moves one space per turn?)
   - How will participants score or gain points? (By landing on the "right" squares? By answering questions? By accumulating points? By making certain decisions?)
   - Will a score sheet be used? (What does it look like? Who records on it? How is the score kept?)
   - How does someone win or finish? (First player to reach finish line? End of 10 minutes? Play to the score of 50? Does there have to be a winner?)
   - What does the player get for winning or finishing? (Tokens, prizes?)
   - How much can the players vary the rules of the game? (Do they have to play "by the book" or can they create their own rules as they go?)

5. What kinds of adaptations can be made for various participant groups?

6. What other kinds of activities or games can be created that use similar (or the same) materials, but have a different intent or overall goal?

Appendix B

Leisure Education Activity Evaluation Sheet (adapted from P. Malik, 1991)

Name of Game/Activity: _____ Designer: _____

Rate each leisure education game/activity on the following 12 points. Modify any part of the game/activity that receives a 3 or 4 rating.

EXCELLENT = 1; GOOD = 2; FAIR = 3; POOR = 4.

	E	G	F	P
1. **GOAL APPROPRIATENESS** (Purpose and goals are appropriate for leisure education activities/games)	1	2	3	4
2. **CONTENT APPROPRIATENESS** (Content covered in the game/activity meets the stated purpose and goals within the description of the game/activity)	1	2	3	4
3. **SIMULATION OF REALITY** (Content, rules, consequences, etc. reflect reality as much as possible)	1	2	3	4
4. **FACILITATION TECHNIQUES** (Suggestions for facilitating game/activity —e.g., discussion questions—are included)	1	2	3	4
5. **DURABLE** (Game/activity can be used repeatedly by participant groups)	1	2	3	4
6. **FEASIBLE** (Game/activity is age- and ability-appropriate for intended participant groups)	1	2	3	4
7. **SELF-EXPLANATORY** (Specialist or participant could start play easily; instructions are clear and easy to understand)	1	2	3	4
8. **SELF-CONTAINED** (All equipment and/or supplies are included in game/activity package)	1	2	3	4
9. **ATTRACTIVE** (Game board, cards, playing pieces, etc. are visually pleasing, neat, and "invite" players to play)	1	2	3	4
10. **ADAPTATIONS/MODIFICATIONS** (Suggestions for how game/activity could be adapted for other settings or participant group are included, as appropriate)	1	2	3	4
11. **CHALLENGE** (Appropriate level of challenge for target participation, i.e., not too easy, not too hard)	1	2	3	4
12. **GAME IS FUN TO PLAY** (Beyond learning content, participants are likely to enjoy playing or being involved in the game/activity)	1	2	3	4

Appendix C

Therapeutic Recreation Resource List (compiled by Norma J. Stumbo and Kari Kensinger)

Resource:	From the Publisher:
Venture Publishing Company 1991 Cato Avenue State College, Pennsylvania 16801-3238 Phone: (814) 234-4561 Fax: (814) 234-1651 Email: vpublish@venturepublish.com Web: www.venturepublish.com	Venture Publishing, Inc. has been offering "Books That Matter" since 1978 to administrators, educators, directors of therapeutic recreation, activity directors, and clinical staff. Their publications cover the areas of therapeutic recreation, activity programming, long-term care, parks and recreation, leisure studies, behavior management skills, advanced CNA training, and private, public, and commercial recreation.
Sagamore Publishing P.O. Box 647 Champaign, Illinois 61824-0647 Phone: (800) 327-5557 or (217) 359-5940 Fax: (217) 359-5975 Email: books@sagamorepub.com Web: www.sagamorepub.com	Sagamore Publishing is committed to providing informative, cutting-edge material in the field of parks, recreation, and leisure education.
Addison-Wesley/Benjamin Cummings 1301 Sansome Street San Francisco, CA 94111 Phone: (415) 402-2500 Fax: (415) 402-2590 Web: www.aw-bc.com	As the premier publisher in computing, economics, finance, mathematics, science, and statistics, their goal is to partner with instructors, authors, and students to create content and tools that take the educational experience forward. They are committed to publishing the best collection of print and electronic content designed to help teachers teach and students learn.
Human Kinetics *United States* Human Kinetics P.O. Box 5076 Champaign, Illinois 61825-5076 Phone: 800-747-4457 Fax: (217) 351-1549 Email: info@hkusa.com Web: www.humankinetics.com *Canada* Human Kinetics 475 Devonshire Rd., Unit 100 Windsor, Ontario N8Y 2L5 Phone: 800-465-7301 (in Canada only) (519) 971-9500 Fax: (519) 971-9797 Email: info@hkcanada.com	At Human Kinetics, our mission is to produce innovative, informative products in all areas of physical activity that help people worldwide lead healthier, more active lives. Human Kinetics is committed to providing quality informational and educational products in the physical activity and health fields that meet the needs of our diverse customers. Within the physical activity field, recreational and organized sports are a major focus. Our customers include scholars who study physical activity and health issues; professionals who apply sport, physical activity, and health knowledge in delivering useful services; and the public who engage in fitness and sports activities in many forms and who benefit from living healthier lifestyles. We are committed to providing not only information but also solutions that help our customers practice their professions better and live healthier, more enjoyable lives. We are committed to providing accurate, useful information and education, packaged and delivered at affordable prices with technology being a key driving force in improving our products and their accessibility. We are committed to being a world leader in our field through innovation and expansion around the world.

Resource:	From the Publisher:
Elsevier, Health Sciences Division *United States* 1600 John F. Kennedy Blvd., Ste 1800 Philadelphia, PA 19103-2899 Phone: (215) 239-3900 Fax: (215) 239-3990 Web: www.elsevier.com *Canada* 1 Goldthorne Avenue Toronto, Ontario Canada M8Z 5S7 Phone: (866) 276-5533 Fax: (888) 359-9534 Email: cs.canada@elsevier.com Web: www.elsevier.ca	Elsevier is a world leading, multiple-media publisher of scientific, technical and health information products and services, with 7,000 employees in 73 locations around the globe. Elsevier publishes more than 20,000 products and services, including journals, books, electronic products, services, databases and portals serving the global scientific, technical and medical (STM) communities.
Aspen Publishers *Corporate Headquarters* 111 Eighth Avenue, 7th Floor New York, NY 10011 Phone: (212) 771-0600 Fax: (212) 771-0885 Web: www.aspenpublishers.com *Customer Care* 7201 McKinney Circle Frederick, MD 21704 Phone: (800)-234-1660 Fax: (800) 901-9075	Aspen Publishers, headquartered in New York City, is a leading information provider for attorneys, business professionals, and law students. Written by preeminent authorities, their products consist of analytical and practical information covering both U.S. and international topics. They publish in the full range of formats, including updated manuals, books, periodicals, CDs, and online products.
Lippincott Williams & Wilkins 530 Walnut Street Philadelphia, PA 19106-3621 Tel: (215) 521-8300 Fax: (215) 521-8902 Web: www.lww.com	Lippincott Williams & Wilkins is a unit of Wolters Kluwer Health, a group of leading information companies offering specialized publications and software for physicians, nurses, students and specialized clinicians. Their products include drug guides, medical journals, nursing journals, medical textbooks and medical PDA software.
Routledge Mental Health 270 Madison Avenue New York, NY 10016, USA America: (Toll Free) (800) 634 7064 Canada: (Toll Free) (877) 226-2237 Web: www.routledgementalhealth.com	The Routledge imprint publishes books and journals on Clinical Psychology, Psychiatry, Psychoanalysis, Analytical Psychology, Psychotherapy, Counseling, Mental Health and other professional subjects.

Resource:	From the Publisher:
Hopkins Technology, LLC 421 Hazel Lane Hopkins, MN 55343-7116 Tel: (952) 931-9376 Fax: (952) 931-9377 Email: infodesk5@hoptechno.com Web: www.hoptechno.com	Hopkins Technology, LLC has been developing software since 1986. They offer about 30 separate software titles to various markets, several of which are available as subscription products on the Internet. In addition, several applications are available on the Internet such as EZ Wedding Planner for planning weddings, EZ Event Planner for planning anything else, and Santé food and recipe lookup. The company maintains the worlds largest food nutrition database compiled from various government and industry sources.
Health Communications, Inc. 3201 S.W. 15th Street Deerfield, Beach, FL 33442 Tel: (800) 441-5569 or (954) 360-0909 Fax: (954) 360-0034 Web: www.hci-online.com	Originally operating as a publisher of informational pamphlets for the recovery community, HCI's moved into mainstream publishing in the 1980s with its first New York Times bestseller, the 1983 *Adult Children of Alcoholics* by Dr. Janet Woititz's. In 1994, HCI published the first *Chicken Soup for the Soul*. HCI has expanded its publishing operations to encompass: Inspiration, Soul/Spirituality, Relationships, Recovery/Healing, Women's Issues, and Self Help. With these themes, HCI represents a broad base in the marketplace of contemporary books.

» CHAPTER 4 »

Planning and Leading Group Activities/ Group Intervention

Marcia J. Carter, Re.D., CTRS, CPRP and
Katherine M. Morse, M.S., CTRS, CPRP

Background and History

Nature of Leadership in Therapeutic Recreation

Leadership in therapeutic recreation is essential to the success of one-on-one, small and large group interventions. Regardless of the nature of the intervention, a therapist uses helper skills to facilitate human interactions and to provide clients with opportunities to improve their health and well-being. The therapist selects and uses specific modalities and facilitation techniques to achieve client goals and objectives. Therapists assume various roles influenced by the nature of the intervention, the group members, and the intended purposes and outcomes of the individual or group experience. Although the history of leadership in therapeutic recreation is limited, one of the initial discussions (Avedon, 1974) outlined the roles of a specialist along a horizontal continuum determined by the client's relative maturity level (which is defined by how much internal or external control is needed in order to function in social situations). At one end of the continuum, the therapist makes all decisions regarding client actions, referred to as a controller role, while at the opposite end, an enabler role is evident when the therapist responds to participants only when assistance is requested. This situational approach to leadership evolved from the realization that as the client, intervention, group members and desired outcomes change, so does the interrelationship among the therapist and these environmental factors (O'Morrow, 1980). Contemporary leadership theories like the servant-leadership approach focus on the relational nature of therapist-client interactions. The therapist's role is one of collaboration and connection with clients through the therapeutic recreation process, known as APIE (assess, plan, implement, and evaluate), to effect growth and development (Carter & O'Morrow, 2006).

The focus of this chapter is planning and leading group experiences to bring about change in the health of group members. Intervention groups rely on effective therapists to give meaning and direction to group experiences (Kraus & Shank, 1992; Shank & Coyle, 2002). Therapists assume roles ranging from being "face-to-face" leaders to facilitators/observers and supervisors who guide and support client-group interactions (Stumbo & Peterson, 2009). Therapists, through their leadership, give structure to group experiences and accurately gauge the group's development and progress toward accomplishing individual and group goals. Therapists also monitor the impact of their leadership on individual and group behavior and the accomplishment of desired goals and objectives (Shank & Coyle, 2002). Ultimately, the effectiveness of the therapist as a leader determines the success of a group experience as an intervention (O'Morrow, 1980). Thus, there are two overarching considerations presented in this chapter. First, planning and leading groups are considered direct or face-to-face leadership and are foundational to engaging clients in group interventions that enable growth and development. Second, group dynamics and processes are discussed to help the reader understand that meaningful group interactions can be created and used as catalysts or change agents toward important therapeutic outcomes (Shank & Coyle, 2002).

Nature of Groups in Therapeutic Recreation

Groups are used as interventions in therapeutic recreation because they are practical, efficient, and effective in accomplishing client outcomes (Shank & Coyle, 2002). The use of the group process as an effective and cost-efficient model of treatment has been accelerated by managed care (Reeve, 2006). With group interventions, therapists realize individual client goals in a timely manner. An intervention group has the purpose of facilitating client change and growth. This occurs through purposeful selection of modalities and facilitation techniques, and through the dynamic processes resulting from interaction among group members and the therapist. Group experiences are therapeutic because cohesion is created—members bond and feel safe, valued, and accepted (Yalom & Leszcz, 2005). Furthermore, as members work together, they develop an identity and shared purpose that allows them to achieve common goals (Shank & Coyle, 2002).

One typology organizes intervention groups into four categories (Shank & Coyle, 2002). *Educational* groups, like leisure education, provide information on the relationships of the client's disability to leisure behavior, health, and quality of life. Second, *functional skills* groups, like social skills training, address clients' needs to improve, regain, or enhance cognitive, physical, social, emotional, and spiritual functioning important to recreation and daily life experiences. Third, *support* groups, like Alcoholics Anonymous or peer counseling groups, provide ongoing social-emotional support, and opportunities for advocacy, and encourage healthy behaviors and appropriate leisure lifestyles. Lastly, *psychoeducational* groups combine education, skill development, and social support to develop practices that will help clients change and monitor their behaviors. Such groups are found in outpatient and outreach clinics with persons who have experienced strokes or with caregivers of clients with Alzheimer's disease. In each of these group formats, therapists' leadership roles vary as they orchestrate group-member involvement in selected modalities and facilitation techniques to achieve therapeutic outcomes.

Intended Client Groups

A number of formal and informal groups are likely to be encountered by the therapeutic recreation specialist (TRS). *Formal treatment groups* are used with inpatient and outpatient interventions, while the leadership and supervision of support groups like a post-traumatic stress disorder (PTSD) group is an *informal group* intervention. Treatment groups are used with: (a) adults with persistent mental illness and children in inpatient psychotherapy; (b) those who have experienced trauma associated with head injuries or abuse; and, (c) inpatient and outpatient services with individuals who have illnesses and physical disabilities with long-term repercussions, like cancer and strokes. Informal groups are usually comprised of individuals who participate voluntarily. Also, a specific intervention may not be prescribed by a physician or used by the therapist. Informal group members are clients, caregivers, and family members. Conditions represented include intellectual deficits, HIV, Alzheimer's disease, substance abuse, traumatic brain injury (TBI), and chronic physical disabilities like Parkinson's disease and spinal cord injuries (SCI).

In therapeutic recreation, group processes are the conduits for implementing other interventions like social skills training, physical activity, adventure therapy, anger and stress management, assertiveness training, leisure education, self-esteem, problem solving, empowerment, reality orientation, reminiscence, remotivation, play therapy, and grief/loss counseling. TRSs will lead and co-lead groups and use group interventions in a variety of formal and informal settings with a full spectrum of individuals having health care issues.

Basic Premises

Planning and Leading Groups

This section of the chapter considers the leader's role as a planner and organizer of groups. Face-to-face or direct leadership is fundamental to engaging clients in group interventions. Structure is brought to a group through a series of tasks intended to enable members to achieve individual outcomes while benefiting from the *esprit de corps*. Even as the leader is influenced by a number of contextual factors and challenges, the therapist motivates, manages, and processes the experience to enable individual growth and group development.

Structure of Group Interventions

The TRS is apt to spend a great deal of time working with groups of various types. The therapist plans, structures, manages, and processes group encounters during a session in order to meet individual and group member needs. Intervention sessions may stand alone or be organized sequentially with several sessions planned to effect desired client outcomes. To illustrate, a TRS may lead a small group in a one-time experience on conflict resolution, while the same clients may practice relaxation techniques during several sequential sessions. Each session is structured or organized in a similar fashion. This facilitates consistency, continuity, and enables documentation of best practices as well as data collection to affirm evidence-based outcomes. Engagement of clients in a session recognizes the intensity of an experience and is visualized as a bell-shaped curve or program wave (refer to Figure 4.1). An acknowledged format organizes a session into an introductory phase, active engagement phase, and closure phase with pre- and post-preparation tasks of group leaders (Carter & LeConey, 2004; Shank & Coyle, 2002). During the introductory phase, the intensity of

Introduction   Active Engagement   Closure

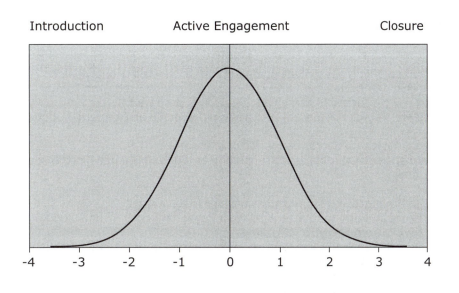

-4   -3   -2   -1   0   1   2   3   4

Figure 4.1. Intensity of Client Engagement during Group Session

interaction commences with minimal client engagement and accelerates as group members become acquainted and familiarized with the intent and structure of the session. In the active phase of engagement, clients' involvements reach "peaks" or climaxes as they engage in group processes, and, as discussion/processing begins, the intensity of the interaction declines. During the closure phase, clients' levels of intensity subsides as debriefing prepares them to transition from the group intervention.

Within a session, the length of each phase varies due to factors like the size of the group, nature of the intervention, total amount of time available, complexity of the experience, intended outcomes, capabilities of clients to manage within the group, and the degree of group cohesiveness. The leadership tasks evident in each of the phases are presented in Table 4.1 (pp. 56–57). *KISS* (or *Keep It Short and Simple*) and *KIP* (or *Keep It Positive*) are guidelines to consider during the preparation, delivery, and closure of experiences. The bell curve represents the flow of effort and energy among clients as they complete an intervention or series of interventions in a session. Transitions within experiences and between experiences are opportunities for debriefing and summarization. As each session ends, the goal is to have clients anticipate future experiences while reflecting on the accomplishments of the session. Immediately prior to session closure, the therapist acknowledges individual and group goal accomplishments and completes a visual assessment of each client to assure they are experiencing closure and are prepared to proceed to the next event.

Factors Influencing Leadership of Intervention Groups

While effectiveness of a group intervention is influenced by the ability of the therapist to structure sessions, outcomes of the intervention are shaped by a number of environmental and personal factors; these include the (a) therapist, (b) clients, (c) situation or environment, and (d) nature of the group. The therapist's leadership skills, experience, self-knowledge, practice, wisdom, and abilities as a therapeutic helper impact factors like selection of specific leadership styles and roles, and comfort with certain client groups, interventions, and co-leaders. Each therapist brings to the group unique behavior and decision-making styles, expertise with particular interventions and clientele, and a professional culture. Likewise, clients have unique backgrounds, needs, and expectations. Clients also may have had different types of group involvement and exposure to various interventions and group processes. Personal factors like culture, gender, age, and literacy level influence group member participation (Shank & Coyle, 2002). Each group member may also have a unique participation reason and goal.

Group interventions take place in particular settings and environments. The climate created by the environment influences, for example, interventions that may be selected, the style and role of the leader(s), the size or number in the group, resources available to the group, physical arrangements, and control of privacy, stimuli, lighting, acoustics, time, and temperature — all elements that impact mood and temperament of

Table 4.1. Leadership Tasks during Each Phase of an Intervention

Preparation
- Prepare materials, equipment, and adaptations prior to client arrival
- Ensure session outcomes encompass client goals and reflect overall group goals
- Choose experiences that can be initiated and completed in the allotted time frame
- Re-check safety and risk protocols as the physical space is prepared
- Assure all therapists are trained, prepared, and assigned specific and general supervisory responsibilities, if appropriate
- Review back-up plans in case resources warrant adjustment
- Rehearse directions/instructions, rules, and transitions among experiences in the session
- Rehearse the experience

Introduction
- Use a consistent signal to start and stop group member involvement
- Welcome or greet clients by name and attend to their personal items, acknowledging any absent group members, and identifying each therapist by name
- Organize members into the desired formation so each client is in the therapist's visual field and their attention is gained through the introduction
- Discuss any previous session experiences and link to the present session, if new members are present, guide past members in summarizing the group experience
- Identify the session outcomes and relate to individual and group goals and the general flow of experiences to occur during the session
- Review safety considerations including behavioral consequences of noncompliance
- Check client readiness by asking questions or making statements like, "let's have each group member identify one outcome they are expecting from today's group" or "what might be the outcome you each would expect from today's experience?"
- Stimulate participation by involving experiences that use as many of the senses as possible and create active involvement of each client, keeping directions to as few words as possible; show outcomes or products of the experience; step-by-step instructions are clear, concise, complete, and compared to a known or familiar experience
- The use of media prompts, handouts, and recognition of previous client experiences complements auditory and visual learners
- Ask clients to either repeat, demonstrate or model directions for successful activity completion, have clients demonstrate what is to occur during the experience, and ask group members if they have any questions
- Engage all group members

Implementation/Active Engagement
- Maintain verbal and visual supervision, monitoring safety and non-goal directed behaviors; stop and redefine outcomes rather than experience unsuccessful outcomes
- Observe and reinforce verbal as well as nonverbal participation, move among clients, use eye contact to reinforce or diminish inappropriate behaviors
- Anticipate conditions and behaviors looking for antecedents and rewards
- Provide group corrective feedback rather than singling out one member
- Provide assistance with social expectations as well as specific activity skills
- Incorporate opportunities for choice, decision-making, and client self-pacing
- Praise positive interaction, restate desired behaviors when unacceptable behaviors occur, practice ignoring behaviors that are not harmful or disruptive to the group
- Reduce waiting and down time with transitions like, "tell me an important fact about today" or "if I had $100.00 I would . . ." or "my favorite leisure experience occurred . . . ."
- Set behavioral expectations prior to implementation; if non-goal-directed behavior or negative group behaviors become evident, prevent escalation by using five steps:
    1. Identify inappropriate behavior
    2. Explain why the behavior, cause and effect, is inappropriate
    3. Present reasonable choices or consequences
    4. Allow client time to choose alternatives, if possible
    5. Follow-through or enforce the consequences
- Reward group progress and monitor intensity of engagement by noting time remaining, individual and group progress toward goals
- Catch experience at its peak or plateau and begin to engage group in processing by using affirmation experiences and recognition of session goals, noting remaining time or tasks

Table 4.1. Leadership Tasks during Each Phase of an Intervention (continued)

Closure/Processing
- Allow decompression or composure time by organizing clients and resources used during the experience, check client well-being, safety, and response to experience
- Reward and recognize cooperation and group goal achievement, all group members are encouraged to work together to acknowledge success and thank each other
- Summarize and clarify observed individual and group outcomes
- Seek feedback through debriefing questions in three areas, what, so what, now what:
- *What* questions:
  1. What happened, behaviors and feelings?
  2. What was accomplished toward individual and group goals?
  3. What communication occurred among group members?
  4. What roles were assumed by group members?
- *So what* questions:
  1. How does the group experience apply to treatment issues?
  2. How does what happened compare with everyday life issues?
  3. What are the consequences of the activity individually and overall for the group?
  4. What outcomes are relevant to the real world?
- *Now what* questions:
  1. What has changed for the client as a result of the experience?
  2. How can group members support and integrate new learning into new skills?
  3. How can group outcomes become part of the client's life?
  4. How will the client maintain the changed behavior?
- A routine is followed so clients recognize a definitive ending
- Clients are thanked and, if appropriate, reminded of the next activity or task
- Homework assignments, if appropriate, are reviewed

Post-closure
- The area is secured/inspected to assure condition of resources
- Experiences are documented with recommendations, adaptations for future sessions
- Team members are debriefed, if appropriate
- Individual client follow-up and needs are documented and planned
- Unanticipated or unplanned outcomes are documented

Adapted from: Carter & LeConey, 2004; Dattilo & Sneegas, 1987; Shank & Coyle, 2002.

therapists and clients. Lastly, the nature of the group affects group dynamics and processes instrumental to achieving individual and group outcomes. Group composition, size, history, relations, gender ratio, culture, and range of ages influence, for example, how the therapist presents information and organizes clients to engage in the experience. Some groups are time-limited with a fixed number of clients, while others are open-ended with a diverse clientele who join/depart at any time (Shank & Coyle, 2002). The degree of group cohesion or "we-ness" varies among these groups, which impacts effectiveness of group intervention. Since the group is the primary agent of change, the therapist's task is to create a group culture conducive to effective group interaction (Yalom & Leszcz, 2005). Thus, as the therapist structures each group intervention, consideration is given to each of these four elements, because the desired end result of the session is impacted by the interplay among these variables. As a consequence, during direct or face-to-face leadership,

therapists' responsibilities include motivating and managing interactions to ensure consistent and safe client outcomes.

Motivating, Managing, Processing Intervention Groups

Motivation is a state of readiness to change (Austin, 2009). The motivation process involves an internal drive that causes behaviors to be directed toward a goal (Jordan, 2007). Therapists use a variety of strategies to establish an environment in which clients are motivated to change and grow. Motivation is enhanced by manipulating physical, psychological, and socioemotional environments and being aware of where the client is in the change process (Austin, 2009; Jordan, 2007).

Client assessment may reveal if the client and support system are aware of the need for change or the degree to which the client/caregiver is able to accept responsibility for or support behavioral change. Thus, therapists may revisit assessment information to identify the client's/caregiver's recognition of the issue and the desired direction of necessary behavioral change. Once identified, the therapist manipulates the physical setting creating a comfortable, pleasant, welcoming environment supportive of affirmation and recognition. The use of food, music, themes, and props creates a special atmosphere. By allowing clients to make choices, receive immediate feedback, participate in the preparing and selecting of familiar activities and ones with compatible levels of skill and challenge, the therapist is encouraging psychological health and achievement (Ellis, Witt, & Aguilar, 1983; Savell, 1986). Likewise, by setting goals and expectations, each group member is made aware of what behaviors are necessary for success. Giving recognition to group members motivates positive reflections and engenders positive self-esteem.

The socioemotional environment of the group is manipulated by attending to group size and composition and by helping group members feel they are valued contributors to individual and group accomplishments. Laughter and humor are motivating, as is the opportunity for a client to assume a leadership role. A primary responsibility of the group leader is to model enthusiasm and readiness to change (Shank & Coyle, 2002). Therapists model such things as giving positive feedback to group members, recognizing individual strengths and group assets, and making everyone feel included during the intervention by identifying each member by name (Shank & Coyle, 2002). By modeling nonjudgmental acceptance as well as recognition of strengths and problem areas, the therapist helps shape a group that is health-oriented (Yalom & Leszcz, 2005). Once the therapist has identified client readiness to change, an environment is created to guide client motivation toward healthier behaviors. This involves carefully structuring the physical setting, creating opportunities for clients to be psychologically connected to the experience, and using the group socioemotional atmosphere to create cohesion and feelings of shared goals.

Motivating group involvement is a primary leader function. Several other leader functions are instrumental to group effectiveness. Whether the therapist completes a risk-management checklist or documents compliance to a physician's orders, client safety is a priority with quality-improvement programs and regulators like Centers for Medicare and Medicaid Services (CMS). A therapist's technical expertise is evident with the selection and instruction of intervention content appropriate to the client's needs and group goals and as a safe experience is delivered. The therapist enforces rules and

relies on written protocols and best practices to guide clients toward safe, relevant outcomes. Therapists are also facilitators, as they connect clients to information, resources, and others in the group (Shank & Coyle, 2002).

The impact of the negotiator is evident when conflict is managed. Therapists also model desirable behaviors and interactions while setting a positive tone through feedback and recognition of progress (Austin, 2009). Because group membership is often fluid, the therapist creates an accepting, nonjudgmental atmosphere by welcoming and acknowledging individual members who join or leave the group. By organizing and consistently monitoring group member participation, therapists bring a sense of direction and stability to the group process (Shank & Coyle, 2002).

A function that continues to become more important to program viability is research and evaluation. A TRS systematically evaluates effectiveness of the group as an intervention; outcomes from various interventions (e.g., social skills training, adventure therapy) that rely on group processes are also documented and evaluated. Managing groups requires the TRS to provide direct leadership, to facilitate and supervise engagements to assure quality, and to set a tone supportive of client change and group growth.

A key function of the therapist is processing experiences. Processing is verbal discussion with group members to consider personal behaviors and the consequences and influences among external or environmental factors (Shank & Coyle, 2002). Processing skills are used to make activities therapeutic: processing is a tool to accelerate the therapeutic change process (Hutchinson & Dattilo, 2001). Behavior change through interventions is achieved with various processing techniques used to help clients focus on their behaviors before, during, and after the experience and then to generalize these behaviors to life functions (Shank & Coyle, 2002).

Frontloading and *framing* the experience occur prior to the activity, *feedback* and *metaphors* are embedded in the activity, and *debriefing* follows the activity (Hutchinson & Dattilo, 2001; Jordan, 2007). Prior to the activity, the therapist helps to focus the group by setting the stage for what learning and group outcomes should result from the experience (called "frontloading the experience"). This occurs by describing what will occur, reflecting on the importance of the experience in group members' lives, and identifying behaviors that will result in success rather than detract from the value of the experience. Review of previous sessions, restating goals, and questions on the importance of the experience to group members' goals are techniques used to frontload. Framing, a subset of frontloading, asks group members to relate the upcoming experience to the real world or their lives outside the group intervention. Questions on how the upcoming activity is similar to their family or work responsibilities "frame" the activity (Jordan, 2007).

During the activity, the therapist provides information about clients' efforts and progress toward goal achievement or uses feedback. Also, therapists connect the experience to clients' lives by using metaphors and analogies. Therapists communicate that successful completion of the experience mirrors successful resolution of life issues (Hutchinson & Dattilo, 2001). Descriptive comments from the therapist reinforce strengths, affirm learning, and create possibilities for transferring behaviors to client real-world responsibilities. To illustrate, when a client or caregiver in a support group identifies optional leisure resources, the therapist acknowledges the validity of the choices, affirms the positive results of decision making, and encourages the use of similar problem-solving behaviors during family discussions on managing time while successfully including the individual in family experiences.

During and following the activity, therapists ask reflective questions to analyze and guide clients to gain understanding and meaning of the experience. A popular form of this debriefing is organized into "what," "so what," and "now what" questions (Shank & Coyle, 2002). The intent is to present clarifying and probing questions so clients reflect on their engagement and are better able to assume ownership for learning and desired changes (Hutchinson & Dattilo, 2001). When clients are asked *what* happened during the session, they are called upon to clarify the various types of learning or behavioral change evident during the activity. *So what* questions that seek the similarities between group experiences and personal lives call upon clients to probe the relevancy of behaviors to real life. Lastly, *now what* questions like, "How will these new behaviors be sustained during family interactions?" involve behavior generalization and transfer and call upon clients to explain in concrete terms what happens after group intervention to maintain behavioral change. While commonly occurring at the conclusion of a session, a therapist may stop a group during intervention to debrief significant outcomes not readily apparent to clients, yet critical to group success.

In addition to clarifying, probing, reflecting, and questioning skills, therapists processing intervention groups encounter behaviors that threaten group cohesiveness and deter the group from becoming an effective change agent. As a consequence, to effectively process group interventions, therapists also use communication skills like focusing, redirecting, and summarizing so support and confrontation build a group culture conducive to effective group interaction (Shank & Coyle, 2002; Yalom & Leszcz, 2005). When clients focus on the physical skills to successfully complete an activity, the therapist asks clients to also consider their socioemotional responses during the experience. Likewise, when group members' comments deviate from the task at hand or focus on unsuccessful attempts, therapists block, link, or redirect discussion and behaviors toward session outcomes. Lastly, prior to, throughout, and at the session conclusion, therapists summarize thoughts and feelings to support bridges and transitions clients make from one session to the next, or from intervention groups to their personal lives. Thus, during processing, a TRS relies on effective communication skills to build group capacity as a therapeutic instrument.

Intervention Group Dynamics and Processes

This section of the chapter considers group dynamics and processes—the essence of what makes groups beneficial as change agents. Every therapy group undergoes a singular development with shifts in member behavior and communication as the group unfolds (Yalom & Leszcz, 2005). For therapists to be effective, they must understand the group's level of maturity, so appropriate leadership strategies are used to create and maintain group cohesion and culture. Each group is also characterized by elements or properties that mold or shape member behavior and interactions among members and the therapist. Consequently, group member roles evolve during engagements and are evident in behaviors and interaction patterns during activities. This chapter section overviews group dynamics and processes affecting the therapist's performance and group member outcomes.

Group Development

A group is a collection of individuals that through their interactions develop interrelatedness, cohesiveness, or unity (Edginton, Hudson, & Scholl, 2005). As a group develops, shifts occur in communication and behavior. Healthy group development results in increased empathy and positive communication (Yalom & Leszcz, 2005). Therapists facilitate development of healthy group norms that promote achievement of individual and group goals. Thus, therapists have a sense of healthy group development that engenders group member confidence and a sense of direction, stability, and connectedness. During each stage of development, the therapist is aware of internal and external forces impacting progress and intervenes to ensure the group serves as an agent of healthy change. A commonly accepted typology of group development is organized into four stages (Tuckman, 1965): forming, storming, norming, and performing.

During the *forming* stage of group development, clients look to the therapist for structure and direction, as well as explanations of "What's in it for me?" "What does this have to do with my issues?" medications, symptoms, and previous therapy experiences (Yalom & Leszcz, 2005). Clients must understand how to achieve their primary tasks (e.g., purpose of the group) while they establish the social relationships critical to accomplishing the primary group objectives and becoming comfortable as group members.

During the *storming* stage, members shift from a search for meaning and guidance to concern for control and power (Yalom & Leszcz, 2005). As members express their needs and pass judgment on others, a struggle among group members for dominance ensues, especially when new clients enter the group. Unrealistic expectations of the therapist result in disappointment and hostility toward the therapist that dissipate as members recognize limitations and begin to examine their group relations and accept feedback. Therapists encourage expression of feelings and acceptance of divergent viewpoints (Jordan, 2007). Gradually group members acquire the capacity to feel emotions expressed among the members and therapist and to reflect on the experience as it relates to individual and group goals (Yalom & Leszcz, 2005).

Resistance to group influence is overcome in the third phase, *norming*, as cohesiveness develops, standards evolve, and clients adopt roles of mutual support and positive relationships with others and the therapist. Personal opinions are expressed as each client begins to struggle with his/her own issues and work as a team member to resolve expressed issues of the group (Tuckman, 1965). Therapists solicit positive and negative feedback and they listen as increasing trust results in member self-disclosure. Norms are solidified, and the group develops a unique culture (Jordan, 2007). Therapists may delegate so the group is allowed to achieve its potential.

During the final stage, *performing,* structural issues are resolved so group energy is channeled into the task (Tuckman, 1965). Interpersonal interactions become the tool to address individual and group goals. Members are aware of each other's assets and liabilities. As feedback is sought from the therapist and

group members, the group becomes self-determining (Jordan, 2007). Through questioning, probing, clarifying, and interpreting, the therapist guides members toward their potential and group goal achievement. The achievement of group maturity is influenced by elements or properties internal and external to the group and therapist; yet these factors influence group development and effectiveness. Consequently, therapists consider these as groups are convened and grow toward maturity as therapeutic agents.

Group Elements

A number of key elements influence the effectiveness of the group as an intervention. Aside from the client characteristics and behaviors, the therapists' competence, the environment or situation in which the group functions, and the nature of the group, several additional factors impact the interrelatedness or "we-ness" developed by the group. Typically, these include goals, norms, cohesiveness, interaction, status or roles of group members, and group task and maintenance functions (Austin, 2009; Edginton, Hudson, & Scholl, 2005; Jordan, 2007).

Goals provide direction and gauge progress of the group as an intervention to achieve individual and group outcomes. Groups with a high degree of cohesion cooperatively pursue group-oriented rather than personally oriented motives; yet, through interactions, members achieve outcomes supportive of individual and group health (Edginton, Hudson, & Scholl, 2005). Conversely, without goals, neither individuals nor the group benefit. Like goals, development of norms is evident in high-functioning groups and absent in groups lacking interrelatedness. Norms are written and unwritten expectations of member behavior. Norms guide interactions. As members grow and change, behaviors are accepted or judged as inappropriate to group functioning and member issue resolution. Cohesion is the forces acting on members that result in attraction and satisfaction derived from the group experience; the stronger the attraction and greater the satisfaction, the higher the degree of bonding and "we-ness" (Edginton, Hudson, & Scholl, 2005; Yalom & Leszcz, 2005). Early cohesion and engagement are critical to group development and capacity to work during later stages (e.g., performing).

The work of the group occurs through verbal and nonverbal communication and interactions among members. With a high degree and equal distribution of communication, interrelatedness and cohesion result. Conversely, without supportive engagements, unity is minimal and movement toward individual and group goals is compromised. Through communication, individual roles of the group members are defined. While norms ascribe similar group behaviors, status or roles of individuals result in unique individual behaviors (Edginton, Hudson, & Scholl, 2005). With a high degree of group consensus about individual roles, interrelatedness results. The behavior, thoughts, and feelings of a member influence the role assumed at any given time. At times, members focus on individual needs or assume self-oriented roles at the expense of group goal achievement and development (Austin, 2009).

Through their roles within the group, individuals assume task and maintenance functions that maintain group health. Task functions relate to accomplishing work to meet group goals, while maintenance functions promote group development. Task roles are evident when members contribute to the group by, for example, identifying or suggesting solutions to member issues. Specific ways members assume task roles include: information seeking or giving, summarizing, evaluating, clarifying, exploring, elaborating, and recording (Austin, 2009; Edginton, Hudson, & Scholl, 2005). Maintenance roles are the socio-emotional activities that build cooperation among members promoting group development. Roles that build interactions include: encouraging, harmonizing, compromising, supporting, following, standard setting, and gate keeping (Austin, 2009; Edginton, Hudson, & Scholl, 2005). Task and maintenance roles are fluid, changing from positive to negative and among group members.

Individuals who assume roles focused on their own rather than the group's goals impede group development. When an individual dominates, protects, blocks, confesses, seeks recognition, or is confused or aggressive and always commits with a "yes," the balance of individual- and group-need satisfaction is tipping toward the individual rather than realization of group outcomes that positively impact all group members (Austin, 2009; Edginton, Hudson, & Scholl, 2005). Effective groups are characterized by, for example, positive behaviors like problem solving and consensus building, while groups become ineffective when negative behaviors like blocking and scapegoating are displayed by group members. Therapists facilitate balance through feedback, modeling, and constructive criticism capitalizing on the strengths of group members. Effective processing contributes to leader and group effectiveness. Recognition of appropriate member roles promotes group synergy and healthy member change.

Group Dynamics and Therapeutic Interventions

Group dynamics is everything that happens within a group and the essence of what makes groups beneficial (Shank & Coyle, 2002). Group dynamics is concerned with factors influencing group communication, interaction internally and externally, and the processes used to influence group behavior and assist the group to achieve its goals (Edginton, Hudson, & Scholl, 2005). This chapter has thus far presented internal and external factors related to the leader, clients, environment, and nature of the group that influence patterns of communication and interaction. These factors create opportunities for change through group cohesion (e.g., shared goals), or are mechanisms for change (e.g., processing). Skilled therapists deliberately use these factors as well as a number of processes to enable growth and change during intervention groups (Shank & Coyle, 2002).

What processes make a group therapeutic? A number of studies have identified therapeutic factors of group therapy to be catharsis, self-understanding, interpersonal input, cohesiveness, and universality (Yalom & Leszcz, 2005). Others add factors like a cluster of hope, acceptance, altruism, self-disclosure, interpersonal learning, modeling, and guidance (Shank & Coyle, 2002). Early in group development, supportive factors that motivate involvement and facilitate connections emerge and include universality, cluster of hope, acceptance and altruism (Shank & Coyle, 2002). Members feel a sense of shared experience, validation of personal feelings, opportunity to turn to others to help, and believe that change and self-improvement are possible. Group cohesion evolves in early stages of group development and sets the stage for greater personal self-disclosure and catharsis (Yalom & Leszcz, 2005). As the group develops, clients are more willing to share their stories (self-disclosure) and receive feedback (interpersonal learning). Self-understanding occurs as clients learn how they are perceived by others (interpersonal input) and they discover and accept previously unknown and unacceptable behaviors. With high-functioning groups, members are willing to learn from others (interpersonal learning) including the therapist, through modeling, guidance, and vicarious experiences in order to find more appropriate ways to interact with others to satisfy their goals. Thus, as members' needs and goals shift, the therapist uses different processes to facilitate change and acceptance of the group as a mechanism for growth. Interpersonal interaction encompassing catharsis, self-understanding, and group cohesion are the *sine qua non* of effective groups, so therapists direct their efforts toward maximal development of these therapeutic factors (Yalom & Leszcz, 2005).

Application to Therapeutic Recreation

Therapeutic recreation professionals work with a number of client groups. Examples of these groups include:

- support groups of caregivers of adults with Alzheimer's disease (Bedini & Phoenix, 1999)
- leisure education strategies used in caregiver groups (Carter, Nezey, Wenzel, & Foret, 1999)
- leisure education groups with adult survivors of childhood abuse (Griffin, 2005)
- leisure education groups for caregivers of persons with Alzheimer's (Keller & Hughes, 1991)
- social skills groups with individuals affected by traumatic brain injury (Richard, Jakobov, Sosowsky, & Leiser, 2008)
- reality orientation groups with individuals with Alzheimer's (Smith-Marchese, 1994)

Related Research

Formal treatment groups with prescribed interventions and informal groups that use group processes are encountered in a number of healthcare settings and among healthcare professionals. Related research is also evident with several client populations.

Terry (2010) introduces the application of interpersonal theories to group treatment in therapeutic recreation practice. As noted earlier, interpersonal interaction is fundamental to effective therapy groups. The author's conceptual paper outlines four principles explaining effectiveness of groups as change agents. Principle one notes the origin of maladaptive interpersonal behaviors (MIPs) in past experiences and posits their presence in current individual and group relations. Second, MIPs are evident when persons become rigid and less able to adapt to interpersonal changes. A model, Maladaptive Transaction Cycle (MTC) helps therapists distinguish between normal and abnormal behaviors during group experiences. The third principle postulates MIPs are enacted between the client and therapist and among clients during group treatment interventions; the MTC is used to assess the presence of normal and maladaptive behaviors during group therapy. Finally, group intervention elicits client change as interpersonal behaviors different than maladaptive patterns are evident during treatment. The therapist focuses on here-and-now interactions. Process illumination and feedback are used to create an environment conducive to change by informing and influencing

group members' MIPs. This conceptual paper presents a theoretical approach to explain effectiveness of group treatment with persons having MIPs while further outlining what makes groups therapeutic.

Caperchione and Mummery (2006) investigated group cohesion as an intervention tool to increase physical activity behavior and adherence among older adults. One-hundred and forty persons over 50 years of age who met the qualifying criteria participated in a 12-week lifestyle intervention program with a 3-, 6-, and 12-month follow-up. Standard groups (total of 5) and enhanced groups (total of 5) participated in instructor-led group walk and group education sessions that incorporated cognitive-behavioral strategies and health-related topics. Additionally, the enhanced groups were exposed to education sessions that focused on participant understanding of the relationship between group development and how increased group cohesion affects physical activity behavior. Physical activity was measured using the Community Healthy Activities Model Program for Seniors Questionnaire (CHAMPS). The Physical Activity Group Environment Questionnaire (PAGEQ) was used to measure perceptions of group cohesion. While there was a significant positive change across time for physical activity behavior, there was no significant difference between intervention groups for cohesion. One reason given for a decrease in perceptions of group cohesion was the lack of physical presence and social interaction between group members post-intervention and throughout the long-term follow-up (Caperchione & Mummery, 2006).

Oei and Browne (2006) investigated the influence of group processes (cohesion, leader support, expressiveness, independence, and self-discovery) on outcomes of clients with anxiety and depression following group cognitive behavior therapy (CBT). For four weeks, 162 clients participated in two four-hour psycho-educational sessions per week with 8 to 14 clients in each therapy group. Clients completed the Beck Anxiety Inventory and the Zung Self-Rating Depression Scale as pre- and post-assessments and the Group Environment Scale as a post-assessment. At the conclusion of treatment patients reported lowered depression and anxiety. Further, within their therapy groups, they benefited from high levels of expressiveness and independence (Oei & Browne, 2006). The researchers concluded that CBT within a group format is an effective form of therapy.

Tomasulo and Razza (2006) described a model of psychotherapy, interactive-behavioral therapy, designed to treat people who are dually diagnosed with intellectual disabilities and psychiatric disorders. This model uses standard techniques from group psychotherapy and psychodrama during ongoing (rather than time-limited) groups to help clients gain a sense of self-efficacy and improved competence. This occurs through support from each other and as "old" group members support "new" group members.

Reeve (2006) described the development of a model, mastery-enhancement group activity (MEGA), which uses community meetings for psychotherapy group intervention with children. Children in inpatient units attend two groups per day. During the initial daily meeting, goals are set for the day. At the end of the day, discussion focuses on how successful children have been in reaching their goals. Staff undergoes group leadership training on the stages of MEGA group development. Reeve (2006) reported that this model appears effective for conducting and understanding group psychotherapy with children having various diagnoses.

Revheim and Marcopulos (2006) reported that psychiatric rehabilitation is primarily delivered using group modalities suitable for persons with serious and persistent mental illness in hospital and community settings. Because cognitive limitations interfere with effective group functioning, the authors propose a cognitive framework for group treatment. Three approaches (integrated psychological therapy, neuropsychological educational approach to rehabilitation and a cognitive adaptive training model) are presented as examples of treatment using remediation and compensatory strategies to change cognitive functioning. Additionally, the authors suggested the role of the therapist, environmental adaptations, and ways to facilitate learning must also be taken into consideration. Best practices are offered for each of these factors.

Social work practice with groups relies on mutual aid, strengths, and empowerment to meet therapeutic needs of individuals with traumatic histories. These individuals include trauma survivors of war, torture, political oppression, and sexual abuse (Knight, 2006). The mutual aid model with groups "has been found to reduce symptoms of (posttraumatic stress syndrome) PTSD and other stress reactions, enhance self-esteem, reduce depression and isolation, and promote more prosocial behaviors" (Knight, 2006, p. 22). This model is based on the assumption that being with others with similar challenges is empowering. As the sense of isolation dissolves, participants discover they are not alone resulting in connections with each other that enhance self-worth. Self-efficacy is also enhanced as members assist and learn from each other's mistakes and successes.

A pilot project field-tested a developmentally specific, psycho-educational group intervention for children with HIV/AIDS. HIV/AIDS information was combined with play therapy techniques for the purpose of increasing the children's self-esteem and control while decreasing their feelings of hopelessness and depression (Bacha, Pomeroy, & Gilbert, 1999). A variety of play therapy experiences were conducted once per week, for two hours during six consecutive weeks, with six children (five after the first session). Following the intervention, interviews with caregivers and the children found participants displayed more positive dispositions in their daily lives and felt they were "not alone" with HIV/AIDS.

Resources

Brigman, G., & Earley, B. (1991). *Group counseling for school counselors: A practical guide*. Portland, ME: J. Weston Walch.

Cavert, C., & Friends. (1999). *Games (& other stuff) for group book 1 revised & expanded* (2nd ed.). Oklahoma City, OK: Wood & Barnes Publishing.

Jones, A. (1996). *The wrecking yard of games and activities*. Ravensdale, WA: Idyll Arbor, Inc.

Stumbo, N. J. (1997). *Leisure education III: More goal-oriented activities*. State College, PA: Venture Publishing, Inc.

Stumbo, N. J. (1998). *Leisure education IV: Activities for individuals with substance addictions*. State College, PA: Venture Publishing, Inc.

Stumbo, N. J. (2002). *Leisure education I: A manual of activities and resources* (2nd ed.). State College, PA: Venture Publishing, Inc.

Stumbo, N. J. (2002). *Leisure education II: More activities and resources* (2nd ed.). State College, PA: Venture Publishing, Inc.

Witman, J. P. (2008). *Taking the initiative: Activities to enhance effectiveness and promote fun*. State College, PA: Venture Publishing, Inc.

Example Activities

Leisure Education III: More Goal-Oriented Activities. (1997). By Stumbo. Venture Publishing, Inc. (Social Skills Activities, pp. 165-283).

Welcoming Newcomers (pp. 219–222)

The intent of the activity is to increase participants' awareness of different responses to newcomers' attempts to join a group, to understand what it feels like to be a newcomer, and what it feels like to be part of a group that either accepts or rejects a newcomer. Three participants are asked to leave the room while others are divided into three groups. Each group will discuss a topic of their choice as each of the three returns to the room and joins one of the three groups. One group ignores the newcomer, the second is rude to the newcomer while the third group accepts the newcomer. Debriefing considers how the newcomer and group members feel, how to properly join groups, and how participants will treat newcomers in future situations.

Taking the initiative: Activities to enhance effectiveness and promote fun. (2008). By Witman. Venture Publishing, Inc.

Consensus (p. 26)

Participants are divided into teams of two or three and form a circle so teams each see one another. All teams have about two minutes to decide on a motion to show the entire group. The leader then tells the group that the goal is to reach consensus with everyone doing the same motion in as few turns as possible, communication is only nonverbal. When the leader says "show us what you've got," each team does their motion for about ten seconds while they look at the motions of the other teams. Teams can only change their motion during the next turn. As the leader repeats "show us what you've got" teams change to someone else's motion until the entire group has reached consensus. Debriefing considers how it felt to have their respective ideas chosen, why teams switched, how it feels if your idea is never accepted, and how the group might function best with future challenges.

References

Austin, D. R. (2009). *Therapeutic recreation processes and techniques* (6th ed.). Champaign, IL: Sagamore Publishing.

Avedon, E. M. (1974). *Therapeutic recreation service: An applied behavioral science approach.* Englewood Cliffs, NJ: Prentice-Hall, Inc.

Bacha, T., Pomeroy, E. C., & Gilbert, D. (1999). A psychoeducational group intervention for HIV-positive children: A pilot study. *Health & Social Work, 24*(4), 303–306.

Bedini, L. A., & Phoenix, T. L. (1999). Recreation programs for caregivers of older adults: A review and analysis of literature from 1990 to 1998. *Activities, Adaptation & Aging, 24*(2), 17–34.

Caperchione, C., & Mummery, K. (2006). The utilisation of group process strategies as an intervention tool for the promotion of health-related physical

activity in older adults. *Activities, Adaptation & Aging, 30*(4), 29–45.

Carter, M. J., & LeConey, S. P. (2004). *Therapeutic recreation in the community: An inclusive approach* (2nd ed.). Champaign, IL: Sagamore Publishing.

Carter, M. J., Nezey, I. O., Wenzel, K., & Foret, C. (1999). Leisure education with caregiver support groups. *Activities, Adaptation & Aging, 24*(2), 67–81.

Carter, M. J., & O'Morrow, G. S. (2006). *Effective management in therapeutic recreation service* (2nd ed.). State College, PA: Venture Publishing, Inc.

Dattilo, J., & Sneegas, J. (1987). Leadership strategies in therapeutic recreation. *Programming Trends in Therapeutic Recreation, 8*(3), 5–8.

Edginton, C. R., Hudson, S. D., & Scholl, K. G. (2005). *Leadership for recreation, parks, and leisure services* (3rd ed.). Champaign, IL: Sagamore Publishing.

Ellis, G. D., Witt, P. A., & Aguilar, T. (1983). Facilitating "flow" through therapeutic recreation services. *Therapeutic Recreation Journal, 17*(2), 6–15.

Griffin, J. (2005). Recreation therapy for adult survivors of childhood abuse: Challenges to professional perspectives and the evolution of a leisure education group. *Therapeutic Recreation Journal, 39*(3), 207–228.

Hutchinson, S. L., & Dattilo, J. (2001). Processing: Possibilities for therapeutic recreation. *Therapeutic Recreation Journal, 35*(1), 43–56.

Jordan, D. J. (2007). *Leadership in leisure services: Making a difference* (3rd ed.). State College, PA: Venture Publishing, Inc.

Keller, M. J., & Hughes, S. (1991). The role of leisure education with family caregivers of persons with Alzheimer's disease and related disorders. *Annual in Therapeutic Recreation, 2*, 1–7.

Knight, C. (2006). Groups for individuals with traumatic histories: Practice considerations for social workers. *Social Work, 51*(1), 20–30.

Kraus, R., & Shank, J. (1992). *Therapeutic recreation service: Principles and practices* (4th ed.). Dubuque, IA: Wm. C. Brown Publishers.

Oei, T. P. S., & Browne, A. (2006). Components of group processes: Have they contributed to the outcome of mood and anxiety disorder patients in a group cognitive-behaviour therapy program? *American Journal of Psychotherapy, 60*(1), 53–70.

O'Morrow, G. S. (1980). *Therapeutic recreation: A helping profession* (2nd ed.). Reston, VA: Reston Publishing Company, Inc.

Reeve, J. (2006). Group psychotherapy with children on an inpatient unit: The MEGA group model. *Journal of Child & Adolescent Psychiatric Nursing, 19*(1), 3–12.

Revheim, N., & Marcopulos, B. A. (2006). Group treatment approaches to address cognitive deficits. *Psychiatric Rehabilitation Journal, 30*(1), 38–45.

Richard, L., Jakobov, N., Sosowsky, B. B., & Leiser, M. (2008). The use of groups as a therapeutic modality with individuals who are brain injured. *American Journal of Recreation Therapy, 7*(2), 9–16.

Savell, K. (1986). Implications for therapeutic recreation leisure-efficacy: Theory and therapy programming. *Therapeutic Recreation Journal, 20*(1), 43–52.

Shank, J., & Coyle, C. (2002). *Therapeutic recreation in health promotion and rehabilitation.* State College, PA: Venture Publishing, Inc.

Smith-Marchese, K. (1994). The effects of participatory music on the reality orientation and sociability of Alzheimer's residents in a long-term-care setting. *Activities, Adaptation & Aging, 18*(2), 41–55.

Stumbo, N. J., & Peterson, C. A. (2009). *Therapeutic recreation program design principles & procedures* (5th ed.). San Francisco, CA: Pearson Benjamin Cummings.

Terry, L. J. (2010). Interpersonal theories and applications to therapeutic recreation. *Therapeutic Recreation Journal, 44*(2), 121–137.

Tomasulo, D. J., & Razza, N. J. (2006). Group psychotherapy for people with intellectual disabilities: The interactive-behavioral model. *Journal of Group Psychotherapy, Psychodrama, & Sociometry, 59*(2), 85–93.

Tuckman, B. W. (1965). Developmental sequence in small groups. *Psychological Bulletin, 63*(6), 384-399.

Yalom, I. D., & Leszcz, M. (2005). *The theory and practice of group psychotherapy* (5th ed.). New York, NY: Basic Books.

» CHAPTER 5 »
Communication Techniques

Norma J. Stumbo, Ph. D., CTRS and Nancy H. Navar, Re.D., CTRS

Communication involves two or more people in exchanging ideas, concepts, and meanings as they attempt to come to a shared understanding. "It is through our communication with others that we learn and affirm who we are" (Worthington, 2008, p. 18). Because communication is so complex, many individuals find communicating well to be troublesome. For example, children who are aggressive (Dumas, Blechman, & Prinz, 1994), individuals with learning disabilities (Kevan, 2003; Mathinos, 1988), individuals with dementia (Davis, 2005), and individuals with schizophrenia (Takahashi, Tanaka, & Miyaoka, 2006) are among the typical clients of therapeutic recreation services who experience systemic difficulties with communication. It is clear that communication skills are closely related to social, anger management, assertion, and problem-solving and coping skills (Mathinos, 1998; Takahashi et al., 2006). However, for the convenience of discussion in this text, we will highlight communication skills as one of the introductory chapters on "professional" skills of therapeutic recreation specialists, while saving social, anger management, assertion, and problem solving and coping skills for the section on important client skills (see Chapters 9, 10, 11, and 12). We recognize that communication skills significantly overlap with the above skills but will use this opportunity to focus on communication skills as a professional instead of client competency.

The Importance of Clear and Effective Communication

Rowan (2008) noted that like other complex skills, such as music and mathematics, communication skills continue to develop over a lifetime given that the individuals involved receive supportive feedback and have opportunities to practice and improve their skills. Communicating accurately and meaningfully requires a diverse and complex set of skills that include expressive skills (sending the message), receptive skills (receiving the message), active and empathic listening,

observing and using body language, as well as analyzing and evaluating the communication message.

At a more demanding level are communication skills needed by therapists and specialists as they work with other treatment team members and clients for whom they provide services. Proficiency in communication skills is a prerequisite to establishing adequate patient-specialist relationships (Berger, 2005). Communication problems in healthcare produce immediate and long-term health risks for consumers (DeWalt, 2007; Fukui, Ogawa, Ohtsuka, & Fukui, 2008; Kreps & Atkin, 1991; Wilson, Baker, Nordstrom, & Legwand, 2008). Advanced communication skills are important for healthcare and human service providers, such as therapeutic recreation specialists, in order to exchange information accurately and compassionately with clients and patients (Worthington, 2008). "Patient-centered communication" involves relationship, partnering, counseling, and communication skills, all deemed integral to effective healthcare and directly relational to patient's satisfaction, adherence, and well being" (Gremigi, Sommaruga, & Peltenburg, 2008, p. 57).

Patients need to be able to uptake health information from professionals that is being communicated to them and develop adequate "health literacy." Reduced or low health literacy, the end result of poor communication between patient and professional, leads to negative health outcomes (DeWalt, 2007; Harper, Cook, & Makoul, 2007; Schwartzberg, Cowett, VanGeest, & Wolf, 2007). Clearly the ways in which healthcare professionals communicate with consumers is crucial. These professional communication skills make up the backbone of this chapter.

The good news is that higher-level communication skills, even those needed, for example, by oncology nurses who are involved in informing patients of a cancer diagnosis, are learnable. Given the proper training and execution, they can have positive effects such as lowering psychological stress and improving coping skills of clients (Fukui et al., 2008) or improving the closeness of staff with patients, as well as improving job satisfaction of healthcare staff (McGilton, Irwin-Robinson,

Boscart, & Spanjevic, 2006). Communication skills needed by healthcare and related specialists are teachable and learnable.

Purpose and Organization of This Chapter

For the purposes of this chapter, the communication skills presented here will emphasize the role of the therapist or specialist. This chapter's topics include:

- Basic Premises of Communication
- Roadblocks or Barriers to Communication
- Aspects of Communication: Pieces of the Interaction Puzzle
- Communication Skills for Healthcare Professionals
- Communication Techniques and Strategies

In the last section several communication techniques, such as active listening, reflection, and restatement, that will improve exchanges with clients are discussed.

Basic Premises of Communication

There are multiple schools of thought about human communication. Among those that may provide insights for therapeutic recreation specialists include Interactional Theory (Watzlawick, Beavin, & Jackson, 1967), and McGuire's (1989) framework for communication planning. Both of these are discussed briefly below; interested readers are encouraged to go to original source materials for further information.

Interactional Theory

Among the most popular is the Interactional Theory of communication presented by Watzlawick et al. (1967). They proposed five axioms of communication:

- **One cannot not communicate.** It is impossible to "not communicate." Even without the use of words, individuals can send messages with nonverbal behaviors or with silence.
- **Every communication has a content and relationship aspect such that the latter classifies the former and is therefore a meta-communication.** The information exchanged is the content of

the message; by relaying information the person is intent on eliciting some reaction and establishing the relationship between the individuals. When the exchange is functional and useful, the focus is on the content; when the exchange is not functional the focus moves to the nature of the relationship. The feedback being returned is also information, so it, too, is filtered.

- **The nature of the relationship is contingent upon the punctuation of the communicational sequences between the communicants.** Every set of individuals develops patterns of communication, sometimes the focus when people "get stuck" in certain untenable patterns. Unless people can rise above the patterns and meta-communicate about their patterns, they often become cemented and habitual. Often, it is not possible to assign a "beginning" to a communication sequence.

- **Human beings communicate both digitally and analogically.** Communicating digitally means that the individual states the emotion he or she is feeling: "I am happy" or "I am upset." Communicating analogically applies more to the relationship aspect; for example, smiling or frowning. The behaviors then can support, extend, or contradict the digital message. Communication on the basic (digital) level is what we say or do (content level). Communication on the relationship (analog) level is what we really mean, what we feel. We cannot use only one level at a time. They coexist at all times.

- **All communicational interchanges are either symmetrical or complementary depending on whether they are based on equality or difference.** Symmetrical interchanges are those that draw out similarities, and the individuals involved tend to reciprocate with like gestures and speech patterns. In complementary communication, the individuals maximize difference and the individuals do not blend speech or behavior patterns. Both patterns of behavior are difficult to change.

Although this is a very brief explanation of the Interactional Theory, it demonstrates that communication, between any two individuals is complex and dependent on many factors. The next section discusses the barriers or roadblocks to effective communication. They are presented here so that the barriers can be reviewed before outlining the solutions to the problem areas.

Roadblocks or Barriers to Communication

Gordon (1970) developed a list of twelve general road-blocks to communication. He has applied these road-blocks to parent training as well as business leadership training. The roadblocks represent barriers that carry a high risk of being negatively received by the target person, who will then tend to escalate in emotion or withdraw. When individuals are stressed and are expressing a great deal of emotion, the roadblocks can become even more destructive. The twelve roadblocks are categorized under three headings in Table 5.1 (p. 70).

It is clear that these barriers to communication can create additional problems, hurt feelings, and misunderstandings. In addition, poor communication can reduce the effectiveness of professionals and treatments in health care and other settings by reducing the patient's ability to understand and utilize needed information.

Jangland, Gunningberg, and Carlsson (2009) conducted a study within a university hospital in Sweden and examined the content of patient complaints to the Patients' Advisory Committee. They found the following as prominent communication complaints:

1. Not receiving information or being given the option to participate
   - Insufficient information
   - Insufficient exchange of information between health professionals
   - Insufficient participation
   - Difficulty speaking and understanding language
2. Not being met in a professional manner
   - Insufficient respect
   - Insufficient empathy
   - Insufficient acknowledgement
   - Poor conversation skills
   - Professionals' abuse of position
3. Not receiving nursing or practical support
   - Insufficient nursing
   - Insufficient practical support

They felt that most of these problems could have been corrected with improved communication skills and attitudes among health professionals.

Booth, Maguire, and Hillier (1999), through their research study of interviewing skills of healthcare providers, noted a number of positive and negative communication behaviors. Table 5.2 (p. 71) provides a quick overview of these problems that become barriers to effective and clear healthcare interviews.

Most communication barriers or problems can be alleviated by learning and using techniques that promote positive, effective, and meaningful communication. The appendix to this chapter provides some examples of common positive ways to communicate and socially reinforce children and youth. The next several sections will start with a broad overview of communication planning, and move toward a more specific level aimed at healthcare providers, to then an even more detailed level of person-to-person communication techniques. In moving from the general to the specific, the chapter moves from broader skill sets that provide a foundational backdrop to more narrow skill sets that can be taught and learned. The reader is encouraged to read through these next sections with an eye toward his or her own skill set and areas of needed skill improvement.

Aspects of Communication: Pieces of the Interaction Puzzle

Communication and interaction can be viewed from a variety of levels, from macro levels (mass communication) to micro levels (person-to-person exchanges). This section reviews some basics of communication planning, especially noteworthy for those individuals who are involved in writing brochures, developing websites, or managing publicity campaigns. After this brief overview, communication skills especially applicable to healthcare professionals will be presented. The ideas presented in this section are listed in Table 5.3 (p. 71).

Communication Planning

A classic model of communication stems from the work of McGuire (1989). He developed a framework for communication planning, especially public campaigns, and noted five types of factors or input variables that influence how communication is received; that is, how effective it is evaluated to be.

The five factors include:

1. **Source:** Credibility plays an important role in the effectiveness of a message. Two dimensions, expertise and trustworthiness, are important in the possibility of the message being accepted by the audience. Kreuter and McClure (2004) noted that both expertise and trustworthiness

Table 5.1. General Roadblocks to Communication (Gordon, 1970; www.gordontraining.com)

I. Judging the Other Person	1. Judging, disagreeing, blaming, criticizing	Making a negative evaluation of the other person, his/her actions, or attitudes. "You brought it on yourself—you've got nobody else to blame for the mess you are in." "You are so lazy. You never follow through with what you say you are going to do."
	2. Namecalling, stereotyping, labeling	"Putting down" or stereotyping the other person. "What a dope!" "Man-hater!" "Just like a woman." "Idiot!" "You hardhats are all alike." "You are just another insensitive male."
	3. Interpreting, analyzing, diagnosing	Analyzing why a person is behaving as he/she is; playing amateur psychiatrist. "I can read you like a book." "You are doing that to irritate me." "You are trying to avoid the topic because you were not listening to me."
	4. Praising evaluatively	Making a positive judgment of the other person, his/her actions, or attitudes. Trying to make the individual feel better or deny there is a problem. "You are always such a good boy. I know you will help me with the lawn tonight." Teacher to teenage student: "You are a great poet." "You are a good student. You can figure out how this assignment needs to be completed." (Many people find it difficult to believe that some of the barriers like praise are high-risk responses.)
II. Sending Solutions—Often compounds a problem or creates new ones without resolving the original dilemma	1. Commanding, directing, ordering	Commanding the other person to do what you want to have done. "Do your homework right now." "Why?!" "Because I said so..." "Stop whining and finish the assignment."
	2. Warning, threatening	Trying to control the other's actions by warning of negative consequences that you will instigate. "You'll do it or else..." "Stop that noise right now or I will keep the whole class after school." "You must finish your peas if you want dessert."
	3. Preaching, moralizing, listing "shoulds" and "oughts"	Telling another person what he/she should do. "Preaching" at the other: "You shouldn't get a divorce; think of what will happen to the children." "You ought to tell him you are sorry." "Instead of this, you should do that."
	4. Excessive/ Inappropriate questioning	Closed-ended questions are often barriers in a relationship; these are those that can usually be answered in a few words, often with a simple yes or no. "When did it happen?" "Are you sorry that you did it?" "Will this be a problem again?" "Why did you wait so long to start this?"
	5. Advising, offering solutions or suggestions	Giving the other person a solution to her problems. "If I were you, I'd sure tell her off." "That's an easy one to solve. First..." "I think you need to stop listening to her."
III. Avoiding the Others' Concerns— Getting conversation off track	1. Withdrawing, distracting, being sarcastic, humoring, diverting	Pushing the other's problems aside through distraction. These messages tend to divert the person or avoid the person altogether: "Seems like you got up on the wrong side of the bed today." "Don't dwell on it, Sarah. Let's talk about something more pleasant." Or "Think you've got it bad?! Let me tell you what happened to me."
	2. Logical argument, teaching, lecturing	Attempting to convince the other with an appeal to facts or logic, without consideration of the emotional factors involved. "Look at the facts: if you hadn't bought that new car, we could have made the down payment on the house." "I don't care if the assignment is hard or you don't know where to start, sit down and do it now."
	3. Reassuring, sympathizing, consoling, supporting	Trying to stop the other person from feeling the negative emotions she is experiencing. "Don't worry, it is always darkest before the dawn. It will all work out OK in the end." "You can get another dog." "Lightning doesn't strike the same place twice."

Table 5.2. Selected Positive and Negative Communication Behaviors (from Booth et al., 1999)

Positive	Negative
Open-ended questions	Leading questions or closed-ended questions
Questions focusing on psychological or physical aspects as indicated by patient	Interviewer moving to opposite focus from patient (called blocking)
Empathy	Giving advice; premature advice

are context dependent; that is, is the person communicating the message an expert and/or trustworthy in regard to this message? In addition, when the "source" is most like the audience, demographically or attitudinally whether real or perceived, the audience is more likely to view the message as favorable.

- If the audience will agree on an early opinion of a speaker, they will probably agree with him or her on subsequent ones.
- High credibility sources have the greatest immediate positive influence.
- "Sleeper effect" positive reactions resulting from high credibility or negative reactions resulting from low credibility tend to disappear over time.

2. **Message:** The content and structure of the message is important as well. Kreuter and McClure (2004) noted that several message factors are important including: approaches, formats, balance, framing, order, and specificity of a call for action. Those interested in communicating a message need to consider a wide variety of dimensions to ensure the message is conducive to its purpose and the audience receiving it.

- A good presentation is as necessary as concrete data; the way it is presented is every bit as important as what is presented.

Table 5.3. Communication Information Important to Healthcare Professionals

- Communication Planning
- Communication Skills for Healthcare Professionals
  - Compassionate Listening and Compassionate Speaking
  - Teach Back
  - Low Health Literacy and Cultural Competence
  - Healthcare Mnemonics
  - Communication Assessment and Analysis Tools

- The message must be designed and delivered to gain attention.
- The speaker must use words, symbols, stereotypes that the receiver understands.
- The message must be interesting to the particular audience.
- Moderate difference of opinion between speaker and audience results in greatest opinion change. Start where people are and change them slowly.
- A speaker must provide a means of action to meet the needs presented.
- Where fear is aroused but not fully relieved by the reassurances contained in the communications, the audience will ignore or minimize the importance of the threat.
- The first impression or presentation is not always the most effective or the one that influences the most.

3. **Channel:** Different modalities carry different characteristics and will reach different audiences. Brochures, television ads, posters, signs, and face-to-face communication all reach different people in different ways. Which channel is the target group most likely to respond to?

4. **Receiver:** Communication messages should be targeted to the end receiver. Language, symbols, length, complexity, and the like are all considerations for designing messages appropriate for the end users. What demographic and cultural characteristics of the audience affect the content and format of the message?

- The receiver tends to expose him- or herself to communications that are of interest and consistent with personal goals and attitudes.
- Humans try to establish harmony or consistency in their opinions.

- If an audience has low self-esteem they will be highly persuadable, if they have a high self-esteem they will be less likely to be persuaded.
  - After a person changes a position or opinion, discussion with those who have also changed tend to reinforce the decision.

5. **Destination:** This translates into the effect that is desired on the person or persons who is receiving the message. What do you want the person or person to do, think, or feel as a result of the message?

Communication Skills for Healthcare Professionals

There is a growing literature on communication skills and assets for healthcare professionals. These also range from general skill sets to more detailed skill sets. This section first starts with three broad communication concepts: (a) compassionate listening and speaking, (b) teach back, and (c) health literacy techniques. After these three techniques, the section will address more definite information with health mnemonics and communication assessment tools. Many of the points brought out in the professional communication for

healthcare literature will be discussed more fully in the section on individual skills.

Compassionate Listening and Speaking

In the 1990s, two women who were interested in improving peaceful relations and humanizing contact between Americans, Israelis, and Palestinians developed the Compassionate Listening Project (compassionatelistening.org). Eventually this work resulted in a set of communication principles to promote peace, and they are listed on Table 5.4. Individuals who promote these principles note that they sound deceptively simple but are extremely difficult to practice in everyday life. "The key is to set aside the urge to respond, to blame, to 'stop the lies' or to blame and to simply let the speaker's words in" (http://www.jewishmuslimdialogue.org/Compassionate%20Listening.htm).

One of the settings in which the Compassionate Listening and Speaking principles have been applied is hospice (Worthington, 2008). She provided these suggestions for hospice volunteers:

- Invite clients to tell their stories.
- Invite clients to teach you about their beliefs.
- Listen to the specific words and expressions used to describe experience and beliefs (and adapt your communication accordingly).

Table 5.4. Guidelines for Compassionate Listening and Compassionate Speaking

---

Compassionate Listening

- Listen to hear, really hear, what is being said.
- Listen to understand.
- Listen to learn.
- Listen without comment, even if you do not agree with what is being said. You don't have to agree. Just listen.
- Listen completely focused on the speaker. Don't try to come up with counter arguments or to frame your reply. Simply focus on what the speaker is saying.
- Listen with respect, no matter whether the speaker is on "your" side or "theirs," regardless of the speaker's status or position.
- Listen to find links between you and the speaker.
- Listen with empathy.
- Listen with your heart, always with your heart.

Compassionate Speaking

- Speak from your heart, neither censoring nor holding back your feelings.
- Speak only from your experiences and of things you directly know about.
- Speak as if all your listeners are your friends, rather than "others" to be persuaded or defeated.
- Speak using "I" statements as much as possible, rather than "you," "they," or "we" statements.
- Speak without labeling or insulting others.
- Speak on topic, avoiding side topics and gratuitous remarks.
- Speak with consideration for your listeners.
- Speak to educate and enlighten your listeners.
- Speak to open their hearts and minds, not to defeat them.
- Speak directly from your heart to theirs.

- Pay attention to the nuances of nonverbal language (both yours and theirs).
- Demonstrate respect for different cultural expressions and practices.
- Balance questions with observations and reflections.
- Only ask questions to which you are ready to receive the response (you have both the time and emotional capacity to listen and give support as needed).
- Use active listening skills (e.g., paraphrasing, empathic responses, summarizing).
- Allow for suffering to be expressed.
- Allow silence to unfold.

Teach Back

Many healthcare references talk about "teach back" as an important technique for improving consumers' understanding of and adherence to treatment (DeWalt, 2007; Oates & Paasche-Orlow, 2009; Schwartzberg et al., 2007). For example, see the following section on low health literacy.

Teach back involves asking the patient to explain or to "teach back" to the healthcare provider the critical action items from intervention (Oates & Paasche-Orlow, 2009). Teach back may focus on questions such as "What steps will you take to _____?" "Tell me how you will explain to your spouse the steps to locating x resource in the community." These types of clarification questions help the professional assess the degree of understanding held by the participant. If the person cannot explain or mixes up the steps or information, the professional has an opportunity to provide immediate feedback and educate the client on information that the person did not understand well. A second round of teach back then can confirm whether the individual has gained new understanding.

Low Health Literacy and Cultural Competence

Health literacy is the ability to uptake, process, and apply health information to one's conditions and lifestyle (Schwartzberg et al., 2007). The opposite, low health literacy, refers to "the condition in which individuals are unable to comprehend health-related information or instructions and may fail to make appropriate decisions regarding their care" (Schwartzberg et al., p. S96). "Basic literacy skills, such as proficiency in reading, writing, listening, interpreting images, and interacting with documents, as well as facility with numeric concepts, and basic computation, are central to the concept of health literacy and greatly affect a patient's level of health literacy" (Oates & Paasche-Orlow, 2009, p. 1049). However, low literacy and low

health literacy are not synonymous. A person might be able to read and converse but not be able to understand medical terminology or concepts in materials or conversations.

Unfortunately, individuals who are older, lower-incomed, from racial or ethnic minorities, or living in rural areas are at the highest risk of low health literacy. These groups might be those with the greatest disease burdens. Importantly, low health literacy predicts poor health outcomes (DeWalt, 2007; Harper et al., 2007; Oates & Paasche-Orlow, 2009; Schwartzberg et al., 2007). Oates and Paasche-Orlow noted that health literacy is a recent cross-cutting priority of the Institute of Medicine, the American College of Physicians, and the Joint Commission. Harper et al. (2007) noted that clear communication strategies should be used with all patients, not singly out those with the above characteristics.

A number of solutions are used by healthcare providers to overcome low health literacy. Oates and Paasche-Orlow (2009) provided a list of clear communications strategies, and these are included in Table 5.5 (p. 74).

The strategies listed on Table 5.5 are similar to those used in the research of Schwarzenberg et al. (2007). They queried 356 healthcare providers and found the following to be the top 14 most used and believed to most efficacious communication techniques:

- use of simple language (avoiding technical jargon)
- asking patient if having a family member present for instructions is wanted
- asking patients to repeat information, using a teach-back strategy
- speaking more slowly
- drawing pictures
- following up with a phone call to check understanding
- empower patient to leave medical encounters knowing the answer to the question "What do I need to do?"
- use of models to explain
- writing out instructions
- reading aloud instructions
- underlining key points in patient information handout
- having patients follow up with office staff to review instructions
- asking patients how they will follow the instructions at home
- presenting two or three concepts at a time and checking for understanding
- handing out printed materials to patients

Table 5.5. Strategies for Improving the Health Literacy of Consumers (Oates & Paasche-Orlow, 2009)

Clinical Skills	Avoid jargon
	Use simple sentences and plain language
	Speak slowly
	Use analogies, if appropriate (e.g., "Getting a pacemaker is like replacing electrical wiring in your house")
	Limit the amount of information discussed; Focus on 2 to 3 key concepts; Repeat often; Use other staff to reinforce
Be Specific	Use clear, action-oriented directives
	Stress action steps the patient should take
	Minimize information about anatomy and physiology
	Focus on the patient's question: "What do I need to do?"
Use Multiple Forms of Communication	Use more than one communication modality to give the most important information
	Use pictures to help convey complex information or explain procedures
	Videos or interactive computer programs may be useful
	Get feedback from patients to make certain materials are understandable
Help Patients Ask Questions	Create an environment conducive to patients asking questions. Instead of asking: "Do you have any questions?" ask "What questions do you have for me?"
Confirm Comprehension	Use teach-back strategies

Table 5.6. Mnemonics Related to Healthcare Communication

Boyle, Dwinnell, & Platt (2005) – **ILS**
- **I** – **I**nvites patient to tell a story ("Tell me a little about yourself")
- **L** – **L**istens avidly and develops rapport
- **S** – **S**ummarizes – "I see, you're feeling more bloating, and it's getting more frequent"

Keller & Carroll (1994) – **4Es**
- **E**ngagement
- **E**mpathy
- **E**ducation
- **E**nlistment

Lieberman (1997) – **BATHE**
- **B** – **B**ackground
- **A** – **A**ffect
- **T** – **T**roubles
- **H** – **H**andling of current situations
- **E** – **E**mpathic responses

Mjaaland & Finset (2009) – **GRIP**
- **G** – **G**et measure of patient's symptoms and complaints
- **R** – **R**espond to and refocus the patient's understanding of his/her complaints
- **I** – **I**dentify resources and solutions
- **P** – **P**romote coping

Fukui et al. (2008) – **SPIKES**
- **S** – **S**etting up the interview
- **P** – Assessing the **P**atient's perception of the illness (in this case, cancer)
- **I** – Obtaining an **I**nvitation by the patient to disclose information
- **K** – Giving **K**nowledge and information to the patient
- **E** – Addressing the patient's **E**motions with empathic responses
- **S** – **S**trategy and summary

Healthcare Mnemonics

A number of mnemonics have been developed to help healthcare professionals remember the steps to better communication. These are included in Table 5.6.

Communication Assessment and Analysis Tools

Makoul, Krupat, and Chang (2007) developed the Communication Assessment Tool (CAT) as a way to allow patients to evaluate residents' and physicians' communication skills. Mercer et al. (2008) adapted the tool for the broader medical team and called it Communication Assessment Tool-Team (CAT-T). Each of the items are rated on a 5-point scale and are included on Table 5.7, as they point to important information when communicating with healthcare patients.

Gremigni et al. (2008) created a similar 15-item survey to test patients' perception of "patient-centered communication" that occurred during outpatient care. Their items were developed in four categories: (a) problem solving (PS), (b) respect (R), (c) lack of hostility (LH), and (d) nonverbal immediacy (NI). Although they do not provide the exact items in their manuscript as does Makoul et al. (2007), the questionnaire started with the general questions: "During the course of the brief encounter with the hospital professional you met just a few minutes ago, to what extent did each of the following events occur?" Examples of two items are: "He/she turned to me with a smile," and "He/she was able to resolve my problems." Table 5.8 contains the basic content of the 15 items and their respective category.

Booth et al. (1999) developed a communication-analysis scheme, somewhat like the one above, but more specific for human-to-human interactions. They noted that every communication, especially healthcare interviews, contain six main domains, as seen in Table 5.9.

It seems appropriate to consider these domains when communicating with clients and important others. Other parts of this chapter, especially in the strategies and techniques section, will address some issues related to these six domains.

A therapeutic recreation specialist, whether designing a brochure or a poster, or opening a session with clients, needs to consider the myriad factors of communication. If communicating a message is important, then paying attention to the content and format of that message are also important.

The information heretofore broadly introduced in this chapter will now be addressed more explicitly in the next section. The skills previously discussed

---

Table 5.7. Items from the Communication Assessment Tool (Makoul et al. 2007)

The health professional:

- Greeted me in a way that made me feel comfortable
- Treated me with respect
- Showed interest in my ideas about my health
- Understood my main health concerns
- Paid attention to me (looked at me, listened carefully)
- Let me talk without interruptions
- Gave me as much information as I wanted
- Talked in terms I could understand
- Checked to be sure I understood everything
- Encouraged me to ask questions
- Involved me in decisions as much as I wanted
- Discussed next steps, including any follow-up plans
- Showed care and concern
- Spent the right amount of time with me

Table 5.8. Item Content from the Health Care Communication Questionnaire (HCCQ) (Gremigni et al., 2008)

- Solved the patient's problem (PS)
- Managed the difficulties (PS)
- Kept calm (PS)
- Considered patient privacy (PS)
- Respectful of patient's needs (R)
- Requests were clear (R)
- Information given was clear (R)
- Courtesy was shown (R)
- Aggressive requests [reversed scaled] (LH)
- Aggressive answers [reversed scaled] (LH)
- Rushed approach [reversed scaled] (LH)
- Eye contact (NI)
- Smiling (NI)

Table 5.9. Six Domains of Interview "Utterances" (Booth et al., 1999)

Form	The grammatical style	e.g., closed or open question, statement
Function	The purpose	e.g., eliciting psychological information
Content	What is being discussed	e.g., the disease, prognosis, social implications, family relationships
Level	The degree of feeling	e.g., explicit mention of feeling
Blocking	Explicit avoidance	e.g., moves topic to something less central; uses distancing
Cue Base	Use made of patient cues	e.g., disclosure from earlier in interview

in somewhat "broad strokes" will be addressed more definitively in the next section. Skills such as empathic listening, reflection, summarization, clarification, and the like will be presented. Again, while they are presented individually for ease of presentation, a skilled specialist needs to synthesize and incorporate these skills into his or her professional "toolkit" in order to communicate with confidence and expertise.

Communication Techniques and Strategies

"To be a good communicator, one must not only express thoughts and feelings in understandable words, but also listen, clarify, and process information as it is intended" (Seaward, 2004, p. 286). It is clear that communication skills can be taught and learned (Levy-Storms, 2008). Levy-Storms found that acquisition and application of skills such as using open-ended questions, positive statements, eye contact, affective touch, and smiling were important to skill improvement of the nursing assistants and improved quality of life for residents.

In fact, Rowan (2008) noted that effective communication skills develop continually over a lifetime. She noted that improvements are most likely to occur when individuals (a) are able to explicitly learn and practice communication skills, (b) have multiple opportunities to observe and mimic model behaviors through role-play from a wide array of skilled individuals, (c) receive repeated feedback on their skill level, (d) are able to build skills slowly and steadily, and (e) take pride in and identify with skill mastery. In summarizing research on therapeutic communication training programs for nursing assistants working with patients with dementia in long-term care settings, Levy-Storms (2008) concluded that programs should (a) emphasize simple, concrete, verbal and nonverbal communication behaviors, (b) have an external, professional trainer lead the instruction, (c) focus the training program on psychosocial aspects of long-term care for all staff with direct-care responsibilities, and (d) design the evaluation and instruction as a quality improvement effort with both in-class and on-the-floor training and feedback with skilled staff supervision.

Communicating well, especially in professional environments, requires (a) considerable skill, (b) practice over many occurrences, and (c) repeated feedback. How the specialist communicates is very important to the client-therapist relationship. It has been noted that the professional has to be careful not to under-participate, over-participate, or to be distractive during any communication exchanges. Table 5.10 provides some examples of under-participating, over-participating, and distracting behaviors of professionals that are detrimental to establishing rapport with clients. Each therapeutic recreation specialist should consider whether any of these behaviors are reducing rapport and detracting from his or her interactions with clients, and possibly seek feedback from colleagues and clients.

The next section introduces a number of communication techniques that are appropriate for use with clients of therapeutic recreation services. The specific skills addressed include: (a) attending to the individual, (b) active listening, (c) the therapeutic use of silence, (d) self-disclosure, (e) communication focus, (f) restatement (g) reflection of feeling, (h) summarization of feeling, (i) request for clarification, (j) probe, (k) accent, (l) I Messages, (m) ability potential response,

---

Table 5.10. Examples of Under-Participation, Over-Participation, and Distractive Patterns

---

Under-Participation by the Professional
Nonverbal Characteristics
- May appear stiff; little body movement
- Body position often pulling away from the client
- Eyes are often averted and downcast, or looking away
- Sometimes evidence of stooped shoulders, shrugging of shoulders

Verbal Characteristics
- Monosyllabic responses or phrases
- Non-continuous speech
- Self-demeaning or "put-down" statements
- Verbal responses are primarily reflective in nature
- Voice is soft and weak; trails into silence

Over-Participation by the Professional
Nonverbal Characteristics
- Excessive body movements; fidgeting, toe-tapping
- Much animation and expression (can be distracting)

Verbal Characteristics
- Too many words
- Much verbal detail and repetition
- Length of response often is longer than client's preceding response
- Fast speech; few pauses between sentences
- High, loud voice

Distracting Participation by the Professional
Nonverbal Characteristics
- Inappropriate smiling
- Frequent nervous laughter
- Nail biting, pencil tapping, gum chewing, etc.

Verbal Characteristics
- Distractions (uh, OK, Say what?)
- Responds to secondary stimulus, not the stimulus of importance
- Frequent shifts in topics
- Focuses on the others rather than the client

(n) confrontation, and (o) conflict resolution. These techniques are listed in Table 5.11.

Attending to the Individual

Paying attention to the individual is of prime importance. Attentiveness is accomplished through facial expressions, bodily posture and movements, and verbal responses, and it lets the client know whether the specialist's reactions are positive, negative, or neutral. It also involves active and empathic listening. For example, how do you know when someone is really listening? How does he or she look or what does he or she do?

Facial Expressions include eye contact, head movements, and facial animations or movements.

- **Eye Contact:** Not too little or too much; should have a balance between directly looking at the individual and breaks in eye contact.
- **Head Movements:** Nodding indicates an affirmation and conveys to the individual he or she is being listened to and understood. Shaking one's head left to right indicates disagreement or disapproval. When head movements are overdone, they become distracting and annoying.
- **Facial Animations or Movements:** Smiling, looking sad, furrowing eyebrows, or other facial expressions of the listener convey messages of happiness, sadness, confusion, puzzlement, and the like to the speaker. When facial expressions mirror the client's feelings, he or she is most likely to feel accepted.

Nonverbal Body Language may include posture, proximity to the other person, position of the arms and legs, touch, head tilts, facial expressions, gestures,

Table 5.11. Selected Communication Strategies and Techniques

- Attending to the Individual
- Active Listening
- The Therapeutic Use of Silence
- Self-Disclosure
- Communication Focus
- Restatement
- Reflection of Feeling
- Summarization of Feeling
- Request for Clarification
- Probe
- Accent
- I-Messages
- Ability Potential Response
- Confrontation
- Conflict Resolution

vocal qualities, and even the style of clothing (Seaward, 2004; Slater, 2008). Insel and Roth (2004) and Slater (2008) reported that as much as 65 to 70% of face-to-face communication is expressed nonverbally. "Nonverbal communication is not only indirect, but often unconscious. . . . Ideally, nonverbal messages support verbal communication, reinforcing words with gestures to promote clearer understanding of the intended message" (Seaward, p. 289). Tensed or "closed" body positions when the arms and legs are crossed convey tension and discomfort of the listener to the speaker. To encourage open communication, the listener should assume and keep a relaxed position, slightly leaning forward, and reflecting the same body position of the client.

Verbal Behavior includes many facets. Tone of voice, amount of talking/responding, interruptions, and type of response either encourage or discourage the speaker from continuing. In general verbal responses need to:

- be evenly modulated with even and comfortable tone
- focus the conversation on the speaker and the immediate present
- minimize interruptions to the flow of thought
- use phrases such as "ah" or "I see" to provide encouragement and reinforcement to continue without changing direction or focus (similar to head nod, eye contact, and smiling)

Active Listening

Active, empathic, or reflective listening is one aspect of attending to the individual (Benson & Stuart, 1993; Seaward, 2004). Worthington (2008) noted that active empathic listening involves sensing, processing, and responding to incoming messages.

> Sensing involves awareness of verbal and nonverbal messages in order to assess both the basic content and the relational overtones of the message. Processing is cognitive in nature and includes understanding, interpreting, evaluating, and remembering the message. Responding may be either verbal or nonverbal, and signals to the speaker that he or she has been heard, subsequently encouraging additional disclosure. (p. 29)

Active listening involves going beyond just "hearing" what is said by asking questions or paraphrasing what the other person said to ensure understanding and should be aimed at gaining a "mutual understanding that is necessary to solve important problems" (Slater, 2008, p. 63). Tenholm and Jensen (2008, as cited in Worthington, 2008) identified three features to empathic listening: (a) respecting others' viewpoints, (b) fully understanding another's message prior to replying, and (c) confirming one's understanding through restatement, paraphrasing, and the like.

Besides facial expression, verbal and nonverbal behaviors mentioned above, active listening also includes using some of the responses below (such as restating, clarifying, and paraphrasing) as well as perception checking. Perception checking involves asking the client whether the specialist's impression or perception of his or her intent is correct. The aim of active listening is building trust and allowing the client to feel free to self-disclose and explore their thoughts and feelings. It is founded on a sense of mutual respect and understanding.

The Therapeutic Use of Silence

Silence can be non-therapeutic or can be used in a therapeutic manner. Silence is non-therapeutic when the client uses it to avoid an uncomfortable situation or to avoid addressing certain issues. It can be also be non-therapeutic when the professional is not involved in the session and is inappropriately silent. However, when used well silence can allow the client time to assimilate information or to allow the client to continue more deeply in the issue at hand.

- **Reflection:** Allows the client to think about what was just said—"like speaking into an echo"—give him or her insight.
- **Pacing the interview:** The specialist paces the interview through strategically timed and placed silent moments. Allows client to bring up what is important if specialist is directing too quickly.
- **Silent focusing:** The specialist uses silence to focus the client's attention on the moment at hand; this allows the statement just made to be reflected upon without interruption.
- **Responding to defenses:** Using silence to respond to a statement by a client may provide the client with insights into how his or her own defenses are working.
- **Silent caring:** This type of silence is used in an emotional moment when words are not adequate to respond to the situation.
- **Making a point:** After remaining silent for several moments what is said may have more impact.

Self-Disclosure

Self-disclosure is an expression of the professional's thoughts, ideas, and feelings that allow the client to see the specialist as a person, not just as a staff member (Corey & Corey, 1998; Insel & Roth, 2004; Seaward, 2004). It involves revealing one's own reactions to the person or group. Self-disclosure should be related to feelings or thoughts about the session or the client, not merely just random information about the professional. If used appropriately, self-disclosure may facilitate deeper levels of interaction and trust, and provide a model to clients about ways in which they might self-disclose.

Corey and Corey (1998) provided an example of an appropriate self-disclosure statement:

> **Therapist:** *I've noticed at times that it's very difficult for me to stay tuned in to what you're telling me. I'm able to be with you when you talk about yourself and your own feelings, but I tend to get lost as you go into great detail about all the things your daughter is doing or not doing.* (p. 74)

They also provided some thought provoking questions that the specialist can ask him or herself to determine is self-disclosure in a certain situation is appropriate:

- Do your disclosures help clients talk more honestly and specifically about themselves?
- Do they help them consider new alternatives for action?
- Do they help them translate their insights into new behavior?

Communication Focus

In every exchange the specialist makes the choice of responding to the *content* of the exchange or the *feeling* of the exchange. Choosing one over the other will guide the discussion is different ways. Some of these effects and limitations are listed below.

Cognitive Content
Effects of Responding to Cognitive Content
- decreases anxiety for people easily threatened by feelings
- assists in developing thought processes involved in decision making and problem solving
- usually client has goal(s) which need an action plan—based on people, events, and objects—may help focus on behavior change

Limitations of Responding Only to Cognitive Content
- fosters intellectualization and possible denial or disregard of feelings
- does not provide opportunity to identify and express feelings in a nonjudgmental/caring environment

Affective Content
Effects of Responding to Affective Content
- decreases anxiety (generally speaking responding to affect diminishes the intensity of feelings)
- expression of feelings (for example, venting of frustration may be an important goal for some clients)
- often the best way to communicate warmth and involvement with clients and establish level of trust

Limitations of Responding Only to Affective Content
- fosters an internal focus to the exclusion of world around client
- can foster cyclical "sick talk," e.g., "I'm no good"

The "trick" with responding to cognitive or affective content is to determine what is necessary to move the client toward his or her goals. Some of the following techniques are helpful in either targeting cognitive content or feeling content of interactions.

Restatement

Restatement or paraphrasing is a repetition of the main thought or feeling expressed by the client's preceding communication and neither adds or detracts from it. It can either be verbatim or in slightly different words (paraphrases) to determine that the professional is actually perceiving what the client is saying (Seaward, 2004). Restatement promotes understanding and rapport. It is important to pick out the primary *thought* or *feeling* of the client when using this technique and it is important not to overuse it.

Elements
- confirms for the client that s/he has been heard
- mirrors (but does not parrot) the client's previous communication
- focuses on most important part of the client's message
- used to:
  - check for accuracy of understanding
  - allow person to think about what he or she just said

Examples:
Client: *I went to a party this weekend and felt really uncomfortable with my old friends.*

Therapist: *You went to a party this weekend and felt uncomfortable with your friends.* Or *You felt uncomfortable with your old friends. . .*

Client: *I don't know whether to talk to my husband about doing more things together or not. He works a lot and gets impatient with me when I tell him that I want more of his time.*

Therapist: *You don't know whether to talk to your husband or not.*

Client: *I'm dissatisfied with my leisure, but I don't know what to do.*

Therapist: *You're dissatisfied with your leisure but don't know what to do.*

Client: *I don't know whether I'm satisfied with my job. I could quit but then I would risk losing all my health benefits.*

Therapist: *You're not sure whether to continue working or quit and lose your benefits.*

Reflection of Feeling

This is a paraphrased response to a feeling expressed by the client, either verbalized or not. The paraphrase should mirror the feelings expressed or implied by the client. Reflection of feelings or emotions convey "being understood" and accepted by the specialist.

Reflection of Overtly Expressed Feelings
Client: *I feel really mad that you interrupted me.*
Therapist: *You're very angry about being interrupted.*
Client: *One of my main problems is that I don't know how to act around girls. Even when I'm with girls I know well I feel uncomfortable and out of place.*
Therapist: *You feel uncomfortable.*

Reflection of Implied Feelings
Client: *I feel really mad that you interrupted me.*
Therapist: *You feel discounted when I don't listen to all of what you have to say.*
Client: *I feel like I have to be so responsible all of the time.*
Therapist: *Sometimes you'd feel relieved just to forget all that responsibility—to say to heck with it.*

Reflection of Nonverbal Feeling: Paraphrased, interpretive response to a feeling expressed by the client either nonverbally or verbally.
Client: *(sitting in a chair in a slumped position, eyes downcast, forlorn look on face)*
Therapist: *From the way you look, you must be feeling pretty sad, pretty wiped out right now.*

Summarization of Feeling

Summarization of feeling is similar to reflection of feeling but it incorporates feelings that have been communicated over several minutes and the professional pulls together several thoughts or statements (Seaward, 2004). Done correctly, it helps to provide meaning and continuity, and may help the client "move on."

Elements:
- integration of affective components throughout a conversation
- bring elements of communication together into meaningful whole
- reflect feelings of client in specialist's own words
- summarization of feelings can:
  - increase interview pace
  - identify a central theme
  - provide direction for interview
  - reaffirm the client

Examples:

Client: *The last few months, I haven't felt like doing any recreation at all . . . I don't know why . . . It just doesn't seem to appeal to me . . . Last night I had to force myself to go to dinner with friends . . . I used to be very active, but now I just don't feel like doing anything.*

Therapist: *You feel uninterested in the things that you used to enjoy—there's no fun in them any more—you don't know why but it seems that way.*

Request for Clarification

This technique is used when the interviewer does not clearly understand what the client is expressing and the interviewer asks the client to rephrase or reword what he or she said. The professional is attempting to grasp the essential elements of the message at both the thinking and feeling levels, and is trying to get to the core of the message. This request may be overused and underused and the professional should strive to balance the use of this technique while maintaining maximum understanding of the client's communications. If at any time, the client's comments are confusing or vague, the professional should ask for clarification and not assume he or she understands what the client is expressing. Requests for clarification may help clients to sort out conflicting and confused feelings and thoughts and arrive at a more meaningful understanding of the message.

Examples:

Therapist: *I'm not sure that I follow what you mean.*

Therapist: *When you say "fuzzy," what is that feeling like?*

Therapist: *I think I got lost in that. Could you go through that sequence again?*

Therapist: *When you say "off the wall," what does that mean?*

Therapist: *Could you please describe that feeling again? I'm not sure I understand what you meant.*

Probe

A conversational probe or open-ended question is used when more than a yes or no answer is desired from the client. A probing question focuses on *what*, *where*, *when*, and *how*, but not *why*. The interviewer should keep the focus on the client and eliciting more information, but yet not bombard the client with endless questions. The idea is to prevent the client from answering questions with a yes or no response. Below are some typical examples of probes.

Examples:

Client: *I really would like to meet some new people.*

Therapist: *Where do you plan on looking?*

Therapist: *How do you plan to do this?*

Therapist: *What are strategies you might use to do this?*

Therapist: *When would be good times to do this?*

Client: *I'd like to learn a new leisure skill.*

Therapist: *Where would be places you could go to learn new skills?*

Therapist: *How would you go about doing this?*

Therapist: *What types of places might offer lessons?*

Therapist: *When do you have time available to go for lessons?*

It should also be noted here that *closed-ended* questions such as "Do you have plans for this weekend?" "Did you get tickets to the ball game?" "Have you heard from your sister?" typically result in yes/no or one-word responses and should be avoided. If the specialist notices that many of his or her questions are being answered with a minimal response, he or she should give consideration to using more *open-ended* questions: "Tell me about your weekend." "What did you like best about going bowling?" "How will you be able to incorporate that into your fitness routine?" If too many probes are being used, examine the types of questions being asked.

Accent

The accent is a one- or two-word restatement that focuses or brings attention to a preceding client response. It is often intonated in a questioning manner. An accent puts emphasis on a particular thought or feeling and encourages the client to clarify or expand on his or her previous statement, since it suggests that the professional does not fully understand the client's intent. Accents are used most appropriately to highlight a word that seems vague, abstract, or misused. The professional's tone of voice indicates the client should elaborate on his or her answer.

Examples

> **Client:** *When I think about trying something new, I feel overwhelmed.*
> **Therapist:** *Overwhelmed?*
> **Client:** *I'd like to feel good about myself, but it's hopeless. . . ."*
> **Therapist:** *Hopeless?*
> **Client:** *After I returned home from therapy, I felt really burned out.*
> **Therapist:** *Burned out?*
> **Client:** *I'd like to develop a better self-image, but then I'm only kidding myself.*
> **Therapist:** *Kidding yourself?*

I-Messages

Another way to build better relationships with others is sharing thoughts and feelings through "I" messages. They are used to honestly communicate the effect of the other person's *behavior* on you. They enable the individual to better express his or her thoughts or feelings without putting down the other person or blaming. The criticism is not leveled at the other individual but at his or her behavior. It enables the person to assume responsibility for and change the problematic behavior. Because the offended person is able to express his or her feelings and how the situation impacts him or her, it helps the other person understand the situation from another perspective and often produces a willingness to change. The other person is more able to look at the speaker as a real person, capable of experiencing different feelings and expressing them. When "you" messages are used ("You are being rude," "You hurt my feelings"), an opposite effect occurs: the other person feels put down and blamed, possibly guilty, and avoids taking responsibility for his or her actions.

"I" messages consist of three parts: behavior, feelings, and effects. These can be expressed in any order. Although the "I" statement can be said in any order, an easy formula to being with is:

> "When you . . . . . ." (state the situation or behavior)
> "I feel . . . . . . " (state your feelings about it)
> "Because . . . . . . " (state the effect it has on you)

Examples:

> "*When you* cancel plans with me at the last minute, *I feel* angry and disappointed, *because* I look forward to being with you and it's too late to make other plans."
> "*When you* take clients out of my small group, it is distracting to the other clients and *I feel* frustrated *because* they are not reaching their goals for the session."

Ability-Potential Response

The Ability-Potential Response is a strategy to help the client understand that he or she has the ability to make choices and the capability to succeed in meeting his or her goals. The therapist reinforces the client's sense of control and ability to engage in a certain behavior or activity that is within the person's capability range. The professional usually expresses his or her belief in the client starting with "you could" or "you can."

Examples:

> **Client:** *I don't know what to do this weekend. I think I'll be bored.*
> **Therapist:** *You could call the YWCA and look into those swimming lessons we have talked about.*
> **Client:** *I sure wish I could participate in sports again.*
> **Therapist:** *You could attend one of the local club's practices and see if you like kayaking.*

Confrontation

Confrontation is not lecturing, arguing, judging, or acting in a punishing manner. It does help the client recognize a discrepancy, contradiction, rationalization, or excuse in regard to his or her behavior and enables the opportunity to face something he or she has previously avoided. Discrepancies are usually between (a) verbal statements and behaviors, (b) expressions of feelings and how his or her behavior suggests he or she might be feeling, and (c) two verbal messages of the client. Confrontation is helpful in four ways: (a) assisting the client in achievement of congruency, (b) establishing the professional as a role model for congruent communication, (c), reflecting back to the individual his or her discrepant behavior, and (d) helping the client explore conflict related to goal setting and change. With confrontation, the client is encouraged to engage in honest self-investigation, to explore his or her barriers to fulfilling his or her potential, and open new doors for achieving goals.

The specialist usually responds with a two-part message: "You said/did this" but "here is the discrepancy."

Examples:

    Client: *I know that exercise helps me physically, but I don't have time for it.*

    Therapist: *You say that fitness is important, but you don't make it a priority.*

    Client: *I wanted to stay sober, but my friends came over with a case of beer and I couldn't help it.*

    Therapist: *You say you want to maintain your sobriety, but are not making that choice.*

    Client: *I want to go to the ball game, but I don't know how to get there.*

    Therapist: *You say you want to go to the game, but you opted out of the session on leisure resources yesterday where you could have learned how to locate transportation.*

Conflict Resolution

"Conflicts often arise due to misunderstanding both verbal and nonverbal messages that are sent and received" (Seaward, 2004, p. 292). Most conflicts result in emotional turmoil and therefore need to be handled quickly (if possible) and with great care. Benson and Stuart (1993) recommended that conflicts be resolved with an aim toward creating win-win situations in which both parties receive benefit.

Seaward (2004) addressed three types of conflict: (a) content conflicts that involve misunderstandings of factual information, definitions of terms, concepts, goals or strategies, (b) value conflicts when one person's or group's values are in opposition with each other on issues such as prayer in schools or gays in the armed forces, and (c) ego conflicts based on win-lose situations that are based on power, competency, identity, and emotional attachment.

There are several styles of conflict management, each having its purpose, depending on the situation, the nature of the conflict, and the relationship of the individuals. According to Seaward (2004), the five major styles of conflict management include:

- *withdrawing* or avoiding the situation or people
- *surrendering* or giving in to avoid unpleasantness
- *hostile aggression* or confronting in a manner to intimidate or manipulate
- *persuading* by attempting to alter the other person's attitude or behavior
- *dialoguing* or negotiating by exchanging ideas and coming to an agreement

Insel and Roth (2004) provided more information about a method to resolve interpersonal conflicts. Their six steps to effective conflict resolution included:

1. Clarify the issue: What is really at issue?
2. Find out what each side wants: What are the desired outcomes?
3. Identify various alternatives for getting each person what he or she wants: What are options to get to the desired outcomes?
4. Decide how to negotiate: What method will be used to get to a resolution?
5. Solidify the agreements: What can both sides agree to?
6. Review and renegotiate: Is the agreement working and what needs to happen if it's not?

Summary

The intent of this chapter was to review some of the most important skills necessary for meaningful interpersonal relationships, especially those between clients and professionals.

- Learning to communicate well is a lifelong process and involves training, practice, feedback, and continued opportunities for growth.
- Communication between clients and healthcare professionals is especially important as poor communication or miscommunication can result in poor health outcomes.
- People are always communicating, intentionally or not.
- Knowing roadblocks or barriers to communication is important so that they may be eliminated or reduced. Patient complaints often result from poor communication with staff.
- There are five factors of planning communication outlets such as brochures, presentations, and websites: (a) source, (b) message, (c) channel, (d) receiver, and (e) destination.
- General communication skills such as compassionate listening and speaking, using teach back, and improving health literacy are important. Some professionals use mnemonics to improve their interaction skills. Some conduct research using communication assessment tools.
- Obtaining and applying practical communication skills is important to building rapport with clients and moving them toward their goals.
- Professionals need to be aware of under-participating, over-participating, and distracting behavior that detracts from an exchange.
- Attending skills include facial expressions, nonverbal body language, and verbal behavior.
- Active, empathic, or reflective listening involves

sensing, processing, and responding to incoming messages.
- The therapeutic use of silence, self-disclosure, and communication focus are skills that need to be used with considerable expertise.
- Specific dialogue skills such as restatement, reflection of feeling, summarization of feeling, request for clarification, probe, accent, I-Messages, Ability-Potential Response, confrontation, and conflict resolution can be learned, and when used in conversations with clients, can improve the specialist's ability to move the client toward his or her targeted outcomes.

References

Benson, H., & Stuart, E. M. (1993). *The wellness book: The comprehensive guide to maintaining health and treating stress-related illnesses*. New York, NY: Fireside.

Berger, C. R. (2005). Interpersonal communication: Theoretical perspectives, future prospects. *Journal of Communication, 55*(3), 415–447.

Booth, K., Maguire, P., & Hillier, V. F. (1999). Measurement of communication skills in cancer care: Myth or reality? *Journal of Advanced Nursing, 30*(5), 1073–1079.

Boyle, D., Dwinnell, B., & Platt, F. (2005). Invite, listen, and summarize: A patient-centered communication technique. *Academic Medicine, 80*(1), 29–32.

Corey, M. S., & Corey, G. (1998). *Becoming a helper* (3rd ed.). Pacific Grove, CA: Brooks/Cole.

Davis, L. A. (2005). Educating individuals with dementia: Perspectives for rehabilitation professionals. *Topics in Geriatric Rehabilitation, 21*(4), 304–314.

DeWalt, D. A. (2007). Low health literacy: Epidemiology and interventions. *North Carolina Medical Journal, 68*(5), 327–330.

Dumas, J. E., Blechman, E. A., & Prinz, R. J. (1994). Aggressive children and effective communication. *Aggressive Behavior, 20*, 347–358.

El Dib, R. P., & Atallah, A. N. (2006). Evidence-based speech, language and hearing therapy and the Cochrane Library's systematic reviews. *Sao Paulo Medical Journal, 124*(2), 51–54.

Fukui, S., Ogawa, K., Ohtsuka, M., & Fukui, N. (2008). A randomized study assessing the efficacy of communication skill training on patients' psychologic distress and coping: Nurses' communication with patients just after being diagnosed with cancer. *Cancer, 113*(6), 1462–1470.

Gordon, T. (1970). Roadblocks to communication. Retrieved September 15, 2009, from: http://www.gordontraining.com

Gremigni, P., Sommaruga, M., & Peltenburg, M. (2008). Validation of the Health Care Communication Questionnaire (HCCQ) to measure outpatients' experience of communication with hospital staff. *Patient Education and Counseling, 71*, 57–64.

Harper, W., Cook, S., & Makoul, G. (2007). Teaching medical students about health literacy: 2 Chicago initiatives. *American Journal of Health Behavior, 31*(Supp 1), S111–S114.

Insel, P. M., & Roth, W. T. (2004). *Core concepts in health* (9th ed.). Boston, MA: McGraw-Hill.

Jangland, E., Gunningberg, L., & Carlsson, M. (2009). Patients' and relatives' complaints about encounters and communication in health care: Evidence for quality improvement. *Patient Education and Counseling, 75*(2), 199–204.

Keller, V. F., & Carroll, J. G. (1994). A new model for physician-patient communication. *Patient Education and Counseling, 23*, 131–140.

Kevan, F. (2003). Challenging behavior and communication difficulties. *British Journal of Learning Disabilities, 31*, 75–80.

Kreps, G. L., & Atkin, C. (1991). Current issues in health communication research. *American Behavioral Scientist, 34*(6), 648–651.

Kreuter, M. W., & McClure, S. M. (2004). The role of culture in health communication. *Annual Review of Public Health, 25*, 439–455.

Levy-Storms, L. (2008). Therapeutic communication training in long-term care institutions: Recommendations for future research. *Patient Education and Counseling, 73*(1), 8–21.

Lieberman, J. A. III. (1997). BATHE: An approach to the interview process in the primary care setting. *Journal of Clinical Psychiatry, 58*(Suppl 3), S3–S6.

Makoul, G., Krupat, E., & Chang, C. H. (2007). Measuring patient views of physician communication skills: Development and testing of the Communication Assessment Tool. *Patient Education and Counseling, 67*(3), 333–342.

Mathinos, D. A. (1988). Communicative competence of children with learning disabilities. *Journal of Learning Disabilities, 21*(7), 437–443.

McGilton, K., Irwin-Robinson, H., Boscart, V., & Spanjevic, L. (2006). Communication enhancement: Nurse and patient satisfaction outcomes in a complex continuing care facility. *Journal of Advanced Nursing, 54*(1), 35–44.

McGuire, W. J. (1989). Theoretical foundations of campaigns. In R. Rice & C. Atkins (Eds.), *Public communication campaigns* (pp. 43–65). Newbury Park, CA: Sage.

Mercer, L. M., Tanabe, P., Pang, P. S., Gisondi, M. A., Courtney, D. M., Engel, K. G., et al. (2008). Patient perspectives on communication with the medical team: Pilot study using the Communication Assessment Tool-Team (CAT-T). *Patient Education and Counseling, 73*(2), 220–223.

Mjaaland, T. A., & Finset, A. (2009). Communication skills training for general practitioners to promote patient coping: The GRIP approach. *Patient Education and Counseling, 76*, 84–90.

Oates, D. J., & Paasche-Orlow, M. K. (2009). Health literacy: Communication strategies to improve patient comprehension of cardiovascular health. *Circulation, 119*(7), 1049–1051.

Rowan, K. E. (2008). Monthly communication skill coaching for healthcare staff. *Patient Education and Counseling, 71*(3), 402–404.

Schwartzberg, J. G., Cowett, A., VanGeest, J., & Wolf, M. S. (2007). Communication techniques for patients with low health literacy: A survey of physicians, nurses, and pharmacists. *American Journal of Health Behavior, 31*(Supp 1), S96–S104.

Seaward, B. L. (2004). *Managing stress: Principles and strategies for health and well-being* (4th ed.). Boston, MA: Jones and Bartlett.

Slater, L. (2008). Pathways to building leadership capacity. *Educational Management Administration & Leadership, 36*(1), 55–69. Retrieved July 16, 2009, from: http://ema.sagepub.com

Takahashi, M., Tanaka, K., & Miyaoka, H. (2006). Reliability and validity of communication skills questionnaire (CSQ). *Psychiatry and Clinical Neurosciences, 60*, 211–218.

Watzlawick, P., Beavin, J. H., & Jackson, D. D. (1967). *Pragmatics of human communication: A study of interactional patterns, pathologies, and paradoxes*. New York, NY: Norton.

Wilson, F. L., Baker, L. M., Nordstrom, C. K., & Legwand, C. (2008). Using the teach-back and Orem's self-care deficit nursing theory to increase childhood immunization communication among low-income mothers. *Issues in Contemporary Pediatric Nursing, 31*(1), 7–22.

Worthington, D. L. (2008). Communication skills training in a hospice volunteer training program. *Journal of Social Work in End-of-Life & Palliative Care, 4*(1), 17–37.

Appendix: Social Reinforcers for Children and Youth
(Sulzer-Azaroff, B., & Mayer, G. R., 1977)
Applying Behavior-Analysis Procedures with Children and Youth, Rinehart and Winston.

Children	Youth
Nod	Nod
Smile	Smile
Tickle	Laugh (with, not at)
Pat on shoulder, head, knee, back	Wink
Hug	Signal or gesture of approval
Wink	Orienting glance directly toward face
Kiss	Assistance when requested
Signal or gesture to signify approval	Positive comment on appearance
Swing around	Pat on the back
Touch on cheek	Handshake
Holding on lap	Asking client to discuss something before group
Fulfillment of requests	Asking client about items of interest to individual
Tickle	Asking client to demonstrate something
Eating with children	
Assistance	
Joining class during recess	
Saying:	Saying:
Yes.	Very good.
Nice.	Okay.
Good.	Beautiful.
Great.	Good for you.
Fine.	Exactly.
Very good.	Thank you.
Fantastic.	That's interesting.
Very fine.	_____ is excellent.
Excellent.	That's great.
Unbelievable.	Yeah.
Marvelous.	Great.
Atta-girl, Atta-boy	Right.
Far out.	I agree.
I like that.	Good job.
Right on.	Good idea.
Right.	Fantastic.
That's right.	Fine.
Correct.	Fine answer.
_____ is really paying attention.	What a clever idea!
Wonderful.	Unbelievable!
You really pay attention well.	You really are creative, innovative, and so on.
You do that well.	See how you're improving.
I'm pleased with (proud of) you.	That looks better than last time.
That was very nice of you.	Keep up the good work.
That's good.	You've apparently got the idea.
That's great.	Little by little we're getting there.
Wow.	See how _____ has improved.
Oh boy.	Mmmm.
Very nice.	You're really becoming an expert at this.
Good work.	Do you see what an effective job _____ has done?
Good job.	You are very patient.
Great going.	That shows a lot of work.
Good for you.	You look great today.
_____ is a good worker today.	It really makes me feel good when I see so many of
That's the way.	you hard at work.
That's interesting.	That's the best job I've seen today.
Much better.	You're paying attention so nicely!
Okay.	The interest you're showing is great.
You should show this to your parents.	It makes me happy to see you working so well.
You're doing better.	That's a thoughtful (courteous) thing to do for _____.
That's perfect.	_____ has gotten his materials and has started to
That's another one you got right.	work already; good going!
You're doing very well.	_____ is ready to start.
See how well _____ is doing?	You're really very considerate of one another.
Look how well he (she) did.	
_____ is really working.	

Appendix: Social Reinforcers for Children and Youth (cont'd)
(Sulzer-Azaroff, B., & Mayer, G. R., 1977)
Applying Behavior-Analysis Procedures with Children and Youth, Rinehart and Winston.

Children	Youth

Watch what he did; do it again.
Show the class your _____.
_____ is really working hard; he is going to be able to _____.
Wow, look at _____ work.
You look nice today.
_____ is working nicely; keep up the good work.
I can really tell _____ is thinking by what she just said.
_____ is sitting quietly and doing his work; good for you.
_____ is listening with such concentration;
  that's very polite, _____ thank you.
You should be proud of the way you're sitting quietly and listening to
  me while I'm giving a lesson.
_____ just earned another point by sitting quietly and listening while
  I was reading; good job
_____ walked quietly to her seat; thanks.
Good, you sharpened your pencil before class; now you're ready to go.
_____ has all of her supplies on her desk and is ready to go, good!
_____ has gotten his materials and has started to work already,
  good going!
It's nice to see the way _____ raises his hand when he wants to
  share something with the class.
The whole class is really being polite in listening to one another.
This whole row is sitting quietly with their chairs on the floor; great!	

» CHAPTER 6 »

Instructional Techniques

Norma J. Stumbo, Ph. D., CTRS

Leisure education, by its very nature, requires a teaching-learning process. Therapeutic recreation specialists need to understand and apply educational techniques and principles so that clients' time is used wisely, their learning is focused, and their outcomes are maximized. Whether clients are learning how to access community resources, perform specific social skills, or search the Internet, learning when supported by well-thought-out instruction can be beneficial and even fun! However, as seasoned therapeutic recreation specialists know, fun is often the result of a tremendous amount of planning and hard work on the part of the professional. Many decisions need to take place so that optimal learning can occur. The aim of this chapter is to provide background information and introduce material related to:

- the teaching-learning process
- principles of learning
- learning styles
- behavioral objectives
- instructional taxonomies
- instructional methods
- application to therapeutic recreation services

Information on these areas will help the therapeutic recreation specialist think through the options that will make instruction more meaningful and useful to clients. Because of the nature of the material, the term "instructor" or "teacher" will be used to denote the professional and "learner" or "student" will be used interchangeably with client or participant.

The Teaching-Learning Process

The teaching-learning process is a delicate dance between the teacher and the learner. "Good teaching includes teaching students how to learn, how to remember, how to think, and how to motivate themselves" (Weinstein & Mayer, 1983). Learning involves four steps on the part of the student:

- receiving information
- processing it (depends on quality and quantity of competing information)
- evaluating it for meaning, worth, and association with other memories
- encoding or storing it

In order for the learner to do these four actions, the teacher must be skilled and be prepared. Beyond being skilled at a variety of instructional techniques, such as lecture, discussion, and simulation, the teacher also needs to make a number of decisions so that learning is enhanced. Below are examples of questions that the instructor must consider while designing and delivering the program:

- What are the objectives of the session?
- What are the expectations of the learners?
- How ready are the clients to learn the material?
- What is the expectation of the agency?
- What is the instructor's comfort level with different techniques?
- What is the instructor's skill level with different techniques?
- How much time is available and is it adequate for meeting the objectives?
- How can different learning styles be accommodated?
- Is there sufficient variety to sustain learner interest?
- Does new learning relate to past learning and experiences?
- How much interaction between learners is desired and necessary?
- What is the appropriate pace of instruction for this group to learn these objectives?
- How active will the participants be during the learning process?
- What resources are available that will enhance learning?

A good instructor must have adequate background in the teaching-learning process to understand how the different answers to these questions impact the ability of the learner to uptake the targeted information. Instructors (therapeutic recreation specialists) need to undertake four steps:

- assessing
  - assessing learners' skills and readiness
  - assessing agency expectations
- planning
  - setting learning objectives
  - considering learning principles and taxonomies
  - deciding the content, instructional method(s), and materials to maximize learning
- implementing
  - managing resources, space, materials, and people
  - inspiring, motivating, and energizing learners
  - collecting formative feedback
- evaluating
  - assessing whether prior steps were successful and objectives were met
  - using feedback (evaluation data) to improve subsequent instruction

When the instructor does not consider the needs, abilities, and desires of the learners and plans inadequately, opportunities for them to uptake, remember, and use information are minimized.

Three general things that hinder learning include: (a) the lack of readiness on the part of the learner, (b) the lack of preparation on the part of the instructor, and (c) an unencouraging environment. Each of these plays a vital role in the teaching-learning process and when they are not adequately considered early on, can greatly detract from the outcomes attained.

Think for a moment about your own past experiences. Think of a teacher who strongly motivated you to learn—what did this person do? How did he or she act? Now think of a teacher who you felt did not motivate you to do your best—what did this person do? What statements or actions made a difference to you? It is clear that "good" teachers propel us to do our best, while others do not. In most cases, the best teachers incorporate some basic principles of learning, which may seem simple at first, but have a lot to do with the motivation and engagement levels of learners.

Principles of Learning

A number of factors affect the degree of learning that will take place (Babcock & Miller, 1994). For our purposes, these are divided into four major headings:

- preparation, structure, and organization
- optimal arousal and focus
- readiness and prioritization
- active engagement and participation

As a number of principles are discussed under each of these four headings, think back to motivating and unmotivating learning experiences mentioned above and see if you can identify which of these were either present or absent during the teaching-learning process. See Table 6.1.

Table 6.1. Principles of Preparation, Structure, and Organization

---

- Structure
- Open Communication/Pleasant Conditions and Consequences
- Feedback

Preparation, Structure, and Organization

Structure

Learning is facilitated when the session is organized, logical, and has an apparent structure, usually from simpler content to more complex content. Teachers should:

- provide clear context/rationale for the program
- explain how it fits into the context of the total treatment plan or program
- outline steps or activities that will be taken
- define basic terms
- provide specific, concise guidelines for each new learning task
- create opportunities for students to rehearse performance-evaluation tasks
- use specific examples from clients' lived experiences
- use prompts as necessary to keep activity progressing
- allow time for repetition and practice, if needed, until task is clear and is accomplished

Open Communication/ Pleasant Conditions and Consequences

Learning is facilitated if the session is structured and instructor's messages are open to students' inspection. Learning is facilitated if instructional conditions are made pleasant, or at least not aversive. Learning spaces should be comfortable, uncluttered, quiet, and conducive to learning. Teachers should:

- portray enthusiasm for subject matter and model appropriate behavior
- inform students of the objectives for each session
- tell students the reasons for his or her actions
- establish a "safe" environment for personal disclosure
- encourage participants to take risks and ask questions
- create pleasant physical conditions
- set challenging but attainable tasks
- give participants feedback as soon as possible
- reward by recognition of participants' efforts
- avoid ridiculing or degrading participants in any way
- establishing a learning framework that includes mutual respect and consideration for others and their perspectives, while acknowledging value of both critique and collaboration

Feedback

Instructors should also consider the feedback and prompts they give to learners. Feedback should be honest, constructive, and immediate.

- Prompts may be needed with new and complex. tasks; then faded gradually as learning progresses
- Feedback should be directed toward behaviors in meeting session objectives.
- Feedback should be constructive and move learner toward improved learning.
- Immediate feedback provides feeling of satisfaction if client is successful.
- Even when correction is necessary, feedback can reduce tension because learner then knows what is learned and what has not yet been mastered.

Optimal Arousal and Focus

Learning is enhanced when the instructor considers factors that put students in their best learning mode. In order to learn, people need to be motivated, focused, find the material meaningful, and have some degree of control. In addition, learning is enhanced if the learners can also enjoy the activity. See Table 6.2.

Table 6.2. Principles of Optimal Arousal and Focus

- Meaningfulness
- Arousal, Novelty, and Diversity
- Focus and Learner Control

Meaningfulness

Meaningfulness, or being personally tied to the content, is important in order to optimize learning. Personally relevant material is more interesting and easier to learn than information that we feel does not pertain to us. Teachers should:

- relate subject matter to the clients as much as possible
- explain benefits to participants in clear and personal terms
- communicate an expectation of success for each learner
- focus on participants' past, present, or future experiences
- consider students' interests, values, aspirations, and goals
- relate to other treatment being received

Arousal, Novelty, and Diversity

Learning can be enhanced when an appropriate amount of arousal or tension is planned. Novelty and diversity of activities aids in getting and keeping learners' attention. Of course, teachers can go too far with this, and the novelty actually becomes distracting, but a good mix of novel, interesting materials and activities is likely to encourage engagement by participants.

Stumbo and Caldwell (2002) proposed that therapeutic recreation specialists be cognizant of the amount of tension experienced by learners during the experience. Too much tension and the person might become anxious yet too little tension and the person might become bored. This relationship is illustrated in Figure 6.1 (p. 90). Teachers should:

- offer a number of materials/activities (such as posters, poems, readings, testimonials, etc.) with a range of complexity to pique learner interest
- anchor each session to learners' goals and future activities, as well as other treatment
- sequence activities within session to build interest
- consider that learners have different learning styles and preferences
- use real-life examples whenever possible
- use a pleasant voice that expresses enthusiasm

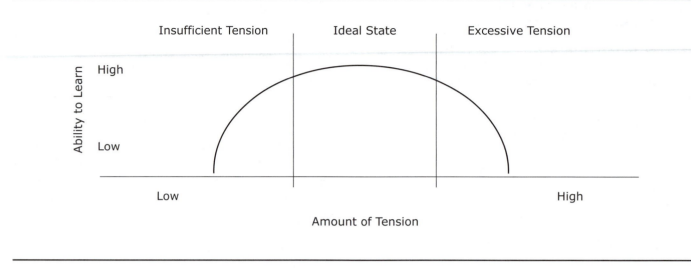

Figure 6.1. Relationship between Tension/Arousal and Ability to Learn (Stumbo & Caldwell, 2002)

- use interesting stimuli, with differing intensity and emotional arousal
- balance appropriate amount of new learning (too much can create anxiety, too little can create boredom)

Focus and Learner Control

The learner must be focused on the task at hand in order to intake information. It is the responsibility of the instructor to structure the experience so that learners can focus and also have a sense of control of their own learning. Teachers should:

- organize materials from simple to complex, known to new, low-risk to high-risk
- give clear, concise directions
- communicate an expectation that each person will participate and take responsibility
- ask participants to set personal goals for the session
- relate each section of the session with other sections and explain overall organization
- use materials that help learners focus, such as flip chart, white board, poster, etc.
- allow learners to have some control or choice over materials and their participation
- use repetition to enhance retention
- ask questions about material being learned
- allow enough time for new information to be synthesized by each participant

Readiness and Prioritization

Learning also depends on a client's readiness and willingness to make learning a priority among competing interests. Teachers should consider if learners have a

grasp of prerequisite knowledge and abilities, as well as concepts such as recency and primacy (see Table 6.3).

Readiness

Learning cannot take place unless learners are ready to learn. For example, when people are uncomfortable (cold, hungry, or in pain), they have a difficult time being ready to absorb information. Similarly, readiness can also relate to developmental progressions. For example, it is hard to learn statistics without first learning mathematical concepts, or difficult to learn advanced physical skills without first learning basic skills. It is clear that the learner must be ready to uptake the information or else learning cannot occur.

This is especially important to consider in healthcare environments. People who are in a medical crisis, or who have severe medical conditions, including experiencing pain, may not be prepared to learn as it is not a high priority to them. Stumbo and Caldwell (2002) proposed the Information Seeking and Health Spectrum Model to illustrate this notion. When people are in critical condition and are in acute care, their need for information is limited to concrete and short-term details, like treatment options, prognoses, survival rates, and the like. As they move to a more rehabilitative type of care, their concerns shift to more specific information about the recovery process, such as treatment regimes and residual effects of the illness/

Table 6.3. Principles of Readiness and Prioritization

- Readiness
- Recency and Primacy

disease/condition. Once individuals are "rehabilitated" they move into the chronic phase of living with the illness/disease/condition and search out information related to incorporating it into their future lifestyle. It is at this phase and beyond that an individual may seek out information about leisure involvement and how they will incorporate leisure and activity into their daily lifestyles.

Although not all illnesses/diseases/conditions progress along this linear path, it serves to remind therapeutic recreation specialists that the participants' readiness to learn is an important consideration in the treatment and rehabilitation process. Optimal learning will occur when people are physically and emotionally able to process the necessary information. Efforts prior to this will not be successful (see Figure 6.2). Teachers should:

- analyze the learning task to determine prerequisite concepts, principles, and skills
- assess and understand learners' current knowledge about the topic, which may include informal questioning about topic
- assist the learner in associating new knowledge with prior knowledge
- consider learner's health, energy level, and ability to concentrate

Recency and Primacy

There is a lot of competing information for the brain to focus on. Often we can remember what we just heard or learned, but with time, that may be replaced by other information. We often recall that which we just learned, while something learned a while ago will not be remembered. Often, over time, our memory of the item becomes less clear and focused, especially as we uptake new information. In addition, most people are better at paying attention to the start of something; sometimes learning can trail off if the session is too long, has too many components, or is too complex. Think of a time when you tried to memorize a list of items. Often we can best remember the first few items on the list and then we get overloaded and experience more difficulty with the remainder of the list. Sessions often promote better learning if they focus on a limited number of items and if those same items are introduced and reinforced throughout the session. Teachers should:

- keep the focus on recently learned information
- limit the number of items (3 to 4) that are to be learned in any one session
- understand that attention is paid and more energy devoted to first items in the session
- introduce the important items first
- add more items to be learned only after the primary ones have been instilled
- add practice with and application of information in order to "imbed" the information more deeply

Active Engagement and Participation

There are two important principles of active engagement. The first is Active Participation, that is getting and keeping the participants actively involved—physically,

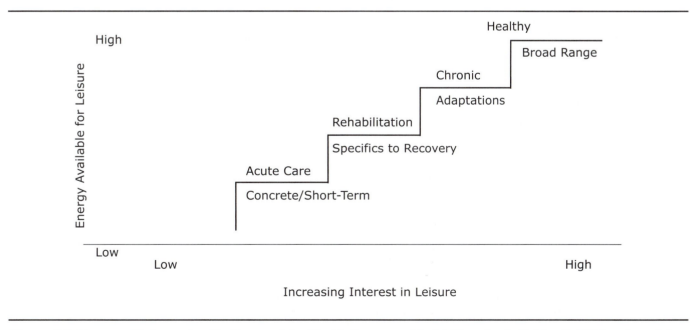

Figure 6.2. Proposed Information Seeking and the Health Spectrum Model (Stumbo & Caldwell, 2002; adapted from Babcock & Miller, 1994)

emotionally, cognitively, and/or socially. The second is Active Appropriate Practice. Both of these involve a great deal of planning on the part of the instructor, to pique participants' interest early and to keep them involved throughout the entire session. Table 6.4 shows the two principles.

Table 6.4. Principles of Active Engagement and Participation

- Active Participation
- Active Appropriate Practice

Active Participation

The best learning occurs when the participants (and instructor, of course) are engaged in the experience. For example, lectures in which the learners are passive are usually much less effective than more active modes such as role-playing, simulations, interviews, problem solving, discussions, debates, games, creative exercises, and other similar activities. Teachers should:

- plan for changes of pace during the session
- use a variety of learning activities during a single session (within reason)
- consider how to get and keep participants engaged, factoring in age, interests, abilities, and skills
- encourage authentic problem solving, self-reflection and evaluation during learning
- be prepared with multiple examples relating to the participants' experiences
- encourage participants to get involved at higher levels of learning (such as application instead of memorization)
- understand that different people have different learning styles so that variety can help enhance learning for each person in the group

Active Appropriate Practice

Learners need to be able to practice skills for several reasons. They need to be able to "go through the motions" enough times to be able to develop competence. For example, think of practice sessions for learning how to interact with strangers or count money back to a cashier. Participants should be able to practice enough times to gain skills and confidence to be able to perform the task in a natural environment without coaching, if possible. Practice, in a "protected" or non-threatening environment, helps the learner to make earnest attempts with the least amount of fear or apprehension. Practice also has the most learning if the task

is as close to the future real task as possible. For example, this is one of the strengths of role-playing—learners practice "real" skills in preparation for real-world application. Teachers should:

- provide authentic experiences in which the learners can practice and hone their skills
- space practice over a period of time
- start with the simplest skills and move to more complex ones
- provide a variety of practice experiences, such as different settings or scenarios, to help broaden the participant's learning and skill application
- intersperse practice times within learning sessions

This section has provided information about four major learning principles that are important to consider when designing and implementing learning experiences or sessions with clients. The principles include:

- Preparation, Structure, and Organization
- Optimal Arousal and Focus
- Readiness and Prioritization
- Active Engagement and Participation

Table 6.5 lists the learning principles discussed in this section. While it may seem like a lot to remember, most individuals can take these principles and apply them relatively easily to designing fun and valuable learning experiences. The principles are mostly straightforward and will produce significant and noticeable results rapidly. And once the principles have been mastered, the design and implementation of learning activities becomes second nature. The best instructors understand that:

Table 6.5. Summary of Learning Principles

Preparation, Structure, and Organization
- Structure
- Open Communication/Pleasant Conditions and Consequences
- Feedback

Optimal Arousal and Focus
- Meaningfulness
- Arousal, Novelty, and Diversity
- Focus and Learner Control

Readiness and Prioritization
- Readiness
- Recency and Primacy

Active Engagement and Participation
- Active Participation
- Active Appropriate Practice

- Deep preparation and organization are important to effective sessions with clients.
- Learners' biological, psychological, sociological, and cultural realities shape perceptions of learning experience.
- The person's current status, such as degree of health, affects the individual's ability to uptake information.
- Application of new learning in variety of contexts broadens generalization of that learning.
- Adequate practice of learning is important since societal norms, self-esteem and previous learning experiences affect willingness to risk, tolerance for temporary failure, and expectation of success.

Learning Styles

Another important consideration in the teaching-learning process is the learning style of the student. Olson (2008) summarized these into three categories: Visual, auditory, and kinesthetic. *Visual learners* depend on seeing and looking. These individuals are likely to prefer charts, posters, signs, and such in order to intake information. *Auditory learners* primarily rely on hearing and listening to learn, and often close their eyes (to reduce visual stimuli) in order to concentrate on better hearing. *Kinesthetic learners* primarily rely on the sense of touching, feeling, and doing. They tend to be "movers" and appreciate where their body is in space and seemingly effortlessly execute physical tasks. Murley (2007) proposed that:

- Visual learners need to see the information in print, with pictures, diagrams, and other models.

- Oral learners need opportunities to talk and discuss.
- Auditory learners need chances to listen to the teacher and to others.
- Tactile or kinesthetic learners need to touch or manipulate materials, as well as move around and see movement, such as demonstration.

While individuals may have a stronger preference for one of these areas, that may shift depending on the demands of the task at hand.

The important piece for specialists to take away from this brief discussion is that people learn differently. People in the same group learn differently. So the best instruction is that which has elements that cater to all three learning styles. Participants, on average, will learn more if the session draws on visual, auditory, and kinesthetic skills. That may mean a brief verbal introduction about the session, perhaps augmented by the goals being written on the board, and culminating in a physical portion, such as a small group discussion or role playing, or similar activity, that relates to the introduction and goals. Pulling from all three sources will help learners imbed the information more deeply and learn more rapidly.

The importance in learning styles lies in the amount of information retained by the learner. Lalley and Miller (2007) created a Learning Pyramid that illustrates seven levels and the average amount of information that is retained in each condition. This has relevance to the selection of behavioral objectives and of teaching methods. For the purpose of this chapter, the Learning Pyramid was a converted into stair steps in which each riser describes the amount of typical learning under each condition (see Figure 6.3). For the original pyramid, see Lalley and Miller (2007).

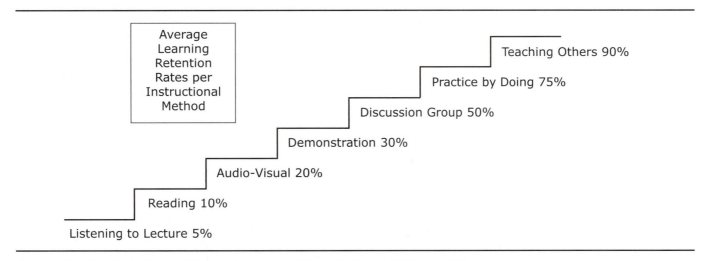

Figure 6.3. The Stair Steps of Learning (adapted from Lalley & Miller, 2007)

Armed with this information, specialists can plan and carry out sessions that will flow more easily and yield better results. This, of course, has significance for clients (learners) as they reach the intended outcomes more quickly while (hopefully) enjoying themselves. When therapeutic recreation specialists document their expectations through behavioral objectives—or client outcomes—their instruction is greatly improved.

Behavioral Objectives

Behavioral objectives are important in every learning environment (Babcock & Miller, 1994). The purpose of behavioral objectives is to specify the exact behavior that will provide evidence that the intent of the objective has been met. As such, the conditions under which the behavior is to be performed, the representative behavior, and the criteria for judging whether the behavior has occurred are all extremely important. Client behavioral objectives help keep the client and specialist focused on the important aspects of behavior, and the intended outcomes of participation. In therapeutic recreation, we might call them client outcomes statements, but they still contain the same three common elements: Condition, behavior, and criterion (Stumbo & Peterson, 2009).

Condition

A *condition* is the circumstance under which the desired behavior will occur. Phrases that indicate common conditions include:

- When given the necessary supplies . . .
- When given a choice of two activities . . .
- After completion of the program . . .
- After one week of active participation . . .

Sometimes conditions are unique to a situation, setting, population, or program. An example follows:

- While involved in a trip in the community with the therapeutic recreation specialist and after completing the program of assertiveness training, the client will . . .

Conditions of a behavioral objective primarily set the stage by identifying necessary equipment, activities, timelines, or other events that are essential to the performance of the desired behavior. Normally, the condition is the first phase of the behavioral objective. It starts with a preposition and is set off from the rest of the behavioral objective by a comma. Occasionally, the conditions are scattered throughout the behavioral

objective. Conditions occur throughout the following behavioral objective and are italicized for identification:

- *On request,* the client will play a game of tennis *with an opponent of equal ability,* staying on task throughout the activity as evidenced by continuous attention to the game and completion of the game within a reasonable amount of time, as judged by the therapeutic recreation specialist.

In this example, some conditions are not mentioned but are implied. The tennis game itself is not specified. Often, when a condition is obvious, it can be eliminated to reduce the length of the complete behavioral objective.

Behavior

The *behavior* identified in the behavioral objective is the central focus. It is the phrase that identifies what action the client will demonstrate to prove that he or she has achieved the desired knowledge, skills, or ability. The behavior must be observable and measurable in order to meet this requirement. Although measurement of the specific action is most often dealt with in the criteria section of the behavioral objective, the behavior focuses the attention of the reader on the behavior of concern. Some examples of the behavioral part of an objective are:

- The client will name one choice . . .
- The client will call . . .
- The client will follow the rules . . .
- The client will verbalize the actions needed to get from his home to the theatre . . .

Note that the wording always includes the phrase "the client will," followed by an *action verb*. The challenge for the therapeutic recreation specialist is to select the most important, representative behavior that would indicate that the client has achieved the targeted outcome. One difficulty of writing good objectives is to stay focused on the important behavior, while making it specific enough to measure it well. The taxonomies that follow help with this task.

Criterion

The *criterion* in the behavioral objective delineates the exact amounts and nature of the behavior that can be taken as evidence that the objective has been met. A criterion is a precise statement or standard that allows individuals to make judgments based on the observable, measurable behavior. Good criterion statements are so clear that two or more different evaluators have no problem making the same decision about whether the desired behavior occurred.

The criterion section defines more specifically the exact act or representation of the behavior stated, along with standards of form, frequency, or other behavioral descriptions. Writing criterion statements requires selection of representative behaviors and then description of the amounts and nature of those behaviors. Criteria can be written in many ways; six of those include:

1. Number of trials.
2. Level of accuracy.
3. Amount of time.
4. Percentages or fractions.
5. Form.
6. Procedures and characteristics.

Stumbo and Peterson (2009) talk more extensively about behavioral objectives in relation to client outcomes in Chapter 11 of their text. Readers are referred there for greater detail.

The above discussion of behavioral objectives frames the information that follows on the three taxonomies of learning (cognitive, affective, and psychomotor). These taxonomies are presented so that therapeutic recreation specialists may understand the levels of learning and consider them when planning sessions with participants. The taxonomies clearly relate to the principle of readiness in that they remind us that learning is often a developmental or somewhat sequential process. Instructors who consider the taxonomies carefully will provide better sessions that enable deeper participants learning.

Again, the taxonomies are helpful for directing instructors to consider at what level their instruction is targeted. For example, if a therapeutic recreation specialist wants a client to learn how to "apply" a piece of knowledge then indicating a lower level of learning, such as simply "knowing" is a mismatch. Therapeutic recreation specialists should consider—and write behavioral objectives/client outcomes—at the desired level.

Instructional Taxonomies

There are three instructional taxonomies, or classification systems, that have become classics in the education literature (Babcock & Miller, 1994). They include Bloom's (1956) Cognitive Taxonomy that has six levels; Krathwohl, Bloom, and Masia's (1964) affective taxonomy that has five levels; and Simpson's (1972) psychomotor taxonomy that has six levels. Each classification system speaks to "levels" of learning that

are normally sequential. A learner usually starts at the lowest level when being introduced to the subject matter and then progresses through the steps (hopefully) to the highest level. The taxonomies are often presented as stair steps, starting with the lowest learning and rising to the highest level of learning. Krathwohl (2002) called this a "cumulative hierarchy" (p. 212). The primary importance of the taxonomies is to help instructors prepare learning materials that are more effective for learners to grasp the information.

Bloom's Cognitive Taxonomy (1956) and Anderson and Krathwohl's Update (2002)

Bloom's original taxonomy has six levels of cognition:

- knowledge
- comprehension
- application
- analysis
- synthesis
- evaluation

Table 6.6 outlines the components of Bloom's original taxonomy, according to Krathwohl (2002). It

---

Table 6.6. Structure of Bloom's Original Taxonomy

1.0 Knowledge
  1.1 Knowledge of specifics
    1.1.1 Knowledge of terminology
    1.1.2 Knowledge of specific facts
  1.2 Knowledge of ways and means of dealing with specifics
    1.2.1 Knowledge of conventions
    1.2.2 Knowledge of trends and sequences
    1.2.3 Knowledge of classifications and categories
    1.2.4 Knowledge of criteria
    1.2.5 Knowledge of methodology
  1.3 Knowledge of universals and abstractions in a field
    1.3.1 Knowledge of principles and generalizations
    1.3.2 Knowledge of theories and structures
2.0 Comprehension
  2.1 Translation
  2.2 Interpretation
  2.3 Extrapolation
3.0 Application
4.0 Analysis
  4.1 Analysis of elements
  4.2 Analysis of relationships
  4.3 Analysis of organizational principles
5.0 Synthesis
  5.1 Production of a unique communication
  5.2 Production of a plan, or proposed set of operations
  5.3 Derivation of a set of abstract relations
6.0 Evaluation
  6.1 Evaluation in terms of internal evidence
  6.2 Judgments in terms of external criteria

---

becomes quickly apparent how important these levels are to cognition and instruction. Each of these levels is explained more fully below.

Knowledge

This level is concerned with memory and recall of specific information, of processes, and of universals. **Examples** (Babcock & Miller, 1994) include:

- recall terminology and demonstrate knowledge of facts
- recall of trends, sequences, conventions, classifications, categories, criteria, and methodologies
- recall of principles and generalizations, theories and structures

Typical verbs used in "knowledge" behavioral objectives are (Gronlund, 1978):

- name, identify, define, list, match, state, tell, mark, indicate, recall

Typical Questions:

- Where is the hospital garden located?
- What equipment is used in soccer?
- What is a trowel used for?

Comprehension

This level is concerned with understanding, a step beyond a simpler ability to recall. Comprehension requires the ability to translate, interpret, and extrapolate. **Examples** (Babcock & Miller, 1994) include:

- knowledge of what is being communicated and has acquired ability to make some use of it
- grasping meaning and intent of material under consideration

Typical verbs used in "comprehension" behavioral objectives are (Gronlund, 1978):

- describe, locate, summarize, explain, discuss, give example, draw, express, outline, restate

Typical Questions:

- When it is important to know how to make change for a dollar?
- Can you explain how to log on to the Internet?
- Can you give an example of an activity that you do in your leisure time?

Application

This level is concerned with applying specific information to a particular situation. **Examples** (Babcock & Miller, 1994) include:

- remembers and makes appropriate generalizations or principles
- can use general rule to particular situation

Typical verbs used in "application" behavioral objectives are (Gronlund, 1978):

- apply, illustrate, demonstrate, solve, utilize, develop, interpret, propose, produce, use

Typical Questions:

- How would you locate a movie theatre in a strange town?
- How would you introduce yourself to a stranger?
- If you were bored, how could you find something fun to do?

Analysis

This level is concerned with analyzing elements, relationships, or organizational principles; that is examining the parts of the whole. **Examples** (Babcock & Miller, 1994) include:

- breakdown of material into parts
- recognize assumptions and distinguish facts from hypotheses
- ability to distinguish between cause-and-effect relationships from coincidences
- detect relationships of parts and the way they are organized

Typical verbs used in "analysis" behavioral objectives are (Gronlund, 1978):

- analyze, arrange, contrast, diagram, dissect, discriminate, separate, sort, compare

Typical Questions:

- What skills contribute to a person's ability to have fun?
- How does knowing leisure skills contribute to your health?
- If you use poor table manners, what is likely to happen?

Synthesis

This level is concerned with using a set of knowledges to produce a plan of some sort; that is putting parts together to create a whole. **Examples** (Babcock & Miller, 1994) include:

- formation of whole by putting parts together
- perform induction and develop a structure or pattern not clearly there before

Typical verbs used in "synthesis" behavioral objectives are (Gronlund, 1978):

- blend, create, integrate, organize, design, revise, propose, teach, simplify

Typical Questions:

- How does calling ahead about the restaurant's accessibility contribute to having a good time Saturday night?
- Given adequate resources, how would you plan a weekend with your family?
- What past behaviors have hindered you from enjoying your leisure?

Evaluation

This level is concerned with being able to judge the worth of something. **Examples** (Babcock & Miller, 1994) include:

- formation of criteria by which to judge value of idea or method
- able to judge value or purpose of an idea or method

Typical verbs used in "evaluation" behavioral objectives are (Gronlund, 1978):

- assess, debate, discriminate, rank, rate, defend, conclude, judge, justify, calibrate

Typical Questions:

- How well did this problem-solving approach work for you in locating low-cost alternatives for this weekend?
- What would have made the leisure experience better?
- How would you rate your satisfaction with your performance in this activity as compared to all other activities?

Table 6.7 (p. 98) is a compilation of many interpretations of Bloom's taxonomy (Arreola, 1998; Chapman, 2006; Huitt, 2004; Lamb, 2001; Touchstone, 2009). Each column is intended to provide clarification and make it easier to use in practice.

Bloom's (1956) original taxonomy held sway over the education community for nearly 45 years. In 2001, two colleagues led a national effort to revise the taxonomy that resulted in changes in the terminology, structure, and emphasis (Anderson & Krathwohl, 2001; Forehand, 2005; Krathwohl, 2002).

The new taxonomy is a matrix that has a knowledge dimension and a cognitive process dimension. The Knowledge dimension has four categories: Factual, Conceptual, Procedural, and Meta-cognitive. Table 6.8 outlines the content with the Knowledge dimension (Krathwohl, 2002).

The Cognitive Process dimension has six categories that resemble the former terms, in their verb format. The Cognitive Process dimension contains: Remember, Understand, Apply, Analyze, Evaluate, and Create. Their new meanings are defined below:

- **Remembering**: Retrieving, recognizing, and recalling relevant knowledge from long-term memory.
- **Understanding**: Constructing meaning from oral, written, and graphic messages through interpreting, exemplifying, classifying, summarizing, inferring, comparing, and explaining.
- **Applying**: Carrying out or using a procedure through executing or implementing.
- **Analyzing**: Breaking material into constituent parts, determining how the parts relate to one another and to an overall structure or purpose through differentiating, organizing, and attributing.
- **Evaluating**: Making judgments based on criteria and standards through checking and critiquing.
- **Creating**: Putting elements together to form a coherent or functional whole; reorganizing elements into a new pattern or structure through generating, planning, or producing. (Anderson & Krathwohl, 2001, pp. 67–68)

Krathwohl (2002) provides the structure of the Cognitive Process dimension of the revised taxonomy that is outlined in Table 6.9 (p. 99).

Although this seems like an overly complex system, it represents the best in current-day thinking and research about learning and cognitive processes. Fisher (2005) provided an online interactive matrix that combines the Knowledge Dimension with the Cognitive Process Dimension. Each of the twenty-four cells contains a

Table 6.7. Cognitive Domain Verbs (Arreola, 1998; Babcock & Miller, 1994; Chapman, 2006; Huitt, 2004; Lamb, 2001; Touchstone, 2009)

Level	Behavior Descriptions	Examples of Activity or Evaluation Evidence	Verbs
Evaluation (highest level)	Assess effectiveness of whole concepts, in relation to values, outputs, efficacy, viability; critical thinking, strategic comparison and review; judgment relating to external criteria	Review strategic options or plans in terms of efficacy, return on investment or cost-effectiveness, practicality; assess sustainability; perform a SWOT analysis in relation to alternatives; produce a financial justification for a proposition or venture; calculate the effects of a plan or strategy; perform a detailed and cost risk analysis with recommendations and justifications	Appraise, argue, assess, audit, calibrate, choose, compute, compare and contrast, conclude, convert, corroborate, convince, criticize, critique, decide, debate, deduct, defend, discriminate, distinguish, estimate, evaluate, explain, gauge, grade, interpret, judge, justify, measure, prove, rank, rate, revise, recommend, score, select, stipulate, summarize, support, test, validate, value, weigh
Synthesis	Develop new unique structures, systems, models, approaches, ideas; creative thinking, operations	Develop plans or procedures, design solutions, integrate methods, resources, ideas, parts, create teams or new approaches, write protocols or contingencies	Adapt, anticipate, arrange, assemble, blend, categorize, collaborate, combine, communicate, compile, compose, condense, confirm, construct, contract, contrast, correlate, conduct, create, defend, define, design, develop, devise, estimate, express, facilitate, formulate, fuse, generate, generalize, integrate, intervene, invent, hypothesize, manage, mix, modify, order, organize, negotiate, paraphrase, perform, plan, predict, prepare, produce, propose, reframe, rearrange, reorganize, revise, rewrite,, simplify, summarize, speculate, structure, substitute, synthesize, teach, transpose, reinforce, rewrite, theorize, validate, write
Analysis	Interpret elements, organizational principles, structure, construction, internal relationships; quality, reliability of individual components	Identify constituent parts and functions of a process or concept, or deconstruct a methodology or process; making qualitative assessment of elements, relationships, values and effects; measure requirements or needs	Analyze, appraise, arrange, assign, associate, break down, calculate, categorize, characterize, classify, compare, connect, contrast, correlate, criticize, debate, delineate, detect, deduce, determine, diagnose, diagram, differentiate, discriminate, distinguish, dissect, explain, focus, illustrate, infer, outline, point out, prioritize, question, relate, research, select, separate out, sort, subdivide, test
Application	Use or apply knowledge, put theory into practice, use knowledge in response to real circumstances	Put a theory into practical effect, demonstrate, solve a problem, manage an activity	Administer, apply, articulate, assess, calculate, change, chart, complete, compute, construct, demonstrate, design, develop, discover, draft, dramatize, draw, edit, eliminate, employ, establish, examine, experiment, formulate, give, illustrate, implement, infer, interpret, investigate, measure, modify, negotiate, operate, organize, order, predict, practice, prepare, present, produce, propose, relate, revise, search, schedule, select, show, shop, solve, teach, transpose, transfer, use, utilize
Comprehension	Understand meaning, restate data in one's own words; interpret, extrapolate, translate	Explain or interpret meaning from a given scenario or statement, suggest treatment, reaction, or solution to given problem, create example or metaphors	Associate, cite, classify, conclude, convert, contrast, defend, describe, discriminate, differentiate, distinguish, discover, discuss, draw, estimate, explain, extend, express, generalize, give example, identify, increase, infer, interpret, group, locate, outline, paraphrase, predict, reiterate, relate, represent, restate, review, rewrite, summarize, trace, translate
Knowledge (lowest level)	Recall or recognize information	Multiple-choice tests, recount facts or statistics, recall a process, rules, definitions; quote law or procedure	Arrange, circle, color, collect, copy, define, describe, enumerate, examine, identify, indicate, label, list, mark, match, name, note, number, outline, point, read, recall, recite, recognize, record, reproduce, retell, report, select, show, state, tabulate, tell, underline, quote, write

Table 6.8. Structure of the Knowledge Dimension of the Revised Taxonomy (Krathwohl, 2002)

A. **Factual Knowledge**—The basic elements that students must know to be acquainted with a discipline or solve problems in it.
    Aa. Knowledge of terminology
    Ab. Knowledge of specific details and elements
B. **Conceptual Knowledge**—The interrelationships among the basic elements within a larger structure that enable them to function together.
    Ba. Knowledge of classifications and categories
    Bb. Knowledge of principles and generalizations
    Bc. Knowledge of theories, models, and structures
C. **Procedural Knowledge**—How to do something; methods of inquiry, and criteria for using skills, algorithms, techniques, and methods.
    Ca. Knowledge of subject-specific skills and algorithms
    Cb. Knowledge of subject-specific techniques and methods
    Cc. Knowledge of criteria for determining when to use appropriate procedures
D. **Metacognitive Knowledge**—Knowledge of cognition in general as well as awareness and knowledge of one's own cognition.
    Da. Strategic knowledge
    Db. Knowledge about cognitive tasks, including appropriate contextual and conditional knowledge
    Dc. Self-knowledge

hyperlink that contains definitions and examples of each of the verbs in the matrix. Although the version printed in this book cannot be interactive, the matrix is included in Table 6.10 (p. 100). Interested readers are encouraged to go to Fisher's original online version to view the interactive format.

The advantage of the updated matrix is that it uses current learning and cognition research and provides a more definitive examination of the entirety of learning complexities and dynamics. Learning and cognitive processes can be pinpointed with greater precision, which helps focus the learning task and better predict the expected outcome. Therapeutic recreation specialists will benefit from using this updated model, which has been widely accepted in the educational community, in defining client outcomes and designing therapeutic interventions.

Krathwohl et al.'s (1964) Affective Taxonomy

It is clear that the "buzz" over the cognitive taxonomy received a great deal of attention in the last five or so decades—much more so than the affective taxonomy developed by the same team of individuals. Some have felt this was due to the complexity of teaching and measuring affective qualities, but others felt it was

just overshadowed by the original Bloom's taxonomy (King, 1984). In any case, it is presented here briefly to draw attention to emotions and feelings in addition to the cognitive domain.

Bloom's original and revised taxonomies list cognitive domains in order of complexity, but the affective domain is listed in order of depth or incorporation into the client's personality and/or value system. Although there is clear consensus that the affective domain is difficult to express and measure, it is also clear that affective learning is important (Babcock & Miller, 1994).

The affective domain contains five levels:

- Receiving
- Responding
- Valuing
- Organization
- Characterization

Receiving

In this level, the person shows awareness, consciousness of a situation, fact, or event. He or she shows movement

Table 6.9. Structure of the Cognitive Process Dimension of the Revised Taxonomy (Krathwohl, 2002)

1.0 Remember—Retrieving relevant knowledge from long-term memory.
    1.1 Recognizing
    1.2 Recalling
2.0 Understand—Determining the meaning of instructional messages, including oral, written, and graphic communication.
    2.1 Interpreting
    2.2 Exemplifying
    2.3 Classifying
    2.4 Summarizing
    2.5 Inferring
    2.6 Comparing
    2.7 Explaining
3.0 Apply—Carrying out or using a procedure in a given situation.
    3.1 Executing
    3.2 Implementing
4.0 Analyze—Breaking material into its constituent parts and detecting how the parts relate to one another and to an overall structure or purpose.
    4.1 Differentiating
    4.2 Organizing
    4.3 Attributing
5.0 Evaluate—Making judgments based on criteria and standards.
    5.1 Checking
    5.2 Critiquing
6.0 Create—Putting elements together to form a novel, coherent whole or make an original product.
    6.1 Generating
    6.2 Planning
    6.3 Producing

Table 6.10. Bloom's Revised Taxonomy with Knowledge Dimension and Cognitive Processing Dimension (Fisher, 2005)

The Cognitive Process Dimension						
The Knowledge Dimension	Remember	Understand	Apply	Analyze	Evaluate	Create
Factual Knowledge	List	Summarize	Classify	Order	Rank	Combine
Conceptual Knowledge	Describe	Interpret	Experiment	Explain	Assess	Plan
Procedural Knowledge	Tabulate	Predict	Calculate	Differentiate	Conclude	Compose
Meta-Cognitive Knowledge	Appropriate Use	Estimate	Construct	Achieve	Action	Actualize

beyond denial by selective attention to the desired field of focus, and a willingness to receive data.

Typical verbs used in "receiving" behavioral objectives are (Gronlund, 1978):

- accept, accommodate, focus, follow, observe, note, allow, attend, listen, look

Examples:

- The client acknowledges the hardships experienced by her family as a result of her drinking.
- The participant adheres to hospital rules.

Responding

Client shows an interest and willingness to respond, and might find satisfaction in responding. May be able to entertain an opposing view.

Typical verbs used in "responding" behavioral objectives are (Gronlund, 1978):

- agree, answer, participate, report, conform, choose, explain, label, practice, react

Examples:

- The client smiles when thinking about the possibilities of being united with her family.
- The participant greets other residents with a smile and a handshake.

Valuing

The person regards a thing or event as having value and shows acceptance of value and willingness to be identified with it. A further progression of valuing is preference for things that have value and an exhibited commitment to those things. He or she demonstrates behavior consistent with this value.

Typical verbs used in "valuing" behavioral objectives are (Gronlund, 1978):

- ask, assert, explain, defend, justify, initiate, help, give, propose, choose

Examples:

- The client is able to verbalize the value of sober leisure and follows through with planning for weekend activities.
- The participant showed a preference for chocolate ice cream by choosing that flavor over others.

Organization

Organization includes conceptualization and classification of the value system. The person considers how the new value fits into his or her current system of functioning and believing. As he or she begins to reorganize priorities and values, the person also attempts to incorporate the value with efforts to resolve any conflicts with previously held values.

Typical verbs used in "organization" behavioral objectives are (Gronlund, 1978):

- adhere, arrange, combine, complete, contrast, modify, synthesize, generalize, integrate, relate

Examples:

- The client remains sober and turns down invitations by old friends to go drinking.
- The participant is integrating her disability into her self-image as a female.

Characterization

The client is consistent in response to related situations. He or she has adopted a basic philosophical position and orientation to the world with regard to the value under consideration. Characterization might involve painful intellectual and affective work. As such, characterization is not easy and takes time and maturity.

Typical verbs used in "characterization" behavioral objectives are (Gronlund, 1978):

- adhere, continue, display, commit, assert, assist, defend, describe, discriminate, explain

Examples:

- The client incorporates more non-drinking and healthy lifestyle behaviors into her daily life.
- The client expresses concern about but conviction for remaining sober.
- The participant believes that all individuals deserve time off work to be at leisure.

It is clear that the affective domain is more difficult to operationalize into neat categories as well as pinpoint for client behavior change. However, it is in the therapeutic recreation specialist's best interests to consider and apply the affective domain when possible. A thorough review of Table 6.11 (p. 102) might help clarify some of the five categories.

Simpson's Psychomotor Taxonomy

As many recreation and leisure activities involve the psychomotor or physical domain, it is important to be able to write good, measurable objectives in this area as well as in the cognitive and affective domains. There are three well-known psychomotor domain taxonomies—Dave (1967), Harrow (1972), and Simpson (1972). For this brief review of the psychomotor domain, Simpson's taxonomy (Kennedy, Hyland, & Ryan, 2006) will be highlighted. Simpson's hierarchy has seven levels:

- perception (awareness)
- set (readiness)
- guided response (attempt)
- mechanism (basic proficiency)
- complex overt response (expert proficiency)
- adaptation (adaptable proficiency)
- origination (creative proficiency)

Perception (Awareness)

In this level, the client has attained sensory awareness of cues associated with task to be performed. The participant has ability to attend to relevant cues and use them to guide physical activity.

Example:

- The client watches as therapist shuffles a deck of cards.

Set (Readiness)

In this level, the client exhibits readiness to undertake a particular action and may display readiness by verbal expressions of willingness to attempt a particular action or body language. This level can involve mental, physical, and emotional disposition.

Example:

- The client picks up deck of cards.

Guided Response (Attempt)

In Guided Response, the client makes his or her first attempts at a physical skill. He or she exerts effort to imitate the behavior observed earlier. He or she attempts to comply with directions and coaching. Trial and error coupled with practice lead to improved performance of the skill.

Example:

- The client tries to shuffle deck of cards and attempts to refine efforts in response to therapist's suggestions.

Mechanism (Basic Proficiency)

At this level, the client has achieved the ability to perform desired skills with a degree of confidence. He or she has mastered each of the steps in the complex task to the point where individual steps are blending into a meaningful whole. The required skill is becoming a habit that is available to the client when it is desired or required. Basic proficiency is gained.

Table 6.11. Affective Domain Explanations and Action Verbs (Babcock & Miller, 1994; Touchstone, 2009)

Level	Definition	Verbs
Receiving (lowest level)	The lowest level. Involves willingness to pay attention, openness to new experience, developing awareness, and selective attention.	Accept, accommodate, admit, allow, ask, attend to, capture, choose, feel, focus, follow, give, heed, hold, identify, listen, locate, look, name, note, obey, observe, pay attention, perceive, point to, pursue, regard, reply, select, sense, sit erect, stay, use
Responding	Refers to active participation and reaction, willingness to respond, showing interest, feeling satisfaction.	Answer, agree, acclaim, approve, assist, attempt, choose, comply, conform, continue, describe, discuss, explain, express, follow along, greet, help, label, participate, present, perform, practice, react, relate, recite, reply, report, select, show, state willingness, try, verbalize, volunteer, write
Valuing	Involves the worth a student attributes to an object, behavior, or phenomenon. Valuing also relates to acceptance of, preference for, or commitment to a particular value.	Appreciate, accept, ask, assert, assist, attempt, argue, believe, challenge, choose, complete, criticize, describe, defend, disagree, explain, follow, form, give, help, initiate, invite, join, justify, prefer, propose, respect, search, persuade, prioritize, read, reconcile, refute, report, seek, select, share, state, study, volunteer, work, write
Organization	Is concerned with resolving conflicts between different values, developing a value system, making judgments, and deciding when faced with alternatives, and comparing, relating and synthesizing values.	Adhere, alter, arrange, build, combine, choose, combine, commit, compare, complete, contrast, defend, develop, explain, express, formulate, generalize, identify, integrate, judge, modify, order, organize, persist, prepare, relate, resolve, synthesize
Characterization (highest level)	Student has a long standing value system that has controlled behavior for a time long enough to develop a "life-style." Behavior is consistent and predictable. Values have been internalized and integrated beliefs, ideas and attitudes form a philosophy of life.	Act, adhere, assert, assist, commit, continue, conclude, defend, describe, discriminate, display, endure, explain, influence, internalize, judge, listen, modify, perform, practice, propose, qualify, question, resolve, review, revise, serve, solve, use, verify

Example:

- The client can shuffle deck of cards with confidence and ease.

Complex Overt Response (Expert Proficiency)

Within Complex Overt Response, the client can perform the desired skill easily and independently. The entire sequence of the complex pattern can be performed without the need for full attention. Responses become even more automatic and proficient; actions are more coordinated with a minimum of wasted effort.

Example:

- The client can shuffle deck of cards while joking with other clients.

Adaptation (Adaptable Proficiency)

The client has achieved such mastery that she or he has the ability to alter the skill to suit various conditions. He or she no longer concentrates on varying responses but performs them automatically as the need arises. Actions are can be taken easily in response to problem situations or to fit special requirements.

Example:

- The client can shuffle two decks of cards at once on an uneven surface.

Origination (Creative Proficiency)

At the highest level, the skills are so well-developed that creativity for special situations is possible.

Example:

- The client can shuffle a deck of overly large cards intermixed with smaller cards.

It is clear that the psychomotor domain, like the cognitive and affective ones, spans from simple tasks to more complex tasks. Learning higher skills is predicated on achieving lower skills. However, unlike the other two taxonomies, the psychomotor one does not have verbs associated strictly within each domain (the reader might have noticed some overlap in the other two taxonomies). Instead, most references (Babcock & Miller, 1994) provide a different kind of chart, that either simplifies and groups some of the seven categories or only lists verbs irrespective of their category. In this chapter, because we believe it simplifies the seven categories, we are adopting the former approach. Table 6.12 outlines the seven areas of Simpson's taxonomy

in a simplified form, along with verbs typically used in each area.

All three taxonomies are important to effective instruction led by solid learning objectives. Knowing the basics about each taxonomy will help therapeutic recreation specialists think more closely about what level they are teaching at and focus in more closely on the appropriate level for writing client objectives or outcomes. Once some of the basic of the teaching-learning process, such as principles of learning, learning styles, behavioral objectives, and learning taxonomies, are gained, then it is also important for the specialist to decide how the information will be delivered. The next section covers the instructional methods of lectures, discussions, and experiential learning activities. Although there are other instructional methods, these three likely form the bulk of most therapeutic recreation practice. Each specialist will benefit from learning and honing their skills in each area, not relying too heavily on

Table 6.12. Simplified Version of Psychomotor Domain

Task	Description	Example	Verbs
Observing (lowest level)	Active mental attending of a physical event	Participant watches a more skilled person complete the physical skill.	Attend, choose, compare, contrast, describe, detect, differentiate, distinguish, focus on, identify, isolate, look, observe, perceive, relate, select, separate
Imitating	Attempted coping of a physical behavior	Participant attempts to copy the physical action. Direction and coaching is needed; movement is not smooth or automatic.	Aim, align, attempt, ask, begin, copy, display, express, get ready, position, prepare, proceed, react, respond, stand up, show, start, try, volunteer
Practicing	Trying a specific physical activity repeatedly	The skill is attempted again and again. The entire sequence is performed over and over. Movement is beginning to become more automatic and smooth.	Align, apply, arise, arrange, assemble, attach, attempt, avoid, balance, boil, breathe, brush, build, change, choose, clean, close, comb, compiled, construct, coordinate, count, connect, cover, crawl, cut, demonstrate, disconnect, discriminate, dissect, examine, find, fold, grasp, guide, hop, hold, insert, join, life, locate, make, manipulate, navigate, open, operate, place, pickup, pinch, pivot, plunge, pour, practice, press, produce, pull, push, raise, read, reassemble, recline, remove, repair, replace, restore, run, secure, separate, shorten, simulate, slide, solve, spread, squeeze, stand, start, stick, stimulate, synchronize, test, turn, transfer, type, walk, wash, weigh
Adapting (highest level)	Fine tuning one's skills; making minor adjustments in the physical skill in attempts to perfect it	The skill is near perfection. A mentor or coach may be needed to provide outside perspective on how to improve or adjust as needed for novel situations.	Adapt, alter, change, convert, correct, create, compose, modify, convert, design, divert, exchange, invert, modify, rearrange, remodel, reorganize, replace, reverse, revise, rotate, shift, reformulate, substitute, swap, switch, vary

one or the other. As has been discussed throughout the beginning parts of this chapter, people learn in different ways, various skills need to be taught in various ways, and variety is most likely to keep people (including the specialist!) interested.

Instructional Methods

Effective instruction involves teaching individuals "how to learn, how to remember, how to think, and how to motivate themselves" (Weinstein & Mayer, 1983, p. 3). An instructional technique "may be defined as a method of presenting content that is designed to bring about specific changes in learners" (Babcock & Miller, 1994, p. 182). Instructional techniques or teaching methods, such as lecture, discussion, demonstration, and simulation, should provide opportunities for individuals to learn, remember, and apply specific information (Davis, 1993; Lalley & Miller, 2007; Murley, 2007). The choice of which method to use in a given situation depends on the content being presented, the abilities and backgrounds of the learners as well as the instructor, the environment in which the teaching/learning process takes place, and the future intended use of the content. As mentioned in the brief discussion about learning styles earlier, different instructional methods result in different rates of retention. According to Lalley and Miller (2007), people retain 10% of what they read, 20% of what they hear, 30% of what they see, 50% of what they hear and see, 70% of what they say or write, and 90% of what they say as they do an activity (see Figure 6.3, p. 93). It is the responsibility of the leader, specialist, or instructor to ensure that retention rates are as high as possible.

In the broadest sense, teaching can be seen as either informal or formal. Informal teaching may involve conversations or role modeling, in that students gain information by paying attention to the appearance, behavior, and language of the "instructor." Formal teaching involves advanced planning, with specific objectives, content to be conveyed, with a known location and time. Although there are many varieties of instructional methods, the key is to look for the best method in which the learner can uptake the necessary information. That requires a thorough understanding of the task to be learned or mastered and the needs and motivations of the learners. The following information is provided as a springboard, but it not intended as a final resource on teaching methods. Many books, websites, and other resources are available for additional information and detail.

Lecture

Lecture is "a verbal disposition by a single individual on a particular body of knowledge in a carefully prepared and well-organized form" (Ekeler, 1994, p. 86). This may include the highly formal lecture in which the instructor presents his or her ideas in a highly structured manner and expects and receives no active participation in the dispersal of knowledge from the student audience, to informal lecture may permit or seek interaction and questions from the audience (Ekeler, 1994).

Advantages of Lectures

Lectures can be advantageous in certain situations, although these are more limited than one might originally think (Ekeler, 1994). Advantages and positive results of lectures include:

- content of the lecture is factual or perceptual in nature
- when variation in viewpoints and scholarly analyses or with multiple points of view that are not readily available or that are presented in inadequate form, such as statistical data and so forth
- the teacher wishes to stimulate the learners to do further research
- when giving a background in history or development of a subject or providing learners with a survey of earlier research that has led to the current situation or development of a discipline
- explaining definitions, labels, and terms essential to understanding a subject
- method is easily understood by all learners; often because they are conditioned to it
- when learners are encouraged to take notes so they have created their own reference materials that they keep
- an ordered approach to a subject is needed
- instructor needs to model correct thinking processes within a discipline, verbally explore possibilities, probability, facts, etc., such as the process of critical thinking and reaching conclusions
- can cover more material than any other method
- used effectively to summarize the results of large numbers of studies or theories
- conveys to the learner that they are receiving information on the "expert level," i.e., that there is a competent basis for the information
- economical mean of teaching large numbers of learners

Problems or Disadvantages of Lectures

There are also a number of cases in which lecture is a problematic or insufficient method of instruction. In these cases, a different instructional method is needed (Ekeler, 1994).

- Lecturing is somewhat inferior to other methods in developing student's problem-solving skills; not well-suited to high-level intellectual skills and attitudes.
- Lecturing does not appear to focus on conceptual learning as well as factual learning.
- Lecturing does not take into account for the differences of interest, knowledge, skills, and intellectual abilities of students; it is "one size fits all."
- Lecturing does not provide immediate feedback about its effectiveness to the instructor.
- The amount of information absorbed by student varies greatly student to student.
- When properly prepared and delivered, the lecture demands an enormous amount of time, energy, and focus.
- Students remain relatively passive.
- Method does not provide for long-term recall of subject matter.

Table 6.13 outlines the DOs and DON'Ts of lectures, adapted from Ekeler (1994).

Table 6.13. DOs and DON'Ts of Lectures

DO:
- Establish and maintain eye contact.
- Get plenty of rest and be ready to lecture well.
- Mix up a lecture with emotion-enhancing words, actions, and behavior.
- Watch good lecturers to learn what they do well.
- Be careful about the environment and make sure it is conducive to lectures and learning.
- Use appropriate humor and wit.
- Remember that the lecturer and learner are in a relationship involving the transmission of knowledge, attitudes, and skills.

DON'T:
- Have complete lecture notes, and never, never read from them.
- Remain in a stationary position.
- Use lecturing when another method is better.
- Over-use lectures, especially formal lectures.
- Repeatedly use the same lectures; frequently freshen the experience with new materials and methods.
- Use lecturing if it does not suit your personality or style.

Anatomy of a Lecture

Every lecture has distinct phases. These include preparation, opening, presentation, application, and evaluation. Preparation is a step that is unfortunately often short-changed. The lecture then becomes less effective and wastes considerable learner time. Better preparation usually leads to better learning. "One must capture the students' imagination, interest, and concern"(Ekeler, 1994, p. 93). Preparation is the key to properly setting the stage, challenging the learners, and guiding them outcome achievement. Table 6.14 (p. 106) outlines a few suggestions in preparing for a lecture.

The opening is important to give the learners an outline of what is to be presented and learned. Learners need to perceive a destination and a basic map to get there. They need to know why they are attending and what the end result will be. The presentation of material is linked to the principles of learning and learning styles mentioned previously in this chapter. For example, the best instructors link new learning to old learning, help make generalizations, encourage transferability and applicability, and generally support learners to do their best. During the actual presentation, it is important to limit the number of points that will be made to only three or four per session, as more than this will tend to confuse and overwhelm most learners. Before the session ends, lecturing also involves the application of the information. Group discussion, debriefing, learning activities, and the like give participants opportunities to apply the information, while still under the guidance of the specialist. In this way, learners can explore, raise questions, share doubts, and seek out new knowledge. Evaluation allows both the learners and the instructor to review and reflect what needs to be modified next time. Done with honesty and openness, evaluation is another key to improving one's ability to give an effective lecture.

After the lecture is prepared, with notes being written and major points being highlighted, there are also a number of considerations in delivering the lecture. Practicing in front of a mirror or friends, or being videotaped, may help detect any major problems that will detract from the participants' learning. Some anxiety is normal and may even help people be more energetic and attuned to the learners. Davis (1993) provided a number of hints to improve the actual act of presenting. They are presented in Table 6.15 (p. 107).

At the end of the lecture, instructors should allow enough time to immediately evaluate the session and make notes. What should be done differently? What were the good points? What needs to be improved? Consider also enlisting a friend or colleague to give

Table 6.14. Suggestions for Preparing for a Lecture (adapted from Davis, 1993)

General Strategies
1. Become comfortable with the material; know it really well.
2. Do not plan to lecture for the whole session.
3. Be clear about what can reasonably be accomplished by lecturing.
4. Budget your own time carefully.

Organizing the Course
1. Decide what content to cover.
2. Organize the topics in a meaningful sequence.
   - Topical
   - Causal
   - Sequential
   - Symbolic or graphic
   - Structural
   - Problem-solution
3. Make the course structure explicitly known to students throughout the session.
4. Vary the types of lectures you deliver.
   - Expository; single question or problem
   - Interactive; orderly brainstorming
   - Problem solving, demonstrations, proofs, and stories; posing questions, answer unfolds during class
   - Case study; realistic situation step-by-step
   - Short lectures framing discussion periods
5. Consider the abilities and interests of your students.
6. Prepare a detailed outline for the learners.
7. Become familiar with the environment before lecturing in it.

Preparing Lecture Notes
1. Carefully prepare your lectures.
2. Avoid lecturing verbatim from a script.
3. Experiment with different formats for your lecture notes.
   - Outline
   - Major points
   - Tree diagram
4. Prepare your notes to aid your delivery.
5. Write down facts and formulas for easy reference.
6. Write down vivid examples.
7. Prepare your lecture for the ear *and* the eye.
8. Rehearse your lecture.

Structuring The Lecture
1. Structure the lecture to suit your audience and the subject matter.
2. Begin by writing out the main theme and why students should learn about it.
3. Provide a logical progression for the materials.
4. Structure your lectures to help students retain the most important material.
   - Attention-getting introduction
   - Brief overview of the main points to be covered ("Tell them what you're going to tell them")
   - Quick statement of background or context
   - Detailed explanation of no more than three major points ("Tell them")
   - Concluding summary of main points; reinforcement ("Tell them what you've told them")
5. Design your lecture in ten or fifteen minute blocks.
6. Budget time for questions.
7. Begin and end with a summary statement.

honest and constructive feedback on points for improvement. Like any other skill, preparing and giving lectures takes reasonable practice, as well as trial and error, to find your style and comfort level.

Two other instructional techniques are discussions and experiential methods. The therapeutic recreation specialist is probably more likely to use these two methods than lecture, since much of therapeutic recreation is active and learner-focused. More information is provided on discussions and experiential learning,

although, again, interested readers are encouraged to explore other resources for more depth.

Discussion

"Effective discussions...hinge on the instructors' learning to become more comfortable with control issues and with their ability to guide students (and themselves) through the minefield of interpersonal interactions, especially those in multicultural classrooms" (Frederick, 1994, p. 99). This quote speaks to

---

Table 6.15. Suggestions for Giving a Lecture (adapted from Davis, 1993)

Opening a Lecture
1. Avoid a "cold start." Talk to participants ahead of time, if possible. Knowing their names and interests during a session will help make them feel more comfortable. Don't make assumptions about what the learners know or do not know.
2. Minimize nervous habits, such as tapping a pencil or foot, or pacing.
3. Grab students' attention with an opening, such as asking a question or making a statement. Place the concept in the larger context of their treatment; perhaps begin with general statement followed by specific examples.
4. Vary your opening, especially if the same participants come to more than one of your sessions.
5. Announce the objectives for each session; consider presenting them visually as well; give the students a "road map" for their learning; create a sense of order.
6. Establish rapport with the learners, by asking about their needs, interests, desired outcomes, experiences, etc.

Capturing Learners' Interest
1. During class, think about and watch your audience—your students. Look for signs of interest as well as boredom in some cases, medical conditions, such as sitting tolerance or pressure ulcers, should be considered.
2. Vary your delivery to keep students' attention; consider asking questions at key junctures, playing devil's advocate, having the students solve a problem, or using visual aids. Draw learners to make discoveries themselves instead of telling them everything they should know.
3. Make the organization of your lecture explicit for the learners at the very beginning of the session; move from the simple to complex, the familiar to unfamiliar.
4. Convey your own enthusiasm for the material; say it and display it.
5. Be conversational. Admit when concepts are complex and difficult to learn.
6. Use concrete, simple, and colorful language; use memorable examples.
7. Incorporate anecdotes and stories into the lecture.
8. Do not talk into or from the lecture notes.
9. Maintain eye contact with individuals in the session. Try to make eye contact with each person in the session.
10. Use movements to hold students' attention. The right amount holds people's attention but is not distracting.
11. Use movements to emphasize an important point.
12. Use facial expression to convey emotions.
13. Admit it and laugh at yourself when you make a mistake.
14. Keep track of time; stay on your schedule if possible; only take more time if it is a "teachable moment" or you really misgauged the timing.
15. Use repetition to enforce key points; state the same thing in different ways which may capture different learners' attention; a certain amount of redundancy is important to enhance learner's uptake of the information.

Mastering Delivery Techniques
1. Vary the pace at which you speak.
2. Project your voice or use a microphone. Everyone in the room should be able to hear you clearly. Ask at the beginning if everyone can hear you, and allow people who can't to move to the front.
3. Vary your voice.
4. Pause; take a breath. What seems to you like a long time, is likely a short time for the learners.
5. Watch out for vocalized pauses—um, well, you know—and minimize these to the greatest degree possible.
6. Adopt a natural speaking stance.
7. Breathe normally.

Closing a Lecture
1. Draw some conclusion for the class; Reiterate the objectives or major points of the session.
2. Finish forcefully, with adequate volume, and on a positive note, if possible.

---

a valuable point: instructors/specialists who are more comfortable with the material and their mastery over it will likely be more comfortable with leading discussions instead of lecturing. The discussion leader has to be equally skilled, and often has to practice to become effective, just as much as in delivering a lecture. Discussions, though, call for a high comfort level with handing control over to the participants. The purpose of small group discussions, according to Davis (1993), is to:

- discuss material or solve a problem
- define a term
- pose "why" or "how" questions from reading or experience
- answer a major question raised by the instructor
- identify major points in the lecture

Learners, to be successful and to retain information, must have some prior knowledge or experience in the area under discussion, and their thoughts cumulate into valuable input. Discussions are particularly helpful when the aim is above the comprehension level, such as application, analysis, synthesis, and evaluation (Babcock & Miller, 1994). Being able to prompt discussion with a critical question or purpose is crucial to the small group discussion's success. As such, discussions have many advantages (Babcock & Miller, 1994; Frederick, 1994):

- Students develop a greater sense of ownership and responsibility for their own learning.
- Discussions further students' appreciation for intellectual complexity (no simple answers).
- Learners develop cognitive skills by participation in discussions.
- Discussions have an affective value—increasing confidence, comfort with topic, and perhaps learning.

But discussions also have limitations as well. Some of these include (Frederick, 1994):

- Discussions should be one approach used among many.
- Discussions can be done poorly and do not guarantee effective learning.
- It is easy to get off course without a clear, purposeful plan.
- Learners must have some prior knowledge, interest, or experience in the topic in order to be motivated to contribute.
- Without clear rules and boundaries, some individuals may dominate the discussion or take it off topic.

Effective discussions have several common characteristics (Davis, 1993; Frederick, 1994). First, they relate to what is happening to the participants. The learners need to have an interest or investment in the discussion topic in order to become engaged. Second, discussions, much like lectures, require a great deal of preparation on part of the instructor, and sometimes on part of the learners. If the latter is the case, learners need to be informed ahead of time about their responsibility within the discussion. Expectations of the participants and ground rules should be made early and explicitly. Third, the purpose of the discussion is clear to all involved. It is focused on an identifiable issue or problem, which may be presented visually to the group as well as throughout the discussion. Fourth, effective discussions have a common focal point; perhaps a handout, a specific quotation, a picture, or a graphic. Fifth, facts or specific pieces of information

are brought out during the discussion, perhaps by the instructor. Sixth, throughout the discussion, it is the responsibility of the leader to intervene and bring the group back to center with comments and questions, such as "Okay, where are we on this discussion?" "Recalling our purpose, where are we?" "Have we made all sides of the issue clear?" Seventh, the instructor is also responsible for moving the discussion beyond basic cognitive (factual knowledge) or affective (receiving) levels to higher levels of learning. Eighth, the instructor is also responsible for the ebb and flow of the discussion, when shifts in energy, voice, and inflection may occur. Ninth, the leader should also consider methods to immediately include everyone in the discussion. For example, using brainstorming, or having each person share one comment, or letting participants think and then share, or having participants move to the sides of the room according to their "vote." This immediate draw-in helps establish that all individuals are expected to contribute and gives everyone an early voice. And tenth, the leader needs to set a comfortable tone and environment, based on mutual trust, acceptance, and respect. These ten strategies go a long way in setting the stage for worthwhile discussion for all participants.

Beyond these ten general strategies, Table 6.16 lists a number of valuable ideas for preparing for, leading, guiding, and evaluating discussions.

A number of authors have also collected and distributed tips for asking good questions that spur effective discussions, and fielding questions from the participants. Asking good questions are an important key to leading better discussions and instructors are encouraged to take adequate time in preparation. Key questions should be decided well in advance and planned out so that the discussion flows naturally and stays on track. The manner in which the beginning question or questions is asked will set the tone for the majority of the discussion.

One popular method within small group discussion is the snowball technique in which a group of two discusses a topic, then groups of four are created for discussion, and then groups of eight. The larger group reports back to the whole, usually presenting a consensus or sides of an issue (Davis, 1993).

Table 6.17 (p. 110) outlines pointers for asking good questions and responding well to questions from the participants.

Role Plays

Experiential strategies, problem-based learning, simulations, and cooperative learning experiences are some of the labels used for instruction that actively engages

Table 6.16. Suggestions for Improving Discussions

Preparing Learners for Discussions
• Help learners prepare
  - Encourage students to learn each other's names and interests (if allowable)
  - Arrange seating to promote discussion
  - Allow the participants time to warm up before launching into the discussion
  - Limit your comments
  - List unfamiliar words or terms and write down the definition
  - Write your version of the main purpose
  - Identify subtopics and design a question for each
  - Indicate what other ideas the issue substantiates, contradicts, or amplifies
  - Summarize your reactions and evaluation of the topic
  - Plan an icebreaker early in the session
• Explain the ground rules for participation; decide if participants can "pass" and under what conditions
• Give pointers about how to participate in discussions
  - Seek the best rather than right answer
  - Try to limit previous thinking from limiting acceptance of new ideas
  - Listen more than you speak
  - Stay with a topic until the group has reached the purpose
  - Avoid long stories, anecdotes, etc.
  - Give encouragement and approval to others
  - Seek out differences of opinion
  - Be sympathetic and understanding of others' views
• Use methods that encourage each person's participation early in the session
  - Ask participants to identify characteristics of an effective discussion
  - Periodically divide clients into small groups
  - Assign roles to students
  - Use poker chips or "comment cards" to encourage discussion
  - Use electronic mail or hallway conversations to start a discussion

Leading Discussions
• Refer to any materials that may have been distributed
• Ask for participants' questions
• Pair participants to discuss materials in a question-and-answer format
• Phrase questions so clients feel comfortable responding to: "What is leisure?" (more difficult question) vs. "What are the major benefits of leisure?" (less difficult question) vs. ("What did you personally learn during the activity that you can use later?") (least difficult question)
• Pose an opening question and give learners a few minutes to write down or think of an answer
• Ask participants to describe a "critical incident"
• Ask students to recall specific images from the materials or from their experience ("What images remain with you after the community out-trip?")
• Ask students to pose the dumbest questions they can think of
• Pose questions based on a shared experience ("What skills did you gain from the community out-trip?")
• Make a list of key points
• Use brainstorming
• Pose a controversial question
• Tactfully correct wrong answers
• Generate "truth" statements
• Have students divide into small groups to discuss a question that has been posed
• Ask students to respond to a brief questionnaire/set of questions
• Use peer group panels
• Use storyboarding

Guiding Discussions
• Take rough notes
• Keep the discussion focused
• Use nonverbal cues to maintain the flow
• Bring the discussion back to key issues
• Listen carefully to what students say
  - Content, logic, and substance
  - Nuance and tone
  - How comment relates to overall discussion
  - Opportunities for moving discussion forward
  - The mood of the class as a whole
  - What is left unsaid
• Clarify students' confusions
• Prevent the discussion from deteriorating into a heated argument; yet allow disagreement to occur
• Prevent the discussion from being dominated by one or a few individuals
  - Break group into small groups or assign tasks to pairs of learners
  - Ask everyone to jot down a response to a question and then choose someone to speak
  - Restate; "I'd like to hear from others"
  - Avoid making eye contact with the talkative
  - Explain the discussion has become too one-sided
  - Assign role to dominant student—like periodic summarizer
  - Set time constraints—"We only have twenty minutes left, let's hear from someone else"
  - Speak to the person after the session
• Change the task if the discussion begins to deteriorate
• Be alert for signs the discussion is breaking down
  - Excessive hair splitting or nit-picking
  - Repetition of points
  - Private conversations
  - Members taking sides and refusing to compromise
  - Ideas being attacked before they are completely expressed
  - Apathetic participation
• Vary the emotional tone of the discussion
• Bring closure to the discussion
• Assign participants responsibility for summarizing major points
• Ask group members to write down a question that is uppermost in their minds

Evaluating Discussions
• Ask participants to write briefly (or verbally explain) on how their thinking has changed as a result of the discussion
• Make your own informal evaluation of the discussion
• Occasionally save time of the end of the session to assess the discussion
• Videotape the discussion and watch it with a mentor or colleague

Table 6.17. Suggestions for Asking Good Questions and Responding to Questions

Asking Good Questions
- Balance the kinds of questions you ask
  - Exploratory questions probe facts and basic knowledge
  - Challenge questions examine assumptions, conclusions, and interpretations
  - Relational questions ask for comparison of themes, ideas, or issues
  - Diagnostic questions probe motives or causes
  - Action questions call for a conclusion or action
  - Cause and effect questions ask for causal relationships between ideas, actions, and events
  - Extension questions expand the discussion
  - Hypothetical questions pose a change in the facts or issues
  - Priority questions seek to identify the most important issue
  - Summary questions elicit syntheses
- Vary the cognitive skills your questions call for (See earlier discussion on Blooms' taxonomy)

Tactics for Effective Questioning
- Ask one question at a time that is focused on the purpose of the discussion
- Avoid yes/no questions; instead ask open-ended questions
- Pose questions that lack a single right answer; avoid leading questions
- After you ask a question, wait silently for the answer
- Search for consensus on responses
- Ask questions that require participants to demonstrate their understanding
- Structure your questions to encourage participant-to-participant interaction
- Draw out reserved and reluctant clients
- Use questions that change the tempo and direction of the discussion
- Use probing strategies
- Move around the room to include various participants in the discussion

Tactics for Handling Students' Responses to Your Questions
- Listen to the questioner
- Use nonverbal gestures to indicate your attention
- Vary your reactions to their responses or questions
  - Restate
  - Ask for clarification
  - Invite speaker to elaborate
  - Expand on the contribution
  - Acknowledge the contribution and ask for another view
  - Acknowledge the originality of the idea
  - Nod or look interested but remain silent
- Praise correct answers
- Tactfully correct wrong answers

Tactics for Answering Questions
- Explicitly request questions from students
- Be aware of how your behavior and offhand remarks set the tone for participants' questions
- Thank or praise the client for having asked a question
- Call on questioners in the order they sought recognition
- Make sure that everyone can hear student's questions; clarify the question if necessary
- Answer students' questions directly, but encourage students to try to answer their own questions
- When responding, talk to the whole group
- When students raise complex or tangential questions, ask them to stop by after the end of the session
- Delay answers to questions that will be covered later
- Check back with the learner to make sure the question has been answered

Tactics for handling Difficult Questions and Questioners
- Be diplomatic
- Admit when you don't know the answer
- Be patient with students who ask questions you have already answered
- Preempt long-winded questioners
- Cut off clients who want an extended dialogue

students (Babcock & Miller, 1994; Nestel & Tierney, 2007; Savery & Duffy, 2001). Although there are many forms of experiential learning, only one—role plays—will be discussed here due to space limitations and its frequent use in therapeutic recreation activities. Role plays are when learners are assigned roles and asked to solve some kind of problem or act out some relevant scenario. They call upon the social environment to improve learning. Therefore, role plays are especially useful for teaching clients cognitive/behavioral skills such as assertion, anger management, and problem solving (Babcock & Miller, 1994). Nestel and Tierney (2007) noted the difference in focus for role plays keyed to knowledge, attitudes, or skills:

> In the acquisition of knowledge, role-plays can be valuable to observe and then discuss—the experience of the role players themselves is less important than the opportunity to observe, understand and assimilate information. For attitude development especially that which focuses on change of affect, then role-plays should be loosely structured so that players experience emotions spontaneously. While for skill acquisition, the opportunity for repeated [instances] with feedback is critical. (p. 2)

In general, when designing and implementing role plays, instructors should (Babcock & Miller, 1994; Davis; Joyner & Young, 2006; Nestel & Tierney, 2007):

- Think deeply about the objectives, tasks, and outcomes of the role play during the design phase.
- Use role play only when the group members have some comfort level and trust among them; children are often more comfortable role playing than adults.
- Develop roles or scenarios or problem that are real, relevant, appropriate, and timely to the client group.
- Consider whether the role play will be fully scripted or partially scripted with details filled in by the participants.
- Consider prior competence or experience when assigning roles; consider also revolving roles so the focus is not on the individuals involved.
- Brief the participants and observers well before the role play begins; relate the role to the larger learning experience.
- Stress the importance of social interactions for learning; highlight the benefits of playing all roles.
- Establish clear boundaries, such as being able to stop if feeling uncomfortable or not participating.

- Use structured feedback guidelines—explore role players' feelings, identify effective skills and those that require more development, seek feedback from each role player, achieve a balance between what has worked and what needs development.
- Allow for sufficient time for preparation of roles.
- Stop the role play only at key junctures; end the role play on a positive note.
- Consider asking participants to write or think about their reactions prior to discussion.
- Understand that the actual role play is less important than the discussion that follows.
- Plan well the debriefing discussion to illuminate key issues raised by the role play.
- Experiment with engaging the entire group in the role play.
- Allow adequate time for debriefing and discussion; re-focusing on the aims of the role play.
- Use audiovisual recording devices for playback as appropriate.

Application to Therapeutic Recreation

Throughout this chapter, application to therapeutic recreation services has been paramount. It is clear that leisure education is largely a teaching-learning enterprise, often making the specialist a teacher or instructor, while the patient or client becomes the learner. In order for learning to take place effectively and efficiently, therapeutic recreation specialists need to fully embrace and gain knowledge and competence in instructional principles and methods. Comprehending the principles of learning and reflecting on one's own learning is important in developing activities for client participation. How do we best engage groups of clients? How ready and able are they to learn? In what environments and conditions do they best learn? What combination of materials will help clients best learn? What are our strengths as instructors? What are our areas of competence and which are our areas of weakness? How will we build on the former and remediate the latter?

In order to plan and implement appropriate learning experiences, specialists also need to know about the three instructional taxonomies (cognitive, affective, and psychomotor) and how they relate to writing targeted behavioral objectives. For most therapeutic recreation specialists, this relates to the development of client outcomes and treatment plans. What exactly do we want clients to learn? At what level? How do we best match this to the learning experiences we provide?

Are we moving clients beyond minimal knowledge to the ability to apply and synthesize information, perhaps even evaluate information? Are our activities designed to match the intended outcomes?

And lastly, but certainly equally important, is the instructional method that is chosen to deliver the content of the session or program. From the discussion of learning styles and the "stair step figure," it is clear that lecture may not be the most effective delivery method for encouraging deep learning. Can we gain comfort and competence in more experiential methods that promote deeper learning? What resources do we need as individuals to gain these skills and experiences?

It is clear that there is a tremendous volume of information about instructional techniques, of which only a fraction has been presented in this chapter. Because there are such volumes of information so widely available, interested readers will have no trouble finding multiple resources to improve their understanding in this area.

Summary

- The teaching-learning process involves (a) receiving information, (b) processing it, (c) evaluating it, and (d) encoding or storing it.
- The principles of learning discussed in this chapter include: (a) preparation, structure, and organization, (b) optimal arousal and focus, (c) readiness and prioritization, and (d) active engagement and participation.
- The primary learning styles are (a) visual, (b) auditory, and (c) kinesthetic.
- Writing clear behavioral objectives that contain (a) condition, (b) behavior, and (c) criterion are important to help clients achieve their outcomes.
- The three instructional taxonomies include: (a) cognitive, (b) affective, and (c) psychomotor.
- The major instructional strategies discussed in this chapter include: (a) lectures, (b) discussions, and (c) role plays.
- Instructional techniques are important for therapeutic recreation specialists to acquire since much of the leisure education process is focused on clients learning the necessary skills, knowledges, and abilities they need to succeed in their leisure.

References

Anderson, L. W., & Krathwohl, D. R. (Eds.). (2001). *A taxonomy for learning, teaching, and assessing: A revision of Bloom's taxonomy of educational objectives: Complete edition*. New York, NY: Longman.

Arreola, R. (1998) Writing learning objectives: A teaching resource document from the Office of the Vice Chancellor for Planning and Academic Support. University of Tennessee, Memphis. Retrieved January 11, 2008 from: http://www.utmem.edu/grad/MISCELLANEOUS/Learning_Objectives.pdf

Babcock, D. E., & Miller, M. A. (1994). *Client education: Theory and practice*. St. Louis, MO: Mosby-Year Book, Inc.

Bloom, B. S. (1956). *Taxonomy of educational objectives: Handbook I: The cognitive domain*. New York, NY: David McKay Co., Inc.

Chapman, A. (2006). Bloom's taxonomy—learning domains. Retrieved May 10, 2009, from: http://www.businessballs.com/bloomstaxonomyoflearningdomains.htm

Dave, R. (1967). *Psychomotor domain*. Berlin: International Conference of Educational Testing.

Davis, B. G. (1993). *Tools for teaching*. San Francisco, CA: Jossey-Bass.

Ekeler, W. J. (1994). The lecture method. In K. W. Prichard & R. McLaran Sawyer (Eds.), *Handbook of college teaching: Theory and applications* (pp. 85-98). Westport, CT: Greenwood Press.

Fisher, D. (2005). Bloom's taxonomy. Retrieved May 10, 2009, from: http://oregonstate.edu/instruct/coursedev/models/id/taxonomy/index.htm

Forehand, M. (2005). Bloom's taxonomy: Original and revised. Retrieved May 1, 2009, from: http://www.coe.uga.edu/epitt/bloom.htm

Frederick, P. J. (1994). Classroom discussions. In K. W. Prichard and R. McLaran Sawyer (Eds.), *Handbook of college teaching: Theory and applications* (pp. 99–109). Westport, CT: Greenwood Press.

Gronlund, N. E. (1978). *Stating behavioral objectives for classroom instruction* (2nd ed.). New York, NY: Macmillan.

Harrow, A. J. (1972). *A taxonomy of the psychomotor domain: A guide for developing behavioral objectives*. New York, NY: David McKay Co., Inc.

Huitt, W. (2004). Bloom et al.'s taxonomy of the cognitive domain. EducationalPsychology Interactive. Valdosta, GA: Valdosta State University. Retrieved February 11, 2005, from: http://www.edpsycinteractive.org/topics/cogsys/bloom.html

Joyner, B., & Young, L. (2006). Teaching medical students using role-play: Twelve tips for successful role-plays. *Medical Teacher, 28*(3), 225–229.

Kennedy, D., Hyland, A., & Ryan, N. (2006). Writing and using learning outcomes: A practical guide. Retrieved May 15, 2009, from: www.bologna.msmt.cz/files/learning-outcomes.pdf

King, E. C. (1984). *Affective education in nursing: A guide to teaching and assessment*. Rockville, MD: Aspen.

Krathwohl, D. R., Bloom, B. S., & Masia, B. B. (1964). *Taxonomy of educational objectives: Handbook II: Affective domain*. New York, NY: David McKay Co., Inc.

Krathwohl, D. R. (2002). A revision of Bloom's taxonomy: An overview. *Theory into Practice, 41*(4), 212–218.

Lalley, J. P., & Miller, R. H. (2007). The learning pyramid: Does it point teachers in the right direction? *Education, 128*(1), 64–79.

Lamb, A. (2001). Creative and critical thinking— Bloom's taxonomy. Retrieved December 6, 2002, from: http://eduscapes.com/tap/topic69.htm

Moore, W. S. (1994). Student and faculty epistemology in the college classroom: The Perry schema of intellectual and ethical development. In K. W. Prichard and R. McLaran Sawyer (Eds.), *Handbook of college teaching: Theory and applications* (pp. 45-67). Westport, CT: Greenwood Press.

Murley, D. (2007). Innovative instructional methods. *Legal Reference Services Quarterly, 26*(1/2), 171–185.

Nestel, D., & Tierney, T. (2007). Role-play for medical students learning about communication: Guidelines for maximizing benefits. *BMC Medical Education, 7*(3), 1–9.

Olson, V. D. (2008). Instruction of competent psychomotor skill. *College Teaching Methods & Styles Journal, 4*(9), 27–30.

Savery, J. R., & Duffy, T. M. (2001). Problem based learning: An instructional model and its constructivist framework. *CRLT Technical Report No. 16-01*. Retrieved March 11, 2005, from: http://crlt.indiana.edu/publications/duffy_pub06.pdf

Simpson, E. (1972). *The classification of educational objectives in the psychomotor domain: The psychomotor domain, Vol. III*. Washington, DC: Gryphon House.

Stumbo, N. J., & Caldwell, L. L. (2002). Leisure education and learning theory. *ADOZ Bulletin, 23*, 29–35 (Spanish version); 35–40 (English version)

Stumbo, N. J., & Peterson, C. A. (2009). *Therapeutic recreation program design: Principles and procedures* (5th ed.). San Francisco, CA: Pearson Benjamin Cummings.

Touchstone, M. (2009). Applications of the taxonomies of learning: Objectives: Part 4. Retrieved May 10, 2009, from: http://www.ems1.com/Columnists/mike-touchstone/articles/453123-Applications-of-the-Taxonomies-of-Learning-Objectives-Part-4/

Weinstein, C. E., & Mayer, R. E. (1983). The teaching of learning strategies. *Innovation Abstracts, 5*(32). ERIC document 237180.

» CHAPTER 7 »

Counseling Theory and Practice: Some Applications for Leisure Education

Carla G. Strassle, Ph.D., Jeffrey P. Witman, Ed.D., CTRS,
Judy S. Kinney, Ph.D., CTRS, LRT, and W. B. Kinney, Ph.D., CTRS, LRT

First we will start with an assumption: you entered the field of therapeutic recreation based on a desire to help others. Wonderful! Desire is great, even essential, but as you probably already know, it is only the start. You then have to translate that desire to help to an *ability* to help others. The counseling psychology field has a rich history to pull from and utilize for understanding how to provide leisure education. As you read this chapter, consider how your efforts to provide leisure education programs of significance can be enhanced by better understanding and applying counseling concepts.

Therapeutic Recreation and Psychology

The field of therapeutic recreation has referenced counseling theory and practice throughout its history. One early application was consideration of pre-discharge counseling, for which Avedon (1974) provided these examples of objectives:

- to enable patients and clients to strengthen existing social ties with individuals and groups, and to form new social ties
- to enable patients and clients to understand how to identify, locate, and use recreation resources
- to enable patients and clients to recognize the meaning of recreation in their lives (p. 97)

As you consider how you might help clients achieve objectives such as these, it's likely both educational and counseling strategies come to mind. Practitioners explored and developed both possibilities. The counseling-vs.-education debate became part of a decades-long discussion of the appropriate role for recreational therapists in providing leisure education services. Stumbo and Peterson (2009) provided some important distinctions in contrasting leisure education and leisure counseling:

> Leisure counseling, as well as other forms of counseling, does not start usually with predetermined content. Rather, the problem or focus of counseling originates from the individual client. This major distinction between counseling and education is an important one. It is, however, common for counselors to use educational techniques within the counseling process. Likewise, educators often use counseling techniques within the educational process. Leisure counseling also has some significant differences when it comes to the issue of qualifications and credentials. In general, it is reasonable to assume that most therapeutic recreation specialists are qualified to use some basic counseling techniques. It is not appropriate to assume that they have sufficient training to utilize the title "counselor." (p. 49)

It is important to remember that while it may be appropriate to utilize counseling techniques and important to gain some basic understandings of counseling theory, the recreational therapist providing leisure education is not a professional counselor. Nonetheless, developing appropriate counseling competence can enhance the ability to promote positive program outcomes.

Comprehensive overviews of counseling theories and their relevance to therapeutic recreation practice have been provided in several texts. Sylvester, Voelkl, and Ellis (2001) detailed existentialist, person-centered therapeutic, behavioral, and cognitive-behavioral approaches. They also provide an extensive review of multicultural considerations. Austin (2009) described five helping theories—psychoanalytic, behavioristic, cognitive-behavioral, growth psychology, and positive psychology (see Table 7.1). He also cited the importance of three related areas—constructivism, feminist therapies, and multicultural perspectives. Austin contends that therapeutic recreation is characterized by eclecticism, or the utilization of approaches from various theories depending on the needs of particular clients. Shank and Coyle (2002) discussed the cognitive-behavioral approach and how it can provide a frame of reference for leisure education. Clients bring a variety of antecedents to their participation in activities. Their participation results in consequences. Reflection on these outcomes can serve to challenge the client's original appraisals. For example, an individual's efficacy expectations, competence, motivation, and behavior all might be altered for subsequent participation in activities.

Additionally, there are non-counseling theories from the psychological field that can be applied to leisure education programming. Carruthers and Hood (2004) provided a thorough review of the potentials and relevance of positive psychology principles (positive emotions, traits, and institutions) to therapeutic recreation services. Individuals are encouraged to pursue experiences that bring enjoyment, develop and expand strengths and passions, and cultivate systems and involvements which maximize fulfillment. Table 7.2 provides information about "positivity."

The Premack principle can be utilized in leisure education programming (Sylvester et al., 2001). Premack (1959) suggested that highly preferred behavior can be used to reinforce a less preferred behavior. For example an individual might make watching a TV show that they enjoy or playing a favorite video game contingent on doing a half-hour of exercise.

Counseling theory and techniques are included in the current areas of competence considered for certification in therapeutic recreation (National Council for Therapeutic Recreation Certification, 2008). They are also a part of the competencies identified by professional organizations. The American Therapeutic Recreation Association *Guidelines for Competency Assessment and Curriculum Planning for Recreational Therapy Practice* (West, Kinney, & Witman, 2008), for example, includes the facilitation techniques/theories identified in Table 7.3 (p. 118). Certainly the practice of therapeutic recreation does not entail mastery of all these techniques. Realistically it might mean knowledge of the various theories and therapies sufficient to complement the treatment program of particular agencies. The sections that follow provide a grounded perspective on the basic process of working with clients and on the use of Motivational Interviewing (MI: Miller & Rollnick, 1991), a technique with particular relevance to leisure education. The final section shares some additional best practices from the counseling literature.

Useful Information from the Counseling Field

Research in the field of counseling psychology (Lambert, 1992) has found that effectiveness of an intervention can be broken down into several main categories, including, in order of importance for change, (a) qualities of the person to whom the intervention is directed, (b) common factors, (c) specific techniques, and (d) expectancy. Hypothetically, these categories can be applied to the field of leisure education to maximize the effectiveness of leisure education interventions as well. We will start our discussion of the intervention with the concepts of common factors and expectation.

When we use the term "common factors," we are referring to a set of things that are inherent to any

Table 7.1. Five Major Theories of Helping

Theory	Concepts
Psychoanalytic	Instincts motivate behaviors. A great deal of significance is given to unconscious factors.
Behavioristic	Behavior is learned. Abnormal behavior is a type of learned behavior and so it can be changed.
Cognitive-Behavioral	People identify thoughts and beliefs they hold about themselves and the world in order to change the way they think about themselves and the world.
Growth Psychology	Sees people as being self-aware, able to deal with environmental influences, and generally in control of their own destinies.
Positive Psychology	People reach optimal functioning through positive emotions, positive traits, and positive institutions.

Table 7.2. A Note on Positivity

Leisure education would appear to have particular relevance to the emerging psychological notion of "positivity." As Fredrickson (2009) detailed it, positivity involves ten forms: joy, gratitude, serenity, interest, hope, pride, amusement, inspiration, awe, and love. In providing background to her discussion of the term, she states the following:

> If the spectrum of life possibilities ranges from -10 to +10, psychology . . . made extraordinary advances in the ability to move people from, say -8 to 0. But we knew little about how to raise people above 0 to +6 or +10. (p. 181)

Her research and notions for self help focus on increasing the ratio of positive to negative emotions and responses. This cultivating of human flourishing (as opposed to just alleviating suffering) is what positivity and perhaps what leisure education can be all about. Recreational therapist Cathy O'Keefe (1991) expressed an aspect of this perspective in the following poem:

A poem on behalf of clients to providers of Therapeutic Recreation

I thank you for listening to me when everyone else was too busy generating fees to spare the time.
I thank you for laughing with me when others simply could not let down their professional guard.
I thank you for having the courage to affirm my need for joy and inner peace, so neglected by others.
I thank you for recognizing that more important than learning to walk is discovering that there is
     someplace you want to go.
That before the desire to speak again must come the need to have something to say.
You recognize that leisure, a state of mind, is an internal place of peace and a bridge that connects
     me in a meaningful way to others.
That no matter how primitive or advanced my level of functioning, you are willing to help me seek out
     and free up the real me, the beautiful, joyful, playful me.
Most of all, the object of your therapy is my spirit and my heart.

---

intervention, regardless of what specific techniques might be used in the intervention (Weinberger, 1995). Thus, thinking about common factors is one way to think about how all interventions are similar. Numerous common factors have been identified (see Frank, 1973; Lambert, 1992; Weinberger, 1995), but none has received more attention than that of the relationship or rapport that a therapist and client form. Different counseling theories define the factors that comprise the relationship differently. For example, the humanistic psychologist Carl Rogers (1957) believed that a relationship encompassing empathy, genuineness, and respect for the client was sufficient for change to take place in treatment. More recent views (e.g., Bozarth, Zimring, & Tausch, 2002) indicate that relationship factors as discussed by Rogers are important in helping to produce change, but that they are not, by themselves, sufficient to produce the change. Other researchers have focused on the concept of the therapeutic alliance, which includes the relationship between client and therapist, the related agreement between the two people on the goals and tasks of the therapy, the client's ability to work in the therapy, and the therapist's understanding of and desire to help with the client's problems (Gaston, 1990). Regardless of how the relationship is defined, simply put, and perhaps

not surprising, a good relationship with the treating professional is important! Think about it. Have you ever learned as much from someone you really *didn't* like as much as you have from someone you did like? Intimately tied to the relationship is expectation, or the client's confidence in the therapy's ability to provide (and the therapist's ability to facilitate) a desired outcome (Frank, 1973), since having good rapport likely increases the positive expectations about the possibility of change that can be instilled in someone. Although Lambert (1992) separated the concept of expectation from common factors per se, it too is a component of all therapies (Frank, 1973); Weinberger (1995) actually listed it as a common factor.

Of course, the client also plays an important role in the success of therapy. Have you ever heard the saying "You can lead a horse to water but you can't make it drink"? This is the idea of individual qualities. Indeed, Lambert (1992) indicated that within the outcome literature, the largest proportion of why someone gets better with therapy has to do preexisting client qualities (such as length of time and level of impairment). Understanding that the person to whom the leisure education intervention is directed is an important part of the equation is vital to a successful intervention.

Table 7.3. Facilitation Techniques in Therapeutic
Recreation (West, Kinney, & Witman, 2008)

- Behavioral theory/therapy/modification
- Behavioral medicine theories
- Cognitive behavioral therapy
- Crisis intervention theory
- Developmental theory
- Dialectical behavior therapy
- Existential theories
- Family treatment theories
- Gestalt therapy
- Group treatment theories
- Helping/counseling theories
  - Behavioristic theories
  - Cognitive-Behavioral
  - Growth or Positive psychology
  - Psychoanalytic
- Learned optimism/positive psychology
- Motivational Interviewing theory
- Person-centered therapy
- Rational-emotive therapy
- Reminiscence theory
- Resiliency/Hardiness theories
- Social learning theory
  - Attribution
  - Learned helplessness
  - Self-concept
  - Social support
  - Self-efficacy, etc.
- Transactional analysis theories
- Validation theory

Transtheoretical Model of Change

With this brief review of several important factors in the success of psychotherapy, we can now introduce a model from the counseling field that encourages active attention to these factors. The Transtheoretical Model (TTM; Prochaska, DiClemente, & Norcross, 1992; see also Prochaska & DiClemente, 1982, 1983, 2005) in the counseling field is a multi-faceted model that harnesses knowledge about specific ways that people change (change processes), based on different levels of readiness to change (stages of change), while attending to relationship factors best suited for differential readiness to change. A brief discussion of these concepts followed by an example of how to use the TTM to provide leisure education will follow. The stages of change will serve as the starting point from which to proceed. (See also Chapter 8 of this text on other health behavior change models applicable to therapeutic recreation.)

Simply put, change and the readiness to change are complex. Two people, both of whom want to change, may still differ in terms of their actual readiness to change (thus the individual qualities of the person). Five stages of changes are generally highlighted, as shown on Table 7.4 (Prochaska et al., 1992; however,

Table 7.4. Stages in the Transtheoretical Model of
Change (Prochaska et al., 1992; Prochaska
& Norcross, 2001)

- Precontemplation
- Contemplation
- Preparation
- Action
- Maintenance
- (Termination)

see Prochaska & Norcross, 2001, for a sixth stage of change entitled "Termination"). First is the Precontemplation stage. This is the first stage, in which there is no intention to change, because the client is not necessarily fully (or at all!) aware of things that need to be changed. The saying "Ignorance is bliss" is a good description of this stage; if you aren't aware of a problem for which change is necessary, then you see no reason to change and are therefore not likely thinking about changing!

Next is the Contemplation stage. In this stage a client is aware of an issue and perhaps of the need to make a change regarding the issue but has taken no steps to change. There are currently many behavioral health issues in our country for which people understand that they *should* do something different (e.g., eat healthily and stop smoking) but don't, and how many times have *you* said "I know I *should* do X" but not done it?!

Following Contemplation is the Preparation stage. In this stage the client both understands the issue and has made a commitment to make a change, including beginner steps that may lead to the desired change. We can think of the steps toward change in this stage as "baby steps"—wobbly at first, but if you keep at it, you can get where you are going.

The fourth stage is Action. This is the most active stage of change. It is often easiest to see change taking place in this stage, but from a TTM perspective this is only one stage in changing behavior, which would not be possible if the previous stages had not also taken place.

Finally, the Maintenance stage acknowledges that just as readiness to change is variable within any given person from day to day (or hour to hour!) the ability to maintain change once it has taken place can also be quite difficult (think of how difficult it is to keep weight off once you have lost it, for example).

The stages of change are conceived to proceed in a nonlinear pattern (Prochaska et al., 1992), which acknowledges that people's ability to maintain a changed pattern of behavior is not constant and setbacks in terms of changing do occur. Additional information related to the stages of change in the counseling literature includes the findings that a client's pretreatment stage of change is an excellent predictor of both outcome (Prochaska et al., 1992), such that the farther along in stages of change a client is at pretreatment predicts positive outcome, and drop out (Prochaska & Norcross, 2001), such that clients in earlier stages are most likely to drop out of treatment.

With an understanding of the stages of change, the TTM then asserts that a professional can intentionally use specific processes of change (Prochaska et al., 1992), defined as actions that an individual takes to change behavior, to best help the client. Prochaska et al. (1992) noted that these change processes are central to leading therapy systems (thus the idea of transtheoretical) even as the techniques to invoke the change processes may differ. These processes of change are typically broken down into two categories of cognitive-affective and behavioral processes that should be applied based on where a client falls within the stages of change. Typically the cognitive-affective change processes in earlier stages and the behavioral change processes in later stages. However, see Rosen (2000) for a discussion of how this differs for different health problems, including the finding pertinent to our focus on leisure education that the highest reliance on cognitive-affective processes for exercise-adoption studies took place during the action and maintenance stages).

In addition to providing information about what change processes to use based on the client's stage of change, Prochaska and Norcross (2001) provided guidance for the common-factor category of relationship based on the stage of change that the client is in. For example, when working with people in the Precontemplation stage, the professional emulates the guidance of a trusted individual who actively helps a client consider options. When working with people in the Contemplation stage, the professional encourages the client to explore and choose his/her own options. When working with people in the Preparation stage, the professional takes on the qualities of a coaching relationship where guidance and ideas are available at regular intervals as the client engages in change. Finally, in the Action and Maintenance stages, the professional is available for consultation.

Using the TTM as an overarching model from which to provide leisure education allows a professional to consider and harness the concepts of relationship, expectation, and individual qualities to best help a client change.

With three of the four categories responsible for therapy effectiveness covered, we can begin discussion of the fourth category (specific techniques) from a TTM perspective and provide an example of how to implement techniques in a leisure education context. The TTM does not provide specific techniques that have been created especially for it. Instead, given the transtheoretical nature of the model, it examines existing methods of therapy to see which ones contain change processes within a certain therapeutic stance to fit specified stages of change. MI (Miller & Rollnick, 1991) is one such therapy that has been identified (Prochaska & Norcross, 2001) as useful/applicable to the TTM and helping clients change.

More on Motivational Interviewing

Many of today's health problems are preventable and can be resolved by changing health behaviors (Rollnick, Miller, & Butler, 2008). This is evident in the obesity epidemic that the U.S. is currently experiencing, which results from poor diet and sedentary lifestyles. Other complications include diabetes, high blood pressure, high cholesterol levels, heart disease, and stroke. The traditional medical model has been unsuccessful in controlling these health issues (e.g., practitioners prescribing changes they feel clients need to make to improve their health). Many practitioners may attribute the inability to change to lack of motivation and view the situation as hopeless. Rollnick et al. (2008) indicated it is a matter of approach. How healthcare professionals approach or talk to clients about behavior change can influence the client's motivation to change. MI can be an effective method in assisting clients to change behavior.

MI has been described as a behavior-change strategy (Rash, 2008), a method (Ravesloot, 2008), a counseling style (Rollnick & Miller, 1995), and an intervention (van Weel-Baumgarten, 2008). It has been defined as "a directive, client-centered counseling style for eliciting behavior change by helping clients to explore and resolve ambivalence" (Rollnick & Miller, 1995, p. 105). The primary purpose of MI is to examine and resolve ambivalence in regards to behavior change. A common example would be an client who, for health reasons, knows he/she should be more physically active. The client knows the reasons why it is important, but does not initiate the prescribed change. It has been documented that educating an client as to the reasons why he/she should engage in a particular behavior or advice giving are not effective in making the behavior change (Rash, 2008; Rollnick & Miller, 1995; van Weel-Baumgarten, 2008). While it is important for the client to know why, it is not sufficient for changing behavior. The client has to be motivated. External motivation is not an effective or long-lasting method of change. Internal motivation is key to getting the client on the path to changing behavior. MI assists the client in exploring the reasons why he/she believes it is important to change the behavior.

MI was first used by Miller (1983) in the treatment of alcohol addictions. Since then there have been "over 140 published randomized controlled trials involving Motivational Interviewing" (Scales, 2008, p. 578). Areas of study have included diet modification, physical activity, managing hypertension, diabetes, obesity, heart disease, medication adherence, and psychiatric illnesses.

There are four guiding principles of MI according to Rollnick, Miller, and Butler (2008) which include "(1) to resist the righting reflex, (2) to understand and explore the client's own motivations, (3) to listen with empathy, and (4) to empower the client, encouraging hope and optimism" (p. 7). The authors suggest using the acronym RULE to assist clinicians in remembering these principles (see Table 7.5).

What follows next is an example where MI (Miller & Rollnick, 1991) may be useful. MI is specified by Prochaska and DiClemente (2005) as especially useful when faced with an client in the Precontemplation or Contemplation stage of the TTM. Choosing to highlight these early stages of change is useful for a number of reasons. First, when looking at a variety of populations, Prochaska and Norcross (2001) estimated that an overwhelming majority of clients are in either the

Contemplation or Precontemplation stage of change. With such high proportions of clients occupying these early stages, it is imperative to understand how leisure education can be successfully applied to this population. Additionally, as discussed previously, these stages have the most challenges both in terms keeping a client in the change cycle and of having positive results related to the desired change, so that providing a concrete method by which to approach such clients should be maximally instructive.

A Case Study

Setting:

A program to promote weight loss and physical activity based on a physician referral for women who are in mid-life and from a low-income socioeconomic status. Referral criteria are a BMI of at least 30, presence of secondary health problem(s) such as Type II diabetes, and being between the ages of 45 and 60. The program, funded by a research grant, is free and consists of 16 weeks of group education, cooking healthy meals, and light exercise with an individualized exercise prescription provided for physical activity outside of the once-per-week meetings. Women start the group at the same time in order to encourage social support and compliance.

Ellie is a 58-year-old woman, 5'5" tall, weighing 221 lbs and with a Body Mass Index of 36.9. She is a county employee working in a mostly rural environment at the centralized government administrative complex. She meets the standards for federal poverty level and works all day at a desk. She was referred by the county medical clinic and attended the weight loss/physical activity program three times (three weeks) when she dropped out. When contacted, she agreed to an interview conducted by Michelle, a state-licensed recreational therapist.

Ellie and Michelle are fictitious characters, but the material is drawn from an actual funded research study being conducted at University of North Carolina, Wilmington, under the direction of a state-licensed recreational therapist. Ellie and Michelle's comments represent actual comments made during research focus groups.

Table 7.5. RULE Acronym for MI (Rollnick, Miller, & Butler, 2008)

Resist the righting reflex: healthcare professionals have the impulse to fix things, prevent harm, etc. Humans have a natural tendency to resist persuasion. This approach by the healthcare provider to the client to prescribe or persuade often leads to resistance on the part of the client, especially when it involves behavior change.

Understand and explore the client's own motivations: Assist the clients to identify their own reasons for change, as these are most likely to trigger behavior change (internal).

Listen with empathy: This implies that the healthcare professional listen at least as much as informing. The answers lie within the client and the role of the healthcare professional is to facilitate this discovery.

Empower the client: The client takes an active role of exploring s/he they can make a difference in his/her own health. This discovery assists the client in understanding s/he has the ability and resources to make this and other health behavior changes.

Michelle (M): Hi Ellie, we've missed you at the healthy eating and physical activity program and thought we would check and make sure everything was OK and if you would be able to rejoin our group. The other women have been asking about you.

Ellie (E): Oh, I'm so sorry I stopped attending. I know it's a great program, everyone says it's so good. I hate to let the other girls down, and God knows I've got to lose some weight, but you know, it's just so hard.

M: What's so hard, Ellie?

E: Well, you know, I mean just sticking with it. I've done all kinds of weight-loss programs in the past and none have worked. This is a great program— good information and all, but I know the head stuff, it's just a matter of getting up and doing it.

M: So you have "been there, done that," but you lose interest or motivation to keep going?

E: There's just so much working against you. Take food. I was doing really well last year before my son and his girlfriend moved in with me for two months. All they ate were chips and dip. Chips and dip all over the house. Do you know how hard it is to eat healthy when chips and dip are staring in your face 24 hours a day? And donuts. My husband brings home donuts. He's no help at all. He's a fatso who intends to die fat.

M: Well we're certainly well aware of how difficult it is to eat healthy and get exercise; that's the whole purpose of our group; we want to help each client find their formula for weight loss and activity and overcome the obstacles they face even in their own homes.

E: I'll tell you my formula – liposuction! (Laughs.)

M: (Laughs.) Sounds kind of like you would like to have an easy way, almost magical and instantaneous solution, although I doubt that liposuction would be much fun.

E: I'm just kidding, I know it takes hard work. But, you know, I'm Italian, I was brought up to eat a lot and with several helpings! I mean it's in my blood.

M: (Laughs.) Sure, but I know some thin Italians.

E: Yeah, they all ride bicycles!!

M: Speaking of which, how about physical activity? You know I gave you that walking schedule and outlined a route near your home that was scenic and with gradual increases of difficulty.

E: Same thing. I don't like doing things alone. I don't want to walk alone, I don't want to do anything alone. Like I said, my husband's lazy. He won't do any exercise at all. Plus, I'm on so many medications that are keeping me alive and when I'm sweating like that it pulls medication out that I need in my system.

M: You really believe that?

E: Well no, my doctor has told me I need the exercise, same as you.

M: What else has your doctor told you about your weight?

E: Well, he says my diabetes is a direct result of my weight and probably my high blood pressure as well. He said if I could lose a significant amount of weight I might not even need the medication and I'd feel a whole lot better. I admit I feel pretty awful and I know I look even worse.

M: So it sounds like you really want to do something about it but just need help. What kind of help would be useful to you?

E: Well since I can't trade in my husband and kids (laughs), probably the best thing is your program. I suppose I could start going back to it. Do the girls really miss me?

M: They ask about you each time we get together. They're really becoming a strong support group and are helping each other face the same kind of obstacles. Several of them even work at the government center where you do. They are now getting together over lunch to walk the loop road. I know they would be ecstatic to have you back.

E: I guess I could give it a try.

M: That's great. Ellie, let's plan some ways to make sure that you get to the group next week. Let's anticipate any distractions or motivation killers and figure out how to deal with them. What do you think we should do?

Case Example Analysis

Note how Michelle followed the basic principles of MI. She approached the session from a collaborative and non-threatening standpoint. Her interactions carefully followed the RULE principles (Rollnick et al., 2008): she resisted the righting reflex by not trying to persuade Ellie to return to the group. Rather she respected her autonomy and understood that the ultimate choice would be Ellie's and that to persuade Ellie would be contra-indicated by the process. "Understand your client's motivations" is the second principle. Michelle demonstrates this when she says, "So you have 'been there, done that,' but you lose interest or motivation to keep going?" Michelle is reassuring Ellie that she understands the difficulty of translating factual knowledge into actual behavior, while at the same time encouraging her to reveal more information. "Listen to your client" is the third principle. Notice how little talking Michelle is doing and how all of her comments are prompting or clarifying messages designed to help Ellie maintain autonomy while allowing Michelle to listen and gain a full understanding of the situation. The final principle, "Empower Your

Client," is demonstrated when Michelle gently prods Ellie about Ellie's statement that sweating pulls medication out of her body. Michelle then prompted Ellie to talk about the benefits of healthy eating and physical activity. Finally, empowerment is reflected when Michelle said, "That's great. Ellie, let's plan some ways to make sure that you get to the group next week. Let's anticipate any distractions or motivation killers and figure out how to deal with them. What do you think we should do?" Michelle recognizes that Ellie may yet decide not to attend the group and that is her right to do so. However, she's gently acting on Ellie's somewhat hesitant interest (indicating Contemplation stage in the TTM) and encouraging Ellie to develop a plan of action for herself. Whether it works or not remains to be seen. You cannot move a client from one stage of the TTM without the client being actively involved in the process. As a final note, recognize how Ellie, much like many extremely obese individuals, uses humor as a coping mechanism. Rather than trying to turn the conversation to a more serious note, Michelle used the humor to either transition to a new statement or to encourage Ellie to say what she really believes.

Additional Best Practices

What has been discussed thus far is work with individual clients. Leisure education programming is often presented through treatment and education groups. Recently the American Group Psychotherapy Association (AGPA, 2007) published evidence-based guidelines for effective practice. Several principles espoused in these guidelines have particular relevance for leisure education programming. First is the importance of conducting pre-group preparation, that sets treatment expectations and defines group roles/responsibilities. Setting group "agreements" for behavior can be an important component of this. Table 7.6 provides an example of such agreements. Having group members agree to follow such guidelines provides a common reference point for subsequent behavior. Another principle for effective groups is displaying clinical judgment that balances intrapersonal (individual member) and intragroup (among group member) considerations. Groups are time-limited so leaders need to ensure that all voices are heard and that the process of the group supports both disclosure and cohesion. A final principle of particular relevance is the need to provide opportunities for feedback and for processing. In regard to feedback, group members need the chance to both give and receive it. With processing the leader can at times speak for the experience, letting group members know, for example, how past participants have related to particu-

Table 7.6. Support Group Agreements

- Don't be afraid to ask for help
- One person at a time talks
- No whining
- Start and end on time
- Don't take yourself too seriously
- Don't be sarcastic
- Take responsibility for your own actions
- Share with one another
- Provide constructive feedback and empathy
- Provide encouragement and avoid judging
- Be open to change
- Everyone participates or lets us know why he or she chooses not to

lar experiences. Additionally, though, the opportunity for participants to share their personal response to and insights from experiences is critical. Several therapeutic factors of group work seem particularly important to establish, including (a) *universality*, where participants can recognize that other members share their feelings, thoughts and problems; (b) *altruism*, where participants can gain a boost to self-concept through extending help to other members; and (c) *hope*, where the success of other members can be instructive and help participants develop optimism for their own improvement (AGPA, 2007).

As another important best practice principle, regardless of whether leisure education is being provided in an individual or group format, multicultural considerations are necessary for effective programming (Sylvester et al., 2001). Facilitators need to demonstrate cultural competence in the development of assessment procedures and in the implementation of programs. Counseling and education approaches need to reflect the audience with which they are being utilized.

In summary, leisure education programming should reflect best practices in counseling. Counseling theories should inform the therapeutic process. "The purposeful use and appropriate selection of modalities and facilitation techniques is essential to successful outcomes for TR interventions" (Kinney, Kinney, & Witman, 2004, p. 59). The recreational therapist who is conversant with counseling theories and able to apply counseling concepts can maximize the impact of leisure education. Greater competence with communicating, motivating, and facilitating can make a difference in program outcomes. Leisure education programming can serve the purpose of promoting fulfilling lifestyles, while at the same time supplementing and complementing the treatment process.

Summary

- Even though therapeutic recreation specialists are not qualified to be counselors, it is helpful to know about counseling techniques in providing therapeutic recreation services.
- There are many theories within counseling, such as existentialism, person-centered therapy, behavioral psychology, growth psychology, and positive psychology, that are important to understand.
- Research shows that being able to build interventions based on counseling principles improves likelihood for success of client outcomes.
- The six stages of the Transtheoretical Model of Change are important to consider when designing programs. The six stages are: (a) Precontemplation, (b) Contemplation, (c) Preparation, (d) Action, (e), Maintenance, and (f) Termination.
- Motivational Interviewing is another behavior-change strategy that is helpful to understand and from which to base interventions.
- Each therapeutic recreation specialist will improve his or her skills by building a "toolkit" of best-practice techniques in leading and guiding groups.

References

American Group Psychotherapy Association. (2007). *Practice guidelines for group psychotherapy*. New York, NY: Author.

Austin, D. R. (2009). *Therapeutic recreation processes and techniques*. (6th ed.). Champaign, IL: Sagamore.

Avedon, E. M. (1974). *Therapeutic recreation service: An applied behavioral science approach*. Englewood Cliffs, NJ: Prentice-Hall.

Bozarth, J. D., Zimring, F. M., & Tausch, R. (2002). Client-centered therapy: The evolution of a revolution. In D. J. Cain & J. Seeman (Eds.), *Humanistic psychotherapies: Handbook of research and practice* (pp. 147–188). Washington, DC: American Psychological Association.

Carruthers, C. P., & Hood, C. D. (2004). The power of the positive: Leisure and well-being. *Therapeutic Recreation Journal, 38*(2), 225–245.

Frank, J. D. (1973). *Persuasion and healing: A comparative study of psychotherapy*. New York: Schocken.

Fredrickson, B. L. (2009). *Positivity*. New York, NY: Crown.

Gaston, L. (1990). The concept of the alliance and its role in psychotherapy: Theoretical and empirical implications. *Psychotherapy, 27*, 143–153.

Kinney, J. S., Kinney, T. & Witman, J. (2004). Therapeutic recreation modalities and facilitation techniques: A national study. *Annual in Therapeutic Recreation, 13*, 59–79.

Lambert, M. J. (1992). Psychotherapy outcome research: Implications for integrative and eclectic therapists. In J. C. Norcross & M. R. Goldfried (Eds.), *Handbook of psychotherapy integration* (pp. 94–129). New York, NY: Basic Books.

Miller, W. R. (1983). Motivational interviewing with problem drinkers. *Behavioural Psychotherapy, 11*, 147–172.

Miller, W. R., & Rollnick, S. (1991). *Motivational interviewing: Preparing people to change addictive behavior*. New York, NY: Guilford.

National Council for Therapeutic Recreation Certification. (2008). *NCTRC national job analysis*. New York, NY: Author. (Available from NCTRC.org).

O'Keefe, C. (1991, October). *Ethics, integrity, and spirituality in therapeutic recreation*. Paper presented at the meeting of the National Recreation and Parks Association Congress for Recreation and Parks/National Therapeutic Recreation Society Institute, Baltimore, Maryland.

Premack, D. (1959). Toward empirical behavior laws: I. Positive reinforcement. *Psychological Review, 66*(4), 219–233.

Prochaska, J. O., & DiClemente, C. C. (1982). Transtheoretical therapy: Toward a more integrative model of change. *Psychotherapy: Theory, Research and Practice, 19*(3), 276–288.

Prochaska, J. O., & DiClemente, C. C. (1983). Stages and processes of self-change of smoking: Toward an integrative model of change. *Journal of Consulting and Clinical Psychology, 51*(3), 390–395.

Prochaska, J. O., & DiClemente, C. C. (2005). The transtheoretical approach. In J. C. Norcross & M. R. Goldfried (Eds.), *Handbook of psychotherapy integration* (2nd ed., pp. 147–171). New York, NY: Oxford University Press.

Prochaska, J. O., DiClemente, C. C., & Norcross, J. C. (1992). In search of how people change: Applications to addictive behaviors. *American Psychologist, 47*, 1102–1114.

Prochaska, J. O., & Norcross, J. C. (2001). Stages of change. *Psychotherapy, 38*(4), 443–448.

Rash, E. M. (2008). Clinicians' perspectives on motivational interviewing-based brief interventions in college health. *Journal of American College Health, 57*(3), 379–380.

Ravesloot, C. (2008). Changing stage of readiness for physical activity in Medicaid beneficiaries with physical impairments. *Health Promotion Practice, 10*(1), 49–57.

Rogers, C. R. (1957). The necessary and sufficient conditions of therapeutic personality change. *Journal of Consulting Psychology, 21*(2), 95–103.

Rollnick, S. & Miller, W. R. (1995). What is Motivational Interviewing? *Behavioural and Cognitive Psychotherapy, 23*, 325–334.

Rollnick, S., Miller, W. R., & Butler, C. C. (2008). *Motivational Interviewing in health care: Helping patients change behavior.* New York, NY: Guilford Press.

Rosen, C. S. (2000). Is the sequencing of change processes by stage consistent across health problems? A meta-analysis. *Health Psychology, 19*(6), 593–604.

Scales, R. (2008). Commentary. *International Journal of Therapy and Rehabilitation, 15*, 578–579.

Shank, J., & Coyle, C. (2002). *Therapeutic recreation in health promotion and rehabilitation.* State College, PA: Venture Publishing, Inc.

Stumbo, N. J., & Peterson, C. A. (2009). *Therapeutic recreation program design: Principles and procedures* (5th ed.). San Francisco, CA: Pearson Benjamin Cummings.

Sylvester, C., Voelkl, J. E., & Ellis, G. D. (2001). *Therapeutic recreation programming: Theory and practice.* State College, PA: Venture Publishing, Inc.

van Weel-Baumgarten, E. (2008). Patient-centred information and interventions: Tools for lifestyle change? Consequences for medical education [Electronic version]. *Family Practice, 25*, i67–i70.

Weinberger, J. (1995). Common factors aren't so common: The common factors dilemma. *Clinical Psychology: Science and Practice, 2*, 45–69.

West, R. E., Kinney, T., & Witman, J. (Eds.). (2008). *Guidelines for competency assessment and curriculum planning for recreational therapy practice.* Hattiesburg, MS: American Therapeutic Recreation Association.

Acknowledgment

We would like to thank Mary Ligon and Laura Steck for their comments on versions of the manuscript.

» CHAPTER 8 »

Health Behavior Change Theories and Models

Norma J. Stumbo, Ph.D., CTRS and Shane Pegg, Ph.D.

Intervention programs are much more likely to succeed when they are founded on tested models and theories that address individual behaviors and the contextual environments in which they occur. Such is the case when the targeted behaviors are those for improving or maintaining health (Glanz & Bishop, 2010; National Cancer Institute [NCI], 2005). Health behavior change is the shift from risky behaviors to the initiation and maintenance of healthful behaviors and functional activities, and the self-management of chronic health conditions (Nieuwenhuijsen, Zemper, Miner, & Epstein, 2006). Health-promoting programs that focus on individual behavior change become more effective when the person's surroundings and environment support the change, when resources are available or provided, and environmental, policy, and political changes are simultaneously made. Behavior change takes a multitude of policies and actions at various levels, such as at the individual, community, and population/societal levels in order to sustain that behavior change (Aro & Absetz, 2009).

Behavior Change Interventions

Interventions that aim to improve some type of health behavior can be designed and assessed by the use of relevant theories of behavior change (Fishbein & Yzer, 2003; Glanz & Bishop, 2010; Michie, Johnston, Francis, Hardeman, & Eccles, 2008). "A growing body of evidence suggests that interventions developed with an explicit theoretical foundation or foundations are more effective than those lacking a theoretical base and that some strategies that combine multiple theories and concepts have larger effects" (Glanz & Bishop, 2010, p. 400). That is, theory-based interventions are more likely to be effective in helping the individual change unhealthful behaviors to more healthful behaviors.

Theories are systematic ways of conceptualizing events or situations and include concepts, definitions, and propositions that explain or predict these events or situations by delineating the relationships between

concepts and variables (Glanz & Bishop, 2010; NCI, 2005). NCI explained that (a) *concepts* and *constructs* are building blocks or the primary elements of a theory, (b) *variables* are more specific operational forms of the constructs in a specific situation, and (c) *models* are logical syntheses of a number of theories that help illuminate a particular problem in a specific context or setting. Theories and models are useful because they give intervention planners strategies beyond just intuition to design, implement, and evaluate programs that can be better tailored to meet individual and situational needs (Fishbein, 2008; Glanz & Bishop, 2010; NCI, 2005). By knowing more about the *patterns* of intentions and actions, better interventions can be designed that eventually lead to sustained health-promoting behaviors (Schwarzer, 2008). "Clearly, the more one knows about the factors that underlie the performance (or nonperformance) of any given behavior, the more likely it is that one can design a successful intervention to change or reinforce that behavior" (Fishbein, 2008, p. 834).

Glanz and Bishop (2010) and Langlois and Hallam (2010) noted that recent research shows that theory-based interventions are more efficacious and that those using multiple theories and concepts have even larger effects or outcomes. They also suggested practitioners and researchers consider health behavior within the individual, interpersonal, community, and environmental contexts in that it affects and is affected by so very many factors. Some of the factors include knowledge, attitudes, reactions to stress, motivation, family history, habits, social relationships, socioeconomic status, culture, geography and the like (Glanz & Bishop, 2010). Clearly, theory-based and model-based programming helps tease out the factors that promote healthful changes and fits well with the current emphasis on evidence-based practice in therapeutic recreation services (see Chapter 1 of this text). As Rothman (2004) emphasized, "Improvements in both health behavior theory and intervention methods depend on one another," implying that theories are needed for improved program development and program evaluation and research is needed to improve the utility and value of theories. Theories help practitioners leverage, or increase the power of, interventions (Spahn et al., 2010).

As always, there are those who caution that theory-based programming may not be what it is cracked up to be because:

- researchers and programmers may not always use the available theories in the right way
- many theories still lack a strong research or evidence foundation
- we tend to over-use theories that are focused on individual and on motivational processes
- we may be too inclined to apply a single-theory approach (Brug, Oenema, & Ferreira, 2005)

The purpose of this chapter is to present a number of health-behavior-change theories and models that are prominent in the health literature and are supported by research. Since therapeutic recreation specialists are often trying to help individuals replace unhealthful or unfulfilling behavior with behaviors that promote health, reduce health risks, and manage chronic conditions, it is felt that health behavior change theories and models are appropriate in the study of therapeutic recreation. Health behavior change models are useful in that they may:

- help explain how individuals view the costs and benefits of making health changes
- help explain the problems or barriers encountered throughout the health behavior change
- direct us to asking the best assessment questions about where people are along the continuum of behavior change
- point to interventions that are most likely to produce behavioral change in the most direct route possible; for example, by specifying what types of communication tools are most effective at what times and for whom
- aid us in evaluating whether our interventions are effective and for whom they were effective

Although there are many others, Glanz and Bishop (2010) and Redding, Rossi, Rossi, Velicer, and Prochaska (2000) noted that a few models in particular were best represented by research and in the literature. They include:

Health Belief Model: One of the oldest and most widely recognized health-behavior-change models is the Health Belief Model developed by Hochbaum,

Rosenstock, Leventhal, and Kegels in the 1950s (Nieuwenhuijsen et al., 2006). It was developed to understand individuals' compliance with preventive services such as vaccinations for polio and considers the "individual's perceptions of the threat posed by the health problem (susceptibility, severity), the benefits of avoiding the threat, and factors influencing the decision to act (barriers, cues to action, and self-efficacy)" (NCI, 2005, p. 12). The key notions of perceived susceptibility and perceived severity, perceived benefits and perceived barriers, cues to action, and the more recent addition of self-efficacy are among the core constructs (Glanz & Bishop, 2010; Nieuwenhuijsen et al., 2006). The addition of self-efficacy indicates a shift from early detection and treatment to primary prevention (Nieuwenhuijsen et al., 2006) and lifestyle behaviors such as sexual risk behaviors (Glanz & Bishop, 2010).

Stages of Change or Transtheoretical Model: The Stages of Change or Transtheoretical Model examines an individual's motivation and readiness to modify a particular behavior (NCI, 2005). The concept of stages of change has been found useful for being able to predict changes in a variety of health behaviors. The model advances five major steps: precontemplation (no recognition of the need for or interest in change); contemplation (thinking about changing), preparation (planning for change), action (using new habits), and maintenance (ongoing efforts at new, healthier behavior). As discussed later in this chapter, people do not always move through the stages in a linear fashion, for example, they may relapse and return to earlier stages. However, the TTM is seen as a very useful tool in identifying an individual's readiness to change and to develop corresponding interventions (Glanz & Bishop, 2010). In fact, Brug et al. (2005) noted that perhaps the most important contribution of the TTM is the separation of the motivational stage and the action stage, in that intention is very different than actual behavior, especially in regard to new health behaviors. Positive intention is no guarantee for a change in behavior. Likewise, many theories focus on *what* needs to be changed rather than *how* to change it.

Theory of Reasoned Action/Planned Behavior: This model proposes relationships between intentions, attitudes, perceived norms, self-efficacy or perceived behavioral control, behavioral beliefs or outcome expectancies, normative beliefs, and control beliefs. The creators believe these seven variables do not account for all the variance of people's health behaviors, but do account for a large portion and "can provide insight into how to intervene to increase the likelihood that people will arrive at informed decisions to engage in health-protective behaviors" (Fishbein, 2008, p. 835).

Social Cognitive Theory: This theory "describes a dynamic, ongoing process in which personal factors, environmental factors, and human behavior exert influence on each other" (NCI, 2005, p. 19). These three factors continually interact and influence one another. Social Cognitive Theory also advances that individuals not only learn through their own experiences, but through observing others' action and the consequences. Concepts such as observational learning, self-control, self-efficacy, goal setting, self-monitoring, and behavioral contracting are all important to SCT (Glanz & Bishop, 2010).

The **Precaution Adoption Process Model** outlines seven steps/stages from awareness and advances through steps of becoming aware, deciding a set of actions, acting, and maintaining the desired behavior (NCI, 2005). It is lesser known and has received fewer research investigations. However, it is included in this chapter since it provides valuable information on the decision-making process that individuals go through when considering health-behavior changes.

Table 8.1 provides a brief overview of the health-behavior-change theories discussed in this chapter. It is clear that all of these theories are important, and no single one holds the key to everyone's behavior change: "There is clearly no single quick-fix solution leading to health behavior change" (Nieuwenhuijsen et al., 2006, p. 248).

Nieuwenhuijsen et al. (2006) noted that each health behavior change theory has a different focus, e.g., the person's belief system, the person's interpersonal experiences, or the person's readiness for change.

Table 8.1. Summary of Theories: Focus and Key Concepts (adapted from NCI, 2005, p. 45)

Theory	Focus	Key Concepts
Health Belief Model	Individuals' perceptions of the threat posed by a health problems, the benefits of avoiding the threat, and factors influencing the decision to act	• Perceived susceptibility • Perceived severity • Perceived benefits • Perceived barriers • Cues to action • Self-efficacy
Stages of Change Model/ Transtheoretical Model	Individuals' motivation and readiness to change a problem behavior	• Precontemplation • Contemplation • Decision • Action • Maintenance
Theory of Planned Behavior/ Theory of Reasoned Action	Individuals' attitudes toward a behavior, perceptions of norms, and beliefs about the ease or difficulty of changing	• Behavioral intention • Attitude • Subjective norm • Perceived behavioral control (Self-efficacy) • Behavioral beliefs • Normative beliefs • Control beliefs
Precaution Adoption Process Model	Individuals' journey from lack of awareness to action and maintenance	• Unaware of issue • Unengaged by issue • Deciding about acting • Deciding not to act • Deciding to act • Acting • Maintenance
Social Cognitive Theory	Personal factors, environmental factors, and human behavior exert influence on each other	• Reciprocal Determinism • Behavioral Capability • Expectations • Self-Efficacy • Self-Reflectiveness • Observational Learning (Modeling) • Reinforcement

However, they all involve the intrapersonal and interpersonal levels, within a contextual environment. They also asserted that recent research, studying many of the health-behavior-change theories, has suggested two factors are the overarching variables of health behavior change: the *intention* to engage in healthy behavior and the degree of *self-efficacy* one has. Schwarzer and Renner (2000) proposed that three factors are important to health behavior change theories: (a) *risk appraisals*, i.e., a person's perceived vulnerability, (b) *outcome expectancies*, e.g., expected benefits outweighing expected barriers, and (c) *self-efficacy* or self-regulation, and belief that one has the ability to control his or her own behavior. Readers should note the prominence of these variables as they read the remainder of this chapter.

As can be seen from Table 8.1, many of the concepts within the different models are quite similar and in many cases the terms are interchangeable (Fried, Bullock, Iannone, & O'Leary, 2009). Noar and Zimmerman (2005) advocated that the health fields develop a stronger consensus on the definition and meaning of each term and acknowledge the degree of overlap and repetition. For example, they felt that "cues from media" used by HBM, "normative beliefs" used by TRA/TPB, and "social support" from SCT were similar, and an integration or merging of terms would be possible. The reader should be aware that while the differences between models are important to program development, so too are the similarities.

The next section will address each of the five health behavior change models selected for this chapter. Description of each model and its variables is provided as is supportive research.

Health Belief Model

The Health Belief Model (HBM) is one of the oldest health-behavior-change models, being created in the 1950s. One group found that the Health Belief Model was the most cited health-behavior-change model from 1974 to 1994 (Clarke, Lovegrove, Williams, & Macpherson, 2000). Janz, Champion, and Strecher (2002) noted the HBM translates values-expectancy theory into health-related behaviors. These include: (a) the desire to avoid illness or to get well (value) and (b) the belief that a specific health action available to the person would prevent or ameliorate the illness (expectation), and specifically that the benefits outweigh the costs.

The individual's health actions are influenced by the perceived threat or risk of the health problem and his or her evaluation of the recommended behavior(s)

for preventing, managing, or eliminating the health problem (Fishbein & Yzer, 2003; Nieuwenhuijsen et al., 2006; Redding et al., 2000). Specifically, the Health Belief Model focuses on *susceptibility*, *severity*, *benefits*, and *barriers* (Clarke et al., 2000).

> In general, it is now believed that people will take action to prevent, to screen for, or to control ill-health conditions if they regard themselves as susceptible to the condition, if they believe it would have potentially serious consequences, if they believe that a course of action available to them would be beneficial in reducing either their susceptibility to or the severity of the condition, and if they believe that the anticipated barriers to (or the costs of) taking the action are outweighed by its benefits. (Janz et al., 2002, pp. 47–48)

The HBM has become widely used to explain change and maintenance of health-related behaviors and as a guiding framework for designing and delivering health behavioral interventions. This model has evolved over the years and now contains six main constructs (see Table 8.2) that are felt to influence people's decisions about taking action to prevent, screen for, or control illness and other health problems. It is believed that individuals are ready to act if they:

- believe they are susceptible to the condition (*perceived susceptibility*)
- believe the condition has serious consequences (*perceived severity*)
- believe taking action would reduce their susceptibility to the condition or its severity (*perceived benefits*)
- believe costs of taking action (*perceived barriers*) are outweighed by the benefits
- are exposed to factors that prompt action (e.g., a television ad or reminder from one's physician to get a mammogram) (*cue to action*)
- are confident in their ability to successfully perform an action (*self-efficacy*) (NCI, 2005, p. 13)

Figure 8.1 (p. 130) outlines the entire Health Belief Model and shows the relationships and interactions between the components. The model outlines individual perceptions, modifying factors, and the resultant likelihood of action. Individual perceptions include perceived susceptibility to the health risk and an assessment of the severity of the health risk. Modifying factors include demographics such as age and sex, knowledge of the health risk, perceived threat of the

Table 8.2. Components of the Health Belief Model (adapted from Janz et al., 2002; NCI, 2005; Redding et al., 2000)

Concept	Definition	Potential Change Strategies
Perceived susceptibility	Beliefs about the likelihood of getting a condition. Includes acceptance of the diagnosis, personal estimates of susceptibility, and susceptibility to illness in general. (People in general tend to underestimate their own susceptibility to disease.)	• Specify the population(s) at risk and their degree of risk • Tailor risk information based on individual's characteristics or behaviors • Assist the individual to develop accurate perception of his or her own risk
Perceived severity	Beliefs about the seriousness of a condition and its consequences or of leaving it untreated; includes both medical and social consequences. Both susceptibility and severity combine to constitute a health threat.	• Specify the consequences of a condition and a course of recommended action
Perceived benefits	Beliefs about the efficacy of taking action to reduce risk or seriousness; may also include additional factors such as social pressure and saving money	• Explain how, where, and when to take action and what the potential positive results will be
Perceived barriers	Beliefs about the material and psychological costs of taking action; Cost-benefit analysis may include weighing effectiveness against financial factors, side effects, resource consumption, and so forth. Benefits must outweigh costs in order for action to be initiated	• Offer reassurance, incentives, and assistance; correct misinformation
Cues to action	Factors that activate "readiness to change"; Triggers to action. Although not yet studied systematically, may include bodily events, media publicity, health problems of friends, etc. More intense stimuli may be needed to initiate action if susceptibility and severity are perceived to be low.	• Provide instructions, promote awareness, and remind as appropriate
Self-efficacy	Confidence in one's ability to take action and achieve the desired outcome(s); most appropriate when the health behavior needing modification requires long-term changes, such as diet and exercise	• Provide training and guidance in performing action • Use progressive goal setting • Provide verbal reinforcement • Demonstrate desired behaviors • Reduce anxiety and other negative emotions

health risk, and cues to action such as media ads. The likelihood of action is affected by the ratio of perceived barriers to perceived benefits.

Since the HBM focuses on health motivation, it is suitable for problem behaviors that evoke health concerns, such as unprotected sexual behavior and the risk of contracting sexually transmitted diseases. The HBM provides a useful framework for both short-term and long-term behavior change strategies when the programmer knows how susceptible the individuals feel regarding the problem, whether they believe it is serious,

and whether they believe action can reduce the threat at an acceptable "cost" (NCI, 2005).

Selected Research Related to the Health Belief Model

Subjects included women from Iowa who participated in a program called WISEWOMAN, which was originally funded by the Centers for Disease Control (Gatewood et al., 2008). Of this larger group, 372 individuals were selected and mailed a survey that contained items on barriers to program participation,

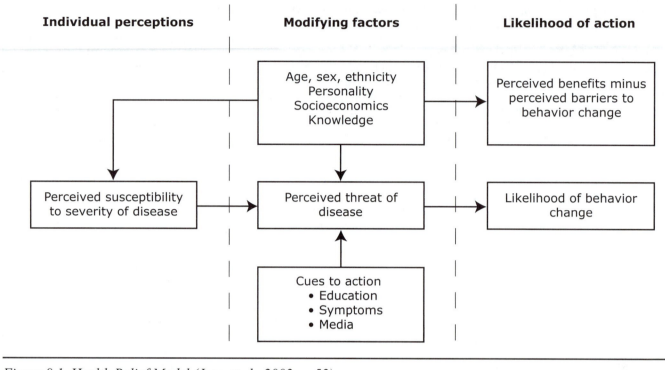

Figure 8.1. Health Belief Model (Janz et al., 2002, p. 52)

barriers to health behavior changes such as nutrition and physical activity, food insecurity, and self-efficacy. The final sample consisted of 147 participants divided into three groups (full, minimal, and no exposure to WISEWOMAN), who were found to be statistically comparable to the larger sample of program participants, except for a higher educational level. Among the most relevant findings to this chapter, it was found that minimal and no participation groups reported "program day and time" and "lack of time" as primary barriers. In addition, anticipated difficulty with behavior change was not different among the three levels of group participation, although the high participation group, whose members were older, more educated and more obese, participated anyway. Lastly, the two strongest barriers to healthful eating and physical activity were lack of nutritional efficacy and physical-activity efficacy.

In 1984, Janz and Becker (1984) conducted a systematic review of 29 HBM studies that were published between 1974 and 1984 and focused on (a) preventive health behaviors such as action to avoid illness or injury (n = 13), (b) sick-role behaviors, for example, actions taken after a specific diagnosis (n = 13), and (c) clinic visits/utilization (n = 3). They found that barriers had the most consistent relationship to results, followed in order by benefits, susceptibility, and severity. They concluded that, "these investigations provide very substantial empirical evidence supporting HBM

dimensions as important contributors to the explanation and prediction of individuals' health-related behavior" (Janz & Becker, 1984, p. 41). While they feted the HBM, they also called for additional research to verify its usefulness and ability to predict health-related actions.

In 1992, Harrison, Mullen, and Green (1992) conducted a meta-analysis of relationships between four HBM dimensions (susceptibility, severity, benefits, costs) and health behavior in 16 studies involving adults. They found that weak effect sizes (small degrees of statistical significance) and lack of homogeneity (the same construct was not being measured in all studies) indicated that reasonable conclusions about the predictability validity of the HBM could not yet be drawn. More recent meta-analyses of the HBM could not be located.

Janz et al. (2002) reported that the HBM enjoys considerable empirical support. They reported that:

- perceived barriers were the single most powerful predictor of the HBM dimensions across all studies and behaviors
- although perceived susceptibility and perceived benefits were important, perceived susceptibility was a stronger predictor of preventive-health behavior and perceived benefits was a stronger predictor of sick-role behavior
- overall perceived severity was the least powerful predictor, although it was strongly related to sick-role behavior

Janz et al. (2002) noted that while a body of research about the HBM has been conducted over the years, future research needs to include: (a) tighter specification of the components of HBM, (b) the relationships between HBM components, and (c) how to apply the HBM to comprehend and alter behaviors that significantly affect public health.

Strategies for Interventions Using the Health Belief Model

Nieuwenhuijsen et al. (2006) outlined these general strategies for the Health Belief Model:

- Explore level of susceptibility, e.g., acquiring secondary health conditions
- Explore benefits and barriers of self-management of health-behavior change
- Create plan to overcome barriers
- Identify and use positive reinforcements as cues for action and to stimulate positive behavior change

Janz et al. (2002) noted the following recommendations for health education and health-promotion practice:

- Programs should be based, at least in part, on knowledge of how susceptible individuals feel regarding a particular health-related outcome, whether they believe the health-related outcome is a serious health problem, and whether they believe that the threat can be reduced by changing their behavior at an acceptable psychological cost.

- Assessment should include the extent to which clients possess adequate self-efficacy to carry out prescribed actions, sometimes over long periods of time.
- Interventions should be designed based on the assessment data collected and, in order to be most effective, likely need to occur over long periods of time.

More information about implementation strategies is presented in the last section of this chapter.

Stages of Change or Transtheoretical Model

Originally published in 1983, Prochaska and DiClemente (1983) developed the Stages of Change or Transtheoretical Model to describe the process of people quitting smoking. In the intervening years, it has been studied with a number of health-behavior changes. Since it uses processes and principles of change from a number of major theories of intervention, the term "*trans*theoretical" is used. It has been called the "most widely used stage model in health psychology" (Weinstein, Rothman, & Sutton, 1998, p. 293). Prochaska, Wright, and Velicer (2008) concurred that the TTM is the most popular health-behavior-change theory in the health literature, and a number of stage-based interventions have been developed and tested.

The model has five stages: precontemplation, contemplation, preparation, action, and maintenance (see Table 8.3). Individuals go through these stages at varying speeds and often cycle through stages in a circular,

Table 8.3. Stages of Change/Transtheoretical Model (Prochaska, Redding, & Evers, 2002, p. 101; Redding et al., 2000, p. 186)

Stage	Definition	Potential Change Strategies
Precontemplation	Has no intention of taking action within the next six months	Increase awareness of need for change: personalize information about risks and benefits
Contemplation	Intends to take action in the next six months	Motivate; encourage making specific plans
Preparation	Intends to take action within the next 30 days and has taken some behavioral steps in this direction	Assist with developing and implementing concrete action plans; help set gradual goals
Action	Has changed overt behavior for less than six months	Assist with feedback, problem solving, social support, and reinforcement
Maintenance	Has changed overt behavior for more than six months	Assist with coping, reminders, finding alternatives, avoiding slips/relapses (as applicable)
Termination	Has long-term control over behavior	N/A

not linear, fashion. The stages are expected to be qualitatively different and mutually exclusive, meaning that different interventions are appropriate at different stages of health-behavior change (Schwarzer, 2008). Also, the distribution across stages may vary for different health-related behaviors. "People do not systematically progress from one stage to the next, ultimately 'graduating' from the behavior change process. Instead, they may enter the change process at any stage, relapse to an earlier stage, and begin the process once more. They may cycle through this process repeatedly, and the process can truncate at any point" (NCI, 2005, p. 15).

As Weinstein et al. (1998) suggested, stage models, when validated, are important because they help programmers target individuals and interventions more precisely. "Thus, if health behavior change proceeds through a series of stages, a theory that correctly describes these stages makes possible the matching of treatments to individuals (because people in different stages have different needs) and the sequencing of treatments (because the stages have a temporal order)" (Weinstein et al., 1998, p. 290).

In *Precontemplation*, individuals are uninformed or underinformed about the need for behavior changes and the consequences of not doing so. They often tend to avoid reading, talking, or thinking about their high-risk behaviors. Often labeled "hard to reach" or "at risk" these individuals lack motivation or are resistant to change. They do not intend to change in the next 6 months (Prochaska et al., 2008).

In *Contemplation*, individuals plan to make a behavioral change in the next six months. They have become more aware of the need for change, but may not be able to do so immediately. These individuals often are characterized as chronic contemplation or behavioral procrastination. They are not ready for immediate action-oriented programs in which they are expected to take quick action. Contemplators do intend to change within the next 6 months (Prochaska et al., 2008).

Preparation is the stage in which people begin to make plans to take action. For example, they may join a health education class, sign up for a personal trainer, or buy a self-help book. They are good candidates for action-oriented health promotion programs and plan to make changes in the next 30 days (Prochaska et al., 2008).

The next stage, *Action*, is the one in which people have made specific, significant, and overt modification in their lifestyles within the past 6 months. The catch is that researchers and health professionals need to agree that the behavior change is significant enough to warrant a reduction in health risk. For example, reducing the amount of cigarettes one smokes is not enough to be considered in the Action stage; one must abstain

from smoking for a designated period, which according to Prochaska et al. is the last 6 months.

Maintenance is the stage in which people strive to prevent relapse into the unhealthful behavior and yet do not have to put forth the same energy as in the Action stage. At this point individuals are less tempted to return to unhealthful behaviors and are more confident in their ability to sustain the change.

Termination is the stage in which individuals no longer succumb to temptation and have total self-efficacy. The individual does not return to the unhealthful behavior.

Table 8.3 (p. 131) lists the Stages of Change, along with their definitions and potential change strategies. A proper assessment of the individual, indicating at which stage he or she is currently, is a must for providing meaningful and outcome-oriented interventions. Individuals at different stages, even within the same program, must be accommodated so that their chances of success are heightened.

Prochaska and colleagues (2002) have provided a number of related concepts to the Transtheoretical Model (see Table 8.4). Among these are the *decisional balance*, which includes the weighing of pros and cons of the behavior change. Until the pros far outweigh the cons, no behavior change will occur. *Self-efficacy* is the "situation-specific confidence that people have that they can cope with high-risk situations without relapsing to their unhealthy or high-risk behavior" (Prochaska et al., 2002, p. 103). This is often weighed against temptation or "the intensity of urges to engage in a specific habit when in the midst of difficult situations" (Prochaska et al., 2002, p. 103). The authors posit that there are three most tempting kinds of situations: negative affect or emotional distress, positive social situations, and craving.

Table 8.4. *Additional Constructs to the Transtheoretical Model (Prochaska et al., 2002, p. 101; Redding et al., 2000, p. 186)*

Constructs		Description
Decisional Balance	Pros	The benefits of changing
	Cons	The costs of changing
Self-efficacy	Confidence	Confidence that one can engage in the healthy behavior across different challenging situations
	Temptation	Temptation to engage in the unhealthy behavior across different challenging situations

In addition, Table 8.5 provides a number of factors that help individuals progress through the stages of change. These ten factors have received the most empirical support (Prochaska et al., 2005).

Marshall and Riddle (2001) noted that these ten concepts can be reduced to three major factors:

- individual's self-efficacy to change
- decisional balance of perceived advantages and disadvantages of change
- strategies and techniques individuals used to alter thoughts, intentions, beliefs, feelings, and actions

Selected Research Related to the Transtheoretical Model

Greaney et al. (2008) studied the efficacy of an intervention designed to address specific needs at each of the TTM stages with regard to physical activity and physical function of 966 community-dwelling older adults in Rhode Island. The intervention consisted of a number of prompts including newsletter, coaching calls, and other print materials. The researchers reported that when individuals who were already at Maintenance at baseline were excluded, individuals' readiness to change improved, although actual physical activity and physical functioning did not improve. They recommended additional research that focused on mediating and moderating variables to the adoption and maintenance of exercise behaviors for community-dwelling older adults and noted that knowing these variables would help in the design of more effective interventions.

Marshall and Riddle (2001) completed a meta-analysis of 80 studies applying the TTM to physical activity and exercise. They found that:

- three of the four stages (all except maintenance) were defined by changes in actual behavior
- self-efficacy increased as individuals moved through the stages (although not in a linear fashion),
- increasing the pros and decreasing the cons of regular exercise are equally important
- individuals use all 10 processes of change (see Table 8.5), most likely during the transitions from Precontemplation to Contemplation and

Table 8.5. Factors that Affect Progress through Stages of Change (Prochaska et al., 2005; Redding et al., 2000, p. 186)

Processes of Change	Consciousness Raising (E)	Finding and learning new facts, ideas, and tips that support the healthy behavior change
	Dramatic Relief (E)	Experiencing the negative emotions (fear, anxiety, worry) that go along with unhealthy behavioral risks
	Self-Reevaluation (E)	Realizing that the behavior change is an important part of one's identity as a person
	Environmental Reevaluation (E)	Realizing the negative impact of the unhealthy behavior or the positive impact of the healthy behavior on one's proximal social and physical environment
	Social Liberation (E)	Realizing that the social norms are changing in the direction of supporting the healthy behavior change
	Self-Liberation (B)	Making a firm commitment to change
	Helping Relationships (B)	Seeking and using social support for the healthy behavior change
	Counterconditioning (B)	Substituting healthier alternative behavior and cognitions for the unhealthy behavior
	Reinforcement Management (B)	Increasing the rewards for the positive behavior change and decreasing the rewards of the unhealthy behavior
	Stimulus Control (B)	Removing reminders or cues to engage in the unhealthy behavior and adding cues or reminders to engage in the healthy behavior

E = Experiential processes; B = Behavioral processes

Preparation to Action, and least likely from Action to Maintenance
- the model holds up reasonably well to meta-analytic scrutiny, most core constructs do differ across the stages, and most changes occur as predicted in the TTM theory

Strategies for Interventions Using the Transtheoretical Model

Spahn et al. (2010) noted that programming strategies depend on the stage of change the person is in, and includes motivational interviewing, skill development training and coaching, demonstration and modeling, reinforcement, self-monitoring, goal setting and behavioral contracting, social support, and stimulus control. Nieuwenhuijsen et al. (2006) outlined these general strategies for the Transtheoretical Model:

- Assess person's readiness for change and sustaining health behaviors.
- Assess individual's awareness of health-related risk factors.
   - If aware, what actions is person taking?
- What are pros and cons of specific treatment modality or intervention?
- Tailor interventions to the person's stage of change.

Prochaska and colleagues (2002) provided a list of five critical assumptions that underlie the Stages of Change model. These include:

1. No single theory can account for all relationships and interactions of behavior change. The best model(s) will likely result from a combination of several well-researched theories.
2. Behavior change is a process that proceeds over time, through a series of stages.

3. Behavior change stages are both stable and open to change.
4. The majority of at-risk populations are not ready for action and will not be well-served (i.e., be motivated) by traditional action-oriented prevention programs.
5. Specific processes and principles should be applied at specific stages to best ensure behavioral change.

To address the prior point, Table 8.6 outlines more specifically the most effective processes to be used within each stage. These processes, when applied at these specific stages, are proven most effective through a number of health-behavior-change research studies.

Subsequent research (Prochaska et al., 2008) has shown how the individual's assessment of pros and cons change over the stages: (a) Cons are greater than Pros in Precontemplation, (b) Pros increase between Precontemplation to Contemplation, (c) Cons decrease from Contemplation to Action, and (d) Pros surpass Cons prior to Action. Knowing these influences over the individual may help the programmer focus on the balance of pros and cons, depending on the person's assessed stage of change.

A TRS can use these supports and strategies to design interventions and aids that help individuals succeed in their behavior change plans. For example, for consciousness raising, the programmer can provide statistics, helpful hints, ideas, and the like in newsletters, on bulletin boards, on websites, in the introduction to the session, and elsewhere to help the individual become more aware of the compelling need for the behavior change. Tailored messages and communications are most likely to be effective. Additional information about generic health behavior change strategies will be presented at the end of this chapter.

Table 8.6. Processes that Mediate Progression between Stages of Change (Prochaska et al., 2002, p. 107)

Stages of Change				
Precontemplation	**Contemplation**	**Preparation**	**Action**	**Maintenance**
Processes	Consciousness raising Dramatic relief Environmental reevaluation			
		Self-evaluation		
			Self-liberation	
				Counterconditioning Helping relationships Reinforcement management Stimulus control

Theory of Reasoned Action/ Theory of Planned Behavior

Fishbein and Ajzen (1975) developed the Theory of Reasoned Action (TRA) to understand the relationships between attitudes and behaviors. They proposed that there was a difference between attitude toward an *object* and an attitude toward a *behavior* with respect to that object. For example, an individual may have an attitude toward the *object* of birth control versus the attitude toward the *behavior* of using contraceptives. Fishbein and colleagues demonstrated that the latter is a much better predictor of actual behavior. Thus, attitude toward birth control is a much weaker predictor of actual behavior than attitude toward the behavior of using contraceptives.

Fishbein demarcated between beliefs, attitudes, intentions, and behavior. According to the TRA, the strongest predictor of behavior is the *behavioral intention*. It is influenced by the individual's *attitude* toward the performance of the behavior, and by *beliefs* about whether others important to the individual approve or disapprove of the behavior (*subjective norm*).

The direct determinants of an individual's behavioral intention are their *attitude* toward performing the behavior and their *subjective norm* associated with the behavior. Attitude is determined by the individual's beliefs about outcomes or attributes of performing the behavior (*behavioral beliefs*) weighted by evaluations of those outcomes or attributes. Thus, a person who holds strong beliefs that positively valued outcomes will result from performing the behavior will have a positive attitude toward the behavior. Conversely a person who holds strong beliefs that negatively valued outcomes will result from the behavior will have a negative attitude toward the behavior. (Montano & Kasprzyk, 2002, p. 70)

TRA specifies that the *intention* to perform a particular behavior is strongly related to the actual performance of the behavior. This comes with two assumptions: (a) behavior is under volitional control (the person has control over his or her own behavior), (b) people are rational beings. That is, people behave in certain ways because we operate with a rational decision-making process in selecting and planning our actions. The TRA was designed to predict behavior from intention and relies on quasi-mathematical relationships between beliefs, attitudes, intentions, and behavior (Redding et al., 2000).

The Theory of Planned Behavior is additive to the Theory of Reasoned Action. Both of these are illustrated in Figure 8.2. The schematic, starting from the right, shows TPB's explanation of how *behavioral intention* determines *behavior*, and how *attitudes toward behavior*, *subjective norm*, and *perceived behavioral*

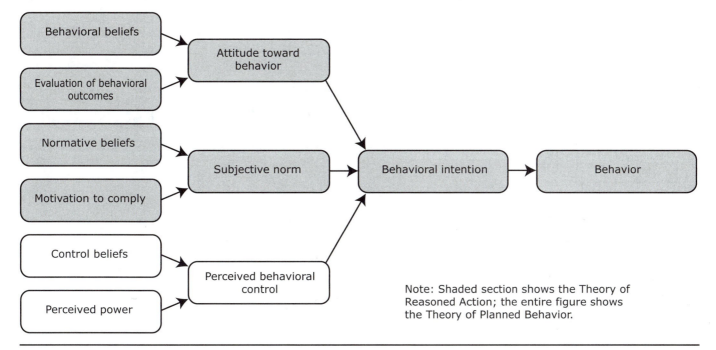

Figure 8.2. Theory of Reasoned Action and Theory of Planned Behavior (Montano & Kasprzyk, 2002, p. 68; NCI, 2005, p. 18)

control affect *behavioral intention*. According to the model, attitudes toward behavior are shaped by beliefs about what is entailed in performing the behavior and the outcomes of the behavior. Beliefs about social standards and motivation to comply with those norms affect *subjective norms*. The presence or lack of factors that will make it easier or more difficult to perform the behavior affect *perceived behavioral control*. "Thus, a causal chain of beliefs, attitudes, and intentions drives *behavior*" (NCI, 2005, p. 18).

The addition of perceived control over the behavior is a key component to the Theory of Planned Behavior (Redding et al., 2000). As such, the TPB is an extension of the TRA. It differs from the TRA in that it includes perceived behavioral control—people's beliefs that they can control a particular behavior. For example, in some situations, people's behavioral intention may be influenced by factors beyond their control (Montano & Kasprzyk, 2002; NCI, 2005).

"As in the original theory of reasoned action, a central factor in the Theory of Planned Behavior is the individual's intention to perform a given behavior. Intentions are assumed to capture the motivational factors that influence a behavior; they are indications of how hard people are willing to try, of how much of an effort they are planning to exert, in order to perform the behavior. As a general rule, the stronger the intention to engage in a behavior, the more likely should be its performance. It should be clear, however, that a behavioral intention can find expression in behavior only if the behavior in question is under volitional control" (Ajzen, 1991, p. 181).

Thus, "behavioral achievement depends jointly on motivation (intention) and ability (behavioral control)" (p. 182). Perceived behavioral control varies across situations and actions.

Both the TPB and the TRA assume that culture, environmental influences, and the like operate but do not independently explain the probability that an individual will behave in a certain way (NCI, 2005). Below is an updated version from Fishbein (2008).

As seen in Figures 8.2 and 8.3, a number of concepts and definitions are important to understanding the TRA and TPB. Table 8.7 provides an overview and gives some examples of measurement items that look at these variables.

Schwarzer (2008), among others, have criticized the TRA/TPB since it is a "continuum model" instead of a "stage model." Continuum models tend to assume that all individuals move through from inaction to action and maintenance in a sequential order. In this way,

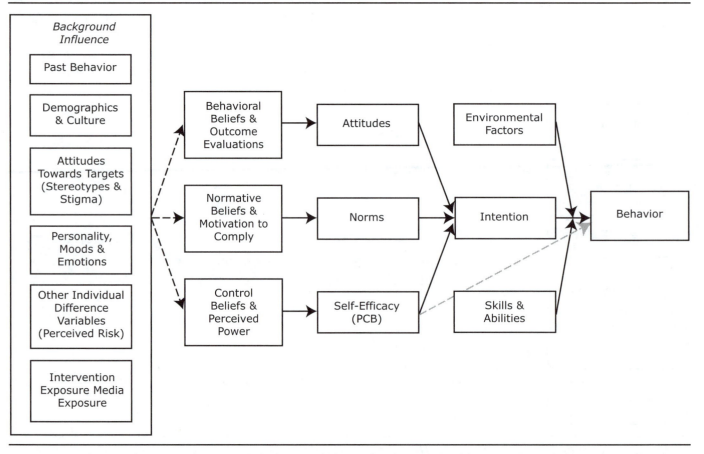

Figure 8.3. Theory of Reasoned Action and Theory of Planned Behavior (Fishbein, 2008, p. 838)

continuum models imply a "one-size-fits-all" type of intervention program, not targeting at which stage the person is in, what barriers might be encountered at specific stages, or other factors that predict failure at moving through the model. Thus, these models do not address the intention-action gap that so many people fall into when trying to change to healthful behaviors.

Research Related to the Theory of Reasoned Action and Theory of Planned Behavior

Three meta-analyses (cf., Armitage & Conner, 2001; Cooke & French, 2008; Sheppard, Hartwick, & Warshaw, 1988) will be highlighted, as they provide a broader picture of the efficacy of TRA/TPB than do single studies. Sheppard et al. (1988) were interested in research that used the TRA/TPB as underlying theory but which did not comply to the conditions of the models. For example, the authors cited three examples of situations in which

the assumptions of the TRA/TPB are violated: (a) the target behavior is not completely under the individual's volitional control, (b) the situation involves a choice not explicitly explored by TRA/TPB, and (c) individuals' intentions are assessed when it is impossible for them to have all the necessary information to form a completely rational intention. One of their major conclusions was that those who had previously conducted research on the TRA had not often used it in the way Fishbein and Ajzen intended. However, much to their surprise,

The model performed extremely well in the prediction of goals and in the prediction of activities involving the explicit choice among alternatives. Thus it would seem that the Fishbein and Ajzen model has strong predictive utility, even when utilized to investigate situations and activities that do not fall within the boundary conditions originally specified by the model (Sheppard et al., 1988, p. 338).

Table 8.7. Theory of Planned Behavior Concepts, Definitions, and Measurement Approaches (Redding et al., 2000)

Concept	Definition	Measurement Approach
Behavioral Intention	Perceived likelihood of performing behavior	Are you likely or unlikely to (perform the behavior)?
Attitude	Personal evaluation of the behavior	Do you see (the behavior) as good, bad, or neutral?
Subjective Norm	Beliefs about whether key people approve or disapprove of the behavior; motivation to behave in a way that gains their approval; the product of normative belief multiplied by motivation to comply	Do you agree or disagree that most people approve/disapprove of (the behavior)?
Perceived Behavioral Control	Belief that one has, and can exercise, control over performing the behavior; Product of control belief multiplied by the perceived power	Do you believe (performing the behavior) is up to you, or not up to you?
Behavioral Belief	Evaluation of likelihood that performance of behavior is associated with certain outcomes	How likely is (behavior) going to produce (outcomes)?
Evaluation of Behavioral Outcomes	How positive or negative those outcomes would be	How positive or negative will the outcomes be?
Motivation to Comply	Motivation to do what each personal contact person wants	Are your friends and family motivators?
Control Belief	Perceived likelihood of each facilitating or constraining condition occurring	Do you feel you have control over what happens?
Perceived Power	Perceived effect of each condition in making the performance of the behavior easier or more difficult	Do you feel you have power to overcome obstacles?
Normative Belief	Perception of how much each personal contact approves or disapproves of the behavior	To what degree do your friends and family influence you?

Armitage and Conner (2001) conducted a meta-analysis and found results similar to prior studies. They summarized their study by saying that the TPB is able to predict intention and behavior, with self-reported behavior being more predictive than observed behavior. In addition, they reported the presence of discriminant validity between desire, intention, and self-prediction, as well as for self-efficacy and perceived control over behavior. In addition, subjective norms, when measured appropriately with multiple-item scales, show a reasonably strong relationship with intention. They felt that additional work on normative variables such as moral and descriptive norms may increase the predictive power of the normative component of the model.

Cooke and French (2008) also completed a meta-analysis on the studies to date of the TRA/TPB. Their meta-analysis was aimed at quantifying how well the TRA and TPB predict intentions to attend screening programs and actual attendance behavior. They found that overall attitudes had a large-sized relationship with intentions, and both subjective norms and perceived behavioral control had a medium-sized relationship with intention. Additionally, intention had a medium-sized relationship with attendance, and these relationships are similar to those found in previous meta-analyses. They concluded that to increase attendance at screening programs, professionals should send people information designed to generate positive attitudes rather than alter subjective norms. They also found that people who were prompted to plan to attend the screening (when, where, and how) were more likely to actually get screened. They called for additional research to tease out increased refinement of the relationships between variables in the TRA/TPB.

Strategies for Interventions Using the TRA/TPB

Fishbein (2008) emphasized that the first step in using a reasoned action intervention approach is to clearly define and describe the behavior(s) of interest. It appears that the more specific the definition/description, the more likely an intervention can be built to impact it. The second step involves recognizing that behavior involves four elements: *action* directed at a *target*, performed in a given *context*, at a certain point of *time*. These help pinpoint whether the individual will have strong intentions to change/modify the behavior. The single best predictor of whether one will or will not perform the behavior in question is that person's intention to perform the behavior. Intentions basically equate with a readiness to engage in a particular behavior. The more the intention and the behavior are

delineated, the more likely the intervention can be targeted and successful. However, if individuals do have the intent and do have information, then it's likely various barriers may be hindering them from going forward. In these cases, reviewing and removing barriers to the healthful behavior will be necessary.

One of the implications of the Theory of Planned Behavior is that it is intended for individuals who mostly do not currently intend to perform the desired target behavior. Interventions are meant to target behavioral, normative, and/or control beliefs to, in turn, affect positive intentions among participants who, prior to the start of the intervention, either did not think about performing the behavior or were not inclined to do so (Fishbein & Ajzen, 2005). These authors mention a number of successful strategies for using TRA or TPB. These include:

- "Reasoned" discussion about erroneous or biased beliefs that are aimed at swaying behavioral, normative, and control beliefs regarding the target behavior
- Instruction in new strategies that are most likely to produce success (e.g., skill-focused workshops).

These conditions point to the fact that a clear and specific assessment needs to be conducted so that the appropriate intervention can be designed and delivered. More about these ideas are presented in the last section of this chapter.

Social Cognitive Theory

The Social Cognitive Theory (SCT) is considered an "interpersonal" theory in that it includes not only the individual but also his or her social environment. The psychosocial dynamics aspect includes opinions, thoughts, behavior, advice, and support of the people surrounding an individual and how they influence his or her feelings and behaviors (NCI, 2005). Simply put, health behavior change is the result of reciprocal and co-existing interactions between personal factors, environmental influences, and behaviors (Nieuwenhuijsen et al., 2006) and has been called *triadic reciprocity* (Redding et al., 2000). A change on any one of these three factors affects the other two.

A prime consideration is the person's agency. The person is considered an agent in that he or she is able to intentionally make things happen by his or her own actions. "Agency embodies the endowments, belief systems, self-regulatory capabilities, and distributed structures and functions through which personal influence is exercised, rather than residing as a discrete entity in a particular place" (Bandura, 2001, p. 2). To be an effective agent, an individual must be able to:

- Develop specific intentions (thoughts about a future course of action)
- Develop and follow through on plans of action
- Carry out appropriate courses of action and motivate and regulate their execution; that is, be self-directed
- Self-reflect or self-examine their own functioning; evaluating their motivation, values, and meaning of their life pursuits; display self-efficacy (Bandura, 2001)

The latter idea of self-efficacy is a pivotal concept in social cognitive theory in that efficacy beliefs affect a person's ability to adapt and to persevere. These kinds of beliefs influence whether people tend to think pessimistically or optimistically and in ways that are self-enhancing or self-defeating (Bandura, 2001). A person who believes that he or she can deliver a desired outcome can lead a more active and self-determined life (Schwarzer & Renner, 2000).

> Efficacy beliefs play a central role in the self-regulation of motivation through goal challenges and outcome expectations. It is partly on the basis of efficacy beliefs that people choose what challenges to undertake, how much effort to expend in the endeavor, how long to persevere in the face of obstacles and failures, and whether failures are motivating or demoralizing. The likelihood that people will act on the outcomes they expect prospective performances to produce depends on their beliefs about whether or not they can produce those performances. A strong sense of coping efficacy reduces vulnerability to stress and depression in taxing situations and strengthens resiliency to adversity. (Bandura, 2001, p. 10)

SCT focuses on the importance of enhancing an individual's behavioral capability (knowledge and skills) and self-confidence (self-efficacy) to engage in a particular health behavior (Lewis, 2002). Additionally, the influences between the individual and his/her environment are considered reciprocal. The person affects the environment in which he/she is located at the same time the environment is also reciprocally affecting him/her (Bandura, 2001).

According to NCI (2005), the SCT is one of the most robust and most frequently used health-behavior-

change theories, because it explores the reciprocal interactions of people and their environments and the psychosocial determinants of health behavior.

Three main variables—(a) self-efficacy, (b) personal goals, and (c) outcome expectancies—play a significant role in the probability that an individual will alter a personal health behavior. If individuals have a high sense of personal control or self-efficacy, behavior change is easier, even though they may face obstacles. "It is partly on the basis of efficacy beliefs that people will choose what challenges to undertake, how much effort to expend in the endeavor, how long to persevere in the face of obstacles and failures, and whether failures are motivating or demoralizing" (Bandura, 2001, p. 10). When the feeling of control is absent, then the motivation to act or persist in the face of challenges is not strong enough to result in changed behavior. Efficacy beliefs also play a key role in shaping one's life course by influencing what types of activities and environments people choose to get into. See Table 8.8 (p. 140) for a description of the major variables in Social Cognitive Theory.

SCT is dynamic in that it holds that the environment and person are constantly interacting and changing one another: "Behavior is not simply a product of the environment and the person, and environment is not simply a product of the person and behavior" (NCI, 2005, p. 20). The social environments that one chooses influence his or her behaviors and choices, which in turn affect the environment. This repetitive, cyclical effect is ongoing—"Thus, by choosing and shaping their environments, people can have a hand in what they become" (Bandura, 2001, p. 11).

Baranowski, Perry, and Parcel (2002) noted that this means SCT addresses both the psychosocial dynamics influencing health behavior and also methods for promoting behavioral change. Bandura (2001) noted that health behavior is similar to other life choices and outcomes:

> Health illustrates self-regulation in another important sphere of life. In recent years, there has been a major change in the conception of health from a disease model to a health model. Human health is heavily influenced by lifestyle habits and environmental conditions. This enables people to exercise some measure of control over their health status. Indeed, through self-management of health habits people reduce major health risks and live healthier and more productive lives (Bandura, 2001, p. 11)

Table 8.8. Social Cognitive Theory (NCI, 2005, p. 20; Nieuwenhuijsen et al., 2006; Redding et al., 2000)

Concept	Definition	Potential Change Strategies
Reciprocal Determinism	The dynamic interaction of the individual, behavior, and the environment in which the behavior is performed	Consider multiple ways to promote behavior change, including making adjustments to the environment or influencing personal attitudes
Behavioral Capability	Knowledge and skill to perform a given behavior; Knowing what to do and how to do it	Promote mastery learning through skills training
Expectations	Anticipated outcomes of a behavior	Model positive outcomes of healthful behavior
Self-Efficacy	Confidence in one's ability to take action and overcome barriers; either self-enhancing or self-hindering; plays central role in self-regulation of motivation through goal challenges and outcome expectations (that is, it mediates between knowledge, attitudes, skills, and behavior)	Approach behavior change in small steps to ensure success; be specific about the desired change
Self-Reflectiveness	Metacognitive ability to reflect upon oneself and the adequacy of one's thoughts and action; Being self-reflective is a precursor to being self-efficacious	Consider pros and cons of certain actions and outcomes
Observational Learning (Modeling)	Behavioral acquisition that occurs by watching the actions and outcomes of others' and one's own behavior; Learning occurs through watching another perform the behavior (modeling) or through personal experience (e.g., trial and error)	Offer credible role models who perform the targeted behavior
Reinforcement	Responses to a person's behavior that increase or decrease the likelihood of reoccurrence. Consequences that affect probability of behavior will be attempted again. People are motivated to perform behaviors through rewards and incentives	Promote self-initiated rewards and incentives

Bandura (2001) also reminds us that besides personal agency, that is the direct choices a person makes individually, there is also collective agency. In collective agency, people turn to others, such as co-workers, relatives, legislators, in an attempt to get those who have access to resources or expertise or who wield influence or power to act at their behest to secure the outcomes they desire. In this way, the individual is conceding a bit of power to another person or group of persons in order to save time, effort, and personal resources. Collective agency is especially important when people have not developed the means to accomplish the task themselves: they believe others can do it better, or they do not want the full responsibility of the outcome. In doing so, they "free themselves of the performance demands and onerous responsibilities that personal control entails" (Bandura, 2001, p. 13).

Nieuwenhuijsen et al. (2006) emphasized three things about self-efficacy. First, they promoted the notion that the impact of self-efficacy on self-management is

paramount and should be a major measure of outcomes. They noted however that enhanced self-efficacy is not equal to functional improvement. Second, they reminded professionals that self-efficacy is specific to a behavior or set of behaviors and is not a personality trait. Likewise, a person might feel self-efficacious toward one behavior and not others.

The concept of reciprocal determinism is also important in SCT. It means that a person can be an agent for change as well as a responder to change. That is, changes in the environment, the persuasion of role models, and positive reinforcement can all be used to promote behavioral changes (Glanz & Bishop, 2010).

Lewis (2002) noted that the most powerful and consistent method of altering self-efficacy is performance attainment (i.e., performing the behavior). Successful interventions engage individuals in incrementally successful structured experiences in which their own self-monitoring of the target behavior, along with feedback from valued others, improves their self-view as being efficacious toward the desired behavior. This involves setting reasonable goals, structured, stepwise interventions, and providing performance feedback to the individual.

Selected Research Related to Social Cognitive Theory

Hundreds of studies involving the Social Cognitive Theory and self-efficacy have been conducted over the years. This section will highlight only two such SCT studies that relate to physical activity for older adults. Kruger (2001) studied self-efficacy as it applies to understanding older adults' likelihood for adhering to preventative health behaviors. She concluded that intervention studies that utilized social cognitive theory to promote behavior change achieved superior results in improving self-efficacy for exercise to those that did not. "Thus, interventions with the goal of promoting regular physical activity in older adults achieved a significant positive effect on self-efficacy, and were considered efficacious in influencing activity behavior through the mediation of self efficacy" (Kruger, 2001, p. viii).

A relationship in the opposite direction was found by another set of researchers. Netz, Wu, Becker and Tenenbaum (2005) conducted a meta-analysis of 36 studies on the effects physical activity on well-being for older adults without clinical conditions. They were looking for the effects that physical activity has on different well-being indicators. They especially found that self-efficacy, overall well-being, and view of self were most significantly and positively affected by physical activity. They suggested that physical activity provided mastery experiences for older adults whose physical self-efficacy might be compromised due to deteriorating physical abilities. In this case, self-efficacy was an important outcome, rather than an intervention input.

Strategies for Interventions Using Social Cognitive Theory

In terms of health, people often turn to educated others, such as therapists and other health-care professionals, to outline choices and consequences of health risks and behaviors. Also, individuals often benefit from group sessions with like-goaled people. Bandura (2001) noted that research shows that the stronger the perceived collective agency, the higher the groups' aspirations and motivational investment in their undertakings, the stronger their staying power in the face of adversity and failures, the higher their morale and resilience to stressors, and the greater their performance accomplishments. One only has to think of

health groups such as the teams on television's "The Biggest Loser" to understand these factors. He further promoted four techniques to improve self-efficacy: (a) mastery experiences, (b) modeling or vicarious experience, (c) persuasion, and (d) physiologically compatible experiences (Bandura, 1997).

Glanz and Bishop (2010) noted that with self-efficacy as the primary focus of SCT, specialists can make deliberate efforts to impact individuals' self-efficacy using three types of strategies:

- Setting small, incremental, and achievable goals
- Using formalized behavioral contracts to establish goals and specify rewards
- Monitoring and reinforcement such as record-keeping and self-monitoring

Nieuwenhuijsen et al. (2006) outlined these general strategies for the Social Cognitive Theory (SCT):

- Discuss with the individual what to do and how to do it (capability building)
- Assess the person's beliefs in his/her ability to control his/her health condition or disability
- Encourage and reward belief in individual's ability to successfully accomplish health actions
- Help the individual set small, incremental goals; reinforce positive behaviors in individual and group settings
- Have person observe others and adopt model behaviors that are desirable

Spahn et al. (2010) noted these strategies for nutritional counseling, which are likely to work in other arenas:

- Testimonials, demonstration, and modeling (Observational learning)
- Skill development training and coaching
- Social support
- Reinforcement
- Sequential goal setting and task breakdown
- Stimulus control
- Motivational interviewing

Additional information about a number of general health behavior change strategies will be presented at the end of this chapter.

Precaution Adoption Process Model

The Precaution Adoption Process Model (PAPM) was presented by Weinstein and Sandman in 1992. It has not received the empirical or pragmatic attention that the prior models have; however it is included in this chapter because it has much to teach therapeutic recreation specialists about the decision-making process of health-behavior change (NCI, 2005). Separate sections about related research and intervention strategies are not included in this chapter for the Precaution Adoption Process Model.

The PAPM delineates seven distinct phases, from unawareness to adoption and/or maintenance of a behavior. In stage 1, Unaware of Issue, the individual may have no idea of a specific hazard, such as lead paint. In stage 2, the person may become aware of the issue, but remain unengaged in any action toward protection. In stage 3, the person makes a decision about acting. If s/he decides to not act, s/he exits the model (stage 4). If s/he decides to act, the individual moves to stage 5. Stage 6 is then acting on the information and stage 7 is maintenance of the new behavior. The PAPM is outlined in Figure 8.4.

The authors felt that a person generally progresses linearly through the model, especially through the first stages. For example, after a person was aware s/he could not again become unaware. However, the person could go backward and forward in the later stages of the model. Weinstein and Sandman (2002) felt that stages 1 (unaware), 2 (unengaged), and 4 (decided not to act) are important to acknowledge.

Those in stage 1 obviously need basic information about the hazard and the recommended precaution. People in stage 2 need something that makes the threat and action personally relevant. Individualized messages and contact with friends and neighbors who have considered action should help these individuals move to the next stage. Another powerful influence on the transition from stage 2 to stage 3 is probably the awareness that others are making up their minds, that one is obliged to have some opinion on this current issue of the day (Weinstein & Sandman, 2002, p. 129).

In addition the authors noted that individuals in stage 4 (decided not to act) are particularly difficult to convince in another direction. They are often well informed and quite tenacious about their beliefs, and will often dispute or ignore information to the contrary (Weinstein & Sandman, 2002).

Like the health-behavior-change models previously introduced in this chapter, it is suggested that health-change messages be tailored to the stages in which the individual or groups of individuals are. Tables 8.9 and 8.10 provide examples of the ways in which health promotion messages can be customized. Specifically modified messages are most likely to be effective and motivate the individual to change from health-harming behavior to health-inducing behavior.

In addition to the guidance provided by Tables 8.9 and 8.10, Weinstein and Sandman (2002) noted a number of suggestions for assessment items to determine an individual's stage. A sampling of these is provided in Table 8.11 (p. 144).

Weinstein et al. (1998) discussed a number of drawbacks in designing and evaluating interventions based on stage models such as this one. First, they noted that a stage model is only useful when it is possible to identify and alter the particular input factors that affect people in moving from one stage to another. Knowing the stages may not be as important as knowing what moves people from one to the next. Second, if determining a person's present stage requires an extensive but problem-fraught assessment process, then the effort expended to know the stage may not be that beneficial. Third, the stages are only as good as the evidence-based interventions that are validated and

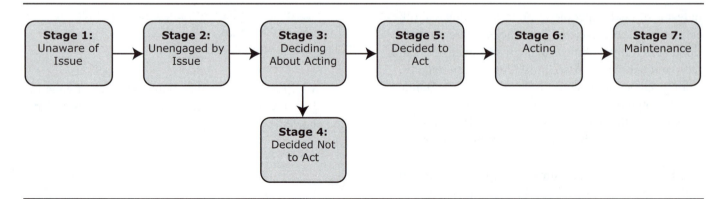

Figure 8.4. Stages of the Precaution Adoption Process Model (NCI, 2005, p. 19)

Table 8.9. Issues Likely to Determine Progress between Stages (adapted from Weinstein & Sandman, 2002, p. 130; Weinstein et al., 1998)

Stage Transition	Important Issues
Stage 1 to Stage 2	• Media messages about the hazard and precaution
Stage 2 to Stage 3	• Communication from significant others • Personal experience with the hazard
Stage 3 to Stage 4 or Stage 5	• Beliefs about likelihood and severity • Beliefs about personal susceptibility • Beliefs about precaution effectiveness and difficulty • Behaviors and recommendations of others • Perceived social norms • Fear and worry
Stage 5 to Stage 6	• Situational obstacles • Time, effort, and resources needed to act • Detailed "how-to" information • Reminders and other cues to action • Assistance in carrying out action

proven to work with people at each stage. Until fairly solid evidence-based treatments are presented, stage-targeted interventions may be no better than generalized interventions at overall health behavior change. Fourth, in all probability, people do not move through the stages at the same pace for all health behaviors, which implies that models should be re-considered as continuums of behavior change rather than as discrete stages. More research on each of these issues will be necessary, but until then, stage models represent one of the best ways to conceptualize how people may move from unhealthful to more healthful behaviors.

Summary of Models

From the previous discussions of the most popular health behavior change models, it is clear that they have multiple overlaps in concepts and yet each adds a unique perspective. The wise professional will acquire the research, consider the possibilities, and use the best information to make informed and conscientious programming choices. Table 8.12 (p. 144) provides an

Table 8.10. Stages of Precaution Adoption Process Model and Communication Strategies (adapted from Weinstein & Sandman, 2002, p. 130; Weinstein et al., 1998)

Stage	Description	Example	General Communication Strategy
Stage 1: Unaware of Issue	Pre-awareness of a health hazard (e.g., not knowing that excessive drinking may cause liver damage)	Never heard that sunscreen is needed before being in the sun	Develop multiple sources of information and make available to individual
Stage 2: Unengaged by Issue	Being aware of a health hazard, but not yet considering whether s/he needs to do anything about it	Never thought about using sunscreen	Materials need to be compelling, personalized, and easily accessible and digestible
Stage 3: Deciding about Acting	Making a decision about what, if any, actions are to be taken regarding the health behavior; Often held onto despite additional information	Undecided about using sunscreen	Materials and instruction should provide facts and compelling arguments about behavior change
Stage 4: Decided Not to Act	Decision is made to "drop out" and not engage in the health-promoting behavior	Decided not to use sunscreen	
Stage 5: Decided to Act	Decision made to "opt in" and engage in health-promoting behavior	Decided to use sunscreen	Materials and instruction should include full disclosure about options for acting, how this is to be accomplished, and the consequences of each option
Stage 6: Acting	Carrying out the intention to act; performing the health-inducing behavior	Uses sunscreen regularly	Support should be provided for initial and subsequent actions
Stage 7: Maintenance	Continuing to carry out the action; performing the health-inducing behavior for a period of time		Support should be provided for maintenance of new behaviors; Supportive atmosphere that aids continued success

Table 8.11. Sample Assessment Items (adapted from Weinstein & Sandman, 2002)

Assessment Item	Stage
Have you ever heard about [health issue]? No Yes (go to item 2) *Example:* Have you heard about the need for weekly physical activity? No Yes (go to item 2)	Stage 1
Have you [dealt with health issue]? Yes No [go to item 3] *Example:* Have you participated in weekly physical activity on a regular basis? Yes No [go to item 3]	Stage 6
Which of the following best describes your thoughts about [health issue]? I've never thought about [health issue] I'm undecided about [health issue] I've decided I don't want to [health issue] I've decided I do want to [health issue] *Example:* Which of the following best describes your thoughts about getting regular physical activity? I've never thought about regular physical activity I'm undecided about regular physical activity I've decided I don't want to be physically active on a regular basis I've decided I do want to be physically active on a regular basis	Stage 2 Stage 3 Stage 4 Stage 5

Table 8.12. Similarities in Different Theories (adapted from Lippke & Ziegelmann, 2008)

Social Cognitive Determinants of Health Behaviors					
	Self-efficacy (Perceived behavioral control)	Outcome expectancies (Behavioral beliefs, subjective norms)	Risk Perception	Intention (Goals)	Planning (Implementation intentions)
HBM	-	X	X	-	-
TRA	-	X	-	X	-
TPB	X	X	-	X	-
SCT	X	X	-	X	-

HBM = Health Belief Model; TRA = Theory of Reasoned Action; TPB = Theory of Planned Behavior; SCT = Social Cognitive Theory

overview of some of the similar concepts used by four of the models.

Webb and Sheeran (2006) conducted a meta-analysis of 47 experimental studies of intention and behavior and found a reasonable link between intention to perform a specific behavior and the actual performance of the behavior. This indicates that models and theories that promote that link are more likely to be used successfully, especially when the behavior is under control of the individual. In fact they found that two theories—the Theory of Reasoned Action/Theory of Planned Behavior and the Protection Motivation Theory (not covered in this chapter)—produce the largest changes in intention and behavior, and thus may be among the most useful of all health-behavior-change theories.

The next section contains a number of different strategies and guidelines to help therapeutic recreation specialists move individuals from unhealthful to more healthful behaviors. Knowing more about how individuals think, feel, make decisions, and act is an important first step in creating interventions that are most impactful.

General Guidelines for Implementation

Change of Approach

The overall approach of using these models differs from historical medical models. Nieuwenhuijsen et al. (2006) noted that under health-behavior-change models, the role of the professional changes from the traditional role under the medical model (see Table 8.13). They also remarked that this might evoke behavioral changes on the part of the professional as well and noted

these changes are mandatory given that the professional is of utmost importance to facilitating functional and behavioral changes within their clientele.

General Implementation Approaches

As can be seen throughout this chapter, many of the health-behavior-change theories have concepts that overlap. Even though different terminology may be used, often, the intention is the same (see Table 8.12). Lippke and Ziegelmann (2008) pointed out that most models also share the notion of three basic stages: 1) individual has not yet decided to act; 2) individual intends to change but has not done so yet; and 3) the individual acts upon his or her intentions to act. Gollwitzer (1999) pointed out that when individuals have implementation intentions (When x barrier occurs, I will initiate y behavior to circumvent it"), they are more likely to overcome the barrier and move forward toward the desired behavior change. Thus, it is important for individuals to have a plan for overcoming barriers that may be placed in their way to reaching their desired state, and will benefit from having a plan on how to restart the pattern if they "relapse" into an unhealthy behavior.

Michie and Abraham (2004), in a broad literature review, cited a number of general techniques to changing unhealthful behaviors including (a) manipulating environmental contingencies and enhancing self-efficacy, (b) introducing cognitive dissonance, (c) introducing strong counter-arguments and creating contrasts between current beliefs and desired states, (d) reinforcing desired behaviors and prompting self-evaluation, (e) scheduling self-rewards and clarifying values, (f) combining fear-induced messages with a health action plan, (g) consciously

Table 8.13. Comparison of Traditional Medical versus Health Behavior Change Intervention (adapted from Nieuwenhuijsen et al., 2006)

Traditional Medical Interventions	Health-Behavior-Change Interventions
Professional is expert, making key decisions	Client is expert; Problems are identified by the client
Patient receives information about the disease, disorder, or injury	Professional is facilitator, providing cues for action and reinforcing positive behavior
Patient received instructions what to do and not to	Client develops skills in self-management of functioning, health, and wellness
Problems are identified by professional	Client identifies key barriers and develops action plan to resolve
Treatment compliance is a personal choice	Treatment adherence is understood within environmental context
Overall theory is that knowledge will lead to change	Overall theory is that shared decision making and increased self-efficacy yield improved outcomes

planning for relapses and developing contingency plans, and (h) unconscious priming.

Aro and Absetz (2009) noted a framework for designing and evaluating health behavior change programs with a series of six steps. These steps include:

- needs assessment including capacities and problems
- definition of evidence-based intervention objectives ranging from the most proximal (close) behavioral targets to health and quality of life outcomes
- theoretically informed selection of determinants of behavior at different levels of influence as well as methods for addressing them
- planning and producing practical program components and materials
- planning for program adoption, implementation, and sustainability by the individual
- developing a framework for process and impact evaluation

Glanz and Bishop (2010) noted that regardless of the health-behavior-change model used by the specialist, a few guidelines help shape and improve the intervention program.

- The most effective interventions are built from multiple theories. In combination, consider the unique contributions of different theories into the model being built.
- Theory, research, and practice are part of a continuum for understanding the determinants of behaviors, testing strategies for change, and disseminating effective treatments.
- There is no substitute for knowing the audience. Participants need to be considered and involved in program planning, design, evaluation, and research.
- Creative interventions that motivate and retain participants not only are theory-driven but entertaining and engaging.
- Consider the social, organizational, and physical environment as important determinants of behavior, as these may constrain or enhance an individual's perceptions (e.g., public walkways, safe parks, accessible facilities and transportation, workplace policies).
- Recognize that behavior change is a process that involves complex relationships among knowledge, awareness of the need to change, intention to change, and actual behavior change. Behavior change is a process, not an event.

- Understand that intentions or contemplation of change are distinct from actual behavior and are, as yet, the best predictors.
- Strategies for initial compliance and maintenance over time may vary. For example, relapse prevention requires self-management and coping skills, as well as new behavior patterns that emphasize perceived control, environmental management, and improved self-efficacy.
- Strategies for rigorous testing of theory-based interventions are needed to delimit the mediators and moderators to health-behavior change.

Langlois and Hallam (2010) suggested the use of a specific planning tool called the PER Worksheet. It distills a number of health behavior change theories and models into a more accessible planning document. For example, it asks about:

- Level of knowledge: What needs to be taught? For example, benefits of physical activity
- Kinds of beliefs: What does the individual believe or value? For example, positive outcomes of physical activity
- Intentions: Does the person intend to be active daily? In what activities?
- What skill set does the individual need? For example, motor skills, assessment of interests and abilities
- What resources does the person have access to? Open areas? Facilities? Equipment? Classes? Personal trainers? Leisure partners?
- What barriers need to be removed? For example, less time playing computer games.
- What reminders does the person need? Scheduling? Prompts?
- What provides positive reinforcement to the individual? Goal attainment? Feeling healthier? Fun? Time spent with friends?
- What stymies the individual by negative reinforcement? Embarrassment? Discomfort?
- What social support systems are available? Teams/Clubs? Family? Peers?

These questions and more like them can help evaluate where the individual or group of individuals are in their particular journey toward better health and health-seeking behaviors. Asking these types of questions will help programmers be able to better target the skill sets, beliefs, and other areas of need that are to be addressed within the intervention.

In October 2007, the National Institute for Health and Clinical Excellence (NICE) published a set of guidelines on implementing behavior change interventions (Yardley & Moss-Morris, 2009, pp. 2–5). Among their recommendations are:

- Plan carefully interventions and programs aimed at changing behavior, taking into account the local and national context and working in partnership with recipients. Interventions and programs should be based on a sound knowledge of community needs and should build upon existing skills and resources within a community.
- Evaluate all behavior-change interventions and programs, either locally or as a part of a larger project. Whenever possible, evaluation should include an economic component.

Planning Interventions

- Work in partnership with individuals, communities, organizations, and populations to plan interventions and programs to change health-related behavior. The plan should:
  - Be based on a needs assessment or knowledge of the target audience
  - Take into account the circumstances in which people live, especially the socioeconomic and cultural context
  - Aim to develop and build upon people strengths or "assets" (that is, their skills, talents, and capacity)
  - Set out how the target population, community, or group will be involved in the development, evaluation, and implementation of the intervention or program
  - Specify the theoretical link between the intervention or program and its outcome
  - Set out which specific behaviors are to be targeted (e.g., increasing levels of physical activity) and why
  - Clearly justify any models that have been used to design and deliver the intervention or program
  - Assess potential barriers to change (e.g., lack of access to affordable opportunities for physical activity, domestic responsibilities, or lack of information or resources) and how these might be addressed
  - Set out which interventions or programs will be delivered and for how long
  - Describe the content of each intervention or program

- Set out which processes and outcomes (at individual, community, or population level) will be measured, and how
- Include provision for evaluation

- Prioritize interventions and programs that:
  - Are based on the best available evidence of efficacy and cost effectiveness
  - Can be tailored to tackle the individual beliefs, attitudes, intentions, skills, and knowledge associated with the target behaviors
  - Are developed in collaboration with the target population, community, or group and take account of lay wisdom about barriers and change (where possible)
  - Are consistent with other local or national interventions and programs (where they are based on the best available evidence)
  - Use key life stages or times when people are more likely to be open to change (such as pregnancy, starting or leaving school, and entering or leaving the workforce)
  - Include provision for evaluation

Individual-Level Interventions and Programs

- Select interventions that motivate and support people to:
  - Understand the short-, medium-, and longer-term consequences of their health-related behaviors, for themselves and others
  - Feel positive about the benefits of health-enhancing behaviors and changing their behavior
  - Plan their changes in terms of easy steps over time
  - Recognize how their social contexts and relationships may affect their behavior, and identify and plan for situations that might undermine the changes they are trying to make
  - Plan explicit "if-then" coping strategies to prevent relapse
  - Make a personal commitment to adopt health-enhancing behaviors by setting (and recording) goals to undertake clearly defined behaviors, in particular contexts, over a specified time
  - Share their behavior change goals with others

Interventions Linked Directly to Theories and Models

Abraham and Michie (2008) conducted a study to develop a list of theory-linked interventions that moved individuals toward behavioral changes, in the areas of physical activity, healthy eating, and a general category of intention/behavior studies. They started with lists from the Transtheoretical Model's processes of change (Prochaska, DiClemente, & Norcross, 1992), a 2000 review of behavior-change methods (Hardeman, Griffin, Johnston, Kinmonth, & Wareham, 2000), and a 2002 review of the same (Conn, Valentine, & Cooper, 2002). They developed a list of 26 behavior-change techniques and plotted them to behavior-change theories or models, when possible. They then conducted a reliability analysis to determine to what degree trained individuals would agree on the techniques' descriptions (see Table 8.14). They found considerable agreement on all but three of the descriptions (#2, #6, and #15). They advocated that the next step would be to precisely categorize interventions by their content and to the theories to which they apply, instead of allowing for multiple interventions to be applied, perhaps, erroneously and without efficacy, to various theories. They then called for adequate testing to ensure that the best interventions are used to promote behavior change.

Michie et al. (2008) had a panel of psychologists indicate the effectiveness of several techniques of behavior change, according to domain constructs. Table 8.15 (p. 150) is a listing of the eleven construct domains, and the techniques the psychologists rated as being likely to be effective. This listing becomes helpful when the specialists knows what domain s/he wishes to effect, and provides strategies that are most likely to work that that domain. For example, if the specialist wants to draw upon social influence, often for the purpose of providing opportunities for social comparison (see #19 in Table 8.14), interactions with the client(s) should include the social processes of encouragement, pressure, and support, as well as modeling/demonstration of behavior by others.

In this continuing line of research, Michie, Abraham, Whittington, McAteer, and Gupta (2009) conducted a meta-regression of 101 studies on physical activity or healthy eating, in order to classify behavior change interventions. First, they found that overall that participants who received behavior-change interventions in fact reported significantly better outcomes than those in control conditions. Second, they found that "prompt self-monitoring of behavior" to have the greatest effect on outcomes. Third, when self-monitoring was used

in combination with one or more of the following, an even greater effect was found: prompting intention formation, prompting specific goal setting, providing feedback on performance, and prompting review of behavioral goals. Again, they called for additional research to clarify these effects, especially for additional areas aside from physical activity and healthy eating.

In 2010, Webb, Joseph, Yardley and Michie (2010) published their results of a meta-analysis of Internet-based behavior-change programs that included 85 investigations and 43,236 participants. They found a number of interesting findings. Among these are: (a) the Internet interventions had a small but significant effect on participants, (b) greater use of theory was associated with greater effect sizes, (c) in particular, interventions based on the Theory of Planned Behavior were found to be most effective, (d) the greater number of behavior-change techniques used, the greater the effects on health-related behavior, and (e) Internet interventions were more effective when they used others modes of communication, such as texts or instant messaging.

In regard to physical rehabilitation, some had advocated for the combination of the International Classification of Functioning, Disability and Health (ICF) and health-behavior-change models as well as the use of health behavior change variables as additional outcome measures in evidence-based rehabilitation research (Nieuwenhuijsen et al., 2006). These authors believe that the synthesis of ICF and HBC models would improve the meaningfulness of outcome measures: "While the ICF provides snapshots of a person's functional abilities within the environmental context at different points in time, HBC theories are essential in understanding how change takes place" (Nieuwenhuijsen et al., 2006, p. 253). In this manner, focusing on the ways in which people with disabilities alter their health habits will eventually provide better and stronger evidence that is needed for improved practice.

Table 8.14. Definitions of Techniques Used in Behavior Change Interventions (Abraham & Michie, 2008)

Technique (Theoretical Framework)	Definition
1. Provide general information (IMB)	General information about behavioral risk, e.g., susceptibility to poor health outcomes or mortality risk in relation to the behavior
2. Provide information on consequences** (TRA, TPB, SCT, IMB)	Information about the benefits and costs of action or inaction, focusing on what will happen if the person does or does not perform the behavior
3. Provide information on others' approval (TRA, TPB, IMB)	Information about what others think about the person's behavior and whether others will approve or disapprove of any proposed behavior change
4. Prompt intention formation (TRA, TPB, SCT, IMB)	Encouraging the person to decide to act or set a general goal, e.g., to make a behavioral resolution such as "I will exercise this week"
5. Prompt barrier identification (SCT)	Identify barriers to performing the behavior and plan ways of overcoming them
6. Provide general encouragement** (SCT)	Praising or rewarding the person for effort or performance without this being contingent on specified behaviors or standards of performance
7. Set graded tasks (SCT)	Set easy tasks, and increase difficulty until target behavior is performed
8. Provide instruction (SCT)	Telling the person how to perform a behavior and/or preparatory behaviors
9. Model or demonstrate the behavior (SCT)	An expert shows the person how to correctly perform a behavior, e.g., in class or on video
10. Prompt specific goal setting (CT)	Involves detailed planning of what the person will do, including a definition of the behavior specifying frequency, intensity, or duration and specification of at least one context, i.e., where, when, how, or with whom
11. Prompt review of behavioral goals (CT)	Review and/or reconsideration of previously set goals or intentions
12. Prompt self-monitoring of behavior (CT)	The person is asked to keep a record of specified behaviors(s), e.g., in a diary
13. Provide feedback on performance (CT)	Providing data about recorded behavior or evaluating performance in relation to a set standard or others' performance, i.e., the person receives feedback on their behavior
14. Provide contingent rewards (OC)	Praise, encouragement, or material rewards that are explicitly linked to the achievement of specified behaviors
15. Teach to use prompts/cues** (OC)	Teach the person to identify environmental cues that can be used to remind them to perform a behavior, including times of day or elements of contexts
16. Agree on behavioral contract (OC)	Agreement, e.g., signing, of a contract specifying behavior to be performed so that there is a written record of the person's resolution witnessed by another
17. Prompt practice (OC)	Prompt the person to rehearse and repeat the behavior or preparatory behaviors
18. Use follow-up prompts	Contacting the person again after the main part of the intervention is complete
19. Provide opportunities for social comparison (SCT)	Facilitate observation of non-expert others' performance, e.g., in a group class or using video or case study
20. Plan social support/social change (social support theories)	Prompting consideration of how others could change their behavior to offer the person help or (instrumental) social support, including "buddy system" and/or providing social support
21. Prompt identification as a role model	Indicating how the person may be an example to others and influence their behavior or provide an opportunity for the person to set a good example
22. Prompt self-talk	Encourage use of self-instruction and self-encouragement (aloud or silently) to support action
23. Relapse prevention (relapse prevention therapy)++	Following initial change, help identify situations likely to result in readopting risk behaviors or failure to maintain new behaviors and help the person plan to avoid or manage those situations
24. Stress management (stress theories)++	May involve a variety of specific techniques, e.g., progressive relaxation, that do not target the behavior but seek to reduce anxiety and stress
25. Motivational interviewing++	Prompting the person to provide self-motivating statements and evaluations of their own behavior to minimize resistance to change
26. Time management++	Helping the person make time for the behavior, e.g., to fit it into a daily schedule

IMB = Information-Motivation-Behavioral Skills Model; TRA = Theory of Reasoned Action; TPB = Theory of Planned Behavior; SCT = Social-Cognitive Theory; CT = Control Theory; OC = Operant Conditioning; ** = lack reliable definitions in this study; ++ = commonly applied sets of techniques

Table 8.15. Behavior Changes Techniques Linked to Determinants of Behavior (Adapted from Michie et al., 2008)

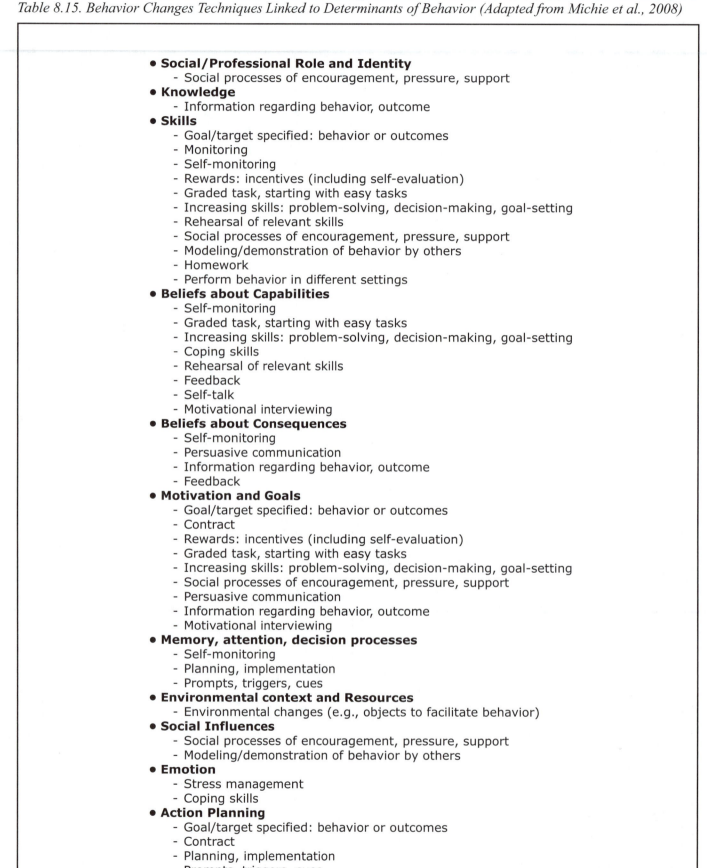

- **Social/Professional Role and Identity**
  - Social processes of encouragement, pressure, support
- **Knowledge**
  - Information regarding behavior, outcome
- **Skills**
  - Goal/target specified: behavior or outcomes
  - Monitoring
  - Self-monitoring
  - Rewards: incentives (including self-evaluation)
  - Graded task, starting with easy tasks
  - Increasing skills: problem-solving, decision-making, goal-setting
  - Rehearsal of relevant skills
  - Social processes of encouragement, pressure, support
  - Modeling/demonstration of behavior by others
  - Homework
  - Perform behavior in different settings
- **Beliefs about Capabilities**
  - Self-monitoring
  - Graded task, starting with easy tasks
  - Increasing skills: problem-solving, decision-making, goal-setting
  - Coping skills
  - Rehearsal of relevant skills
  - Feedback
  - Self-talk
  - Motivational interviewing
- **Beliefs about Consequences**
  - Self-monitoring
  - Persuasive communication
  - Information regarding behavior, outcome
  - Feedback
- **Motivation and Goals**
  - Goal/target specified: behavior or outcomes
  - Contract
  - Rewards: incentives (including self-evaluation)
  - Graded task, starting with easy tasks
  - Increasing skills: problem-solving, decision-making, goal-setting
  - Social processes of encouragement, pressure, support
  - Persuasive communication
  - Information regarding behavior, outcome
  - Motivational interviewing
- **Memory, attention, decision processes**
  - Self-monitoring
  - Planning, implementation
  - Prompts, triggers, cues
- **Environmental context and Resources**
  - Environmental changes (e.g., objects to facilitate behavior)
- **Social Influences**
  - Social processes of encouragement, pressure, support
  - Modeling/demonstration of behavior by others
- **Emotion**
  - Stress management
  - Coping skills
- **Action Planning**
  - Goal/target specified: behavior or outcomes
  - Contract
  - Planning, implementation
  - Prompts, triggers, cues
  - Use of imagery

References

Abraham, C., & Michie, S. (2008). A taxonomy of behavior change techniques used in interventions. *Health Psychology, 27*(3), 379–387.

Ajzen, I. (1991). The theory of planned behavior. *Organizational Behavior and Human Decision Processes, 50*, 179–211.

Armitage, C. J., & Conner, M. (2001). Efficacy of the theory of planned behavior: A meta-analytic review. *British Journal of Social Psychology, 40*, 471–499.

Aro, A. R., & Absetz, P. (2009). Guidance for professionals in health promotion: Keeping it simple—but not too simple. *Psychology & Health, 24*(2), 125–129.

Bandura, A. (1997) *Self-efficacy: The exercise of control.* New York, NY: Freeman.

Bandura, A. (2001). Social cognitive theory: An agentic perspective. *Annual Review of Psychology, 52*, 1–26.

Baranowski, T., Perry, C. L., & Parcel, G. S. (2002). How individuals, environments, and health behavior interact: Social cognitive theory. In K. Glanz, B. K. Rimer, & F. M. Lewis (Eds.), *Health behavior and health education: Theory, research, and practice* (3rd ed.) (pp. 165–184). San Francisco, CA: Jossey-Bass.

Brug, J., Oenema, A., & Ferreira, I. (2005). Theory, evidence, and Intervention Mapping to improve behavior nutrition and physical activity interventions. *International Journal of Behavioral Nutrition and Physical Activity, 2*(1), 2, Retrieved from: http://www.ijbnpa.org/content/2/1/2.

Clarke, V. A., Lovegrove, H., Williams, A., & Macpherson, M. (2000). Unrealistic optimism and the health belief model. *Journal of Behavioral Medicine, 23*(4), 367–376.

Conn, V. S., Valentine, J. C., & Cooper, H. M. (2002). Interventions to increase physical activity among aging adults: A meta-analysis. *Annals of Behavioral Medicine, 24*(3), 190–200.

Cooke, R., & French, D. P. (2008). How well do the theory of reasoned action and theory of planned behavior predict intentions and attendance at screening programmes? A meta-analysis. *Psychology and Health, 23*(7), 745–765.

Fishbein, M. (2008). A reasoned action approach to health promotion. *Medical Decision Making, 28*(6), 834–844.

Fishbein, M. & Ajzen, I. (1975). *Belief, attitude, intention, and behavior: An introduction to theory and research.* Reading, MA: Addison-Wesley.

Fishbein, M., & Ajzen, I. (2005). Theory-based behavior change interventions: Comments on Hobbis and Sutton. *Journal of Health Psychology, 10*(1), 27–31.

Fishbein, M., & Yzer, M. C. (2003). Using theory to design effective health behavior interventions. *Communication Theory, 13*(2), 164–183.

Fried, T. R., Bullock, K., Iannone, L., & O'Leary, J. R. (2009). Understanding advance care planning as a process of health behavior change. *Journal of the American Geriatrics Society, 57*, 1547–1555.

Gatewood, J. G., Litchfield, R. E., Ryan, S. J., Geadelmann, J. D. M., Pendergast, J. F., & Ullom, K. K. (2008). Perceived barriers to community-based health promotion program participation. *American Journal of Health Behavior, 32*(3), 260–271.

Glanz, K., & Bishop, D. B. (2010). The role of behavioral science theory in development and implementation of public health interventions. *Annual Review of Public Health, 31*, 399–418.

Glasgow, R. E., Klesges, L. M., Dzewaltowski, D. A., Bull, S. S., & Estabrooks, P. (2004). The future of health behavior change research: What is needed to improve translation of research into health promotion practice? *Annals of Behavioral Medicine, 27*(1), 3–12.

Gollwitzer, P. M. (1999). Implementation intentions: Strong effects of simple plans. *American Psychologist, 54*(7), 493–503.

Greaney, M. L., Riebe, D., Garber, C. E., Rossi, J. S., Lees, F. D., Burbank, P. A., Nigg, C. R., Ferrone, C. L., & Clark, P. G. (2008). Long-term effects of a stage-based intervention for changing exercise intentions and behavior in older adults. *The Gerontologist, 48*(3), 358–367.

Hardeman, W., Griffin, S., Johnston, M., Kinmonth, A. L., & Wareham, N. J. (2000). Interventions to prevent weight gain: A systematic review of psychological models and behaviour change methods. *International Journal of Obesity, 24*(2), 131–143.

Harrison, J. A., Mullen, P. D., & Green, L. W. (1992). A meta-analysis of studies of the Health Belief Model with adults. *Health Education Research, 7*(1), 107–116.

Janz, N. K., & Becker, M. H. (1984). The Health Belief Model: A decade later. *Health Education Quarterly, 11*(1), 1–47.

Janz, N. K., Champion, V. L., & Strecher, V. J. (2002). The Health Belief Model. In K. Glanz, B. K. Rimer, F. M. & Lewis (Eds.), *Health behavior and health education: Theory, research, and practice* (3rd ed.) (pp. 45–66). San Francisco, CA: Jossey-Bass.

Kruger, J. (2001). A meta-analysis of factors related to self-efficacy for exercise in older adults. Doctoral dissertation, University of Illinois at Chicago. UMI: 3008081

Langlois, M. A., & Hallam, J. S., (2010). Integrating multiple health behavior theories into program planning: The PER worksheet. *Health Promotion Practice, 11*(2), 282–288.

Lewis, F. M. (2002). Perspectives on models of interpersonal health behavior. In K. Glanz, B. K. Rimer, & F. M. Lewis (Eds.), *Health behavior and health education: Theory, research, and practice* (3rd ed.) (pp. 265–273). San Francisco, CA: Jossey-Bass.

Lippke, S. & Ziegelmann, J. P. (2008). Theory-based health behavior change: Developing, testing, and applying theories for evidence-based interventions. *Applied Psychology, 57*(4), 698–716.

Marshall, S. J., & Riddle, S. J. H. (2001). The transtheoretical model of change: A meta-analysis of applications to physical activity and exercise. *Annals of Behavioral Medicine, 23*(4), 229-246.

Michie, S., & Abraham, C. (2004). Interventions to change health behaviours: Evidence-based or evidence-inspired? *Psychology & Health, 19*(1), 29–49.

Michie, S., Abraham, C., Whittington, C., McAteer, J., & Gupta, S. (2009). Effective techniques in healthy eating and physical activity interventions: A meta-regression. *Health Psychology, 28*(6), 690–701.

Michie, S., Johnston, M., Francis, J., Hardeman, W. & Eccles, M. (2008). From theory to intervention: Mapping theoretically derived behavioural determinants to behaviour change techniques. *Applied Psychology, 57*(4), 660–680.

Montano, D. E., & Kasprzyk, D. (2002). The theory of reasoned action and the theory of planned behavior. In K. Glanz, B. K. Rimer, & F. M. Lewis (Eds.), *Health behavior and health education: Theory, research, and practice* (3rd ed.) (pp. 67–98). San Francisco, CA: Jossey-Bass.

National Cancer Institute. (2005). *Theory at a glance: A guide for health promotion practice* (2nd Ed.). Bethesda, MD: U. S. Department of Health and Human Services, National Institutes of Health.

Netz, Y., Wu, M-J., Becker, B. J., & Tenenbaum, G. (2005). Physical activity and psychological well-being in advanced age: A meta-analysis of intervention studies. *Psychology and Aging, 20*(2), 272–284.

Nieuwenhuijsen, E. R., Zemper, E., Miner, K. R., & Epstein, M. (2006). Health behavior change models and theories: Contributions to rehabilitation. *Disability and Rehabilitation, 28*(5), 245–256.

Noar, S. M., & Zimmerman, R. S. (2005). Health Behavior Theory and cumulative knowledge regarding health behaviors: Are we moving in the right direction? *Health Education Research, 20*(3), 275–290.

Prochaska, J. O., & DiClemente, C. C. (1983). Stages and processes of self-change of smoking: Toward an integrative model of change. *Journal of Consulting and Clinical Psychology, 51*(3), 390–395.

Prochaska, J. O., DiClemente, C. C., & Norcross, J. C. (1992). In search of how people change: Applications to addictive behaviors. *American Psychologist, 47*(9), 1102–1114.

Prochaska, J. O., Redding, C. A., & Evers, K. E. (2002). The transtheoretical model and stages of change. In K. Glanz, B. K. Rimer, & F. M. Lewis (Eds.), *Health behavior and health education: Theory, research, and practice* (3rd ed.) (pp. 99–120). San Francisco, CA: Jossey-Bass.

Prochaska, J. O., Wright, J. A., & Velicer, W. F. (2008). Evaluating theories of health behavior change: A hierarchy of criteria applied to the transtheoretical model. *Applied Psychology, 57*(4), 561–588.

Redding, C. A., Rossi, J. S., Rossi, S. R., Velicer, W. F., & Prochaska, J. O. (2000). Health behavior models. *The International Journal of Health Education, 3*, 180–193.

Rimer, B. K. (2002). Perspectives on intrapersonal theories of health behavior. In K. Glanz, B. K. Rimer, & F. M. Lewis (Eds.), *Health behavior and health education: Theory, research, and practice* (3rd ed.) (pp. 144–159). San Francisco, CA: Jossey-Bass.

Rothman, A. J. (2004). "Is there nothing more practical than a good theory?": Why innovations and advances in health behavior change will arise if interventions are used to test and refine theory. *International Journal of Behavioral Nutrition and Physical Activity, 1*, 11. Retrieved from: http://www.ijbnpa.org/content/2/1/2.

Schwarzer, R. (2008). Modeling health behavior change: How to predict and modify the adoption and maintenance of health behaviors. *Applied Psychology, 57*(1), 1–29.

Schwarzer, R., & Renner, B. (2000). Social-cognitive predictors of health behavior: Action self-efficacy and coping self-efficacy. *Health Psychology, 19*(5), 487–495.

Sheppard, B. H., Hartwick, J., & Warshaw, P. R. (1988). The theory of reasoned action: A meta-analysis of past research with recommendations for modification and future research. *Journal of Consumer Research, 15*, 325–343.

Spahn, J. M., Reeves, R. S., Keim, K. S., Laquatra, I., Kellogg, M., Jortberg, B., & Clark, N. A. (2010). State of the evidence regarding behavior change theories and strategies in nutrition counseling to facilitate health and food behavior change. *Journal of the American Dietetic Association, 110*(6), 879–891.

Webb, T. L., Joseph, J., Yardley, L., & Michie, S. (2010). Using the Internet to promote healthy behavior change: A systematic review and meta-analysis of the impact of theoretical basis, use of behavior change techniques, and the mode of delivery on efficacy. *Journal of Medical Internet Research, 12*(1), e4.

Webb, T. L., & Sheeran, P. (2006). Does changing behavioral intentions engender behavior change? A meta-analysis of the experimental evidence. *Psychological Bulletin, 132*(2), 249–268.

Weinstein, N. D., Rothman, A. J., Sutton, S. R. (1998). Stage theories of health behavior: Conceptual and methodological issues. *Health Psychology, 17*(3), 290–299.

Weinstein, N. D., Sandman, P. M. (2002). The precaution adoption process model. In K. Glanz, B. K. Rimer, & F. M. Lewis (Eds.), *Health behavior and health education: Theory, research, and practice* (3rd ed.) (pp. 121–143). San Francisco, CA: Jossey-Bass.

Yardley, L., & Moss-Morris, R. (2009). Current issues and new directions in Psychology and Health: Introducing the NICE guidance on behaviour change interventions. *Psychology and Health, 24*(2), 119–123.

» CHAPTER 9 »
Problem-Solving Therapy

Norma J. Stumbo, Ph.D., CTRS

Being able to solve problems and cope with everyday and significant life events is considered an important developmental asset and contributor to health and well-being (Clarke, 2006). Being able to problem-solve actively (versus avoiding problems or irrationally adapting to the problem) is considered a key skill for exerting personal control over one's environment and one's emotions. Clearly, problem solving is important to social interaction and emotional and physical health. Several authors have noted that programs, such as problem-solving interventions, provide the dual benefit of significantly reducing problems and significantly improving competencies (Durlak & Wells, 1997; Liang, Tracy, Kenny, & Brogan, 2008). Although there is some controversy about the "transferability" of specific skills such as these to a variety of different situations (Dirks, Treat, & Weersing, 2007), there is little question about the importance of being able to problem-solve and cope with life stressors.

Problem Solving and Coping

Problem solving is related to a number of other concepts that are useful in therapeutic recreation services, and which are also discussed in this book. These include coping, resilience, assertiveness, social skills, anger management, stress management, and adaptation. Ebata and Moos (1991, 1994) noted there is an approach-avoidance model of coping, and a problem- and emotion-focused model of coping. In *approach coping*, the individual uses cognitive attempts to understand the problem and uses behavioral strategies to deal with the problem or its consequences. *Avoidance* is used when an individual attempts to withdraw or avert the situation and its consequences. *Problem-focused coping* involves efforts to modify a stressor while *emotion-based coping* is managing or regulating emotional states that accompany or result from the stressor. Ebata and Moos noted that approach and problem-based coping strategies are similar and have been associated

with better adjustment. Proactive and problem-based coping form the basis of the strategies outlined in this chapter.

There are a number of ways to think about how to structure problem-solving interventions or training. For example, Bielaczyc, Pirolli, and Brown (1995) promoted the use of modeling and scaffolding techniques when teaching complex problem-solving skills. *Modeling* requires the leader to consistently demonstrate positive problem-solving skills in his or her interactions with learners. *Scaffolding* is a common term in cognitive psychology and, much like construction, scaffolding involves "hanging" new thoughts close to old thoughts to build a schema that makes sense to the individual. For example, relating the new problem to an old problem that has been solved successfully would be an appropriate strategy.

As an overview, one can think of problem solving in three layers, with increasing need for competence and complexity. The first level is cognitions (thoughts) or a general orientation to problem solving. The second is specific problem-solving skills related to a specific decision. And the third is a larger set of skills that are more generally called into use as needed. Table 9.1 (p. 156) outlines these three levels and therapeutic recreation specialists should consider these levels in designing and implementing problem-solving programs.

Social skills training and interpersonal problem solving became popular in the early 1970s. Key authors included:

- Burglass and Duffy (1974), who created a decision-making model for educating inmates about making better choices
- Blechman (1974), who created a family therapy game to teach decision making
- Shure and Spivack (1972, 1978, 1982; Spivack & Shure, 1974), who created problem-solving materials for children (I Can Problem Solve; see Resource section of this chapter)

Table 9.1. Three Levels of Problem Solving

Problem-Orientation Cognitions:
- Generalized or nonspecific effects on problem-solving performance
- General orientation to problem-solving (how person attends to and thinks about problems in general, independent of any particular problematic situation)
- Includes: problem perception (recognition and labeling of problems), causal attributions, problem appraisal, beliefs about personal control, values concerning commitment of time and effort to independent problem-solving, person's past performance history related to independent problem solving variables
- Whether these cognitions are facilitative or inhibitive influence the initiation and generalization of problem-solving activity, the amount of effort expended, and persistence in the face of obstacles

Specific Problem-Solving Skills:
- Relatively specific problem solving skills, each making distinct contribution to successful outcomes
- Includes tasks of defining and formulating the problem, generating a list of alternative solutions, making a decision, implementing the solution, and evaluating the solution outcome
- Behavioral chain to problem solution

Related Problem-Solving Abilities:
- Basic set of problem-solving abilities that underline and affect ability to learn and implement problem-solving operations at the general and intermediate level
- Includes:
  - sensitivity to problems (ability to recognize that a problem exists)
  - alternative thinking (ability to generate alternative solutions)
  - means-ends thinking (ability to conceptualize relevant means to a goal)
  - consequential thinking (ability to anticipate consequences)
  - perspective taking (ability to perceive a situation from another person's perspective)
  - causal thinking (relating one event to precipitating event)

Table 9.2 outlines the steps in each of these problem-solving models. Although they are useful for outlining problem-solving interventions, they have not received the same level of scrutiny and research that D'Zurilla and Goldfried (1971) model has received. Because their model has been tested in scores of investigations in several countries over several decades, the D'Zurilla model is discussed more extensively in this chapter.

Table 9.2. Early Problem-Solving and Decision-Making Models

Blechman, 1974
1. Definition of the Problem
2. Collection of Relevant Information
3. Examination of Alternatives
4. Selection of Course of Action
5. Evaluation of Consequences

Burglass & Duffy, 1974
1. Defining the Situation
2. Expanding Possibilities
3. Evaluating Possibilities
4. Establishing Decisional Criteria
5. Making a Decision
6. Acting on the Decision
7. Ratifying the Decision

Shure & Spivack, 1978
(Combined with the six related problem-solving skills in Table 9.1, e.g., consequential thinking)
1. Recognition of the Problem
2. Definition of the Problem
3. Alternative Ways to Solve Problems
4. Deciding Which Solution is Best Way to Solve Problem

Problem-Solving Therapy

The concept of Problem-Solving Therapy (PST) was originated by D'Zurilla and Goldfried (1971) and has since gained significant attention in the cognitive psychology fields (Bell & D'Zurilla, 2009a, 2009b; D'Zurilla & Nezu, 2007, 2010; D'Zurilla & Maydeu-Olivares, 1995, 1998; D'Zurilla, Nezu, & Maydeu-Olivares, 2002, 2004). PST is a positive clinical intervention aimed at reducing and preventing psychopathology and enhancing positive well-being. It does so by helping individuals develop coping skills to deal with stressful everyday living situations (Bell & D'Zurilla, 2009a, 2009b; Nezu, 2004). It is based on a relational problem-solving model of stress and well-being (including psychological, social, and health functioning) in which "social problem solving (i.e., real-life problem solving) is assumed to play an important role as a mediator and a moderator of the relationship between stressful life events (major negative events as well as daily problems) and well-being" (Bell & D'Zurilla, 2009b, p. 348). These authors explain the differences between ineffective and effective problem solving: "*Effective* problem solving is expected to reduce the negative impact of stress on well-being and to enhance positive functioning. *Ineffective* problem solving is expected to increase negative impact of stress on well-being" (Bell & D'Zurilla, 2009b, p. 348, italics in original). Effective problem solving has been associated with optimism, hope, greater self-confidence and self-esteem, and improved health, well-being, and overall life satisfaction (D'Zurilla & Nezu, 2007). More details about PST will be discussed in the Basic Premises portion of this chapter.

Related Definitions

Below are some of the formal definitions located in the literature.

- Problem Solving:
  Cognitive-affective-behavioral process through which an individual or group identifies or discovers effective means of coping with problems encountered in everyday living; Involves generation of alternative solutions and decision-making or choice behavior; *Process* by which an individual or group discovers a solution to a problem (D'Zurilla & Goldfried, 1971; D'Zurilla & Nezu, 1982, 1999; Nezu, 2002, 2004)

- Social Problem Solving:
  Real-life problem solving (same as interpersonal problem solving, interpersonal cognitive problem solving, personal problem solving, and applied problem solving); Is at the same time:
    (a) a social learning process, resulting in changed performance;
    (b) a self-management technique, through independent and internal control; and
    (c) a general coping strategy, to help maintain and generalize the effects of treatment (D'Zurilla, 1986)

- Problem:
  Life situation that demands response for effective functioning, but for which no effective response is immediately apparent or available to the individual or group confronted with the situation; Difference between "what is" and "what should be," without apparent, immediate resources (e.g., obstacles), that causes conflict, uncertainty, and/or perceived lack of control. May originate in environment (e.g., task demands) or within the person (e.g., personal goals), but seen as combination because of transactional view (Nezu, 2004)

- Solution:
  Coping response or response pattern that is effective in altering a problematic situation and/or one's own personal reactions to it so that it is no longer seen as a problem, while at the same time

maximizing other positive consequences (benefits) and minimizing negative consequences (costs) (D'Zurilla & Goldfried, 1971; Nezu, 2004)

- Solution Implementation:
  Performance of the solution response, which is a function not only of problem solving, but also other factors in individual's learning history (performance skill deficits, emotional inhibitions, motivation deficits)

- Social Competence:
  Wide range of social skills, behavioral competencies, and coping behaviors, which enable an individual to deal effectively with the demands of everyday living. Problem solving being a significant component of social competence (D'Zurilla, 1986, p. 13)

- Coping:
  Reaction to drastic change, problem or difficult condition that defies regular ways of behaving, requires production of new behavior, gives rise to new feelings like anxiety, despair, guilt, shame, grief

- Coping Style:
  General life stance, including ways of thinking about and dealing with the world (anticipatory or reactionary); either cognitively or emotionally based

- Coping Effectiveness:
  Adaptational outcome of specific, individual stressful encounters

- Coping Competence:
  Summation of coping effectiveness, based on history of coping effectiveness; the longer the history of effectiveness, the more known about strength or vulnerability

Intended Client Groups

Problem-solving therapy has been promoted and researched for a number of groups that are served by therapeutic recreation. These include:

- individuals with depression (Bell & D'Zurilla, 2009b; Cuijpers, van Straten, & Warmerdam, 2007)
- children with ADHD (Aberson, Shure, & Goldstein, 2007)

- children and adolescents (with no known difficulties) (Clarke, 2006; Elias et al., 1986; Kraag, Zeegers, Kok, Hosman, & Abu-Saad, 2006)
- family caregivers (Elliott, Brossart, Berry, & Fine, 2008)
- individuals with spinal cord injuries (Elliott, Bush, & Chen, 2006)
- survivors of domestic abuse (Baker & Hutchinson, 2005)

Basic Premises/How It Works

Therapeutic recreation specialists can think of problem solving in two broad strokes: formal problem solving and informal problem solving. *Formal problem solving*—Problem-Solving Therapy (or intervention) is a reasonably structured experience in which clients or participants are taken through structured, purposeful activities and allowed to practice in order to gain skills. D'Zurilla and Nezu's (as well as the historical authors noted in Table 9.2) model provides a formalized problem-solving approach. After this is discussed, a more *informal approach* to client interaction will be highlighted.

In general, the purpose of problem-solving intervention is to:

- gather as much relevant, factual information about the problem as possible
- clarify the nature of the problem
- set a realistic problem-solving goal
- reappraise the significance of the problem for personal-social well-being

Problem solving helps people apply a logical (cognitive) process and hopefully get to a workable solution. In some cases, participants in therapeutic recreation services have been unable to make successful decisions in their lives and have experienced negative repercussions from those less-than-optimal decisions. Formal problem-solving training helps individuals view and make new choices and experience new outcomes. Rita Mae Brown is attributed to saying: "The definition of insanity is doing the same thing over and over again and expecting different results." The purpose of problem-solving instruction is to help clients chart new paths to achieve new outcomes.

Formal Approach— Problem-Solving Therapy (PST)

D'Zurilla has been the consistent anchor for Problem-Solving Therapy for the last 40 years. He has been joined by colleagues in developing, refining, and test-ing PST (see the reference list at the end of this chapter for scores of materials by D'Zurilla and colleagues). Over time, PST has merged with "new" trends in psychology, such as cognitive behavioral therapy, positive psychology, strengths-based psychology, and self-efficacy. Readers familiar with these concepts will find they form the foundation of PST.

The primary goals of PST (Nezu, 2004) are to:

- enhance the adoption of a positive problem orientation
- decrease one's negative orientation
- improve one's rational problem-solving skills
- decrease one's impulsive/careless style
- decrease one's avoidance

The authors expand on their notions of PST being a positive and rational set of choices and behaviors. Bell and D'Zurilla (2009b) indicated that PST consists of two partially independent components: (1) problem orientation and (2) problem-solving style. "*Problem orientation* is a metacognitive process that primarily serves a motivational function in social problem solving. This process utilizes a set of cognitive-emotional schemas that reflects a person's general awareness and appraisals of problems in living as well as his or her own problem-solving ability" (p. 349). A slightly different definition is offered by Nezu (2004): "*Problem orientation* is the set of relatively stable cognitive-affective schemas that represents a person's generalized beliefs, attitudes, and emotional reactions about problems in living and one's ability to successfully cope with such problems" (p. 3). The concept of problem orientation is predicated on Bandura's (1997) self-efficacy theory and outcome expectancies and spawns two terms: (a) *generalized problem-solving self-efficacy*—the general belief that one is capable of solving problems and implementing solutions effectively, and (b) *generalized positive problem-solving outcome expectancy*—or the general belief that daily problems encountered in life are solvable (Nezu, 2004).

An individual's problem orientation can be either positive or negative. A *positive* orientation involves a person's ability to:

(a) appraise problems as challenges
(b) be optimistic in believing that problems are solvable
(c) perceive one's own ability to solve problems is strong
(d) believe that successful problem solving involves time and effort (Bell & D'Zurilla, 2009a; Nezu, 2004)

A *negative* orientation may result in negative affect and in avoidance, which can subsequently lead to even more negative thinking about future problem-solving attempts. Both of these orientations are "tendencies" and may change, depending on the problem and the circumstances.

"*Problem-solving style* . . . refers to the cognitive and behavioral activities by which a person attempts to understand problems in living and find effective 'solutions' or ways of coping with them" (Bell & D'Zurilla, 2009b, p. 349). Problem-solving styles can either be adaptive (rational) or maladaptive (impulsive/careless or avoidance). A *rational problem-solving style* is a constructive style that involves the systematic and considered application of certain skills, each of which contributes to an adaptive solution or coping response. A rational problem-solving style has four skills:

(a) problem definition and formulation
(b) generation of alternatives
(c) decision making
(d) solution implementation and verification

These four considerations are teachable and are outlined on Table 9.3 (pp. 160–161). A greater level of detail is provided about these four steps, as they can provide the basis for problem-solving educational sessions led by therapeutic recreation specialists.

There are also two maladaptive problem-solving styles: (a) impulsive/careless and (b) avoidance. A person using the first kind of style may be hurried or wanting a quick solution, and therefore does not consider all options and chooses a solution unwisely. Instead of solving a problem, this often creates new ones (Nezu, 2004). A second maladaptive style is avoidance; that is, using procrastination, being passive, or pushing the solution on to someone else. Again, this style is ineffective and unsuccessful for resolving most problems and tends create new difficulties.

Figure 9.1 (p. 162) was created by this chapter author (not the PST originators) and is provided so that specialists can visualize the entirety of the above information. Depending on the cognitive level of participants, the material may or may not be covered during therapeutic recreation sessions.

Informal Approach

Therapeutic recreation specialists can see that there are many different options included in this chapter for formally teaching problem solving to clients and participants. Direct instruction with the pre-determined outcome of measurably improving problem-solving abilities is appropriate and desired. In addition, informal approaches to teaching problem solving are also well-suited to therapeutic recreation services. This is along the lines of "buy a person a fish and she eats for a day, teach a person how to fish and she eats for a lifetime."

Informal problem solving involves everyday conversations. Instead of solving a person's problems for him or her, the therapist engages the person in a dialogue that involves a problem-solving approach (Shure, 1981, 2001; Shure & Aberson, 2006; Shure & Spivack, 1978). It involves teaching:

- the person's view of the problem
- how each person involved feels about it
- what happened during the situation (including consequences)
- what else the person could do to resolve the problem without negative consequences

Table 9.4 (p. 162) contains two example of conversations. The first uses a direct approach that implies that the therapist is the decision maker and authority; the second uses a problem-solving approach that leads the person through the problem-solving process and allows him or her to develop personal solutions.

In most settings (although not all), clients would benefit from being led through this decision-making process. They then "own" their own personal solutions, rather than being passive and receiving instructions or directives from others.

Clients are likely to gain the most from a combined approach that uses both formal and informal problem-solving approaches. Formal approaches can be used in leisure education sessions and informal approaches can be used in all client interactions. The next section addresses the direct application of PST to therapeutic recreation services.

Related Research

Bell and D'Zurilla (2009b) conducted a meta-analysis of 20 studies on PST interventions for individuals with depression. The meta-analysis used only studies with D'Zurilla's pure form of PST and found that it is an effective intervention for reducing depressive symptomatology. Most studies indicated that follow-up reductions were also noted. The investigators noted, "PST was found to be equally effective as alternative psychosocial therapies and medication treatments and significantly more effective than support/attention and waiting-list controls. They noted the studies included

Table 9.3. Four Skills for Rational Problem Solving (Bell & D'Zurilla, 2009a; D'Zurilla, 1986; Nezu, 2004)

I. Problem Definition and Formulation: Well-defined problems are likely to facilitate generation of relevant solutions, improve decision-making effectiveness, and contribute to accuracy of solution verification.

    A. Gathering Information: Must know what kind of information to look for and what cues to attend to: Task information (demands and requirements associated with various tasks to function effectively in different life roles), and social-behavioral information (problem solver's own behavioral characteristics and those of interactants—words, actions, beliefs, values, goals and feelings)

        Barriers:
        (a) arbitrary inference: person draws conclusion without sufficient facts to support it or to rule out alternative interpretations
        (b) selective abstraction: attends to selected information while ignoring other data
        (c) overgeneralization: makes assumptions about general characteristics of people or situations within a given class
        (d) magnification and minimization: exaggerating or devaluing value, intensity, or significance of an event
        (e) under- or overestimation: exaggeration of probability that particular effect will follow antecedent event

    B. Understanding Problem: Organize information to comprehend or understand nature of problem. Need to specify:
        (a) what present conditions are unacceptable (tasks, characteristics, and/or social-behavioral characteristics)
        (b) what changes or additions are demanded or desired
        (c) what obstacle(s) are preventing one from meeting these demands (e.g., emotional obstacles, informational deficit, ability deficit, skill deficit, ambiguity, uncertainty, conflicting demands)

    C. Setting Goals: Provides direction for generation of alternative solutions as well as performance standards for evaluation of solutions. Two rules:
        (a) state the goals in specific, concrete terms (identify relevant, appropriate solutions and helps decision-making effectiveness)
        (b) avoid stating unrealistic or unattainable goals

        Ask "how" or "what" questions to:
        (a) meet task demands (How can I increase client contact by 10%?)
        (b) overcome specific obstacle to meeting those demands (How can I make more time?)
        (c) reducing or changing task demands (How can I reduce my boss's unreasonable demands?)
        (d) some combination of above

    D. Getting at "Real" Problem: Since different ways to formulate goals will affect how problem is attacked, it is important to generate alternative problem formulations. One needs to define original cause of problem (chain of events) and other "umbrella" problems.

    E. Dealing with Complex Problems: Break into small sub-problems, unless causally related to each other—then primary problem should be solved first.

    F. Reappraising Problem: Checking significance of problem to personal/social well-being. May involve considering likely benefits and costs (long-term and short-term) of solving vs. not solving problem. Appraisals: interpretive process representing how person views situation; either cognitively or emotionally-based
        (a) primary appraisals: initial interpretation of threat
        (b) secondary appraisals: coping resources and options are evaluated; what is happening, what will happen and what could happen; as situation progresses, appraisals also shift

        Three ways to appraise stress or problems:
        (a) positive-challenge: transaction noninjurious or positive—emphasizes benefits
        (b) irrelevant-benign: transaction judged to have no bearing on person's well-being—few costs
        (c) stressful-threat: actual or potential outcome is construed as either already harmful or threatening (future harm)—emphasizes costs

Table 9.3. Four Skills for Rational Problem Solving (Bell & D'Zurilla, 2009a; D'Zurilla, 1986; Nezu, 2004) (cont'd)

II. Generation of Alternative Solutions: Generate as many solution alternatives as possible, to maximize likelihood that best/most preferred solution will be among them.

Barriers: Habit and convention. To be effective, one needs different approaches and creativity. Three rules:
(a) quantity: more produced, more good quality ideas will be available, increasing likelihood best solution will be discovered
(b) deferment of judgment: more good quality ideas will be available if evaluation of ideas is suspended until later in PST sequence
(c) variety: greater range or variety of good quality ideas. To increase:
(1) group above ideas into categories
(2) generate more specific solutions that are underrepresented
(3) generate more new strategies that are not represented
(4) generate specific alternative solutions for new strategies
(5) generate combinations, modifications, and elaborations

III. Decision-Making: Evaluate (compare and judge) available solution alternatives to select best one(s) for implementation. Eliminate those that are not feasible or acceptable. Two theories:

(a) Expected Utility Theory: Effectiveness of given solution alternative based on joint consideration of value and likelihood of anticipated consequences. Estimates of costs and benefits of each alternative then compares alternatives on:
(1) problem resolution (likelihood of achieving the problem-solving goal)
(2) emotional well-being (quality of expected emotional outcome)
(3) time/effort (amount of time and effort expected to be required)
(4) overall personal/social well-being (total expected benefit/cost ratio)

(b) Prospect Theory: Two phases:
(1) initial phase in which solution alternatives, solution outcomes, and contingencies are formulated
(2) subsequent phase of evaluation involving generalized expected utility process

Procedures:
(1) review list of alternatives and change any vaguely stated terms into more behavioral terms
(2) view problem from different perspective to generate alternatives
(3) generate as many solutions as possible and consider alternative conceptions
(4) consider all outcomes by anticipating as many gains and losses as possible for each alternative (both subjective and objective gains/losses)

Questions:
(1) is the problematic situation changeable or unchangeable?
(2) do I need more information before I can decide on a course of action?
(3) what solution or combination should I choose to implement?

Solution Plans:
(1) simple: single course of action
(2) solution combination: combination implemented concurrently
(3) contingency plan: if solution A does not work, implement solution B

IV. Solution Implementation and Verification: Assess solution outcome; verify effectiveness of chosen solution strategy in real-life problematic situation.

Behavioral Self-Control:
(a) performance: action toward resolution of problem
(b) self-monitoring: observation of one's own behavior and outcomes—keep records
(c) self-evaluation: compare actual outcome with expected outcome
(d) self-reinforcement: reward for job well done through
(1) reduction of aversive stimulation
(2) occurrence of positive social reinforcement
(3) removal of obstacle to desired goal
(4) resolution of conflict
If unsuccessful:
(a) troubleshoot or determine source of difficulty—return to beginning stages
(b) watch for perfectionistic attitudes—Type A behavior
(c) get help or advice

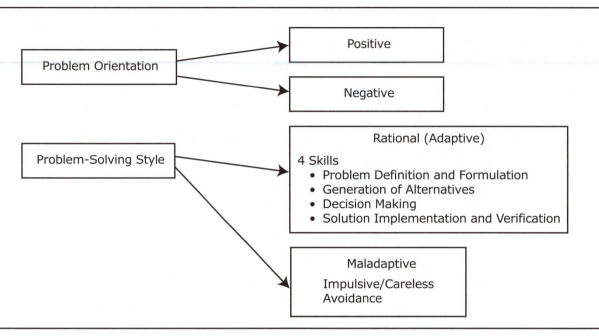

Figure 9.1. A Visual Representation of the Components of Problem-Solving Therapy (Bell & D'Zurilla, 2009a; Nezu, 2004)

family caregivers, nursing home residents, individuals being treated for cancer, and individuals with mental health concerns. They concluded that providers can maximize efficacy of PST by including (a) training in problem orientation as well as the four major problem-solving skills, and (b) assessment of a person's social problem-solving abilities before treatment so that instruction can be tailored to the person's problem-solving deficits. However, PST was not more successful than the placebo when an intention-to-treat method of analysis was used.

Robinson et al. (2008) conducted a study on 176 individuals with stroke who were divided into three groups: those who received escitalopram (anti-depressant); those who received a placebo, and those who received PST. After one year, the results showed that both the drug and the PST were more successful than the placebo for lowering the incidence of depression.

Arean et al. (1993) studied older individuals with depression in a 12-week program comparing reminiscence therapy with PST. Both reminiscence and problem solving were effective in reducing depressive symptoms over the wait-list control group scores. Individuals in the problem-solving treatment group, that closely followed D'Zurilla's PST, were significantly less depressed at the conclusion and a later follow-up than individuals in the reminiscence group.

Malouff, Thorsteinsson, and Schutte (2007) used a meta-analysis technique to examine the efficacy of problem-solving therapy. They reviewed 31 studies that had a combination of 2,895 participants. The

Table 9.4. Two Conversations Using a Direct and a Problem-Solving Approach

Example #1: Direct Approach

Therapist: Daniel, why did you grab that shovel from Jamie?
Child: He never shares.
Therapist: You can't grab toys. Jamie doesn't like that. You should ask.
Child: It's not fair. He won't give it to me.
Therapist: If you grab like that, he won't play with you anymore.
Child: I don't care.
Therapist: Daniel, I told you to ask him for it.
(Daniel asked, was refused, and either in frustration, or by decision, hit Jamie.)

Example #2: Problem-Solving Approach

Therapist: Shelly, what happened when you grabbed that doll from Tasha?
Child: She snatched it back.
Therapist: And what else happened?
Child: She hit me.
(Therapist guides child to consider consequences.)
Therapist: How did that make you feel?
Child: Mad.
Therapist: How do you think Tasha feels?
Child: Mad.
(Therapist guides child to think of own and other's feelings.)
Therapist: You're mad and Tasha's mad. Can you think of a different way to get Tasha to let you have that doll?
Child: But she said no. And I want it!
Therapist: If you try real hard, I bet you can think of an idea.
(Therapist encouraging child not to give up.)
Child: *(to Tasha)* Let's have a puppet show. We can take turns holding it [the doll].
(Tasha agreed, if she could go first.)

investigators determined that PST is statistically significantly more effective than no treatment (waiting list), treatment as usual, or a treatment placebo. However, they also found that it was not more effective than other bona fide treatments offered in the reviewed studies. They reported three mains reasons for these effects: (1) inclusion of "problem orientation" (see Nezu & D'Zurilla, 2007), (2) homework assignments, and (3) participation in the study of one of the original developers of PST (in all cases Arthur Nezu). Among the factors that did not produce differences were (1) individual versus group/family PST, (2) whether participants were clinically diagnosed or from the general population, (3) whether the problem involved some specific type of disorder, and (4) assessment format (e.g., self-report, objective, or mixed).

Cuijpers, van Straten, and Warmerdam (2007) also conducted a meta-analysis on 13 studies of PST for individuals with depression. They defined PST as a psychological treatment in which the following components had to be included: "definition of personal problems, generation of multiple solutions to each problem, selection of the best solution, the working out of a systematic plan for this solution, and evaluation as to whether the solution has resolved the problem" (p. 10; this being a larger definition than Bell and D'Zurilla above.) They found mostly positive effects, although the degree of effect depended on the type and format of training, diagnosis (studies of subjects with major depression had smaller effects), type of analysis, and type of control group. They found that D'Zurilla and Nezu's Social Problem-Solving Therapy to be the most effective of the treatments, although they caution that more needs to be studied to confirm this.

Clarke (2006) included 40 studies in a meta-analysis of child and adolescent coping with interpersonal stress indicated that the mean effect for the relationship between active coping and psychosocial functioning is small but positive. Youth who are taught active coping and problem-solving skills do exhibit better psychosocial functioning that peers who do not receive the training. Although those differences may be small, they are likely to be important to the individuals. One of the most important findings of this study was the conclusion that "context" must be an important part of the training. When stressors were controllable (such as deciding to argue with a sibling) active coping and problem solving were positive, but when stressors were uncontrollable (such as parental illness) the results for the youth were not positive. Therapeutic recreation specialists would do well to consider this important finding.

Elliott et al. (2008) studied the effectiveness of an individualized problem-solving intervention delivered via video conferencing to family caregivers of persons with spinal cord injuries. After a large number of participants discontinued participation with the study, 33 subjects remained for the 6-month and 12-month follow-ups. Although the results are complicated, caregivers in the treatment group reported less depression at the 6-month follow-up but became equal to the control group by 12 months. Individuals who received care in the treatment group reported a significant increase in social functioning over time, while the control group experienced a steady decline in social functioning. Another interesting finding is that while at baseline, both the treatment and control groups of caregivers generated equal solutions to a sample problem, by the fifth session, the treatment group nearly doubled the proposed solutions as the control group. The problem-solving training used in this study positively affected both caregivers and individuals with spinal cord injury.

Elias et al. (1986) found that a yearlong social problem-solving program with 158 fifth-graders to prepare them for a transition to middle school was effective in reducing difficulties coping with stressors, as compared to partial treatment or no treatment. The investigators found this effect to hold even after posttesting following an intervening summer with no contact or further intervention. They concluded that problem analysis and action were important coping skills for individuals to possess, as they related to how intense or problematic events in these children's lives continued to be. They noted that these might be considered "building blocks" to develop appropriate schema for ongoing and more complex problem-solving skills.

Kraag et al. (2006) completed a meta-analysis on the effects of school programs that targeted stress management or coping skills for school children. They analyzed 19 completed studies and found that school programs that focused on stress management or coping skills were effective in reducing stress symptoms and increasing coping skills.

Liang et al. (2008) conducted a study on the Open Circle social competency program with 153 Caucasian middle school children that explored the impact of this social problem-solving curriculum on the relationships of boys and girls transitioning from grade school to middle school. They found that the curriculum helped boys develop higher-quality relationships with peers, mentors, and communities. The same was not true for girls, whom the authors felt already had developed relationships of high quality (authentic, mutually engaging, empowering, and with the ability to negotiate differences) even without the program. Readers can locate information on the curriculum in the Resources section of this chapter.

Elliott, Bush, and Chen (2006) prospectively studied 188 individuals with spinal cord injuries to determine the extent to which problem-solving ability was related to pressure-sore occurrence up to three years post-injury. Through the use of advanced statistics, they developed a model that concludes that some demographic characteristics influence problem-solving abilities and injury severity, and through them, influences pressure-sore occurrence. For example, one of the major findings was that greater problem-solving abilities (as measured by two assessments) resulted in lower pressure-sore occurrence. The findings of this study could be used by rehabilitation personnel to justify the development and implementation of problem-solving programs for individuals with new or recent spinal cord injuries.

Application to Therapeutic Recreation

As mentioned in a prior section of this chapter, problem solving is related to decision making and coping. How people view problems and act toward their resolution (if they do), affect the decisions they make, and ultimately how they cope with the world and their life in it (Heppner, 2008). Clearly, the ability to problem solve is important; however it is not an innate characteristic—it must be taught and learned. Problem solving, decision making, coping, and adaptation skills are assets that many clients of therapeutic recreation services would benefit from gaining. However, therapeutic recreation literature does not enjoy an overabundance of research reports that quantify and validate the need for such skills training per se. For the most part, these skill sets are embedded into larger theoretical frameworks such as family resiliency and life skills education. Rones and Hoagwood (2000) conducted a research review of school-based mental health services and reinforced the idea of multiple program aims and techniques. They found the following characteristics improved the probability of service sustainability and maintenance:

- consistent program implementation
- inclusion of parents, teachers, or peers
- use of multiple modalities
- integration of program content into general classroom curriculum

- developmentally appropriate program components

The primary client groups, as seen in the therapeutic recreation and related literature, include the following:

- at-risk youth (Autry & Anderson, 2007; Caldwell, 2004; Caldwell & Darling, 1999; Caldwell, Darling, Payne, & Dowdy, 1999; Caldwell, Baldwin, Walls, & Smith, 2004; Caldwell & Smith, 1995, 2004, 2006; Caldwell et al., 2004; Darling, Caldwell, & Smith, 2005; Hill, Gomez, & Jeppesen, 2007; LeCroy, 1984; Smith et al., 2008; Ungar, Dumond, & McDonald, 2005; Wegner, Flisher, Caldwell, Vergnani, & Smith, 2008; Wells, Widmer, & McCoy, 2004)
- people with depression (Arean et al., 1993; Bell & D'Zurilla, 2009b; Robinson et al., 2008)
- children with attention deficit/hyperactivity disorder (de Boo & Prins, 2007)
- individuals with spinal cord injury (Hammell, 2007; Johnson & Klaas, 1997)
- individuals with traumatic brain injury (deHope & Finegan, 1999)
- adolescents in substance abuse treatment (Nation, Benshoff, & Malkin, 1996)
- individuals in mental health services (Pegg & Moxham, 2000; Pegg & Patterson, 2002)
- individuals in alcohol treatment (Carruthers & Hood, 2002; Hood & Carruthers, 2002)
- older individuals (Johnson, 1999)
- caregivers (Bedini & Phoenix, 2001; Carter, Nezey, Wenzel, & Foret, 2001; Charters, 2005; Charters, Hutchinson, & Murray, 2006)
- families in outdoor recreation/camping environments (Freeman & Zabriskie, 2002)
- therapeutic recreation specialists as they use clinical reasoning (Hutchinson, LeBlanc, & Booth, 2002)

The following are a few of the therapeutic recreation programs in the literature that have included problem solving as part of their program content. Often, problem solving is part of a larger program aimed at leisure skill building and capacity building. No program that used D'Zurilla's Problem-Solving Therapy was located during a literature search.

The *TimeWise: Taking Charge of Leisure Time* Program, developed by Linda Caldwell (2004) and colleagues, is a five-lesson leisure-education program that aims to increase at-risk adolescents' use of positive free time and reduce the risk and occurrence of substance abuse. A theory-based program, the five lessons include:

Lesson 1: Time use and benefits of leisure
Lesson 2: Reasons for participating in free-time activities
Lesson 3: Developing interests and managing boredom
Lesson 4: Planning and decision making
Lesson 5: Managing free time for balance and variety

Lesson 4 focuses on reviewing enjoyable activities, the constraints to participation (real or perceived), and problem-solving ways to negotiate these constraints. In discussing a number of study results, Caldwell et al. (2004) noted the following:

> Furthermore, reporting higher levels of initiative meant that youth persisted in pursuing activities of choice despite constraints. Thus, not only did students report being more interested in their activities, behaviorally they acted on those interests. These findings combined suggested that *TimeWise* was possibly effective in helping students select, optimize, and compensate in their leisure. They displayed initiative and the ability to self-regulate. These skills were behaviorally manifested as *TimeWise* students spent more time in activities and had higher rates of participation in new activities. They also reported higher awareness of community opportunities and planning and decision-making skills. (p. 329)

The *TimeWise* program has undergone additional research and interested readers are referred to Caldwell (2004), Caldwell and Darling (1999), Caldwell, Darling, Payne, and Dowdy (1999), and Caldwell and Smith (1995, 2004) for further information.

Carruthers and Hood (2002) and Hood and Carruthers (2002) outline the rationale and conceptual framework for a coping-skills program for individuals with alcoholism. They emphasize that effective coping involves cognitive skills (such as restructuring or distraction), behavioral skills (such as decision making and problem solving), and acceptance or tenacity to see the problem to a solution. They promote two main tenets: to decrease negative demands, and to increase positive resources. Decreasing negative demands includes identifying the problem and working toward a solution, cognitive reinterpretations, and distraction from worry. Increasing positive resources include relaxation skills, enjoyable experiences, positive hedonic (joy-building activities), and social support. They developed a 7-session coping-skills program that contains:

Session 1: Recognizing and changing negative thoughts; focusing and enjoying the present
Session 2: Increasing stress-management skills and relaxation skills
Session 3: Focusing on progress, self-acceptance, and social interaction skills
Session 4: Developing friendship skills and assertion skills
Session 5: Developing coping strategies for high-risk leisure activities
Session 6: Developing constructive leisure decision-making skills
Session 7: Identifying leisure interests and overcoming barriers to involvement

The program is outlined in more depth in their *Therapeutic Recreation Journal* articles and a book that will be forthcoming.

Charters (2005; Charters, Hutchinson, & Murray, 2006) conducted research on a leisure-education program for caregivers of older adults. The program consisted of six components: (a) leisure awareness, (b) leisure benefits, (c) leisure values, (d), leisure barriers, (e) leisure resources, and (f) leisure planning. Both leisure barriers and leisure planning contained problem-solving aspects to the content and instruction. Participants at the end of the program improved in many areas, although they did not improve in solutions to general leisure barriers. One aspect the investigator modified during the implementation of the program was to allow the individuals to work in pairs to complete a problem-solving worksheet on leisure barriers. The investigator concluded that the participants gained valuable information about their leisure and about taking care of themselves, and she suggested future implementation of the program.

Hill, Gomez, and Jeppesen (2007) conducted an evaluation of an interdisciplinary program, Staying Off Substances (SOS), with therapeutic recreation and social work for adolescents in substance abuse treatment and their parents. Founded on resiliency theory and seven resiliency traits, the program was operated for 3-hour sessions, 4 days a week for 10 weeks with follow-up in aftercare for 3 months. "Included in this chemical dependency program were such topics as self-esteem enhancement, stress management, relapse prevention planning, anger management, coping skills, and leisure education, along with an intensive focus on substance abuse issues and education" (p. 64). The authors concluded:

There was a significant increase of resiliency from pre-test to post-test among adolescents and parents. Theoretically speaking, these results may indicate that the participants may have a higher perception of resiliency after the intervention and should be able to more effectively cope with daily struggles without substance abuse. There was a significant increase of resiliency over time . . . and by group. . . . This means that overall, the SOS Program fostered resiliency, over the 10-week period. (p. 67)

Summary

- Problem solving is related to a number of other skills such as stress management, anger management, resilience, assertiveness, and social skills, which are topics of other chapters in this text.
- Problem-solving skills range from very general adaptation skills to very specific skills. Problem-solving skills can be taught and learned by using the proper systematic techniques.
- Most individuals who are clients of therapeutic recreation services would benefit from acquisition and application of problem-solving skills.
- D'Zurilla and colleagues developed Problem-Solving Therapy, one of the most popular and well-researched techniques.
- Formal problem solving can be achieved through instruction and informal problem solving can be applied to most conversations with clients.
- Therapeutic recreation enjoys a relatively rich history of focus on problem-solving interventions and research with various client groups.
- There is a significant body of research supporting Problem-Solving Therapy as an appropriate intervention.

Resources

TimeWise: Taking Charge of Leisure Time. (2004). By Caldwell. ETR Associates. (Grades 6–9) http://pub.etr.org, (800) 321-4407

- includes Teacher Guide and 1 Student Workbook
- reduces risks and boredom associated with unstructured free time
- helps students identify and pursue satisfying and healthy leisure interests
- builds skills in decision making, planning, and self-management

- empowers youth to clarify personal values, find new leisure interests, overcome obstacles and take personal responsibility for their free time
- increases intrinsic motivation and initiative to help students make healthy choices and avoid substance use

Games to Enhance Social and Emotional Skills: Sixty-Six Games that Teach Children, Adolescents, and Adults Skills Crucial to Success in Life. (1998). By Malouff & Schutte. Charles C. Thomas. By using a game-centered approach, mental health professionals can help teach social and emotional skills to their clients. The 66 games described in this book are presented using a standard format that includes suggestions for how to help players use their skills in daily life. The games were field-tested using an evaluation strategy that focused on the extent to which players enjoyed the game and the extent to which the game produced the types of experiences that occur in sophisticated training or counseling. The games are organized according to the type of social-emotional goals desired. Chapters are: (1) "Introduction to Social-Emotional Skills and Games"; (2) "Playing the Games"; (3) "Games that Teach How to Identify and Talk about Emotions"; (4) "Games that Foster Self-Confidence"; (5) "Games that Foster a Positive Outlook"; (6) "Games that Foster Value Clarification, Goal Setting, and Planning"; (7) "Games that Teach Problem-Solving Methods"; (8) "Games that Foster Persistence"; (9) "Games that Teach Coping Methods"; and (10) "Games that Enhance Social Skills. An appendix discusses commercial games. Contains 129 references.

Open Circle Curriculum. Open Circle is a comprehensive, grade-differentiated social and emotional learning program for children grades K–5, their teachers, administrators, other school staff, parents, and other caregivers. http://www.open-circle.org

I Can Problem Solve (ICPS): An Interpersonal Cognitive Problem Solving Program for Children (available for various grade levels) (1992). By Shure. Research Press. Interactive activities in the ICPS program develop students' sequential, consequential, and alternative thinking skills. Three volumes: Preschool (59 lessons), Primary (83 lessons), and Elementary (77 lessons). Students begin by learning the vocabulary necessary to understand cause-and-effect relationships. Students work through a series of activities applying these skills to stories and situations that strengthen their problem-solving competencies. This enables them to manage and solve everyday problems more effectively. Tips for integrating lessons into other subject areas, extension activities, activity sheets, parent letters, and blackline masters are included. Published research on this program has shown positive behavioral impacts. www.researchpress.com, (217) 352-3273, (800) 519-2707, Fax: (217) 352-1221

Raising a Thinking Child Workbook: Teaching Young Children How to Resolve Everyday Conflicts and Get Along with Others. (1996). By Shure. Research Press. (English and Spanish versions); Activities, games, exercises.
www.researchpress.com, (800) 519-2707

Raising a Thinking Preteen: The I Can Problem Solve Program for 8–12 Year Olds. (2000). By Shure. Research Press.
Activities, games, exercises.
www.researchpress.com, (800) 519-2707

Thinking Parent, Thinking Child: How to Turn Your Most Challenging Everyday Problems into Solutions. (2005). By Shure. Research Press.
Activities, games, exercises.
www.researchpress.com, (800) 519-2707

Early Coping Inventory. (1988). By Zeitlin, Williamson, & Szczepanski. Scholastic Testing Service. Observation instrument for assessing coping related behaviors used in everyday situations. 48 items in three categories: Sensorimotor organization, reactive behaviors, and self-initiated behaviors. Intended for children 4 months to 3 years old.
www.ststesting.com, (800) 642-6787

Coping Inventory. (1985). By Zeitlin Scholastic Testing Service.
Assesses behavior patterns and skills used by children ages 3 to 16 (observation) and 15 to adult (self-report) to meet personal needs and to adapt to the environment. Two categories of coping behavior: self and environment; and three types of coping: productive/non-productive; active/passive; flexible/rigid.
www.ststesting.com, (800) 642-6787

Ways of Coping Questionnaire. (1988). By Folkman & Lazarus. Mind Garden Publishing.
Measures coping processes in eight categories: such as confrontive, seeking social support, accepting responsibility, planful problem solving, and positive reapprais-

al. Intended for adults. 10 minute administration time. Participants can also take the inventory online.
www.mindgarden.com, (650) 322-6300

Hassles and Uplifts Scale Manual: Research Edition. (1989). By Lazarus & Folkman. Mind Garden Publishing. Identifies sources of stress and helps develop new strategies for coping. Contains three scales: Hassles Scale (117 items), Uplifts Scale (135 items), and Combined Scale (53 items). Intended for adults. 10 minute administration time.
www.mindgarden.com, (650) 322-6300

Stress Processing Report. (1986). By Cook. Human Synergistics.
Stress is not caused by events but rather how people react to events. 160 items used to profile 19 distinct "styles"categorized into four clusters: self, others, process, and goals. Helps to identify thinking and behavior that needs to be changed to reduce stress.
www.hscar.com, (800) 590-0995

Occupational Stress Inventory—Revised. (1988). By Osipow. Psychological Assessment Resources Measures occupational stress, psychological stress, and coping resources with 140 items in three scales: occupational roles questionnaire, personal strain questionnaire, and personal resources questionnaire. Intended for adults.
www.parinc.com, (800) 331-8328

Thinking, Feeling, Behaving: An Emotional Education Curriculum for Children. (2006). By Vernon. Research Press.
Thinking, Feeling, Behaving: An Emotional Education Curriculum for Adolescents. (2006). By Vernon. Research Press.
Curriculum based on principles of Rational Emotive Therapy; activities grouped into five major areas: self-acceptance, feelings, beliefs and behavior, problem solving and decision making, and interpersonal relationships. Ninety activities for each in grades 1 to 6 and grades 7 to 12. Simulations, role playing, stories, writing activities, brainstorming, etc.
www.researchpress.com, (800) 519-2707

Adolescent Coping with Depression Course. (1990). By Clarke, Lewinsohn, & Hops. Castalia Publishing Company.
Treatment program that covers areas of social skills, communication and problems solving for adolescents in mental health treatment.
(541) 343-4433

The Coping with Depression Course: Review and Future Directions. (1989). By Lewinsohn, Clarke, & Hoberman.
This helpful article can be found at: *Canadian Journal of Behavioural Science/Revue canadienne des sciences du comportement, 21*(4), 470-493.

Fighting Invisible Tigers: A Stress Management Guide for Teens (3rd ed.). (2008). By Hipp. Free Spirit Publishing.
Book gives solid advice to individuals ages 11 to 18 on everything from coping with stress to being assertive.
www.freespirit.com

Out of Print but Available through Online Booksellers

Growing Up on Purpose. (1985). By Parkinson. Research Press.
Book for pre-teens to prepare for challenges of adolescence. Decision making, responsibility, self-control, and independent thinking are stressed.
www.researchpress.com

Skills for Living: Group Counseling Activities for Young Adolescents. (1990). By Morganett. Research Press.
Book is divided into two sections: Designing group activities and procedures for conducting activities. Designed for middle or junior high students. Eight topics covered such as: dealing with divorce, meeting, making, and keeping friends, developing self-esteem, anger management skills, coping with grief and loss.
www.researchpress.com

Thinking It Through: Teaching Problem-Solving Strategy for Community Living. (1989). By Foxx & Bittle. Research Press.
Training program for teaching problem solving to four specific groups of individuals: Those with developmental disabilities, chronic mental illnesses, brain injuries, or emotional problems, small group discussion has participants draw situation cards, offer responses, and receive feedback.
www.researchpress.com

Effective Decision Making for the Developmentally Disabled. (1985). By Tymchuk. EDNICK Communications.
Book to be used by parents and professionals who are responsible for training individuals with developmental disabilities in the process of decision making. Helpful in areas such as health, recreation, job, family, social situations, finances, sexual encounters, and psychological needs.

Talking It Out: A Guide to Effective Communication and Problem Solving. (1977). By Strayhorn. Research Press.
Book provides communication techniques for effectively solving problems in family, social, or work settings.
www.researchpress.com

Social Stress and the Family. (1983). By McCubbin, Sussman, & Patterson (Eds.). Routledge.
Soft-bound book on the recent advances and developments in family stress therapy.

Think Aloud: Increasing Social, Cognitive, and Problems Solving Skills. (1985). By Camp & Bash (1985). Research Press.
Combines training in both cognitive and social problem-solving skills through verbal mediation.
www.researchpress.com

Out of Production Videos but Still in Many University Libraries

Why Is It Always Me? By Cisek & George. Research Press.
Video training program ($260.00, 14 minutes) designed to teach young children differences between poor problem-solving skills and more effective techniques. Viewers learn five-step IDEAL problem solving: Identify the Problem, Describe the possibilities, Evaluate the ideas, Act out a plan, Learn for the future. Focuses on consequences and decision-making skills.
www.researchpress.com

The Self-Management Training Program: Teaching Individuals with Developmental Disabilities to Manage Their Disruptive Behavior. (1985). By Cole, Pflugrad, Gardner, & Karan. Research Press.
Video training program teaches specific coping skills necessary to function in vocational setting. Teaches viewers to recognize particular behavior, and either reward or punish themselves for that behavior. Includes modeling, prompting, and reinforcers. Includes detailed training manual that discusses rationale.
www.researchpress.com

Decisions, Decisions: What's a Teenager To Do! (1989). Films Media Group.
Video and book take multi-step approach: Identify problem, gather all data, examine options, weigh consequences, make decision, accept responsibility for decision, and evaluate and learn from decision.

Example Activities

Group Problem-Solving Scenarios

Develop scenarios that are appropriate to the group. For example, attending a party where alcohol is served, wanting to ask someone for a date, wanting to learn a new leisure skill, ending a friendship. Divide the group into pairs or triads. Use D'Zurilla's problem-solving steps to work through the problems toward a workable solution. Discuss the solutions.

Group Problem-Solving Role Playing

Same as above, but ask individuals to role play what they would do toward a workable solution, and ask other group members to critique and come up with alternative solutions.

Dear Abby

Develop "letters to Dear Abby" that present some type of social or leisure problem, such as entering a new group of people for the first time, or traveling to an unfamiliar destination. Have participants respond back to the "letter writer" using a problem-solving approach (not giving them a solution).

Leisure Conflicts

Give people scenarios of conflicts that may occur during recreation and leisure activities; for example, being asked by a friend who has considerably fewer skills to participate in a game of chess, someone cheating at a game of cards, or two people who want to go to different activities held at the same time. Ask participants to use the problem-solving steps to work toward solutions.

References

Aberson, B., Shure, M. B., & Goldstein, S. (2007). Social problem-solving intervention can help children with ADHD. *Journal of Attention Disorders, 11*(1), 4–7.

Arean, P. A., Perri, M. G., Nezu, A. M., Schein, R. L., Christopher, F., & Joseph, T. X. (1993). Comparative effectiveness of social problem-solving therapy and reminiscence therapy as treatments for depression in older adults. *Journal of Consulting and Clinical Psychology, 61*(6), 1003–1010.

Autry, C. E., & Anderson, S. C. (2007). Recreation and the Glenview neighborhood: Implications for youth and community development. *Leisure Sciences, 29*(3), 267–285.

Baker, B. L., & Hutchinson, S. (2005, May). Recreation as a treatment modality and coping resource for survivors of domestic violence. In T. Delamere, D. McDonald, C. Randall, R. Rollins, and D. Robinson (Eds.), *Abstracts of papers presented at the eleventh Canadian Congress on Leisure Research,* Malaspina University-College, Nanaimo, British Columbia.

Bandura, A. (1997). *Self-efficacy: The exercise of control.* New York, NY: W. H. Putnam.

Bedini, L. A., & Phoenix, T. (2001). Recreation programs for caregivers of older adults: A review and analysis of the literature from 1990 to 1998. *Activities, Adaptation & Aging, 24*(2), 17–34.

Bell, A. C., & D'Zurilla, T. J. (2009a). The influence of social problem-solving ability on the relationship between daily stress and adjustment. *Cognitive Therapy Research, 33,* 439–448.

Bell, A. C., & D'Zurilla, T. J. (2009b). Problem-solving therapy for depression: A meta-analysis. *Clinical Psychology Review, 29*(4), 348–353.

Bielczyc, K., Pirolli, P. L., & Brown, A. L. (1995). Training in self-explanation and self-regulation strategies: Investigating the effects of knowledge acquisition activities on problem solving. *Cognition and Instruction, 13*(2), 221–252.

Blechman, E. A. (1974). The family contract game. *The Family Coordinator, 23*(3), 269–281.

Burglass, M. E., & Duffy, M. G. (1974). *Thresholds: Teacher's manual.* Cambridge, MA: Correctional Solutions Foundation.

Caldwell, L. L. (2004). *TimeWise: Taking charge of leisure time.* Scotts Valley, CA: ETR Associates.

Caldwell, L. L. Baldwin, C. K., Walls, T., & Smith, E. (2004). Preliminary effects of a leisure education program to promote health use of free time among middle school adolescents. *Journal of Leisure Research, 36*(3), 310–335.

Caldwell, L. L., & Darling, N. (1999). Leisure context, parental control, and resistance to peer pressure as predictors of adolescent partying and substance use: An ecological perspective. *Journal of Leisure Research, 31,* 57–77.

Caldwell, L. L., Darling, N., Payne, L., & Dowdy, B. (1999). "Why are you bored?": An examination of psychological and social control causes of boredom among adolescents. *Journal of Leisure Research, 31*(2), 103–121.

Caldwell, L. L., & Smith, E. A. (1995). Health behaviors of leisure alienated youth. *Loisir & Societe/ Leisure and Society, 18,* 143–156.

Caldwell, L. L., & Smith, E. A. (2004, May). Role of leisure mediators in preventing substance use among adolescents: A longitudinal analysis. *Society for Research on Adolescents, 11*–13.

Caldwell, L. L., & Smith, E. A. (2006). Leisure as a context for youth development and delinquency prevention. *The Australian and New Zealand Journal of Criminology, 39*(3), 398–418.

Caldwell, L. L., Smith, E. A., Wegner, L., Vergnani, T., Mpofu, E., Flisher, A. J., et al. (2004). HealthWise South Africa: Development of a life skills curriculum for young adults. *World Leisure Journal, 46*(3), 4–17.

Carruthers, C. P., & Hood, C. D. (2002). Coping skills program for individuals with alcoholism. *Therapeutic Recreation Journal, 34*(2), 154–171.

Carter, M. J., Nezey, I. O., Wenzel, K., & Foret, C. (2001). Leisure education with caregiver support groups. *Activities, Adaptation, and Aging, 24*(2), 67–81.

Charters, J. (2005, May). Design and evaluation of a leisure education program for caregivers of institutionalized care recipients. In Abstracts of papers presented at the Eleventh Canadian Congress on Leisure Research, Malaspina University-College, Nanaimo, British Columbia.

Charters, J., & Murray, S. (2006). Design and evaluation of a leisure education program for caregivers of institutionalized care recipients. *Topics in Geriatric Rehabilitation, 22*(4), 334–347.

Clarke, A. T. (2006). Coping with interpersonal stress and psychosocial health among children and adolescents: A meta-analysis. *Journal of Youth and Adolescence, 35*(1), 11–24.

Cuijpers, P., van Straten, A., & Warmerdam, L. (2007). Problem-solving therapies for depression: A meta-analysis. *European Psychiatry, 22*(1), 9–15.

Darling, N., Caldwell, L. L., & Smith, R. (2005). Participation in school-based extracurricular activities and adolescent adjustment. *Journal of Leisure Research, 37*(1), 51–76.

de Boo, G. M., & Prins, P. J. M. (2007). Social incompetence in children with ADHD: Possible moderators and mediators in social-skills training. *Clinical Psychology Review, 27*, 78–97.

deHope, E., & Finegan, J. (1999). The self determination model: An approach to develop awareness for survivors of traumatic brain injury. *NeuroRehabilitation, 13*(1), 3–12.

Dirks, M. A., Treat, T. A., & Weersing, V. R. (2007). Integrating theoretical, measurement, and intervention models of youth social competence. *Clinical Psychology Review, 27*, 327–347.

Durlak, J. A., & Wells, A. M. (1997). Primary prevention mental health programs for children and adolescents: A meta-analytic review. *American Journal of Community Psychology, 25*(2), 115–152.

D'Zurilla, T. J. (1986). *Problem-solving therapy: A social competence approach to clinical intervention.* New York, NY: Springer.

D'Zurilla, T. J., & Goldfried, M. R. (1971). Problem solving and behavior modification. *Journal of Abnormal Psychology, 78*, 107–126.

D'Zurilla, T. J., & Maydeu-Olivares, A. (1995). Conceptual and methodological issues in social problem-solving assessment. *Behavior Therapy, 26*, 409–432.

D'Zurilla, T. J., Maydeu-Olivares, A., & Kant, G. L. (1998). Age and gender differences in social problem solving in college students, middle age, and elderly adults. *Personality and Individual Differences, 25*(2), 241–252.

D'Zurilla, T. J., & Nezu, A. M. (1982). Social problem solving in adults. In P. C. Kendall (Ed.), *Advances in cognitive-behavioral research and therapy* (1st ed.; pp. 201–274). New York, NY: Academic Press.

D'Zurilla, T. J., & Nezu, A. M. (1999). *Problem-solving therapy: A social competence approach to clinical intervention* (2nd ed.). New York, NY: Springer.

D'Zurilla, T. J., & Nezu, A. M. (2007). *Problem-solving therapy: A positive approach to clinical intervention* (3rd ed.). New York, NY: Springer.

D'Zurilla, T. J., & Nezu, A. M. (2010). Problem-solving therapy. In K. S. Dobson (Ed.), *Handbook of cognitive-behavioral therapies* (3rd ed.). New York, NY: Guilford.

D'Zurilla, T. J., Nezu, A. M., & Maydeu-Olivares, A. (2002). *Social problem-solving inventory-Revised (SPSI-R). Technical manual.* North Tonawanda, NY: Multi-Health Systems.

D'Zurilla, T. J., Nezu, A. M., & Maydeu-Olivares, A. (2004). What is social problem solving?: Meaning, models, and measures. In E. C. Chang, T. J. D'Zurilla & L. Sanna, (Eds.) *Social problem solving: Theory, research, and training* (pp. 11–27). Washington, DC: American Psychological Association.

Ebata A. T., & Moos, R. H. (1991). Coping and adjustment in distressed and health adolescents. *Journal of Applied Developmental Psychology, 12*(1), 33–54.

Ebata, A. T., & Moos, R. H. (1994). Personal, situational, and contextual correlates of coping in adolescence. *Journal of Research on Adolescence, 4*(1), 99–125.

Elias, M. J., Gara, M., Ubriaco, M., Rothbaum, P. A., Clabby, J. F., & Schuyler, T. (1986). Impact of a preventive social problem solving intervention on children's coping with middle-school stressors. *American Journal of Community Psychology, 14*(3), 259–275.

Elliott, T. R., Brossart, D., Berry, J. W., & Fine, P. R. (2008). Problem-solving training via video-conferencing for family caregivers of persons with spinal cord injuries: A randomized controlled trial. *Behaviour Research and Therapy, 46*, 1220–1229.

Elliott, T. R., Bush, B. A., & Chen, Y. (2006). Social problem-solving abilities predict pressure sore occurrence in the first 3 years of spinal cord injury. *Rehabilitation Psychology, 51*(1), 69–77.

Freeman, P., & Zabriskie, R. (2002). The role of outdoor recreation in family enrichment. *Journal of Adventure Education and Outdoor Learning, 2*(2), 131–145.

Hammell, K. W. (2007). Experience of rehabilitation following spinal cord injury: A meta-synthesis of qualitative findings. *Spinal Cord, 45*, 260–274.

Heppner, P. P. (2008). Expanding the conceptualization and measurement of applied problem solving and coping: From stages to dimensions to the almost forgotten cultural context. *American Psychologist, 63*(8), 805–816.

Hill, E., Gomez, E., & Jeppesen, G. L. (2007). Adolescent resiliency: A multidisciplinary approach. *Annual in Therapeutic Recreation, 14*, 59–84.

Hood, C. D., & Carruthers, C. P. (2002). Coping skills theory as an underlying framework for therapeutic recreation services. *Therapeutic Recreation Journal, 34*(2), 137–153.

Hutchinson, S. L., LeBlanc, A., & Booth, R. (2002). "Perpetual problem solving": An ethnographic study of clinical reasoning in a therapeutic recreation setting. *Therapeutic Recreation Journal, 36*(1), 18–34.

Johnson, C. D. (1999). Therapeutic recreation treats depression in the elderly. *Home Health Care Services Quarterly, 18*(2), 79–90.

Johnson, K. A., & Klaas, S. J. (1999). Recreation involvement and play in pediatric spinal cord injury. *Topics in Spinal Cord Injury Rehabilitation, 3*(2), 105–109.

Kraag, G., Zeegers, M. P., Kok, G., Hosman, C., & Abu-Saad, H. H. (2006). School programs targeting stress management in children and adolescents: A meta-analysis. *Journal of School Psychology, 44*(6), 449–472.

LeCroy, C. W. (1984). Residential treatment services: A review of some current trends. *Child Care Quarterly, 13*(2), 83–97.

Liang, B., Tracy, A., Kenny, M., & Brogan, D. (2008). Gender differences in relational health of youth participating in a social competence program. *Journal of Community Psychology, 36*(4), 499–514.

Malouff, J. M., & Schutte, N. S. (1998). *Games to enhance social and emotional skills: sixty-six games that teach children, adolescents, and adults skills crucial to success in life*. Springfield, IL: Charles C. Thomas.

Malouff, J. M., Thorsteinsson, E. B., & Schutte, N. S. (2007). The efficacy of problem-solving therapy in reducing mental and physical health problems: A meta-analysis. *Clinical Psychology Review, 27*(1), 46–57.

Nation, J. M., Benshoff, J. J., & Malkin, M. M. (1996). Therapeutic recreation programs for adolescents in substance abuse treatment facilities. *Journal of Rehabilitation, 62*, 10–16.

Nezu, A. M. (2002). Problem-solving therapy. In T. Scimali & L. Grimaldi (Eds.), *Cognitive psychotherapy toward a new millennium: Scientific foundations and clinical practice* (pp. 89–94). New York, NY: Kluwer Academic Publishers.

Nezu, A. M. (2004). Problem solving and behavior therapy revisited. *Behavior Therapy, 35*, 1–33.

Nezu, A. M., & D'Zurilla, T. M. (2007). The psychometric validation of the social problem-solving inventory—Revised with UK incarcerated sexual offenders. *Sexual Abuse: A Journal of Research and Treatment, 19*(3), 217–236.

Pegg, S., & Moxham, L. (2000). Getting it right: Appropriate therapeutic recreation programs for community-based consumers of mental health services. *Contemporary Nurse, 9*(3–4), 295–302.

Pegg, S., & Patterson, I. (2002). The impact of a therapeutic recreation program on community-based consumers of a regional mental health service. *Journal of Park and Recreation Administration, 20*(4), 65–89.

Robinson, R. G., Jorge, R. E., Moser, D. J., Acion, L., Solodkin, A., Small, S. L., et al. (2008). Escitalopram and problem-solving therapy for prevention of poststroke depression: A randomized control trial. *Journal of the American Medical Association, 299*(20), 2391–2400.

Rones, M., & Hoagwood, K. (2000). School-based mental health services: A research review. *Clinical Child and Family Psychology Review, 3*(4), 223–241.

Shure, M. B. (1981). Social competence as a problem-solving skill. In J. D. Wine and M. D. Smye (Eds.), *Social competence* (pp. 158–185). New York, NY: Guilford Press.

Shure, M. B. (2001). I Can Problem Solve (ICPS): An interpersonal cognitive problem-solving program for children. *Residential Treatment for Children and Youth, 18*(3), 3–14.

Shure, M. B., & Aberson, B. (2006). Enhancing the process of resilience through effective thinking. In S. Goldstein & R. B. Brooks (Eds.), *Handbook of resilience in children* (pp. 373–394). New York, NY: Springer.

Shure, M. B., & Spivack, G. (1972). Means-ends thinking, adjustment, and social class among elementary-aged children. *Journal of Consulting and Clinical Psychology, 38,* 348–353.

Shure, M. B., & Spivack, G. (1978). *Problem-solving techniques in child-rearing.* San Francisco, CA: Jossey-Bass.

Shure, M. B., & Spivack, G. (1982). Interpersonal problem solving in young children: A cognitive approach to prevention. *American Journal of Community Psychology, 10,* 341–356.

Smith, E. A., Palen, L. A., Caldwell, L. L. Flisher, A. J., Graham, J. W., Mathews, C., et al. (2008). Substance use and sexual risk prevention in Cape Town, South Africa: An evaluation of the HealthWise program. *Preventive Sciences, 9*(4), 311–321.

Spivack, G., & Shure, M. B. (1974). *Social adjustment of young children.* San Francisco, CA: Jossey-Bass.

Ungar, M., Dumond, C., & McDonald, W. (2005). Risk, resilience and outdoor programmes for at-risk children. *Journal of Social Work, 5*(3), 319–338.

Wegner, L., Flisher, A. J., Caldwell, L. L., Vergnani, T., & Smith, E. A. (2008). HealthWise South Africa: Cultural adaptation of a school-based risk prevention programme. *Health Education Research, 23*(6), 1085–1096.

Wells, M. S., Widmer, M. A., & McCoy, J. K. (2004). Grubs and grasshoppers: Challenge-based recreation and the collective efficacy of families with at-risk youth. *Family Relations, 53*(3), 326–333.

» CHAPTER 10 »

Anger Management

Norma J. Stumbo, Ph.D., CTRS

Background/History

Anger is a range of emotional/affective states of vary-ing intensity, from aggression and annoyance to rage and fury (Hagiliassis, Gulbenkoglu, DiMarco, Young, & Hudson, 2005; Howells & Day, 2003; Spielberger, 1991). From a cognitive-behavorial perspective, Thomas and Jefferson (1996, p. 12) noted that anger is a "strong, uncomfortable emotional reaction to another person or event that offends our beliefs about the way things should be in a particular situation." For example, Levinson (2006) suggested that anger was the result of dissonance between irrational beliefs and reality. Levinson listed these as typical irrational beliefs that provoke anger responses when reality is different:

- Things should be quick and easy.
- People should love and approve of me.
- Other people make me angry.
- I must have certainty in my life.
- I must do well in everything that I try.
- I must seek revenge for past harms.

Deffenbacher (1999), a psychologist who has spent his career studying anger, went a step further and ar-gued that anger is interactional:

Anger can be viewed as arising from interac-tions among (i) one or more eliciting [external] events, (ii) the individual's pre-anger state, including both momentary and enduring char-acteristics [such as anger-related memories and images], and (iii) the person's appraisals, not only of eliciting events, but also of his or her coping resources (primary and secondary appraisals, respectively). . . . Anger is an expe-riential state consisting of emotional, cognitive, and physiological components that co-occur, rapidly interacting with and influencing each other in such a way that they tend to be experi-enced as a singular phenomenon. The individual

also behaves in reaction to precipitating events and to experienced anger. (pp. 295–296)

How one responds to anger is important and takes considerable effort to reshape what might seem as automatic and natural responses. Joseph and Strain (2003) believed that "controlling anger and impulse is perhaps the most difficult task of emotional literacy. . . . Remaining calm in the presence of adverse situations is not about the suppression of emotions, but the dy-namic engagement of affective, cognitive, and behav-ioral processes" (p. 1).

Deffenbacher (1999) explained that an angry reac-tion depends on the surrounding circumstances, such as being tied up in a traffic jam, as well as the individ-ual's cognitive characteristics. He noted that anger is often the result when a person's sense of internal integ-rity or code of conduct is violated, or a goal-directed behavior has been thwarted. He further noted that anger becomes dysfunctional when these cognitive processes become rigid, arbitrary, and over-generalized: "Values cease to be preferences, but become sanctified dogma imposed on others. Personal desires take the form of commandments. Expectations and promises become absolute, never to be unfulfilled" (Deffenbacher, 1999, p. 296).

Deffenbacher also believed that a person's primary appraisal of the situation is key to evoking an anger response. If the individual believes the "attack" on his or her personal integrity or code of conduct is (a) un-warranted, (b) intentional, (c) preventable, and/or (d) blameworthy (the other person is responsible), anger will be the primary result. A secondary appraisal then occurs, in which the individual assesses whether he or she has the resources to cope with the original "attack" and whether aggression is the sanctified response. "Anger is likely when individuals assess themselves experiencing something they should not have experienced and with which they are unable to cope or should not have to cope, and/or for which they believe attack and aggression are appropriate" (p. 297).

Gaines and Barry (2008) focus on the physiological arousal that comes with the increase of angry thoughts, and note that helping individuals increase their awareness of this arousal and their ability to self-regulate it is key to anger management.

Willner and Tomlinson (2007) discussed the Novaco model, which views anger as an emotion with three components (physiological, behavioral, and cognitive); thus, therapy should address relaxation, behavioral coping skills, and cognitive restructuring. They report that many studies have been conducted and (although many are small case studies) provide evidence that programs in which participants are taught techniques for coping with anger-provoking situations are effective and useful in decreasing the expression of anger by clients with intellectual disabilities.

Men, as reported by Thomas (2003), have different anger responses than women. Using healthcare examples, the author noted that her research had shown that men are more angered by loss of control, inefficiency of the system, and/or lack of staff professionalism. Women become more angry and hurt when they perceive staff as uncaring and/or unwilling to take time to listen to them and form a relationship. Thomas (2001) further explained that men may benefit more from anger management programs that involve cognitive behavioral training and rational-emotive therapy, while women will benefit more from anger expression training involving skill development that helps them eradicate their sense of powerlessness (e.g., assertiveness training, conflict resolution, problem solving). Interestingly, Phillips, Henry, Hosie, and Milne (2006), in their study of 286 older adults, reported that improved management of emotions (especially anger) as one ages is a significant factor in maintaining well-being into old age.

Anger is a normal, natural, universal emotion, and is not in itself problematic. In fact, Thomas and Jefferson noted the numerous benefits of anger (pp. 13–14):

- can lead to personal and/or situational insight
- grabs other people's attention because it is an unmistakably clear form of communication
- enhances one's ego, boosts personal competence, and increases self-esteem
- protects against domination, control, or being taken advantage of
- serves as a warning signal that one's stressors are exceeding one's resources
- signals one's rights are being violated or values are being compromised
- signals key relationship problems, like when a significant other is doing too much or too little

- encourages exploration of new approaches and options, from job changes to divorce
- helps one fight disease (if managed well)
- encourages efforts to correct injustices, to improve one's life and the lives of others

Conversely, anger can be the source of many drawbacks as well. Some of these are physical. The American Psychological Association (APA, 2006) noted that anger is accompanied by physiological and biological reactions, such as increased heart rate, blood pressure, energy hormones, adrenaline, and noradrenaline. Levinson (2006) added that anger increased stomach acid secretions as well as weakened a person's immune system, making it more difficult to ward off diseases. In the short term, these bodily reactions can help the individual "fight back" to correct the problem; in the longer term, these responses can cause significant bodily damage.

Other drawbacks are social or psychological. The APA (2006) stated that individuals consciously and unconsciously use three main approaches to dealing with anger: (a) expressing, (b) suppressing, and (c) calming. Anger becomes problematic when its intensity, frequency, duration, and behavioral effects are viewed as inappropriate and cause distress for the individual and/or others. People who do not control how they express their anger may do so in ways which produce harmful results, ranging from conviction and incarceration to being labeled as socially incompetent and isolative (Hagiliassis et al., 2005; Howells & Day, 2003). These individuals may exhibit aggressive (e.g., causing injury to self or others) or passive-aggressive behaviors (e.g., being cynical, hostile, critical).

Suppressing anger happens when the individual holds in his or her anger and tries to concentrate on something positive. While in some cases, this approach works well, in others, when anger festers inside, it is often turned inward and becomes self-destructive.

The third approach is to calm down through intentional physical control and thought patterns. These include relaxation, cognitive restructuring (changing irrational thoughts to rational ones), problem solving, improved communication, using appropriate humor, changing external circumstances, avoidance, counseling, and assertiveness training. Many of these techniques are discussed more fully in other chapters in this text.

Thomas (2003) noted that research has supported two productive anger-management strategies: (a) taking constructive action on the antecedents to anger whenever possible, and (b) when no constructive action is possible, finding healthy ways to discharge the strong physiological arousal of anger though exercise, laughter, or calming techniques, such as meditation and talking with a confidante. She also noted that improved skills in conflict resolution, assertiveness, bargaining, and negotiating helped with anger-coping, as well as counseling and cognitive-restructuring.

Singh et al. (2007) noted that especially for individuals with long-term aggression issues, such as those with persistent mental illness, the etiology is multifaceted, so treatment must be multifaceted as well, often including both pharmacological and behavioral treatments. They noted that anger management treatment often includes training in problem solving, social skills, relaxation, and cognitive behavioral therapy. They noted that "mindfulness," awareness and non-judgmental acceptance with a clear, calm mind focusing on the present moment, is often added to cognitive behavioral therapy.

Intended Client Groups

Anger management programs have been developed and studied for a variety of populations, such as:

- at-risk youth who demonstrate severe aggression, antisocial behavior, conduct disorders, and delinquency (Deffenbacher, Lynch, Oetting, & Kemper, 1996; Gaines & Barry, 2008; Raymond, 2005; Woolgar & Scott, 2005)
- youth with Asperger's syndrome (Sofronoff, Attwood, Hinton, & Levin, 2007)
- adult offenders (Bourke & van Hasselt, 2001; Duncan, Nicol, Ager, & Dalgleish, 2006; Hornsveld, 2005; Howells et al., 2005; Ireland, 2004; Serin, Gobeil, & Preston, 2009; Watt & Howells, 1999)
- individuals with cognitive and communication disabilities (Hagiliassis et al., 2005)
- individuals, especially armed forces veterans, who have post-traumatic stress disorder (Reilly, Clark, & Shopshire, 1996; Reilly et al., 1994)
- adults with mild intellectual disability (Hassiotis & Hall, 2004; King, Lancaster, Wynne, Nettleton, & Davis, 1999; Nickerson & Coleman, 2006; Sturmey, 2004; Willner, Brace, & Phillips, 2005)
- adults with developmental disabilities (Benson, Rice, & Miranti, 1986; McLain & Lewis, 1998a, 1998b)
- individuals with acquired brain injury (Demark & Gemeinhardt, 2002)

- individuals with mental health problems, especially depression (Tang, 2001)

Basic Premises

As noted above, individuals respond to anger in a variety of ways. While some individuals are actually more "hot-headed" than others (APA, 2006), others withdraw socially and sulk or pout, and still others become chronically irritable or cranky. While some individuals show signs of quick anger at a very early age, oftentimes, reactions to anger are sociocultural; that is, learned from disruptive, chaotic, or emotionally stunted families or peers. But whatever behaviors and thoughts can be learned can be unlearned as well. Bourke and van Hasselt (2001) also provided important reminders that many ethnic cultures respond to anger in different ways, and those differences need to be acknowledged and respected.

How people react when angry depends on many factors, such as situational context, cultural norms, intensity of the anger, prior history in such situations and their results, the person's pre-anger state, and the like. One of the primary goals of anger management programs is to assess how the person behaves, the consequences of such behavior, and the variability of adaptive and maladaptive behaviors across anger episodes, and to incorporate that information into treatment planning (Deffenbacher, 1999).

In anger-management programs, clients learn to reduce the reactions to emotional triggers and the physiological arousal that anger causes. Anger management clients learn that they cannot get rid of, totally avoid, or change all the things or people that trigger an anger response. But these clients can learn to control their reactions and responses to these triggers, and use a variety of techniques to positively manage the situation. Cognitive therapy is one of the most popular interventions in the treatment of anger (Deffenbacher, 1999; Deffenbacher, Dahlen, Lynch, Morris, & Gowensmith, 2000).

Thomas (2001) noted that most anger-management programs typically range from three to eight sessions, depending on the clients and resources available. Sessions usually include lectures on content, role-playing, targeted activities and exercises, small and large group discussions, and homework assignments. In many cases, clients are undergoing individual psychotherapy in addition to the anger-management program. Because individuals learn in different ways, Bourke and van Hasselt (2001) suggested that a variety of teaching techniques be used. Among the techniques they used in the anger-management program for adult offenders were direct instruction, modeling, role-playing, performance feedback and positive reinforcement, homework assignments, and prompting sheets. Additionally, Raymond (2005) advocated physical exercises, active discussions, inter-group challenges, and periods of reflection. Sturmey (2004) emphasized that most anger management programs were implemented in three basic stages: (1) education about anger and anger management, (2) interventions for anger, and (3) applying strategies for progressively more realistic life situations.

Thomas (2001, p. 44) offered 20 questions to aid in assessing how well individuals manage their anger. These questions included:

1. What is the client's usual proneness to respond angrily (hot-headed vs. slow to respond)?
2. How intense is the angry emotionality?
3. What is the duration of a typical anger episode? Minutes, hours, days?
4. How does the client usually express anger? Is it suppressed or directed outward in physical actions or verbal behavior? How does the client feel about his/her style of anger expressions? What are some of the consequences?
5. Does the person ruminate about the grievance, rekindling anger again and again?
6. Are there irrational beliefs fueling the anger (beliefs about the way other people should behave or about the way a fair world ought to operate)?
7. If the anger is kept to oneself, what barriers prevent its expression?
8. If the anger is directed outward, does the person make a clear forthright declaration of the anger to the person who provoked it?
9. Does the person engage in yelling, screaming, threats, or profanity when angry?
10. What triggers the anger? What is it about? What are the recurrent themes, patterns?
11. What strategies are used to control temper and cool down? Humor? Meditation? Physical exercise?
12. To what degree is anger creating problems for this client in the workplace or intimate relationships? Has the client ever harmed self or others when angry?
13. What defense mechanisms come into play? Intellectualization, projection, isolation?
14. How does the current angry behavior compare to the person's usual pattern?

15. What did the client learn about anger while growing up? Rules for anger display vary greatly among cultures. Gender role socialization is another strong influence.
16. Is the anger somatized in headaches, gastric distress, and other physical symptoms?
17. Is the discomfort of anger medicated through alcohol, drugs, or cigarettes, or food binges?
18. With whom does anger most frequently occur? Are there any commonalities among the provocateurs? Are transference phenomena evident?
19. In a situation of recurrent conflict, what would the client like to be different? Is it possible for the client to understand the other person's position on the issue?
20. Who will support the client's efforts to try new anger behaviors? Who will attempt sabotage? How will the client respond to saboteurs?

Thomas and Jefferson (1996) suggested teaching clients a number of rules that can be applied in anger-invoking situations. These include:

1. You have the right to become angry if the wrongdoing you've experienced is correctable.
2. You should not get angry at events or misdeeds that can be corrected in more standard ways.
3. Your anger should only be directed at those who can be held responsible for their actions.
4. Your anger should begin with an explanation of the harm done.
5. The aim of your anger should be to correct the situation, not to inflict pain on others.
6. Your anger should be proportional to its cause.
7. Your anger should not exceed what is necessary to correct the situation or prevent the instigation from recurring.
8. Your anger should include a commitment to appropriate follow-through.
9. Terminate your anger whenever the target apologizes or makes amends.
10. Do not displace your anger on an innocent party.
11. Your anger should not last for more than a few hours or days at most.
12. An angry person should not be held completely responsible for his or her actions. (This is not a license to kill, but a plea for compassion for people who bungle their anger expression.)

Deffenbacher (1999) noted a variety of cognitive-behavioral approaches to anger management, many of which are described in more detail in other chapters in this book. These approaches to anger management include:

- Self-awareness: Keeping an anger journal (see Example Activities, p. 184), role-plays, and behavioral experiments
- Appropriate avoidance: Avoiding anger-provoking events, distancing oneself by delaying a response, and taking a time-out
- Relaxation: Focusing on emotional and physiological arousal to evoke sense of calm and control, as well as sense of coping
- Cognitive therapy/cognitive restructuring: Focusing on dysfunctional cognitive and cultural components of the pre-anger state, biased appraisal processes, and the cognitive component of experienced anger; helping the individual to identify and alter anger-provoking cognitive appraisals
- Silly humor: Magnifying the situation and the person's reaction to the point it becomes silly
- Problem solving: Looking for viable alternatives that produce the desired consequences
- Communication, assertion, and conflict management skills: Changing the person's appraisals of their ability to cope and dysfunctional ways of responding to inevitable personal conflict by teaching them new replacement skills
- Counseling: One-on-one or small group therapy to discuss anger issues and their impact on the person's personal and professional life, and to design successful solutions

Willner et al. (2005) concluded that since anger is an emotion with three components—physiological, behavioral, and cognitive—the anger-management program should be constructed using relaxation, coping skills, and cognitive restructuring. They delineated eight predominant anger-management strategies for use with individuals with intellectual disability:

1. Relax: using relaxation skills to reduce anger (e.g., physical muscle relaxation and deep breathing)
2. Count to 10: pausing before expressing anger, giving the individual time to think
3. Walk away: This means without becoming angry, without storming off in a temper
4. Do something else: examples are provided of other things the individual might do in order to diffuse their potential anger (e.g., getting on

with work, looking for someone else to share time with, choosing another activity)
5. Ask for help: either from a staff member or another client
6. Rethink the situation: examples are provided of ways in which the client might reformulate the situation. These could represent either spontaneous accounts or acceptance of a reasonable argument put to the client, typically by a staff member. Some examples: "That's Bob, and he can't see very well," "She missed breakfast this morning, so it's understandable," "Actually she's right about that," "He's been upset for some time now, so I'll let that go."
7. Use humor: making a joke about the issue, which could be client-led or could be as a response to someone else.
8. Be assertive: The interviewer may need to explain the difference between aggressiveness and assertiveness (standing up for your rights, without infringing on others). Some discussion may be needed to decide whether raised voices are assertive or aggressive in a particular case.

Gulbenkoglu and Hagiliassis (2006) authored an anger-management training program specifically for individuals with disabilities. Their training package, available for purchase (see Resources, p. 184), included 12 sessions:

1–2. Introduction to anger management
3. Learning about feelings and anger
4. Learning about helpful and unhelpful ways
5–6. Learning to relax
7–9. Learning to think calmly
10. Learning to handle problems
11. Learning to speak up for ourselves
12. Putting it all together.

An anger-management program for adults with developmental disabilities, created by McLain and Lewis (1998a, 1998b), contained 11 sessions. The topics included:

1–2. Rationales for improving anger management
3–4. Identifying patterns and antecedents to temper outbursts, recognizing internal cues, and developing relaxation skills
5. Physiological responses to anger and need for self-regulatory behavior
6. Review of previous sessions
7. Advanced cognitive-behavioral aspects of

temper control (e.g., irrational thoughts, thought-stopping)
8. Assertiveness skills
9. Problem-solving skills, strategies for identifying and defining problems, generating alternatives, and evaluating outcomes
10. Subtle aspects of assertiveness skills (e.g., active listening) and social skills development (such as responding to criticism, taking responsibility)
11. Review through role-plays and personal goal setting

Ireland (2004) reported on a 12-session anger-management program that was developed for young male offenders in the United Kingdom and that included the following components:

1. Overview of the sessions, rules of the course, importance of using anger diaries
2. Triggers for angry behavior, understanding the consequences of anger loss
3. Cycle of angry behavior, importance of body language in signaling anger
4. Replacing aggressive body language with non-aggressive body language
5. Importance of thoughts, using "non-angry" thoughts, the parts of an angry incident, i.e., before, during, and after
6. Using non-angry thoughts before, during and after angry incidents, important of self-praise following avoidance of anger-loss
7. Importance of bodily arousal in relation to angry behavior, learning how to wind down
8. Relaxation techniques to help cope with feeling wound up
9. Choosing how you behave toward others
10. Learning to express anger assertively
11. Recognizing and dealing with criticisms and insults, peer group pressure and how to deal with it
12. Identifying high-risk situations and lapse/relapse

Reilly et al. (1994) outlined a 12-week anger management program that used with individuals who were experiencing post-traumatic stress disorder as well as substance abuse. Their sessions included:

1–2. Cues to anger and the anger meter
3. Anger control plans and anger as a secondary emotion (as a reaction to fear, insecurity, jealousy, etc.)

4. Time out and the aggression cycle (escalation, explosion, post-explosion)
5. Self-talk model (beliefs and expectations that produce emotional responses)
6. Relaxation training
7. Conflict resolution
8–9. Analysis of most violent incident (re-evaluate prior violent behavior)
9–10. Anger in family of origin (how clients influenced by family's expression of anger)
11. Assertiveness training
12. Review of anger control plans

Snyder, Kymissis, and Kessler (1999) implemented a brief (4-session) anger management program for adolescent inpatients of a psychiatric unit who demonstrated high levels of anger. Their 4-session program included:

1. Introduction to concepts
   a. Orientation to the group
   b. Provide structure: reducing anxiety and resistance
   c. Discuss general concepts of anger What does anger feel like in the body? Where is it felt?
   d. Anger as interpretations/perceptions of situations
   e. Styles of handling anger are learned from role models (parents, siblings, older peers, etc.)
   f. Participation from group on each of these points, examples
   g. Stay with major ideas: Don't delve too deeply into underlying dynamics

2. Anger management concepts: More in-depth
   a. Reiterate: anger as interpretations/perceptions of situations
   b. Discussion of social misperceptions, misinterpretations, hostile stances
   c. Interpretations of other people's behaviors—are they accurate?
   d. Alternative explanations for others' behaviors (person was just rude, jealous, having a bad day, etc.)
   e. Hostile stances protect us, but are they realistic?
   f. Sometimes anger is appropriate, but how to express it?
   g. Concrete strategies for checking one's own perceptions, controlling angry reactions, choosing more appropriate behaviors

h. Group members begin to develop individualized strategies for dealing with anger (taking it out on a basketball court, walking away, talking it over, using humor, etc.)

3. Practice
   a. The Anger Control Game (Berg, 1995)—a game designed for this population
   b. Provides concrete opportunities for practice, structured role-plays, naturalistic in vivo provocations, feedback from peers and co-therapists

4. Review and Integration
   a. Review of strategies
   b. Hassle logs (Feindler & Guttman, 1994)—concrete format to bring in personal examples
   c. Role-plays, practiced, reviews of the adolescents' actual social situations
   d. Peer feedback to each other (with co-therapist guidance) on how effective each person's responses were, how well they controlled anger
   e. Discussion, opinions about the group, what each person liked about the group

Nickerson and Coleman (2006) briefly outlined a 6-session anger-coping program for youths with emotional disorders. The 40-minute sessions included:

Session 1: Introduction, icebreaker, group rules, discussion of confidentiality; conversation about behavior management and incentive system (penny jar).

Session 2: Review of session 1. Discussion of feelings and connections between thoughts, feelings, and behaviors. Book of faces (emotions) introduced; homework to identify feelings.

Session 3: Review of sessions 1 and 2. Discussion of anger and anger thermometers; story read about angry child; homework about rating feelings throughout the week.

Session 4: Review of previous sessions. Discussion of anger, triggers, and consequences; alternatives and problem solving for solutions; inappropriate and appropriate ways to handle anger; homework included blank cartoon to be filled in with positive coping skills.

Session 5: Review. Stoplight highlighting—"Stop-think-act"—as strategy for anger-arousing situations; Homework included identifying situation in which stop-think-act could be used.

Session 6: Review. role plays practicing stopping, thinking, acting about alternatives and getting to appropriate response. Group closure and pizza party.

Sofronoff, Attwood, Hinton, and Levin (2007) developed a cognitive behavioral therapy anger management program for youth with Asperger's syndrome. Their 6-session program is as follows:

Session 1: Exploration of positive emotions: happiness and relaxation; range of group and individual activities to measure, experience, and compare emotions in specific scenarios.

Session 2: Exploration of anger; recognition of changes that occur in physiology, thinking, behaving, and speech. Toolbox concept used to equate a number of "tools to fix the feeling" are explored.

Session 3: Social "tools" explored; how other can help restore positive feelings and how avoidance can be beneficial; thinking "tools" (problem solving) also explored.

Session 4: Focus on measuring emotion, such as thermometer or rope laid on floor with each person standing where he or she falls in degree of anger at a situation; successful solutions for managing anger.

Session 5: How "social stories" can be used for emotional management, with each person creating an "antidote" to poisonous or noxious thoughts.

Session 6: Participants worked together to design individualized anger-management programs.

Thomas (2001, p. 46) outlined a specific 4-week anger management program for women living in the community. The detailed agenda included:

Week I: Introduction to anger and the relational nature of women's anger

1. Didactic components
   a. Definition of anger, distinction among irritation, anger, hostility, aggression, and violence
   b. Brief overview of the research findings on anger's causes and unhealthy manifestations (e.g., overeating, substance abuse, headaches)
2. Experiential components
   a. Get acquainted exercises
   b. Self-assessment of anger, using paper-and-pencil test
   c. Sharing personal anger situations in dyads
   d. Goal setting
3. Homework: Begin by keeping anger log, reflect on core values being violated, meaning to recurring anger in relationships

Week II: Anger expression styles and empowerment styles
1. Didactic components
   a. Reframing anger as a catalyst for personal and professional empowerment (i.e., enhanced ability to take action and resolve problems)
   b. Anger management techniques for women who suppress and for those who too readily express anger
   c. Tactics for lowering physiological anger arousal (e.g., relaxation or vigorous activity) and decreasing rumination (e.g., thought-stopping)
   d. Assertiveness, negotiation, and bargaining strategies
2. Experiential components
   a. Sharing incidents from anger logs with the group
   b. Behavioral practice of new approaches to handling these incidents (e.g., discussion in triads, selected exemplars discussed in larger group as well)
3. Homework: Select one thing to address assertively in the coming week; record experience and outcomes in journal

Week III: Women's anger at work (omitted if most women in the class are homemakers)
1. Didactic components
   a. Factors involved in women's anger at work
   b. Passive-aggressive behavior in the workplace
   c. How to defuse angry situations with customers, colleagues, students, etc.
   d. How to take productive action on grievances or harassment through assertiveness and coalition forming
2. Experiential components
   a. Reports on homework (success as well as failures)
   b. Role-playing work-related situations in triads
   c. Selected exemplars discussed in larger group
3. Homework: Use principles presented in class in a workplace situation

Week IV: Women's anger in intimate relationships (can be tailored to need of the group)
1. Didactic components
   a. Factors involved in women's anger at significant others (e.g., spouses, ex-spouses, friends, relatives, children)
   b. Strategies for achieving conflict resolution and relationship reciprocity
   c. Releasing old anger (from childhood, divorce, etc.) through forgiveness, peace talks, and healing rituals
2. Experiential components
   a. Review of homework assignment outcomes
   b. Termination activities (each woman shares one thing she learned in the class and a goal for continued skill practice)

Hornsveld (2005) described a 15-week program (with three follow-ups at weeks 20, 25, and 30) developed in the Netherlands for violent forensic psychiatric patients. The program focused on self-control, deficiencies in social skills, and antisocial attitudes, and was designed as follows:

A. Anger management (weeks 1–5): recognizing and adequately handling emotions such as irritation, anger, and rage;
B. Social skills (weeks 6–10): enhancing or expanding existing relevant social skills;
C. Moral reasoning (weeks 11–15): becoming familiar with common values and norms and learning to solve moral issues;
D. Self-regulation skills (weeks 6–15): altering inadequate aspiration levels, self-reinforcement for results achieved, and developing programs for new behavior;
E. Follow-up sessions (weeks 20, 25, 30): evaluation and reporting.

Deffenbacher (1999) added that it is important for the individual to "own" his or her anger before any real and lasting behavioral changes can occur. Interventions need to identify the individual's stage of readiness and be matched to it in order to be successful. He suggested exploration of the consequences of anger and whether anger is helping the person achieve all of his or her short- and long-term goals. Deffenbacher believed that such interventions could provide motivation for and movement toward actual changes in the person's thoughts and behaviors.

Related Research

Unfortunately, some studies have found that aggressive students in first-grade classrooms that are not well managed tend to sustain that problematic behavior into middle school. This especially is found in classrooms in which teachers respond to these challenging behaviors with strategies that reinforce and sustain the problem behaviors (Farmer et al., 2006; Kellam, Rebok, Ialongo, & Mayer, 1994; Sutherland, 2000). Aggression usually inspires returned aggression, and teachers and clinicians are not exempt from this natural response to perceived threats.

In a study of 49 classrooms involving 790 second- and third-graders, Frey, Hirschstein, and Guzzo (2000) reported that in an experimental violence prevention program that included empathy, social problem solving and anger management, especially in non-structured settings like the playground and lunch time, students in the treatment group greatly reduced aggressive behavior. The researchers also reported that physical aggression was significantly lower, and higher levels of positive interaction were maintained at follow-up, six months later. Bourke and van Hasselt (2001) developed a program for incarcerated adults similar to that of Frey, Hirschstein, and Guzzo. Their program included anger management, empathy training, stress inoculation, and social-skills training.

Nickerson and Coleman (2006) conducted a study on anger-coping with six children aged 10 to 12 with emotional disturbances in the northeastern U.S. The results indicated that the students exhibited more engagement and less avoidance with other group members following the treatment. In addition, the children, their parents, and their teachers noted marked behavioral improvements. The authors noted that this limited, brief treatment seemed to work and may have implications for improving the anger control and social skills of children with emotional disturbances.

Sofronoff, Attwood, Hinton, and Levin (2007) used cognitive behavioral therapy in an anger-management program for 52 Australian children with Asperger's syndrome. At completion of the 6-session program, they found that children had learned a number of effective strategies and had fewer anger episodes, as reported by both parents and teachers. The treatment also increased parents' confidence in their ability to improve their child's anger behavior, and gave parents and teachers a common language to help the children both at home and in the classroom.

Deffenbacher, Lynch, Oetting, and Kemper (1996), in a study of 120 high-anger sixth- through eighth-graders, found that both interventions—social skills training and cognitive-relaxation training—were equally effective in reducing anger and its outward negative expression as well as increasing a calmer, more controlled expression. They also found that cognitive-relaxation training lowered anxiety, depression, shyness, and deviant behavior, whereas social skills training did not. They reported that not only were the programs successful in immediate improvement of emotional and behavioral control, but also provided secondary prevention effects by lowering future aggression, delinquency, and substance abuse.

Gavita and Joyce (2008) completed a meta-analysis of five studies that provided parenting programs in the treatment of conduct problems with their children. They found that cognitive-behavioral programs are effective to improve the parents' mental health, improve their parenting practices, and decrease the children's disruptive behaviors. They found these improvements held at follow-ups, ranging from 3 months to 3 years. These researchers emphasized that the cognitive component of the parenting programs was essential to their success.

Deffenbacher and Stark (1992), in a study of 55 college psychology students, found that a combination of cognitive therapy and relaxation techniques was effective in reducing general anger, anger across varied situations, anger from worst ongoing personal situation, anger suppression, anger-related physiological arousal, state anger, and dysfunctional coping tendencies. Although they found that individually both cognitive and relaxation techniques were equally effective, they felt the most meaningful strategy was introducing relaxation first, so that participants were calmer when the cognitive strategies were introduced.

King et al. (1999) conducted research on 11 adults with intellectual disabilities in Australia. The group met for 15 weekly 90-minute sessions. The anger management program contained training on identification of anger-provoking situations, coping skills, relaxation training, and probem solving. They found significant improvements in anger control scores both in self-reports and caregiver reports. They felt that greater involvement of caregivers during the program and a more robust research design (e.g., treatment/control group) would have improved the long-term generalization of the program results.

Seventeen individuals with intellectual disabilities in a day-treatment program in the United Kingdom were the subjects of an anger-management program discussed by Willner, Brace, and Phillips (2005). The program was offered over 12 weekly, 2-hour sessions, facilitated by two staff members. Although the group reported slightly less tendency to be angry (although not a statistical difference), they did show marked improvements in anger-coping skills, as measured by the Profile of Anger-Coping Skills instrument. The clients especially showed improvements in their ability to ask for help and in assertiveness, which may have seen improvement due to the use of role-playing. The authors felt one advantage of their study was the program's implementation by day staff, which would likely result in longer generalization of skills for the clients.

A systematic review of the anger management literature for individuals with learning disabilities was conducted by Hassiotis and Hall (2004). These authors, while remarking on a severe lack of high-quality and controlled research in this area, declared that cognitive-behavorial methods (modified relaxation, assertiveness training with problem solving, and anger management) were effective in reducing aggressive behavior for individuals with learning disabilities by the end of the treatment period. They also noted, in the reviewed studies, that the effect was significant at the end of treatment but was not found in 6-month follow-ups.

Howells et al. (2005) studied 418 adult male offenders in Australia. At the conclusion of a 10-session anger-management program, they concluded that the participants improved knowledge of anger management but that the knowledge did not necessarily translate to improved behavior. The gains were sustained over a 6-month period, however. They importantly noted that individual gains were substantially related to an individual's readiness to change—a concept noted by Deffenbacher (1999). Since the studied population had low motivation and multiple problems, the authors suggested that the intensity and duration of the program be increased.

Likewise, Ireland (2004) studied 87 young male offenders in a prison in the United Kingdom in a 12-hour intervention over a 3-day period, with small groups of 10 facilitated by two staff. Ireland found that this brief, group-based intervention had positive effects on 92% of the treatment group in the anger-management program, both in unit reports and self-reports by the participants. The 8% within the treatment group who did not make positive changes after the intervention included those who were younger, less violent, and who had lower anger scores at the start of the program.

Hornsveld (2005) completed research with violent male offenders, with 109 forensic inpatients and 44 outpatients, in the Netherlands. Reduced hostility and aggressive behavior were reported in both inpatients and outpatients who completed the treatment, at the end and at follow-ups. Those with the most anger in the beginning were those most likely to benefit. Higher than average and lower than average social skills were not a result. The authors noted that forensic offenders may need to learn "prosocial" behavior and unlearn "antisocial" behaviors in order to see score changes.

Howells and Day (2003) noted that readiness for real anger containment and management is often difficult for individuals in these programs because of many factors, among which are:

a. multiplicity of the person's problems (e.g., lack of resources, poor role models, family dysfunction, personality disorders),
b. setting in which anger management programs are conducted (institutional programs are less effective than community programs),
c. the individual's inferences about his or her anger (e.g., low personal responsibility, blaming others, self-righteousness),
d. coerced or mandatory treatment (e.g., compulsory, coerced, or mandatory treatment does not ensure client readiness),
e. inadequate attention paid to the individual's goals (i.e., some individuals feel that anger nets them positive results, such as being seen as strong or intimidating),
f. ethnic and cultural differences (e.g., one culture with unique expectations and norms being judged by individuals from another culture), and
g. gender (i.e., both genders have unique anger experiences, expressions, and triggers).

Howells and Day (2003) recommended that programmers consider the client's readiness to change, his or her level of self-determination, and degree of responsiveness to treatment. Instead of only looking for ways to modify the client and his or her behavior, the authors suggested also thinking about ways in which interventions can be structured to be most effective, as well how the social climate of the setting can be modified.

Application to Therapeutic Recreation

Therapeutic recreation professionals work with a number of client groups that have anger as a prime characteristic. These groups include:

- individuals with AIDS (Bonadies, 2004; Grossman, 1993)
- heart transplant patients (Holt & Ashton-Shaeffer, 2001)
- individuals with grief from losing a loved one (Sorenson & King, 1999)
- individuals in hospice care (Hodges, 1998), women with multiple sclerosis (Broach & Dattilo, 2003)
- individuals with traumatic brain injury (Gongora, McKenney, & Godinez, 2005)
- children with attention deficit disorder (Kennison, 1996)
- individuals with physical disabilities (Bedini, 2000)

While anger management is not usually a primary component of leisure education, it is one of many complementary skill sets targeted during leisure education programs. As Gongora et al. (2005) noted, anger management may be a prerequisite to developing additional social skills:

> Therapeutic recreation (TR) professionals are in the position of not only helping improve a person's functional abilities, but assisting in improving that person's life-skills, as well . . . helping individuals develop anger coping strategies, which in turn could help individuals to learn or relearn social skills necessary for success in their personal or professional lives. (Gongora et al., 2005, p. 230)

Gongora et al. (2005) offered an 8-session anger-coping program that is to be implemented by therapeutic recreation specialists with, in this particular case, individuals with traumatic (acquired) brain injury. The eight sessions included:

1. Identifying anger (defining anger, identifying and categorizing stressors)
2. Reacting to anger (identifying emotional and physical reactions to stress/anger)
3. The boiling point (identifying triggers)
4. Coping with anger (identifying alternative strategies)
5. Discussing assertive reactions (expressing feelings directly and honestly)
6. Modeling assertive behavior (role playing by the specialist)
7. Role-playing assertive behavior (role playing by the participant)
8. Processing feelings (summarizing successful alternatives for expressing anger)

While this anger-coping program was seen as successful with one individual in a case study, it would appear that additional research is needed—and easily accomplished—with other populations who have difficulties expressing anger appropriately.

Summary

- Anger is a natural emotion that ranges in intensity and appropriateness.
- When people are angry, they often feel at risk and without adequate resources to surmount the problem or accomplish the task.
- Anger is a cognitive, affective, behavioral, and physiological phenomenon.
- Many client groups served by therapeutic recreation would benefit from anger-management training.
- There are many anger-management programs available, most relying on similar concepts and activities to provide instruction.
- Research demonstrates that problem-solving therapy and instruction is mostly effective with a variety of groups; the training program must be well-conceived to be effective.
- Although there are not large amounts of research on anger management in therapeutic recreation, the studies that have been completed are promising.

Resources

Anger Toolkit. By Ingram.
www.angermgmt.com/measure.asp

Anger Management: An anger management training package for individuals with disabilities. (2006). By Hrepsime Gulbenkoglu & Hagioliassis. Jessica Kingsley Publishers.

Anger-Free: Ten basic steps to managing your anger. (2000). By Gentry. HarperCollins Publishers.

Full Catastrophe Living: Using the wisdom of your body and mind to face stress. (1990). By Kabat-Zinn. Dell Publishing.

Anger Management Resources. A wide variety of games, books, videos, and other resources on anger management are available for purchase. www.therapeuticresources.com/anger.html

Angry Monster Machine Game. www.addwarehouse.com

Example Activities

Anger Journal. (1996). By Thomas & Jefferson. Have clients use a daily anger journal or diary to collect information on anger trigger and responses. Have them record:

- the precipitating incident
- their first reaction
- their secondary behavioral reactions (e.g., suppressing, venting outwardly, talking with a friend, vigorously exercising, pouting, sulking)
- their physical reactions (e.g., crying, knotted stomach, headaches)
- their anger intensity, duration, and aftermath (e.g., feelings, actions)
- the "cause"of their anger (e.g., powerlessness, disrespectful treatment)
- whether they followed the Anger Rules (see p. 176)

The last step is to develop a new strategy for the next time a similar situation occurs. The journal is kept for a specific amount of time (week or month) and at the end of the period, clients then summarize what they've learned from their Anger Journal.

Anger Exercise. (2006). By Ingram; (1996). By Reilly, Clark, & Shopshire.
Have participants work through four steps, either on paper or verbally. First, have participants identify mistaken attitudes and convictions that predispose them to being angry (for example, that they are responsible for someone else's behavior, or that people will always do things that please them, or that other people should know what they want without telling them). Second, identify barriers or impediments from childhood that impair the adequate expression of anger toward others. For example, fear, denial, or ignorance of feelings. Third, have clients brainstorm "legitimate" ways for expressing anger at others. Fourth, forgive individuals, so that residual anger can be replaced with relief as well as proactive and positive emotions.

Turtle Technique. (2003). By Joseph & Strain. Especially for young children, teach them to recognize when they feel angry and to think "stop." Then they are to go into their "shell," take three deep breaths, and think calming, coping thoughts. They can come out of their shell when they are calm and can think of some solutions to the original problem. The authors suggest a turtle puppet be used to demonstrate the technique, as well as having the children make a paper-plate turtle to practice on before they try it for themselves.

Anger Thermometer. (2006). By Nickerson & Coleman. Ask clients to use anger thermometers to identify the degree of their anger. Discussion could follow about how often each level of anger is felt, what appropriate reactions might be, and how to reduce anger intensity and well as occurrences.

Anger Role Plays. (2006). By Nickerson & Coleman. Develop written scenarios in which anger might be provoked and ask participants to "finish" the role plays with appropriate and inappropriate ways of responding to anger. Discuss triggers and consequences, problem solving and alternatives.

References

American Psychological Association. (2006). Controlling anger—before it controls you. Available online at: http://www.apa.org/topics/anger/control.aspx

Bedini, L. (2000). "Just sit down so we can talk": Perceived stigma and community recreation pursuits of people with disabilities. *Therapeutic Recreation Journal, 34*(1), 55–68.

Benson, B. A., Rice, C. J., & Miranti, V. S. (1986). Effects of anger management training with mentally retarded adults in group treatment. *Journal of Consulting and Clinical Psychology, 54*(5), 728–729.

Berg, B. (1995). Anger control game. Available from: http://www.creativetherapystore.com/Anger-Control/Game/W-410

Bonadies, V. (2004). A yoga therapy program for AIDS-related pain and anxiety: Implications for therapeutic recreation. *Therapeutic Recreation Journal, 38*(2), 148–166.

Bourke, M. L., & van Hasselt, V. B. (2001). Social problem-solving skills training for incarcerated offenders: A treatment manual. *Behavior Modification, 25*(2), 163–188.

Broach, E., & Dattilo, J. (2003). Effect of aquatic therapy on strength of adults with multiple sclerosis, *Therapeutic Recreation Journal, 37*(3), 224–239.

Deffenbacher, J. L. (1999). Cognitive-behavioral conceptualization and treatment of anger. *Journal of Clinical Psychology, 55*(3), 295–309.

Deffenbacher, J. L., Dahlen, E. R., Lynch, R. S., Morris, C. D., & Gowensmith, W. N. (2000). An application of Beck's cognitive therapy to general anger reduction. *Cognitive Therapy and Research, 24*(6), 689–697.

Deffenbacher, J. L., Lynch, R. S., Oetting, E. R., & Kemper, C. C. (1996). Anger reduction in early adolescents. *Journal of Counseling Psychology, 43*(2), 149–157.

Deffenbacher, J. L., & Stark, R. S. (1992). Relaxation and cognitive-relaxation treatments of general anger. *Journal of Counseling Psychology, 39*(2), 158–167.

Demark, J., & Gemeinhardt, M. (2002). Anger and its management for survivors of acquired brain injury. *Brain Injury, 16*(2), 91–108.

Duncan, E. A. S., Nicol, M. M., Ager, A., & Dalgleish, L. (2006). A systematic review of structured group interventions with mentally disordered offenders. *Criminal Behaviour and Mental Health, 16*(4), 217–241.

Farmer, T. W., Goforth, J. B., Hives, J., Aaron, A., Jackson, F., & Sgammato, A. (2006). Competence enhancement behavior management. *Preventing School Failure, 50*(3), 39–44.

Feindler, E. L., & Guttman, J. (1994). Cognitive-behavioral anger control training for groups of adolescents: A treatment manual. In C. W. LeCroy (Ed.), *Handbook of child and adolescent treatment manuals* (pp. 170–199). New York, NY: Lexington Books.

Frey, K. S., Hirschstein, M. K., & Guzzo, G. (2000). Second Step: Preventing aggression by promoting social competence. *Journal of Emotional and Behavioral Disorders, 8*(2), 102–112.

Gaines, T., & Barry, L. M. (2008). The effect of a self-monitored relaxation breathing exercise on male adolescent aggressive behavior. *Adolescence, 43*(170), 291–302.

Gavita, O., & Joyce, M. (2008). A review of the effectiveness of group cognitively enhanced behavioral based parent programs designed for reducing disruptive behavior in children. *Journal of Cognitive and Behavioral Psychotherapies, 8*(2), 185–199.

Gongora, E. L., McKenney, A., & Godinez, C. (2005). A multidisciplinary approach to teaching anger coping after sustaining a traumatic brain injury: A case report. *Therapeutic Recreation Journal, 39*(3), 229–240.

Grossman, A. H. (1993). Psychosocial issues confronting health care professionals working with people with AIDS. *Loss, Grief & Care, 6*(4), 39–49.

Gulbenkoglu, H., & Hagiliassis, N. (2006). *Anger management: An anger management training package for individuals with disabilities*. Melbourne, Australia: Scope.

Hagiliassis, N., Gulbenkoglu, H., DiMarco, M., Young, S., & Hudson, A. (2005). The anger management project: A group intervention for anger in people with physical and multiple disabilities. *Journal of Intellectual & Developmental Disability, 30*(2), 86–96.

Hassiotis, A., & Hall, I. (2004). Behavioural and cognitive-behavioural interventions for outwardly-directed aggressive behaviour in people with learning disabilities. Cochrane Database of Systematic Reviews. Available online from: http://www.cochrane.org.

Hodges, J. (1998). Quality during the end of life—Therapeutic recreation in hospice care. *Parks & Recreation, 33*(5), 72–79.

Holt, M., & Ashton-Shaeffer, C. (2001). Therapeutic recreation's role in meeting the needs of heart transplant patients. *Parks & Recreation, 36*(5), 58–65.

Hornsveld, R. H. J. (2005). Evaluation of Aggression Control Therapy for violent forensic psychiatric patients. *Psychology, Crime, & Law, 11*(4), 403–410.

Howells, K., & Day, A. (2003). Readiness for anger management: Clinical and theoretical issues. *Clinical Psychology Review, 23*, 319–337.

Howells, K., Day, A., Williamson, P., Bubner, S., Jauncey, S., Parker, A., & Heseltine, K. (2005). Brief anger management programs with offenders: Outcomes and predictors of change. *The Journal of Forensic Psychiatry & Psychology, 16*(2), 296–311.

Ingram, L. (2006). Anger Toolkit: Four proven techniques for managing anger. Available online from: http://www.angermgmt.com/techniques.asp

Ireland, J. L. (2004). Anger management therapy with young male offenders: An evaluation of treatment outcome. *Aggressive Behavior, 30*(2), 174–185.

Joseph, G. E., & Strain, P. E. (2003). Helping young children control anger and handle disappointment. Available online from: http://csefel.vanderbilt.edu

Kellam, S. G., Rebok, G. W., Ialongo, N. S., & Mayer, L. S. (1994). The course and malleability of aggressive behavior from early first grade into middle school: Results of a developmental epidemiologically based preventive trial. *Journal of Child Psychology and Psychiatry and Allied Disciplines, 35*, 259–281.

Kennison, J. A. (1996). Therapy in the mountains. ERIC document 020925.

King, N., Lancaster, N., Wynne, G., Nettleton, N., & Davis, R. (1999). Cognitive-behavioral anger management training for adults with mild intellectual disability. *Scandinavian Journal of Behavior Therapy, 28*(1), 19–22.

Levinson, M. H. (2006). Anger management and violence prevention: A holistic solution. *ETC: A Review of General Semantics, 63*(2), 187–199.

McLain, W., & Lewis, E. (1998a). Anger management and assertiveness skills. *Positive Practices, 3*(4), 1, 13–26.

McLain, W., & Lewis, E. (1998b). Anger management and assertiveness skills: Use of a curriculum in supported living services. *Positive Practices, 3*(3), 1, 10–18.

Nickerson, A. B., & Coleman, M. N. (2006). An exploratory study of member attraction, climate, and behavioral outcomes of anger-coping group therapy for children with emotional disturbance. *Small Group Research, 37*(2), 115–139.

Phillips, L. H., Henry, J. D., Hosie, J. A., & Milne, A. B. (2006). Age, anger regulation, and well-being. *Aging & Mental Health, 10*(3), 250–256.

Raymond, I. (2005). The rock and water program: Empowering youth workers and clients. *Youth Studies Australia, 24*(4), 34–39.

Reilly, P. M., Clark, H. W., Shopshire, M. S. (1996). Anger management and PTSD: Engaging substance abuse patients in long-term treatment. *NCP Clinical Quarterly, 6*(3). Available online from: http://www.ncptsd.va.gov

Reilly, P. M., Clark, H. W., Shopshire, M. S., Lewis, E. W., & Sorensen, D. J. (1994). Anger management and temper control: Critical components of a

posttraumatic stress disorder and substance abuse treatment. *Journal of Psychoactive Drugs, 26*(4), 401–407.

Serin, R. C., Gobeil, R., & Preston, D. L. (2009). Evaluation of the persistently violent offender treatment program. *International Journal of Offender Therapy and Comparative Criminology, 53*(1), 57–73.

Singh, N. N., Lancioni, G. E., Winton, A. S. W., Adkins, A. D., Wahler, R. G., Sabaawi, M. et al. (2007). Individuals with mental illness can control their aggressive behavior through mindfulness training. *Behavior Modification, 31*(3), 313–328.

Sofronoff, K., Attwood, T., Hinton, S., & Levin, I. (2007). A randomized controlled trial of a cognitive behavioural intervention for anger management in children diagnosed with Asperger syndrome. *Journal of Autism and Developmental Disorders, 37*(7), 1203–1214.

Sorenson, B., & King, K. (1999). Play and healing: Therapeutic recreation's role in coping with grief. *Camping Magazine, 72*(2), 29–33.

Snyder, K. V., Kymissis, P., Kessler, K. (1999). Anger management for adolescents: Efficacy of brief group therapy. *Journal of the American Academy of Child and Adolescent Psychiatry, 38*(11), 1409–1416.

Spielberger, C. D. (1991). State-trait anger expression inventory: Revised research edition professional manual. Odessa, FL: Psychological Assessment Resources.

Sturmey, P. (2004). Cognitive therapy with people with intellectual disabilities: A selective review and critique. *Clinical Psychology and Psychotherapy, 11*(4), 222–232.

Sutherland, K. S. (2000). Promoting positive interactions between teachers and students with emotional/behavioral disorders. *Preventing School Failure, 44*, 110–115.

Tang, M. (2001). Clinical outcome and client satisfaction of an anger management group program. *Canadian Journal of Occupational Therapy, 68*, 228–236.

Thomas, S. P. (2001). Teaching healthy anger management. *Perspectives in Psychiatric Care, 37*(2), 41–48.

Thomas, S. P. (2003). Anger: The mismanaged emotion. *Dermatological Nursing, 15*(4), 351–357.

Thomas, S., & Jefferson, C. (1996). *A woman's guide to empowerment: Use your anger.* New York, NY: Pocket Books.

Watt, B. D., & Howells, K. (1999). Skills training for aggression control: Evaluation of an anger management program for violent offenders. *Legal and Criminological Psychology, 4*(2), 285–300.

Willner, P., Brace, N., & Phillips, J. (2005). Assessment of anger coping skills in individuals with intellectual disabilities. *Journal of Intellectual Disability Research, 49*(5), 329–339.

Willner, P., & Tomlinson, S. (2007). Generalization of anger-coping skills from day-service to residential settings. *Journal of Applied Research in Intellectual Disabilities, 20*(6), 553–562.

Woolgar, M., & Scott, S. (2005). Evidence-based management of conduct disorders. *Current Opinions in Psychiatry, 18*(4), 392–396.

» CHAPTER 11 »
Social Skills Training

Norma J. Stumbo, Ph.D., CTRS and Brad Wardlaw, Ph.D., CTRS

Background/History

Social interaction plays a large role in most people's leisure (Kelly, 1975). Leisure behavior often occurs within social contexts and environments (Iso-Ahola, 1980). Because many leisure situations require the presence of others and the results of these interactions produce pleasant experiences, "social interaction can be both a cause and effect of leisure involvement" (Iso-Ahola, 1980, p. 242). Leisure often activates social interaction and social interaction often produces the positive feelings associated with leisure. Most activities can either be classified as those that are primarily social in nature (such as family gatherings) or those that have social "byproducts" (such as attending sporting events with friends). Stumbo and Peterson (2009) suggested there are four scenarios for social interaction in leisure:

- Activity is the reason for getting together, but social interaction has real meaning (e.g., social dancing).
- Activity has significant meaning, but interaction is essential for successful involvement (e.g., playing bridge)
- Some activities require little social interaction, but enjoyment is increased by interaction (e.g., bowling)
- Activity may be entirely social (e.g., a party).

It is clear in all four situations that adequate and appropriate social interaction skills are necessary for satisfactory leisure participation.

There seems to be consensus among writers in the field that social interaction plays a major role in an individual's perception and evaluation of a leisure experience (Ashton-Schaeffer & Kleiber, 1990; Crandall, 1979; Iso-Ahola, 1980; Kelly, 1975; Peterson & Gunn, 1984; Sneegas, 1989). It follows, then, that an individual must have adequate and appropriate social

skills in order to perform within a leisure or larger life context. However, several authors (Dattilo & Murphy, 1991; Sneegas, 1989; Stumbo, 1995a, 1995b) note that for many individuals with disabilities and/or illnesses, a prevalent problem may be the lack of appropriate social interaction skills. These deficits may affect negatively how they are treated by others and the quality of interpersonal interactions, as well as interfere with other assessments, such as tests of cognitive ability (Gresham, 1983). Thus, direct intervention or treatment is necessary to intervene in what could become a negative downward spiral of reactions and actions (McEvoy, Shores, Wehby, Johnson, & Fox, 1990; Sneegas, 1989; Gresham, 1983). Vandercook (1991) notes that leisure activities provide a natural environment in which to provide social skills instruction.

Social interaction is often a major motivator for participation in leisure activities as well as a great source of satisfaction (Sneegas, 1989). Participation in social leisure activities contributes to overall leisure satisfaction (Crandall, 1979). Because social interaction is such a central part of most leisure experiences, possessing adequate social skills can be seen as a prerequisite for other leisure and life behaviors.

Social Competence Defined

Social competence implies a complex set of skills that can be defined from a variety of viewpoints. There are five basic categories of definitions of social competence. The first kind of definitions of social competence are considered *cognitive-based*, in that they tend to emphasize knowledge or understanding of social relationships, ability to assume other social perspectives or roles, or awareness of interpersonal goals. Cognitive-based definitions tend to emphasize problem solving in social situations (Odom & McConnell, 1985; Shure, 1981). The second type of definitions are *behaviorally based*, implying that people who engage in mutually satisfying social interactions, exhibit social behavior that prevents psychopathology, and display responses that produce positive effects for the interactors are viewed as socially competent (Foster & Ritchey, 1979; Odom & McConnell, 1985, p. 8). The third type of definitions are considered *performance-based* in that a person's social competence is a summary of multiple judgments about that person's behavior in a variety of contexts (Odom & McConnell, 1985, p. 9). The fourth kind of definitions are some *combination* of the above three, such as the one offered by Bailey and Simeonsson (1985, pp. 21–22): "Social competence is thus defined as the infant or preschooler's ability to engage with adults or peers in interactions that (a) either elicit nurturing environmental responses or achieve desired effects; (b) are mutually satisfying to both the child and the person with whom he or she is interacting, and (c) are consistent with the adult expectations for socially competent behavior." Spence (2003) cited Bierman and Welsh (2000) in another combination definition of social competence as "an organizational construct that reflects the child's capacity to integrate behavioral, cognitive, and affective skills to adapt flexibly to diverse social contexts and demands" (p. 84). Lastly, the fifth category advocates *mastery definitions* of social competence. It is important for each therapeutic recreation specialist to understand that the definition s/he selects as most appropriate, impacts the skills to be taught and the method used to teach them. In these, like other forms of life adaptations, the individual makes attempts, learns from what works and what does not, and adjusts his or her attempts until he or she achieves mastery. Regardless of the definition use, it is clear that social skills and social competence are complex notions that need due consideration prior to designing and implementing programs.

Spence (2003, p. 84) noted the complexity of social competence:

> Success in social interactions is determined by many factors relating to the individual, the response of others, and the social context. Social skills represent the ability to perform those behaviors that are important in enabling a person to achieve social competence. . . . These skills include a range of verbal and nonverbal responses that influence the perception and response of other people during social interactions. It is important that individuals are able to adjust the quantity and quality of nonverbal responses such as eye-contact, facial expression, posture, social distance and use of gesture, according to the demands of different social situations. Similarly, verbal qualities such as tone of voice, volume, rate and clarity

of speech significantly influence the impression we make upon others and their reaction to us. These micro-level aspects of social skills are highly important in determining the success of social interactions.

The above remarks begin to shed light on the complexity of social micro-skills, such as nonverbal responses and verbal qualities, that a person must demonstrate to be socially successful. However, she also noted that possession and execution of these micro-skills are not enough to be considered truly socially competent. She continues:

> At the more macro-level, individuals need to be able to integrate these micro-level skills within appropriate strategies for dealing with specific social tasks. For example, success in starting a conversation involves many micro-level social skills in addition to more complex skills such as identifying appropriate moments to initiate the conversation, and so on. The ability to perform these important behavioral social skills is a necessary but insufficient determinant of competent social functioning. (pp. 84–85)

Definitions and observations about the nature of social competence are important in selecting the instructional content and method to teach these skills and assets to clients. In Table 11.1, the examples of therapeutic recreation assessment methods and program delivery are provided to highlight these differences. Each definition focuses on a different set of social skills or evaluations of social interactions that imply distinctive service delivery practices.

There seems to be growing consensus that social competence involves: possessing a variety of knowledges and behaviors that can be utilized and displayed when and where necessary, to engage in meaningful and reciprocal social exchanges, and that result in the person being deemed socially competent (or at least not socially incompetent) (Odom & McConnell, 1985; Trower, 1984). That is, a collection of social skills alone is not sufficient to define social competence, but must also include the person's ability to use them at the "right" time, in the "right" way, and with the "right" people (Odom & McConnell, 1985; Schlundt & McFall, 1985; Trower, 1984). Gresham, Sugai, and Horner (2001), noted: "Social skills are behaviors that must be taught, learned, and performed whereas social competence represents judgments or evaluations of these behaviors [by others] within and across settings" (p. 333, explanation added).

Table 11.1. Five Views of Social Competence

1. Cognitive-based definitions emphasize:	• knowledge or understanding of social relationships • ability to assume other social perspectives or roles or awareness of interpersonal goals • problem-solving in social situations TR would focus on: • social knowledge or awareness • observational ratings of role-played behavior • content including: perspective or role taking, empathic listening, or attainment of interpersonal goals
2. Behavior-based definitions emphasize:	• effectiveness or outcomes of personal interactions • encouraging reciprocal social actions TR would focus on: • behavioral observations of social interactions • outcomes of the interactions and the behaviors or verbal exchanges occurring on the path to these outcomes • helping individuals understand the dynamic nature of interactions and the impact of individual interactions on the outcome of exchanges • helping clients define acceptable ranges of behaviors both for themselves and others
3. Performance- or judgment-based definitions emphasize:	• social competence as a summary of multiple judgments about a person's behavior in a variety of contexts TR would focus on: • recording and comparison of the informed judgment of familiar others who compare the person's demonstration of social behaviors to mastery criteria or normative groups
4. Combination definitions emphasize:	• multiple combinations of above; (e.g., "Social competence is thus defined as the infant or preschooler's ability to engage with adults or peers in interactions that either elicit nurturing environmental responses or achieve desired effects; are mutually satisfying to both the child and the person with whom he or she is interacting; and are consistent with the adult expectations for socially competent behavior," p. 21–22). TR would focus on: • tools and services that contain multiple approaches/goals, in alignment with combination approaches
5. Adaptive behavior or mastery definitions emphasize:	• the individual using defenses and eventually gaining mastery by coping with a variety of individual, stressful situations • gaining mastery by overcoming social frustrations or new events through repeated application of successful adaptive efforts. TR would focus on: • the individual's ability to interact "successfully" by obtaining information, making decisions, interacting with others, and making some degree of independence • assisting the individual in making repeated efforts at some social task, with ongoing modifications, until a successful outcome (mastery) is achieved

Intended Client Groups

Importance of Social Skills Instruction for Individuals with Disabilities

Many individuals with disabilities and/or illnesses lack adequate social interaction skills. For example, they may (a) have low levels of interaction through communication disorders or difficulties; (b) display inappropriate behavior such as loudness or talking to strangers; (c) exhibit high levels of aggression while not being able to channel that anger differently; (d) be viewed as "unskilled," such as not knowing how to ask or what to ask in conversations; or (e) exhibit stereotypic or unusual behaviors, such as private behaviors in public places. As such, this lack (either real or perceived) of social interaction skills puts them at higher risk of future failure because of the interrelationship between social competence and other long-term functions, such as work and leisure participation. The lack of social competence decreases the potential of positives such as (a) landing a job, (b) meeting and socializing with others, (c) social acceptance and friendships, and (d) positive self-regard. It also increases the likelihood of negatives such as (a) mental health problems, (b) dropping out of school, (c) juvenile delinquency, and (d) school maladjustment. This likely is due to the lack of social acceptance by others of individuals who do not provide the *regular, expected patterns of social exchanges* and behaviors (Durlak & Wells, 1997; Sabornie, 1985).

Think about it: on average, society accepts a certain range of social behaviors, but outliers (those outside of the usual patterns) are not usually well accepted. It is hard to identify exactly what constitutes social competence and the lack of social competence, but we know it when we see it. This lack of social acceptance may lead to further outright rejection and social isolation or withdrawal.

Therefore, individuals who lack appropriate social skills may need direct instruction in those skills. Social skills are, in fact, quite teachable in the vast majority of circumstances. Social skills can be taught through a variety of instructional strategies such as positive reinforcement, demonstration, modeling, role-playing, discussion groups, video feedback, homework assignments, etc. Before instruction is designed, a review of the reasons for the original lack of social skills is important. A review of the literature has documented several of these reasons that can be classified under four major headings: (a) lack of social skills in general; (b) inadequate friendship/participation patterns; (c) inadequate life adjustment; and (d) inadequate school/work adjustment. Under each heading, characteristics that may prevent or hinder social competence are given.

Lack of Social Skills in General

Individuals with disabilities:

- may experience skill deficits (i.e., not possessing the skills to interact appropriately with others) and performance-skill deficits (i.e., having the necessary skills but not performing them at the appropriate levels) (Baker & Donelly, 2001; Bullis, Walker, & Sprague, 2001; Chronis, Jones, & Raggi, 2006; Gresham, 1986)
- may lack motivation and cognitive abilities to apply positive social behaviors (Perlmutter, 1986)
- may misread nonverbal communication (Bryan, 1977)

- may lack prerequisite social behavior to be successful with peers (Baker & Donelly, 2001; Kronick, 1978)

Inadequate Friendship/ Participation Patterns

Individuals with disabilities:

- experience low social status among peers without disabilities (Bryan, 1974, 1976; Bruininks, 1978; Chronis et al., 2006; Ray, 1985; Sabornie & Kauffman, 1985, 1987)
- are not well accepted by their class peers without disabilities (Bullis et al., 2001; Sabornie, 1985)
- have fewer friendships than cohorts without disabilities (Zetlin & Murtaugh, 1988)
- experience more loneliness and isolation in school than their peers without disabilities (Luftig, 1988; Sabornie & Thomas, 1989)
- have low participation rates in school-related and out-of-school activities (Deshler & Schumaker, 1983; Sabornie, Thomas, & Coffman, 1989)
- are more likely to express dissatisfaction with their social lives (White, Schumaker, Warner, Alley, & Deshler, 1980)
- are identified as "handicapped" largely because of social skills deficits (Chronis et al., 2006; Epstein, Kauffman, & Cullinan, 1985)
- are denied full integration, even when learning difficulties are taken care of, because of social skills deficits (Chronis et al., 2006; Nelson, 1988)
- (a) interact less frequently and more negatively than children without disabilities; (b) are poorly accepted by their peers without disabilities; and (c) do not model the behaviors of children without disabilities as a result of increased exposure to them (Gresham, 1983).
- can be helped through social skills training as one way to increase the odds that children with disabilities will interact with and be socially accepted by their peers without disabilities (Chronis et al., 2006; Gresham, 1982, p. 430)
- should learn certain social behaviors, such as cooperation, positive peer interaction, sharing, greeting others, asking for and giving information, and making conversation, which are predictive of social acceptance (Asher & Hymel, 1981; Asher, Oden, & Gottman, 1977)

Inadequate Life Adjustment

Children with disabilities and poor interpersonal skills:

- do not generally outgrow their social deficits without direction and extensive intervention and are likely to develop more life-adjustment problems (Michelson & Wood, 1980)
- usually demonstrate academic underachievement, delinquency, poor self-concept, and a variety of other maladaptive processes (Conger & Keane, 1981; Michelson & Wood, 1980)
- may face psychological problems in adulthood (Cowen, Pederson, Babigian, Izzo, & Trost, 1973)
- show tendencies toward juvenile delinquency, dropping out of school, military discharges for bad conduct, adult mental health problems (Goldsmith & McFall, 1975; Roff, Sells, & Golden, 1972; Van Hasselt, Hersen, Whitehill, & Bellack, 1979)

Inadequate School/Work Adjustment

A variety of authors have discussed social skills in relation to school and work adjustment including the following points:

- Poor social skills are often correlated with academic underachievement. (Moote, Smyth, & Wodarski, 1999; Milsom & Glanville, 2010)
- Children with disabilities should be provided with the social skills necessary for peer acceptance before being integrated. (Gresham, 1982)
- Inclusion decisions should be based more upon a child's level of social skills than IQ or academic achievement levels. The bulk of research evidence suggests that social skills are perhaps the most critical variable in evaluating the social outcomes of mainstreaming and inclusion (Asher & Taylor, 1981; Gresham, 1981a, 1982)
- Social skills play a large part in occupational success (hiring and maintaining). (Johnson & Mithaug, 1978)
- Specific social-behavioral competencies such as coping skills, work habits, and peer relationships are clearly linked to students' performance in the mainstream or inclusive environment. (Fad, 1990)
- Research evidence bears out the importance of effective social interaction skills. School, home, and community success are contingent upon the ability to control behavioral excesses and to interact appropriately with other people. (Green, Forehand, Beck, & Vosk, 1980; Ullman, 1957)
- The degree to which pupils with disabilities or disorders interact successfully with individuals without similar disabilities and/or disorders is dependent upon former pupils' behavior improvements and environmental conditions, including public attitudes toward deviant behavior. (Gaylord-Ross & Haring, 1987)

To the greatest degree possible, improving a person's social skills allows him or her to intermingle in society as others do. Dever (1983, 1989) called this "independence":

> Independence is exhibiting behavior patterns appropriate to the behavior settings that are frequented by others of the person's age and social status in such a manner that the individual is not perceived as requiring assistance because of his behavior. In other words, if a person can go where others go, do what they do there, and not look out of place because of his or her behavior, that person would be seen by others as part of the fabric of the community. (Dever, 1989, p. 397)

However, we also acknowledge that work is needed within the larger community for a wider acceptance of "different" social behaviors. Toward this end, Baker and Donelly (2001) suggested that ecological, environmental approaches be given high priority so that all the emphasis is not always or only placed on "remediating" the individual.

> All too often a child's deficits are blamed for unsuccessful friendships and social interactions. Such attitudes contribute to the unsupportive environment that sets many children up for school failure. . . . Knowledge of environmental factors, which are often overlooked when determining the success of an inclusive placement, would assist teachers, principals, and families in creating optimum social and learning opportunities. (p. 82)

Given these criteria and observations, social skills instruction is indicated for a variety of groups. Among these are:

- children without identified disabilities (Lane, Menzies, Barton-Arwood, Doukas, & Munton, 2005; Meier, DiPerna, & Oster, 2006; Durlak, Weissberg, & Pachan, 2010)
- children with disruptive behavior disorders (such as ADHD, conduct disorder, autism spectrum disorders, emotional and behavior disorders, and oppositional defiant disorder) (Cheney, Flower, & Templeton, 2008; Chronis et al., 2006; Cook

et al., 2008; de Boo & Prins, 2007; Gresham, Sugai, & Horner, 2001; Maag, 2005; Preece & Mellor, 2009; Sim, Whiteside, Dittner, & Mellon, 2006)

- children with autism spectrum disorders and Asperger's Syndrome (Beauchamp & Anderson, 2010; Rao, Beidel, & Murray, 2008; White, Koenig, & Scahill, 2007)
- individuals with schizophrenia (Beauchamp & Anderson, 2010; Bellack, 2004; Kurtz & Mueser, 2008)
- individuals with intellectual disabilities (Bielecki & Swender, 2004)
- individuals with traumatic brain injury (Beauchamp & Anderson, 2010; Ylvisaker, Turkstra, & Coelho, 2005)
- young individuals in residential treatment centers (Zimmerman, 2002)
- young individuals who possess social skills but use them in violent, antisocial, and destructive ways (Bullis et al., 2001)

Basic Premises

Like other leisure-related skills mentioned throughout this book, social skills are highly teachable to most individuals and can be taught using the instructional principles and techniques covered in Chapter 6. Carter and Sugai (1988, p. 68) stated: "we must teach many children how to become more socially competent using the same strategies that we use to teach academic skills." Lovitt (1987, p. 213), in speaking about children with learning disabilities [LD], explains "many teachers agree that we can no longer assume that some LD students will acquire social competencies as do some others, therefore, they must be taught those behaviors, just as they are instructed to read, write, and do math."

Elliott and Gresham (1991) identified five reasons for deficient social skills functioning: (a) lack of knowledge, (b) lack of practice/feedback, (c) lack of cues, (d) lack of reinforcement, and (e) interfering problem behaviors. Social skills deficiencies may be due to a *lack of knowledge* necessary to behave in socially appropriate and acceptable ways. There are three types of knowledge deficits: (a) not recognizing appropriate goals for the interaction (e.g., trying to win instead of cooperate); (b) lacking related skills and behavior strategies to reach socially appropriate goals (e.g., lacking group-entry skills); and (c) lacking knowledge of behavior appropriate in special contexts (e.g., lacking ability to read nonverbal social cues).

Lack of opportunities to practice or receive feedback is another reason for social skills deficits. Many interventions may not allow enough practice time for the behavior to be naturalized into the person's repertoire. *Lack of cues or opportunities to exhibit the skills* may also be a problem. Individuals who learn a skill within a certain context (e.g., in training) may not be able to generalize the skill to another context where the cues are different. *Lack of reinforcement* means that individuals do not choose to exhibit a behavior because the environment does not reinforce them for doing so. For example, people may become withdrawn because others in the environment do not react positively to their attempts at interaction. *Presence of interfering behaviors*, such as anxiety, impulsivity, and low self-esteem, may prevent an individual from adequately learning and displaying appropriate social skills.

Smith (1988) emphasizes the role to be played by therapeutic recreation in helping individuals overcome deficits in social skills: "Many learning-disabled children and adults require social tutoring similar to reading tutoring. They also require small-group experiences in social activities, led by a teacher, social worker, drama specialist, or therapeutic recreation leader" (p. 32). Again, many individuals with disabilities do not have the opportunity or means to learn social interaction skills in the same way as their peers without disabilities or illnesses, so direct instruction, often provided by therapeutic recreation specialists must be provided.

The therapeutic recreation specialist has two options for social skills instruction: (1) creating their own, customized social skills activities/programs/curricula, or (2) utilizing commercially available resources or curricula. Before examining this decision, there are multiple decisions that need to be considered and made. For example, one of the factors important to consider before making that decision is reviewing exactly what social skills need to be taught. Previous research and literature may be helpful in guiding that decision.

Cautions and Consideration in Teaching Social Skills

It is clear that often individuals with disabilities and/or illnesses may need assistance and training in learning appropriate social skills for use in school, work, and life environments. However, there are certain cautions and considerations for developing and providing such training. Therapeutic recreation specialists can benefit from the research and experience of other professionals as documented throughout the literature. Some of these cautions and considerations are noted below, with a discussion of devising a training program to follow.

- Research has little evidence that instruction directed at improving student's social competence works over time and across settings. This is often due to the brevity of training (Gresham, Sugai, & Horner, 2001; Maag, 2005; Schloss, Schloss, Wood, & Kiehl, 1986)
- Social interaction is reciprocal and involves social exchanges among individuals. Individuals with disabilities lack socially competent peer models (Nelson, 1988)
- Training must take place in settings with appropriate peers for newly acquired skills to generalize and be maintained (Shores, 1987; Simpson, 1987)
- Exposure to peer models is insufficient—peers without disabilities must be taught to interact back (Hollinger, 1987; McEvoy & Odom, 1987)
- Teaching social skills is very complex. Some considerations include:
  - characteristics of individuals with disabilities including their attitude toward individuals without disabilities
  - characteristics of faculty and staff including attitudes toward inclusion and social interaction programs
  - parent and family variables, including attitudes of parents of children without disabilities
  - environmental characteristics including physical structure and arrangement of schools, homes, and communities
  - social interaction opportunities, programs, curricula, and activities for individuals with disabilities
  - behavioral and social characteristics (e.g., social skills, aberrant responses, management strategies, etc.) of individuals with disabilities (Simpson, 1987)
- The instruction of social skills should target those behaviors that are most likely to generalize to other settings and can be maintained after instruction has ended (Nelson, 1988; Shores, 1987; Simpson, 1987)
- Simply providing for social integration opportunities (physical integration) and informing normally developing peers about disabling conditions and methods of interacting with students with disabilities will not ensure social integration. Teachers must provide direct instruction during

the interaction to increase desired social interaction among normally developing children and those who have disabilities and/or are socially withdrawn (Shores, 1987)
- When peers are taught to initiate and teach social skills to children with disabilities, peers might perceive themselves as teachers instead of friends. The resultant differences in perceived status and power may adversely affect attitudes in social/leisure interactions. This is a vertical rather than horizontal social relationship. Horizontal/equal relationships are needed (Certo & Kohl, 1984; Gaylord-Ross & Haring, 1987)
- Noted problems with simple social skill training and research include:
  - Absence of behaviors equated with absence of skill but act differently in different environments
  - Assumption that person lacking skill is one for targeted intervention alone; probably not paying attention to responses gained from interactions/initiations; teaching individual skills alone may have no enduring effect on the person's ability to use them in other circumstances
  - Most training programs focus on discrete behavior categories, which teacher reinforces, but in fact, teacher may interrupt social exchange (Strain, Odom, & McConnell, 1984)

In general then, for social-skill training to be most effective, it needs to include instruction: (a) that is directed to the most frequently used and important social skills; (b) with individuals likely to be equal, co-interactants; (c) in multiple, naturalized environments; and (d) with a dual focus on both social actions and reactions, as well as (e) generalization and future maintenance of the skills.

Designing Social Skills Interventions

It is clear that a variety of authors agree that direct intervention to improve the social skills of individuals with disabilities often is needed (Andersen, Nelson, Fox, & Gruber, 1988; Gunter, Fox, & Brady, 1984; Howell, 1985; Nelson, 1988; Rule, Stowitschek, Innocenti, Striefel, Killoran, Swezey, & Boswell, 1987; Sabornie, 1985; Simpson, 1987; Vandercook, 1991). Gresham (1982) stated that it is unlikely that individuals with disabilities will experience full social integration and social acceptance without direct intervention from professionals, and he advocated that this intervention happen prior to the inclusion of the individuals with disabilities into the community. Carter and Sugai (1988), Lovitt (1987), and Smith (1988) indicated that the social skills intervention must be treated very much like "academic skills." This implies that individuals with disabilities do not tend to learn social skills through just observation or just from modeling (Gresham, 1982, 1984), and need specific, targeted, and sequential instruction (Carter & Sugai, 1988; Lovitt, 1987; Simpson, 1987; Smith, 1988). Caldarella and Merrell (1997) designed a taxonomy of five broad dimensions of social skills:

- peer relations skills
- self-management skills
- academic skills
- compliance skills
- assertion skills

These five skills areas can be important for delineating which social skills need to be taught to which individuals. In addition, Gresham (1981a, 1981b) noted that there is a difference among acquisition, performance, and fluency deficits. *Acquisition deficits* occur when the person had difficulty uptaking the information. In *performance deficits*, the person has difficulty in demonstrating the behavior. *Fluency deficits* result when a person knows how and wants to perform a given social skill but appears awkward and unpolished in the action. De Boo and Prins (2007), for example, suggested that children with ADHD are "well able to perform social skills, but fail to do so in specific situations" (p. 84), highlighting the difference between acquisition of skills and performance of those same skills. Gresham et al. (2001) also noted that more severe social skills deficits need significantly more intensity, duration, and frequency of training.

Dirks, Treat, and Weersing (2007) reminded social skills instructors that there are four primary factors that influence the assessment and instruction of social skills: person, behavior, situation, and judge. One important consideration when looking at these is that social skills cannot be taught in a vacuum, but must be contextualized within settings, situations, and people. For example, it is not always appropriate to greet unfamiliar people, and training is improved when contextual factors are part of the instruction.

According to Maag (1989, p. 6), the "efficacy of social skills training is related directly to the degree to which assessment methodology promotes a functional analysis of observed performance deficits." In other words, provision of an intervention program mandates: (a) an assessment of social skill deficits, and (b) a

logical link between the assessment and the intervention. At least three models for linking social skill assessment and training exist in the literature.

Elliot and Gresham's Model (1991). The first model was created by Elliott and Gresham (1991). These authors created both an assessment (Social Skills Ratings System [SSRS]) (Gresham & Elliott, 1990) and an intervention package for students with disabilities (Elliott & Gresham, 1991). Their model provides a general framework for streamlining and connecting social skills assessment and training. Using the acronym of DATE, their model includes the following steps for training: Define, Assess, Teach, and Evaluate.

- **Define** and state behaviors in observable terms. In addition, define the conditions (antecedent and consequent) that surround the behavior.
- **Assess** behaviors by using multiple forms of the Social Skills Ratings System (SSRS). Supplement this assessment by direct observations of the student, interviews with teachers and/or parents, and occasionally a structured role-play to confirm deficits and to refine intervention plans.
- **Teach** treatment units and use strategies that fit the student's needs as determined by the assessment results and the classification that best characterizes the student's social skills deficiencies.
- **Evaluate** the effects of the teaching procedures empirically by using the assessment methods by which were selected students for training (Elliott & Gresham, 1991, p. 24)

Accompanying this model is a five-step process that links the assessment procedure and the provision of the training (Elliott & Gresham, 1991). These steps help to explain methods of implementing DATE and include:

1. Establish the need for performing the behavior.
2. Identify the specific behavioral components of the skill or perform task analysis.
3. Model the behavior by using either live or filmed procedures (symbolic modeling or coaching the behavior).
4. Provide behavior rehearsal and response feedback.
5. Generalize training [to other settings and with other people]. (p. 24)

The combination of these two guides helps to identify the types of social skills to be taught, and the methods to be used to teach and generalize the skills.

Sugai and Fabre's Model (1987). Secondly, Sugai and Fabre (1987) provide a Systematic Instructional Model as part of their Behavior Teaching Plan for students with behavior disorders. The model is helpful in designing a systematic, logical plan of instruction and includes the following steps:

1. Assess relevant behaviors.
2. Establish long-term objectives.
3. Establish short-term objectives.
4. Develop and write an instructional plan.
5. Develop and write measurement procedures.
6. Implement the instructional plan and measurement procedures.
7. Modify the plan based on data.
8. Evaluate overall progress.

Two initial concerns of the total model (Sugai & Fabre, 1987) are to provide an operational or measurable description of the major behaviors to be targeted, and then a description of the measurement system used to assess and record behaviors. This model focuses on the ability to appropriately target the skill to be taught and then continually measure the progress of the learner in obtaining the skill. Again, defining the target skill or behavior is important to the implementation of the remainder of the steps.

Stephens' Model (1992). Stephens (1992) provided a third model specifically for assessing and teaching social skills. Although the model is presented visually in Stephens' work as an interactive systems model, the following summarized steps capture the essence of the model.

1. Define the social skill objective.
2. Assess the level of skill either in a natural or contrived situation.
3. If the learner has mastered the skill, move to next skill; if not, move to 3-stage intervention.
4. Intervention: Select a teaching strategy (including social modeling, social reinforcement or contingency contracting)
5. Intervention: Implement teaching strategy.
6. Intervention: Reassess skill level; if at acceptable level, move to next skill; if not select another teaching strategy and re-teach.

Stephens (1992) also concurred that the first step is defining and examining the target behavior. However simplistic this may sound, it is indeed a difficult process to delineate what is meant by social skills and social competence, and conversely, social skills deficits and social incompetence.

These three models can be very useful to the therapeutic recreation specialist. They can help delineate the targeted behavior, both to assess and to teach. Although little research has been conducted by therapeutic recreation professionals concerning social skills programs, we can benefit from incorporating the ideas and research of other disciplines.

At least two process models have been documented in the literature that outline the steps of creating social skills instruction programs. The first is by Lane, Menzies, Barton-Arwood, Doukas, and Munton (2005) and involves six steps. Their six steps, which they propose as an empirically validated method, include:

1. Identify students for participation
2. Identify specific skill deficits and design the intervention program
3. Organize intervention groups
4. Prepare intervention leaders
5. Implement the intervention
6. Monitor student progress

The steps, as suggested by Lane et al. (2005), are useful but they are not as explicit as those provided by Stephens (1978). In Stephens' process model, eight steps are spelled out and provide more detail for fine-tuning instruction. Stephens' model is visually depicted in Figure 11.1 (p. 198) and outlined in Table 11.2 (p. 199). What follows below is a logical process of social-skills design and instruction, suggested by Stephens, infused with comments and research results from other fields. The eight-step process includes:

1. Selecting the group targeted for social skills instruction
2. Selecting the behaviors/skills to be taught
3. Task analyzing the selecting behavior
4. Assessing the degree to which the targeted person(s) possesses the targeted skills
5. If the skill is not exhibited, selecting a teaching strategy
6. Implementing the teaching strategy
7. Reassessing the skill achievement of the person(s)
8. If mastered, targeting the next skill to be learned

Step 1. Select those individuals or groups of clients who:
- demonstrate low levels of social interaction with peers, family, or authority figures
- exhibit abnormally high rates of aggressive or other negative behaviors

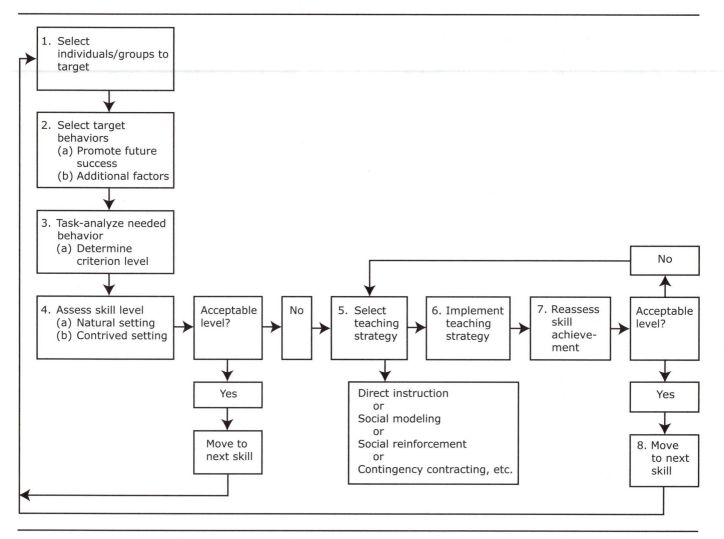

Figure 11.1. Selecting and Teaching Social Skills (adapted from Nelson, 1988; Stephens, 1987; Strain, Odom, & McConnell, 1984)

- are viewed by others as generally "unskilled," "not socially competent," or "socially immature"
- exhibit unusual or stereotypic behavior in social settings (Strain, Odom, & McConnell, 1984)

Step 2. Select target behaviors for social skills instruction that:

- can be acquired or learned in a reasonable period of time (Strain, Odom, & McConnell, 1984)
- can be used when interacting with peers/family outside of agency setting (Strain, Odom, & McConnell, 1984)
- will be effective in gaining positive responses from peers/family (sharing, suggesting play ideas, offering physical assistance, affection behavior) (Shores, 1987; Strain, Odom, & McConnell, 1984)

- terminated past interactions (looking for reducing negative behaviors) (Shores, 1987)
- are group-entry or group-approach behaviors (e.g., identifies a group member, moves close to the group member, imitates the member's behavior; shares an item, asks if can join, suggests a relevant idea) (Strain, Odom, & McConnell, 1984)
- increase the person's social acceptance (asking questions, teaching, offering support) (Strain, Odom, & McConnell, 1984)
- are similar to those of peers without disabilities that are useful and acceptable (Nelson, 1988; Strain, Odom, & McConnell, 1984)
- are considered important to "hopeful friend"—then train in those skills after making behavior template (Strain, Odom, & McConnell, 1984)
- that can be maintained after intervention is terminated (McConnell, 1987; Nelson, 1988)

Table 11.2. Steps to Designing Social Skills Instruction Programs

Step 1. Select those individuals or groups of clients
Step 2. Select target behaviors for social skills instruction
Step 3. Task analyze the selected behavior
Step 4. Assess whether person possesses skills to criterion level
Step 5. If not, select teaching strategy (social modeling, social reinforcement, contingency contracting, demonstration, role playing, etc.)
Step 6. Implement the teaching strategy
Step 7. Reassess person's skill achievement
Step 8. If competent/mastered, move to next skill

- generalize across settings (McConnell, 1987; Nelson, 1988)
- co-vary with specific social behaviors of peers in different situations (McConnell, 1987; Nelson, 1988)
- are not socially acceptable at any level for persons with disabilities (considered deviant behavior) (Nelson, 1988)

Additional factors to consider:

- developmental level of the individual—chronological vs. adaptive age
- primary or secondary disability problems (e.g., communication or speech delays)
- magnitude and type of social skills problems (e.g., withdrawn to aggressive)
- appropriateness to clients' peer group
- appropriateness to clients' culture
- socioeconomic or social class determinants
- gender
- physical environment and orientation of the instructional setting
- continuance of reinforcement from peers (Strain, Odom, & McConnell, 1984)

Step 3. Task-analyze the selected behavior

- determine the specific component tasks of the behavior(s) to be taught
- determine criterion level need to achieve/master social skill

Step 4. Assess whether person possesses skills to criterion level

- in natural setting
- in contrived setting

If the skill level is adequate, the training moves on to the next skill and starts at Step 1 for the new skill (see Figure 11.1)

Step 5. If not, select teaching strategy (social modeling, social reinforcement, contingency contracting, demonstration, role-playing, etc.)

If the skill level is not adequate, a teaching strategy (such as direct instruction, social modeling, social reinforcement or contingency contracting) is devised to teach the social skill.

Step 6. Implement teaching strategy

After the instruction is designed, the program is then implemented and the skill is taught to the client.

Step 7. Reassess person's skill achievement

After the instruction has been implemented for an adequate length of time, the client's skill level is reassessed. If the skill is not mastered, the professional re-creates a teaching strategy that will change (i.e., improve positive or decrease negative) skill(s).

Step 8. If competent/mastered, move to next skill

If the individual skill is mastered at the criterion level, the instruction for that skill is complete, and another skill is selected for instruction. This process may continue until the individual has adequate social skills to interact with peers, family, friends, and people in the community at large.

Appendix 11A (pp. 218–219) of this chapter provides a self-guided worksheet for using the above process in developing a social skills training program. Readers are invited to complete the worksheet in order to more fully comprehend the process.

Packaged Social Skills Programs

The second option is to adhere to pre-packaged social skills programs. While these are generally aimed at children, the therapeutic recreation specialist in any setting may benefit from reviewing their content. Again, a number of factors should be considered prior to use.

For example, the therapeutic recreation programmer needs to determine if the target outcomes of intervention is to eliminate behavioral excesses or remediate social deficits. Does the client need to extinguish certain current behaviors (excesses) or learn to incorporate new behaviors (deficits)? According to Sabornie and Beard (1990), most training programs or curricula focus on providing basic social skills to those individuals with few appropriate responses, by strengthening social behaviors that are not displayed with regularity, and through teaching individuals that situational social problems can be resolved in acceptable ways. However, Lovitt (1987) cautions that many curricula are "one size fits all" and may not contain skills that the instructor considers important, are aimed at children or individuals with specific disabilities, and are designed as discrete instructional units that are taught individually instead of incorporated into a variety of living situations.

Several other selection criteria are found throughout the literature. According to various authorities, considerations for selecting training packages include:

Skills. Skills to be taught are appropriate to group targeted for training (Sabornie & Beard, 1990); are reciprocal and produce positive responses from peers (Nelson, 1988); and are comprehensive enough to have meaning (that is, a great enough variety of social skills to be taught) (Sabornie & Beard, 1990). For example, "Getting Along with Others" (Jackson, Jackson & Monroe, 1983) teaches 17 core social skills, while "Skillstreaming the Adolescent" (Goldstein, Sprafkin, Gershaw, & Klein, 1980) teaches 50 skills.

Approach or Method. Training packages should have a demonstrated research base (Sabornie & Beard, 1990); provide practice sessions and feedback opportunities (Schumaker & Hazel, 1984); and consider the learning characteristics of and the most effective instructional methodologies for the intended user group (Schumaker, Pederson, Hazel, & Meyen, 1983). "Stacking the Deck" (Foxx & McMorrow, 1983) promotes the learning of skills through a game board, while "ASSET" (Hazel, Schumaker, Sherman, Sheldon-Wildgen, 1982) is a more comprehensive program that uses modeling, practice, feedback, reinforcement, and generalization as well as homework, progress notes, and parental evaluation.

Setting. Skills should be taught in the most normalized setting possible; and should be generalized to and maintained in a variety of environments (Nelson, 1988; Sabornie & Beard, 1990). While all resources focus in varying degrees on integrated or naturalized environments, ones such as "Social Skills on the Job (Macro Systems, Inc., 1989) focus specifically on specialized environments like the work place.

Logistics. Packages should be priced at a reasonable cost and be user-friendly (Sabornie & Beard, 1990). Costs of the resources range from under $30,

such as "Skillstreaming in Early Childhood (McGinnis & Goldstein, 1990) to $1,400 for the eight videotape program of "ASSET" (Hazel, Schumaker, Sherman, & Sheldon-Wildgen, 1982).

When possible, the above information has been included in the resource descriptions provided in Appendices 11B through 11D (pp. 220–236), while attempting to maintain page restrictions. The descriptions may be a combination of publisher information and author evaluation. An attempt was made to include a variety of resources to complement the variety of needs in the field; several packages for children and for individuals without disabilities are included as it was felt that most social skills are common among population sub-groups. In all cases, there is more to the package than the content presented, however, the basic premises and ideas are easy to discern. Reviewing these packaged programs may be helpful in developing one's own social skills instruction package and task-analyzing skills to be taught and learned.

The inclusion of a package in the appendix does not imply any approval or quality rating of the source. Likewise, there may be other packages available that are not in the table, and this does not imply disapproval or lack of quality. The best known information at the time of this writing is given with regard to descriptions, publisher location, and price. Potential buyers and reviewers are encouraged to request catalogs and related materials from the companies prior to purchasing. Epstein and Cullinan (1987) suggest that, until more research can be conducted on each of these resources, purchasers use their experience and common sense as the best guidelines.

Related Research

Meier, DiPerna, and Oster (2006) conducted a study to determine which social skills teachers felt were important for elementary school children. The result of the 50 teachers' ratings indicated that cooperation and self-control were more important than assertion. The 11 specific skills they rated highly included: (a) controls temper with peers, (b) gets along with people, (c) responds appropriately when hit, (d) ignores peer distractions, (e) responds to peer pressure, (f) follows directions, (g) attends to instructions, (h) cooperates with peers, (i) controls temper with adults, (j) uses free time acceptably, and (k) uses time appropriately. For those therapeutic recreation specialists working with children, these eleven skills may be priorities for social skills instruction.

Cowart, Saylor, Dingle, and Mainor (2004) studied 196 public school students from kindergarten to eighth grade. For analyses, they divided their sample into three groups, those with no diagnosis, those with ADHD, and those with a disability other than ADHD, and queried their parents about the students' social skills and recreation preferences. Their results demonstrated that all three groups significantly differed from one another in all four social skills (responsibility, assertiveness, cooperation, and self-control), with those students with no diagnosis rating higher than student disabilities other than ADHD, who rated higher than students with ADHD. No significant differences in recreation preferences were found between the three groups of children. In the total sample, more positive social skills scores were associated with more active recreation, arts, volunteer work, and clubs/camps. Volunteer work is the one activity preference that most strongly related to better social skills. Several other relationships were found for the three sub-samples.

The following short descriptions represent just a tip of the iceberg of a multitude of social skills research studies. Each study that follows was included because it sheds some light on how to better design, implement and/or evaluate social skills instruction.

Children with Behavior Disorders

Mikami (2010) conducted an analysis of 7 studies about friendship in ADHD. In 5 of the 7 studies analyzed, the researcher reported that youth with ADHD had fewer friendships or lower friendship stability than those in comparison groups. The researcher suggested that developing social skills in regards to self-disclosure, expressing caring and admiration, and feeling comfortable with intimacy in fostering close friendships would improve stability in developing friendships. The researcher identified 3 components that need to be addressed in friendship intervention strategies to improve the likelihood that it is successful. These include (a) consideration of selection of friends, (b) focus on specific friendship behaviors in key situations, and (c) high parental involvement.

Corkum, Corbin, and Pike (2010) conducted an evaluation of a school based social skills program for children with ADHD. The program, called Working Together: Building Children's Social Skills Through Folk Literature, was delivered in 3 schools to 16 children over a 10-week period. Students, parents and teachers were used as data sources. Intervention skills addressed in the program included: (a) making conversation, (b) introducing oneself, (c) making positive statements about others, (d) speaking assertively, (e) using courtesy words, (f) asking for help, (g) offering and giving help, (h) giving and accepting criticism, (i) joining a play activity, and (j) negotiating conflict. Results of the study demonstrated that the program was effective in improving social skills in students with ADHD.

Cook et al. (2008) conducted a meta-analysis of several meta-analyses studies, involving thousands of children. They found that social skills training is an effective intervention in that two-thirds of students with emotional/behavioral disorders (EBD) benefit significantly from the training. Without the social skills instruction, only a third of children with EBD improved. They concluded that social skills training needed to be customized to the skill deficits of the individuals, but given the future implications of gaining social competence and living a more successful life, instruction was warranted and important.

Maag (2006) conducted an analysis of 13 studies on social skills training for youth with emotional and behavioral disorders. He concluded that studies often showed a lack of generalization past the training time and environment, lack of valid and reliable social skills assessment instruments and techniques, and lack of treatment fidelity (organization and consistency). He concludes with six recommendations for future research: (a) development of social skills training that can be conducted by school personnel without outside assistance, (b) focus on students who are neglected as well as those rejected by peers, (c) generalization strategies should be built into the program itself, (d) implementing assessments that focus on performance deficits of the individuals under study, (e) extending intervention duration, and (f) studying the differential efficacy on students of various academic deficiencies.

Preece and Mellor (2009) conducted a two-treatment group study with adolescents with severe behavior disorders. "The Tough Kid" program was utilized but extended from the original 8-week program to a 14-week, 1-hour-per-week program. The children were assessed prior to start-up, at weeks 5 and 10, immediately following the conclusion of the program, and at a 6-month follow-up. Four sources (parents, teachers, independent observers, and the children themselves) were used as data sources. They found that learning, over time, was not consistent nor in an upward angle, with some children's learning declining, some increasing, and some hitting peaks and valleys. They concluded that this study, while not suggesting an ideal length or number of training sessions, did verify the need for using various sources, settings, and methods of evaluation of social skills, as well as further research.

De Boo and Prins (2007) conducted a systematic review of social skills intervention programs for children with ADHD. They used six studies to conclude that social skills training for this group, while not being empirically validated, is promising but needs to acknowledge that social skills deficits are cognitively, socially, behaviorally, and emotionally based.

> The social problems of children with ADHD cannot be fully understood as the result of a lack of social skills. They are associated with a wide range of cognitive and emotional deficiencies, including cognitive distortions in social information processing . . . executive dysfunctions . . . and emotional deregulations. . . . Therefore, cognitive behavioral interventions (i.e., problem solving, self-control, emotional regulation) are conceptually better linked to the social problems of children with ADHD than purely behavioral interventions. (p. 91)

Sim et al. (2006) completed a study on the effects of a social skills and anger management program for 71 children with identified mental health difficulties. They found the 12-week therapy program, which included sessions with parents, decreased outward displays of poor social skills and improved their ability to play well with other children. They suggested that treatments be focused on specific social skill deficits, that instruction include parents, and that additional work be conducted on assessments to improve their reliability and validity.

Olmeda and Kauffman (2003) conducted a systematic review of research related to racial/ethnic differences and their impact on social skills training outcomes for African American youth with emotional and behavioral disturbances. Even though they document many ways in which social behaviors of African Americans differ from Caucasians, they noted that no study specifically addressed these differences in assessment, design, implementation, and outcome measurement. They suggested that researchers pay closer attention to the sociocultural *contextual* factors of the trainees. Instead of combining trainees of all backgrounds together, they encouraged researchers also to delineate factors that "will help improve their ability to understand both cultural minority and majority social norms" (p. 118). Among the differences in norms they noted was that verbal expressions of African Americans is more likely to be emotional, confrontational, and interpersonal; typical nonverbal expressions were less eye contact, more emphasis placed on physical expressiveness, and preference for closer personal space.

Again, these are just a few of the factors they recommended to be considered in creating and researching social skills studies.

Durlak and Wells (1997) performed a meta-analysis on 177 outcome studies of social skills training programs involving youth with mental health difficulties. They found that the treatment conditions produced beneficial, positive outcomes and reduced negative, disruptive behaviors. One of their conclusions focused on the fact that most social skills training programs produced positive effects for the participants and resulted in few, if any, negative side effects.

Individuals with Schizophrenia

A meta-analysis of social skills training effects for people with schizophrenia was conducted by Kurtz and Mueser (2008). Their study supported the use of social skills training and reported that effect sizes of performing positive social skills were highly significant, in the moderate range, and consistent across studies. They also found that negative symptoms were also reduced. "Taken together, these findings show strong evidence for the generalization of social skills training interventions from the training environment to the more complex spheres of everyday living" (p. 495). They also concluded that social skills instruction did not reduce psychiatric symptoms and that better designed training programs had larger effects.

Bellack (2004), in investigating the efficacy of social skills training as one intervention among others for individuals with schizophrenia, concluded that such training has the most support, although it targets a byproduct, not the actual cause of schizophrenia. His review suggested that the most successful interventions were those that included: (a) emphasis on behavioral rehearsal, rather than conversation to change behavior, (b) shaping behavior toward more competent performance, and (c) adjusting therapeutic goals and interactions to align with cognitive impairment and various degrees of motivation.

Individuals with Intellectual Disabilities

Cheng and Chen (2010) studied the effects of using a three-dimensional emotion system intervention on subjects with intellectual and developmental disabilities in learning socially based emotions in social contexts. The intervention program provides three-dimensional character representations of four emotions (happiness, anger, sadness, and fear). The program works in three stages. Stage 1 allows the participant to recognizes the emotion the three-dimensional character is representing. In Stage 2, the three-dimensional character is placed in a social context and with thinking bubbles providing hints, the subject tries to identify the emotion that is occurring. Stage 3 allows the participants to determine in what social situation the emotion displayed by the three-dimensional character most likely would occur. The three subjects participated in the training one day a week for 40 minutes for a period of five weeks. Results showed that each of three subjects improved social-emotional competence during the intervention, however two subjects were unable to maintain the improvement in follow up sessions.

Bielekci and Swender (2004) conducted a literature review of promising practices in assessment of social skills for individuals with intellectual disabilities. They noted that:

> Research demonstrates that there is an established relationship between social skills and maladaptive behaviors, but because the data is correlational, it is unclear if social skills deficits result in problem behaviors or if the presence of maladaptive behaviors results in social impairments. (p. 695)

They further reviewed the strengths and weaknesses of behavioral observations, role-playing scenarios, and checklists and rating scales, such as:

- American Association of Mental Deficiency's (AAMD—now the American Association of Intellectual and Developmental Disability, AAIDD) Adaptive Behavior Scale [this scale was newly released in 2010, see Resources section of this chapter],
- Vineland Adaptive Behavior Scales (VABS; Sparrow, Galla, & Cicchetti, 1984a, 1984b, 1985),

and social skills measures such as:

- Social Performance Survey Schedule (SPSS) (Lowe & Cautela, 1978; Matson, Helsel, Bellack, & Senatore, 1983)
- the Matson Evaluation of Social Skills for Individuals with Severe Retardation (MESSIER) (Matson, 1994), and the
- Assessment of Social Competence (ASC) (Meyers, Schleser, Cooke, & Cuvillier, 1985)

Bielecki and Swender (2004) advocated the use of scales such as the MESSIER and the SPSS, while advocating for more and better research, especially in the area of developing assessment norms for children with intellectual disability.

Individuals with Learning Disabilities

Kavale and Mostert (2004) completed a meta-analysis of 53 studies that examined 2,113 subjects, with an average age of 11.5 years old. In the reviewed studies, students with learning disabilities evaluated their gain in social skills higher than peers or teachers did. The authors noted that students with learning disabilities felt their social status was elevated due to the training, but actual interaction with peers was not increased. Likewise, peers without learning disabilities did not appear to alter their perspectives about the lowered social status of the peers with learning disabilities, although they did report being more open to integration. Teachers rated the students with learning disabilities as better adjusted and less dependent, although hyperactivity and academic success were not positively affected. Like other investigators using meta-analysis, they commented on the variability of social skills programs, differing assessment measures, and multiple conceptual limitations in social skills training programs. They noted that social skills training needs to become more systematic to move from being 'promising' to 'efficacious.'

Children with Autism Spectrum Disorders

White et al. (2010) examines a cognitive-behavioral intervention program geared towards reducing anxiety and social deficits in youth with ASD. The Multimodal Anxiety and Social Skills Intervention (MASSI) is designed for youth aged 12–17 with ASD and anxiety. The program is divided into three treatment modalities: individual therapy, group therapy, and parental involvement. The researchers also review the nine essential elements of the program which include: (a) parent and family involvement, (b) regular practice, (c) immediate, direct, and specific feedback, (d) emphasis on corrective, positive social learning experiences, (e) modeling new skills, (f) psychoeducational and explicit teaching about ASD and anxiety, (g) structured delivery, (h) therapeutic rapport, and (i) integration of creative, alternative, and varied teaching strategies.

Duncan and Klinger (2010) discussed effective social skill strategies for youth with ASD and implementation in group, school, and community settings. Strategies included: incidental teaching, social stories and scripts, role plays, self-monitoring, peer education, and peer buddies. After reviewing each strategy in depth, they recommend that research is needed to develop and assess efficacy of these intervention strategies.

Lu, Peterson, Lacroix, and Rousseau (2010) investigated the effects of a sandplay program on communication and social interaction in children with ASD.

Twenty-five subjects with an average age of 9.9 took part in the 10 week program. Each session occurred one time a week and lasted 60 minutes. Sessions consisted of an opening ritual, a sandplay period, a storytelling period and closing ritual. Findings showed the participants increased verbal communication, engaged and sustained social interaction, and increased play interactions.

Video modeling is an another intervention strategy used to improve social skills in youth with ASD. Tetreault and Lerman (2010) examined the use of video modeling to teach three youth with ASD to initiate and maintain a conversation. Results of the study showed that video modeling was effective for two of the participants while the third participant needed additional prompts to increase social initiation.

Walker, Barry, and Bader (2010) studied parental and therapist perception changes in social skill behaviors in youth with ASD following a summer treatment camp. The study examined social skills ratings of 12 children diagnosed with ASD who attended a four-week summer camp that focused on peer interaction and social skill development. Findings revealed that parents and therapists perceived improvement in verbal communication, social interaction, attention to task, and transitions.

Rao et al. (2008) noted a number of social skill difficulties for children with autism or Asperger's Syndrome. These include: lack of orientation towards a social stimuli and inadequate use of eye contact, problems initiating social interactions, difficulty interpreting both verbal and nonverbal social cues, inappropriate emotional response, lack of empathy toward others' distress, sharing affective experiences, and understanding the perspective of others. After systematically reviewing a number of other studies, they recommended that tighter treatment protocols and stronger research designs are needed to demonstrate efficacy and generalizations outside of the treatment setting.

White et al. (2007) conducted a systematic review of 14 studies that met their inclusion criteria and came up with a number of promising social skills instruction practices. Table 11.3 lists the goals and accompanying strategies. Chronis et al. (2006) also conducted a systematic review of interventions that work with individuals with ADHD and concluded also that social skills training programs, while not completely "evidence-based," should be considered as promising practices.

Table 11.3. Promising Social Skills Instruction Strategies for Children with Autism Spectrum Disorders (White et al., 2007, p. 1864)

Goal	Strategies
Increase social motivation	• Foster self-awareness and self-esteem • Develop nurturing, fun environment • Intersperse new skills with previously mastered skills • Start with simple, easily learned skills (errorless teaching)
Increase social initiation	• Make social rules clear and concrete (e.g., stay one arm's length from other person) • Model age-appropriate initiation strategies • Use natural reinforcers for social initiations (e.g., follow child's conversation lead/interest) • Teach simple social scripts for common situations
Improve appropriate social responding	• Teach social response scripts • Reinforce response attempts • Use modeling and role-play to teach social skills
Reduce interfering behaviors	• Making teaching structured and predictable • Differentially reinforce positive behaviors • Keep behavior charts (e.g., checkmarks or stars) for positive behavior • Review socially appropriate and inappropriate behaviors of the participants as a group, via video or audiotape segments
Promote skill generalization	• Orchestrate peer involvement (e.g., prompting and initiating social interactions, physical proximity) • Use multiple trainers and individuals with which to practice skills • Involve parents in training • Provide opportunities to practice skills in safe, natural settings (e.g., field trips) • Use time between sessions to practice skills (e.g., via homework)

Application to Therapeutic Recreation

Discussions about the necessity of teaching social skills for successful participation are found often in the therapeutic recreation literature, including service models, articles, and textbooks. For example, Sneegas (1989) discussed the complexities of social skills within leisure contexts and provided examples of client goals and interventions using the Leisure Ability Model as a foundation. Stumbo (1994/95, 1995a, 1995b) provided extensive listings of resources on social skills assessment and instruction that could be applied to therapeutic recreation programs. Schleien, Green, and Stone (2003) discussed the need for true friendship among those with and without disabilities and the need for inclusive community recreation programs and facilities that are inviting, accessible, and advocate true inclusion.

Others, such as Bedini and Henderson (1993/94), Mactavish and Schleien (2000), and Khemthong, Packer, Passmore, and Dhaliwal (2008) studied social support or social leisure as a larger concept within individuals' lives, but not the effects of social skills instruction/intervention specifically.

Among the groups for which social skills training is advocated include:

- individuals with intellectual disabilities (Coyne, 1980a, 1980b; Kleinert, Miracle, & Sheppard-Jones, 2007; LeConey, Devine, Bunker, & Montgomery, 2000)
- individuals with autism spectrum disorders (Coyne & Fullerton, 2004; Fullerton & Coyne, 1999; Schleien, Heyne, & Berken, 1988)
- individuals with schizophrenia (Finnell, Card, & Menditto, 1997; Pestle, Card, & Menditto, 1998; Mueller & Roder, 2005)
- individuals with persistent mental illnesses (Skalko, 1991)
- individuals with intellectual disabilities (Ashton-Shaeffer & Kleiber, 1990; Green & Schleien, 1991)
- children with behavior disorders (Rothwell, Piatt, & Mattingly, 2006)

Green and Schleien (1991) reported on a study of friendships involving 11 adults with intellectual disabilities residing in an intermediate-care facility. Their results concluded that:

- Adults with intellectual disabilities living in community residential facilities often do not develop meaningful, reciprocal relationships with peers without disabilities.
- The individuals in the study did not make new friends during recreation participation in the community.
- Social skills shown by these individuals in this investigation were likely not the same skills that need to be exhibited to be successfully integrated into community environments.

They concluded:

The development of friendships should be considered a high priority. Not only does friendship contribute to one's quality of life, but the intimacy and support provided through friendship has been demonstrated to contribute to physical and mental well-being. It is through recreation, however, with an emphasis on freedom of choice, that friendship development can flourish. For these reasons, therapeutic recreation specialists and community recreation professionals have an obligation to serve as catalysts for social integration. (p. 38)

Ashton-Shaeffer and Kleiber (1990) conducted a study of the parents and/or caregivers of individuals with intellectual disabilities who participated in the special recreation programs in Illinois. The results showed that individuals involved in the special recreation programs scored higher on social and communication skills, as well as personal living, and community living skills. However, in general they did not find that additional participation significantly increased these scores. Overall they concluded that participation in special recreation programs did improve the functional skills of the participants.

Loy and Dattilo (2000) used a single-subject research design to study the social interactions between a boy with Asperger's Syndrome and six of his peers in free play, cooperative games, and competitive games. They found that cooperative games yielded the highest rates of both positive and negative social interactions. They noted that simple involvement in games and activities did not teach social skills (that is, they are not direct instruction), but games and activities, especially those that promote social interaction, could be used as a context for children's practice of social interaction skills.

Dattilo, Williams, and Cory (2003) conducted research on the effects of a computerized leisure education program on the attainment of social skills by three boys (ages 6-15 years) with intellectual disabilities.

The researchers used a single-subject multiple baseline across participant study design. At the beginning of the study, the participants tested below 60% on the social skills criteria. During the program, the participants experiences a gradual acceleration in scores until they achieved at least two consecutive sessions at 80% of the criteria. Follow-up scores were taken at six weeks post-intervention and found to be similar to the post-test scores (80%). The study provided support for the computerized leisure education program, showing adequate skill retention at six-weeks post-intervention.

Rothwell, Piatt, and Mattingly (2006) conducted an evaluation of an outpatient program aimed at improving the social competence of children with behavior disorders. The recreation therapy program included social skills instruction, leisure education, and self-esteem. They concluded that the program had a positive impact on the social skills of the 15 individuals involved over the nine-month duration of the data collection. They also noted that, since social skills are so fundamental to leisure involvement and peer acceptance, instruction in appropriate social interactions "may be one of the most important interventions for children with mental disorders" (p. 251).

McKenney, Dattilo, Cory, and Williams (2004) studied the effects of a computerized therapeutic recreation social skills program on the knowledge acquisition of four adolescent males (ages 11–12 years) with emotional and/or behavioral disorders. A computerized game, featuring a cavewoman confronted with various social situations, was used as the intervention and the Social Interaction in Leisure Assessment was used for pre and post-test, and follow-up testing purposes. Three of the four boys improved their scores almost immediately, with the fourth participant gaining knowledge by the ninth day. Follow-up scores at five weeks nearly mirrored post-test scores. The authors reported that the intervention was successful for gaining immediate knowledge for three of the boys, with eventual achievement and maintenance (at five weeks) of the learning criteria.

Mueller and Roder (2005) conducted a treatment-control group study of 70 inpatients and outpatients with schizophrenia, examining functional skills, recreation skills, neurocognition, general social skills, and well-being. The recreation therapy program consisted of group therapy, individual therapy, in vivo exercises, and homework assignments. They used a specific "manualized" program (that is, one that has a very specific implementation strategy laid out in manual form) that contained four areas of content: (a) cognitive orientation, (b) individual goal attainment, (c) training in specific social skills, and (d) coping with difficulties. They found that, after the intervention, the treatment group scored better on psychopathology and recreation skill measures, and both treatment and control groups scored better on neurocognition, general social skills, and well-being. They also concluded that recreation skills were significantly associated with therapy motivation, general social functioning, negative symptoms, and intelligence. Among other results, the authors summarized their findings: "It is evident that the recreational therapy program targets unmet needs of schizophrenia patients, such as leisure activities and contacts. Additionally, increased leisure activities are strongly associated with higher quality of life" (p. 18).

Pestle, Card, and Menditto (1998) completed a study using a time-series design with repeated measures in evaluating the effects of a social-learning program that took place over five, 3-month periods, for a total of 15 months for six individuals with chronic schizophrenia. They found the social learning program improved residents' appropriate social behavior over time, and they advocated these skills as foundational for future participation and success in community life.

Resources

The Tough Kids. (1995). By Sheridan. *Social skills training program* [book]. Longmont: Sopris West.

Student Risk Screening Scale. (1994). By Drummond. Mass screening tool used to identify elementary students at risk for antisocial behavior. Items in seven categories: (a) steals, (b) lies, cheats, sneaks, (c) behavior problems, (d) peer rejection, (e) low achievement, (f) negative attitude, (g) aggressive behavior.

Social Skills Rating System. (1990). By Gresham & Elliott. Method to identify first-grade students who lack social skills; comprehensive approach to assess social skills.

Social Skills Intervention Guide: Practical Strategies for Social Skills Training (1991). By Elliott & Gresham. Provides lesson plans.

The following is from the AAIDD website:

Diagnostic Adaptive Behavior Scale
AAIDD's new Diagnostic Adaptive Behavior Scale (DABS) will provide a comprehensive standardized assessment of adaptive behavior. Designed for use with individuals from 4 to 21 years old, DABS provides precise diagnostic information around the cutoff point

where an individual is deemed to have "significant limitations" in adaptive behavior. The presence of such limitations is one of the measures of intellectual disability.

- AAIDD is seeking volunteers to conduct interviews and help with the development of DABS!
- Download a recruitment response form.
- Adaptive behavior is the collection of conceptual, social, and practical skills that all people learn in order to function in their daily lives. DABS measures these three domains:
  - Conceptual skills: literacy; self-direction; and concepts of number, money, and time
  - Social skills: interpersonal skills, social responsibility, self-esteem, gullibility, naïveté (i.e., lack of wariness), social problem solving, following rules, obeying laws, and avoiding being victimized
  - Practical skills: activities of daily living (personal care), occupational skills, use of money, safety, health care, travel/transportation, schedules/routines, and use of the telephone

The DABS focuses on the critical "cut-off area" for the purpose of ruling in or ruling out a diagnosis of intellectual disability or related developmental disability. Professionals likely to use it include school psychologists, forensic psychologists, clinical psychologists, psychometricians, social workers, occupational therapists, and pediatricians, as well as officials in disability-related government agencies.

The purpose of establishing a diagnosis of intellectual disability is to determine eligibility for:

- special education services
- home and community-based waiver services
- social Security Administration benefits
- specific treatment within the criminal justice system (e.g., In 2002, the U.S. Supreme Court ruled in *Atkins v. Virginia* that executing the mentally retarded violates the Eighth Amendment's ban on cruel and unusual punishment)

Example Activities

Social Skills Scenarios and Role-Plays

Create several leisure scenarios that require the application of social skills, and after initial instruction, ask clients to role-play to display both appropriate and inappropriate social skills. Have the small group discuss each role-play, guiding them toward positive and assertive interactions. Two example of scenarios include:

1. You and a close friend are going out to a movie. The friend selects a new movie that just opened. When you arrive, you see the movie is rated R and you would rather not see it. What would you do? What actions would you take?
2. You have just been out of substance abuse treatment for two weeks and your friends ask you to go out Saturday night to the local club, a place for singles to meet. You do not think you are ready to resist the temptation of drinking; what is your response? What actions do you take?

Social Skills Grid
(Jackson, Jackson, & Monroe, 1983)

Create a 4 by 4 grid on a large sheet of paper or on a white board. Down the left hand side, write four leisure skills, such as "greet a person," "offer to help," or "take turns." Across the top, write different groups of people, such as family, friends, peers, and the community at large. Ask individuals or a small group to fill in the boxes with how they would perform the skill with that particular group. For example, how would the person "greet" a "family member?" This is especially useful when the individual or small group needs to learn that social skills sometimes co-vary by the situation or persons involved.

References

Andersen, M., Nelson, L. R., Fox, R. G., & Gruber, S. E. (1988). Integrating cooperative learning and structured learning: Effective approaches to teaching social skills. *Focus on Exceptional Children, 20*(9), 1–8.

Armstrong, S. W., & McPherson, A. (1991). Homework as a critical component in social skills instruction. *Teaching Exceptional Children, 24*(1), 45–47.

Armstrong, S. W., Mulkerne, S., & McPherson, A. (1988). *Socially appropriate and inappropriate development (SAID): Social skills assessment and instructional program.* Birmingham, AL: EBSCO Curriculum Materials.

Asher, S. R., & Hymel, S. (1981). Children's social competence in peer relations: Sociometric and behavioral assessment. In J. D. Wine & M. D. Smye (Eds.), *Social competence*, (pp. 125–157). New York, NY: Guilford Press.

Asher, S. R., Oden, S. L., & Gottman, J. M. (1977). Children's friendships in school settings. In L. G. Katz (Ed.), *Current topics in early childhood education* (Vol. 1, pp. 33–61). Norwood, NJ: Albex.

Asher, S. R., & Taylor, A. R. (1981). The social outcomes of mainstreaming: Sociometric assessment and beyond. *Exceptional Education Quarterly, 1*(4), 13–30.

Ashton-Schaeffer, C., & Kleiber, D. A. (1990). The relationship between recreation participation and functional skill development in young people with mental retardation. *Annual in Therapeutic Recreation, 1*, 75–81.

Bailey, D. B., & Simeonsson, R. J. (1985). A functional model of social competence. *Topics in Early Childhood Special Education, 4*(4), 20–31.

Baker, K., & Donelly, M. (2001). The social experiences of children with disability and the influence of environment: A framework for intervention. *Disability and Society, 16*(1), 71–85.

Beauchamp, M. H., & Anderson, V. (2010). SOCIAL: An integrative framework for the development of social skills. *Psychological Bulletin, 136*(1), 39–64.

Bedini, L. A., & Henderson, K. A. (1993/94). Interdependence, social support, and leisure: Describing the experiences of women with physical disabilities. *Annual in Therapeutic Recreation, 4*, 96–107.

Bellack, A. S. (2004). Skills training for people with severe mental illness. *Psychiatric Rehabilitation Journal, 27*(4), 375–391.

Bellack, A. S., Mueser, K. T., Gingerich, S., & Agresta, J. (2004). *Social skills training for schizophrenia: A step-by-step guide* (2nd ed.). New York, NY: Guilford Press.

Bielecki, J., & Swender, S. L. (2004). The assessment of social functioning in individuals with mental retardation: A review. *Behavior Modification, 28*(5), 694–708.

Bierman, K. L., & Welsh, J. A. (2000). Assessing social dysfunction: The contributions of laboratory and performance-based measures. *Journal of Clinical Child Psychology, 29*, 526–539.

Bond, G. R., & Campbell, K. (2008). Evidence-based practices for individuals with severe mental illness. *Journal of Rehabilitation, 74*(2), 33–44.

Bormaster, J. S., & Treat, C. L. (1982). *Talking, listening, communicating: Building interpersonal relationships.* Austin, TX: Pro-Ed.

Brown, L., & Hammill, D. D. (1990). *Behavior rating profile* (2nd ed.). Austin, TX: Pro-Ed.

Brown, L., & Leigh, J. E. (1986). *Adaptive behavior inventory.* Odessa, FL: Psychological Assessment Resources.

Bruininks, R. H., Rynders, J. E., & Gross, J. C. (1974). Social acceptance of mildly retarded pupils in resource rooms and regular classes. *American Journal of Mental Deficiency, 78*, 377–383.

Bruininks, V. L. (1978). Actual and perceived peer status of learning disabled students in mainstream programs. *The Journal of Special Education, 12*(1), 51–58.

Bryan, T. (1974). Peer popularity of learning disabled children. *Journal of Learning Disabilities, 7*, 621–625.

Bryan, T. (1976). Peer popularity of learning disabled children: A replication. *Journal of Learning Disabilities, 9*, 307–311.

Bryan, T. (1977). Learning disabled children's comprehension of nonverbal communication. *Journal of Learning Disabilities, 10*(8), 501–506.

Bullis, M., Walker, H. M., & Sprague, J. R. (2001). A promise unfulfilled: Social skills training with at-risk and antisocial children and youth. *Exceptionality, 9*(1&2), 67–90.

Burns, M. K., & Ysseldyke, J. E. (2009). Reported prevalence of evidence-based instructional practices in special education. *Journal of Special Education, 43*(1), 3–11.

Burstein, N.D. (1986). The effects of classroom organization on mainstreamed preschool children. *Exceptional Children, 52*(5), 425–434.

Caldarella, P., & Merrell, K. (1997). Common dimensions of social skills of children and adolescents: A taxonomy of positive behaviors. *School Psychology Review, 26*(2), 264–278.

Camp, B. W., & Bash, M. A. S. (1985a). *Think aloud: Increasing social and cognitive skills—A problem-solving program for children—Classroom program.* Champaign, IL: Research Press.

Camp, B. W., & Bash, M. A. S. (1985b). *Think aloud: Increasing social and cognitive skills—A problem-solving program for children—Small group program.* Champaign, IL: Research Press.

Carter, J., & Sugai, G. (1988). Teaching social skills. *Teaching Exceptional Children, 20*(3), 68–71.

Cartledge, G., & Kleefeld, J. (1991). *Taking part: Introducing social skills to children.* Circle Pines, MN: American Guidance Service.

Cartledge, G., & Milburn, J. F. (1986). (Eds.). *Teaching social skills to children: Innovative approaches.* (2nd ed.). Boston, MA: Allyn and Bacon.

Cautela, J. R., Cautela, J., & Esonis, S. (n.d.). *Forms for behavioral analysis with children.* Champaign, IL: Research Press.

Certo, N., & Kohl, F. L. (1984). A strategy for developing interpersonal interaction instructional content for severely handicapped students. In N. Certo, N. Haring, & R. York (Eds.), *Public school integration of severely handicapped students: Rational issues and progressive alternatives* (pp. 221–224). Baltimore, MD: Brookes.

Cheney, D., Flower, A., & Templeton, T. (2008). Applying response to intervention metrics in the social domain for students at risk of developing emotional or behavioral disorders. *Journal of Special Education, 42*(2), 108–126.

Cheng, Y., & Chen, S. (2010). Improving social understanding of individuals of intellectual and developmental disabilities through a 3D-facial expression intervention program. *Research in Developmental Disabilities, 31*(6), 1434–1442.

Chronis, A. M., Jones, H. A., & Raggi, V. L. (2006). Evidence-based psychosocial treatments for children and adolescents with attention-deficit/hyperactivity disorder. *Clinical Psychology Review, 26*(4), 486–502.

Cone, J. D. (1984). *Pyramid scales: Criterion-referenced measures of adaptive behavior in severely handicapped persons.* Austin, TX: Pro-Ed.

Conger, J. C., & Keane, S. P. (1981). Social skills intervention in the treatment of isolated or withdrawn children. *Psychological Bulletin, 90*(3), 478–495.

Consulting Psychologists Press. (n.d.). *Factor tests of social intelligence.* Palo Alto, CA: Author.

Cook, C. R., Gresham, F. M., Kern, L., Barreras, R. B., Thornton, S. & Crews, S. D. (2008). Social skills training for secondary students with emotional and/or behavioral disorders. *Journal of Emotional and Behavioral Disorders, 16*(3), 131–144.

Corkum, P., Corbin, N., & Pike, M. (2010). Evaluation of a school-based social skills program for children with attention deficit/hyperactivity disorder. *Child and Family Behavior Therapy, 32*(2), 139–151.

Cowart, B. L., Saylor, C. F., Dingle, A., & Mainor, M. (2004). Social skills and recreational preferences of children with and without disabilities. *North American Journal of Psychology, 6*(1), 27–41.

Cowen, E. L., Pederson, A., Babigian, H., Izzo, L. D., & Trost, M. A. (1973). Long-term follow-up of early detected vulnerable children. *Journal of Consulting and Clinical Psychology, 41*(3), 438–446.

Coyne, P. (1980a). Developing social skills in the developmentally disabled adolescent and young adult: A recreation and social/sexual approach. *Journal of Leisurability, 7*(3), 70–76.

Coyne, P. (1980b). Social skills training: A three-pronged approach for developmentally disabled adolescents and young adults. Portland, OR: Oregon University Health Sciences Center. ERIC # ED222015

Coyne, P., & Fullerton, A. (2004). *Supporting individuals with autism spectrum disorder in recreation.* Champaign, IL: Sagamore.

Crandall, R. (1979). Social interaction, affect and leisure. *Journal of Leisure Research, 11*(3), 165–181.

Crouch, P. (1980). *Adaptation of the social behavior assessment scale for parents.* Ames, IA: Department of Psychology, Iowa State University.

Dattilo, J., & Murphy, W. D. (1991). *Leisure education program planning: A systematic approach.* State College, PA: Venture Publishing, Inc.

Dattilo, J., Williams, R., & Cory, L. (1993). Effects of computerized leisure education on knowledge of social skills of youth with intellectual disabilities. *Therapeutic Recreation Journal, 37*(2), 142–155.

Davis, D. E. (1977). *My friends and me.* Circle Pines, MN: American Guidance Service.

Day, R. M., Fox, J. J., Shores, R. E., Lindeman, D. P., & Stowitschek, J. J. (1983). The social competence intervention project: Developing educational procedures for teaching social interaction skills to handicapped children. *Behavior Disorders, 8*(2), 120–127.

Day, R. M., Powell, T. H., & Stowitschek, J. (1980). *SCIP training package.* Nashville, TN: George Peabody College for Teachers, Vanderbilt University.

de Boo, G. M., & Prins, P. J. M. (2007). Social incompetence in children with ADHD: Possible moderators and mediators in social-skills training. *Clinical Psychology Review, 27*(1), 78–97.

deMille, R., O'Sullivan, M., & Guilford, J. P. (1965). *Missing cartoons.* Palo Alto, CA: Consulting Psychologists Press.

Deshler, D. D., & Schumaker, J. B. (1983). Social skills of learning disabled adolescents: Characteristics and intervention. *Topics in Learning and Learning Disabilities, 3*(2), 15–23.

Dever, R. B. (1983). *Muscatatuck state hospital and training center curriculum.* Butlerville, IN: Muscatatuck State Hospital and Training Center.

Dever, R. B. (1989). A taxonomy of community living skills. *Exceptional Children, 55*(5), 395–404.

Dinkmeyer, D., & Dinkmeyer, D., Jr. (1982a). *DUSO-1: Developing understanding of self and others.* Circle Pines, MN: American Guidance Service.

Dinkmeyer, D., & Dinkmeyer, D., Jr. (1982b). *DUSO-2: Developing understanding of self and others.* Circle Pines, MN: American Guidance Service.

Dirks, M. A., Treat, T. A., & Weersing, V. R. (2007). Integrating theoretical, measurement, and intervention models of youth social competence. *Clinical Psychology Review, 27*, 327–347.

Dodge, K. A., McClaskey, C. L., & Feldman, E. (1985). Situational approach to the assessment of social competence in children. *Journal of Consulting and Clinical Psychology, 53*(3), 344–353.

Drummond, T. (1994). The Student Risk Screening Scale (SRSS). Grants Pass, OR: Josephine County Mental Health Program.

Duncan, A. W., & Klinger, L. G. (2010). Autism spectrum disorders: Building social skills in group, school, and community settings. *Social Work With Groups, 33*(2 & 3), 175–193.

Dunn, J. K. (1983). Improving client assessment procedures in therapeutic recreation programming. In G.L. Hitzhusen (Ed.), *Expanding horizons in therapeutic recreation 10* (pp. 61–84). Columbia, MO: University of Missouri.

Dunn, J. (1984). Assessment. In C. A. Peterson & S. L. Gunn (Eds.), *Therapeutic recreation program design: Principles and procedures*. (2nd ed.) (pp. 267–320). Englewood Cliffs, NJ: Prentice-Hall, Inc.

Dunn, J. K. (1989). Guidelines for using published assessment procedures. *Therapeutic Recreation Journal, 23*(2), 59–69.

Durlak, J. A., Weissberg, R. P., & Pachan, M. (2010). A meta-analysis of after school programs that seek to promote personal and social skills in children and adolescents. *American Journal of Community Psychology, 45*(3–4), 294–309.

Durlak, J. A., & Wells, A. M. (1997). Preliminary prevention mental health programs for children and adolescents: A meta-analytic review. *American Journal of Community Psychology, 25*(2), 115–152.

Dykes, M. K. (1980). *Developmental assessment for the severely handicapped*. Austin, TX: Pro-Ed.

Edwards, J. (n.d.). *Behavior management of social/sexual behaviors videotape*. Austin, TX: Pro-Ed.

Edwards, J. P. (n.d.). *Overview: Social/sexual training videotape*. Austin, TX: Pro-Ed.

Edwards, J., & Wapnick, S. (1988). *Being me: A social/sexual training program for the developmentally disabled*. Austin, TX: Pro-Ed.

Edwards, J., Wapnick, S., Mock, P., & Whitson, L. (n.d.). *Feeling free: A social/sexual training program for the hearing and visually impaired*. Austin, TX: Pro-Ed.

Elias, M. J., & Maher, C. A. (1983). Social and affective development of children: A programmatic perspective. *Exceptional Children, 49*(4), 339–346.

Elliott, S. N., & Gresham, F. M. (1991). *Social skills intervention guide: Practical strategies for social skills training*. Circle Pines, MN: American Guidance Service.

Epstein, M. H. (1982). Special education programs for the handicapped adolescent. *School Psychology Bulletin, 11*(4), 384–390.

Epstein, M. H., & Cullinan, D. (1987). Effective social skills curricula for behaviorally disordered students. *Pointer, 31*(2), 21–24.

Epstein, M. H., Kauffman, J. M., & Cullinan, D. (1985). Patterns of maladjustment among the behaviorally disordered, II: Boys aged 6–11, boys aged 12–18, girls aged 6–11, and girls aged 12–18. *Behavior Disorders, 10*, 125–135.

Fad, K. S. (1990). The fast track to success: Social-behavioral skills. *Intervention in School and Clinic, 26*(1), 39–43.

Feigin, J., & Meisgeier, C. (1987). Learning disabilities and critical social and behavioral issues: A review. *Journal of Reading, Writing and Learning Disabilities, 3*, 259–274.

Finnell, A., Card, J., & Menditto, A. (1997). A comparison of appropriate behavior scores of residents with chronic schizophrenia participating in therapeutic recreation services and vocational rehabilitation services. *Therapeutic Recreation Journal, 31*(1), 10–21.

Folkman, S. (2008). The case for positive emotions in the stress process. *Anxiety, Stress, and Coping, 21*(1), 3–14.

Fordyce, W. G., Yauck, W. A., & Raths, L. (1946). A manual for the Ohio guidance tests for the elementary grades. Columbus, OH: Ohio State Department of Education.

Foster, S. L., & Ritchey, W. L. (1979). Issues in the assessment of social competence in children. *Journal of Applied Behavior Analysis, 12*(4), 625–638.

Foxx, R. M., & Bittle, R. G. (1989). *Thinking it through: Teaching a problem-solving strategy for community living—Curriculum for individuals with brain injuries*. Champaign, IL: Research Press.

Foxx, R. M., & McMorrow, M. J. (1983). *Stacking the deck: A social skills game for adults with developmental disabilities*. Champaign, IL: Research Press.

Fullerton, A., & Coyne, P. (1999). Developing skills and concepts for self-determination in young adults with autism. *Focus on Autism and Other Developmental Disabilities, 14*(1), 42–52.

Gaylord-Ross, R., & Haring, T. (1987). Social interaction research for adolescents with severe handicaps. *Behavioral Disorders, 12*(4), 264–275.

Goldsmith, J. B., & McFall, R. M. (1975). Development and evaluation of an interpersonal skill-training program for psychiatric inpatients. *Journal of Abnormal Psychology, 84*, 51–58.

Goldstein, A. P. (1988). *The PREPARE curriculum: Teaching prosocial competencies*. Champaign, IL: Research Press.

Goldstein, A. P., Glick, B., Reiner, S., Zimmerman, D., & Coultry, T .M. (1987). *Aggression replacement training: A comprehensive intervention for aggressive youth*. Champaign, IL: Research Press.

Goldstein, A. P., & McGinnis, E. (n.d.). *The skillstreaming video: How to teach students prosocial skills*. Champaign, IL: Research Press.

Goldstein, A. P., Sprafkin, R. P., Gershaw, N. J., & Klein, P. (1980). *Skillstreaming the adolescent: A structured learning approach to teaching prosocial skills*. Champaign, IL: Research Press.

Green F. P., & Schleien, S. J. (1991). Understanding friendship and recreation: A theoretical sampling. *Therapeutic Recreation Journal, 25*(4), 29–40.

Green, K., Forehand, R., Beck, S., & Vosk, B. (1980). An assessment of the relationship among measures of children's competence and children's academic achievement. *Child Development, 51*, 1149–1156.

Gresham, F. M. (1981a). Assessment of children's social skills. *Journal of School Psychology, 19*(2), 120–133.

Gresham, F. M. (1981b). Social skills training with handicapped children: A review. *Review of Educational Research, 51*(1), 139–176.

Gresham, F. M. (1982). Misguided mainstreaming: The case for social skills training with handicapped children. *Exceptional Children, 48*(5), 422–433.

Gresham, F. M. (1983). Social skills assessment as a component of mainstreaming placement decisions. *Exceptional Children, 49*(4), 331–336.

Gresham, F. M. (1984). Social skills and self-efficacy for exceptional children. *Exceptional Children, 51*(3), 253–261.

Gresham, F. M. (1986). Conceptual and definitional issues in the assessment of children's social skills: Implications for classifications and training. *Journal of Clinical Child & Adolescent Psychology, 15*(1), 3–15.

Gresham, F. M., & Elliott, S. N. (1990). *Social skills rating system*. Circle Pines, MN: American Guidance Service.

Gresham, F. M., Elliott, S. N., & Black, F. L. (1987). Teacher-rated social skills of mainstreamed mildly handicapped and nonhandicapped children. *School Psychology Review, 16*(1), 78–88.

Gresham, F. M., Elliott, S. N., & Evans-Fernandez, S. (1993). *Student self-concept scale*. Circle Pines, MN: American Guidance Service.

Gresham, F. M., Sugai, G., & Horner, R. H. (2001). Interpreting outcomes of social skills training for students with high-incidence disabilities. *Exceptional Children, 67*(3), 331–344.

Gronlund, H., & Anderson, L. (1963). Personality characteristics of socially accepted, socially neglected and socially rejected junior high school pupils. In J. Sederman (Ed.), *Educating for mental health*. New York, NY: Cromwell.

Gunter, P., Fox, J. J., & Brady, M. P. (1984). Social skills training of handicapped children in less restrictive environments: Research implications for classroom teachers. *Pointer, 29*(1), 8–10.

Guralnick, M. J. (1990). Social competence and early intervention. *Journal of Early Intervention, 14*(1), 3–14.

Hammell, K. W. (2007). Experience of rehabilitation following spinal cord injury: A meta-synthesis of qualitative findings. *Spinal Cord, 45*, 260–274.

Hazel, J. S., Schumaker, J. B., Sherman, J. A., & Sheldon-Wildgen, J. (1982). *ASSET: A social skills program for adolescents*. Champaign: IL: Research Press.

Hoier, T. S., & Foster, S. L. (1985). Methods of assessing children's social skills: Current status and future directions. *Journal of Special Education Technology, 7*(2), 18–27.

Honig, A. S., & McCarron, P. A. (1988). Prosocial behaviors of handicapped and typical peers in an integrated preschool. *Early Child Development and Care, 33*(1–4), 113–125.

Hops, H., Guild, J. J., Fleishman, D. H., Paine, S. C., Street, A., Walker, H. W., & Greenwood, C. R. (1978). *PEERS: (Procedures for establishing effective relationship skills): Manual for consultants*. Unpublished manuscript, Center for Behavioral Education of the Handicapped, University of Oregon, Eugene.

Howell, K. W. (1985). A task-analytical approach to social behavior. *Remedial and Special Education, 6*(2), 24–30.

Hollinger, J. D. (1987). Social skills for behaviorally disordered children as preparation for mainstreaming: Theory, practice, and new directions. *Remedial and Special Education, 8*(4), 17–27.

Hundert, J., & Houghton, A. (1992). Promoting social integration of children with disabilities in integrated preschools: A failure to generalize. *Exceptional Children, 58*(4), 311–320.

Innocenti, M., Rule, S., Killoran, J., Stowitschek, J. J., Striefel, S., & Boswell, C. (1982). *Let's be social parents' manual*. Logan, UT: Outreach and Development Division, Exceptional Child Center.

Innocenti, M., Rule, S., Stowitschek, JJ., Striefel, S., & Boswell, C. (1983). *Let's be social home liaison manual. Logan*, UT: Outreach and Development Division, Exceptional Child Center.

Iso-Ahola, S. E. (1980). *The social psychology of leisure and recreation*. Dubuque, IA: Wm. C. Brown Company.

Jackson, D. A., Jackson, N. F., Bennett, M. L., Bynum, D. M., & Faryna, E. (1991). *Learning to get along: Social effectiveness training for people with developmental disabilities*. Champaign, IL: Research Press.

Jackson, N. F., Jackson, D. A., & Monroe, C. (1983). *Getting along with others: Teaching social effectiveness to children*. Champaign, IL: Research Press.

Jenkins, J. R., Odom, S. L., & Speltz, M. L. (1989). Effects of social integration on preschool children with handicaps. *Exceptional Children, 55*(5), 420–428.

Johnson, J. C., & Mithaug, D. E. (1978). A replication survey of sheltered workshop entry requirements. *AAESPH Review, 3*, 116–122.

Junttila, N., Voeten, M., Kaukiainen, A., & Vauras, M. (2006). Multisource assessment of children's social competence. *Educational and Psychological Measurement, 66*(5), 874–895.

Kavale, K. A., & Mostert, M.P. (2004). Social skills interventions for individuals with learning disabilities. *Learning Disability Quarterly, 27*(1), 31–43.

Kelly, J. R. (1975). Three leisure locales: Exploring role stability and environmental change. In B. van der Smissen (compiler), *Indicators of change in the recreation environment—A national research symposium*. HPER Series No. 6, University Park, PA: The Pennsylvania State University.

Khemthong, S., Packer, T. L., Passmore, A., & Dhaliwal, S. S. (2008). Does social leisure contribute to physical health in multiple sclerosis related fatigue? *Annual in Therapeutic Recreation, 16*, 71–80.

Killoran, J., Rule, S., Stowitschek, J. J., Innocenti, M., Striefel, S., & Boswell, C. (1982). *Let's be social*. Logan, UT: Outreach and Development Division, Exceptional Child Center.

Kleinert, H., Miracle, S., & Sheppard-Jones, K. (2007). Including students with moderate and severe disabilities in extracurricular and community recreation activities: Steps to success! *Teaching Exceptional Children, 39*(6), 33–38.

Kronick, D. (1978). An examination of psychosocial aspects of learning disabled adolescents. *Learning Disabilities Quarterly, 1*(4), 86–93.

Kurtz, M. M., & Mueser, K. T. (2008). A meta-analysis of controlled research on social skills training for schizophrenia. *Journal of Consulting and Clinical Psychology, 76*(3), 491–504.

Lane, K. L., Menzies, H. M., Barton-Arwood, S. M., Doukas, G. L., & Munton, S. M. (2005). Designing, implementing, and evaluating social skills interventions for elementary students: Step-by-step procedures based on actual school-based investigations. *Preventing School Failure, 49*(2), 18–26.

LeConey, S., Devine, M. A., Bunker, H., & Montgomery, S. (2000). Utilizing the therapeutic recreation process in community settings: The case of Sue. *Parks & Recreation, 35*(5), 70–77.

LeCroy, C. W. (1983). (Ed.). *Social skills training for children and youth*. New York, NY: Haworth Press.

Lovitt, T. C. (1987). Social skills training: Which ones and where to do it? *Journal of Reading, Writing, and Learning Disabilities, 3*, 213–221.

Lowe, M. R., & Cautela, J. R. (1978). A self-report measure of social skill. *Behavior Therapy, 9*(4), 535–544.

Loy, D. P., & Dattilo, J. (2000). Effects of different play structures on social interactions between a boy with Asperger's Syndrome and his peers. *Therapeutic Recreation Journal, 34*(3), 190–210.

Lu, L., Petersen, F., Lacroix, L., & Rousseau, C. (2010). Stimulating creative play in children with autism through sandplay. *The Arts in Psychotherapy, 37*(1), 56–64.

Luftig, R. L. (1988). Assessment of perceived school loneliness and isolation of mentally retarded and nonretarded students. *American Journal on Mental Retardation, 92*(5), 472–475.

Maag, J. W. (1989). Assessment in social skills training: Methodological and conceptual issues for research and practice. *Remedial and Special Education, 10*(4), 6–17.

Maag, J. W. (2005). Social skills training for youth with emotional and behavioral disorders and learning disabilities: Problems, conclusions, and suggestions. *Exceptionality, 13*(3), 155–172.

Maag, J. W. (2006). Social skills training for students with emotional and behavioral disorders: A review of the reviews. *Behavioral Disorders, 32*(1), 5–17.

Macro Systems, Inc. (1989). *Social skills on the job*. Circle Pines, MN: American Guidance Service.

Mactavish, J. B., & Schleien, S. J. (2000). Exploring family recreation activities in families that include children with developmental disabilities. *Therapeutic Recreation Journal, 34*(2), 132–153.

Mannix, D. S. (1986). *I can behave: A classroom management curriculum for elementary students*. Austin, TX: Pro-Ed.

Matson, J. L. (1994). *Autism in children and adults: Etiology, assessment, and intervention*. Pacific Grove, CA: Brooks/Cole.

Matson, J. L., Fee, V. E., Coe, D. A., & Smith, D. (1991). A social skills program for developmentally delayed preschoolers. *Journal of Clinical Child & Adolescent Psychology, 20*(4), 428–433.

Matson, J. L., Helsel, W. J., Bellack, A. S., & Senatore, V. (1983). Development of a rating scale to assess social skills deficits in mentally retarded adults. *Applied Research in Mental Retardation, 4*(4), 399–407.

Matson, J. L. Rotatori, A. F., & Helsel, W. J. (1983). Development of a rating scale to measure social skills in children: The Matson evaluation of social skills with youngsters (MESSY). *Behaviour Research and Therapy, 21*(4), 335–340.

McCallum, R. S., Herrin, M. S., Wheeler, J. P., & Edwards, J. R. (1984). *Brief index of adaptive behavior.* Bensenville, IL: Scholastic Testing Service.

McClennen, S. E., Hoekstra, R. R., & Bryan, J. E. (1980). *Social skills for severely retarded adults: An inventory and training program.* Champaign, IL: Research Press.

McConnell, S. R. (1987). Entrapment effects and the generalization and maintenance of social skills training for elementary school students with behavioral disorders. *Behavioral Disorders, 12*(4), 252–263.

McCormick, B. P. (1999). Contribution of social support and recreation companionship to the life satisfaction of people with persistent mental illness. *Therapeutic Recreation Journal, 33*(4), 320–332.

McEvoy, M. A., & Odom, S. L. (1987). Social interaction training for preschool children with behavioral disorders. *Behavioral Disorders, 12*(4), 242–251.

McEvoy, M. A., Shores, R. E., Wehby, J. H., Johnson, S. M., & Fox, J. J. (1990). Special education teachers' implementation of procedures to promote social interaction among children in integrated settings. *Education and Training in Mental Retardation, 25*(3), 267–276.

McFall, R. M. (1982). A review and reformulation of the concept of social skills. *Behavioral Assessment, 4*(1), 1–33.

McGinnis, E. & Goldstein, A. P. (1990). *Skillstreaming in early childhood: Teaching prosocial skills to the preschool and kindergarten child.* Champaign, IL: Research Press.

McGinnis, E., Goldstein, A. P., Sprafkin, R. P., & Gershaw, N. J. (1984). *Skillstreaming the elementary school child: A guide for teaching prosocial skills.* Champaign, IL: Research Press.

McGinnis, E., Sauerbry, L., & Nichols, P. (1985). Skillstreaming: Teaching social skills to children with behavior disorders. *Teaching Exceptional Children, 17*(3), 160–167.

McKenney, A., Dattilo, J., Cory, L., & Williams, R. (2004). Effects of computerized therapeutic recreation program on knowledge of social skills of male youth with emotional and behavioral disorders. *Annual in Therapeutic Recreation, 13,* 12–23.

Meadows, N., Neel, R. S., Parker, G., & Timo, K. (1991). A validation of social skills for students with behavioral disorders. *Behavioral Disorders, 16*(3), 200–210.

Mechanic, D. (1974). Social structure and personal adaptation: Some neglected dimensions. In G. V. Coelho, D. A. Hamburg, & J. E. Adams (Eds.), *Coping and adaptation* (pp. 32–46). New York, NY: Basic Books, Inc.

Meier, C. R., DiPerna, J. C., & Oster, M. M. (2006). Importance of social skills in the elementary grades. *Education and Treatment of Children, 29*(3), 409–419.

Meyers, A. W., Schleser, R., Cooke, C. J., & Cuvillier, C. (1979). Cognitive contributions to the development of gymnastic skills. *Cognitive Therapy & Research, 3*(1), 75–85.

Michelson, L., & Wood, R. (1980). Behavioral assessment and training of children's social skills. In M. Hersen, R. M. Eisler, & P. M. Miller (Eds.), *Progress in behavior modification* (Vol. 9). New York, NY: Academic Press.

Mikami, A.Y. (2010). The importance of friendship for youth with attention-deficit/hyperactivity disorder. *Clinical Child and Family Psychological Review, 13,* 181–198.

Milsom, A., & Glanville, J. L. (2010). Factors mediating the relationship between social skills and academic grades in a sample of students diagnosed with learning disabilities or emotional disturbance. *Remedial and Special Education, 31*(4), 241–251.

Moote, G. T., Smyth, N. J., & Wodarski, J. S. (1999). Social skills training with youth in school settings: A review. *Research on Social Work Practice, 9*(4), 427–465.

Mueller, D. R., & Roder, V. (2005). Social skills training in recreational rehabilitation of schizophrenia patients. *American Journal of Recreation Therapy, 4*(5), 11–19.

Mueser, K. T., & Bellack, A. S. (2007). Social skills training: Alive and well? *Journal of Mental Health, 16*(5), 549–552.

Nelson, C. M. (1988). Social skills training for handicapped students. *Teaching Exceptional Children, 20*(4), 19–23.

Nihira, K., Foster, R., Shellhaas, M., & Leland, H. (n.d.). *AAMD Adaptive behavior scale: Residential and community edition*. Austin, TX: Pro–Ed.

Nihira, K., Foster, R., Shellhaas, M., Leland, H., Lambert, N. M., & Windmiller, M. (n.d.). *AAMD Adaptive behavior scale: School edition*. Odessa, FL: Psychological Assessment Resources.

Novak, M. A., Olley, J. G., & Kearney, D. S. (1980). Social skills of children with special needs in integrated and separate preschools. In T. Field, S. Goldberg, D. Stern, & A. M. Sostek (Eds.), *High-risk infants and children* (pp. 327–346). New York, NY: Academic Press.

Odom, S. L., & McConnell, S. R. (1985). A performance-based conceptualization of social competence of handicapped preschool children: Implications for assessment. *Topics in Early Childhood Special Education Quarterly, 4*(4), 1–19.

Olmeda, R. E., & Kauffman, J. M. (2003). Sociocultural considerations in social skills training research with African American students with emotional or behavioral disorders. *Journal of Developmental and Physical Disabilities, 15*(2), 101–121.

O'Sullivan, M., & Guilford, J. P. (1965). *Social translations*. Palo Alto, CA: Consulting Psychologists Press.

Page, P., Cieloha, D., & Suid, M. (n.d.). *Getting along*. Circle Pines, MN: American Guidance Service.

Personal care program. (n.d.). Flaghouse, Inc.

Perlmutter, B. (1986). Personality variables and peer relations of children and adolescents with learning disabilities. In S. J. Ceci (Ed.), *Handbook of cognitive, social and neuropsychological aspects of learning disabilities* (Vol 1, pp. 339–359). Hillsdale, NJ: Erlbaum.

Pestle, K., Card, J., & Menditto, A. (1998). Therapeutic recreation in a social-learning program: Effect over time on appropriate behaviours of residents with schizophrenia. *Therapeutic Recreation Journal, 32*(1), 28–41.

Peterson, C. A., & Gunn, S. L. (1984). *Therapeutic recreation program design: Principles and procedures* (2nd ed.). Englewood Cliffs, NJ: Prentice-Hall, Inc.

Popovich, D., & Lahan, S. (1981). *Adaptive behavior curriculum*. Baltimore, MD: Paul H. Brookes.

Preece, S., & Mellor, D. (2009). Learning patterns in social skills training programs: An exploratory study. *Children and Adolescent Social Work Journal, 26*, 87–101.

Rao, P. A., Beidel, D. C., & Murray, M. J. (2008). Social skills interventions for children with Asperger's Syndrome or high-functioning autism: A review

and recommendations. *Journal of Autism and Developmental Disorders, 38*, 353–361.

Ray, B. M. (1985). Measuring the social position of the mainstreamed handicapped child. *Exceptional Children, 52*(1), 57–62.

Riggio, R. E. (n.d.). *The social skills inventory: Research edition*. Palo Alto, CA: Consulting Psychologists Press.

Roff, M., Sells, S. B., & Golden, M. M. (1972). *Social adjustment and personality development in children*. Minneapolis, MN: University of Minnesota.

Rothwell, E., Piatt, J., & Mattingly, K. (2006). Social competence: Evaluation of an outpatient recreation therapy treatment program for children with behavioral disorders. *Therapeutic Recreation Journal, 40*(4), 241–254.

Rule, S., Stowitschek, J. J., Innocenti, M., Striefel, S., Killoran, J., Swezey, K., & Boswell, C. (1987). The social integration program: An analysis of the effects of mainstreaming handicapped children into day care centers. *Education and Treatment of Children, 10*(2), 175–192.

Sabornie, E. J. (1985). Social mainstreaming of handicapped students: Facing an unpleasant reality. *Remedial and Special Education, 6*(2), 12–16.

Sabornie, E. J., & Beard, G. H. (1990). Teaching social skills to students with mild handicaps. *Teaching Exceptional Children, 23*(1), 35–38.

Sabornie, E. J., & Kauffman, J. M. (1985). Regular classroom sociometric status of behaviorally disordered adolescents. *Behavioral Disorders, 10*, 268–274.

Sabornie, E. J., & Kauffman, J. M. (1987). Assigned, received, and reciprocal social status of adolescents with and without mild mental retardation. *Education and Training in Mental Retardation, 22*, 139–149.

Sabornie, E. J., & Thomas, V. (1989). Adjustment and intimacy of mildly handicapped and nonhandicapped students. Paper presented at the annual meeting of the American Educational Research Association, San Francisco, CA.

Sabornie, E. J., Thomas, V., & Coffman, R. M. (1989). Assessment of social/affective measures to discriminate between BD and nonhandicapped early adolescents. *Monograph in Behavior Disorders: Severe Behavior Disorders in Children and Youth, 12*, 21–32.

Schleien, S. J., Heyne, L. A., & Berken, S. B. (1988). Integrating physical education to teach appropriate play skills to learners with autism: A pilot study. *Adapted Physical Activity Quarterly, 5*(3), 182–192.

Schloss, P. J., Schloss, C. N., Wood, C. E., & Kiehl, W. S. (1986). A critical review of social skills research with behaviorally disordered students. *Behavioral Disorders, 12*, 1–14.

Schlundt, D. G., & McFall, R. M. (1985). New directions in the assessment of social competence and social skills. In L. L'Abate & M. A. Milan (Eds.), *Handbook of social skills training and research* (pp. 22–49). New York, NY: John Wiley & Sons.

Schumaker, J. B., & Hazel, J. B. (1984). Social skills assessment and training for the learning disabled: Who's on first and what's on second? Part II. *Journal of Learning Disabilities, 17*(8), 492–499.

Schumaker, J., Hazel, J. S., & Pederson, C .S. (n.d.). *Social skills for daily living*. Circle Pines, MN: American Guidance Service.

Schumaker, J. B., Pederson, C. S., Hazel, J. S., & Meyen, E. L. (1983). Social skills curricula for mildly handicapped adolescents: A review. *Focus on Exceptional Children, 16*(4), 1–16.

Shores, R. E. (1987). Overview of research on social interaction: A historical and personal perspective. *Behavioral Disorders, 12*(4), 233–241.

Shure, M. B. (1981). Social competence as a problem-solving skill. In J. D. Wine & M. D. Smye (Eds.), *Social competence* (pp. 158–185). New York, NY: Guilford Press.

Sim, L., Whiteside, S. P., Dittner, C. A., & Mellon, M. (2006). Effectiveness of a social skills training program for school age children: Transition to the clinical setting. *Journal of Child and Family Studies, 15*, 409–418.

Simpson, R. L. (1987). Social interactions of behaviorally disordered children and youth: Where are we and where do we need to go? *Behavioral Disorders, 12*(4), 292–298.

Skalko, T. K. (1991). Social skills training for persons with chronic mental illnesses. *The Journal of Physical Education, Recreation, & Dance, 62*(4), 31–33.

Smith, S. L. (1988). Teaching the fourth R—Relationships. *Pointer, 32*(3), 23–33.

Sneegas, J. J. (1989). Social skills: An integral component of leisure participation and therapeutic recreation services. *Therapeutic Recreation Journal, 23*(2), 30–40.

Sparrow, S. S., Galla, D. A., & Cicchetti, D. V. (1984a). *Vineland Adaptive Behavior Scales: Survey form manual*. Circle Pines, MN: American Guidance Service.

Sparrow, S. S., Galla, D. A., & Cicchetti, D. V. (1984b). *Vineland Adaptive Behavior Scales: Expanded Forma manual*. Circle Pines, MN: American Guidance Service.

Sparrow, S. S., Galla, D. A., & Cicchetti, D. V. (1985). *Vineland Adaptive Behavior Scales: Classroom edition*. Circle Pines, MN: American Guidance Service.

Spence, S. (1981). *Social skills training with children and adolescents: A counselor's manual*. Windsor, Berks, London: NFER-Nelson Publishing Company.

Spence, S. H. (2003). Social skills training with children and young people: Theory, evidence, and practice. *Child and Adolescent Mental Health, 8*(2), 84–96.

Startline: Social education/communication. (1987). Allen, TX: DLM.

Stephens, T. (1978). *Social skills in the classroom*. Columbus, OH: Cedars Press.

Stephens, T. M. (1992). *Social skills in the classroom* (2nd ed.). Columbus, OH: Cedars Press.

Stephens, T. M. & Arnold, K. D. (n.d.). *Social behavior assessment inventory* (2nd ed.). Odessa, FL: Psychological Assessment Resources.

Stowitschek, J. J., Killoran, J., Rule, S., Innocenti, M., Striefel, S., & Boswell, C. (1982). *Let's be social: teachers' guide*. Logan, UT: Outreach and Development Division, Exceptional Child Center.

Strain, P. S ., & Odom, S. L. (1986). Peer social initiations: Effective intervention for social skills development of exceptional children. *Exceptional Children, 52*(6), 543–551.

Strain, P. S., Odom, S. L., & McConnell, S. (1984). Promoting social reciprocity of exceptional children: Identification, target behavior selection, and intervention. *Remedial and Special Education, 5*(1), 21–28.

Strayhorn, J. M., Jr. (1977). *Talking it out: A guide to effective communication and problem solving*. Champaign, IL: Research Press.

Strayhorn, J. M., & Strain, P. S. (1986). Social and language skills for preventive mental health: What, how, who, and when. In P. S. Strain, M. J. Guralnick, & H. M. Walker (Eds.), *Children's social behavior: Development, assessment and modification* (pp. 287–323). Orlando, FL: Academic Press.

Stumbo, N. J. (1994/95). Assessment of social skills in therapeutic recreation practice. *Annual in Therapeutic Recreation, 5*, 68–82.

Stumbo, N. J. (1995a). The importance of social skills to therapeutic recreation services. In G.L. Hitzhusen & L. Thomas (Eds.), *Expanding horizons in therapeutic recreation XVI* (pp. 7–90). Columbia, MO: Curators University of Missouri.

Stumbo, N. J. (1995b). Social skill instruction through commercially available resources. *Therapeutic Recreation Journal, 29*(1), 30–55.

Sugai, G., & Fabre, T. R. (1987). The behavior teaching plan: A model for developing and implementing behavior change programs. *Education and Treatment of Children, 10*(3), 279–290.

Taylor, A. R. (1982). Social competence and interpersonal relations between retarded and nonretarded children. In N. Ellis (Ed.), *International review of research in mental retardation*, Vol. II, (pp.247–283). New York, NY: Academic Press.

Tetreault, A. S., & Lerman, D. C. (2010). Teaching social skills to children with autism using point-of-view video modeling. *Education and Treatment of Children, 33*(3), 395–419.

Torrey, G. K., Vasa, S. F., Maag, J. W., & Kramer, J. J. (1992). Social skills interventions across school settings: Case study reviews of students with mild disabilities. *Psychology in the Schools, 29*(3), 248–255.

Trower, P. (1984). A radical critique and reformulation: From organism to agent. In P. Trower (Ed.), *Radical approaches to social skills training* (pp. 48–88). New York, NY: Methuen.

Trower, P., Bryant, B., & Argyle, M. (1978). *Social skills and mental health*. London, UK: Methuen.

Ullman, C. A. (1957). Teachers, peers, and tests and predictors of adjustment. *Journal of Educational Psychology, 48*, 257–267.

Valletutti, P. J., & Bender, M. (1982). *Teaching interpersonal and community living skills: A curriculum model for handicapped adolescents and adults*. Austin, TX: Pro–Ed.

Van Hasselt, V. B., Hersen, M., Whitehill, M. B., & Bellack, A. S. (1979). Social skill assessment and training for children: An evaluative review. *Behavior Research and Therapy, 17*(5), 413–437.

Vandercook, T. (1991). Leisure instruction outcomes: Criterion performance, positive interactions, and acceptance by typical high school peers. *Journal of Special Education, 25*(3), 320–339.

Waksman, S. A. (n.d.). *Waksman social skills rating scale (WSSRS)*. Odessa, FL: Psychological Assessment Resources.

Waksman, S. A., & Messmer, C. L. (1985). *Assertive behavior: A program for teaching social skills to children and adolescents*. Portland, OR: Enrichment Press.

Waksman, S., Messmer, C. L., & Waksman, D. D. (1988). *The Waksman social skills curriculum: An assertive behavior program for adolescents* (3rd ed.). Austin, TX: Pro-Ed.

Walker, A. N., Barry, T. D., & Bader. S. H. (2010). Therapist and parent rating of changes in adaptive social skills following a summer treatment camp

for children with autism spectrum disorders: A preliminary study. *Child & Youth Care Forum, 39*(5), 305–322.

Walker, H. M. (1983). The social behavior survival program (SBS): A systematic approach to the integration of handicapped children into less restrictive settings. *Education and Treatment of Children, 6*(4), 421–441.

Walker, H. M. & McConnell, S. R. (1988). *Walker-McConnell scale of social competence and school adjustment*. Austin, TX: Pro-Ed.

Walker, H. M., McConnell, S., Holmes, D., Todis, B., Walker, J., & Golden, N. (1988). *The Walker social skills curriculum: The ACCEPTS Program*. Austin, TX: Pro-Ed

Walker, H. M., Todis, B., Holmes, D., & Horton, G. (1988). *The Walker social skills curriculum: The ACCESS program*. Austin, TX: Pro-Ed.

Wells, R. H. (n.d.). *Personal power*. Austin, TX: Pro-Ed.

White, B. N. (1980). Mainstreaming in grade school and preschool: How the child with special needs interacts with peers. In T. Field (Ed.), *High-risk infants and children* (pp. 347–371). New York, NY: Academic Press.

White, R. W. (1974). Strategies of adaptation: An attempt at systematic description. In G. V. Coelho, D. A. Hamburg, & J. E. Adams (Eds.), *Coping and adaptation* (pp. 47–68). New York, NY: Basic Books, Inc.

White, S. W., Albano, A. M., Johnson, C. R., Kasari, C., Ollendick, T., Klin, A., Oswald, D., & Scahill, L. (2010). Development of a cognitive-behavioral intervention program to treat anxiety and social deficits in teens with high-functioning autism. *Clinical Child and Family Psychological Review, 13*(1), 77–90.

White, S. W., Koenig, K., & Scahill, L. (2007). Social skills development in children with autism spectrum disorders: A review of the intervention research. *Journal of Autism and Developmental Disorders, 37*(10), 1858–1868.

White, W. J., Schumaker, J. B., Warner, M. M., Alley, G. R., & Deshler, D. D. (1980). *The current status of young adults identified as learning disabled during their school career*. (Research Report No. 21). Lawrence, KS: University of Kansas Institute for Research in Learning Disabilities.

Wilkinson, J., & Canter, S. (1982). *Social skills training manual: Assessment, program design, and management of training*. New York, NY: Wiley.

Williams, S. L., & Bloomer, J. (1987). *Bay area functional performance evaluation* (2nd ed.). Palo Alto, CA: Psychologists Press.

Williams, S. L., Walker, H. M., Holmes, D., Todis, B., & Fabre, T. R. (1989). Social validation of adolescent social skills by teachers and students. *Remedial and Special Education, 10*(4), 18–27, 37.

Wrubel, J., Benner, P., & Lazarus, R. S. (1981). Social competence from the perspective of stress and coping. In J. D. Wine & M. D. Smye (Eds.), *Social competence* (pp. 61–99). New York, NY: Guilford Press.

Ylvisaker, M., Turkstra, L. S., & Coelho, C. (2005). Behavioral and social interventions for individuals with traumatic brain injury: A summary of the research with clinical implications. *Seminars in Speech and Language, 26*(4), 256–267.

Zetlin, A. G., & Murtaugh, M. (1988). Friendship patterns of mildly learning handicapped and nonhandicapped high school students. *American Journal on Mental Retardation, 92*(5), 447–454.

Zimmerman, D. P. (2002). Research and practice in social- and life-skills training. *Residential Treatment for Children and Youth, 20*(2), 51–75.

Zirkelbach, T. (n.d.) *PLUSS: Putting language to use in social situations*. Mt. Vernon, NY: Flaghouse.

Appendices 11A–11D

Appendix 11A Designing Social Skills Instructional Activities

1. Select one group of clients who meet one or more of the criteria from Step 1a–d in text.

For example: clients who are aggressive, clients who lack social initiation skills for community re-entry, clients who are self-injurious in new social situations, etc.

Client Group _____

2. Select one category of social skills for the above group of clients that meet the criteria from Step 2 in text. (These will be task-analyzed in the next step.)

For example:

     clients who are aggressive = alternatives to aggression in new situations;

     clients who lack social initiation skills for community re-entry = how to enter a new group of people,

     clients who are self-injurious in new social situations = alternatives to self-injurious behavior.

Target Behavior to Change

Client Group _____

3. Task-analyze the above category of behavior, including criterion levels.

For example: clients who lack social initiation skills = how to enter a new group of people.

Task-Analysis of Entering New Group of People:	Criterion Level:
1. enters room/situation in which people are gathered	can identify when interruption is okay
2. approaches individuals in group	stands within two feet of group, makes eye contact
3. listens to conversation	attends to conversation of group without immediate interruption
4. greets individuals in group	says hello to known person(s), makes eye contact, uses appropriate gestures in greeting
5. enters into conversation	adds to topic, asks questions, offers to help, appropriate gestures, body space

Task Analysis of: _____   Criterion Level: _____

4. Assess whether Person Possesses Skill to Criterion Level

Example: Entering New Group of People

Plan to assess:

     Assess Joe's skills in Social Skills Group Monday afternoon (contrived)

     Assess Joe's skills in open recreation hour on Tuesday (natural)

     Assess using the Group Entry Social Skills checklist

Target Behavior: _____

Plan to Assess: (contrived) _____

                  (natural) _____

                  (assessment tool) _____

Appendix 11A Designing Social Skills Instructional Activities (cont'd)

5. Select Teaching Strategy

Examples: Direct Instruction, Modeling, Positive Reinforcement, Contingency Contracting, Role Playing, Token Reinforcement, Rehearsal and Practice, Simulations, Prompting, etc.

Example: Entering New Group of People

Teaching Strategies: Role Playing, Prompting and Fading, Positive Reinforcement

Target Behavior: _____

Teaching Strategies: _____

6. Implement Teaching Strategy

Example: Entering New Group of People

Planned Intervention: 15 minutes at beginning of Social Skills Group on Monday afternoons for four weeks, reassess at the end of four weeks.

Target Behavior: _____

Planned Intervention: _____

7. Reassess Person's Skill Achievement

Example: Entering New Group of People

Reassessment: Assess at end of four weeks of training, using Group Entry Social Skills checklist

Target Behavior: _____

Reassessment: _____

8. If Competent/Mastered, Move to New Skill; If not, Select Another Teaching Strategy and Retrain

Example: Entering New Group of People

Reassessment Results: Joe attained criterion level of group entry skills on Group Entry Skills checklist

Target Behavior: _____

Reassessment Results: _____

Appendix 11B-a. Description of Social Skills Curricula and Resources

CURRICULUM NAME/AUTHOR(S)	BRIEF DESCRIPTION OF CURRICULUM	PUBLISHER
1. ACCEPTS (A Curriculum for Children's Effective Peer and Teacher Skills) (Walker, McConnell, Holmes, Todis, Walker, & Golden, 1988)	Increases occurrence of appropriate social responses in all environments to enhance social competence. 28 skills in five groups: (a) classroom skills/adjustment; (b) interaction; (c) getting along, (d) making friends, and (e) coping. Scripts and videotape; individual, small and large group, 5–10 week program. Mainstreamed K–6th graders. Program (a) defines skill to be learned, (b) provides examples and nonexamples of behavior, (c) allows for active practice, (d) offers performance feedback, and (e) provides generalization of skills.	PRO-ED, Inc. 8700 Shoal Creek Boulevard Austin, TX 78757-6897 (512) 451-3246 Cost: $237 plus S & H (Optional video is $198 of total cost)
2. ACCESS: Adolescent Curriculum for Communication and Effective Social Skills (Walker, Todis, Holmes, & Horton, 1988)	Similar to above program. Mainstreamed adolescents and high school students. 30 social skills grouped into three major categories: (a) relating to peers, (b) relating to adults, and (c) relating to yourself. Eight-step instructional process. Social scripts included in student guide and curriculum manual. Also available from Psychological Assessment Resources.	PRO-ED, Inc. 8700 Shoal Creek Boulevard Austin, TX 78757-6897 (512) 451-3246 Cost: $50 plus S & H
3. Personal Power (Wells)	3-volume series: (a) succeeding in school/developing appropriate teacher interaction skills; (b) succeeding with self/gaining self-control; and (c) succeeding with others/peer interaction skills. Grades 6–12. Extensive lesson plans include games, role-playing, group exercises, contests, artwork and stories.	PRO-ED, Inc. 8700 Shoal Creek Boulevard Austin, TX 78757-6897 Cost: $79 each, plus S & H
4. I Can Behave: A Classroom Self-Management Curriculum for Elementary Students (Mannix, 1986)	10 stories, each focusing on specific classroom dilemma like sharing, taking turns, etc. Program includes story book, manual with lesson plans, student workbooks, pre-post tests, placement inventories. Disabled or non-disabled.	PRO-ED, Inc. 8700 Shoal Creek Boulevard Austin, TX 78757-6897 Cost: $139 plus S & H
5. Waksman Social Skills Curriculum: An Assertive Behavior Program for Adolescents (3rd. ed.) (Waksman, Messmer, & Waksman, 1988)	Program based on 9-week, 18-lesson format with instructions, activities, worksheets, and homework assignments. Each lesson plan includes goals, objectives, and procedures. Disabled or non-disabled, but helpful for those with behavior disorders, hyperactivity and emotional problems. Research-based.	PRO-ED, Inc. 8700 Shoal Creek Boulevard Austin, TX 78757-6897 Cost: $59 plus S & H
6. Social Skills in the Classroom (2nd. ed.) (Stephens, 1992)	Strengthens social skills of students found to lack appropriate social responses. Direct instructional approach using modeling, role-playing, behavior rehearsal. Any age student. 136 skills in four major categories: (a) environmental, (b) interpersonal, (c) self-related, and (d) task-related. Program format: (a) define skill, (b) assess performance of skill; (c) use the recommended teaching strategy, and (d) evaluate the outcome of instruction. See Social Behavior Assessment.	Psychological Assess. Resources P.O. Box 998 Odessa, FL 33556 (800) 331-8378 Cost: $38.95 plus S & H
7. Getting Along with Others: Teaching Social Effectiveness to Children (Jackson, Jackson, & Monroe, 1983)	Presents 17 core social skills and 18 common target behaviors. Elementary age. Program guide includes step-by-step process of program development, second guide with lesson plans to teach 17 skills. Individual skill lesson format: (a) labeling and defining skill to be taught, (b) demonstrating instances and non-instances of the skill, (c) practicing the skill through role playing (d) reviewing rationales for using the skills, and (e) discussing the problems of when skills do not bring desired outcomes in real-life. Uses positive feedback, ignore-attend praise, teaching interaction, direct prompt, and sit and watch (i.e., a procedure that combines time-out and overcorrection).	Research Press Department G, P.O. Box 9177 2612 N. Mattis Avenue Champaign, IL 61826 (217) 352-3273 Cost: $33.95 plus S & H

Appendix 11B-b. Description of Social Skills Curricula and Resources (cont'd)

CURRICULUM NAME/AUTHOR(S)	BRIEF DESCRIPTION OF CURRICULUM	PUBLISHER
8. Learning to Get Along: Social Effectiveness Training for People with Developmental Disabilities (Jackson, Jackson, Bennett, Bynum & Faryna)	Comprehensive training program for teaching appropriate social behavior for adolescents and adults with mild to moderate developmental disabilities. Provides structured lesson plans and guidelines for naturally occurring opportunities. Program Guide helps staff master program methods. Group Training Manual contains 21 core social skills, such as compromising, interrupting, etc.	Research Press Department G, P.O. Box 9177 2612 N. Mattis Avenue Champaign, IL 61826 Cost: $35.95 plus S & H
9. Skillstreaming in Early Childhood (McGinnis & Goldstein, 1990)	Group training program. 40 skills, such as: Trying when it's hard, joining in, dealing with fear, knowing when to tell, waiting your turn. Includes 29 reproducible forms such as homework reports, checklists, recording forms, and awards. For children ages 3 to 6. Illustrated for non-readers.	Research Press Department G, P.O. Box 9177 2612 N. Mattis Avenue Champaign, IL 61826 Cost: $28.90 plus S & H
10. Skillstreaming the Elementary School Child (McGinnis, Goldstein, Sprafkin, Gershaw, 1984)	Group training program. 60 skills in five categories: (a) classroom survival, (b) friendship-making, (c) dealing with feelings, (d) alternatives to aggression, and (e) dealing with stress. Manual includes: planning and organizing structured learning groups, curriculum guide, suggestions to integrate skills into daily school program, managing individual and group behavior problems. Audio cassettes and skill cards available, in addition to manual.	Research Press Department G, P.O. Box 9177 2612 N. Mattis Avenue Champaign, IL 61826 (217) 352-3273 Cost: $(variable) plus S & H
11. Skillstreaming the Adolescent (Goldstein, Sprafkin, Gershaw, & Klein, 1980)	Group training program. 50 skills grouped into six categories: (a) beginning social skills, (b) advanced social skills, (c) dealing with feelings, (d) alternatives to aggression, (e) dealing with stress, and (f) planning skills. Designed for aggressive, immature or withdrawn adolescent students.	Research Press Department G, P.O. Box 9177 2612 N. Mattis Avenue Champaign, IL 61826 Cost: $70.00 plus S & H
12. The Skillstreaming Video: How to Teach Students Prosocial Skills (Goldstein & McGinnis)	Video that provides training to teachers in order for them to implement Skillstreaming curricula (see above). Viewers shown how to conduct groups and apply teaching methods of modeling, role playing, performance feedback, and transfer training. Purchase of video includes Skillstreaming the Adolescent and Skillstreaming the Elementary School Child below. Video is 26 minutes.	Research Press Department G, P.O. Box 9177 Champaign, IL 61826 Cost: $365.00 purchase, +S & H Rental: $55/3 days
13. Social Skills for Severely Retarded Adults: An Inventory and Training Program (McClennen, Hoekstra, & Bryan, 1980)	Social skills inventory and training program for teaching skills essential for living independently: social interaction, leisure skills, and group interaction. Specific skills, such as: appropriate physical interactions, social smiling, waiting, sharing, taking turns, reaction to name, eye contact, etc.	Research Press Department G., P.O. Box 9177 2612 N. Mattis Avenue Champaign, Il 61826 Cost: $49.95 plus S & H
14. Stacking the Deck: A Social Skills Game for Adults with Developmental Disabilities (Foxx & McMorrow, 1983)	Training program designed as activity using game board. Individuals play by drawing cards and reacting to specific social situations. Three areas: general social skills, social/vocational skills, and social/sexual skills. Includes 144 training cards, detailed instructions, reproducible forms and manual.	Research Press Department G., P.O. Box 9177 2612 N. Mattis Avenue Champaign, IL 61826 Cost: $19.95 plus S & H
15. The PREPARE Curriculum: Teaching Prosocial Competencies (Goldstein, 1988)	Well-researched book provides comprehensive training program for junior and senior high students who display problem behaviors. Includes 10 interventions, such as: Problem-solving, interpersonal skills, situational perception, anger control, stress management, cooperation. Involves games, simulations, role plays, group discussion, etc.	Research Press Department G., P.O. Box 9177 2612 N. Mattis Avenue Champaign, IL 61826 Cost: $29.95 plus S & H

Appendix 11B-c. Description of Social Skills Curricula and Resources (cont'd)

CURRICULUM NAME/AUTHOR(S)	BRIEF DESCRIPTION OF CURRICULUM	PUBLISHER
16. Think Aloud: Increasing Social and Cognitive Skills: A Problem Solving Program for Children *Small Group Program* (Camp & Bash, 1985)	Designed to teach problem-solving skills to individuals 6 to 8 years old. Originates from cognitive self-control base in that students are taught series of questions: 1. What is my problem? 2. What am I supposed to do? 3. What is my plan? 4. Am I using my plan? Uses modeling, overpractice, fading. Found useful with aggressive students. Small group program.	Research Press Department G, P.O. Box 9177 2612 N. Mattis Avenue Champaign, IL 61826 Cost: $49.95 plus S & H
17. Think Aloud: Increasing Social and Cognitive Skills: A Problem Solving Program for Children *Classroom Program* (Camp & Bash, 1985)	Program used for all children within class. Separate programs for grades 1-2 (30 lessons), grades 3-4 (31 lessons), and grades 5-6 (23 lessons). Structured lessons based on verbal mediation, self-monitoring and self-evaluation skills. Each lesson includes teaching strategies, prerequisites, objectives, necessary materials. Scripts and program forms included.	Research Press Department G, P.O. Box 9177 2612 N. Mattis Avenue Champaign, IL 61826 Cost: $39.95 each plus S & H
18. Aggression Replacement Training: A Comprehensive Intervention for Aggressive Youth (Goldstein, Glick, Reiner, Zimmerman, & Coultry, 1987)	Three-part training approach designed to teach adolescents to understand and replace aggression and antisocial behavior with positive alternatives. Three parts include prosocial skills (e.g., expressing a complaint), anger control, and moral reasoning. Designed for at-risk or delinquent adolescents.	Research Press Department G, P.O. Box 9177 2612 N. Mattis Avenue Champaign, IL 61826 Cost: $18.95 each plus S & H
19. Talking It Out: A Guide to Effective Communication and Problem Solving (Strayhorn, 1977)	Provides communication techniques for effectively solving problems in family, social or work settings. Book has many helpful examples and role playing exercises.	Research Press Department G, P.O. Box 9177 Champaign, IL 61826 Cost: $9.95 plus S & H
20. Social Skills Training for Children and Youth (Lecroy, 1983)	Book synthesizes practical knowledge and research in the development of social skills with an emphasis on application to practitioners.	Haworth Press 28 East 22 Street New York, New York 10010 Cost: $11.95 plus S & H
21. Let's Be Social (Killoran, Rule, Stowitschek, Innocenti, Striefel, & Boswell, 1982)	26-unit curriculum designed to increase social interaction through daily whole-group "warm-up" sessions and coincidental teaching sessions. (Instruction in specific skill on the occasion when it should be applied, such as saying hello upon entering the classroom for the first time that day.)	Outreach and Development Ctr. Developmental Center for Handicapped Persons Utah State University Logan, UT
22. ASSET (Hazel, Schumaker, Sherman, & Sheldon-Wildgen, 1982–1983)	Enhances specific behaviors of wide range of older adolescents who are lacking social skills. Increases social interaction skills in eight different areas: (a) giving negative feedback, (b) giving positive feedback, (c) accepting negative feedback, (d) resisting peer pressure, (e) solving problems, (f) negotiating, (g) following instructions, and (h) conversing. 8 videotapes of social situations prompt discussion. Uses modeling, practice, feedback, reinforcement and generalization. Homework, progress notes, and parental evaluation.	Research Press Department G, P.O. Box 9177 Champaign, IL 61826 Cost: $1400.00, plus S & H (One-day free preview available)
23. My Friends and Me (Davis, 1977)	Curriculum of 87 lessons. Topics includes personal identity (social identity, emotional identity, physical identity, and intellectual and creative identity) and social skills and understanding (cooperation, consideration of others, ownership and sharing, and dependence and help). Intended for ages 4–5. Includes activity manual, dolls, audio cassettes, activity board, etc. Related materials available.	American Guidance Service 4201 Woodland, P.O. Box 99 Circle Pines, MN 55014-1796 (800) 328-2560 Cost: $340 (free sample)

Appendix 11B-d. Description of Social Skills Curricula and Resources (cont'd)

CURRICULUM NAME/AUTHOR(S)	BRIEF DESCRIPTION OF CURRICULUM	PUBLISHER
24. DUSO-1: Developing Understanding of Self and Others (Dinkmeyer & Dinkmeyer, Jr., 1982)	Activities intended to help children practice social skills; become aware of feelings, priorities, and choices; and develop positive self-image and an appreciation of individual strengths. Intended for grades K–2. Includes teacher's guide, storybooks, puppets, activity cards, audio cassettes, and other materials.	American Guidance Service 4201 Woodland, P.O. Box 99 Circle Pines, MN 55014-1796 (800) 328-2560 Cost: $315, plus S & H
25. DUSO-2: Developing Understanding of Self and Others (Dinkmeyer & Dinkmeyer, Jr., 1982)	Activities intended to provide children with greater understanding of feelings; opportunities to choose solutions, suggest alternatives, and predict and understand consequences; and ways to build communication and decision-making skills. Intended for grades 3–4. Includes teacher's guide, activity cards, audio cassettes and other materials.	American Guidance Service 4201 Woodland, P.O. Box 99 Circle Pines, MN 55014-1796 (800) 328-2560 Cost: $199, plus S & H
26. Getting Along (Page, Cieloha, & Suid)	Activities help children deal with ten problem behaviors: teasing, bossiness, bullying, overcompetitiveness and poor sportsmanship, fighting, intolerance, violent play, disrespect for others' and public property, and selfishness. Two levels: K–1 and grades 2–4. Includes teacher's guide, topic cards, posters, audio cassette, and student activity sheets. Available in Spanish.	American Guidance Service 4201 Woodland, P.O. Box 99 Circle Pines, MN 55014-1796 (800) 328-2560 Cost: $162 each level, plus S & H
27. Taking Part: Introducing Social Skills to Children (Cartledge & Kleefeld, 1991)	Curriculum includes 30 lessons within six units: Making conversation, expressing oneself, communicating nonverbally, cooperating with peers, playing with peers, and responding to aggression. Intended for preschool to grade 3. Focuses on motivation, practice, and maintenance and generalization. Manual, puppets, stickers, etc. See Social Skills Rating System (assessment).	American Guidance Service 4201 Woodland, P.O. Box 99 Circle Pines, MN 55014-1796 (800) 328-2560 Cost: $140, plus S & H
28. Social Skills Intervention Guide: Practical Strategies for Social Skill Training (Elliott & Gresham, 1991)	Intervention includes 43 lessons grouped by: cooperation, assertion, responsibility, empathy, and self-control. Intended for grades 3–12. Remediation directly tied to assessment (Social Skills Rating System). Book includes practical tips and actual case studies of using this intervention approach.	American Guidance Service 4201 Woodland, P.O. Box 99 Circle Pines, MN 55014-1796 (800) 328-2560 Cost: $59.50, plus S & H
29. Teaching Social Skills to Children: Innovative Approaches (Second Edition) (Cartledge & Milburn, 1986)	Widely accepted book includes Part I: selecting social skills, assessment and evaluation of skills, the teaching process, generalization and maintenance of social skills, and integrating the steps—issues in application. Part II: cognitive-affective approach, teaching severely handicapped children; coaching techniques; using activities to teach social skills; and teaching the adolescent.	American Guidance Service 4201 Woodland, P.O. Box 99 Circle Pines, MN 55014-1796 (800) 328-2560 Cost: $23.50, plus S & H
30. Social Skills for Daily Living (Schumaker, Hazel, & Pederson)	Package includes four modules: Program Basics (prerequisite social skills); Conversation and Friendship Skills; Skills for Getting Along with Others; and Problem-Solving Skills. Intended for ages 12–21 with mild or no disabilities. Includes instructor's manual, workbooks, skills books, practice cards, comic books, etc. Each module sold separately.	American Guidance Service 4201 Woodland, P.O. Box 99 Circle Pines, MN 55014-1796 Cost: $81 Basic Module, + S & H Other Modules: $265 each
31. Social Skills on the Job (Macro Systems, Inc., 1989)	Curriculum focuses on job skills, such as appropriate dress, good hygiene, getting to work on time, greeting authority figures, breaktime behavior, admitting mistakes, etc. Intended for individuals ages 15 and up, with mild retardation or emotional disturbances. Includes teacher's guide, videotape, handouts, computer disks (Apple), and software manual.	American Guidance Service 4201 Woodland, P.O. Box 99 Circle Pines, MN 55014-1796 (800) 328-2560 Cost: $490, plus S & H

Appendix 11B-e. Description of Social Skills Curricula and Resources (cont'd)

CURRICULUM NAME/AUTHOR(S)	BRIEF DESCRIPTION OF CURRICULUM	PUBLISHER
32. Talking, Listening, Communicating: Building Interpersonal Relationships (Bormaster & Treat, 1982)	Curriculum for helping students build positive interpersonal relationships through group activities. Content includes: developing self-understanding, relating and working with others, developing creativity, problem solving skills, and decision-making skills through group processes. Activities require less than 30 minutes each. Sequential lesson plans.	PRO-ED, Inc. 8700 Shoal Creek Boulevard Austin, TX 78757-3246 (512-451-3246 Cost: $21, plus S & H
33. Teaching Interpersonal and Community Living Skills: A Curriculum Model for Handicapped Adolescents and Adults (Vallentutti & Bender, 1982)	Book that provides model for teaching interpersonal and community living skills from sociological and functional perspective. Features curriculum objectives, lesson plans, illustrations, resources, and dimensions of the learning task. Emphasizes role as worker, consumer, resident, citizen, learner and participant in leisure activities.	PRO-ED, Inc. 8700 Shoal Creek Boulevard Austin, TX 78757-6897 (512) 451-3246 Cost: $29, plus S & H
34. PLUSS: Putting Language to Use in Social Situations (Zirkelbach)	Program consisting of 10 units including games, home activities and classroom presentations. Users learn to request, inform, inquire, express feelings, introduce and participate in discussions. Language goals included. Appropriate for language-delayed grades 3–6. Package includes posters, manual, flashcards, photo cards, student handbook, and parent guides. Also available from Pro-Ed.	Flaghouse, Inc. 150 N. MacQuesten Parkway Mt. Vernon, NY 10550 (800) 221-5185 Cost: $163, plus S & H
35. Personal Care Program	Program teaches 10 important areas of personal care for daily living. Includes comprehensive manual of teaching strategies and performance objectives. Audio cassette included. Intended for children. Also available from Pro-Ed.	Flaghouse, Inc. 150 N. MacQuesten Parkway Mt. Vernon, NY 10550 $152, plus S & H
36. Being Me: A Social/Sexual Training Program for the Developmentally Disabled (Edwards & Wapnick, 1988)	Curriculum contains four elements used in combination or individually. Intended for individuals with mild to severe disabilities, ages 6 to adults. Promotes normalization in the community. Includes teacher's guide, slides, assessment record form, photo cards, and book.	PRO-ED, Inc. 8700 Shoal Creek Boulevard Austin, TX 78757-6897 (512) 451-3246 Cost: $139, plus S & H
37. Feeling Free: A Social/Sexual Training Program for the Hearing and Visually Impaired (Edwards, Wapnick, Mock, & Whitson)	Curriculum on social/sexual training for individuals with hearing or visual impairments. Intended for children to adults. Includes teacher's guide, picture cards, cut-out patterns.	PRO-ED, Inc. 8700 Shoal Creek Boulevard Austin, TX 78757-6897 (512) 451-3246 Cost: $39, plus S & H
38. Behavior Management of Social/Sexual Behaviors Videotape (Edwards)	30-minute video for trainers using above two programs. Subjects include handling behaviors such as inappropriate touching, hugging, kissing, approaching, exposure, and self-stimulation.	PRO-ED, Inc. 8700 Shoal Creek Boulevard Austin, TX 78757-6897 (512) 451-3246 Cost: $98, plus S & H
39. Overview: Social/Sexual Training Videotape (Edwards)	50-minute video for trainers providing social/sexual training. Instructs on how to set up class, implementing above curriculum, teaching techniques, etc. Demonstrations and applications shown throughout videotape.	PRO-ED, Inc. 8700 Shoal Creek Boulevard Austin, TX 78757-6897 (512) 451-3246 Cost: $98, plus S & H

Appendix 11B-f. Description of Social Skills Curricula and Resources (cont'd)

CURRICULUM NAME/AUTHOR(S)	BRIEF DESCRIPTION OF CURRICULUM	PUBLISHER
40. Social Competence Intervention Package for Preschool Youngsters (SCIPPY) (Day, Powell, & Stowitschek, 1980)	Major goals of program: identify critical social initiations likely to produce positive responses, evaluate functionality of these responses for mildly and moderately handicapped children, develop instructional procedures for teaching these responses, and develop empirically validated teacher training materials. For 3, 4, & 5 year olds. Self-initiations identified: initiations of rough/tumble play, sharing, verbally organizing play, physical assistance, and affection.	
41. Social Skills Training (Spence, 1981)	Social skills training with children and adolescents: A counselor's manual. Windsor, Berks, London	NFER-Nelson Publishing Company
42. Assertive Behavior (Waksman & Messmer, 1985)	Reference: Waksman, S.A., & Messmer, C.L. (1985). Assertive behavior: A program for teaching social skills to children and adolescents. Portland, OR	Enrichment Press
43. Social Skills Training (Wilkinson & Canter, 1982)	Reference: Wilkinson, J., & Canter, S. (1982). Social skills training manual: Assessment, program design, and management of training. New York	Wiley
44. PEERS (Hops, Guild, Fleishman, Paine, Street, Walker, & Greenwood, 1978)	Reference: Hops, H., Guild, J.J., Fleishman, D.H., Paine, S.C., Street, A., Walker, H.W., & Greenwood, C.R. (1978). PEERS (Procedures for establishing effective relationship skills): Manual for consultants. Unpublished manuscript, Center for Behavioral Education of the Handicapped, University of Oregon, Eugene.	Unpublished
45. Startline: Social Education/ Communication	Reference: Startline: Social education/communication. (1987). Allen, TX	DLM
46. The Adaptive Behavior Curriculum (Popovich & Laham, 1981)	Reference: Popovich, D., & Laham, S. (1981). Adaptive behavior curriculum. Baltimore	Paul H. Brookes
47. Socially Appropriate and Inappropriate Development (SAID): Social Skills Assessment and Instruction Program (Armstrong, Mulkerne, & McPherson, 1988)	Reference: Armstrong, S.W., Mulkerne, S., & McPherson, A. (1988). Socially appropriate and inappropriate development (SAID): Social skills assessment and instructional program. Birmingham, AL	EBSCO Curriculum Materials

Appendix 11C-a. Description of Social Skills Assessments and Resources

ASSESSMENT NAME/AUTHOR(S)	BRIEF DESCRIPTION OF ASSESSMENT	PUBLISHER
1. Social Behavior Assessment Inventory (2nd ed.) (Stephens & Arnold)	136 items describing 136 social skills in four categories: environmental, inter-personal, self-related, and task-related. 30 subscales rated on 6-point scale from 0 (not observed or not applicable) to 3 (behavior is never exhibited). Higher scores represent lower levels of social skills. Includes teaching techniques. See Social Skills in the Classroom (curriculum).	Psychological Assess. Resources P.O. Box 998 Odessa, FL 33556 Cost: $78, plus S & H
2. Social Behavior Assessment Inventory (Adapted for Parents) (Crouch, 1980)	Reference: Crouch, P. (1980). Adaptation of the social behavior assessment scale for parents. Ames, IA: Department of Psychology, Iowa State University.	
3. Waksman Social Skills Rating Scale (WSSRS) (Waksman)	Identifies specific social skills deficits for students grades K-12. Assesses both aggressive and passive domains for both males and females. Information allows for social skills training or special counseling programs to be designed. See Waksman Social Skills Curriculum. Also available from PRO-ED, Inc.	Psychological Assess. Resources P.O. Box 998 Odessa, FL 33556 Cost: $49, plus S & H
4. Forms for Behavioral Analysis with Children (Cautela, Cautela, & Esonis)	Unique collection of 42 behavior assessment forms for pinpointing target behaviors. Includes observational forms, interviews, informant ratings, and self-reports. Three categories: Intake packet, intervention development, and intervention recording and guidelines. Examples include: Children's Reinforce-ment Schedule, Fear Inventory, School Behavior Status Checklist, etc.	Research Press Department G. P.O. Box 9177 2612 N. Mattis Avenue Champaign, IL 61826 Cost: $39.95, plus S & H
5. Walker-McConnell Scale of Social Competence and School Adjustment (Walker & McConnell, 1988)	43-item teacher rating scale of social skills for students in K to 6 grades. Three subscales: teacher-preferred social behavior, peer-preferred social behavior, and school adjustment. 5-point scale. Nationally normed.	PRO-ED, Inc. 8700 Shoal Creek Boulevard Austin, TX 78757-6897 Cost: $ 54, plus S & H
6. The Social Skills Inventory—Research Edition (Riggio)	Assesses communication skills as they relate to overall social competence. 90 items with 5-point scale, evaluates verbal and nonverbal skills and evaluates strengths and weaknesses. Key areas: Emotional expressivity; emotional sensitivity; emotional control; social expressivity; social sensitivity and social control. Intended for adults.	Consulting Psychologists Press 3803 E. Bayshore, P.O. Box 10096 Palo Alto, CA 94303 (800) 624-1765 Cost: $22 sample set, plus S & H
7. Factor Tests of Social Intelligence	Four tests, available separately, measure person's ability to understand the thoughts, feelings, and intentions of other people expressed in behavior and communicated by pictures. Multiple-choice format. Intended for adults.	Consulting Psychologists Press 3803 E. Bayshore, P.O. Box 10096 Palo Alto, CA 94303 (800) 624-1765 Cost: $12 sample set, plus S & H
8. Social Translations (O'Sullivan & Guilford, 1965)	24-item inventory assesses person's ability to evaluate interpersonal relation-ships as well as verbal and behavioral cues which have different meanings in different contexts. Intended for adults. May be group administered. 10-minute administration time.	Consulting Psychologists Press 3803 E. Bayshore, P.O. Box 10096 Palo Alto, CA 94303 (800) 624-1765 Cost: $22, plus S & H

Appendix 11C-b. Description of Social Skills Assessments and Resources (cont'd)

ASSESSMENT NAME/AUTHOR(S)	BRIEF DESCRIPTION OF ASSESSMENT	PUBLISHER
9. Missing Cartoons (deMille, O'Sullivan, & Guilford, 1965)	Each of 28 items consists of 4-part cartoon strip that must be completed by respondent. Measures ability to perceive others' feelings and intentions. Intended for adults. May be group administered. 16-minute administration time.	Consulting Psychologists Press 3803 E. Bayshore, P.O. Box 10096 Palo Alto, CA 94303 (800) 624-1765 Cost: $45, plus S & H
10. Bay Area Functional Performance Evaluation (Second Edition) (Williams & Bloomer, 1987)	Consists of two separately scored evaluations: Task Oriented Assessment (five specific goal-directed tasks scored on 12 functional parameters); and Social Interaction Scale (evaluates behavior in five specific settings on seven functional parameters). Intended for adults in mental health or developmental disability facilities. Administration time ranges from 30 to 60 minutes.	Consulting Psychologists Press 3803 E. Bayshore, P.O. Box 10096 Palo Alto, CA 94303 (800) 624-1765 Cost: $45, plus S & H
11. Vineland Adaptive Behavior Scales (Sparrow, Galla, & Cicchetti, 1984, 1985)	Assesses personal and social skills in four areas: Communication (e.g., receptive), Daily Living Skills (e.g., domestic), Socialization (e.g., interpersonal relationships), and Motor Skills (e.g., gross). Three versions: Interview Edition, Survey Form; Interview Edition, Expanded Form; and Classroom Edition. Standardized, norms available. Children to adults.	American Guidance Service 4201 Woodland Road, P.O. Box 99 Circle Pines, MN 55014-1796 (800) 328-2560 Cost: $115 Starter Set, plus S & H
12. Adaptive Behavior Inventory (ABI) (Brown & Leigh, 1986)	Inventory contains five, 30-item scales: Self-Care Skills; Communication Skills, Social Skills, Academic Skills, and Occupational Skills. Completed by teacher or other professional. Intended for individuals ages 5 to 18, with mental retardation or emotional disturbances. Standardized, norms provided. Short Form of 50 items available. Also available from PRO-ED, Inc.	Psychological Assess. Resources P.O. Box 998 Odessa, FL 33556 (800) 331-8378 Cost: $62 Kit, plus S & H
13. AAMD Adaptive Behavior Scale, School Edition (Nihira, Foster, Shellhaas, Leland, Lambert, & Windmiller)	Observational rating scale assess behavior and social adjustment of children whose behavior suggests possible mental retardation, emotional disturbance, or other learning disabilities. 95 scale items divided into two parts, that cover 21 domains of adaptive behavior. Intended for children ages 3–16. Standardized norms, aids in planning, placement and diagnostic procedures. Also available from PRO-ED, Inc.	Psychological Assess. Resources P.O. Box 998 Odessa, FL 33556 (800) 331-8378 Cost: $40 Kit, plus S & H
14. AAMD Adaptive Behavior Scale, Residential and Community Edition (Nihira, Foster, Shallhaas, & Leland)	Similar to above, for individuals ages 3 to adult. 100 scale items in two parts: Personal Independence and Maladaptive Behaviors.	PRO-ED, Inc. 8700 Shoal Creek Boulevard Austin, TX 78757-6897 Cost: $24 starter kit, plus S & H
15. Developmental Assessment for the Severely Handicapped (Dykes, 1980)	Consists of five Pinpoint scales which assess performance in language, sensory motor skills, activities of daily living, preacademic skills, and social-emotional skills. Sensitive to small changes in skills. Identifies skills as present, emerging, task resistive, nonrelevant or unknown. Aids in development of intervention and training programs.	PRO-ED, Inc. 8700 Shoal Creek Boulevard Austin, TX 78757-6897 (512) 451-3246 Cost: $98 kit, plus S & H
16. Pyramid Scales: Criteria Referenced Measures of Adaptive Behavior in Severely Handicapped Persons (Cone, 1984)	Assesses adaptive behavior in moderately to severely handicapped persons from birth to 78 years. Can be administered by interview, through informant, or by direct observation. 30–45 minutes administration time. Elementary language.	PRO-ED, Inc. 8700 Shoal Creek Boulevard Austin, TX 78757-6897 Cost: $46 kit, plus S & H

Appendix 11C-c. Description of Social Skills Assessments and Resources (cont'd)

ASSESSMENT NAME/AUTHOR(S)	BRIEF DESCRIPTION OF ASSESSMENT	PUBLISHER
17. Behavior Rating Profile (Second Edition) (Brown & Hammill, 1990)	Unique battery of six norm-referenced instruments that provide different evaluations of person's behavior at school, home and in interpersonal relationships. Evaluated from perspectives of parents, teachers, peers and individuals. Uses sociogram to evaluate individual's sociometric status in the classroom. Extensively researched.	PRO-ED, Inc. 8700 Shoal Creek Boulevard Austin, TX 78757-6897 (512) 451-3246 Cost: $114 kit, plus S & H
18. Student Self-Concept Scale (SSCS) (Gresham, Elliott, & Evans-Fernandez, 1993)	75 item measure of three areas: Academic Self-Concept; Social Self-Concept; and Self-Image. Confidence, Importance and Outcomes ratings relate to Bandura's theory of self-efficacy. Intended for grades 3–12. Includes Lie Scale. Gender norms available by grade. (Included because of Gresham & Elliott's well-known work in social skills.)	American Guidance Service 4201 Woodland Road, P.O. Box 99 Circle Pines, MN 55014-1796 (800) 328-2560 Cost: $95 total set, plus S & H
19. Social Skills Rating System (SSRS) (Gresham & Elliott, 1990)	Comprehensive system includes three rating forms (teacher, parent and student). Three scales: Social Skills Scale (cooperation, empathy, assertion, self-control, and responsibility), Problem Behaviors Scale (externalizing or internalizing problems, and hyperactivity), and Academic Competence Scale (academic functioning). Gender norms available by grade. Computer scoring and planning.	American Guidance Service 4201 Woodland Road, P.O. Box 99 Circle Pines, MN 55014-1796 (800) 328-2560 Cost: $178 for two starter sets, plus S & H
20. Brief Index of Adaptive Behavior (BIAB) (McCallum, Herrin, Wheeler, & Edwards, 1984)	Inventory of 39 items which assess three domains: independent functioning, socialization, and communication. Used to screen individuals 5 to 17 years of age who may need complete evaluation of behavior disorders. Provides profile of potential disorders, identifying those areas of behavior that deviate from the norm. Manual and forms.	Scholastic Testing Service 480 Meyer Road Bensenville, IL 60106-1617 (708) 766-7150 Cost: Specimen set $13, plus S & H
21. Peer Acceptance Scale (Bruininks, Rynders, & Gross, 1974)	Reference: Bruininks, R.H., Rynders, J.E., & Gross, J.C. (1974). Social acceptance of mildly retarded pupils in resource rooms and regular classes. American Journal of Mental Deficiency, 78, 377–383.	
22. Ohio Social Acceptance Scale (Fordyce, Yauck, & Raths, 1946)	Reference: Fordyce, W.G., Yauck, W.A., Raths, L. (1946). A manual for the Ohio guidance tests for the elementary grades. Columbus, OH: Ohio State Department of Education.	

Appendix 11D-a

McGinnis, E., & Goldstein, A. P. (1990). *Skillstreaming in early childhood: Teaching prosocial skills to the preschool and kindergarten child.* Champaign, IL: Research Press.

Group I: Beginning Social Skills
1. Listening
2. Using Nice Talk
3. Using Brave Talk
4. Saying Thank You
5. Rewarding Yourself
6. Asking for Help
7. Asking for a Favor
8. Ignoring

Group II: School-Related Skills
9. Asking a Question
10. Following Directions
11. Trying When It's Hard
12. Interrupting

Group III: Friendship-Making Skills
13. Greeting Others
14. Reading Others
15. Joining In
16. Waiting Your Turn
17. Sharing
18. Offering Help
19. Asking Someone to Play
20. Playing a Game

Group IV: Dealing with Feelings
21. Knowing Your Feelings
22. Feeling Left Out
23. Asking to Talk
24. Dealing with Fear
25. Deciding How Someone Feels
26. Showing Affection

Group V: Alternatives to Aggression
27. Dealing with Teasing
28. Dealing with Feeling Mad
29. Deciding If It's Fair
30. Solving a Problem
31. Accepting Consequences

Group VI: Dealing with Stress
32. Relaxing
33. Dealing with Mistakes
34. Being Honest
35. Knowing When to Tell
36. Dealing with Losing
37. Wanting to be First
38. Saying No
39. Accepting No
40. Deciding What to Do

Appendix 11D-b

Goldstein, A. P., Sprafkin, R.P. Gershaw, N.J., & Klein, P. (1980). *Skillstreaming the adolescent: A structured learning approach to teaching prosocial skills.* Champaign, IL: Research Press.

Group I: Beginning Social Skills
1. Listening
2. Starting a Conversation
3. Having a Conversation
4. Asking a Question
5. Saying Thank You
6. Introducing Yourself
7. Introducing Other People
8. Giving a Compliment

Group II: Advanced Social Skills
9. Asking for Help
10. Joining In
11. Giving Instructions
12. Following Instructions
13. Apologizing
14. Convincing Others

Group III: Skills for Dealing with Feelings
15. Knowing Your Feelings
16. Expressing Your Feelings
17. Understanding the Feelings of Others
18. Dealing with Someone Else's Anger
19. Expressing Affection
20. Dealing with Fear
21. Rewarding Yourself

Group IV: Skill Alternatives to Aggression
22. Asking Permission
23. Sharing Something
24. Helping Others
25. Negotiation
26. Using Self-Control
27. Standing Up for Your Rights
28. Responding to Teasing
29. Avoiding Trouble with Others
30. Keeping Out of Fights

Group V: Skills for Dealing with Stress
31. Making a Complaint
32. Answering a Complaint
33. Sportsmanship After the Game
34. Dealing with Embarrassment
35. Dealing with Being Left Out
36. Standing Up for a Friend
37. Responding to Persuasion
38. Responding to Failure
39. Dealing with Contradictory Messages
40. Dealing with an Accusation
41. Getting Ready for a Difficult Conversation
42. Dealing with Group Pressure

Group VI: Planning Skills
43. Deciding on Something to Do
44. Deciding What Caused a Problem
45. Setting a Goal
46. Deciding on Your Abilities
47. Gathering Information
48. Arranging Problems by Importance
49. Making a Decision
50. Concentrating on a Task

Appendix 11D-c

Goldstein, A. P., Sprafkin, R.P. Gershaw, N.J., & Klein, P. (1980). *Skillstreaming the adolescent: A structured learning approach to teaching prosocial skills.* Champaign, IL: Research Press.

Group I: Beginning Social Skills
Skill 1: Listening

Steps	*Trainer Notes*
1. Look at the person who is talking.	Face the person; establish eye contact.
2. Think about what is being said.	Show this by nodding your head, saying "mm-hm."
3. Wait your turn to talk.	Don't fidget; don't shuffle your feet.
4. Say what you want to say.	Ask question; express feelings; express your ideas.

Suggested Content for Modeling Displays:
A. School, neighborhood or work: Person A explains directions to another person.
B. Home: Family member feels sad; client listens.
C. Peer Group: Friend describes interesting movie to client.
==

Group I: Beginning Social Skills
Skill 2: Starting a Conversation

Steps	*Trainer Notes*
1. Greet the other person.	Say "hi"; shake hands; choose the right time and place.
2. Make small talk.	
3. Decide if the other person is listening.	Check to see if the other person is listening; looking at you, nodding, saying "mm-hm."
4. Bring up the main topic.	

Suggested Content for Modeling Displays:
A. School, neighborhood or work: Client starts conversation with person in store.
B. Home: Client discusses news item with family member.
C. Peer Group: Client suggests weekend plans to friend.
==

Group I: Beginning Social Skills
Skill 3: Having a Conversation

Steps	*Trainer Notes*
1. Say what you want to say.	
2. Ask the other person what he/she thinks.	
3. Listen to what the other person says.	
4. Say what you think.	Respond to the other person; add new information; ask questions.
5. Make a closing remark.	Steps #1 - 4 can be repeated many times before #5.

Suggested Content for Modeling Displays:
A: School, neighborhood, work: Client talks with co-worker about upcoming shift change.
B: Home: Client talks with brother or sister about school experiences.
C: Peer Group: Client discusses vacation plans with friend.

Appendix 11D-d

Stephens, T.M. (1992). *Social skills in the classroom (2nd ed.).* Odessa, FL: Psychological Assessment Resources.

Self-Related Behaviors
    Accepting Consequences
    Ethical Behavior
    Expressing Feelings
    Positive Attitude Toward Self
    Responsive Behavior
    Self Care

Task Related Behaviors
    Asking and Answering Questions
    Attending Behavior
    Classroom Discussion
    Completing Tasks
    Following Directions
    Group Activities
    Independent Work
    On-Task Behavior
    Performing Before Others
    Quality of Work

Environmental Behaviors
    Care for the Environment
    Dealing with Emergencies
    Lunchroom Behavior
    Movement Around the Environment

Interpersonal Behaviors
    Accepting Authority
    Coping with Conflict
    Gaining Attention
    Greeting Others
    Helping Others
    Making Conversation
    Organized Play
    Positive Attitude Toward Others
    Playing Informally
    Property: Own and Others

Appendix 11D-e

Stephens, T.M. (1992). *Social skills in the classroom (2nd ed.).* Odessa, FL: Psychological Assessment Resources.

Major Category:	INTERPERSONAL BEHAVIOR
Subcategory:	**Accepting Authority**
Skills:	To comply with request of adult in position of authority.
	To comply with request of peer in position of authority.
	To know and follow classroom rules.
	To follow classroom rules in the absence of the teacher.
	To question rules which may be unjust.

Major Category:	INTERPERSONAL BEHAVIOR
Subcategory:	**Coping with Conflict**
Skills:	To respond to teasing or name calling by ignoring, changing the subject, or using some other constructive means.
	To respond to physical assault by leaving the situation, calling for help, or using some other constructive means.
	To walk away from peer when angry to avoid hitting.
	To refuse request of another politely.
	To express anger with nonaggressive words rather than physical action or aggressive words.
	To handle constructive criticism or punishment perceived as undeserved.

Major Category:	INTERPERSONAL BEHAVIOR
Subcategory:	**Gaining Attention**
Skills:	To gain teacher's attention in class by raising hand.
	To wait quietly for recognition before speaking out in class.
	To use "please" and "thank you" when making requests of others.
	To approach teacher and ask appropriately for help, explanation, instructions, etc.
	To gain attention from peers in appropriate ways.
	To ask a peer for help.

Major Category:	INTERPERSONAL BEHAVIOR
Subcategory:	**Greeting Others**
Skills:	To look others in the eye when greeting them.
	To state one's name when asked.
	To smile when encountering a friend or acquaintance.
	To greet adults and peers by name.
	To respond to an introduction by shaking hands and saying "How do you do?"
	To introduce oneself to another person.
	To introduce two people to each other.

Appendix 11D-f

Walker, H.M., Todis, B., Holmes, D., & Horton, G. (1988). *The Walker social skills curriculum: The ACCESS program—adolescent curriculum for communication and effective social skills.* Austin, TX: Pro-Ed.

Triple-A Strategy
1. Assess
2. Amend
3. Act

Listening
1. Maintaining eye contact
2. Let others do most of the talking
3. Pay attention
4. Avoid interruptions

Greeting Other People
1. Look at and acknowledge the person
2. Introduce others
3. Show interest

Joining In with Others
1. Find a person or group you would like to join
2. Approach confidently
3. Watch and wait for a good time to join
4. Decide on the best way to join
5. Join in and participate

Having Conversations
1. Listen about as much as you talk
2. Show enthusiasm and interest
3. Make sense; stay on the topic
4. Keep the conversation going; ask/answer questions

Borrowing
1. Ask permission politely
2. Don't become angry/disappointed when turned down
3. Treat what you borrow as if it was your own
4. If you borrow, be ready to lend

Offering Assistance
1. Decide whether the person needs help
2. Listen to what the person needs
3. Decide whether you can help or whether you know someone who can
4. Offer to help and follow through

Complimenting
1. Recognize the value of a compliment
2. Notice what you can compliment about others
3. Express what you have noticed
4. Be sincere

Showing a Sense of Humor
1. Have fun and enjoy yourself
2. Try to find something funny in a difficult situation
3. Be able to laugh at yourself
4. Be able to take a joke
5. Know when to show a sense of humor and when to be serious

Keeping Friends
1. Stay in contact
2. Demonstrate thoughtfulness
3. Be a good listener
4. Compliment your friend
5. Offer assistance
5. Borrow the right way

Interacting with the Opposite Sex
1. Carry on good conversations
2. Extend invitations
3. Read the other person's signals
4. Act thoughtfully

Negotiating with Others
1. State your position calmly
2. Let others state their positions
3. Evaluate, fairly, the other person's position
4. Compromise

Being Left Out
1. Try to decide why you were left out
2. Try to resolve the problem
   A. Apologize for your behavior
   B. Ask to be included
3. If you are still left out, find other friends or something else to do

Handling Group Pressure
1. Ask yourself "Is this something I should do or really want to do?"
2. If it is something you shouldn't or don't want to do, choose a way to say no:
   A. Give a reason
   B. Suggest something else to do
   C. Change the subject
   D. Stall
   E. Give permission to someone else
3. If you are still feeling pressured, say "no" and leave

Appendix 11D-g

Walker, H.M., McConnell, S., Holmes, D., Todis, B., Walker, J., & Golden, N. (1988). *The Walker social skills curriculum: The ACCEPTS Program.* Austin, TX: Pro-Ed.

Classroom Skills
Listening to the teacher when you are told to do something
Doing your best work
Following classroom rules

Basic Interaction Skills
Eye contact
Using the right voice
Starting
Listening
Answering
Making sense
Taking turns talking
Asking a question

Getting Along Skills
Using polite words
Sharing
Following the rules
Assisting others
Touching the right way
Grooming
Smiling
Compliments
Making friends

Coping Skills
When someone says "no"
Expressing anger
When someone teases you
When someone tries to hurt you
When someone asks you do to something you can't do
When things don't go right

Appendix 11D-h

Jackson, N.F., Jackson, D.A., & Monroe, C. (1983). Getting along with others: Teaching social effectiveness to children. Champaign, IL: Research Press.

Skill 1: Introducing
To introduce yourself to someone, you:
- Use a pleasant face and voice
- Look at the person
- Tell the person your name
- Ask for the person's name

To introduce two people who don't know each other, you:
- Use a pleasant face and voice
- Look at each person
- Tell each person the other's name

Skill 2: Following Directions
To follow directions, you:
- Use a pleasant face and voice
- Look at the person giving the directions
- Say "OK"
- Start to do what was asked right away
- Do it satisfactorily

Skill 3: Giving and Receiving Positive Feedback
To give positive feedback, you:
- Use a pleasant face and voice
- Look at the person
- Tell exactly what you like about what the person did
- Tell the person right after it was done

To receive positive feedback, you:
- Use a pleasant face and voice
- Look at the person
- Acknowledge the feedback by saying, "Thanks" or "You're welcome"

Skill 4: Sending an "I'm Interested" Message
To send an "I'm Interested" message, you:
- Use a pleasant face
- Look at the person
- Keep your hands and body still

Skill 5: Sending an Ignoring Message
To send an ignoring message, you:
- Keep a pleasant face
- Look away or walk away from the person
- Keep a quiet mouth
- Pretend you're not listening

Skill 6: Interrupting a Conversation
To interrupt the right way, you:
- Use a pleasant face and voice
- Wait for a pause in the conversation
- Say "excuse me"
- Look directly at the person
- Then talk

Skill 7: Joining a Conversation
To join a conversation, you:
- Use a pleasant face and voice
- Look at the person
- Wait for a pause
- Say something on the topic

Skill 8: Starting Conversation/Keeping It Going
To start a conversation and keep it going, you:
- Use a pleasant face and voice
- Look at the person
- Ask a question about the other person
- Tell about yourself

Skill 9: Sharing
To share, you:
- Use a pleasant face and voice
- Divide up something there's not much of, so others can also have some (if appropriate)
- Take turns (if appropriate)

Skill 10: Offering to Help
To offer to help, you:
- Use a pleasant face and voice
- Notice something you can do for someone
- Ask if you can help
- If that person says "yes," then you do it

Skill 11: Compromising
To compromise, you:
- Use a pleasant face and voice
- Think of a way both people can get something that they want
- Suggest it

Skill 12: Asking for Clear Directions
To ask for clear directions, you:
- Use a pleasant face and voice
- Look at the person
- Ask for more information
- Repeat the directions to the person

Skill 13: Problem Solving
To solve a problem, you:
- Take a deep breath to get a calm body and good attitude
- Think of at least three different things you can do
- Pick the best one for you
- Try that one first

Skill 14: Using Positive Consequences
To reward someone, you:
- Use a pleasant face and voice
- Do something nice for the person
  For example, you could do the person a favor, thank the person, give the person a hug, or share something

Skill 15: Giving/Receiving Suggestion for Improvement
To give a suggestion for improvement, you:
- Use a pleasant face and voice
- Say something nice on the topic
- Make a suggestion
- Thank the person for listening

Skill 16: Handling Name Calling and Teasing
To handle name calling and teasing, you:
- Keep a pleasant face
- Take a deep breath to get calm
- Look away, or walk away if you can
- Use positive self-talk (say to self, "I am calm," etc.)

Skill 17: Saying "No" to Stay Out of Trouble
To say "no," you:
- Use a pleasant face and voice
- Take a deep breath to get calm
- Look at the person
- Keep saying "no"
- Suggest something else to do

If suggesting doesn't work, you:
- Ignore and walk away

» CHAPTER 12 »

Assertiveness Training

Deborah Hutchins, Ph.D., CTRS

Background/History

Assertiveness has been described as a trait, a behavioral style, a communication style, and a skill to promote positive relations and self-esteem. Salter (1949) described assertiveness as a trait someone was born with. However, scholars later acknowledged that assertiveness is a skill that can be learned. Bedell and Lennox (1996) define assertiveness as an interpersonal behavioral approach "that simultaneously attempts to maximize the person's satisfaction of wants while considering the wants of other people, thus promoting respect of self and others" (p. 132). Alberti and Emmons (2001) defined assertiveness as a behavior which "enables a person to act in his or her own best interest, to stand up for himself or herself without undue anxiety, to express honest feelings comfortably, or to exercise personal rights without denying the rights of others" (p. 13). They also distinguish assertive responding behavior from nonassertive and aggressive styles of responding. Paterson (2000) described assertiveness as one of several styles of interpersonal communication. The other styles he described include passive, aggressive, and passive-aggressive.

Assertiveness is a concept that has its roots in early behavioral therapy. Salter (1949) and Wolpe (1958) both recognized that some individuals had specific difficulties standing up for their rights. Assertiveness skill-development strategies were used to help these individuals function better in everyday life (Bedell & Lennox, 1996, p. 268). In his 1949 publication, *Conditioned Reflex Therapy*, Salter described several prescribed response styles. He called these styles the "excitatory reflexes." These reflexes, or responses, were used in the treatment of a wide variety of symptoms, such as claustrophobia, shyness, low self-sufficiency, depression, sexual problems, psychosomatic problems, stuttering, and alcohol addiction (Colter & Guerra, 1976; Salter, 2002). Wolpe, a behavioral therapy pioneer, recognized assertiveness training for its ability to

reciprocally reduce anxiety (Bedell & Lennox, 1996). Assertiveness training became popular with women in the 1970s as a way for them to be informed about their interpersonal rights, overcome their internal barriers to change, and negative socialization ("Assertiveness Training," 2003; Enns, 1992).

Alberti and Emmons (2001) noted that in terms of assertiveness, individuals are characterized as either "situational nonassertive/aggressive" or "generalized nonassertive/aggressive." The situational nonassertive/aggressive individual can be a relatively healthy person who, with or without professional help, may learn to successfully initiate more assertive behaviors. However, the generalized nonassertive/aggressive individual will probably require some form of professional attention in order to overcome his or her behavioral deficits related to assertion. Therefore, the generalized nonassertive/aggressive type person is the best candidate for assertiveness training.

Intended Client Groups

Assertiveness as a behavioral or communication response and assertive training programs have been utilized and studied for a variety of populations, such as:

- individuals with physical disabilities and wheelchair users (Glueckauf & Quittner, 1992; Page, Holland, Rand, Gartin, & Dowling, 1981)
- individuals with visual impairments (Hersen & Kabacoff, 1995; Kim, 2003; Kolb, 1985)
- individuals with chronic pain (Winterowd, Beck, & Gruender, 2003; Zelik, 1984)
- individuals with eating disorders (Shiina et al., 2005)
- at-risk youth who demonstrate difficulties with interpersonal communication (Laxton, Gray, & Watts, 1997; Shannon, 1999)
- victims of violence and abuse (Brecklin & Ullman, 2005; Meyer, 1999; Ticoll, 1994)

- marginalized groups such as women and the elderly (Doty, 1987; Ryan, Anas, & Friedman, 2006; Davidson, 1997; Jakubowski-Spector, 1973)
- individuals with mental illness, especially those who have depressed or suicidal ideation (Douglas, 1980; Lin et al., 2008; Arean, Nezu, & Nezu, 1991; Weinhardt, Carey, Carey, & Verdecias, 1998)
- adolescents susceptible to peer pressure to drink alcohol, smoke, ingest illegal drugs (Goldberg-Lillehoj, Spoth, & Trudeau, 2005)
- individuals with substance addictions (Clark, 2000; Heinemann, 1993)
- participants with disabilities in a sheltered workshop (Page et al., 1981)
- residents of institutions such as nursing homes and hospitals (Segal, 2005)
- school children at-risk for bullying (Crothers & Kolbert, 2004)

Basic Premises

Assertiveness Training (AT) is a form of behavioral therapy with a long history of use in personal growth groups and mental health treatment ("Assertiveness Training," 2003). AT has roots in the women's movement and in treating individuals with various mental health conditions. During the 1970s, the use of assertiveness training with people with disabilities broadened. The recognition of assertiveness training as a method to build self-esteem, to improve communication of needs, and to empower people with disabilities facilitated the increased use of assertiveness training with diverse populations and in a variety of service settings ("Assertiveness Training," 2003; Ruben & Ruben, 1989).

Assertiveness training has been described as an intervention that explores and develops personal techniques for positive verbal communication and preferred behavioral responses which lead to better interpersonal relations (Dombeck & Wells-Moran, 2006; Kim, 2003). It has been touted as a process for communicating feelings, improving self-esteem, and empowering individuals who have traditionally been marginalized (Austin, 2004; Davidson, 1997; Kolb, 1985; Shiina et al., 2005). As a treatment intervention, assertiveness training provides a mechanism for coping with the social anxiety and the emotional barriers that may interfere with recovery and successful community reintegration (Douglas, 1980; Glueckauf & Quittner, 1992; Heinemann, 1993; Lin et al., 2008; Zelik, 1984). According to the *Encyclopedia of Mental Disorders*,

the main premise of assertiveness training is "to teach people strategies for acting on their desires, needs, and opinions while remaining respectful of others" ("Assertiveness Training," 2003).

Wolpe and Lazarus (1966) described methods of assertiveness training as including behavioral methods such as modeling, shaping, and autofeedback. In their *Handbook for Communication and Problem-Solving Skills Training*, Bedell and Lennox (1996) outlined a framework for assertiveness training that includes sections on the verbal and nonverbal components of assertiveness, in addition to addressing the consequences of assertive responses. They describe a four-component process of training including (a) instruction, (b) supervised practice, (c) feedback, and (d) independent practice. Alberti and Emmons (2001) recommend that the content of an assertiveness-training program contain both behavioral rehearsal and cognitive rehearsal components. The behavioral rehearsal components include definitive behaviors that lead to assertive response (e.g., refusing a request, expressing emotions, and defending oneself). Cognitive rehearsal modifies attitudes and beliefs that could undermine assertiveness (e.g., self-defeating descriptions, reasoning, and thought modification).

"Being There" is an assertiveness program designed by professionals at Changeways Clinics in Vancover, Canada that uses a psychoeducational group therapy approach. This program consists of 8 to 10 sessions (2 1/2 hours each) addressing a range of 12 topics on assertiveness. The topics include: (a) definitions of assertive, passive, aggressive, and passive-aggressive; (b) barriers to assertiveness; (c) assertiveness rights; (d) nonverbal behavioral styles; (e) giving opinions; (f) accepting compliments; (g) coping with criticism; (h) giving constructive negative feedback; (i) saying no; (j) making effective requests; and (k) dealing with confrontations. *The Assertiveness Workbook* (2000), authored by Randy Paterson, is based in part on the "Being There" program. He provided information, self-assessments, writing exercises, and practice suggestions to the reader for a self-help approach to assertiveness training.

Zelik (1984) described an assertiveness program for patients with chronic pain. The goals of this program include: (a) to enhance patient understanding of the role of stress in their lives and how assertiveness can reduce stress, (b) to teach assertiveness concepts and role-playing situations that they can incorporate these concepts into their lives, and (c) to assist patients in recognizing their behavioral response styles and how to change negative behaviors to assertive behaviors. The program consisted of 6 hours of classroom instruction, including theory, discussion, and practice through role-playing. Assertiveness training was introduced after 2 weeks of a 5-week inpatient admission. The program incorporated handouts, practice sheets, and a bibliography of readings. The content of the training included defining key concepts such as passive, assertive, aggressive behaviors; discussing the relationship of stress and pain; the importance of nonverbal communication and listening skills; dealing with potential anger issues through conflict resolution; and role-playing specific situations where assertive responses would be the preferred. As part of an interdisciplinary plan of treatment, this program was rated favorably by patients in terms of gaining control over their pain, increasing their ability to handle stress, and improving communication skills.

Teaching assertiveness skills to people with learning disabilities was the goal of a program implemented by Laxton, Gray, and Watts (1997). This program consisted of 24 group sessions covering five main areas: (a) improving self-esteem, (b) identifying and labeling feelings, (c) rights and responsibilities, (d) passive, aggressive, and assertive behavior, and (e) presentation of knowledge and skills to others. Activities utilized in the training program included self-drawings, audio tape recordings, videos, behavioral rehearsal, feedback, games, relaxation sessions, role plays, and open discussions. A unique feature of this program was that, at the conclusion of their sessions, the participants planned and implemented a presentation on assertiveness to their family members and the agency staff. The intent of this presentation was to facilitate the support of family and staff for practicing and maintaining the assertive skills they learned through the program. Pre- and post-questionnaires, along with weekly session evaluations, were used to evaluate the program. These sources of evaluation indicated overall program success with the final presentation being rated as the most positive aspect of the program.

Several models of response have been used to teach assertiveness strategies. The assertive model DESK described by Shannon (1999) is proposed as part of a program to teach children to effectively express themselves. DESK is an acronym: "D," describe the behavior; "E," express feelings using the "I" message; "S," state what the complainant wants the listener to change; "K," know what the listener will not change. To be most effective, it is recommended that both the complainant and listener are trained in the use of this model. In a similar vein, Davis (1998) proposed the use of the formula DESC as a format for assertion. This formula directs the use of "I messages" in a

systematic and detailed way. DESC is an acronym for "D," describe the situation; "E," express your feelings regarding the situation; "S," specify the change that you desire; "C," identify the consequences that could occur. These are important strategies for individuals to organize an assertive response.

Another common assertiveness-training strategy is to teach individuals about their "rights" and how to stand up for their rights without infringing on the rights of others (Alberti & Emmons, 2001; Hermes, 1997; Paterson, 2000; Smith, 1975). The application of the "I" message versus the "you" message is a concept used to reinforce this strategy. An "I" message focuses on the person taking responsibility for their feelings and needs and expressing them. The "I" message is preferred to a "you" message that puts responsibility for feelings on others and begets blame. Hermes (1998, p. 21) proposed the use of the "Assertiveness Formula" as a tool in reinforcing the use of "I" messages. The formula is as follows:

I feel _____

When you _____

Because _____

I want/need _____

In her book *Assertiveness: Practical skills for positive communication*, Hermes provides worksheets to practice applying this formula in various life circumstances (1998, pp. 21–24). The focus on "I messages" is an important aspect of providing assertive responses. (See also Chapter 5 on Communication Techniques in this text.)

Related Research

Aspects of assertiveness training are often incorporated into interdisciplinary treatment programs and/or TR interventions, such as social-skill training, anger management, stress management, and/or community reintegration programs (Clark, 2000). However, more specific AT programs have been described in the literature and in research studies testing its efficacy.

Glueckauf and Quittner (1992) designed an assertiveness-training program for individuals who use wheelchairs. The program consisted of 11 sessions addressing a variety of topics: (a) introduction; (b) distinguishing among passive, aggressive, and assertive behaviors; (c) practice of basic listening skills; (d) providing feedback and managing awkward disability-related situations; (e) ineffective thinking and identification of assertive rights; (f) practice of autogenic and progressive relaxation techniques; (g) expressing frustration and anger in an assertive fashion; (h) implementation and practice of individual assertion goals; (i) group practice of assertion goals; and (j) social networks and termination. These topics were addressed through both group and individualized sessions. The training program included reading the book, *Your Perfect Right: Assertiveness and Equality in Your Life and Relationships,* by Alberti and Emmons (2008). In addition, participants participated in video reviews, discussion, role plays, writing exercises, and homework. An efficacy research study of this program showed that individuals participating in the assertiveness training reported significantly higher assertiveness responses in both general and disability-related interactions (Glueckauf & Quittner, 1992).

An outpatient treatment program for individuals with bulimic disorders combined behavioral therapy with assertive training and self-esteem enhancement. The program consisted of 10 1-hour sessions held weekly. Each group consisted of three to six patients. The psychoeducation topics included: (a) diet and eating behavior and lifestyle; (b) cognitive restructuring regarding their dieting and body shaping and behavioral therapy for acquiring a healthy diet and lifestyle; (c) assertiveness training for coping with interpersonal problems; (d) social-skills training based on problem-solving therapy; and (e) self-esteem enhancement. This study demonstrated that the treatment program resulted in less binge-eating behavior and improved social function of patients with eating disorders (Shiina et al., 2005).

A study that assessed the relationships of assertiveness, depression, and social support among 50 older nursing home residents found a significant correlation between assertiveness and depression. The subjects in this study were older adults (mean age 75), 75% female and 95% Caucasian, free of cognitive impairments. Several measures were administered, including the Wolpe-Lazarus Assertiveness Scale (WLAS), the Geriatric Depression Scale (GDS), and the Social Support List of Interactions (SSL12-1). Correlations between the mean scores were completed. The most significant findings were the correlations between assertiveness and depression, and between overall physical health and depression. Despite limitations, this study supports the use of interventions designed to increase assertiveness and improve physical health

among nursing home residents as a strategy for reducing depression (Segal, 2005). Similar methods were used in a study completed with 100 older adults in a rehabilitation facility (Hersen & Kabacoff, 1995). Study results supported similar findings regarding the correlation between assertiveness and depression. The researchers concluded that older people with visual impairments need "new assertive response strategies to have their needs met successfully" (p. 528).

In 2005, a study to evaluate the effects of an assertiveness training program was conducted in an acute psychiatric unit of a military hospital in Taiwan (Lin et al., 2008). There were 68 subjects who participated in the study, which used a quasi-experimental design. The patients in the study were diagnosed with depression, bipolar disorder, anxiety disorder, or adjustment disorder. They were placed in an experimental group or a diagnosis-matched comparison group. The 40 patients who were in the experimental group were divided into subgroups of 5–8 individuals who participated in eight 2-hour assertiveness-training sessions conducted twice a week. The assertiveness-training sessions included: (a) an introduction to concepts of assertiveness theory and behaviors; (b) the presentation of information related to individual rights; (c) skill development related to listening and questioning behaviors; (d) definition and discussion regarding the relationship of self-esteem and assertiveness; (e) dealing with criticism; (f) the refusal of requests; (g) practicing both verbal and nonverbal assertiveness techniques; and (g) the giving of empathy and praise. The sessions included the use of various training strategies including "teaching, demonstration, feedback, role-playing, coaching, reinforcement, homework, group discussions, and self-directed learning" (Lin et al., 2008, p. 2878). The efficacy of the training was measured by assertiveness, social anxiety, and self-esteem inventories. After training, the results indicated that the experimental group subjects had a significant increase in assertiveness and a significant decrease in social anxiety. However, self-esteem did not increase significantly as a result of training, and no improvement was observed in the control group.

A study that compared views on bullying and anti-bullying interventions between middle school students (n = 285) and teachers (n = 37) was completed using quantitative and qualitative methods. The results of the study showed that both teachers and students strongly supported the teaching of assertiveness as a strategy for dealing with bullying (Crothers & Kolbert, 2004).

Research focusing on adolescents in a rural environment studied the relationship of assertiveness and alcohol use. This longitudinal preventative intervention study collected data from 470 adolescents from the Midwest. A modified version of the Assertion Inventory (developed by Gambrill & Richey, 1975) was administered, as was the Alcohol Use Composite Index (AUCI). The results of data analysis indicated that several dimensions of assertiveness were found to have significant influence on the alcohol-use index. These findings support the use of multidimensional assertiveness training, offered over time, as a preventive intervention for adolescents residing in a rural setting (Goldberg-Lillehoj et al., 2005).

The use of assertiveness training to reduce the risk of HIV among women with severe mental illness was studied by Weinhardt, Carey, Carey, and Verdecias (1998). This study focused on "sexual assertiveness" training. Twenty female outpatients with primary diagnosis of schizophrenia, bipolar disorder, and major depressive disorder were screened using the HIV-Risk Behavior Screening Instrument (HRBS). Once admitted to the assertiveness program the subjects received 10 treatment sessions during a two-week period, co-facilitated by a male and a female. Sessions included HIV information, condom use, sexual assertiveness (negotiation of condom use with resistant partners and refusing to engage in unsafe sexual behaviors). Sessions focused on education and skill development. The results of this study found that women who participated in the sexual assertiveness program improved their sexual assertiveness skills through the 4-month follow-up and indicated an increased frequency of protected sex at a 2-month follow-up.

Studies related to older adults have supported the use of assertiveness in the context of receiving health-related services. In general, older adults are less assertive than the younger population because of their unfamiliarity with assertive behavior and due to their loss of confidence in using an assertive approach. After studying several conversation scenarios within a healthcare context, it was determined that assertiveness can be a positive option for older adults to utilize when communicating with their physician or other healthcare professionals (Ryan, Anas, & Friedman, 2006).

Whether designed as a separate intervention or as part of a larger program of leisure education, social-skills development, and/or anger management, assertiveness training has application as a TR intervention with a number of different client populations in a variety of practice settings.

Application to Therapeutic Recreation

The concept of assertiveness training has been described as being founded in behavioral therapy (Austin, 2004), cognitive-behavior therapy, and social-cognitive theory (Goldberg-Lillehoj, Spoth, & Trudeau, 2005). It involves behavioral, cognitive, affective, and social aspects (Moore, Hudson, & Smith, 2007) and occurs within a context that is influenced by the environment (Goldberg-Lillehoj, Spoth, & Trudeau, 2005; Ruben & Ruben, 1989). Assertiveness training reflects aspects of behavior when clients are able to express their emotions and needs in specific situations and can utilize behaviors that enhance communication and establish positive interpersonal skills. The cognitive and affective aspects of assertiveness are reflected when clients are able to express and react to positive and negative emotions without excessive anxiety and/or aggression (Colter & Guerra, 1976; Moore et al., 2007). The development of assertive response skills occurs within a social context and is influenced by a dynamic environment.

Therapeutic recreation services commonly utilize interventions that are founded in cognitive-behavioral and social-cognitive theory to address the various needs of the clients. In fact these theories are the basis for commonly used therapeutic recreation (TR) interventions such as leisure education/counseling, social skills development, and stress management (Austin, 2004; Malkin & Kastrinos, 1997; Shank & Coyle, 2002).

Therapeutic recreation practitioners often focus on the clients' social interaction skills as an important aspect of leisure participation and quality of life (Stumbo & Peterson, 2009; Carter, Van Andel, & Robb, 2003). Social interaction as a construct is comprised of several aspects, including: communication skills, relationship-building skills, and self-presentation skills (Stumbo & Peterson, 2009). Many clients served in TR have difficulties with aspects of social interaction, and these difficulties are often addressed through interventions such as leisure education/counseling, social skills programs, community reintegration programs, and anger management (Austin, 2004; Carter et al., 2003). Given the focus of assertiveness training in the development of communication skills, relationship skills, and self-presentation skills, AT appears as a viable option for TR intervention (Austin, 2004; Glueckauf & Quittner, 1992; Malkin & Kastrinos,1997; Shank & Coyle, 2002).

Although somewhat varied dependent on the characteristics of the population being served, the process of conducting assertiveness training programs utilizes several common approaches. The "typical" assertiveness training program includes an introduction of the key concepts of assertive, passive, aggressive, and passive-aggressive behaviors/responses. These concepts are defined and the verbal and nonverbal aspects of these concepts introduced. This introductory information is typically presented using readings, worksheets, discussions, and/or video examples. This introduction leads to the identification of specific situations in which the clients might use these behaviors/responses to improve communication, enhance self-esteem, and/or decrease anxiety. It is important that the clients apply the concepts to situations that are "real" for them. The clients are also exposed to the consequences of using the various behaviors/responses in specific situations. Although the assertive behavior/response is generally preferred, clients are shown that behavioral responses are a choice and that sometimes no response is the best response. This notion is sometimes referred to as "selective assertion" (Dombeck & Wells-Moran, 2006; Doty, 1987).

Typically, assertive behaviors/responses are practiced in carefully designed role-playing that includes feedback from the therapist to the client. These role plays can be videotaped for more careful analysis and detailed feedback. Eventually, practice in the community or in "real life" situations usually occurs and the client evaluates his or her behavior/responses as part of "homework" and/or "self-assessment" (Austin, 2004; Hermes, 1998; Kolb, 1985; Paterson, 2000). Given the complexity of learning and applying assertiveness behaviors/responses, it is recommended that training be "tailored to the needs of specific participants and situations they find particularly challenging" ("Assertiveness Training," 2003). It is also important to note that assertive responses learned in a training environment are not automatically generalized to different situations (Doty, 1987; Ruben & Ruben, 1989).

The research on assertiveness training supports the use of a group format for assertiveness training over the individual approach (Lange & Jakubowski, 1978; Laxton, Gray, & Watts, 1997; Lin et al., 2008). The group format provides the opportunity for participants to practice assertiveness techniques with others and to share feedback that will reinforce the continued use of assertive responses (Lin et al., 2008). The frequency of assertiveness training sessions and the duration of sessions will depend on the needs of clients, setting of service, and resources available to the leader. It is generally recommended that sessions be held once or twice a week with time in between sessions for

clients to complete "homework" and/or practice skills (Hermes, 1998).

As noted previously, assertiveness training can be a valuable TR intervention for clients who have difficulty expressing their needs, clients who could benefit from increased self-esteem, clients who have difficulty with interpersonal relationships, clients whose anxiety levels limit their satisfaction with social situations, and/or clients who lack skills in other areas of social interaction. However, participation in assertiveness training does not guarantee that clients will be successful in using these skills in all environments or that their assertive behavior/response will produce the outcomes they desire. This important point reinforces the need for therapists to discuss/practice the consequences of choosing assertive behaviors/responses so that clients are prepared for unexpected outcomes ("Assertiveness Training," 2003; Brecklin & Ullman, 2005; Dombeck & Wells-Moran, 2006; Doty, 1987).

Summary

- Assertiveness can be described as a trait, a behavior style, a communication style, and as a skill.
- Behaviors are usually sorted into assertive, aggressive, passive, and sometimes passive-aggressive. Assertive is preferred, as it expresses one person's right, but not at the expense of the other person's rights.
- Assertiveness training is appropriate for a number of client groups, such as individuals with physical disabilities, at-risk youth, marginalized groups, individuals with substance addictions, and older adults.
- Most assertiveness training programs include topics such as definitions (see the second bullet above), emotions, and communication skills, practiced through role-plays, simulations, independent practice, and group training.
- Research on assertiveness training indicates that most programs are effective in increasing participants' skill levels, which may further decrease social anxiety and improve self-esteem for some groups.
- Assertiveness skills are often taught in therapeutic recreation programs within larger social-skills training programs.
- There are many assertiveness training resources available for purchase or online.

Resources

Assertiveness: Practical Skills for Positive Communication. (1998). [Workbook and accompanying video]. By Hermes. Hazelden Publishing.

Life Management Skills I, II, & II. (1993–1994). By Korb-Khalsa & Leutenberg. The Guidance Group. www.idyllarbor.com

The Assertiveness Workbook. (2000). By Paterson. New Harbinger Publishers, Inc.

The Complete Idiot's Guide to Assertiveness. (1997). By Davidson. Alpha Books.

Listen to Me, Listen to You. (2007). By Kotzman & Kotzman. Penguin Books.

Your Perfect Right: Assertiveness and Equality in your Life and Relationships. (2001). By Alberti & Emmons. Impact Publishers, Inc.

Example Activities

Self-Assessment of Communication Styles. (1998). By Hermes.

- Checklist for identifying individual's communication style (passive, assertive, aggressive)
- Results in a score that identifies your predominant style
- Self-assessment results can be used to set goals and/or to facilitate discussion

Barriers to Assertiveness Worksheet. (2007). By Kotzman & Kotzman.

- Worksheet with questions related to the barriers to assertion
- Completed worksheet can guide discussion related to reducing these barriers

Assertiveness Scorecards. (2000). By Paterson.

- The scorecard provides an outline for recording challenging situations that one might encounter and helps one to commit to using assertive behaviors
- Can be reproduced for ongoing use as new situations arise

References

Alberti, R. E., & Emmons, M. L. (2008). *Your perfect right: Assertiveness and equality in your life and relationships* (9th ed.). Atascadero, CA: Impact Publishers, Inc.

Assertiveness Training. (2003). In *Encyclopedia of mental disorders* [Web]. Gale Cengage. Retrieved Jan 1, 2009, from: http://www.enotes.com/mental-disorders-encyclopedia

Austin, D. (2004). *Therapeutic recreation: Processes and techniques* (5th ed.). Champaign, IL: Sagamore.

Bedell, J. R., & Lennox, S. S. (1996). *Handbook for communication and problem-solving skills training*. New York, NY: John Wiley & Sons.

Brecklin, L. R., & Ullman, S. E. (2005). Self-defense or assertiveness training and women's responses to sexual attacks. *Journal of Interpersonal Violence*, *20*(6), 738–762.

Carter, M. J., Van Andel, G., & Robb, G. (2003). *Therapeutic recreation: A practical approach* (3rd ed.) Prospect Heights, IL: Waveland Press.

Clark, C. (2000). *Integrating complementary health procedures into practice*. New York, NY: Springer.

Colter, S. B., & Guerra, J. J. (1976). *Assertion training: A humanistic-behavioral guide to self-dignity*. Champaign, IL: Research Press.

Crothers, L. M. & Kolbert, J. B. (2004). Comparing middle school teachers' and students' views on bullying and anti-bully interventions. *Journal of School Violence*, *3*(1), 17–32.

Davis, C. (1998). *Patient practitioner interaction: An experiential manual for developing the art of health care* (3rd ed.). Thorofare, NJ: SLACK, Inc.

Davidson, J. (1997). *The complete idiot's guide to assertiveness*. New York, NY: Alpha Books.

Dombeck, M., & Wells-Moran, J. (2006). Setting boundaries appropriately: Assertiveness training. Retrieved December 12, 2008, from: http://www.mentalhelp.net

Doty, L. (1987). *Communication and assertion skills for older persons*. Washington, DC: Hemisphere Publishing.

Douglas, R. R. (1980). Assertiveness training for emotionally disturbed clients. *Journal of Rehabilitation*, *46*(1), 46–47.

Enns, C. Z. (1992). Self-esteem groups: A synthesis of consciousness-raising and assertiveness training. *Journal of Counseling & Development*, *71*, 7–13.

Gambrill, E. D., & Richey, C. (1975). An assertion inventory for use in assessment and research. *Behavior Therapy*, *6*(4), 550–561.

Goldberg-Lillehoj, C. J., Spoth, R., & Trudeau, L. (2005). Assertiveness among young rural adolescents: Relationship to alcohol use. *Journal of Child & Adolescent Substance Abuse, 14*(3), 39–68.

Glueckauf, R. L., & Quittner, A. L (1992). Assertiveness training for disabled adults in wheelchairs: Self-report, role-play, and activity pattern outcomes. *Journal of Consulting and Clinical Psychology, 60*(3), 419–425.

Hargie, O., Saunders, C., & Dickson, D. (1994). *Social skills in interpersonal communication.* New York, NY: Routledge.

Heinemann, A. (Ed.). (1993). *Substance abuse and physical disability.* Philadelphia, PA: Haworth Press.

Hermes, S. (1998). *Assertiveness: Practical skills for positive communication.* Center City, MN: Hazelden.

Hersen, M., Kabacoff, R. I., Van Hasselt, V. B., Null, J. A., Ryan, C. F., Melton, M. A., & Segal, D. L. (1995). Assertiveness, depression, and social support in older visually impaired adults. *Journal of Visual Impairment & Blindness, 89*(6), 524–531.

Jakubowski-Spector, P. (1973). Facilitating the growth of women through assertive training. *The Counseling Psychologist, 4*(1), 75–86.

Kim, Y. (2003). The effects of assertiveness training on enhancing the social skills of adolescents with visual impairments. *Journal of Visual Impairments & Blindness, 97*(5), 285–298.

Kolb, C. (1985). Assertiveness training for women with visual impairments. In M. J. Deegan & N. Brooks (Eds.), *Women & disability: The double handicap* (pp. 87–94). Edison, NJ: Transaction.

Kotzman, A., & Kotzman, M. (2007). *Listen to me, listen to you.* New York, NY: Penguin.

Lange, A., & Jakubowski, P. (1978). *The assertive option.* Champaign, IL: Research Press.

Laxton, M., Gray, C. J., & Watts, S. M. (1997). Teaching assertiveness skills to people with learning disabilities: A brief report of a training programme. *Journal of Intellectual Disabilities, 1*(2), 71–76.

Lin, Y., Wu, M., Yang, C., Chen, T., Hsu, C., Chang, Y., et al. (2008). Evaluation of assertiveness training for psychiatric patients. *Journal of Clinical Nursing, 17*(21), 2875–2883.

Malkin, M., & Kastrinos, G. (1997). Integration of cognitive therapy techniques with recreational therapy. In D. M. Compton (Ed.), *Issues in therapeutic recreation: Toward the new millennium* (2nd ed.) (pp. 445–460). Champaign, IL: Sagamore.

Meyer, L. (1999). People with disabilities and abuse. Retrieved January 10, 2009, from: http://www.ilru.org/html/publications/readings_in_IL/abuse.html

Moore, K. A., Hudson, E. E., & Smith, B. F. (2007). The relationship between assertiveness and social anxiety in college students. *Undergraduate Research Journal for the Human Sciences, 6,* Article 0000001016. Retrieved on August 8, 2008, from: http://www.kon.org/ure/v6/moore.html

Nezu, C. M., Nezu, A. M., & Arean, P. (1991). Assertiveness and problem-solving training for mildly mentally retarded persons with dual diagnoses. *Research in Developmental Disabilities, 12,* 371–386.

Page, E. C., Holland, B., Rand, M. E., Gartin, B. C., & Dowling, D. A. (1981). Assertiveness training groups with the disabled: A pilot study. *Journal of Rehabilitation, 47*(2), 52–55.

Paterson, R. J. (2000). *The assertiveness workbook.* Oakland, CA: New Harbinger.

Ruben, D. H. & Ruben, M. J. (1989). Why assertiveness training programs fail. *Small Group Behavior, 20*(3), 367–380.

Ryan, E. B., Anas, A. P., & Friedman, D. B. (2006). Evaluations of older adult assertiveness in problematic clinical encounters. *Journal of Language and Social Psychology, 25,* 129–145.

Salter, A. (1949). *Conditioned reflex therapy: A direct approach to reconstruction of personality* (1st ed.). New York, NY: Creative Age Press.

Salter, A. (2002). *Conditioned reflex therapy: A direct approach to the reconstruction of personality* (50th anniversary printing). Gretna, LA: Wellness Institute, Inc.

Segal, D. (2005). Relationships of assertiveness, depression, and social support among older nursing home residents. *Behavior Modification, 29*(4), 689–695.

Shank, J., & Coyle, C. (2002). *Therapeutic recreation in health promotion and rehabilitation.* State College, PA: Venture Publishing, Inc.

Shannon, J. W. (1999). Teaching children healthy responses to anger with assertiveness training. *Brown University Child and Adolescent Behavior Letter, 15*(7), 1–3.

Shiina, A., Nakazato, M., Mitsumori, M., Koizumi, H., Shimizu, E., Fujisaki, M., et al. (2005). An open trial of outpatient group therapy for bulimic disorders: Combination program of cognitive behavioral therapy with assertive training and self-esteem enhancement. *Psychiatry and Clinical Neurosciences, 59*(6), 690–696.

Smith, M. J. (1975). *When I say no, I feel guilty.* New York, NY: Bantam Books.

Stumbo, N. J., & Peterson, C. A. (2009). *Therapeutic recreation program design: Principles and procedures* (5th ed.). San Francisco, CA: Pearson Benjamin Cummings Publishing.

Ticoll, M. (1994). *Family violence prevention unit*. Ottawa, Ontario: National Clearinghouse on Family Violence.

Weinhardt, L. S., Carey, M. P., Carey, K. B., & Verdecias, R. N. (1998). Increasing assertiveness skills to reduce HIV risk among women living with a severe and persistent mental illness. *Journal of Consulting and Clinical Psychology, 66*(4), 680–684.

Winterowd, C., Beck, A.T., & Gruener, D. (2003). *Cognitive therapy with chronic pain patients*. New York, NY: Springer.

Wolpe, J. (1958). *Psychotherapy by reciprocal inhibition*. Stanford, CA: Stanford University Press.

Wolpe, J., & Lazarus, A. (1966). *Behavior therapy techniques: A guide to the treatment of neuroses*. Oxford, UK: Pergamon Press.

Zelik, L. (1984). The use of assertiveness training with chronic pain patients. In Cromwell, F. (Ed.), *Occupational therapy and the patient with pain* (pp. 109–118). New York, NY: Routledge.

» CHAPTER 13 »
Physical Activity

Kenneth E. Mobily, Ph.D.

Background/History

Austin (2002) noted that physical activity and exercise was a usual and customary part of therapeutic recreation (TR) practice prior to the last 20 years of the 20th century. One may speculate on the reasons for inclusion of physical activity as an aspect of TR service in the past (e.g., many TR professional preparation programs were administratively housed within physical education; physical education often served as the original source for TR; some mental health afflictions are easier to manage if those afflicted participate in exercise, etc.), but regardless of the cause, its use by TR professionals has sparked controversy.

In an effort to find its uniqueness, the field, perhaps subconsciously, began to distance itself from the use of exercise as a modality. The TR literature of the 1980s and 1990s reveals a marked absence of research and program papers pertaining to the use of exercise by TR. All manner of other interventions served as topics for research papers, including hippo-therapy, horticulture, and various relaxation techniques.

The use of physical activity as a TR technique re-emerged during the latter part of the 1990s and the first decade of the 21st century. There are many reasons that physical activity has started to attract more interest from the TR field. Among these reasons are the rise in chronic conditions, the recent focus on holistic health, and the recommendations for physical activity by the medical field.

Chronic Conditions

As lifespan increased in the 20th century, the causes of morbidity and mortality changed as well, from infectious diseases and acute illnesses to diseases associated with lifestyle and poor health habits (Centers for Disease Control and Prevention [CDC], 2007). In fact, three poor lifestyle factors—smoking, obesity, and physical inactivity—were associated with one third of deaths in the United States in 2000 (CDC, 2007).

Chronic conditions were less visible throughout most of human history because people simply did not live long enough (the average life expectancy in 1900 was 47 years) to manifest the negative consequences of smoking, sedentary lifestyle, and poor diet (CDC, 2007). Likewise, the early history of TR practice did not focus on chronic conditions (and arguably, TR practice still does not). Instead, service to persons with developmental disabilities and traumatic injuries attracted the most interest. However, better health care and longer life spans make chronic conditions difficult to ignore today. But chronic conditions usually do not cause mortality or even morbidity right away. Instead, they gradually erode the person's life quality and lead to increased dependency, eventually predisposing the person to an acute event—e.g., untreated or undiagnosed high blood pressure often leads to a heart attack or stroke.

Heart disease, cancer, and stroke continue to be the leading causes of death in the United States (CDC, 2007). Chronic conditions can be a direct cause of death (e.g., congestive heart failure, diabetes) or a contributing factor (e.g., osteoporosis, hypertension, frailty), or both (e.g., diabetes). Even survival from a disease or traumatic event can make the person vulnerable to developing a chronic condition. For instance, a person who sustains a spinal cord injury is at greater risk for developing osteoporosis, urinary and kidney problems, and skin lesions.

Holistic Health

Because TR has been so very involved in mental health, a significant amount of attention has been paid to holistic health in recent years (Austin, 1998; Van Andel, 1998; Wilhite, Keller, & Caldwell, 1999), emphasizing the notion that mind and body interact. How one feels physically affects mental health and mental disposition and one's mental condition can affect physical health (see the stress management chapter of this text.) Therefore, it is not surprising to find that some assessments of mental health, such as depression, also evaluate the presence/absence of somatic signs of depression (e.g., poor posture, excessive sleep, physical lethargy).

Hans Selye (1956) was among the first to suggest that mind and body interaction was more than a metaphor—actual physiologic and anatomical connections existed. His focus was on how stress affected health. He also chronicled "diseases of adaptation," which result from pathological coping strategies, such as excess drinking, eating, and smoking.

The actual connection between mind and body occurs between two structures, the hypothalamus and the pituitary gland. The two structures are largely responsible for regulating all manner of internal physiology, from fluid volumes to electrolyte balance. An upsetting or threatening stimulus (physical of psychological threat) provokes a series of interactions between mind (hypothalamus) and body (endocrine system) that, if chronic, can lead directly (ulcer in the digestive system) or indirectly (hypertension) to a stress-related disorder.

Recommendations for Physical Activity

When members of the former National Therapeutic Recreation Society (NTRS) were questioned about areas of research priority by Wilhite, Keller, Collins, and Jacobson (2003), exercise and physical activity was ranked ninth on a list of the 25 most important topics for research. This finding may indicate that the TR field is prepared to reconsider exercise and physical activity as a viable program option.

Recently, most TR practice models have included health in some form, often as health promotion. Exercise, of course, is one health promotion option. Notably, Austin's (1998) Health Protection/Health Promotion model; Van Andel's (1998) Service Delivery/Outcomes models; and Wilhite, Keller, and Caldwell's (1999) Lifelong Health and Well-Being Model have been explicit about including health promotion as a TR service area.

Intended Client Groups

Most causes of morbidity and mortality can be favorably affected by a regular exercise habit. Not only does exercise prevent, it also has been associated with improved function and quality of life among persons with chronic conditions. In this section, some of the most common disorders that may benefit from physical activity and the likely mechanisms of benefit are explained.

Cardiovascular conditions, such as heart disease and hypertension, stand to benefit from regular exercise, especially if it is of the aerobic type. (Aerobic

exercise is endurance exercise involving repeated submaximal muscle contractions over a prolonged period of time, usually 20–30 minutes minimum). Benefits of exercise are associated with several factors. Endurance exercise (such as walking at a brisk pace, swimming, cycling, etc.) strengthens the heart, resulting in more blood being pumped per beat. This means the heart does not have to work as hard or contract as frequently to pump the needed amount of blood. Endurance exercise also increases the muscle tone of involuntary muscle that lines blood vessels, resulting in an improvement in its ability to manage blood flow to various parts of the body.

Voluntary muscle (skeletal muscle) also benefits from regular exercise. Strength training, for example, among frail (low-muscle fitness) older adults has been routinely shown to improve functional fitness and reduce the risk of falls. Falls and the resulting injuries, such as hip fractures and brain injuries, are unfortunately too common. Moderate intensity resistance strength training two times per week has improved muscle tone and strength among vulnerable older adults.

Diabetes is the inability to absorb simple sugar (glucose) from the blood stream into muscles and the liver for later use in energy formation. Diabetes is especially hard on the body, increasing the risk of kidney disease, heart disease, blindness, skin lesions and necrosis, and infections. Regular exercise in conjunction with diet management has been shown to help manage the damaging effects of diabetes. Exercise appears to accomplish this benefit because it makes cells more responsive to the insulin (the hormone that causes absorption of glucose), especially in the case for Type II diabetes.

Arthritis, in general, refers to a joint disease that actually represents hundreds of different joint and bone disorders. The most common type of arthritis is osteoarthritis, the deterioration of a joint because of trauma, excess stress on the joint because of load bearing, or a combination of the two. It is positively correlated with aging, with older adults much more apt to report osteoarthritis.

Osteoporosis is a joint/bone-related disorder that is served by the Arthritis Foundation and its programs. Osteoporosis refers to an excessive loss of mineral content in bone, causing diminished bone density. Among older adults, osteoporosis is a significant problem that puts them at risk for a variety of fractures, most importantly, fractures of the hip and skull. Commonly, weight-bearing activity, such as walking, has produced improvement in bone density among younger subjects. But results with older adults are mixed.

Part of the difficulty in attempting to reverse or slow the progress of osteoporosis is that the remedy, weight-bearing activity, also puts the client at risk for fracture because of excess stress on an already weakened skeletal system. The accommodation to this dilemma has been to use safer weight-bearing activities, such as aquatic exercise and strength training (often in a seated position) to minimize the risk of fracture.

Cancer is the second leading cause of death in the United States. Epidemiological studies have demonstrated a negative correlation between regular exercise and some forms of cancer. But the mechanism behind the lower cancer risk among exercisers is not well understood.

Likewise, the relationship between exercise and mental health, especially depression and depressive symptoms, is favorable but not easily explained. Various hypotheses (see Mobily et al., 1996) to explain the beneficial effect of exercise on depression include the fact that exercise is commonly something done in a group setting and the social support results in a positive effect on mental health. Physiologic explanations for the psychological benefits of exercise have included stimulation of beneficial neurotransmitters and endorphins, and habituation to stress associated with the hypothalamic-pituitary-adreno-cortical axis. Another physiologic explanation relates to improved vascular profusion to the brain that may result in better mood. From a psychological perspective, exercise may promote positive mental health because it promotes a perception of mastery and control on the part of the participant, and improves self-concept and self-confidence.

Basic Premises

The American College of Sports Medicine and American Heart Association recommendations have served as the "gold standard" guidelines for practitioners delivering exercise and physical activity programs. The most recent recommendations for adults 18–64 years of age are:

- perform moderate intensity exercise (equivalent to a brisk walk, about three miles per hour on a flat surface) for 30 minutes, five days per week (or vigorous aerobic activity for 20 minutes, three times per week)
- moderate intensity aerobic activities are in addition to regular and routine activities and should be completed in bouts of at least 10 minutes or longer

- strength train at least two times per week (on non-consecutive days), employing 8–10 exercises that work all major muscle groups and to a point that produces "substantial fatigue" (Haskell et al., 2007)

Further, the American College of Sports Medicine and American Heart Association clarified their exercise recommendations for persons aged 65 and older or those aged 50–64 with clinically significant chronic conditions or functional limitations (Nelson et al., 2007). Although the basic recommendations remained the same, for these groups the definition of "moderate intensity" may be adjusted according to the individual's ability and fitness. In addition, older adults and those with significant chronic conditions should strength train using more repetitions (implying less resistance) at a level of moderate intensity. In addition to the baseline recommendations for moderate aerobic exercise and strength training, older adults should practice flexibility and balance exercises.

From a theoretical viewpoint, the absence of exercise has been reliably associated with increased risk for several chronic conditions, such as heart disease, high blood pressure, and diabetes. Conversely, the practice of regular exercise has been associated with increased longevity, better physical health, and improved mental health. Physical health benefits from exercise are attributable to "overload," a concept based on "stressing" the body (in a positive manner) with more physical work. Mechanisms for improvement in mental health are less clear, although less depression and anxiety are consistent outcomes associated with regular exercise. Perhaps the best news is that improvements in physical health and mental health indicators usually do not require maximal exertion, but moderate intensity exercise instead.

The overload principle applies broadly across many physiologic systems in the human body. Because the human body is adaptable, favorable adjustments to overload in physiological mechanisms result. Endurance training through repetitious sub-maximal effort, such as brisk walking, stationary cycling, and swimming, stresses the cardiovascular system by demanding more effort than routine daily activities. Cardiac output is determined by two factors, heart rate and the force of contraction. If the heart is strengthened through endurance training, then it is able to exert more force with every beat. The body's need for blood is relatively constant (assuming there is no significant change in weight and tissue demand for blood), and if more blood is pumped with every beat of a well-conditioned heart, then the result is that resting heart rate will gradually decline over the course of endurance training. Resting heart rate is generally taken as an indicator of better cardiovascular health.

Overload is also applicable to the muscle system: improved muscle strength results when muscles must adapt to extra loads associated with a progressive resistance exercise program (e.g., weight training, resistance bands, medicine balls, hydraulic resistance machines, etc.). The functional unit of muscle contraction is called a sarcomere. Within the sarcomere are contractile proteins. Repeated exposure to resistance greater than that encountered in one's daily routine causes a gradual increase in the amount of contractile proteins within each sarcomere. Muscles hypertrophy (increase in size) as a result. Generally, bigger muscles are stronger muscles.[1]

The skeletal system demonstrates a favorable response to exercise, especially resistance training and weight-bearing exercise. Bones represent a type of connective tissue known for its hard character. The "hardness" of bone is a result of minerals being deposited between bone cells that solidify the intercellular matrix. The reason exercise is associated with enhanced bone health is again overload. If the skeleton is asked to bear more weight (as in a regular walking program) or resistance (as in a progressive resistance training program), then it adapts by depositing more minerals in between the bone cells and increasing bone density—the relative amount of mineral content in the skeleton. Enhanced bone density means that bones are not as susceptible to fractures, exactly the opposite physiologic response that is associated with osteoporosis. And, of course, hip fractures and other skeletal injuries have been increasing among older adults over the last decade or so at an alarming rate.

Related Research

Aquatic exercise programs have been the most common exercise intervention reported in the TR literature. Generally, these have been small sample studies and have demonstrated functional improvements among persons with arthritis, fibromyalgia, and neurological impairments (e.g., spinal cord injury, multiple sclerosis).

Parallel improvements in physiologic concomitants of functional improvement have not been evident though.

Psycho-social improvements associated with physical activity, typically sports of various types, have been mixed. In some studies, manipulation of another independent variable (e.g., choice, inclusion) was more apt to be the cause of any observed improvements in function (e.g., increase in appropriate play, compliance with treatment, anger management).

A few studies used land-oriented exercise to produce functional improvement or favorable increments in health-related variables. Strength training has been associated with functional improvement; walking and strength training have been correlated with fewer respiratory infections. Gardening, however, failed to produce functional improvement.

Secondary analysis of existing data and studies that rely on self-report of past behavior have been relatively rare in the TR literature, although such studies have started to appear in the TR literature. Secondary analysis of data pertaining to older adults shows that persons with disabilities are physically inactive, similar to the balance of the US population, especially the older adult population. Of course, retrospective studies are limited by the nature of the original data set and/or the reliability and validity of subject recall over a significant period of time.

Application to Therapeutic Recreation

The traditional acronym for the TR process is APIE—assessment, planning, implementation, and evaluation. Although most would acknowledge that practice is rarely as simple as APIE, the framework is employed in this section as the foundation for application of physical activity and exercise to TR practice.

Assessment

As a general rule, questionnaires are used to assess mental entities of interest to TR practice—attitudes, perceptions, beliefs or levels of satisfaction. Observation is commonly used to assess behavior (e.g., see Burlingame & Blaschko, 2002). For baseline and outcome measures related to exercise and physical activity, the types of assessment employed usually come in the form of a hybrid of observation—functional and performance testing. With functional and performance testing the client is typically asked to execute a physical task that represents a function of interest (e.g., lower extremity strength).

---

[1] However, the excess hypertrophy often seen in body builders is NOT typical of hypertrophy in normal individuals who strength train. There is some reluctance, especially on the part of women, to strength train because of the exaggerated hypertrophy seen in body builders. This has often been associated with substance abuse. The excesses of body builders do not represent a normal response to strength training. Women who strength train do NOT become excessively muscular.

The desirable attributes of field measures of function and performance include the following:

1) The assessments should be valid—most good field measures of function are correlated with more controlled, laboratory measures to establish concurrent validity. For example, one field measure commonly used to assess cardiovascular function in high school students is a 12-minute run/walk; it correlates with maximum exhaustion tests on a bicycle ergometer in a laboratory settings (these typically gauge cardiovascular function by measuring maximum oxygen expenditure to exhaustion).

2) The assessments should be reliable—functional tests used in the field should measure consistently from one time to the next, assuming the subject does not do anything between administrations to markedly improve or detract from functional performance (e.g., the subject catches a bad case of influenza between first and second administrations). In addition, the TR specialist should be prepared to administer the measure over several trials because of "learning effect." Learning effect is a characteristic that affects some measures, both cognitive and motor. It involves a linear improvement in performance on consecutive trials of any given task. For instance, a test of agility might involve the subject walking a small obstacle course for time. Chances are reasonably good that if the subject was given a second and even a third trial on the obstacle course his or her performance would improve. This is learning effect, the subject "learned" the course and the map of the course was registered in motor memory, leading to an improvement of performance in subsequent trials on the course. The way practitioners can control for learning effect is to administer multiple trials until performance no longer continues to improve. This is usually a matter of three to four trials at all but the most fatiguing tasks. Following administration of repeated trials the "best" score (in repetitions or time) is recorded. Using a multiple trial testing protocol for most performance of functional measures will produce better reliability (and validity).

3) The assessments should be practical—administration of the test(s) should not be highly technical and should not involve the use of expensive and complicated equipment. What the practitioner seeks in a field measure of function is a measure that is "low tech" but valid. Results should be easy to interpret (e.g., more repetitions of an arm curl with a light weight are an indication of upper extremity strength/endurance). Practical also means inexpensive because most practitioners do not have the finances to underwrite the expense involved in purchasing "high tech" testing equipment. The testing materials should also be "transportable;" that is, easy to move from one location to the next without damaging or having to re-calibrate the testing equipment from site to site.

The American Alliance for Health, Physical Education, Recreation and Dance has (AAHPERD) developed a simple and inexpensive functional assessment battery for older adults that is available for field use (see Osness under "resources" below). The AAHPERD functional fitness battery assesses upper extremity strength, hand-eye coordination, flexibility, agility, endurance, and body composition. The battery is highly valid and reliable (Bravo et al., 1994; Mobily & Mobily, 1997; Shaulis, Golding, & Tandy, 1994).

In addition, other functional measures for static balance and lower extremity strength are highly recommended to assure a comprehensive evaluation at baseline and at follow-up. Static balance may be easily assessed using a "stork stand" (see Berg et al., 1992). The stork stand involves the client balancing on one (preferred) foot for up to 30–60 seconds; the time of the task may be adjusted according to the functional ability of the subject.

Lower extremity strength assessment among persons with low muscle fitness (frailty) and older adults at risk (e.g., vertigo and other balance issues) is vital to conducting a safe (fall-free) exercise program and to determine if the participant's lower extremity strength has improved after a period of participation. A simple test of lower extremity strength involves is the timed-stands test, wherein the subject is timed while standing-up and sitting-down ten times (Csuka & McCarty, 1985).

Planning and Implementation

Program plans for exercise within a TR framework differ little from planning for any other activity or program. Goals and objectives still have to be developed. Length of the program still has to be determined. Leadership skills still have to be applied. Finally, space and equipment requirements need to be determined.

Nevertheless, there are aspects of each of the above fundamental planning tasks that are unique to the use of exercise in TR. Some goals relate to physical outcomes and are clear, objective, and measurable; for example, arm curl repetitions, length of time of 'stork stand,' etc. But perhaps the more interesting goals lie in the behavioral domain. Changing behavior has long been the mantra of TR, and exercise, like other health behaviors (e.g., smoking cessation), is always well intentioned but seldom adopted on a long-term basis. Goals appropriate to exercise within TR service include any or all of the following:

1) Learning how to exercise—something we rarely think about, but should, is that many of our participants are apprehensive about exercise because they have never been taught how to exercise properly and correctly. The appliances and equipment associated with exercise are foreign to them. They may not know how to interpret labored breathing and sweating ("Am I exercising too hard?"; "Will I have a heart attack?"). Or they may perceive barriers to exercise ("Older ladies are not supposed to exercise; it's undignified!"). Cognitive and attitudinal goals and outcomes relative to physical activity programs are often overlooked. Clearly, learning how to exercise safely could involve a considerable number of learning and performance goals, such as knowing what resistance to use, how many repetitions to perform, how many sets to execute, why muscles get stronger, demonstrating proper exercise techniques, knowing how fast/how far/how often to walk to achieve benefit, and so on. All of the foregoing and more represent goals that TR specialists could focus on depending on the ages and impairments represented among exercise participants.

2) Cross-training—exercise should be fun, interesting, and stimulating. One time-honored means of perpetuating intrinsic interest in an activity class is to vary the stimulus array (e.g., Iso-Ahola, 1980). More plainly, changing the type and nature of exercise can keep it interesting from a psychological point of view. In addition, cross-training may prevent overuse injuries associated with excess repetition of the same motoric action. Many soft-tissue injuries, such as tendonitis, inflamed ligaments, muscle strains, and skeletal irritations may be avoided by spreading the stress of exercise across systems, joints, and muscle types. By walking, biking, and strength training on different days, no one system, joint, or muscle group bears all the stress associated with daily exercise. Hence, it makes sense to teach a variety of types of exercise and exercise techniques both across exercise modes (e.g., walking, biking, strength training) and within each exercise mode (e.g., one may strength train using free weights, thera-bands, hydraulic equipment, stationary resistance machines, etc.).

3) Exercise compliance—perhaps even more important than the intensity of exercise is the ability to persist at regular exercise over a protracted period of time, to make exercise part of one's normal, daily schedule. This is the case because the beneficial physiologic effects of exercise become manifest only after months or years of practice. Furthermore, to retain the beneficial effects of exercise one must continue a regular program of physical activity throughout life. Fortunately for TR, one factor that promotes compliance is enjoyment (Wankel, 1993). TR specialists conducting exercise programs for persons with chronic conditions and other disabilities should therefore encourage goals that promote building of a social support group that exercises together, knowledge of various exercise sites that are accessible and available in the event of inclement weather, and educate significant others of the importance of exercise (Dishman, 1988 and 1994, suggests that support from significant others promotes exercise compliance).

Professional Ethics

The most apparent ethical principles that apply to physical activity and exercise programs led by TR specialists are non-malfeasance (do no harm) and veracity (truthfulness). Appropriate screening for participation should be conducted before consumers begin an exercise program. This is true because many of the groups that would benefit from exercise are also among those most at risk for unintended consequences—injuries or worse resulting from participation. Hence, administration of a screening tool helps avoid negligence and assures participants are safe to engage in mild to moderate, "recreational level" exercise. One such screening tool is the revised Physical Activity Readiness Questionnaire (rPARQ) developed by Shephard and his colleagues (1991) for use nationwide use in Canada. The screening consists of seven simple, yes/

no questions. If the subject answers "yes" to any of the questions, she should be required to check with her physician before beginning any program of exercise.[2] The questions on the rPARQ survey inquire about heart health and blood pressure issues, joint problems, and vertigo.

A second ethical issue is veracity—truthfulness. One should not misrepresent exercise at a mild to moderate level as "therapy." Indeed, functional improvement may result. In fact, abundant literature suggests that significant improvement in function will be associated with a regular habit of mild to moderate exercise, similar in character to the program recommended by the CDC (noted above). Such a program, though beneficial, does not meet the specifications for "therapy" in the same sense as an exercise prescription would, and it is simply wrong to mislead the consumer. Misrepresentation of recreational-level exercise as therapy may lead the individual to assume he no longer needs to participate in any physical therapy that may be prescribed (resulting from the lower expense associated with the provision of mild to moderate exercise by a TR specialist). Such a decision would not serve the client best and could produce more harm than good. With that said, however, working closely with physical therapy or others responsible for implementing an exercise prescription is a wise step toward maximizing the benefits of exercise for the client. Such a partnership would avoid duplication, ensure a smoother transition from a controlled-exercise setting to a community-based one, and be more likely to result in long-term compliance with an exercise habit.

Time, Space/Place, and Equipment

The length of time for recreation programs for persons with limitations varies according to a number of variables, such as length of hospitalization, intent of the intervention, degree of impairment, and so on. However, the general rule for manifesting functional fitness improvement among persons with chronic conditions ranges from six to eight weeks of exercise—for endurance/cardiovascular improvement, five or more bouts of exercise of about a half an hour each; for strength improvement, two or three times per week of 8 to 12 exercises involving all body parts (i.e., upper and lower extremities and core body strength). Flexibility and stretching should be practiced daily; balance exercise may be combined with stretching at a daily or almost daily rate.

Space for exercise is important. Locations should be accessible and accommodating. A variety of exercise venues should be selected to adjust for inclement weather. For example, walking outdoors can move to an indoor mall during cold months. Strength training on an individual basis can be done in the comfort of one's own home in minimal space, but a group strength-training program needs adequate space to prevent injuries.

Equipment needed to exercise depends on the economic resources of the agency providing the service and the participant. Really, minimal equipment is necessary. Comfortable, loose-fitting clothing that allows for free movement trumps designer dress. A comfortable, good-fitting pair of walking shoes may be the most expensive financial outlay and can last for months. Strength training may take additional equipment, although many strength-training exercises require little equipment (e.g., a folding chair and an exercise mat). Of course, if a senior center or recreation center already has more expensive equipment such as free weights, weight machines, stationary bicycles and treadmills, then membership is a cost that may be involved as an indirect equipment cost to the participant.

Continuing Education

Few TR specialists currently practicing graduated with the technical skills to run an exercise program for persons with disabilities or chronic conditions. However, options to acquire skills necessary to safely conduct exercise for various groups are available through training programs offered by condition-specific organizations, such as the Arthritis Foundation. The Arthritis Foundation offers training for professionals interested in running land-based and/or aquatic exercise programs for persons with arthritis and arthritis-related syndromes. Other nonprofit groups do as well.

Leadership Skills

The TR professional intent on leading exercise groups and facilitating physical activity should practice several important leadership techniques. First, the practitioner should be a role model, demonstrating a personal commitment to a regular program of exercise allows the professional to speak with more credibility; he/she should "practice what they preach." Second, the exercise leader must show enthusiasm for the content and program of exercise. If the leader is not excited and enthusiastic about exercise, how can he/she expect the consumer to be, especially if the latter party is not entirely convinced it would not just be easier to "rest"? One cannot expect the participant to be highly motivated to exercise each time a group meets.

---

[2] This author's experience with pre-participation screening is that no query to a physician that has resulted from answering "yes" to a rPARQ question has led to a contra-indication for exercise at a mild to moderate intensity level.

Although enthusiasm and commitment tend to run high among participants early in exercise programs, it later tends to wane with redundancy (if exercise is not varied as in "cross training" above), small aches and pains, and other conflicts and barriers (e.g., vacations, fear of crime, low income, inaccessible facilities). Third, the leader should give clear instructions so that the novice exerciser understands exactly what to do. Instructions may include demonstration, mirroring, one-to-one attention, and adaptations for those who cannot complete the exercise in the typical manner. Last, the practitioner needs to be able to "read" his/her participants to—most importantly—avoid injury, but also to sense when the person is exercising too intensely or unsafely, when the participant is hesitant about an exercise, or when the client seems to be in pain.

Evaluation

The final step in the TR process is evaluation, in this case specifically client evaluation. The simplest approaches are often the best. Pre-test (at baseline) and post-test comparison of functional fitness measures, such as balance, strength and endurance, will yield a straightforward indication of progress. Secondly, achievement of learning goals and objectives also serve as a rather direct measure of client attainment. Third, follow-up with participants will acquire compliance data, another indicator of success. In addition, the three outcomes defined here can be used as indirect evidence of teaching/program effectiveness. If the participant improves function, achieves learning goals and objectives, and complies with the recommended exercise program, then the preponderance of data suggest that the exercise program and instruction were likely sources of the favorable changes.

Resources

Arthritis Foundation Training Programs for professionals interested in leading aquatic exercise and land-based exercise programs for persons with arthritis and arthritis-related impairments (including osteoporosis) http://www.arthritis.org.

Mobily, K. E. (2008). *Strength training for older adults: Workshop manual.* University of Iowa.

Mobily, K. E., & Mobily, P. R. (1997). *Progressive resistance training—A research based protocol.* (Available from the University of Iowa Gerontological Nursing Intervention Research Center Development and Dissemination Core, UIHC Department of Nursing, 200 Hawkins DR, T100 GH, Iowa City, IA 52242).

Osness, W. H., Adrian, M., Clark, B., Hoeger, W., Raab, D., & Wiswell, R. (1996). *Functional fitness assessment for adults over 60 years: A field based assessment* (2nd ed.). Dubuque, IA: Kendall Hunt.

References

Austin, D. R. (2002). A call for training in physical activity. In D. R. Austin, J. Dattilo, & B. P. McCormick (Eds.), *Conceptual foundations for therapeutic recreation* (pp. 225–234). State College, PA: Venture Publishing, Inc.

Austin, D. R. (1998). The health protection/health promotion model. *Therapeutic Recreation Journal, 32*(2), 109–117.

Berg, K., Wood-Dauphinee, S., Williams, J. I., & Maki, B. (1992). Measuring balance in the elderly: Validation of an instrument. *Canadian Journal of Public Health*, July/August supplement 2: S7–11.

Bravo, G., Gauthier, P., Roy, P., Tessier, D., Gaulin, P., Dubois, M., & Peloquin, L. (1994). The functional fitness assessment battery: Reliability and validity for elderly women. *Journal of Aging and Physical Activity, 2*, 67–79.

Burlingame, J., & Blaschko, T. M. (2002). *Assessment tools for recreational therapy and related fields* (3rd ed.). Ravensdale, WA: Idyll Arbor.

Centers for Disease Control and Prevention. (2007). Improving the health of older Americans. *Chronic Disease Notes and Reports, 18*(2), 1, 3–7.

Csuka, M., & McCarty, D. J. (1985). Simple method for measurement of lower extremity muscle strength. *The American Journal of Medicine, 78*(1), 77–81.

Dishman, R. K. (1988). Determinants of physical activity and exercise for persons 65 years of age and older. *American Academy of Physical Education Papers, 22*, 140–162.

Dishman, R. K. (1994). Motivating older adults to exercise. *Southern Medical Journal, 87*, S79–82.

Haskell, W. L., Lee, I., Pate, R. R., Powell, K. E., Blair, S. N., Franklin, B. A., et al. (2007). Physical activity and public health: Updated recommendation for adults from the American College of Sports Medicine and American Heart Association. *Circulation, 116*(9), 1081–1093.

Iso-Ahola, S. E. (1980). *Social psychology of leisure and recreation.* Dubuque, IA: Brown.

Mobily, K. E., & Mobily, P. R. (1997). Reliability of the 60+ functional fitness test battery for older adults. *Journal of Aging and Physical Activity, 5*(2), 150–162.

Mobily, K. E., Rubenstein, L. M., Lemke, J. H., O'Hara, M. W., & Wallace, R. B. (1996). Walking and depression in a cohort of older adults: The Iowa 65+ rural health study. *Journal of Aging and Physical Activity, 4*(2), 119–135.

Nelson, M. E., Rejeski, W. J., Blair, S. N., Duncan, P. W., Judge, J. O., King, A. C., et al. (2007). Physical activity and public health in older adults: Recommendation from the American College of Sports Medicine and the American Heart Association. *Medicine and Science in Sports and Exercise, 39*(8), 1435–1445.

Selye, H. (1956). *The stress of life*. NY: McGraw-Hill.

Shaulis, D., Golding, L. A., & Tandy, R. D. (1994). Reliability of the AAHPERD functional fitness assessment across multiple practice sessions in older men and women. *Journal of Aging and Physical Activity, 2*, 273–279.

Shephard, R. J., Thomas, S., & Weller, I. (1991). The Canadian home fitness test. *Sport Medicine, 1*, 359.

Van Andel, G. (1998). TR service delivery and TR outcomes models. *Therapeutic Recreation Journal, 32*(3), 180–192.

Wankel, L. M. (1993). The importance of enjoyment to adherence and psychological benefits from physical activity. *International Journal of Sport Psychology, 24*, 151–169.

Wilhite, B., Keller, M. J., & Caldwell, L. (1999). Optimizing lifelong health and well-being: A health enhancing model of therapeutic recreation. *Therapeutic Recreation Journal, 33*, 98–108.

Wilhite, B., Keller, M. J., Collins, J. R., & Jacobson, S. (2003). A research agenda for therapeutic recreation revisited. *Therapeutic Recreation Journal, 37*, 207–223.

» CHAPTER 14 »

Pain Management

Norma J. Stumbo, Ph.D., CTRS and Judy S. Kinney, Ph.D., CTRS, LRT

Background/History

The majority of medical appointments made by Americans are due to pain (Crook, Rideout, & Browne, 1984). In 1995, the National Institutes of Health (NIH) cited pain as a critical national health problem that has serious, detrimental effects on mobility, overall functional status, immune function, sleeping and eating patterns, and psychological well-being (Crook et al., 1984; Gureje, Von korff, Simon, & Gater, 1998; Liebeskind, 1991; National Institutes of Health [NIH], 1995; Scudds & Robertson, 1998). The estimated annual cost of chronic pain in the U.S. is around $100 billion (American Pain Foundation [APF], 2008). Untreated pain increases length of hospital stays and also increases use of emergency room and clinic visits. Despite the high number of people who experience pain and the cost to society, pain management does not seem to be a priority. The APF reported that regardless of these staggering costs, "less than 2% of the NIH research budget is dedicated to pain" (2008, p. 2).

The International Association for the Study of Pain defined pain as "an unpleasant sensory and emotional experience arising from actual or potential tissue damage or described in terms of such damage" (Carr, 1993, p. 1). Pain is no longer considered a simple neural activation within the body, and is instead seen as an individualized experience, interpreted through one's culture, previous experience and anticipation, emotional and cognitive contributions, and the context of the situation in which the pain occurs (Bonica, 1990; Cleland & Gebhart, 1997; Hawthorn & Redmond, 1998; Kingdon, Stanley, & Kizior, 1998; Main & Spanswick, 2000; Melzack & Casey, 1968; Nurmikko, Nash, & Wiles, 1998; Springhouse Corporation, 1997; Turk, 1997). "Pain is a subjective experience reflecting a dynamic interaction between sensory, affective, motivational, and cognitive systems" (Fiset et al., 1997, p. 291). Pain can be operationally defined as whatever the individual says it is (McCaffery, 2001). When assessing pain, a multitude of variables need to be considered, including intensity, frequency, duration, how pain is interpreted by the individual, and the burden experienced as a result of the painful experience. Because pain is such a common occurrence, many have suggested that pain be assessed as the fifth vital sign, along with temperature, pulse, blood pressure, and respiratory rate (Carpenter, 1997; Cohen, 2007; Curtiss, 2001). Pain can be classified according to *duration* (acute, prolonged, or chronic), *source* (somatic or visceral; Cleland & Gebhart, 1997), and *transmission* (nociceptive and neuropathic; Kingdon et al., 1998). According to Gold, Townsend, Jury, Kant, Gallardo, and Joseph (2006) "as a profession, we no longer refer to pain as 'real' or 'psychosomatic.' Pain is now categorized as 'structural pain,' 'pain associated with tissue damage,' or 'functional pain,' pathological pain not associated with ongoing tissue damage" (p. 160).

Incidence of Pain and Inadequate Pain Relief

Americans annually incur about 65 million traumatic injuries, including 2 million burns, and millions more have diseases that produce acute pain (Phillips, 2000). According to the National Centers for Health Statistics, 76.2 million people over the age of 20 suffer from pain (APF, 2008). This figure does not account for acute pain but only pain that endured for more than 24 hours. According to Richard Chapman, former president of the American Pain Society, only 25% of individuals who have surgical operations receive adequate acute pain relief (Phillips, 2000). Curtiss (2001) provided similar estimates, stating that 50–80% of surgical patients do not receive adequate acute pain relief. More Americans deal with pain than "diabetes, heart disease, and cancer *combined*" according to the National Institutes of Health (NIH, 2007, p. 1) and the APF (2008).

Of the 50 million people in this country with chronic pain, between 40% and 67% are misdiagnosed (Meisler,

2002), and 4 in 10 with moderate to severe pain cannot find adequate pain control. More than 26 million people 20 to 64 years of age have frequent or persistent back pain, and one in six has painful arthritis. Only about 30% of all cancer patients with pain get enough relief according to Chapman (as cited in Phillips, 2000). Only 25% of patients with moderate or severe chronic pain are referred to a pain specialist, with the majority of those with chronic pain being women (Meisler, 2002). "Chronic pain is the most common cause of long-term disability" (NIH, 2007, p. 1). More than two in five (42%) individuals who reported having chronic pain indicated the pain lasted longer than 1 year (APF, 2008).

Curtiss (2001) noted that among patients who reported pain, 34% characterized it as very severe, 23% as severe, and 43% as moderate. Only half of those with very severe pain and 39% of those with severe pain reported controlling it successfully, even though pain occurred an average of 5.7 days per week. Among those with controlled, very severe pain, 70% reported that it took more than 6 months to gain control, while for the remainder it took more than a year. At all levels of pain, respondents reported a diminished quality of life with respect to physical activity (81%), sleep (79%), domestic chores (65%), hobbies and leisure activities (67%), social activities (65%), walking (59%), and sexual activity (54%). Emotional well-being similarly was affected (Curtiss, 2001).

Types of Pain

It is important to realize that there are multiple types of pain, including: (a) acute pain, (b) chronic pain, (c) recurring pain, (d) procedure-related pain, and (e) pain associated with terminal illness (American Academy of Pediatrics, 2001; Lotan et al., 2009). The committee addressed the multidimensional aspects of pain including "…sensory, emotional, cognitive, and behavioral components that are interrelated with environmental, developmental, sociocultural, and contextual factors" (p. 793). *Acute pain* is defined as pain that lasts "between three to five days and is attributed to a specific cause such as surgery or an injury" (Obrecht & Andreoni, 2007, p. 521). *Chronic pain* "is characterized by its prolonged and persistent nature, lasting 3 months or longer" (Dell'Api, Rennick, & Rosmus, 2007, p. 270); some define chronic pain lasting for 6 months or longer. *Intermittent pain* is pain that lasts for a period of time, goes away, then comes back.

Barriers to Pain Management

JCAHO's implementation of pain-management standards in January 2001 focused a spotlight on the inadequate treatment of pain. Healthcare institutions were caught between the requirement to fulfill every patient's right to pain assessment and adequate treatment on the one hand, and a widespread knowledge and competence deficit among clinicians regarding pain and pain management on the other hand (Stegman, 2001). Many reasons converged to create this contrast. Some of the barriers to adequate pain management and control documented in the literature are included in Table 14.1.

Joint Commission's (2001) Pain Standards

There is no area of clinical practice in which administrators' and clinicians' obligations to patients have evolved more dramatically in the last 10 years than pain management. In that time, several important forces converged to highlight adequate analgesic therapy as an integral part of clinical practice in all illnesses and conditions and throughout the healthcare system (American Pain Society, 2001, p. 27).

In 2001, as a response to pain emerging as a critical national health issue, the Joint Commission (2001, 2006) created pain-management standards requiring "a comprehensive pain assessment [be] conducted as appropriate to the individual's condition and the scope of care, treatment, and services provided."

Table 14.2 (p. 260) highlights the six guidelines that form the Joint Commission's pain standards, to be used by all care providers.

Understanding and following national pain management standards and clinical practice guidelines ensures higher quality care, which benefits both the patient and professionals. The major aim of any form of pain treatment is to eliminate pain-associated suffering and increase function. Specifically, the notion is to increase pain control, decrease analgesic use when possible, increase activity and function, decrease depression and anxiety, and increase family involvement in care (Ardery, Herr, Titler, Sorofman, & Schmitt, 2003). "Suffering occurs when the pain leads the person to feel out of control, the pain is overwhelming, the source of the pain is unknown, the meaning of the pain is perceived to be dire, and/or the pain is chronic" (American Pain Society [APS], 2001, p. 793).

Additional goals are to provide comfort, inhibit pain impulses to diminish reflex responses to pain, and prevent future episodes ("Living with cancer," 1998;

Table 14.1. Barriers to Adequate Pain Management

Problems Related To Healthcare Professionals	• Inadequate knowledge of and competence with pain management in both medical training and practice (Bonica, 1985; Cleeland, Cleeland, Dar, & Rinehardt, 1986; Ferrell, Nash, & Warfield, 1992; Hawthorn & Redmond, 1998; Kingdon et al., 1998; Phillips, 2000; Von Roenn, Cleeland, Gonin, Hatfield, & Pandya, 1993) • Poor assessment of pain and inadequate prescribing (Grossman, Sheidler, Swedeen, Mucenski, & Piantadosi, 1991; Hawthorn & Redmond, 1998; Meyers, 1997; Von Roenn et al., 1993) • Concern about regulation of controlled substances (Gebhart, 1997; Hawthorn & Redmond, 1998; Joranson, Cleeland, Weissman, & Gilson, 1992; Miller, 2000; Phillips, 2000; Von Roenn et al., 1993; Weissman, Joranson, & Hopwood, 1991) • Fear of patient addiction (Bonica, 1985; Ferrell et al., 1992; Hawthorn & Redmond, 1998; Kingdon et al., 1998; Marks & Sachar, 1973; Miller, 2000; Phillips, 2000) • Pain control offers physicians little in the way of reimbursement and financial incentives (Phillips, 2000) • Patients who complain of pain are seen as whiners (Phillips, 2000) • Pain control takes back seat to other specialties and is not well respected in the medical community or within medical training. Some doctors feel that if they deal with a patient's pain, they lose objectivity (Beresford, 1998; Phillips, 2000) • Concern about the side effects of analgesics as well as patient addiction (Cleeland et al., 1986; Kingdon et al., 1998; Von Roenn et al., 1993)
Problems Related To Patients	• Reluctance to report pain for fear of distracting doctors from underlying disease (Dar, Beach, Barden, & Cleeland, 1992; Levin, Cleeland, & Dar, 1985; Hawthorn & Redmond, 1998; Von Roenn et al., 1993; Ward et al., 1993) • Fear that pain means that disease is worse (Dar et al., 1992; Levin et al., 1985; Von Roenn et al., 1993; Ward et al., 1993; Weissman et al., 1991) • Concern about being a "good patient" (Dar et al., 1992; Hawthorn & Redmond, 1998; Levin et al., 1985; McCaffrey, 2001; Von Roenn et al., 1993; Ward et al., 1993) • Reluctance to take pain medications; fear of addiction or of being thought of as an addict (although addiction is rarely seen [O'Neill & Fallon, 1997], worries about unmanageable side effects, concern about becoming tolerant to pain medications (Cleeland, 1989; Dar et al., 1992; Kingdon et al., 1998; Meyers, 1997; O'Neill & Fallon, 1997; Rimer et al., 1987; Von Roenn et al., 1993; Ward et al., 1993)
Problems Related To the Health-care System	• Low priority given to cancer pain treatment (Bonica, 1985; Hawthorn & Redmond, 1998; Kingdon, et al., 1998; Max, 1990) • Inadequate reimbursement (Joranson et al., 1992) • Most appropriate treatment may not be reimbursed or may be too costly for patients and families (Joranson et al., 1992) • Restrictive regulation of controlled substances (Foley, 1985; Hawthorn & Redmond, 1998; Joranson, et al., 1992; Weissman, et al., 1991) • Problems of availability of treatment or access to it (Foley, 1985; Hawthorn & Redmond, 1998) • Older individuals at the end-of-life in long-term-care settings receive no or inadequate pain relief when compared to their end-of-life hospice care peers who fare better for pain management (Miller, Mor, Wu, Gozalo, & Lapane, 2002)

Roberge & McEwen, 1998). Pain relief enhances a patient's restoration of function and enables the patient to breathe and move about more easily. After complete pain assessment information is gathered, a wide variety of pharmacological and nonpharmacological treatment options can be explored to alleviate, relieve, or eliminate pain (Blumstein & Gorevic, 2005; Goldstein & Morrison, 2005; Helmrich, 2001; Schofield & Dunham, 2005). Untreated, there are numerous cumulative effects of unmanaged pain.

Many healthcare professionals, including therapeutic recreation specialists (Finch, 2006; Kuntsler, Greenblatt, & Moreno, 2004; Mobily & Verburg, 2001; Schofield, 2005; Stumbo, 2002, 2006a, 2006b), lack a thorough understanding of pain mechanisms as well as competence with pain interventions (Stegman, 2001). This chapter provides information for therapeutic recreation specialists on pharmacological and nonpharmacological strategies for pain management, especially for older individuals and children, with a focus on physical activity and cognitive behavioral therapy.

Table 14.2. Overview of Joint Commission's (2001) Pain-Management Standards (Phillips, 2000)

1. Recognize the right of an individual to appropriate assessment and management of pain.
2. Assess the existence and, if so, the nature and intensity of pain in all patients, residents, or clients.
3. Establish policies and procedures that support the appropriate prescribing or ordering of effective pain medications.
4. Educate patients, residents, clients, and their families about effective pain management.
5. Address the individual's need for symptom management in the discharge planning process.
6. Incorporate pain management into the organization's performance measurement and improvement plan.
7. Evaluate staff competency in pain assessment and management.
8. Establish policies and procedures on prescription pain medications.
9. Ensure pain does not hinder participation in rehabilitation services.

Overview of Pain Management and Older Individuals

As individuals reach 65 years of age and over, they are more likely to experience pain (Davis & Srivastava, 2003; Gloth, 2000) but be unable to report pain (Brummel-Smith et al., 2002). It is estimated that 40–50% of older adults suffer from chronic pain (Harkins, Kwentus, & Price, 1990; Klippel, 2000). Even though they receive a disproportionately higher percentage of medications compared to their representation in the general population (Sloane, Zimmerman, Brown, Ives, & Walsh, 2002), they are less likely to receive adequate pain management and relief (American Pain Society, 2001; Boughton et al., 1998; Gloth, 2000; Zalon, 1997). Without adequate pain management, older individuals are more likely to experience related physical decline; cognitive failure; depression and mood disturbance; and reduction in mobility, activities of daily living, participation in hobbies and recreation, and quality of life (Blomqvist & Edberg, 2002; Brummel-Smith et al., 2002; Davis & Srivastava, 2003; Lewis, 2002; Mobily, Herr, Clark, & Wallace, 1994). However, Fishman (2001, p. 13) noted, "Pain is not an expected or acceptable consequence of aging."

Pain management, especially for older adults, has come to the forefront of healthcare in recent years. It is well documented that without adequate pain control, individuals with pain are at risk for increased complications and a lower quality of life

(Blumstein & Gorevic, 2005; Goldstein & Morrison, 2005; Schofield & Dunham, 2005). Table 14.3 gives the American Geriatrics Society (AGS, 2002) guidelines for older adults.

It is important to focus specifically on pain in the elderly for at least six reasons. The first is that this segment of the American population experiences chronic pain quantitatively and qualitatively more than younger adults. Second, this segment of the population is growing at an increasing proportion, resulting in more Americans experiencing pain than ever before. Third, older adults are much less likely to seek assistance for pain; most notably, they are less likely to seek pharmacological solutions. Fourth, because of the complexities of their health comorbidities, it may be more difficult to assess their pain accurately. Fifth, aside from assessment difficulties, older adults are much less likely to receive adequate treatment for pain for a number of reasons. And sixth, the consequences of inadequate pain relief are greater for older adults than those who are younger. These six issues have been explored in depth elsewhere in the therapeutic recreation literature (Stumbo, 2006a, 2006b) and are overviewed in Table 14.4.

The National Institute of Neurological Disorders and Stroke (NINDS, 2001) commented that the sometimes unrelenting nature of pain forms "the terrible triad" of suffering, sleeplessness, and sadness. Although the causes of untreated or unrelenting pain are numerous, Cleeland et al. (1994) found that the most powerful predictor of poor pain management was the discrepancy between the patient's perception of pain and that of the clinician.

Overview of Pain Management and Children

According to Claar & Scharff (2007) "...pediatric recurrent pain is a significant problem and is estimated to affect more than 25% of children and adolescents" (p.

Table 14.3. Overview of the American Geriatric Society's (2002) Pain Management for Older Adults

- Reassess regularly for improvement, deterioration, or complications.
- Evaluate significant issues identified in the initial evaluation.
- Repeat the same quantitative assessment scales in follow-up.
- Evaluate analgesic use, side effects, and compliance.
- Assess effects of nonpharmacological interventions.

Table 14.4. Special Concerns of Pain Management in Older Adults

Pervasiveness of Pain in Older Adults	• 25–50% experience major pain problems on a daily basis (Blomqvist & Edberg, 2002; Brochet, Michel, Barberger-Gateau, & Dartigues, 1998; Chodosh, Ferrell, Shekelle, & Wenger, 2001; Grimby et al., 1999; Kedziera, 2001; Klippel, 2000; Lewis, 2002; Mobily et al., 1994). • Pain incidence doubles for individuals over the age of 60, and 59% of those have multiple pains (Chodosh et al., 2001) and take multiple medications (Gloth, 2001) • For those living in nursing homes, the prevalence of pain increases to 45–80% (Chodosh et al., 2001; Gloth, 2000, 2001; Kedziera, 2001; Lewis, 2002). • Nursing staff rated pain complaints as the second most frequent behavior problem among nursing home residents, surpassed only by depressed mood (Haly, as cited in Cook, 1998).
Proportion of Older Adults Growing in United States	• 12.4% of Americans of 281 million Americans were 65 years of age or older in 2000. • By 2020, 16.4% (53 million of 324 million) will be 65 or over. • By 2030, 20.3% will be 65 or older (U.S. Census Bureau, 2000). • Number of elderly persons, especially 85 and older, growing at faster rates than rest of population (U.S. DHHS and U.S. DoC, 2001).
Older Adults are Less Likely to Seek Pain Treatment	• Older adults do not want to be seen as complainers, think pain is a natural part of aging (Kedziera, 2001), feel it may indicate a more serious problem, or may lead to addiction (Pitkala, Strandberg, & Tilvis, 2002). • Persons in residential care felt that nursing staff was too busy and would be unable to reduce pain (Blomqvist & Edberg, 2002; Yates, Dewar, & Fentiman, 1995). • Some also do not have economic resources to pay for continued pain medications (Kedziera, 2001).
Older Adults' Pain is More Difficult to Assess	• Pain in older patients is more difficult to assess due to (a) complications of comorbid diseases that may influence pain, (b) insufficient training of healthcare providers in both geriatrics and pain management, (c) inadequate assessments for pain in older adults, and (d) a reluctance by both healthcare providers and patients to use opioid pain medications (Gloth, 2000). • Individuals with moderate dementia were able to answer only 40% of the questions on a pain assessment interview, while those with severe dementia answered 0–20% of the time (Duke, 1997). • Many individuals with dementia who are irritable and show inappropriate emotional reactions may be signaling underlying pain that is not being treated adequately (Duke, 1997), although Brummel-Smith et al. (2002) found that individuals with dementia and in moderate to severe pain were no more likely than those without dementia to display verbal outbursts. • Other comorbid conditions may affect written, verbal, and functional pain assessment in older adults: lessened communication skills; sensory impairments, such as hearing and vision problems; failing memory; and decreased motor function. Alternative pain-assessment tools and scales may be necessary, in addition to assessing nonverbal cues, such as grimacing, inactivity, or excessive activity (Hicks, 2000; Kedziera, 2001).
Older Adults Receive Inadequate Pain Management and Relief	• Adverse drug reactions occur in older patients at twice the frequency of younger persons, and the risk rises and the number of medications increases. An older individual taking six medications is 14 times more likely to have an adverse reaction than a younger person taking the same number of medications (Gloth, 2000). • Adverse drug events occur for up to 74% of those living in residential care facilities, largely due to multiple medication prescriptions. In their four-state study of 193 residential and assisted care facilities, the majority of the 2,014 individuals took over 5 medications, with prescriptions for 10 or more not being uncommon (Sloane et al., 2002). • Persons who had dementia received fewer narcotic pain medications and received pain medications for fewer months. In part, the researchers concluded that this may be due to the subjects' inability to use conventional pain-rating scales (Brummel-Smith et al., 2002). • Only 34% of nursing home residents in the Houston area had routine medication orders for chronic pain, well below the estimated range of 45–80% of residents suspected of suffering from pain (McClaugherty, 2002). • Older adults also experience age-related alterations in physiologic factors, pharmacodynamics of drug distribution and metabolism, and pain perception (Gloth, 2000, 2001; Sloane et al., 2002).
Consequences of Inadequate Pain Management are Significant	• Experiencing pain, especially on a persistent basis, reduces the person's quality of life physically, socially, psychologically, spiritually, and economically (Johnson, 2003). • Unrelieved pain may increase morbidity, length of stay, use and cost of medical resources, mortality, delayed healing, and prolonged rehabilitation (Carpenter, 1997; Cheever, 1999; Curtiss, 2001). • Social isolation was often associated with pain in older adults (Chodosh et al., 2001; Hicks, 2000). • Psychologically, NINDS (2001) found that diminished leisure and enjoyment, difficulty concentrating, decreased sexual function and affection, increased anxiety and fear, depression, personal distress, somatic preoccupation, altered appearance, and increased caregiver burden (Ferrell & Ferrell, 1997; NINDS, 2001). • Financially, pain results in an increased use of health care facilities that often are expensive (Chodosh et al., 2001; Hicks, 2000).

285). Children experience pain differently than adults. Children are not miniature adults, therefore pain management for children should be different. Due to an immature immune system, treatment (especially pharmacological) is of concern. Pediatric pain research has provided a wealth of information in the last 25 years regarding the unique issues regarding treatment of pain in children, the causes, mechanisms, treatment, and management of pain. Despite these changes, pain is still undertreated in children (Cohen, 2007) and a gap between "knowledge and everyday clinical practice remains a major difficulty" (Howard, 2003, p. 2464). He acknowledges the complexities of the issue:

> The study of pain in children requires considerable ingenuity and innovation. The diversity and developmental range of the pediatric population have enormous implications for the design and conduct of clinical research and the interpretation of research findings. . .There is a lack of comparable randomized, controlled trials of children's pain management. . .There are many reasons: difficulties in the measurement of pain, developmental differences that can confound comparisons between ages... (p. 2465).

Prevalence rates for hospitalized children who experience "clinically significant pain" range from 20% to 49% but some experts believe it could be as high as 60% (Walker & Wagner, 2003). A 1990 study conducted by Selbst and Clark on analgesic use in the emergency room found that children received half the amount of analgesics as adults with similar traumas (in Gold et al., 2006). Pain remains undertreated in children despite the fact that it creates unnecessary suffering in children (Gimbler-Berglund, Ljusegren, & Enskar, 2008).

Historically, children were not treated for their pain. The belief was that young infants did not experience pain, or if they did, they would not remember the painful experience. Because of this belief, they did not use anesthesia on infants undergoing circumcision. Many myths existed regarding pain and children including: (a) children do not experience pain, (b) pain medications cause addictions, (c) children do not feel as much pain as adults, (d) children will get used to pain, (e) they cannot reliably explain their pain, (f) if the child can be distracted, they are not in pain, and (g) if a child says he or she is in pain but does not appear to be in pain, he or she does not need relief (Zeltzer, Bush, Chen, & Riveral, 1997). Despite increased research on pain in children that resulted in refuting

many of these myths, unfortunately some of these misconceptions still persist. Each of these myths will be discussed below.

Children do not experience pain

It was believed, not long ago, that young infants either do not experience pain (Davis, 2008; Kuttner, 1996; Obrecht & Andreoni, 2007; Schechter, Blankson, Pachter, Sullivan, & Costa, 1997), or if they did, they would not remember the painful experiences. The medical community believed that infants had premature brains, so they either did not experience pain or would not remember painful experiences. Experts also thought that because children could not physiologically process pain experiences, they were insensitive to pain.

> The rationale for this belief was that the physiological immaturity of infants—specifically the lack of myelination (a protein sheath that surrounds the nerves and enables the nerve impulse to travel very rapidly) of the nervous system—meant that providing these babies with pain medication for painful invasive procedures was unnecessary. (Kuttner, 1996, p. 12)

The fact is infants, do indeed, experience pain—they demonstrate this behaviorally and physiologically. There are hormonal changes that occur that are directly associated with pain (Gold, et.al, 2006, Kuttner, 1996). "Evidence is growing that pediatric patients of all ages, even the most extremely premature neonates, are capable of experiencing pain as a result of tissue injuries due to medical illnesses, therapeutic and diagnostic procedures, trauma and surgery" (Kraemer & Rose, 2009, p. 241).

Fear of addiction to pain medications

Health care professionals were reluctant to use pain medication for fear of addiction (Schechter et al., 1997). This thinking hinders the proper management of pain: "when a child is in severe pain, the use of opioids will not create an addiction" (Kuttner, 1996, p. 16). When children receive the weight-appropriate dose of pain medication, they are not more susceptible to undesired effects of the medication (Kuttner, 1996). Many professionals still have this concern today.

Children tolerate pain better than adults

Another prevailing thought was that children did not feel as much pain as adults (Kuttner, 1996; Schechter, et al., 1997). It is now known that pain tolerance increases with age. Children feel as much or more pain than adults. Ignoring a child's fears will usually lead to greater fear on the child's part. Individuals who perform painful procedures to help children recover "tend to either provide a supportive and understanding climate . . . or emotionally cut themselves off from the experience . . . downplaying children's experience of pain" (Kuttner, 1996, p. 14). Some expect the child to struggle or fight. Proper intervention and preparation can prevent this emotionally draining experience for all parties (child, health care providers, and parents).

Children become accustomed to pain and/or painful procedures

The fact is that many children become more sensitive and/or anxious to painful procedures (Kraemer & Rose, 2009). Animal studies indicated that painful experiences as an infant increased pain sensitivity as an adult. According to Kuttner (1996), "prolonged pain also causes changes in the nervous system, along with increased sensitivity and irritability. Thus, achieving relief becomes more and more difficult for children over time . . ." (p. 14). When children undergo multiple painful experiences, they become *more* sensitive to pain (Anand, 2001; Mowery, Suddaby, & Kang, 2008). Sensitization (an increased reaction to subsequent procedures) may occur when a child is exposed to repeated procedures and a child may develop a lower pain threshold (von Baeyer, Marche, Rocha, & Salmon, 2004).

Children are not accurate reporters of pain

Many believed that children were not accurate reporters of pain due to their cognitive limitations. The fact is "if children are asked with non-leading questions where they hurt and how much they hurt, young children (even at 20 months) will answer by pointing to the site of their pain" (Kuttner, 1996, p. 15). Even in children, self-reports are "considered the most reliable indicators of pain" (Griffin, Polit, & Byrne, 2008, p. 297). The "gold standard" for pain assessment is self-report (Blount, Piira, Cohen, & Cheng, 2006; Walker & Wagner, 2003).

If they can be distracted, they are not in pain

Distraction is a healthy coping mechanism. This "...in no way indicates that the child is no longer experiencing pain. It merely indicates that the child is capable at the moment of using his cognitive capacities to move away from the pain" (Kuttner, 1996, pp. 16–17). Healthcare professionals should ask the child if there is any question about whether he/she is experiencing pain.

If a child says they are in pain but it does not appear that they are in pain, the child does not need relief

As stated earlier, pain is what the person says it is and pain experiences vary from person to person. Each child reacts to pain differently—some will complain, some pretend it is not there, some give hints, and some try to hide it because they fear further painful encounters (Kuttner, 1996).

Table 14.5 provides the 2000 American Academy of Pediatrics and the Canadian Paediatric Society Pain Guidelines for Newborns (Anand, 2001, p. 174). These guidelines can be generalized for working with children of any age who are in pain or have to undergo painful medical procedures.

Developmental Considerations

Children do not experience and express pain the same as adults. They tend to regress behaviorally when in pain (Wong, 1999). It is critical to establish the current developmental level of the child as cognitive abilities and skills will dictate how the healthcare professional intervenes with the child. The child's cognitive stage of development will provide information about how the child processes information and on how best to approach the child. This allows the therapist to provide

Table 14.5. General Principles for the Prevention and Management of Pain in Newborns

- Pain in newborns is often unrecognized and undertreated. Neonates do feel pain, and analgesia should be prescribed when indicated during their medical care.
- If a procedure is painful in adults, it should be considered painful in newborns, even if they are preterm.
- Compared with older age groups, newborns may experience a greater sensitivity to pain and are more susceptible to the long-term effects of painful stimulation.
- Adequate treatment of pain may be associated with decreased clinical complications and decreased mortality.
- The appropriate use of environmental, behavioral, and pharmacological interventions can prevent, reduce, or eliminate neonatal pain in many clinical situations.
- Sedation does not provide pain relief and may mask the neonate's response to pain.
- Healthcare professionals have the responsibility for assessment, prevention, and management of pain in neonates.
- Clinical units providing health care to newborns should develop written guidelines and protocols for the management of neonatal pain.

developmentally appropriate information and instruction to the child and family members.

> The age and developmental status of the child are critical components of the plan to manage painful procedures. Younger children who have limited cognitive ability to understand what is being done and the rationale for it experience increased fear and anxiety. Therefore, the plan should include anticipated use of maximum levels of medications as well as use of non-pharmacological supports. (Mowery, Suddaby, Kang, & Cooper, 2008, p. 491)

The gold standard of measuring pain is self-report; neonates, infants, some toddlers, and children with limited cognitive abilities are at a disadvantage (Howard, 2003).

> When a self-report cannot be obtained or its validity is questionable, other more indirect measures must be used. Infants, preverbal children, and individuals with communication difficulties may be among the most vulnerable to unrecognized pain, and yet they are unable to describe or rate it. (Howard, 2003, p. 2465)

Other methods are used to measure pain especially for those unable to communicate about pain. Methods include physiologic measures such as sensory reflexes, heart rate, and blood pressure; behavioral observations; or a combination of these methods. The findings from a study of 44 children ages 4 to 11 found that young children "can communicate their pain experiences competently. The words used by the children give a good indication of the severity of pain" (Kortesluoma & Nikkonen, 2006, p. 224). Using qualitative interviews, the researchers discovered that:

> ... [the children in the study] regarded pain as a multidimensional phenomenon. In their descriptions, they introduced its physical dimensions such as location, quality, thermal, and autonomic responses as well as the weakness induced by pain. Further, they mentioned the psychological dimension of pain ... also generated evaluative descriptions expressing duration. (p. 218)

Altered pain

Neonates and infants who undergo painful and repetitive painful procedures may actually have altered pain perceptions later in life. "Pain and its management,

especially in infancy, may have consequences for later pain-related behavior and perception. Studies revealed that infants who experienced repeated heel lancing showed behavioral and other effects that outlasted the painful stimulus by hours or days" (Howard, 2003, p. 2466). Howard discusses the long term potential impact of multiple painful procedures:

> ...repeated needle prick in the neonatal period causes complex and persistent behavioral effects later, including reduced pain thresholds. More severe injury in the form of inflammation is capable of permanent alterations in sensory processing; some but not all, of these effects appear to be modified by analgesia. (p. 2466)

Some studies suggested that early painful experiences "might permanently alter the neuronal circuits that process pain in the spinal cord" (Blount, Piira, Cohen, & Cheng, 2006). According to Walker and Wagner (2003), during infancy and early childhood, the pain pathways continue to develop which:

> ...involves the refinement of the sensory modalities and the intracortical connections with the limbic system and the affective and associative areas of the cortex ... this is a "critical period" of plasticity during which the central nervous system is susceptible to substantial remodeling in response to various inputs. This has raised concerns about the effects of repeated painful stimuli and stress on brain development. (p. 262)

Another consequence of repeated painful procedures for infants is the development of "windup," which describes an infant's response to "non-noxious stimuli (such as handling, physical examination, nursing care, etc.) as painful because of the heightened activity in nociceptive pathways. These typically non-noxious stimuli may now provoke the physiologic, systemic stress response..." (Walker & Wagner, 2003, p. 263). Carbajal, Rousset, Danan, et al. (2008) stated that "multiple lines of evidence suggest that repeated and prolonged pain exposure alters their subsequent pain processing, long-term development, and behavior" in neonates (p. 60). Investigators observed 430 neonates in intensive care units, and recorded all painful and stressful procedures that occurred during the first 14 days of admission for the neonates. The frequency of painful or stressful procedures (including heel sticks, venipuncture, arterial puncture) did not decrease substantially over time. The average number of painful procedures per day was 12 and the average number of painful plus stressful procedures was 16. Some neonates had as many as 62 procedures per day (Carbajal et al., 2008). Think about the possibility of experiencing 62 painful procedures in a day; it seems improbable that an adult would tolerate that amount of painful procedures. An infant, who cannot understand why these procedures are being done, has little defense against these very painful procedures and the consequences of this exposure are long term.

Chronic Pain

Acute illnesses in children have remained fairly stable in the U.S., but "the prevalence of chronic illness in American children has risen over the past several decades" (Wise, 2007, p. S6). Chronic pain affects a large number of children with some estimates of more than 25% (Claar & Scharff, 2007). According to Howard (2003), "...epidemiologic studies suggest that many children do not receive appropriate help or treatment" (p. 2467). Meldrum, Tsao, and Zeltzer (2008) stated, "...chronic intractable non-malignant pain, with associated limitations in physical, academic and social functioning, is a significant problem in children and adolescents" (p. 131). Children with chronic illnesses require far more services "... an average of more than 7 times as many days in the hospital than children without such conditions" (Wise, p. S7). It is estimated that chronic illness accounts for "60% of admissions and more than 90% of all childhood medical causes of death" (Wise, p. S7).

Functional limitations are associated with limited activities of daily living, decreased quality of life, and psychosocial distress (Meldrum et al., 2008). This study interviewed 45 children; predominant themes that emerged focused on functional limitations such as missing school and participating in a favorite activity. The children's responses were categorized according to how they reported handling their pain—adaptive, passive, and stressed. The adaptive children reported the highest level of functioning.

Procedural Pain

Pain children experience from procedures "has been reported to be a greater problem than the pain from the malignant disease itself" (Nilsson, Finnström, Kokinski, & Enskar, 2009, p. 102). In order to manage procedural pain, anticipation is crucial (American Academy of Pediatrics, 2001). "Procedural pain is unique because it tends to involve anticipatory anxiety, which in turn may increase the likelihood of experiencing more pain and distress during the procedures" (Lotan et al., 2009,

p. 404). Children who have extensive burns require "extensive painful wound-care procedures that must be performed daily or even several times a day" (Blount et al., 2006, p. 28). Children quickly remember the painful, daily cycle of anticipation of the procedure, feelings of distress, the pain of the actual dressing changes, and additional pain. See discussion below on the use of virtual reality programs as an effective distraction tool. The American Academy of Pediatrics (2001) suggests using cognitive behavioral strategies (e.g., relaxation, imagery) as interventions for pain that can be employed independently or with analgesics. One example of painful procedures is the routine skin care of children who experienced burns.

Intended Client Groups

Pain management has been investigated for literally every population seen in community and health care settings, such as:

- injured soldiers (Gallagher & Polomano, 2006)
- comparisons of younger (under 60) and older (over 60) adults (Wittink et al., 2006)
- persons with dementia (Snow, Rapp, & Kunik, 2005)
- older adults (Schneider, 2005)
- children (Gerik, 2005; Kortesluoma & Nikkonen, 2006)
- people with chronic nonmalignant pain syndrome (Adams, Poole, & Richardson, 2006; Richardson, Adams, & Poole, 2006; Sanders, Harden, & Vicente, 2005)

Basic Premises

Beyond a single pharmacologic or analgesic approach, the focus of pain management and control has broadened to include a variety of modalities that are designed to alleviate, relieve, or eliminate pain. It is well documented that without adequate pain control, individuals with pain are at risk for increased complications and a lower quality of life. The next section will review general guidelines as well as pharmacological and nonpharmacological treatment options for pain.

General Guidelines for Pain Management

The major aim of any form of pain treatment is to eliminate pain-associated suffering and increase function. Specifically, the notion is to increase pain control, decrease analgesic use, increase activity and function, decrease depression and anxiety, and increase family involvement in care (Ardery et al., 2003). "Suffering occurs when the pain leads the person to feel out of control, the pain is overwhelming, the source of the pain is unknown, the meaning of the pain is perceived to be dire, and/or the pain is chronic" (American Pain Society, 2001, p. 793). Additional goals are to provide comfort, inhibit pain impulses to diminish reflex responses to pain, and prevent future episodes (Living with cancer, 1998; Roberge & McEwen, 1998). Pain relief enhances a patient's restoration of function and enables the patient to breathe and move about more easily.

Healthcare professionals and family members should, above all, respect the pain-control method preferred by the person and additionally encourage continued use of his or her typical coping methods (such as prayer). Basic comfort measures, such as decreased lighting, noise, and environmental distractions; soothing foods and beverages; increased privacy; adherence to usual routines; movement and repositioning for pressure-relief; and visitor restrictions should be first-order considerations. In addition, staff and family should remember that patient fatigue interferes with many pain-management techniques (Ardery et al., 2003).

A three-pronged approach to assessing pain that focuses not on the relative level of pain but rather the functional limitations caused by the pain has been suggested (Meisler, 2002). These three considerations are:

- Identify pain characteristics: location, temporal features, quality, severity, and factors that may make the pain worse or better.
- Clarify pain-related constructs, such as:
  - Etiology (presence of disease in the body that can account for pain)
  - Syndrome (e.g., fibromyalgia)
  - Inferred pathophysiology (mechanisms of pain may fit a certain constellation), which can be subdivided as neuropathic (pain occurs due to dysfunction or disorder of the nervous system), nociceptive (ongoing injury in the body is activating a normal nervous system), and psychogenic (predominantly psychological factors) pain. These pains are not mutually exclusive, as multiple pathophysiologies are common.
- Determine pain-related functional impairment (impact of pain on mood, energy/physical activity level, level of stress, relationships) and comorbidities, including physical, medical, and psychosocial conditions, such as diabetes or major depressive disorder. (Meisler, 2002, p. 343)

Lewis (2002) noted that treatment protocols for pain management in the elderly should be slightly different than those for younger individuals. Drug reactions and side effects need to be monitored more closely, since older individuals are more sensitive to NSAIDS. Their condition may need more effective treatment than NSAIDS can offer, since less than 1% of all pain studies focus on elderly individuals.

After the assessment information is gathered, treatment options can be explored. In general, pain-management options include pharmacological or non-pharmacological approaches (Helmrich, 2001). Non-pharmacological approaches include:

- neurostimulation (transcutaneous electric nerve stimulation [TENS] and deep brain stimulation)
- physical techniques (physical and occupational manipulation, application of heat and cold, ultrasound, massage, acupuncture)
- anesthesiologic therapies (nerve blocks and use of implanted pumps and stimulators to direct medication to the spine)
- psychological interventions (cognitive-behavioral approaches, such as biofeedback, hypnosis, guided imagery, relaxation, breathing, aromatherapy, and distraction) (Helmrich, 2001; Johnson, 2003; Meisler, 2002)

Goodman (2003) noted that pain-management treatments should be holistic, involving several healthcare disciplines, rather than disease-specific, while Ross, Carswell, Hing, Hollingworth, and Dalziel (2001) noted that older Canadians used self-management techniques such as ignoring the pain, using distraction, exercising, resting, and using heat and cold, turning to medications only as a last resort.

The American Geriatrics Society (2002) advised the following when reassessing pain in the elderly:

- Reassess regularly for improvement, deterioration, or complications.
- Evaluate significant issues identified in the initial evaluation.
- Repeat the same quantitative assessment scales in follow-up.
- Evaluate analgesic use, side effects, and compliance.
- Assess effects of nonpharmacological interventions.

The next section briefly discusses pharmacological and psychological approaches to pain management.

Pharmacological Approaches to Pain Management

Acute and chronic pain management depends on the patient's presenting problem, co-morbidity, magnitude of the pain, previous opioid use, overall health, mental capacity, ethnic customs, and the like. Surgery, radiation, nerve blocks, and medications are examples of various ways to reduce, and hopefully eliminate the patient's pain. Analgesic drugs often are first considered because of their relative low cost, few side effects, and immediate effect. The overall aim of pain management is to "achieve constant pain relief while minimizing side effects" (Meyers, 1997, p. 100).

Carpenter (1997) reported that analgesia is "best provided by a combination of two or more analgesic agents or techniques. This appears to be particularly valuable when analgesic is produced by an action at two different sites or through different mechanisms of action, or when analgesics effects are synergistic" (p. 836). That is, a multi-delivery method or multi-drug combination often is the best for adequate relief of moderate to severe pain (Kehlet, 1995). Delivery methods depend on the type of drug being administered, but may include:

- orally (by mouth)
- intravenously (either nurse- or patient-controlled [PCA])
- intramuscularly (injection directly into muscle tissue)
- transdermally (adhesive patches on skin)
- epidurally (catheter into the spinal column)
- intrathecally (spinal)
- subcutaneously (under the skin)

- topically (on the skin)
- parenterally (within food mixture directly into vein)
- rectally (suppositories)
- sublingually (under the tongue)
- intranasally (nasal spray) (Carpenter, 1997; Cheever, 1999; Cherny et al., 1995; Hawthorn & Redmond, 1998; McQuay, 1999; Meyers, 1997; Miller, Miller, & Jolley, 2001; Stegman, 2001)

The World Health Organization (1996) created a three-step ladder for the administration of drugs for pain management:

1. Nonopioids (NSAIDS [nonsteroidal anti-inflammatory drugs] or acetaminophen) for mild pain.
2. Weak opioids (such as codeine) for moderate to severe pain.
3. Strong opioids (such as morphine, methadone, or fentanyl) for severe pain.

Pain relief drugs can be classified into four broad categories: acetaminophen, NSAIDS, opioids, and adjuvant drugs. Common drugs under each of the four categories are included on Table 14.6.

Pharmacological Pain Management and Older Adults

Davis and Srivastava (2003) extended the aim for pain management in the elderly to include reduction of pain and optimization of activities of daily living, not complete eradication of pain nor the lowest possible dosages of pain medications. Johnson (2000) noted older individuals are at higher risk for adverse drug

---

Table 14.6. Common Pain Relief Drugs

1. Acetaminophen: Tylenol, Excedrin
2. NSAIDS: Aspirin, Ibuprofen (Advil, Nuprin, Motrin), Ketorolac (Toradol), Naproxen (Naprosyn, Anaprox, Naprelan), Naproxen Sodium (Aleve), and Piroxicam (Feldeme)
3. Opioids (best for nociceptive pain): Mu-agonists (full agonists): Codeine (Tylenol #3), Fentanyl (Duragesic patch), Hydrocone (Vivodin), Hydrocodone (Vicoden, Lortab), Hydromorphone (Dilaudid), Mereridine (Demerol), Oxycodone (Percodan, Percocet, Tylox); Agonists-antagonists: Pentazocine HCI (Talwin), Butorphanol (Stadol)
4. Adjuvants (best for neuropathic pain; a drug whose primary indication is other than pain but which has an analgesic effect in some painful conditions): Multipurpose: Methylprednisolone (Medrol), Dexamethasone (Decadron), Dextroamphetamine (Dexadrine), Methylphendate (Ritalin); Tricyclic antidepressants: Amitriptyline (Elavil), (Norpramin), Imipramine (Tofranil), Doxepin (Sinequan), Clomipramine (Anafamil), Desipramine (Norpramin); Nortriptyline (Pamelor): Anticonvulsants: Carbamazepine (Tegretol), Clonazepam (Klonopin), Phenytoin (Dilantin), Gabapentin (Neurontin); Anti-histamine: Hydroxyzine

(Adam, 1997; Carpenter, 1997; Hawthorn & Redmond, 1998; McCaffrey, 1997; Meyers, 1997; Miller et al., 2001; Montauk & Martin, 1997; O'Neill & Fallon, 1997; Ruoff, 1999; Stegman, 2001)

events. Among the reasons are number of medications, number of chronic, active medical problems, decreased renal function from certain types of medication, lower medication compliance, failure to receive information about medication's adverse effects, and lower body mass index. Consequently, adverse drug events often result in a concurrent decrease in desired health outcomes.

When using a pharmacological approach, drug reactions and side effects need to be monitored more closely, since older individuals are more sensitive to NSAIDS, their condition may need more effective treatment than NSAIDS can offer, and—since less than 1% of all pain studies focus on elderly individuals—their difficulties with pain medication are less easily predicted (Blumstein & Gorevic, 2005; Lewis, 2002). Gloth (2001) and Johnson (2000) provided nine principles for prescribing pain medications to older individuals:

1. Determine if drug therapy is really necessary.
2. Decide that drugs are most appropriate given the patient's age and other concurrent medication.
3. Avoid medications with a high incidence of adverse effects in the elderly.
4. Consider whether the total number of medications will be tolerable and manageable for the patient.
5. Decide which dosage formulation is most appropriate for patients with difficulty swallowing.
6. Choose medications that require fewer numbers of doses per day to improve compliance.
7. Avoid use of intermittent schedules, such as alternate day therapy, since they are rarely followed accurately.
8. Assess whether the patient may need a smaller dose than a younger person.
9. Routinely assess the need for continued use of each medication and discontinue drugs that are no longer needed.

Pharmacological Pain Management and Children

The types of pharmacological options listed above in Table 14.6 are similar for children, except for dosages. According to Walker and Wagner (2003):

> . . . mild to moderate pain is best managed by using mild to moderate nonopioid analgesics . . . If pain control is not achieved with nonopioids, weak opioids may be added to the regimen. Use of opioid-nonopioid combina-

tions is generally helpful is generally helpful in maximizing analgesia while reducing opioids requirements . . . For moderate to severe pain, moderate to strong opioids are the drugs of first choice; they are used alone or in combination with nonopioid analgesics. (p. 264)

Walker and Wagner (2003) provided general guidelines for pain management that utilized information from the acute Pain Management Guideline Panel, the American Academy of Pediatrics and American Pain Society, and the International Evidenced-Based Group for Neonatal Pain. See Table 14.7.

Alternative Approaches to Pain Management

Because pharmacological approaches are sometimes less than satisfactory or increase the patient's burden by increasing undesired side effects (American Pain Society, 2001; Chodosh et al., 2001; Johnson, 2003; Meisler, 2002; Buchanan, Voigtman, & Mills, 1997) many healthcare professionals continue to look for complementary, holistic, synergistic, cost-effective, nonpharmacologic strategies to reduce and control pain. Nonpharmacologic strategies should be selected to complement, not replace, analgesics (Ardery et al., 2003; Nicholson, 2003). "Although pharmacologic treatment is the most common form of pain treatment . . . the use of complementary and alternative medications and nonpharmacologic interventions also must be considered, especially when results with the former are felt to be less than satisfactory or the burden of potential adverse effects outweigh the benefits" (Chodosh et al., 2001, p. 731). Gloth (2001) also advocated the use of nonpharmacological options due to lower overall cost and few side effects, noting they provide a "high benefit-to-risk ratio" and are likely to "lead to the release of endogenous opioids [internally created feel-good chemicals]" (2001, p. 189). According to Blumstein and Gorevic (2005), nonpharmacological approaches are always preferred over drug therapies for pain management.

However, the research on the provision of interdisciplinary, nonpharmacologic pain management is less than encouraging. Retrospective research on the medical records at a Veterans Health Administration center found that the initiative "Pain as the 5th Vital Sign" was unsuccessful in improving the quality of pain management for patients. Most patients in this study continued to have substantial pain without adequate pain control (Mularski et al., 2006). Similarly, a second retrospective study at a suburban teaching hospital also found that pain-management standards had no affect on practice nor on the pain experienced by patients (Narasimhaswamy, Vedi, Xavier, Tseng, & Shine, 2006). One survey of 220 hospitals in New York state noted that a collaborative, interdisciplinary approach to pain control was used in only 42% of the hospitals and underutilization of nonpharmacologic therapies to pain control was widespread (Jiang, Lagasse, Ciccone, Jakubowski, & Kitain, 2001). Another reported that nurses found that the benefits of non-drug therapies included improved pain management, feelings of self-control, enhanced nurse-patient relationships, and improved patient satisfaction. However, the nurses reported that barriers included lack of time and the ambivalence of other staff and administrators toward alternative pain therapies (Helmrich, 2001). In another study of 100 older persons, the investigators found that care providers, such as nurses, physical therapists, and occupational therapists, perceived pain-management methods to be more effective than their older patient counterparts (Blomqvist & Hallberg, 2002).

Nonetheless, complementary strategies are being more widely explored (Tan, Alvarez, & Jensen, 2006). Goodman (2003) noted that pain-management treatments should be holistic, involving several healthcare disciplines. It also it worthwhile to note that many adults used self-management techniques such as ignoring the pain, using distraction, exercising, resting, and using heat and cold, turning to healthcare professionals and medications only as a last resort.

Nonpharmacological approaches include:

- neurostimulation (transcutaneous electric nerve stimulation [TENS] and deep brain stimulation)
- physical techniques (exercise and physical activity, physical and occupational manipulation, application of heat and cold, ultrasound, massage, acupuncture)
- anesthesiologic therapies (nerve blocks and use of implanted pumps and stimulators to direct medication to the spine)
- psychological or cognitive interventions (patient education, cognitive-behavioral approaches, such as biofeedback, hypnosis, guided imagery, psychotherapy, structured or peer support, coping skills training, relaxation, breathing, aromatherapy, and distraction) (Blomqvist & Hallberg, 2002; Blumstein & Gorevic, 2005; Helmrich, 2001; Johnson, 2003; Kingdon et al., 1998; Ross et al., 2001)

Blomqvist and Hallberg (2002) cited several research studies that found TENS, exercise and physical activity, and rest were more effective for people

---

Table 14.7. General Guidelines for Management of Pain in Neonates, Infants, and Children (Walker & Wagner, 2003, p. 264)

- Anticipate predictable painful experiences and intervene accordingly. Prevention is better than treatment.
- Involve the family in the child's care, as family insights are very helpful.
- Use multimodal approaches to pain management, incorporating pharmacologic and non-pharmacologic interventions when possible.
- Proper early treatment is safer and more efficacious than delayed treatment. Early effective treatment results in improved patient comfort and may be associated with decreased clinical complications and decreased mortality.
- Analgesics should be administered on a scheduled, around-the-clock basis for moderate to severe pain, rather than on an as-needed basis.
- Use intravenous medications for severe, acute pain; avoid intramuscular injections.
- Oral medications are preferred for mild to moderate pain. If the child can tolerate orals, oral analgesics may be more convenient (and less expensive) than parenteral therapy.
- Base the initial choice of analgesic on the severity and type of pain.
- Adjust the analgesic dose and dosing interval based on regular, systematic pain assessments.
- Titrate the dose as necessary until pain relief is achieved, side effects become unmanageable, or maximum recommended dosages are reached. There is no maximum dose of opioids unless the opioid is a combination product containing acetaminophen or aspirin, in which case the maximum acetaminophen or aspirin daily dose must not be exceeded.
- Monitor and manage any side effects. Side effects that can be anticipated (e.g., constipation) should be prevented or treated promptly.
- When selecting a dose of an opioid, consider whether the patient is opioids-naïve or opioids-tolerant. Patients who have used opioids regularly for approximately 7 days or more are considered opioids tolerant and will require higher doses for acute pain control.
- Provide rescue analgesics for breakthrough pain. Increase the maintenance dose of the opioids if more than two rescue doses per day are needed.

with arthritis. Cold, joint protection, TENS, and massage were less common for hip and joint pain. They also noted that group interventions, talking, and distractions were more frequently used than specific techniques such as biofeedback and participation in support groups. Older individuals also used informal techniques, such as listening to music, praying, using humor, going on outings, or visiting with friends.

Two strategies often employed by therapeutic recreation specialists, physical activity and cognitive behavioral interventions, are commonly provided as complementary pain-management treatments with "high benefit-to-risk ratio" and "feel good" factors. Several authors have noted the prevalence of these two programs to aid in pain relief (Blumstein & Gorevic, 2005; "Finding the right care," 1996; Holdcroft & Power, 2003; Nurmikko et al., 1998; Schneider, 2005; Schofield & Dunham, 2005; Talbot, Gaines, Huynh, & Metter, 2003).

Physical Activity as Part of a Pain-Management Program

One monumental change in pain-management therapies is the swing away from bed rest toward active movement to the greatest degree possible (Talbot et al., 2003). Previously, pain was thought to be caused by tissue damage and be purely an anatomical or bodily function. Now it is recognized that pain involves altered sensation and cognitive appraisal (Holdcroft & Power, 2003). While bed rest was the preferred method of treatment when tissue damage was thought to be the cause, activity is now seen as the best route to restoring normal sensation. Activity, especially for back pain, leads to more rapid recovery of mobility, less chronic disability, reduced stress, and shorter return-to-work time (Chakravarthy, Joyner, & Booth, 2002; Holdcroft & Power; Schneider, 2005).

The medical and healthcare literature is inundated with the message that individuals who perform even minimal physical activity have important reductions in chronic disease (Chakravarthy et al., 2002). The same literature also noted that physical activity prescriptions should be highly individualized, contingent on the individual's family health history, disease history, current condition, and current activity level. However, it is recommended that physicians and other healthcare providers adhere to the national guidelines established by the American College of Sports Medicine (ACSM) (2005) and the Centers for Disease Control and Prevention (CDC) (2006) and the U.S. Surgeon General's Office (SGO).

The ACSM (2005) and the CDC (2006) recommended at least moderate physical activity for a minimum of 30 minutes on most, if not all, days of the week. They further emphasized that shorter bursts of activity, such as three 10-minute walks throughout the day, were equal in health benefits to 30 minutes of continuous activity. These guidelines should be followed, unless the assessment finds the individual sedentary or with other presenting problems, and then a slower but steady start is recommended. Chakravarthy et al. (2002) added:

> The health gain obtained by completely sedentary patients who undertake moderate physical activity is equal to or greater than the gains experienced by individuals who are already physically active and increase their level of activity . . . It is difficult to imagine a more effective approach to improving our nation's health. (p. 169)

Physical Activity Program Recommendations For Older Adults

The American Geriatrics Society (AGS, 2002), the American Medical Directors Association (AMDA, 2006), and the American College of Sports Medicine (ACSM, 2005) are among many organizations that have documented that physical activity programs help individuals control persistent diseases and lessen the clinical impact of the biological aspects of aging. They also noted that systematic reviews and randomized, controlled clinical trials (the strongest forms of practice evidence) showed strong support for physical activity as a method of pain reduction and functional enhancement (reversing effects of previous deconditioning). They also found that physical activity enhanced psychological health, in addition to physical health.

The AGS (2002) suggested that, after an assessment that includes comorbidities, medications, and physical impairments, an exercise program should include activities to improve joint range of motion, increase muscle strength and power, enhance postural and gait stability, and restore cardiovascular fitness. They noted that patient preference was an important consideration for continued participation. In addition, they stated that effective combinations of nonpharmacological approaches might reduce drug dosages. Complete recommendations for physical activity programs for older adults with pain are located in the AGS's (2002) clinical practice guideline, *The Management of Persistent Pain in Older Persons*.

Koltyn (2002) examined the research literature on exercise as a pain-management technique for older adults and arrived at several conclusions:

- A wide variety of exercise-training programs (e.g., stretching, range of motion exercises, walking, cycling, aerobic dance, Tai Chi, and resistance exercise) have been employed in research studies.
- Most studies have recorded pain improvement for the community-dwelling research subjects, especially those with osteoarthritis pain.
- It is not known which form of exercise-training is most effective for pain management of older adults.
- Further research is needed to determine the optimal mode, intensity, duration, and frequency of exercise that is safe and effective for pain management, especially for individuals living in long-term and assisted-care facilities.
- Further research is needed to determine the bio-physiological mechanism that operates to reduce pain as a result of exercise.

Physical Activity Program Recommendations For Children

Children who restrict their level of activity because they fear their pain will increase can actually "cause or exacerbate pain as a consequence of the physical changes associated with their altered behaviors" (McGrath, 1991, p. 98). Play "mediates reactions to stress and has beneficial physiological benefits as well" (Sheridan, 2007, p. 463). Play helps a child work through experiences; many types of play are used as therapeutic interventions for children who are hospitalized. Medical play provides the child with opportunities to "perform" medical procedures on anatomically correct dolls, and "buddy" dolls have procedures performed on the doll before they are completed on the child. Education takes place during these types of intervention and provide a window into how the child is interpreting what will be done to her or him. Any misconceptions can be dispelled during the play session. Through play, the child can manipulate their world and regain some sense of control over their life. Playrooms are considered "pain-free," where no procedures, tests, injections, or medications are given. Children work off the anxieties they have from their experiences during the day. The recreation therapist and/or child life-specialist can assist in facilitating healthy coping skills while children undergo therapeutic procedures.

It is important that the child maintain some sense of routine. Inactivity creates a host of potential medical problems. "The deleterious effects of prolonged bed rest and sustained inactivity have well been documented" (Hacker et al., 2006, p. 615) and include potential cardiopulmonary effects, pneumonia, loss of muscle mass and strength, increased risk of joint contractures, and the negative effects of immobility on mood. The study found that patients who underwent stem cell transplants had a 58% reduction in physical activity and concluded that "the prolonged physical inactivity may result in more serious complications and hamper recovery" (p. 622).

Cognitive-Behavioral Approaches to Pain Management

Self-efficacy (Bandura, 1977) and stress coping theories are synergistic with the cognitive behavioral interventions used in most modern pain-management programs (DeGood, 2000). Cognitive behavioral interventions are aimed at helping patients increase coping skills regarding pain and its threat to their functioning, and reduce associated emotional distress. The overall goal of cognitive behavioral interventions is to "improve quality of life by changing the way the patient perceives and responds to pain" (Kingdon et al., 1998, p. 117). As mentioned earlier, pain is more than a physiological response to trauma; it is a subjective, individualized experience unique to each person. As such, cognitive behavioral approaches assume that the pain experience includes cognitive, affective, and behavioral components, and help patients respond to the total experience by taking an active role in reassessing and controlling the pain (Turk & Meichenbaum, 1994; Turk, Meichenbaum, & Genest, 1983; Turk & Rudy, 1992).

Hawthorn and Redmond (1998) indicated "cognitive behavioral strategies include a range of different interventions which are aimed at changing the patient's perception of pain, altering, dysfunctional pain behaviors, and fostering a sense of control over pain" (p. 204). Cognitive coping strategies may include distraction activities to divert attention away from pain (e.g., imagery, focal point, counting methods), mindfulness methods to accept pain (e.g., meditation), and methods for altering self-defeating thought patterns that contribute to pain and distress (e.g., thought-stopping). Behavioral strategies noted by the AGS (2002) included pacing of activities according to level of pain, increasing involvement in pleasurable activities, and using relaxation methods. Relaxation and distraction often are cited as effective methods, except for those older individuals who are cognitively impaired (Ardery et al., 2003; Gloth, 2001). The effects of CBT (cognitive-behavioral therapy) with those with cognitive impairments are not known at this time (AGS, 2002). Combined approaches using both cognitive and behavioral are the most effective, and usually focus on stress-coping strategies. These skills can be taught by a trained specialist, either with individuals or groups, and usually run 60 to 90 minutes over 6 to 10 sessions. Involvement of spouses or significant others improves effectiveness (AGS, 2002).

Keefe, Jacobs, and Underwood-Gordon (1997) outlined a general format that most cognitive-behavioral interventions follow. These interventions are intended to be an adjunct rather than replacement for biomedical pain treatments (Pearl, 2001). The intervention typically begins with an educational component that explains the role of situations, thoughts, emotions, and behaviors in the pain experience. These patient-education sessions cover the mind-body connections during the pain experience. Second, patients are encouraged to recognize and challenge the dysfunctional thoughts, beliefs, and attitudes that may contribute to their pain and suffering. For example, patients are asked to examine their attitudes and beliefs about pain that may be contributing negatively to their experience and slowing their recovery or rehabilitation.

Third, the patient is instructed in some combination of specific, nonpharmacologic behavioral skills that emphasize the mind-body connection between emotions, thoughts, and feelings with bodily reactions. Techniques include self-relaxation, deep breathing, guided imagery, meditation, distraction techniques, exercise, music, pacing of activities, assertiveness, support groups, positive self-talk, hypnosis, behavior modification, and biofeedback. These skills are first practiced and rehearsed in the treatment session and then in everyday situations. Self-monitoring and self-reinforcement are typically encouraged (American Society of Anesthesiologists [ASA], 1999; Ashburn & Staats, 1999; DeGood, 2000; Friedrich, 1999; Kwekkeboom, 1999; NINDS, 2001; Pearl, 2001).

Fourth, patients are asked to identify high-risk situations (pain flare-ups, work or home stressors, emotional upsets) and to plan and rehearse strategies to meet these challenges. Again, patients are asked to practice the skills they have learned and apply them to situations that are most likely to produce the most stress, and therefore be associated with pain. Rehearsing behaviors ahead of when they are needed helps the person in improving efficacy expectations and emotion-focused coping skills.

The final stage often involves decision making or problem solving in relationship to employment, rehabilitation, and leisure activities necessary to return to prior daily life or to adapt to a new lifestyle. For example, a person with chronic pain may need assistance prioritizing and accomplishing life and leisure activities around a pain medication schedule. Another individual may need instruction in adaptive techniques that help reduce the physical strain on a painful joint.

Use of Distraction Techniques

"Distraction is a cognitive coping strategy that works by diverting attention from a painful stimulus by passively redirecting the subject's attention or actively involving the subject with a task" (Murphy, 2009, p. 18). The premise of distraction is to divert the child's attention from the painful procedure to something that is of interest to the child, therefore decreasing the amount of pain experienced; this also includes anticipatory reactions to the event. "The principal rationale for distraction methods derives from 'fixed capacity' theories of attentional processing" (Piira, Hayes, & Goodenough, 2002, p. 2). This non-pharmacological intervention ". . . can bring measurable benefits, is free of risk, and can be provided at low cost" (Murphy, p. 18). VR ideally lures attention into the computer-generated world, leaving less attention available to process incoming nociceptive signals" (p. 834).

The use of distraction is based on two theoretical constructs: the Gate Control Theory (Melzack & Wall, 1965) and the limited capacity of attention (Gold, Kant, Kim, & Rizzo, 2005). "The basic theory behind distraction dictates that attention is diverted away from a noxious stimulus and is instead focused on more pleasant stimuli, resulting in a reduction in the perception and experience of pain" (Gold, et al., 2005, p. 204). Hoffman (2004) uses the analogy of a spotlight in explaining the limited capacity of attention in that individuals ". . . select some information to process and ignore everything else, because there is a limit to how many sources of information we can handle at one time" (p. 62). Recently the use of virtual reality (VR) programs has been researched for their efficacy as distracters and reducing the pain experience. According to Patterson, Hoffman, Palacios, and Jensen (2006) "pain requires conscious attention to process. Hoffman (2004) explains the connection between attention and the use of virtual reality programs:

> While a patient is engaged in a virtual-reality program, the spotlight of his or her attention is no longer focused on the wound and the pain

but drawn into the virtual world. Because less attention is available to proves incoming pain signals, patients often experience dramatic drops in how much pain they feel and spend much less time thinking about their pain during wound care." (p. 62)

Many studies on the efficacy of virtual reality focus on the subjective evaluation of pain which is supported by the pain literature and current pain theories. However, Hoffman (2004) also used physiological measures in his study; he ". . . measured pain-related brain activity using functional magnetic resonance imaging (fMRI)" (p. 63). This measurement used healthy volunteers using an electrically heated element that was applied to the foot for a brief time to simulate pain. Volunteers

> . . . reported severe pain intensity and unpleasantness and spent most of the time thinking about their pain . . . their fMRI scans showed a large increase in pain-related activity in five regions of the brain that are known to be involved in the perception of pain: the insula, the thalamus, the primary and secondary somatosensory cortex, and the affective division of the anterior cingulated cortex. (p. 63)

When the volunteers used the VR program, there was a significant decrease in the "pain related activity in their brains" (p. 63) as well as lower subjective self-reports of pain. According to Hoffman, findings suggest that VR is ". . . not just changing the way patients interpret incoming pain signals; the programs actually reduce the amount of pain-related brain activity" (p. 63). According to Gold et al. (2005), the use of VR as a potential tool in managing pain:

> . . . has considerable promise. Specifically, VR anesthesia may hold promise for a diversity of routine medical interventions that traditionally require significant pharmacological intervention. Although VR anesthesia has demonstrated promise for decreasing pain, fear, and anxiety, it may also decrease additional pharmacological needs, such as sedatives and anxiolytics, therefore decreasing overall risks associated with sedation. (p. 208)

Related Research

Physical Activity as a Pain-Management Technique for Older Adults

The following are seven, typical examples of physical activity and pain research conducted with older adults. Frost, Moffett, Moser, and Fairbank (1995) conducted a study in the United Kingdom of 81 older adults with chronic low back pain. While both groups were taught specific exercises and sent to "back-school," the randomly assigned treatment group attended eight fitness program classes over four weeks. The treatment group reported less disability and pain, and higher self-efficacy and walking distances than the control group, even six months after the initial study. The investigators noted that simply advising people to exercise was not as effective as having them attend exercise classes.

In their studies of elderly Canadians, Ross et al. (2001) found that exercise was among the most used self-management modalities for managing pain. The subjects included in their daily regimes gardening, cooking, walking, stretching, bicycling, swimming, getting out of the house, breathing fresh air, and meeting new people. The subjects reported the most benefits when exercise was enjoyable, a variety of activities were employed, and it resulted in contact with others. They felt exercise reduced the need for both prescription and non-prescription medication, prevented additional irritation of muscles and joints, strengthened muscles, and improved circulation. They noted the need for exercise moderation and acceptance of one's true limitations.

Ettinger et al. (1997) studied the effects of structured exercise programs on 439 community-dwelling older adults with knee osteoarthritis and found that modest effects resulted from both the aerobic exercise and resistance exercise programs. The results included improvements in measures of disability, physical performance, and reductions in pain perception. They recommended that physical activity (aerobic exercise and resistance training) be included in the treatment of older individuals experiencing pain from knee osteoarthritis. Talbot et al. (2003) instituted a "Walk+" program (arthritis self-management and pedometer training) for 34 community-dwelling older adults (60 and older) with knee osteoarthritis, and they reported that the treatment group took more steps, became more efficient in their gait as well as faster and stronger when compared to the control group. They recommended additional research using pedometer-monitored walking for older adults.

In addition, Bartha and Petrella (1999) found, in a study involving 172 older individuals with knee osteoarthritis, that the combination of an analgesic (oxaprozin) and physical exercise was additive. However, they called for more research before any definitive conclusions could be made about dose-response relationships between analgesics and physical activity.

van Tulder et al. (2001) conducted a systematic review of randomized controlled trials. They further explored the 39 studies that met the quality criteria and rated the evidence as strong, moderate, limited, or none. They reported strong evidence that exercise therapy was not more effective for acute low back pain than inactive or other active treatments with which it was compared. They reported conflicting results with regard to the effectiveness of exercise therapy compared to inactive treatments for low back pain. In addition, they explained that exercise therapy was more effective than usual care by the general practitioner and just as effective as conventional physiotherapy for chronic low back pain. The researchers concluded that the research does not indicate specific exercises that are effective for the treatment of low back pain; however, exercise may be helpful to people with low back pain to expedite return to typical daily activities and work.

Lastly, Tak, Staats, Van Hespen, and Hopman-Rock (2005) conducted a similar study on 109 participants with hip osteoarthritis by evaluating the effects of an eight-week exercise program of strength training and lifestyle advice and found that the treatment group reported less pain and disability, greater hip function, and better timed "Up & Go" test scores. Although they found no improvement in quality of life, observed disability, or body mass index scores, they felt the reductions in pain and increases in hip function warranted further exploration of exercise programs for the management of osteoarthritis in older adults.

All of these studies found that exercise for older individuals in pain produced positive results, primarily with those in the treatment groups reporting less pain and disability. Without clear-cut conclusions on which physical activities are most beneficial to which groups, therapeutic recreation specialists are reminded to consult the ASCM and CDC guidelines for exercise prescription.

Physical Activity as a Pain-Management Technique for Children

Walters and Williamson (1999) investigated the relationship between pain, activity restriction, and depression in children with chronic illnesses (cancer, sickle cell, hemophilia, JRA, bone and muscle disorders). Activity restriction was defined as "the extent to which

illness interfered with a child's social, physical, and school-related activities" (p. 36). Parents and children rated the level of restriction in daily activities (e.g., eating, sleeping, school, homework, sports, playing with friends). The daily activity most disrupted was play or activity (90%), then school (80%), and difficulty eating (55%). Children spontaneously indicated that the limitations to social or competitive activities were the most distressing to them.

Hacker et al. (2006) concluded, "maintaining or increasing levels of physical activity may play a role in reducing fatigue and improving health status perceptions and quality of life" (p. 623). Blyth, March, Nicholas, and Cousins (2005) found that individuals with chronic pain who used "active strategies substantially reduced the likelihood of having high levels of pain-related disability" (p. 285) and they found that those who used active strategies had:

- 4 times less pain disability and 2 times fewer sites
- less need for help at home
- less sleep disruption

Yoga was found to significantly reduce "self-reported disability and pain, and reduced use of pain medication" (Williams et al., 2005, p. 114); these improvements were also maintained on a 3-month follow-up "indicating that the yoga intervention is associated with longer lasting reductions in disability and pain outcomes than an educational intervention" (p. 114).

Cognitive Behavioral Therapies as a Pain-Management Technique for Older Adults

Although cognitive-behavioral interventions are widely used, most are supported through anecdotal reports rather than efficacy research. DeGood (2000) reported that the outcomes associated with cognitive behavioral interventions include improved coping skills that help modify the pain experience, mood elevation, and improved overall quality of life. Curtiss (2001) indicated outcomes for pain management include "decreased pain intensity and increased level of function; improved sleep and mood; improved ability to work, socialize, and play; generally improved quality of life; and other similar patient-directed outcomes" (p. 30). According to Saunders (1998), cognitive-behavioral treatment has been found to be more effective than medical care alone in improving medium-term functioning, and optimal treatment requires multiple one-hour individual sessions over several months.

Cook (1998) reported research on the effectiveness of a cognitive-behavioral treatment program for nursing home residents modeled after Turk et al. (1983). Subjects met for 10 weekly sessions of approximately 60 to 75 minutes duration. A treatment manual was developed, incorporating: (a) education and reconceptualization of pain (two sessions); (b) training in behavioral and cognitive coping skills, including progressive relaxation, imagery, attention diversion, and cognitive restructuring (five sessions); and (c) consolidation of skills and follow-through using planning, practice, and role playing (three sessions). The general format of each session was (a) review of previously discussed material and homework assignments, (b) presentation and practice of new information and skills, (c) discussion of the application of new skills using a problem-solving framework, and (d) review of the session and assignments for home practice. The study was shown to be effective in reducing pain and pain-related disability in elderly nursing home residents with chronic pain. The results were clinically significant in both frequency and magnitude.

Stanley, Diefenbach, and Hopko (2004) used applicable research to develop an evidence-based cognitive-behavioral intervention program for older individuals with generalized anxiety disorders. Their research is mentioned here because they also indicate its usefulness for older individuals with depression, insomnia, and specific fears, common secondary conditions to chronic pain for the elderly. They developed an eight-session intervention that included: (a) motivation, education, and breathing skills; (b) progressive muscle relaxation; (c) changing thoughts; (d) problem solving; (e) changing behavior and teaching sleep skills; and (f) coping skills. An evaluation of their preliminary work "suggested promise" in that it led to "significant improvements in worry and depression relative to usual care" (p. 75).

Okifuji and Turk (1999), in reviewing a number of efficacy studies on cognitive-behavioral interventions, summarized that while approximately 40% of patients could be considered to have meaningful changes after treatment, more information is needed about the variance among individuals. They and their colleagues (Turk, Okifuji, Sinclair, & Starz, 1996, 1998) reported that treatment differences varied significantly across sub-groups of fibromyalgia patients. Patients who tended to have high levels of pain, poor coping, emotional distress, and perceived disability benefited most from the treatment, whereas those whose distress and disability were associated with interpersonal problems did not improve, suggesting that an additional treatment component was needed. In addition, a group of patients who were coping relatively well showed minimal changes, probably due to the floor effect, raising the question of whether these patients needed comprehensive treatment at all.

More clinical efficacy research is needed on the types of services most beneficial for different categories of clients. Kwekkeboom (1999) and NINDS (2001) concurred with Turk and his colleagues that additional research is needed to create a model that delineates individual factors that influence the selection of cognitive-behavioral interventions so that successful patient outcomes can be predicted with greater confidence.

Cognitive-Behavioral Therapies as a Pain-Management Technique for Children

Cognitive-Behavioral Therapy (CBT) empowers individuals to manage their own care; "self-management of chronic pain is one of the central tenets of CBT and pain-management programs" (Smith & Elliott, 2005, p. 249). Those with active strategies (Blyth et al., 2005) saw significant improvement in the management of their pain. Active strategies included exercise, working, using correct postures, use of prayer, relaxation/meditation, and/or mental distraction. Smith and Elliott (2005) stated if further studies support the findings in the Blyth et al. study, there will be a need to promote active self-management as an effective pain-management tool. The key in these approaches is "adopting an active internal approach to illness" (p. 250) and that healthcare professionals are in a position to influence this shift to self-management.

Research has provided "strong evidence that psychological treatments, particularly relaxation, biofeedback, and cognitive behavioral therapy, are highly effective in treating chronic pain in children and adolescents . . . . Use of active pain coping strategies has been associated with more favorable pain outcomes than reliance on passive strategies" (Claar & Scharff, 2007, pp. 285, 298).

Application to Therapeutic Recreation

At present, therapeutic recreation specialists are developing a growing body of knowledge about the design and effectiveness of pain-management programs for a variety of client groups. Professionals have combined concepts from physical activity and cognitive-behavioral interventions, self-efficacy theory, and stress-coping models to provide effective and meaningful pain-management programs under the umbrella of therapeutic recreation services. Mobily and MacNeil (2002) advocated that therapeutic recreation specialists use exercise and physical activity in addressing older patients with pain. They noted that physical activity's contributions may include increased flexibility, strength, endurance, and range of motion, as well as cognitive and psychological benefits. They also noted that pain should be used as the upper limit of safe participation for clients within therapeutic recreation programs; that is, specialists should adjust the requirements of physical activity according to the person's capacity to tolerate pain and benefit from the activity. According to Carter, Van Andel, and Robb (2003), within the auspices of therapeutic recreation, typical cognitive-behavioral training programs for pain management may include content on stress management, time management, problem solving, decision making, imagery, cognitive restructuring, relaxation, assertiveness training, activity pacing, leisure skill development, and communication strategies.

Stumbo (2002) provided an overview of types of pain, pain-management initiatives, pain assessment and treatments, and therapeutic recreation's role in pain-control programs. Stumbo extended this information with two articles on pain management specifically for older adults (2006a, 2006b). Finch (2006) provided additional insights into pain management and evidence-based practice for individuals with osteoarthritis. She specifically promoted exercise and physical activity as a prescription for osteoarthritis-related pain. Richeson (2004) described the role of therapeutic recreation specialists on the pain-management team, especially for older individuals with dementia. She discusses several nondrug treatment options for persons with dementia.

Beyond these overviews, the next step of systematically documenting success cases and conducting efficacy research is just now gaining momentum. The following three articles represent recent research on therapeutic recreation's role in pain management.

Schofield (2005) conducted a study to evaluate the use of Snoezelen, or sensory stimulation and relaxation, as a therapeutic intervention for use in the management of chronic-pain patients. The study compared the use of Snoezelen to traditional relaxation within the pain clinic setting. Seventy-three adult patients were recruited from a convenience sample and then randomly assigned into control and experimental groups. The control group was given access to a relaxation program within a pain-clinic setting; the experimental group was given access to a Snoezelen environment for the same amount of time. Assessments were carried out at three time intervals on a range of symptoms designed to reflect the multidimensional nature of the chronic pain experience, including pain intensity,

quality, anxiety, depression, coping, confidence, and quality of life. Although both groups demonstrated some improvements in their outcome measures, the experimental group appeared to do better, thus suggesting that Snoezelen is as good as, if not slightly better, than a traditional relaxation environment.

Mobily and Verburg (2001) completed a case study to describe the effects of an aquatic exercise program an individual with fibromyalgia. A 59-year-old female school teacher with fibromyalgia participated in an aquatic therapy program for 4.5 months in a community-based therapeutic recreation setting. Shortly after participation was initiated, she reported relief from acute pain. Improvement in the degree to which pain interfered with functional activities was noted. She reported returning to work on a half-time basis and regained the stamina to participate in her favorite recreation and social activities. Findings from this case are consistent with those obtained from larger clinical trials using exercise interventions with persons diagnosed with fibromyalgia. Implications for community-based therapeutic recreation are discussed.

Kunstler, Greenblatt, and Moreno (2004) conducted a study on four older women in a long-term care facility using a single-subject research design. They used both aromatherapy and hand massage as treatments for pain management and found them both to be effective in reducing pain. They also noted additional benefits such as better sleep patterns. They recommended that multiple strategies be used for multiple effects.

Bonadies (2004) reported on the quantitative and qualitative evaluation results of a yoga program for individuals with AIDS-related pain. During and after the 8-week program the four participants had lower pain ratings, lower anxiety scores, and lowered use of PRN drugs. Both the participants and staff noted improved physical functioning and less reduction on nonprescribed drugs for pain. Although Bonadies noted continued problems with participation compliance by the clients, three of the four requested continuation of the program after the 8-week trial.

Resources

www.partnersagainstpain.com/
For individuals in pain, caregivers, and health professionals. Offers toolkit for pain management and other resources. Sponsored by pharmaceutical company.

www.painedu.org/
For healthcare professionals, including courses for CEUs. Sponsored by pharmaceutical company.

www.pain.com/
For healthcare professionals and individuals in pain.

American Alliance of Cancer Pain Initiatives
The Resource Center
1300 University Avenue Room 4720
Madison, Wisconsin 53706
(608) 265-4013

American Chronic Pain Association
P.O. Box 850
Rocklin, California 95677-0850
T: (916) 632-0992
F: (916) 632-3208
ACPA@pacbell.net
www.theacpa.org

American Council for Headache Education Associates
19 Mantua Road
Mt. Royal, NJ 08061
T: (856) 423-0258
F: (856) 423-0082
achehq@talley.com
www.achenet.org

American Pain Society
4700 West Lake Avenue
Glenview, Illinois 60025
T: (847) 375-4715
www.ampainsoc.org/

American Society of Pain Management Nurses
2755 Bristol Street Suite 110
Costa Mesa, California 92628
T: (714) 545-1305

Mayday Pain Resources Center
City of Hope Medical Center
1500 East Duarte Road
Duarte, California 91010
T: (818) 359-8111 ext. 3829
prc.coh.org

National Chronic Pain Outreach Association, Inc.
P.O. Box 274
Millboro, VA 24460
T: (540) 862-9437
www.chronicpain.org

National Headache Foundation
428 West St. James Place
2nd floor
Chicago, IL 60614-2750
T: (773) 388-6399
F: (773) 525-7357
info@headaches.org
www.headaches.org

Example Activities

Unlike other chapters in which this section suggests a few activities, the following pages provide protocols for working with children in pain, due to Dr. Kinney's expertise and prior work. The protocols include: (a) distraction, (b) medical preparation, (c) play, (d) play therapy, and (e) relaxation (pp. 278–281).

Title	Distraction for Painful Procedures for Children and Adolescents Protocol By Judy S. Kinney
Purpose	To reduce the trauma experienced by children/adolescents and increase tolerance of painful procedures.
Staff Requirements	The CTRS must be knowledgeable about distraction techniques and have available resources to provide a variety of distraction techniques.
Entrance Requirements	Child/Adolescent who is scheduled to undergo medical procedures. RT must assess child/adolescent prior to procedure. RT has identified coping strategies of C/A and effective distraction methods. C/A & family practiced skills prior to procedure C/A engaged in play therapy/recreation therapy prior to procedure.
Exit Requirements	Completion of medical procedure and when C/A appears to be calm. May be ongoing depending on treatment requirements—will vary by individual.
Group Size	1:1 for distraction during medical procedure. Involve family if possible.
Duration	Variable, depending on procedure. RT to schedule time with client prior to, during and after procedure.
Safety Considerations	Type of distraction must be appropriate to the setting and/or procedure (must not impede ability of medical staff to successfully complete procedure). Medical staff should approve items prior to introducing item to client. No items that could trigger a reaction (allergic/asthmatic or otherwise) in an individual should be used (e.g., scented items, liquids). Alternative methods/equipment should be available so that if initial distractor is not effective, an alternative method can be used.
Facility and Equipment	Environment should be quiet and as stimulus-free as possible (see medical preparation/education protocol). Equipment—a variety of distraction items should be available. Small items should be kept in a bag. Room should be equipped with video/TV, music, or other devices used.
Methods	1. Preparation/education about procedure should occur prior to scheduled event with child or adolescent and family members if appropriate. 2. Child/parents should be familiar with setting (room & equipment) as well as the actual procedure prior to the scheduled event. 3. RT and child should select several methods that may provide relief during the procedure (identify primary method and alternative backups). C/A should demonstrate ability to successfully utilize intervention. 4. RT to check with medical staff prior to meeting with family and child to determine whether the procedure will occur on time. RT to provide as much information as possible about any potential delays and reasons for delay. 5. RT will meet with family and child prior to scheduled event to review procedure and reduce anxiety. 6. RT to be present in room during procedure to facilitate distraction if that was the role planned, otherwise encourage child/family member to utilize methods. RT to provide encouragement and praise positive behaviors. 7. Provide additional time after procedure to debrief child and/or family and work through any reactions that may have occurred as a result of the procedure. 8. Provide feedback and problem solve with client and family about effectiveness of plan for future use.
Possible Client Objectives or Outcomes	C/A and family will experience a decrease in distress and anticipation anxiety. C/A will experience an increase in pain tolerance (decrease in pain perception) of medical procedures. C/A will increase self-regulation skills (sense of control, use of positive coping skills). C/A will experience a reduction in pain experienced during procedure. C/A will increase self-esteem.
References	American Academy of Pediatrics. (2001). The assessment and management of acute pain in infants, children, and adolescents. *Pediatrics, 108*(3), 793–797. Claflin, C. J., & Barbarin, O. A. (1991). Does "telling" less protect more? Relationships among age, information disclosure, and what children with cancer see and feel. *Journal of Pediatric Psychology, 16*(2), 169–191. Piira, T., Hayes, B., & Goodenough, B. (2002). Distraction methods in the management of children's pain: An approach based on evidence or intuition? *The Suffering Child, 1*, 1–10. Retrieved from http://thesufferingchild.net Zempsky, W. T., Cravero, J. P., & the Committee on Pediatric Emergency Medicine and Section on Anesthesiology and Pain Medicine. (2004). Relief of pain and anxiety in pediatric patients in emergency medical systems. *Pediatrics, 114*(5), 1348–1356.

Title	Medical Preparation/Education Children & Adolescents Protocol By Judy S. Kinney
Purpose	To provide education regarding procedures to enable C/A to cope effectively with pain.
Staff Requirements	RT and/or a Certified Child Life Specialist will prepare/educate C/A and family on the treatments/interventions scheduled as part of the treatment.
Entrance Requirements	Child/Adolescent who is in pain and/or scheduled for procedures. Child/Adolescent referred by treatment team or RT.
Exit Requirements	Child/Adolescent demonstrates understanding of disease/illness/understanding of pain. Child/Adolescent expresses and/or displays a reduction in stress and/or anxiety regarding his/her situation. Child/Adolescent able to use strategies independently or with prompting.
Group Size	Individual sessions or small groups of C/A scheduled for similar procedures.
Duration	Length of each session will vary according to age and developmental level of child (especially attention span). RT should monitor C/A for signs of fatigue. Number of sessions to be determined by TR and based upon progress made by the child/adolescent. Sessions should be about 30–45 minutes in length. The number of sessions will be determined by the progress made by the C/A and parents.
Safety Considerations	RT should note any restrictions in movement or positions prior to working with the C/A. Modifications can be made to accommodate restrictions. Frequent informal assessments of C/A's toleration of activity for signs of pain should be made. C/A should be given opportunity to continue at a later time after rest and/or request for pain relief. No items that could trigger a reaction (allergic/asthmatic or otherwise) in an individual should be used (e.g., scented items, liquids). RT to sterilize equipment after use by clients. Some equipment may not be used again after use by a client. RTs should refer to their agency's infection-control standards to identify correct standards of use.
Facility and Equipment	Sessions can occur at bedside if a client is unable to leave room. Teaching materials should be developmentally appropriate and utilize a variety of media (visual, sound, tactile, etc.). Realistic replicas or the actual equipment used in procedures should be available for the C/A to manipulate, explore, and try out.
Methods	1. Assess level of understanding of C/A and parents about what they think will happen regarding the procedure. 2. Provide a variety of materials and objects that are appropriate to age and developmental level of C/A to assist in the learning process. 3. A picture book, video, or book describing procedures and instruments can be used as teaching devices for the RT. 4. Pictures of the environment and detailed description of what they will see, hear, and feel is critical in reducing anxiety about the experience. 5. Use of dolls—both anatomically correct and cloth dolls ("buddy dolls") can be used as tools to demonstrate procedures and use of equipment. Child can manipulate tools and practice procedure on doll. This is not only therapeutic for child but allows the RT to assess level of understanding on the part of the child and correct any misconceptions that the child may have. 6. Tours of the actual room (or pictures) where procedure will occur are encouraged to increase comfort level and familiarity with the procedure.
Possible Client Objectives or Outcomes	C/A and family will experience a decrease in distress and anxiety. C/A will increase knowledge of procedure. C/A will experience an increase in sense of control over situation. C/A will utilize positive coping skills for dealing with the procedure and possible pain associated with the procedure.
References	Claflin, C. J., & Barbarin, O. A. (1991). Does "telling" less protect more? Relationships among age, information disclosure, and what children with cancer see and feel. *Journal of Pediatric Psychology, 16*(2), 169–191. Committee on Hospital Care. (2000). Child life services. *Pediatrics, 106*, 1156–1159. Nelson, C. C., & Allen, J. (1999). Reduction of healthy children's fears related to hospitalization and medical procedures: The effectiveness of multimedia computer instruction in pediatric psychology. *Children's Health Care, 28*(1), 1–13. Piira, T., Hayes, B., & Goodenough, B. (2002). Distraction methods in the management of children's pain: An approach based on evidence or intuition? *The Suffering Child, 1*, 1–10. Retrieved from http://www.thesufferingchild.net Stacey, D. W. (1990). Children in pain: An overview for child life workers. *Journal of Child and Youth Care, 4*(1), 43–53. Wong, D. L. (1999). *Nursing care of infants and children* (6th ed.). St. Louis, MO: Mosby.

Title	Play Therapy/Medical Play for Children and Adolescents Protocol By Judy S. Kinney
Purpose	Child/Adolescent and family (if indicated) will utilize a variety of play methods to learn effective coping skills about pain, illness, hospitalization, and/or medical procedures.
Staff Requirements	CTRS trained in play-therapy interventions and medical play to address pediatric issues regarding pain, illness/hospitalization and/or medical procedures.
Entrance Requirements	Child/Adolescent who is scheduled to undergo medical procedures, management of pain, hospitalization, and/or adjustment to illness/disability. Child/Adolescent referred by treatment team or RT. RT assessed child/adolescent and identified play therapy/medical play as an appropriate intervention.
Exit Requirements	Child/Adolescent demonstrates use of positive coping skills for pain, illness, hospitalization, and/or medical procedures. Child/Adolescent demonstrates knowledge and/or adequate preparation for procedures (good understanding based on developmental age and cognitive abilities). Child/Adolescent expresses and/or displays a reduction in pain, stress and/or anxiety regarding his/her situation.
Group Size	Variable; 1:1 with C/A and/or family or up to four children to one CTRS.
Duration	Length of each session will vary according to age and developmental level of child (especially attention span). Length usually between 30 and 60 minutes. Number of sessions to be determined by TR and based upon progress made by the child/adolescent. Opportunities for play therapy should be made available after procedures to work though any additional issues that occurred as a result of the procedure.
Safety Considerations	Type of play materials made available must be appropriate to the setting and/or procedure and determined to be safe for individual use. For example, if using syringes, needles should be removed. Items that could trigger a reaction (allergic/asthmatic or otherwise) in an individual should not be used (e.g., scented items, liquids). RT to sterilize play equipment after use. Some equipment may not be used again after use. RTs should refer to their agency's infection-control standards to identify correct standards of use.
Facility and Equipment	Environment should be quiet and as stimulus-free as possible. Sessions can occur at bedside if a client is unable to leave room. Toys and materials should be appropriate to age and developmental stage of each child/adolescent. Toys and equipment should be of sturdy and safe materials.
Methods	1. Provide a variety of play materials and objects that are appropriate to age and developmental level of C/A. Variety allows C/A to explore concerns or issues they may not have previously identified by RT and/or treatment team. 2. Through play, dolls, or use of objects, RT may identify previously unknown issues about the intensity and/or duration of pain that the child is experiencing and/or range of coping strategies that the child utilizes. 3. Explore evidence of child's fears of reporting pain because they fear it will keep them from going home or further restrict their movements. 4. If possible, include realistic medical equipment that can be manipulated by the C/A. 5. Allow C/A to be the "doer" or medical professional with the RT or a doll as the "patient." 6. Provide medical dolls or anatomically correct dolls that can be explored and manipulated by the child. 7. Provide art materials—use of "medical art" activities such as syringe painting or use of medical supplies (tongue depressors, cups, gloves, cotton, etc.). 8. Provide clothing that can be tried on/worn by clients including hats, gloves, masks, gowns, etc. 9. RT can plan play sessions to either be directed or non-directed in nature, depending on the goals set for the client.
Possible Client Objectives or Outcomes	C/A and family will experience a decrease in distress and anticipation anxiety regarding upcoming medical/procedural treatments. C/A will provide an accurate report of pain experienced; reduce fear that expressing pain will prevent them from going home. Child will increase knowledge of what the pain means and decrease unrealistic fears about punishment for their behavior, or about body mutilation and death that they may have developed. C/A will experience a decrease in the intensity of their fears or anxiety regarding pain. C/A will experience an increase in sense of control over situation. C/A will utilize positive coping skills during procedures.
References	American Academy of Pediatrics. (2001). The assessment and management of acute pain in infants, children, and adolescents. *Pediatrics, 108*(3), 793–797. Bennett, S. M., Huntsman, E., & Lilley, C. M. (2001). Parent perceptions of the impact of chronic pain in children and adolescents. *Children's Health Care, 29*(3), 147–159. Claflin, C. J., & Barbarin, O. A. (1991). Does "telling" less protect more? Relationships among age, information disclosure, and what children with cancer see and feel. *Journal of Pediatric Psychology, 16*(2), 169–191. Piira, T., Hayes, B., & Goodenough, B. (2002). Distraction methods in the management of children's pain: An approach based on evidence or intuition? *The Suffering Child, 1,* 1–10. Retrieved from http://thesufferingchild.net Walters, A. S., & Williamson, G. M. (1999). The role of activity restriction in the association between pain and depression: A study of pediatric patients with chronic pain. *Children's Health Care, 28*(1), 33–50.

Title	Play/Recreation as Stress Reduction for Children & Adolescents Protocol By Judy S. Kinney
Purpose	Use of play and/or recreation activities to reduce stress and provide opportunities for sense of mastery and control.
Staff Requirements	CTRS should be skilled in a variety of activity skills and have experience in processing the activity to determine skills learned.
Entrance Requirements	Child/Adolescent who is experiencing pain. Child/Adolescent referred by treatment team or RT. RT assessed child/adolescent and identified play/recreation as an appropriate intervention to manage pain and/or relieve stress.
Exit Requirements	Child/Adolescent demonstrates use of positive coping skills for managing pain. Child/Adolescent expresses and/or displays a reduction in stress and/or anxiety regarding his/her situation.
Group Size	Variable; four to six children to one CTRS, depending on age and activity.
Duration	Length of each session will vary according to age and developmental level of child (especially attention span). RT should monitor C/A for signs of fatigue. Number of sessions to be determined by RT and based upon progress made by the child/adolescent.
Safety Considerations	RT should note any restrictions in movement or positions prior to engaging C/A in an activity. Modifications to the activity can be made to accommodate restrictions. Frequent informal assessments of C/A's toleration of activity for signs of pain should be made. C/A should be given opportunity to continue at a later time after rest and/or request for pain relief. Items that could trigger a reaction (allergic/asthmatic or otherwise) in an individual should not be used (e.g., scented items, liquids). RT to sterilize play equipment after use by clients. Some equipment may not be used again after use by a client. RTs should refer to their agency's infection control standards to identify correct standards of use.
Facility and Equipment	Sessions can occur at bedside if a client is unable to leave room. Bedside activities, use of music, video games, computers, books, etc. can be made available to C/A that is unable to go to the activity room. Toys and materials should be appropriate to age and developmental stage of each child/adolescent. Toys and equipment should be of sturdy and safe materials.
Methods	1. Provide a variety of play/recreation materials and objects that are appropriate to age and developmental level of C/A. Variety allows C/A to engage in activities that they enjoy. 2. Provide games and materials that promote interaction among peers. 3. Activities can avert attention away from pain and give a moderate sense of relief for periods of time. This does not mean that the child is not in pain, but rather is an opportunity not to dwell on discomfort. 4. Play/recreation provides opportunities for the C/A to make choices, and to have a sense of control over what happens to them. 5. Activity room should be a "pain-free" room. This means that no painful procedures shall take place in this room. This policy allows C/A a sense of security while in the room. 6. Play/recreation activities provide opportunities for self-expression and interaction with peers (socialization). It can also provide a cathartic opportunity. 7. Play/recreation opportunities provide some sense of routine for C/A, which is especially important for young children. 8. For young children, play can provide opportunities to encourage normal development and prevent developmental delay due to restrictions in movement and routines. 9. RT can structure interactions to involve C/A to express frustrations and identify healthy methods to deal with pain, frustrations, and lack of control over situations.
Possible Client Objectives or Outcomes	C/A and family will experience a decrease in distress and anxiety. C/A will experience some relief from pain through the use of activities. C/A will experience an increase in sense of control over situation. C/A will utilize positive coping skills for dealing with pain. C/A will maintain and/or increase developmental and social skills.
References	Committee on Hospital Care. (2000). Child life services. *Pediatrics, 106*, 1156–1159. Walters, A. S., & Williamson, G. M. (1999). The role of activity restriction in the association between pain and depression: A study of pediatric patients with chronic pain. *Children's Health Care, 28*(1), 33–50. Wong, D. L. (1999). *Nursing care of infants and children* (6th ed.). St. Louis, MO: Mosby.

References

Adam, J. (1997). The last 48 hours. *British Medical Journal, 315*(712), 1600–1604.

Adams, N., Poole, H., & Richardson, C. (2006). Psychological approaches to chronic pain management: Part 1. *Journal of Clinical Nursing, 15*(3), 290–300.

American Academy of Pediatrics. (2001). The assessment and management of acute pain in infants, children, and adolescents. *Pediatrics, 108*(3), 793–797.

American College of Sports Medicine (ACSM) (2005). *ACSM's guidelines for exercise testing and prescription* (7th ed.). Baltimore, MD: Lippincott Williams & Wilkins.

American Geriatrics Society (AGS) (2002). The management of persistent pain in older persons. *Journal of the American Geriatrics Society, 50*(S6), 5205–5224.

American Medical Directors Association (AMDA) (2006). Clinical practice guideline: Pain management in the long term care setting. Retrieved April 16, 2006, from: http://www.amda.com/info/cpg/chronicpain.htm

American Pain Foundation (APF) (Nov 2008). Pain Facts and Statistics. Retrieved June 16, 2009, from: http://www.painfoundation.org/Publications/PainFactsandStats.pdf

American Pain Society (APS) (2001). The assessment and management of acute pain in infants, children, and adolescents. *Pediatrics, 108*(3), 793.

American Society of Anesthesiologists (ASA) (1999). The management of pain. Retrieved April 16, 2006, from: http://www.ASAhq.org/PublicEducation/pain_manage.html

Anand, K. J. S. (2001). Consensus statement for the prevention and management of pain in the newborn. *Archives of Pediatric and Adolescent Medicine, 155*, 173–180.

Ardery, G., Herr, K. A., Titler, M. G., Sorofman, B. A., & Schmitt, M. B. (2003). Assessing and managing acute pain in older adults: A research base to guide practice. *Medsurg Nursing, 12*(1), 7–18.

Ashburn, M. A., & Staats, P. S. (1999). Management of chronic pain. *Lancet, 353*(9167), 1865–1869.

Bandura, A. (1977). Self-efficacy: Toward a unifying theory of behavioral change. *Psychological Review, 84*, 191–215.

Bartha, C., & Petrella, R. J. (1999). Randomized trial of home-based exercise treatment for osteoarthritis of the knee. *Medicine, Sports Science, and Exercise, 31*(5 suppl.), S209.

Beresford, L. (1998). Palliative care, Gain on pain: Two new initiatives bring long-overlooked pain control issues front and center. *Hospitals & Health Networks, 72*(15–16), 72.

Blomqvist, K., & Edberg, A. (2002). Living with persistent pain: Experiences of older people receiving home care. *Journal of Advanced Nursing, 40*(3), 297–306.

Blomqvist, K., & Hallberg, I. R. (2002). Managing pain in older persons who receive home-help for their daily living: Perceptions by older persons and care providers. *Scandinavian Journal of Caring Sciences, 16*(3), 319–328.

Blount, R. L., Piira, T., Cohen, L. L., & Cheng, P. S. (2006). Pediatric procedural pain. *Behavior Modification, 30*, 24–49.

Blumstein, H., & Gorevic, P. D (2005). Rheumatologic illnesses: Treatment strategies for older adults. *Geriatrics, 60*(6), 28–35.

Blyth, F. M., March, L. M., Nicholas, M. K., & Cousins, M. J. (2005). Self-management of chronic pain: a population-based study. *Pain, 113*(3), 285–292.

Bonadies, V. (2004). A yoga therapy program for AIDS-related pain and anxiety: Implications for therapeutic recreation. *Therapeutic Recreation Journal, 38*(2), 148–166.

Bonica, J. J. (1985). Treatment of cancer pain: Current status and future need. In H. L. Fields, R. Dubner, & R. Cervero (Eds.), *Proceedings of the Fourth World Congress on Pain* (pp. 589–616). Seattle, WA: Raven Press.

Bonica, J. J. (1990). Cancer pain. In J. J. Bonica (Ed.), *The management of pain* (2nd ed., Vol. 1, 400–460). Philadelphia, PA: Lea and Febiger.

Boughton, K., Blower, C., Chartrand, C., Dircks, P., Stone, T., Youwe, G., et al. (1998). Impact of research on pediatric pain assessment and outcome. *Pediatric Nursing, 24*(1), 31–35, 62.

Brochet, B., Michel, P., Barberger-Gateau, P., & Dartigues, J. F. (1998). Population-based study of pain in elderly people: A descriptive study. *Age and Ageing, 27*(3), 279–284.

Brummel-Smith, K., London, M. R., Drew, N., Krulewitch, H., Singer, C., & Hanson, L. (2002). Outcomes of pain in frail older adults with dementia. *Journal of the American Geriatrics Society, 50*(11), 1847–1851.

Buchanan, L., Voigtman, J., & Mills, H. (1997). Implementing the agency for health care policy and research pain management pediatric guideline in a multicultural practice setting. *Journal of Nursing Care Quality, 11*(3), 23–36.

Carbajal, R., Rousset, A., Danan, C., Coquery, S., Nolent, P., Ducrocq, S., et al. (2008). Epidemiology and treatment of painful procedures in neonates in intensive care units. *JAMA, 300*(1), 60–70.

Carpenter, R. L. (1997). Optimizing postoperative pain management. *American Family Physician, 56*(3), 835–849.

Carr, D. B. (1993). Pain control: The new "whys" and "hows." *Pain: Clinical Updates, 1*(1), 1–9.

Carter, M. J., Van Andel, G. E., & Robb, G. M. (2003). *Therapeutic recreation: A practical approach.* Prospect Heights, IL: Waveland.

Centers for Disease Control and Prevention (CDC) (2006). Physical activity and health: A report of the surgeon general. Retrieved April 16, 2006, from: http://www.cdc.gov/mmwr/preview/mmwrhtml/00042984.htm

Chakravarthy, M. V., Joyner, M. J., & Booth, F. W. (2002). An obligation for primary care physicians to prescribe physical activity to sedentary patients to reduce the risk of chronic health conditions. *Mayo Clinical Procedures, 77*, 165–173.

Cheever, K. H. (1999). Control critically ill patients' acute pain. *Nursing Management, 30*(8), 40–43.

Cherny, N. J., Chang, V., Frager, G., Ingham, J. M., Tiseo, P. J. Popp, B., Portenoy, R. K., & Foley, K. M. (1995). Opioid pharmacotherapy in the management of cancer pain: A survey of strategies used by pain physicians for the selection of analgesic drugs and routes of administration. *Cancer, 76*(7), 1283–1293.

Chodosh, J., Ferrell, B. A., Shekelle, P. G., & Wenger, N. S. (2001). Quality indicators for pain management in vulnerable elders. *Annals of Internal Medicine, 135*(8), 731–735.

Claar, R. L. & Scharff, L. (2007). Parent and child perceptions of chronic pain treatments. *Children's Healthcare, 36*(3), 285–301.

Cleland, C. S. (1989). Pain control: Public and physicians' attitudes. In C. S. Hill, Jr. & W. S. Fields (Eds.), *Drug treatment of cancer pain in a drug-oriented society: Advances in pain research and therapy* (Vol. 11: pp. 81–89). New York, NY: Raven Press, Ltd.

Cleland, C. S., Cleland, L. M., Dar, R., & Rinehardt, L. C. (1986). Factors influencing physician management of cancer pain, *Cancer, 58*(3), 796–800.

Cleland, C. S., Gonin, R., Hatfield, A. K., Edmonson, J. H., Blum, R. H., Stewart, J. A., et al. (1994). Pain and its treatment in outpatients with metastatic cancer. *New England Journal of Medicine, 330*, 592–596.

Cleland, C. L., & Gebhart, G. F. (1997). Principles of nociception and pain. In Springhouse Corporation (Ed.), *Expert pain management* (pp. 1–30). Springhouse, PA: Author.

Cohen, L. L. (2007). Introduction to the special issue on pediatric pain: Contextual issues in children's pain management. *Children's Healthcare, 36*(3), 197–202.

Cook, A. J. (1998). Cognitive-behavioral pain management for elderly nursing home residents. *Journals of Gerontology—Series B: Psychological Sciences & Social Sciences, 53*(1), 51–59.

Crook, J., Rideout, E., & Browne, G. (1984). The prevalence of pain complaints in a general population. *Pain, 18*(3), 299–314.

Curtiss, C. P. (2001). JCAHO: Meeting the standards for pain management. *Orthopaedic Nursing, 20*(2), 27.

Dar, R., Beach, C. M., Barden, P. L., & Cleland, C. S. (1992). Cancer pain in the marital system: A study of patients and their spouses. *Journal of Pain and Symptom Management, 7*(2), 87–93.

Davis, C. L. (2008). Does your facility have a pediatric sedation team? If not, why not? *Pediatric Nursing, 34*(4), 308–309.

Davis, M. P., & Srivastava, M. (2003). Demographics, assessment, and management of pain in the elderly. *Drugs and Aging, 20*(1), 23–57.

DeGood, D. E. (2000). Relationship of pain-coping strategies to adjustment and functioning. In R. J. Gatchel & J. N. Weisberg (Eds.), *Personality characteristics of patients with pain* (pp. 129–164). Washington, DC: American Psychological Association.

Dell'Api, M., Rennick, J. E., & Rosmus, C. (2007). Childhood chronic pain and health care professional interactions: Shaping the chronic pain experiences in children. *Journal of Child HealthCare, 11*(4), 269–286.

Duke, D. (1997). Elderly with dementia having trouble reporting pain, according to study. Retrieved April 16, 2006, from: http://record.wustl.edu/archive/1997/02-20-97/1700.html

Ettinger, W. H., Burns, R., Messier, S. P., Applegate, W., Rejeski, W. J., Morgan, T., et al. (1997). A randomized trial comparing aerobic exercise and resistance exercise with a health education program in older adults with knee osteoarthritis: The fitness arthritis and seniors trial (FAST). *The Journal of the American Medical Association, 277*(1), 25–31.

Ferrell, B. R., Nash, C. C., & Warfield, C. (1992). The role of patient-controlled analgesia in the management of cancer pain. *Journal of Pain and Symptom Management, 7*(3), 149–154.

Ferrell, B. R., & Ferrell, B. A. (1997). Care of elderly patients with pain. In Springhouse Corporation (Ed.), *Expert pain management* (pp. 375–396). Springhouse, PA: Author.

Finch, K. M. (2006). Recreational therapy: Relieving pain in older adults with osteoarthritis. *American Journal of Recreation Therapy, 5*(1), 27–39.

Finding the right care for chronic pain: The team approach to pain management enables chronic pain sufferers to resume work and reduces their use of health care services. (1996). *Business & Health, 14*(11A), 17–23.

Fiset, L., Leroux, B., Rothen, M., Prall, C., Zhu, C., & Ramsay, D. S. (1997). Pain control in recovering alcoholics: Effects of local anesthesia. *Journal of Studies on Alcohol, 58*(3), 291–295.

Fishman, S. M. (2001). Pain and the older patient: Pain management may be big news, but it doesn't always get delivered. *Geriatrics, 56*(10), 13.

Foley, K. M. (1985). The treatment of cancer pain. *New England Journal of Medicine, 313*(2), 84–95.

Friedrich, M. J. (1999). Experts describe optimal symptom management for hospice patients. *JAMA: The Journal of the American Medical Association, 282*(13), 1213–1214.

Frost, H., Moffett, J. A. K., Moser, J. S., & Fairbank, J. C. T. (1995). Randomised controlled trial for evaluation of fitness programme for patients with chronic low back pain. *British Medical Journal, 310*, 151–154.

Gallagher, R. M., & Polomano, R. (2006). Early, continuous, and restorative pain management in injured soldiers: The challenge ahead. *Pain Medicine, 7*(4), 284–286.

Gebhart, F. (1997). California leads way to pain control with opioid guide (state medical board publishes guide for chronic pain management). *Drug Topics, 141*(1), 84.

Gerik, S. M. (2005). Pain management in children: Developmental considerations and mind-body therapies. *Southern Medical Journal, 98*(3), 295–302.

Gimbler-Berglund, I., Ljusegren, G., & Enskar, K. (2008). Factors influencing pain management in children. *Paediatric Nursing, 20*(10), 21–24.

Gloth, F. M. (2000). Geriatric pain. *Geriatrics, 55*(10), 46–51.

Gloth, F. M. (2001). Pain management in older adults: Prevention and treatment. *Journal of the American Geriatric Society, 49*(2), 188–199.

Gold, J. I., Kant, A. J., Kim, S. H., & Rizzo, A. (2005). Virtual anesthesia: The use of virtual reality for pain distraction during acute medical interventions.

Seminars in Anesthesia, Perioperative Medicine and Pain, 24(4), 203–210.

Gold, J. I., Townsend, J., Jury, D. L., Kant, A. J., Gallardo, C. C., & Joseph, M. H. (2006). Current trends in pediatric pain management: From preoperative to the postoperative bedside and beyond. *Perioperative Medicine and Pain, 25*(3), 159–171.

Goldstein, N. E., & Morrison, R. S. (2005). Treatment of pain in older adults. *Critical Reviews in Oncology/ Hematology, 54*(2), 157–164.

Goodman, G. R. (2003). Outcomes measurement in pain management: Issues of disease complexity and uncertain outcomes. *Journal of Nursing Care Quality, 18*(2), 105–111.

Griffin, R. A., Polit, D. F., & Byrne, M. W. (2008). Nurse characteristics and inferences about children's pain. *Pediatric Nursing, 34*(4), 297–305.

Grimby, C., Fastbom, J., Forsell, Y., Thorslund, M., Claesson, C. B., & Winblad, B. (1999). Musculo-skeletal pain and analgesic therapy in a very old population. *Archives of Gerontology and Geriatrics, 29*, 29–43.

Grossman, S. A. Sheidler, V. R. Swedeen, K., Mucenski, J., & Piantadosi, S. (1991). Correlation of patient and caregiver ratings of cancer pain. *Journal of Pain and Symptom Management, 6*(2), 53–57.

Gureje, O., Von Korff, M., Simon, G. E., & Gater, R. (1998). Persistent pain and well-being. *Journal of the American Medical Association, 280*(2), 147–151.

Hacker, E. D., Ferrans, C., Verlen, E., Ravandi, F., van Besien, K., Gelms, J. & Dieterle, N. (2006). Fatigue and physical activity in patients undergoing hematopoietic stem cell transplant. *Oncology Nursing Forum, 33*(3), 614–624.

Haley, W. E. (1983). Priorities for behavioral intervention with nursing home residents. *International Journal of Behavioral Geriatrics, 1*(4), 47–51.

Harkins, S. W., Kwentus, J., & Price, D. D. (1990). Pain and suffering in the elderly. In J. T. Bonica (Ed.), *The clinical management of pain* (pp. 552–559). Philadelphia, PA: Lea & Febiger.

Hawthorn, J., & Redmond, K. (1998). *Pain: Causes and management*. Oxford, UK: Blackwell Science.

Helmrich, S. (2001). Factors influencing nurses' decisions to use non-pharmacological therapies to manage patients' pain. *Australian Journal of Advanced Nursing, 19*(1), 27–35.

Hicks, T. J. (2000). Ethical implications of pain management in a nursing home: A discussion. *Nursing Ethics, 7*(5), 392–396.

Hoffman, H. G. (2004). Virtual-reality therapy. *Scientific American*, 58–65.

Holdcroft, A., & Power, I. (2003). Management of pain. *British Medical Journal, 326*(7390), 635–639.

Howard, R. F. (2003). Current status of pain management in children. *Journal of the American Medical Association, 290*(18), 2464–2469.

Jiang, H. J., Lagasse, R. S., Ciccone, K., Jakubowski, M. S., & Kitain, E. M. (2001). Factors influencing hospital implementation of acute pain management practice guidelines. *Journal of Clinical Anesthesia, 13*(4), 268–276.

Johnson, M. (2003, March 3). Managing chronic pain the elderly. *GP: General Practitioner, 59.*

Johnson, N. (2000). Improving outcomes in the elderly. *Formulary, 35*(11), 904–908.

Joint Commission on Accreditation of Healthcare Organizations (2001). Pain standards for 2001. Retrieved June 02, 2004, from: http://www.jcaho.org/standard/pm.html

Joint Commission on Accreditation of Healthcare Organizations: (2006). Assessment. Retrieved April 16, 2006, from: http://www.jointcommission.org

Joranson, D. E., Cleeland, C. S., Weissman, D. E., & Gilson, A. M. (1992). Opioids for chronic cancer and non-cancer pain: A survey of state medical board members. *Federation Bulletin: The Journal of Medical Licensure and Discipline, 79*(4), 15–49.

Kedziera, P. L. (2001). Easing elders' pain. *Holistic Nursing Practice, 15*(2), 4–16.

Keefe, F. J., Jacobs, N. M., & Underwood-Gordon, L. (1997). Biobehavioral pain research: A multi-institute assessment of cross-cutting issues and research needs. *Clinical Journal of Pain, 13,* 91–103.

Kehlet, H. (1995). Synergism between analgesics. *Annals of Medicine, 27,* 259–262.

Kingdon, R. T., Stanley, K. J., & Kizior, R. J. (1998). *Handbook for pain management.* Philadelphia, PA: Saunders.

Klippel, J. (2000). *Pain in America. Gallup survey for the Arthritis Foundation.* Atlanta, GA: The Arthritis Foundation.

Koltyn, K. F. (2002). Using physical activity to manage pain in older adults. *Journal of Aging & Physical Activity, 10*(2), 226–240.

Kortesluoma, R.L., & Nikkonen, M. (2006). 'The most disgusting ever': Children's pain descriptions and views of the purpose of pain. *Journal of Child HealthCare, 10,* 213–227).

Kraemer, F. W. & Rose, J. B. (2009). Pharmacologic management of acute pediatric pain. *Anesthesiology Clinics, 27*(2), 241–268.

Kunstler, R., Greenblatt, F., & Moreno, N. (2004). Aromatherapy and hand massage: Therapeutic recreation interventions for pain management. *Therapeutic Recreation Journal, 38*(2), 133–147.

Kuttner, L. (1996). *A child in pain: How to help, what to do.* Berkeley, CA: Hartley and Marks.

Kwekkeboom, K. L. (1999). A model for cognitive-behavioral interventions in cancer pain management. *Image: Journal of Nursing Scholarship, 31*(2), 151.

Levin, D. N., Cleeland, C. S., & Dar, R. (1985). Public attitudes toward cancer pain, *Cancer, 56*(9), 2337–2339.

Lewis, T. (2002). Pain management for the elderly. *William Mitchell Law Review, 29*(1), 223–244.

Liebeskind, J. C., (1991). Pain can kill. *Pain, 44*(1), 3–4.

Living with cancer but not the pain. (1998). *Harvard Health Letter, 23*(12), 6–7.

Lotan, M., Ljunggren, E. A., Johnsen, T. B., Defrin, R., Pick, C. G., & Strand, L. I. (2009). A modified version of the Non-Communicating Children Pain Checklist-Revised, adapted to adults with intellectual and developmental disabilities: Sensitivity to pain and internal consistency. *The Journal of Pain, 10*(4), 398–407.

Main, C. J., & Spanswick, C. C. (2000). Models of pain. In C. J. Main & C. C. Spanswick (Eds.), *Pain management: An interdisciplinary approach* (pp. 1–114). New York, NY: Churchill Livingstone.

Marks, R. M., & Sachar, E. J. (1973). Undertreatment of medical inpatients with narcotic analgesics. *Annals of Internal Medicine, 78*(2), 173–181.

Max, M. B. (1990). Improving outcome of analgesic treatment: Is education enough? *Annals of Internal Medicine, 113*(11), 885–889.

McCaffery, M. (1997). Pain management handbook: Practical tips for relieving your patient's pain. *Nursing, 27*(4), 42–46.

McCaffery, M. (2001). Overcoming barriers to pain management. *Nursing, 31*(4), 18.

McClaugherty, L. (2002). Chronic pain: We're undertreating the elderly. *Nursing Homes Long Term Care Management, 51*(8), 58–59.

McGrath, P. A. (1991). Intervention and Management. In J. P. Bush & S. W. Harkins (Eds.), *Children in pain: Clinical and research issues from a developmental perspective.* New York, NY: Springer-Verlag, pp. 83–116.

McQuay, H. (1999). Opioids in pain management. *Lancet, 353*(9171), 2229–2232.

Meisler, J. G. (2002). Toward optimal health: The experts discuss chronic pain. *Journal of Women's Health and Gender-Based Medicine, 11*(4), 341–345.

Meldrum, M. L., Tsao, J. C., & Zeltzer, L. K. (2008). "Just be in pain and just move on": Functioning limitations and strategies in the lives of children with chronic pain. *Journal of Pain Management,* *1*(2), 131–141.

Melzack, R., & Casey, K. L. (1968). Sensory, motivational, and central control determinants of pain: A new conceptual model. In D. Kenshalo (Ed.), *The skin senses* (pp. 423–443). Springfield, IL: Charles C. Thomas Publishers.

Melzack, R. & Wall, P. D. (1965). Pain mechanisms: A new theory. *Science, 150,* 971–979.

Meyers, J. C. (1997). The pharmacist's role in palliative care and chronic pain management. *Drug Topics, 141*(1), 98–106.

Miller, K. E. (2000). Physician attitudes a barrier to pain management. *American Family Physician, 62*(10), 2317.

Miller, K. E., Miller, M., & Jolley, M. R. (2001). Challenges in pain management at the end of life. *American Family Physician, 64*(7), 1227.

Miller, S. C., Mor, V., Wu, N., Gozalo, P., & Lapane, K. (2002). Does receipt of hospice care in nursing homes improve the management of pain at the end of life? *Journal of the American Geriatrics Society, 50*(3), 507–515.

Mobily, K. E., & MacNeil, R. D. (2002). *Therapeutic recreation and the nature of disabilities.* State College, PA: Venture Publishing, Inc.

Mobily, K. E., & Verburg, M. D. (2001). Aquatic therapy in community-based therapeutic recreation: pain management in a case of fibromyalgia. *Therapeutic Recreation Journal, 35*(1), 57–69.

Mobily, P. R., Herr, K. A., Clark, M. K., & Wallace, R. B. (1994). An epidemiologic analysis of pain in the elderly: The Iowa 65+ health study. *Journal of Aging and Health, 6,* 139–154.

Montauk, S. L., & Martin, J. (1997). Treating chronic pain. *American Family Physician, 55*(4), 1151–1163.

Mowery, B. D., Suddaby, E., Kang, K. A., & Cooper, L. (2008). The art of procedural sedation and analgesia. *Pediatric Nursing, 34*(6), 490–492.

Mularski, R. A., White-Chu, F., Overbay, D., Miller, L., Asch, S. M., & Ganzini, L. (2006). Measuring pain as the 5th vital sign does not improve quality of pain management. *Journal of General Internal Medicine, 21*(6), 607–612.

Murphy, G. (2009). Distraction techniques for venepuncture: A review. *Paediatric Nursing, 21*(3), 18–20.

Narasimhaswamy, S., Vedi, C., Xavier, Y., Tseng, C., & Shine, D. (2006). Effect of implementing pain management standards. *Journal of General Internal Medicine, 21*(7), 689–693.

National Institute of Neurological Disorders and Stroke (NINDS) (2001). *Chronic pain: Hope through research.* Retrieved April 16, 2006, from: http://www.ninds.nih.gov/health_and_medical/pubs/chronic_pain_htr.htm

National Institutes of Health (NIH). (1995, 1998). Biobehavioral pain research program announcement. *NIH Guide, 24*(5).

National Institutes of Health (NIH). (2007). Pain Management Fact Sheet. Retrieved June 16, 2009, from: http://www.ninr.nih.gov/NR/rdonlyres/DC0351A6-7029-4FE0-BEEA-7EFC3D1B23AE/0/Pain.pdf

Nicholson, B. D. (2003). Diagnosis and management of neuropathic pain: A balanced approach to treatment. *Journal of the American Academy of Nurse Practitioners, 15*(12), 3–9.

Nilsson, S., Finnstrom, B., Kokinsky, E., & Enskar, K. (2009). The use of virtual reality for needle-related procedural pain and distress in children and adolescents in a paediatric oncology unit. *European Journal of Oncology Nursing, 13*(2), 102–109.

Nurmikko, T. J., Nash, T. P., & Wiles, J. R. (1998). Control of chronic pain. *British Medical Journal, 317,* 1438–1441.

Obrecht, J., & Andreoni, V. M. (2007). Pain Management. In N. L. Potts & B. L. Mandleco *Pediatric nursing: Caring for children and their families* (2nd ed., pp. 521–545). Clifton Park, NY: Thomson Delmar Learning.

Okifuji, A., & Turk, D. C. (1999). Fibromyalgia: Search for mechanisms and effective treatments. In R. J. Gatchel & D. C. Turk (Eds.), *Psychosocial factors in pain: Critical perspective* (pp. 227–246). New York, NY: Guilford Press.

O'Neill, B., & Fallon, M. (1997). ABC of palliative care. Principles of palliative care and pain control. *British Medical Journal, 315*(7111), 801–806.

Patterson, D. R., Hoffman, H. G., Palacios, A. G., & Jensen, M. J. (2006). Analgesic effects of posthypnotic suggestions and virtual reality distraction on thermal pain. *Journal of Abnormal Psychology, 115*(4), 834–841.

Pearl, T. S. (2001). Nonpharmacological pain management is also an effective tool. *Pediatric Nursing, 27*(3), 307.

Phillips, D. M. (2000). JCAHO pain management standards are unveiled. *Journal of the American Medical Association, 284*(4), 428.

Piira, T., Hayes, B., & Goodenough, B. (2002). Distraction methods in the management of children's pain: An approach based on evidence or intuition? *The Suffering Child, 1*(10), 15–20.

Pitkala, K. H., Strandberg, T. E., Tilvis, R. S. (2002). Management of nonmalignant pain in home-dwelling older people: A population-based survey. *Journal of the American Geriatrics Society, 50*(11), 1861–1865.

Richardson, C., Adams, N., & Poole, H. (2006). Psychological approaches for the nursing management of chronic pain: Part 2. *Journal of Clinical Nursing, 15*(9), 1196–1202.

Richeson, N. E. (2004). Recreation therapy as a non-drug approach to pain management in older adults with dementia. *American Journal of Recreation Therapy,* 31–36.

Rimer, B., Levy, M. H., Keintz, M. K., Fox, L., Engsrom, P. F., & MacElwee, N. (1987). Enhancing cancer pain control regimens through patient education. *Patient Education & Counseling, 10*(3), 267–277.

Roberge, C. W., & McEwen, M. (1998). The effects of local anesthetics on postoperative pain. *AORN Journal, 68*(6), 1003–1012.

Ross, M. M., Carswell, A., Hing, M., Hollingworth, G., & Dalziel, W. B. (2001). Seniors' decision making about pain management. *Journal of Advanced Nursing, 35*(3), 442–451.

Ruoff, G. E. (1999). Strategies to control musculoskeletal pain: A guide to drug therapy. *Consultant, 39*(10), 2773–2778.

Sanders, S. H., Harden, R. N., & Vicente, P. J. (2005). Evidence-based clinical practice guidelines for interdisciplinary rehabilitation of chronic nonmalignant pain syndrome patients. *Pain Practice, 5*(4), 303–315.

Saunders, C. S. (1998). New directions in chronic fatigue syndrome, *Patient Care, 32*(14), 101–110.

Schechter, N. L., Blankson, V., Pachter, L. M., Sullivan, C. M., & Costa, L. (1997). The ouchless place: No pain, children's gain. *Pediatrics, 99*(6), 890–894.

Schneider, J. P. (2005). Chronic pain management in older adults: With coxibs under fire, what now? *Geriatrics, 60*(5), 26–31.

Schofield, P. A. (2005). A pilot study comparing environments in which relaxation is taught: Investigating the potential of Snoezelen for chronic pain management. *American Journal of Recreation Therapy, 3,* 17–27.

Schofield, P., & Dunham, M. (2005, December). Clinical: Factors to consider in pain management for older people. *GP: General Practitioner,* 19–24.

Scudds, R. J., & Robertson, J. M. (1998). Empirical evidence of the association between the presence of musculoskeletal pain and physical disability in community-dwelling senior citizens. *Pain, 75*(2–3), 229–235.

Sheridan, E.A. (2007). Care of children who are hospitalized. In N. L. Potts & B. L. Mandleco *Pediatric nursing: Caring for children and their families* (2nd ed., pp. 451–495). Canada: Thomson Delmar Learning.

Sloane, P. D., Zimmerman, S., Brown, L. C., Ives, T. J., & Walsh, J. F. (2002). Inappropriate medication prescribing in residential care/assisted living facilities. *Journal of the American Geriatrics Society, 50*(6), 1001–1011.

Smith, B. H. & Elliott, A. M. (2005). Active self-management of chronic pain in the community. *Pain, 113*(3), 249–250.

Snow, L., Rapp, M. P., & Kunik, M. (2005). Pain management in persons with dementia: BODIES mnemonic helps caregivers relay pain-related signs, symptoms to physicians and nursing staff. *Geriatrics, 60*(5), 22–25.

Springhouse Corporation (1997). *Expert pain management.* Springhouse, PA: Author.

Stanley, M. A., Diefenbach, G. J., & Hopko, D. R. (2004). Cognitive behavioral treatment for older adults with a generalized anxiety disorder: A therapist manual for primary care settings. *Behavior Modification, 28*(1), 73–117.

Stegman, M. B. (2001). Control of pain: Every person's right. *Orthopaedic Nursing, 20*(2), 31–36.

Stumbo, N. J. (2002). Implications of pain management for therapeutic recreation services. *Annual in Therapeutic Recreation, 11,* 11–32.

Stumbo, N. J. (2006a). An evidence-based approach to providing physical activity and cognitive behavioral therapy to older adults with pain. *American Journal of Recreation Therapy, 5*(3), 13–25.

Stumbo, N. J. (2006b). Unique issues in pain management for older individuals. *American Journal of Recreation Therapy, 5*(2), 37–47.

Tak, E., Staats, P., Van Hespen, A., & Hopman-Rock, M. (2005). The effects of an exercise program for older adults with osteoarthritis of the hip. *Journal of Rheumatology, 32*(6), 1106–1113.

Talbot, L. A., Gaines, J. M., Huynh, T. N., & Metter, E. J. (2003). A home-based pedometer-driven walking program to increase physical activity in older adults with osteoarthritis of the knee: A preliminary study. *Journal of the American Geriatrics Society, 51*(3), 387–392.

Tan, G., Alvarez, J. A., & Jensen, M. P. (2006). Complementary and alternative medicine approaches to pain management. *Journal of Clinical Psychology, 62*(11), 1419–1431.

Turk, D. C. (1997). Psychological aspects of pain. In Springhouse Corporation (Ed.), *Expert pain management* (pp. 124–178). Springhouse, PA: Author.

Turk, D .C, & Meichenbaum, D. (1994). Cognitive-behavioral approach to the management of chronic pain. In P. D. Wall & R. Melzack (Eds.), *Textbook of pain* (3rd ed.). New York, NY: Churchill Livingstone.

Turk, D. C., Meichenbaum, D., & Genest, M. (1983). *Pain and behavioral medicine: A cognitive-behavioral perspective*. New York, NY: Guilford Press.

Turk, D. C., Okifuji, A., Starz, T. W., & Sinclair, J. D. (1996). Effects of type of symptom onset on psychological distress and disability in fibromyalgia syndrome patients. *Pain, 68*, 423–430.

Turk, D. C., Okifuji, A., Sinclair, J. D., & Starz, T. W. (1998). Differential responses by psychosocial sub-groups of fibromyalgia syndrome patients to an interdisciplinary treatment. *Arthritis Care and Research, 11*, 397–404.

Turk, D. C., & Rudy, T. (1992). Classification, logic, and strategies in chronic pain. In D. C. Turk and R. Melzack (Eds.), *Handbook of pain assessment* (pp. 409–428). New York, NY: Guilford Press.

U.S. Census Bureau (2000). Census 2000 summary file 1. Retrieved April 16, 2006, from: http://factfinder.census.gov

U.S. Department of Health and Human Services and U.S. Department of Commerce (2001). *An Aging World: 2001: International Population Reports*. Washington, DC: Authors.

van Tulder, M. W., Ostelo, R., Vlaeyen, J. W. S., Linton, S. J., Morley, S. J., & Assendelft, W. J. (2001). Behavioral treatment for chronic low back pain: A systematic review within the framework of the Cochrane back review group. *Spine, 26*(3), 270–281.

von Baeyer, C. L., Marche, T. A., Rocha, E. M., & Salmon, K. (2004). Children's memory for pain: Overview and implications for practice. *The Journal of Pain, 5*(5), 241–249.

Von Roenn, J. H., Cleeland, C. S., Gonin, R., Hatfield, A. K., & Pandya, K. J. (1993). Physician attitudes and practice in cancer pain management: A survey from the Eastern Cooperative Oncology Group. *Annals of Internal Medicine, 119*(2), 121–126.

Walker, P. C., & Wagner, D. S. (2003). Treatment of pain in pediatric patients. *Journal of Pharmacy Practice, 16*(4), 261–275.

Walters, A. S. & Williamson, G. M. (1999). The role of activity restriction in the association between pain and depression: A study of pediatric patients with chronic pain. *Children's Health Care, 28*(1), 33–50.

Ward, S. E., Goldberg, N., Miller-McCauley, V., Mueller, C., Nolan, A., Pawlik-Plank, D., et al. (1993). Patient-related barriers to management of cancer pain. *Pain, 52*(3), 319–324.

Weissman, D. E., Joranson, D. E., & Hopwood, M. B. (1991). Wisconsin physicians' knowledge and attitudes about opioid analgesic regulations. *Wisconsin Medical Journal, 90*(12), 671–675.

Wise, P. H. (2007). The future pediatrician: The challenge of chronic illness. *The Journal of Pediatrics, 151*(5), Suppl, S6–S10.

Williams, K. A., Petronis, J., Smith, D., Goodrich, D., Wu, J., Ravi, N., Doyle, E. J., Jr., Jucjett, R. G., Kolar, M. M., Gross, R., & Steinberg, L. (2008). Effect of Iyengar yoga therapy for chronic low back pain. *Pain, 115*(1), 107–117.

Wittink, H. M., Rogers, W. H., Lipman, A. G., McCarberg, B. H., Ashburn, M. A., Oderda, G. M., et al. (2006). Older and younger adults in pain management programs in the United States: Differences and similarities. *Pain Medicine, 7*(2), 151–163.

World Health Organization (1996). *Cancer pain relief: With a guide to opioid availability* (2nd ed.). Geneva: Author.

World Health Organization (n.d.). *WHO's pain ladder*. Retrieved April 16, 2006, from: http://www.who.int/cancer/palliative/painladder/en/

Wong, D. L. (1999). *Whaley and Wong's nursing care of infants and children* (6th ed.). St. Louis, MO: Mosby.

Yates, P., Dewar, A., & Fentiman, B. (1995). Pain: The views of elderly people living in long-term residential care settings. *Journal of Advanced Nursing, 21*, 667–674.

Zalon, M. L. (1997). Pain in frail, elderly women after surgery. *Journal of Nursing Scholarship, 29*(1), 21–27.

Zeltzer, L.K., Bush, J.P., Chen, E., & Riveral, A. (1997). A psychobiologic approach to pediatric pain: Part 1. History, physiology, and assessment strategies. *Current Problems in Pediatrics, 27 (6)*, 225–253.

» CHAPTER 15 »

Cognitive-Behavioral Approaches to Therapeutic Recreation

Terry Long, Ph.D.

Therapeutic recreation (TR) professionals must be familiar with the nature of the various theoretical frameworks for providing therapeutic recreation services. Utilizing theory to guide practice is a critical aspect of ensuring predictable outcomes when implementing any therapeutic intervention. Good theories allow us to predict what the consequences of a therapeutic recreation program will be, assuming the program is built on the associated principles.

One theoretical approach that can be applied to the therapeutic recreation environment is cognitive-behavioral theory (CBT). As the name suggests, this approach is based on the integration of earlier behavioral and cognitive explanations of human behavior and mental illness (Ledley, Marx, & Heimberg, 2005). The purpose of this chapter is to describe key theoretical concepts and therapeutic mechanisms associated with CBT, as well as potential applications of this information to therapeutic recreation practice.

Basic Premises

Cognitive-behavioral theory is based on the idea that a person's thoughts, or cognitions, dictate how he or she reacts emotionally and behaviorally to any particular situation (Alford & Beck, 1997; Beck, 1995; Corey, 2008; Leahy, 1996). Feelings are a direct result of the thoughts a person has about a situation. For example, a wife who believes that her husband's late arrival is due to an automobile accident is likely to experience worry, anxiety, and fear. If she believes the husband is late because he is drinking with his buddies, she might feel abandoned or angry. If she simply attributes his tardiness to the likelihood of heavy traffic on the highway, she may have no emotional reaction at all. These three scenarios illustrate how the same situation can evoke different emotional responses based on the thoughts that a person has about the given situation.

Theorists who support this viewpoint not only would argue that emotions such as fear and anxiety are a result of how a person interprets a situation, but

also that the strength of the belief impacts the strength of the emotion (Alford & Beck, 1997; Ledley et al., 2005). Furthermore, when people have irrational or inaccurate cognitive interpretations of a situation, it can lead to extreme emotional response or mental illness.

Based on the premise that thoughts dictate emotions, cognitive-behavioral interventions are designed to help clients recognize how thinking impacts emotions and to teach them techniques for monitoring and re-evaluating their thinking (Leichsenring, Hiller, Weissberg, & Leibing, 2006). This identification and reframing of maladaptive thought is the primary tool for therapeutic intervention (Ledley et al., 2005). Cognition is the focus of intervention, but various other humanistic and behavioristic mechanisms and approaches are commonly utilized to reinforce understanding and change (Alford & Beck; 1997; Cave, 1999; Corey, 2008; Leahy, 1996).

Intended Client Groups

Cognitive-behavioral theory offers a broad array of techniques that have been applied to many different client groups across various clinical settings. Such techniques can also be a core part of maintaining health and wellness outside of the clinical care environment. Reviewing the evidence of effectiveness for the different cognitive behavioral theories and associated interventions goes beyond the focus of this chapter. Instead, this section talks about the applicability of cognitive behavioral interventions in the context of generally accepted applications and intellectual capacity of the client.

Early on, Aaron Beck's Cognitive Therapy and Albert Ellis' Rational Emotive Therapy (RET) were established as successful in treating conditions of depression and anxiety (Corey, 2008). As these techniques have become more popular and more advanced, they have been applied to a variety of conditions, such as phobias, eating disorders, personality disorders, adjustment disorders, hostility and anger, as well as pain management, social skills training, and various other forms of self-management (Corey, 2008; Leahy, 1996, 2003). Corey has pointed out that, when describing the applicability of RET, Albert Ellis tends to focus not so much on the condition or symptom, but on the capacity of the client to participate successfully in logic-driven therapies. While this "one cure fits all who are intellectually capable" approach might be a bit ambitious, a valid point is made here in that a critical prerequisite for successful implementation of such interventions is the capability of the client to intellectually perform the primarily cognitive tasks associated with therapy (i.e., thinking and self monitoring). Clients who are detached from reality, who struggle with logic, who are philosophically opposed to logic, or who refuse to make basic changes will not react well to cognitive-behavioral interventions

This general principle is supported by recent studies verifying the effectiveness of CBT as a useful intervention for individuals with unipolar depression (Butler, Chapman, Forman, & Beck, 2006; Chu & Harrison, 2007; Rupke, Blecke, & Renfrow, 2006), anxiety-related disorders (Butler et al.; Chu & Harrison, 2007), anger (Butler et al.; Sukhodolsky, Kassinove, & Gorman, 2004), and pain management (Eccleston, Morely, Williams, Yorke, & Mastroyannopoulou, 2002). Other studies have demonstrated that CBT interventions are ineffective for certain conditions such as schizophrenia and bipolar disorder (e.g., Lynch, Laws, & Mckenna, 2010). The latter findings reiterate the fact

that CBT does not provide a blanket cure that covers all conditions, but can serve as an effective intervention for those whose condition is significantly influenced by learned cognitive tendencies.

Relatively speaking, there have been very few studies that directly examine CBT-based interventions in therapeutic recreation practice. In addition, these studies have used a variety of different theories or approaches; therefore, it is difficult to draw specific conclusions about the effectiveness of CBT in therapeutic recreation practice. Still, there is research that demonstrates specific mechanisms and techniques can lead to therapeutic change across a variety of settings. As such, the potential for effective application in therapeutic recreation practice exists. Examples of research supporting the use CBT-based interventions within the therapeutic recreation realm can be seen in Table 15.1. In addition, there are countless studies that allude to the use of CBT-based principles, but do not directly identify the interventions as such. This fact reiterates the importance of considering theory when developing interventions, and identifying the theoretical foundation of an intervention when disseminating related research findings.

Background

The latter half of the 20th century brought with it the birth and evolution of what is generally referred to as cognitive-behavioral theory. Psychoanalytic and behavioral theories had dominated all areas of psychology

Table 15.1. Examples of Therapeutic Recreation Investigations Supporting the Use of Cognitive-Behavioral Therapy

Author(s)	Technique	Application/Population
Bonadies, 2009	Guided imagery	Chronic back pain
Richeson, Croteau, Jones, and Farmer, 2006	Self-monitoring	Physical performance, mobility-related self-efficacy/seniors
Wise, Ellis, & Trunnell, 2002	Provision of efficacy-related information during weight training	Generalization of self-efficacy to ADLs/spinal cord injury
Long, 2001	Constructivist-based leisure education program	Leisure knowledge, meaning, and behavioral intentions/youth w/emotional, behavioral difficulty
Mahon, 1994	Decision-making and self-control instruction and strategies via leisure education	Decision making in leisure/mild to moderate intellectual disability
Ellis Maughan-Pritchett, & Ruddell, 1993	Attribution-based verbal persuasion	Self-efficacy judgments and video game performance/adolescents with depression
Maughan & Ellis, 1991	Provision of efficacy-related information	Perceptions of freedom and control/adolescents with depression

up until the 1950s, but the acceptance of social and cognitive influences on learning, motivation, and behavior grew as the limitations of these earlier frameworks became apparent (Blackburn & Davidson, 1995; Cave, 1999). Because the emergence of cognitive-behavioral theory was occurring on many fronts and in many different forms, it is impossible to pinpoint a "beginning" of CBT. Instead, several different, and often simultaneously occurring, developments need to be considered. Much of the early development of CBT was done in the realm of psychotherapy. Albert Ellis (1962) and Aaron Beck (1967, 1976) laid the foundation for what are now two well-established schools of thought regarding cognitive-behavioral counseling principles and techniques. As these approaches developed, a broad array of techniques for therapeutic intervention also developed. Many of these techniques are applicable to and can be implemented within therapeutic recreation practice. Before discussing these applications, it is helpful to review the basic premises of these two counseling approaches.

Rational Emotive Therapy

Albert Ellis' rational emotive therapy (RET) is based on the assumption that people are very capable of rational thinking, but they also have a tendency to use unrealistic or illogical thinking when dealing with life demands (Corey, 2008; Ellis, 1994; Ellis & Bernard, 1986). Emotional disturbance comes from irrational thinking that is characterized by "should," "ought to," and "must" cognitions that leave no room for compromise. Beliefs such as "I must succeed," "I should have been a better wife," or "I ought to be able to do better" lead to severe emotional reactions when there is a failure to achieve such extreme and persistent standards. The goal of RET is to identify the basic rules and assumptions that clients hold and regularly use in their cognitive interpretations of the world (Corey, 2008). These thinking tendencies, or habits, and the resulting conclusions drawn from them are evaluated and challenged through a dialogue with the therapist (Blackburn & Davidson, 1995). Through this process, the client becomes aware of how absolutes negatively impact the interpretation of life events, and the resulting emotional reaction.

At the core of RET is the A-B-C theory of personality (Ellis & Bernard, 1986). The letter "A" represents an activating event, which can come in the form of a behavior, a fact, or an attitude of the individual (e.g., forgetting to take out the trash). The activating event triggers a belief ("B"), such as "I *have to* get that trash out today." The belief creates an emotional or behavioral

consequence ("C"), such as rage, panic, and leaving work without permission to go home and take out the trash (all of which would be unreasonable reactions unless your trash contains something extremely disgusting or extremely illegal).

The primary mechanism for change that is used in RET is the introduction of a disputing intervention ("D"). The purpose of this intervention is to challenge irrational beliefs that are causing emotional distress and to encourage alternative perspectives such as "I *would like* to get the trash out, but I don't have to...the world won't end, my house might just stink a little."

The disputing intervention is meant to induce "E" and "F". The "E" refers to the establishment of an effective philosophy, resulting in "F", or a new set of feelings (Corey, 2008). This process consists of engaging clients in a manner that counters their irrational beliefs and self-defeating behaviors.

Figure 15.1 (p. 292) illustrates another example of the A-B-Cs of RET. In this figure, the primary activating event is "job loss." The top portion of the figure represents a typical maladaptive response that might occur, leading to feelings of depression and hopelessness. The lower portion depicts the introduction of a disputing intervention, and the resulting change in beliefs. This change in cognitive interpretation results in additional changes in associated beliefs and behaviors.

Corey (2008) suggested that the rational emotive therapist's role consists of four steps:

1. Teaching clients to identify irrational beliefs and separate them from rational ones.
2. Working to recognize how persistent irrationalities feed emotional disturbance.
3. Working toward modification of thinking and abandonment of irrational ideas.
4. Challenging clients to develop a rational philosophy to enable permanent change.

It should also be pointed out that the RET process uses a combination of cognitive, emotive, and behavioral techniques to assist the client in making a cognitive paradigm shift. Corey provided a more detailed discussion of such techniques, a few of which are described in Table 15.2 (p. 292). Note that, while the focus and depth may be different, these techniques are commonly seen in therapeutic recreation modalities. What is useful about CBT is that it provides a framework for implementing commonly used therapeutic recreation modalities, such as mental rehearsal and role-play experiences (metaphorical or actual). Also note that the previous sentence referred to using CBT (theory) and not RET (psychotherapy), which is a

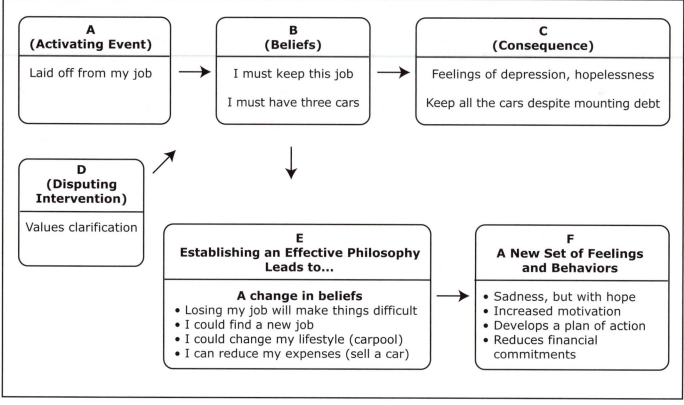

Figure 15.1. The ABCs of Rational Emotive Therapy

Table 15.2. Techniques Utilized in Rational Emotive Therapy for Challenging Irrational Thoughts and Beliefs

Technique	Role-Playing	Changing Language	Shame Attacking	Imagery
Description	Acting out or talking through behaviors that typically lead to negative emotional reactions	Therapist monitors language patterns, because language and thinking shape one another. Imprecise language	Exercises and home works are conducted to get over feeling ashamed for behaving in a certain way	Clients imagine themselves thinking, feeling, or behaving as they would like to
Goal	To trigger emotions and identify irrational thoughts that drive them	Help clients develop language patterns that discourage distorted thinking	To realize feelings of shame are self-created, unjustified, and inhibiting	Establish new emotional patterns through mental rehearsal
Example	Role-play a conversation with parents about career choice Monitor client thoughts and emotions during the role play Challenge the belief that the client must choose a career that pleases others	In conversations with the client, point out absolute statements like: • I *have to* get a job in my hometown • I *can't* change majors, my dad will kill me • I'll *never* get a job Encourage alternative language like: • I would *like to* get a job near home • Getting a job *will be* tough in this economy	Client is given tasks of: • Refusing to tip a rude waitress • Wearing a wig to work • Singing in public place • Wearing a shirt that says "I'm a recreation major"	Client vividly imagines: • Going to an exam and taking the exam with no anxiety • Last semester's grade card, the resulting emotional reactions, and how to change emotions about these grades

counseling approach that goes well beyond the typical education and credentials of therapeutic recreation professionals. This issue of staying within one's area of practice, and not overstepping professional qualifications, will be further addressed in later sections. Still, the applicability of this approach within therapeutic recreation practice clearly exists. For example, consider that initiative-based interventions that are frequently used in therapeutic recreation serve the purpose of challenging current interpretations or viewpoints of clients so that they can explore alternatives.

Beck's "Cognitive Therapy"

Often referred to as cognitive therapy, Aaron Beck's approach has many similarities with Ellis' RET. Despite the name, this approach is a cognitive-behavioral approach, utilizing behavioral techniques throughout the therapy process. Both approaches emphasize that thoughts dictate emotions and both work on helping the client examine those cognitive interpretations of the world that lead to emotional difficulties.

Alford and Beck (1997) divided the theoretical principles associated with cognitive therapy into 10 axioms. These axioms lay the foundation for Beck's cognitive therapy and also illustrate some of the core differences between the two approaches. Axiom 1 posits that meaning-making structures of cognition, known as schemas, are the "central pathway to psychological functioning or adaptation" (Alford & Beck, 1997, p. 15). Leahy (1996) described schemas as the "concepts the patient habitually uses in viewing reality" (p. 25). Negative schemas relating to rejection, abandonment, and unrelenting standards influence focus and retrieval of information (Leahy, 1996). A person who has a negative schema of rejection will constantly seek evidence that they are being rejected, and ignore evidence that opposes this assumption. Schemas are operationalized, or defined, based on the specific bias that they create (e.g., rejection), and are often formed at an early age. When addressing this bias, however, one does so in the present, with a retrospective view (Leahy, 1996).

Axiom 2 states that the resulting meanings associated with schemas control psychological systems and, therefore, activate strategies for coping (adaptation). The way we interpret the world will influence how we cope with it. Emotions are part of this adaptation system. As a result, our schemas determine our emotional and behavioral reactions. A biased perspective that encourages a person to inaccurately and consistently interpret interactions with others as indications of rejection will lead that person to react in a maladaptive way. In general, both axiom 1 and 2 are consistent

with the RET model, placing the focus of intervention on cognitive interpretations and understandings of the world. Beck's conceptualization of schemas and how they operate is much more elaborate than the RET approach, as can be seen in axioms 3–10.

Axiom 3 acknowledges the importance of cognitive systems interacting with other systems, and being fully aware of how emotions impact these often unconscious systems is an important part of the cognitive behavioral stratey. Beck's approach differs somewhat from Ellis in this area, as RET tends to be more rigid and less open to acknowledging these unconscious or emotional influences on the client.

"Schema" and "core belief" are terms that are used interchangeably by some scholars; however, Beck (1964) differentiates a core belief from a schema, with the former being a specific belief and the latter being a mental representation that might include several core beliefs (e.g., "I am certain to be abandoned" is a core belief under the schema "rejection"). Judith Beck (1995), Aaron Beck's daughter, pointed out that core beliefs can be about others as well, and lists examples such as "other people are untrustworthy" and "the world is a rotten place" (p. 166).

Furthermore, axiom 4 states that meanings derived from schemas are "translated into specific patterns of emotion, attention, memory, and behavior" (Alford & Beck, 1997, p. 16). This process is called cognitive content specificity and essentially means that the way people interpret the world leads them to engage in certain patterns of functioning as human beings.

Axiom 5 points out that core beliefs, and the resulting schemas, are "correct or incorrect" depending on the goal they are meant to achieve within the context of a particular situation. Cognitive distortions or bias in the meanings we derive from situations leads to maladaptive activation of systems (i.e., physical, emotional, and cognitive systems). For example, a person who misinterprets the meaning of casual small talk at a birthday party ("Susie, you are as quiet as a mouse, loosen up a bit!") as a personal attack related her own self-perceived inadequacies ("These people think I'm weird; I feel so stupid; I want to leave; I'm shaking") is likely to inappropriately activate certain physical or emotional responses that are unwarranted (isolating, leaving the party, embarrassment, anxiety, crying). All of these unpleasant reactions are a result of a schema, or cognitive understanding, that provides an incorrect interpretation of meaning. This person's emotions and behaviors are driven by schemas that do not reflect reality.

Likewise, axiom 6 states that people are predisposed to certain patterns of maladaptive, or inaccurate, cognition. Certain types of "cognitive vulnerabilities" put a person at risk of developing certain mental illnesses. As such, the cognitive distortions typically associated with depression will follow a unique pattern that is distinguishable from patterns associated with other conditions (e.g., anxiety). This concept differs from Ellis' RET model, which essentially used a more general explanation of thinking errors to explain all syndromes.

Axiom 7 asserts, "psychopathology results from maladaptive meanings that have been constructed regarding the *self*, the environmental *context* (experience), and the *future* (goals)" (Alford & Beck, 1997, p. 16). These three elements make up the "cognitive triad." The patterns mentioned under axiom 6 are directly relevant to these aspects of the triad. Consider the above example of the anxious girl at a party (see axiom 5 discussion). According to Alford and Beck, anxiety disorders are characterized by the following pattern: the self is inadequate, the context is dangerous, and the future is uncertain (see Figure 15.2). Intervention for this client would, therefore, focus on cognitive distortions pertaining to her self-perceived social inadequacy, her misinterpretation of others as a threat, and her tendency to imagine the worst in regard to outcome.

Axiom 8 points out that there are two levels of meaning to consider in regard to events or circumstances in one's life. The first is public meaning, which has very little influence or impact on an individual. The second, which is strongly demonstrated in the birthday party example depicted in Figure 15.2, is personal or private meaning. This aspect of meaning includes all of the cognitive interpretations a person draws pertaining to implications, significance, and generalizations (Alford & Beck, 1997; Beck, 1976).

Axiom 9 establishes that there are three levels of cognition, each representing a different level of awareness for the person. The preconscious level is characterized by automatic thoughts. These automatic thoughts manifest as a result of deeper intermediate beliefs, and even deeper core beliefs (see Figure 15.3).

Psycho-pathology	Cognitive Triad		
	Self	Environmental Context	Future
Depression	Inadequate	Inadequate	Inadequate
Anxiety	Inadequate	Threatening	Uncertain
Paranoia	Mistreated	Unfair	Threatened by Others

Figure 15.2. Common Patterns of Maladaptive Meaning (created from Alford & Beck, 1997)

These three elements are represented in the lower portion of Figure 15.3, which is a further illustration of the birthday-party example mentioned earlier. Deeply rooted schemas impact how Susie interprets the world, resulting in negative reactions to the situation across emotional, behavioral, and physical domains. Therapy often starts by focusing on preconscious attitudes, beliefs, and tendencies, as they are most accessible to the client and the therapist. Note that this is also represented in Figure 15.3.

The second level, referred to as the conscious level, is characterized by the ability to report and discuss cognitive content. The third level, or metacognitive level, involves actively selecting, evaluating, and monitoring the development of schemas. These levels of thought are also represented in Figure 15.3, and reflect processes that can be facilitated through therapeutic intervention.

Finally, axiom 10 states that schemas serve the purpose of facilitating adaptation to the environment. Emotions, or psychological states, can only be judged as adaptive or maladaptive within the environmental context in which they occur. Anger, for example, may be considered adaptive in one situation but maladaptive in another. Intervention should be centered on schemas as the mechanism for activating emotion and behavior. Likewise, the context of emotions and behaviors must also be considered as these interventions are put into place.

Table 15.3 (p. 296) describes a number of additional techniques that are often associated with cognitive behavioral therapy.

Other Cognitive Theories

In addition to the cognitive behavioral theories that have developed from the work of Beck and Ellis, there are several other cognitively oriented frameworks that have direct relevance to therapeutic recreation practice. All of these theories, at least to some extent, are rooted in the principles of cognitive behavioral theory. Many of the modalities used by TR practitioners are grounded in these theories. Unfortunately, this connection is often overlooked, which can lead to ineffective application of the modality. Several of these theories will be briefly mentioned here, particularly because they have had a significant influence on the development of therapeutic recreation modalities, and because they still have great potential for additional influence.

Constructivism

Constructivism is a theory that explains how people learn and is based on the later works of Jean Piaget

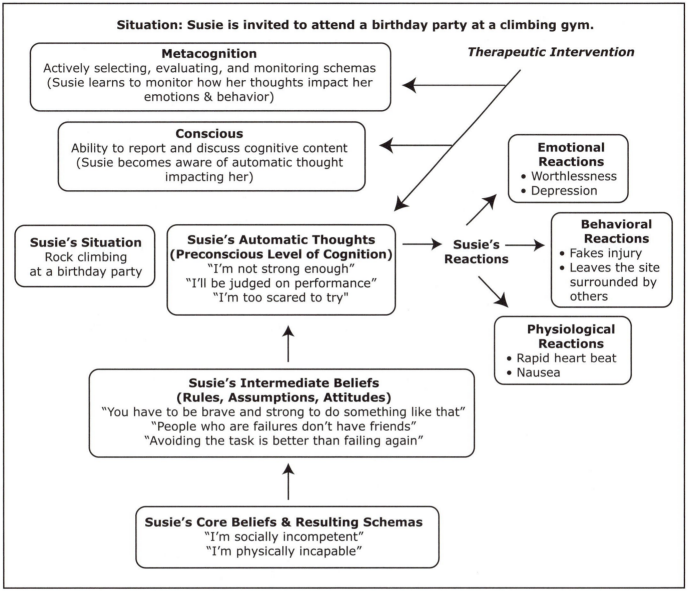

Figure 15.3. A Case Example of Beck's Three Levels of Cognition (adapted from Beck, 1995)

(1970, 1977). Piaget's work grew out of his frustration with the defining of "knowledge" as a reflection of the real world, independent of the knower (von Glasersfeld, 1996). Under this traditional definition, knowledge can be measured based on the extent to which one has accumulated, or memorized, facts or concepts. The more you can memorize and regurgitate, the more you know.

In contrast, Piaget proposed that knowledge consists of a person's individualized cognitive understanding of the world and is only significant within the context of the mind (von Glasersfeld, 1995, 1996). The existence of a "true reality" of the world seems both logical and likely; however, facts and natural laws are related to knowledge only in that a person develops his or her own interpretation of how such phenomena operate. This interpretation, or perception, directly affects an individual's ability to function in daily life (e.g., is your interpretation of how to fix a leaky toilet or how to iron a shirt effective or ineffective?). Thus, a person who is knowledgeable about a specific phenomenon has more than the ability to reproduce facts. This person has a useful understanding of how these facts operate and interact, and can apply this understanding in ways that allow for creative problem solving.

The basic learning process underlying constructivism can be explained through Piaget's concepts of accommodation and assimilation (Piaget, 1977; von Glasersfeld, 1995). Similar to Beck, Piaget asserts that a person's knowledge is made up of schemas, or mental representations of how the world functions. When a new concept is introduced, our current schemas are challenged and they must accommodate this new information.

Table 15.3. Additional CBT Techniques

Technique	Description	Examples for Practice
Thought Recording (Real Time)	Asking clients to record absolute/maladaptive thoughts, beliefs, and associated emotions as they occur, noting details such as when, where, why, intensity	As you observe clients acting on self defeating thoughts regarding an activity, ask them to acknowledge and record the thoughts and associated emotions
Thought Diaries (Homework)	Tracking thoughts as they occur provides specific opportunities to challenge irrational beliefs	Clients journal their thoughts and associated emotions prior to, during, or after a ropes course activity
Goal Setting	Goals specifically oriented around maladaptive thinking patterns (schemas) are established with client	Work with clients to develop a personal development plan, focusing on leisure related achievements
Activity Scheduling	Provides opportunity for schemas to be tested/practiced in a real world setting Provides opportunity to reward healthy thoughts and behaviors	Scheduling a trip to an amusement park where self-efficacy beliefs regarding social skills can be observed and challenged, new skills can be practiced
Examining Evidence	Looking for evidence to support client beliefs challenges irrational assumptions	Clients examine their ropes course experience for evidence to support/refute their thought diary
Pros and Cons Exercises	Exploring both sides of a possibility is used to challenge absolute thinking and create a balanced, realistic perspective	Exploring values and associated beliefs about behavioral choices with a substance abuser
Imagery/ Visualization	Client is taught to manipulate mental images in a way that impacts emotional or biological reactions to the associated thoughts	Using a mental image to stop stress provoking thoughts and/or control pain
Role Play	Thought patterns and associated behaviors are acted out in a way that explores alternative outcomes	Allowing an adolescent son to act as the decision maker on an adventure trip with parents
Rehearsal	Thought patterns and associated behaviors are practiced in a safe environment	Practicing various aspects a community outing before actually leaving the rehab facility
Use of Metaphors	Metaphors allow for clients to challenge their own understanding of a situation by considering it within an alternative world	Bibliotherapy, Cinematherapy can be used to reflect on specific issues that pertain to the client
Experiential Learning	Create opportunities for clients to learn and explore concepts in an unstructured, exploratory manner	Asking a group of first time campers to set up their tents for the first time with no/minimal instruction

The person copes with this new concept by trying to fit it into his or her current schema set. Often, new concepts challenge current knowledge, resulting in disequilibrium. To reestablish equilibrium, there is an attempt to understand how the new concepts interact with previous knowledge. This process is called assimilation and is achieved by mentally or physically experimenting with concepts until a new and more effective understanding of the world is established. By successfully assimilating a new concept into previous understanding, equilibrium is reestablished. Through this experimentation, learning occurs. In other words, we learn more effectively by doing, not by memorizing.

To add to this theory, Vygotsky (1962) has proposed that learning in groups is more effective than individual learning. This "social constructivism" is based on the premise that sharing ideas and possible explanations to a problem with one another enhances everyone's ability to explore concepts and come up with solutions.

The work of both Piaget and Vygotsky can be seen in the foundations of CBT. Intervention is built upon challenging the client's current cognitive understanding and interpretation of circumstances. When inconsistencies surface, they are pointed out and the client is encouraged to work through, or experiment with, the nature of these inconsistencies. Furthermore, it is the interpersonal (social) interactions between the therapist and client that induce disequilibrium and open the door to alternative understanding of life's circumstances.

Self-Efficacy Theory

Another theory that exemplifies the interaction between cognitive processes and social phenomena is self-efficacy theory. "Self-efficacy" refers to the extent to which one is confident that he or she can complete a given task so as to achieve a given outcome (Bandura, 1986). Self-efficacy theory is relevant to therapeutic recreation in a variety of contexts and has been repeatedly acknowledged as a theoretical framework upon which practice can be based (Ellis, Morris, & Trunnell, 1995; Long, Ellis, Trunnell, Tatsugawa, & Freeman, 2001; Wise, 2003, 2004). A further explanation of the elements of self-efficacy theory will illustrate its usefulness.

According to this theory, self-efficacy can be influenced by four factors: (a) performance accomplishments, (b) verbal persuasion, (c) vicarious experience (i.e., observation or visualization), and (d) emotional arousal (Bandura, 1986, 1997). To illustrate these four factors, imagine that you are in the car on your way to go hang-gliding with friends (no really, take a second and imagine this scenario). How confident are you that you will be able to successfully hang-glide and avoid falling like a rock off the side of a cliff? If you have been hang-gliding many times in the past without incident, your self-efficacy will be bolstered (i.e., performance accomplishments). It also might increase your self-efficacy if your friends are "psyching you up" on the way to the cliff (i.e., verbal persuasion and emotional arousal). Once you get there, it also might help if you observe an instructional video and imagine yourself successfully using the techniques observed in the video (vicarious experience). Of course, if you are scared of heights and standing on the edge of the cliff terrorizes you, your level of self-efficacy may plummet as you prepare to take off (emotional arousal).

Of course, high self-efficacy does not guarantee success. Low self-efficacy, however, can lead to avoidance behaviors and negative self-perceptions. Manipulation of these four factors can, therefore, be used as a therapeutic intervention, with the goal being to influence beliefs, or expectancies, of the client. These expectancies can exist in two forms. The first is outcomes expectancies, which refers to beliefs regarding whether or not an action will lead to a given outcome. The second is efficacy expectancies, or beliefs one holds about his or her ability to perform the task at hand.

Wise (2004) has provided additional insight into self-efficacy within the context of the Knowledge-and-Appraisal Personality Architecture (KAPA) matrix (for more on this theory of human behavior, see Cervone, 1997, 2004; Wise, 2004). Within the broader KAPA framework, schemas about the self and schemas about situations contribute to a person's knowledge structure. Self-efficacy is a result of comparisons made between beliefs, the self, and situation (Wise, 2004).

Self-efficacy related beliefs have significant implications for how therapeutic recreation clients perceive their own capabilities within the context of society. Furthermore, the theory provides a foundation for how to assist individuals who may be experiencing difficulty due to their perception of self-efficacy (Bandura, 1986). By enabling client successes, enhancing motivation through appropriate levels of arousal, providing verbal persuasion, and creating opportunities to observe or imagine successful completion of behaviors, the therapeutic recreation professional can facilitate growth and accomplishment among clients. Wise (2004) pointed out that, under the KAPA framework, changes in self-efficacy can result from adding new beliefs or altering or eliminating existing beliefs about the self and environment. Furthermore, self-efficacy can also be strengthened by helping clients understand the relationship between self-schemas and situational-schemas. In other words, clients recognize the skills they have as relevant to the situation they face. This aspect of KAPA highlights the cognitive mechanism for change. Inset 15.1 (p. 298) provides an explanation of this theory.

Attribution Theory

Attribution theory is a cognitive theory of motivation that focuses on a person's explanations for why events occur, and in particular, whether or not that person had a role in producing the event. These beliefs are significant because they will directly impact motivation for future behavior. For example, if a person believes that his or her past success as a gambler is due to personal talent, they are going to be more likely to keep gambling in the future. On the other hand, if they have consistently lost money, but attribute this loss to "just a string of bad luck," they may continue to gamble despite persistent losses. In the first scenario, the talent belief drives behavior, whereas the bad luck belief drives behavior in the second scenario.

There are three important factors that determine how a particular belief, or causal attribution, will influence future behavior (Weiner, 1985, 1992). The first factor to consider is if a given behavioral outcome is attributed to an internal or external factor. Talent and effort are internal factors, whereas luck or the influence

Inset 15.1. The Tommy Boy Effect

As a scholar and researcher, I am proud to say that I (Terry Long) named the "Tommy Boy Effect" myself. This phenomenon explains how self-efficacy can be strengthened when a person realizes the connection between existing personal schemas and existing situational schemas. What were previously viewed as two unrelated beliefs suddenly become relevant to one another, bolstering self-efficacy. Here's how it works.

•••••

In the movie Tommy Boy, Chris Farley plays an aspiring car parts salesman. In one particular scene, Tommy sits at a roadside diner with his sidekick Richard (David Spade) sulking over their failed efforts to sell brake pads and save the family business. Feeling a bit down on himself, Tommy decides to have some hot wings for lunch. When the waitress reports that the grill is closed, Tommy cleverly sweet-talks her into firing up the grill and cooking the wings. Surprised by Tommy's stunning combination of wit and sincerity, Richard points out to Tommy that if he could sell brakes like he sold the waitress on cooking his hot wings, he would be a great salesman. Up to this point, Tommy knew that he was excellent at having a good time, telling jokes, and engaging pleasant conversation, but he didn't realize these skills were relevant to being a salesman. At that moment, assisted by his observant friend, Tommy went from being a sure failure to a potential success, both in his mind and in reality. All he had to do was realize his belief in his ability to get along with others was relevant to his belief that he needed to sell some brake pads to save the business. Making this connection increased his self-efficacy related to salesmanship. You probably know the rest of the story.

of others are external factors. The second factor is whether or not the causal attribution is stable or unstable. An unstable attribution is a belief that the outcome of a particular behavior will change in the future, whereas stable attributions are an expectation of a consistent outcome. In the gambling example above, the "luck" belief is unstable, because luck can change at any time. This provides hope for future success. This second factor is important as it often influences client beliefs regarding the potential for change. Third is whether the causal attribution is specific to the task at hand or generalizes to other tasks (global). A specific causal attribution (e.g., "I lost the game because I'm not good at basketball.") limits generalizability of motivation to similar tasks, but a global attribution (e.g., "I lost the game because I'm not good at sports.") has the potential to impact motivation pertaining to many behaviors.

Attribution theory asserts that people may tend to display specific attribution styles, and these styles can significantly influence motivation. For example, it has been proposed that an external, stable, specific attribution style regarding successes, in combination with an internal, unstable, global attribution style regarding failures, can lead to learned helplessness and depression (Abramson, Alloy, & Metalsky, 1995; Abramson,

Seligman, & Teasdale, 1978). When considering how recreation, leisure, and therapeutic recreation are philosophically tied to intrinsic motivation and perceived freedom, the relevance of this theory and the potential application to practice becomes even more apparent.

Also notable is the close relationship between self-efficacy and attribution. Attribution style certainly can impact self-efficacy. Likewise, providing verbal persuasion that encourages healthy attribution patterns (e.g., intrinsic, stable, global attribution statements about a client's successful performance) can have a positive effect (Ellis, Maughan-Pritchett, & Ruddell, 1993; Long et al., 2001; Wise, Ellis, & Trunnell, 2002).

Generally speaking, a healthy attribution pattern is one that portrays reality. For the gambler, banking on talent or luck is maladaptive in either case. The reality of this situation is that casino games are in the house's favor, and winning on a consistent basis is an impossibility in most cases. Thus, a more healthy attribution pattern would be "I won because I got lucky" or "I lost because the odds were against me and there is little I can do about it." Maladaptive beliefs such as those portrayed in this example often drive gamblers to continue to lose money despite significant negative impacts on their lives.

Applications to Therapeutic Recreation

The ideal scenario for development of therapeutic recreation programs is that the process be conducted under the guidance of an appropriate theoretical framework. Doing so provides consistency in how assessments are conducted, how programs are developed and implemented, how client experiences are facilitated, and how outcomes are measured. Theory is important because it points us to underlying principles that guide program design and outcomes. Every element of the program is driven by a common and well-defined purpose, ensuring consistency and avoiding the arbitrary.

Cognitive-behavioral theory, including all of the theories mentioned above, provides a series of theoretical frameworks for therapeutic recreation practice. In some cases, therapeutic recreation programs may be operating within a larger therapy milieu that is already utilizing an approach such as Beck's cognitive therapy or RET. This point is supported by the observations of Rupke et al. (2006) regarding the role of leisure-related, or pleasurable, activity for patients participating in cognitive-behavioral therapy. Rupke states, "An important part of CBT for depression is scheduling pleasurable activities, especially with others, that usually give positive reinforcement" (p. 84).

In such situations, therapeutic recreation staff should familiarize themselves with the specific nature of the approach being utilized, and built their own programs in manner that contributes to the overall theoretical framework of the client's treatment. In other cases, the therapeutic recreation program may be "on their own" in regard to treatment philosophy, but can utilize these same theoretical concepts and associated techniques to guide their work.

In either case, CBT can be used by the therapeutic recreation professional as a foundation for work within therapeutic recreation practice. Goals and objectives falling within the realm of therapeutic recreation services can be addressed through interventions that are consistent with CBT.

The ultimate test for determining if a therapeutic recreation intervention or program is grounded in a cognitive-behavioral philosophy is to ask the question: "*Is the change agent of our program built around how clients think about, or interpret, their experiences?*" Be careful with this question. It says nothing about how clients feel. Emotions are important to acknowledge, and they should not be disputed or discounted, but the key to addressing emotional, behavioral, and even physical problems is focusing on cognition. As previously mentioned, the potential applications of CBT within therapeutic recreation practice are very broad; however, it is useful to review several common areas of application.

Application 1: Clinical Reasoning

Terms like "briefing," "leading," "facilitation," "processing," and "debriefing" are commonly used among therapeutic recreation professionals to describe the interactions they have with clients. Techniques such as the outward-bound approach ("what, so what, and now what"; see Chapter 4 for more detail) or "the Five Questions" model (Jacobson & Ruddy, 2004) are commonly used to provide structure to this process (Long, 2008). These systems give us guidance in determining what to say to clients and when to say it, which is often the most difficult part of being a therapeutic recreation professional. Still, even these models are rather generic in regard to the content of such interactions. Theory, however, can provide more detailed direction within these frameworks.

At the core of facilitation and processing of client experiences is *clinical reasoning*. Clinical reasoning has been described by Hutchinson, LeBlanc, and Booth (2002) as "the thinking and decision-making process-

es (that) are integral to clinical practice" (p. 19). This mental monitoring takes place at all times throughout the therapeutic recreation process (i.e., assessment, planning, implementation, and evaluation), but can be especially intense during and just after therapeutic recreation sessions (i.e., while leading, facilitating, and processing experiences).

As a practitioner dealing with various scenarios, dilemmas, or problems, choosing the appropriate response or action can be difficult, and should not be improvised. Such decisions require immediate attention within the context of complex situations, and utilizing a theoretical framework for such decision making is critical. Cognitive-behavioral models can be used as a beacon for clinical reasoning in such situations. The therapeutic recreation professional is not a psychotherapist, and must be cognizant of his or her professional limitations; however, utilizing cognitive-behavioral approaches to facilitate the achievement of goals within the context of an accepted therapeutic recreation modality is both acceptable and desirable. Furthermore, clinical reasoning is a constant process when working with clients and is an inherent part of applying any cognitive-behavioral technique in therapeutic recreation practice.

Scenario for Clinical Reasoning

Implementation of the therapeutic recreation process requires ongoing clinical reasoning. As an example of how CBT can be part of this process, consider "Joe," a client receiving treatment in a mental-health day-treatment program for adults. Joe has difficulty in confronting anxiety, which provokes interpersonal conflicts. For example, his inability to maintain composure during job interviews has been a major problem for him, leading to long-term unemployment. Joe also avoids participating in social activities for fear of embarrassing himself in front of others. He has not gone on a date for seven years. Joe has limited financial resources, but has been unable to say no to repeated requests for money from his siblings. Joe believes he has to continue to support his siblings whenever asked because "they are family."

In a scenario such as this, the Certified Therapeutic Recreation Specialist (CTRS) can utilize CBT in several ways as she works to determine how to best provide services to Joe. First, the CTRS might attempt to set "performance accomplishments" for Joe that measure his ability to navigate challenging interpersonal situations (self-efficacy theory). To do this, the CTRS would work with Joe to establish a series of increasingly challenging goals to work toward during his participation in a social assertiveness group. Joe's first goal may be to identify, through an expressive writing activity, how he might handle unreasonable requests from his family. Next, he may identify and role-play past scenarios where he has done poorly on job interviews. These role-plays would allow Joe to practice some of the cognitive self-monitoring strategies being taught to him by his psychotherapist in an emotionally safe environment. Joe's final goal may be to ask a long-time acquaintance to go on a date with him.

Of course, the CTRS would provide information to Joe about how to master these skills, but the CTRS also knows that it is essential that Joe actually practice being more assertive and socially engaged rather than just hear about it (this is the premise of constructivism). To provide this opportunity, the CTRS might arrange for a mock job fair where clients can practice inquiring about and interviewing for jobs.

As Joe participates in all of these activities, the CTRS would work to facilitate client progress through active listening and processing. For example, in anticipation of his attending a Christmas party for which he has set a goal to interact with at least five strangers, he may make comments like: "I always look stupid when I talk to strangers," "There's no way I'm dancing, I'm the worst dancer in the world," or "I know I'm going to chicken out before I get there, I'm scared out of my mind." The CTRS is responsible for helping Joe recognize the self-defeating nature of his comments. Sometimes this will just be a matter of prompting Joe to recognize what he has said. Other times it might require a more skilled discussion to help Joe recognize the irrational logic he is implementing. In response to the latter comment about "being scared," it might be necessary to explore what beliefs are making Joe scared, and discussing if these beliefs are true or untrue.

Again, clinical reasoning is the ongoing and challenging process of constant decision making on the part of a therapist regarding client care. Basing such decisions on a framework such as CBT can greatly increase one's ability to consistently and effectively implement a therapeutic recreation program, as well as the overall treatment program.

Application 2: Teaching Clients the ABCs

Because cognitive behavioral interventions are based on reframing how clients think or interpret their life situation, it is necessary to teach them about the relationship between thoughts, feelings, and behaviors (Beck & Weishaar, 2005; Corey, 2008; Ellis & Bernard, 1986; Lam & Gale, 2000). Therapeutic recreation programs

built on CBT principles should include a direct explanation of this relationship (or whatever framework is being taught to the client; see p. 291). Likewise, clients can be educated about how the causal attributions they make influence their thinking. Clients need to understand how their thinking influences their emotions, and how it can be altered, as they will ultimately be responsible for monitoring their own thoughts. This process can be addressed through structured leisure education, focusing on an explanation of how people's interpretation of their leisure experiences will influence feelings or emotions regarding those experiences (e.g., satisfied, embarrassed, frustrated). Leisure awareness programs can be tailored to explore current leisure patterns, associated thoughts, and resulting feelings. Establishing this knowledge will set the groundwork for facilitation and processing of therapeutic recreation experiences that are to occur in later sessions.

Application 3: Identifying and Evaluating Cognitive Distortions

In order to address cognitive distortions or thinking errors, the therapeutic recreation professional must somehow create situations where these errors are notable or observable. Sometimes this is easy, because the client's thinking is so affected by cognitive distortions that they are persistently expressed. Other times, detrimental thinking patterns or tendencies are more subtle. Still, careful program planning can help engineer experiences where cognitive distortions manifest more easily. Such circumstances, when paired with competent clinical reasoning, are at the core of therapeutic change.

At times, the focus on cognitive distortions can be very directive. For example, several commonly used therapeutic recreation tools or modalities have been designed specifically to challenge current cognitive understandings. Probably the best example of this is the therapy workbook entitled *Crossing the Bridge: A Journey in Self-Esteem, Relationships, and Life Balance* (Negley, 1997). This resource consists of several journaling based activities designed to help clients identify core beliefs that influence them and reframe those beliefs as a means of addressing issues of esteem and emotion.

Bibliotherapy (use of reading materials) and cinematherapy (use of movies) have also been identified as potentially effective mechanisms for assisting clients in examining maladaptive thinking processes (Austin, 2009; Yang & Lee, 2002, 2005). In both cases the storyline (or other content) is used to elicit discussion that taps into rigid cognitive frameworks, creating an opportunity for assimilation and accommodation of new information. Role-play activities and journal analysis present similar opportunities.

Application 4: Coping with Emotional Distress and Pain

One element of cognitive behavioral interventions that has yet to be mentioned is the fact that it can be used to help people cope with emotional distress and even physical pain. The truth is that many people who are receiving therapeutic recreation services have a significant amount of stress and trauma occurring in their lives. One aspect of the therapeutic recreation is helping people cope with this distress. In some cases, their distress may be in the form of worry: "Will I ever be able to go home?" "Will I ever walk again?" "Am I going to die?" These are the realities with which clients must deal. At the same time, they may be experiencing significant physical pain, which has an extensive psychological impact as well. There are cognitive-behavioral interventions that can significantly relieve emotional and physical distress.

In regard to pain management, there appear to be several areas of potential application to therapeutic recreation practice. First, patients can be provided with intervention and training related to relaxation strategies, meditation, biofeedback, redirection (distraction) strategies, regulation of ruminating thoughts (thought-stopping), and other techniques designed to ensure physical pain is not exacerbated by other controllable cognitive functions (Stumbo, 2006a). In addition, Stumbo (2002, 2006b) has repeatedly pointed out the need to promote self-efficacy among clients in regard to using resources and strategies for pain management. Feelings helplessness in this area only exacerbates the existing pain and distress. (See also Chapter 17, on stress management, for more detail.)

One example of how cognitive exercises can be used to help reduce pain was presented by Bonadies (2009). In this case report, integrated guided imagery was successfully implemented by a CTRS to reduce chronic back pain in a 52-year-old Hispanic male with a diagnosis of AIDS, multiple substance abuse, and depression. This scenario involved the CTRS facilitating a guided imagery session in which the client had significant liberty to choose his own imagery as a symbolic representation of his pain, as well as its gradual reduction.

When utilizing integrated guided imagery, the CTRS first works to induce an optimal state of relaxation for the client (in this case the CTRS used the "body scan" technique, during which the CTRS verbally instructs the client on how to progressively relax muscle groups throughout the body). Next, the CTRS provides a general imagery concept. In the case study, the imagery concept was "a scale." The client is then allowed to imagine whatever type of scale they want, and how it operates. The CTRS then asks the client to imagine on the scale the current level of pain, and then, gradually, to imagine the scale moving downward as his pain decreases. Through this process, the client learns to cognitively reduce his pain levels.

Not all clients are appropriate for guided imagery, nor will all respond positively. As with many modalities available to the CTRS, guided imagery offers various levels of complexity. Certifications are available for more advanced forms of guided imagery, including integrated guided imagery. Therapeutic recreation professionals should always adequately research any technique they consider utilizing to ensure they are remaining within their professional capabilities.

Application 5: Clarification of Values

One area of therapeutic recreation practice where addressing a client's cognitive interpretation of his or her life circumstances may play a major role is the clarification of values. As noted by Austin (2009), values clarification is a technique that allows clients to examine the beliefs and principles by which they live. These personally held beliefs are extremely powerful in determining client action. If clients hold values that are impacted by cognitive distortions, the consequences can be devastating. For example, a parent who strongly values "unconditional love" of her children may have good intentions, but if that unconditional love is grounded in core beliefs such as "I must give my child whatever he desires" and "I should always take my child's side to show I love him," the parent's core beliefs most likely contradict the long-term outcome the parent would want for the child. Exploring contradictions and opposing core beliefs can help clients work through the clarification of their core values and allow for behavior to change if necessary.

Bibliotherapy and cinematherapy are excellent tools for values clarification. Value-laden scenarios can be presented through these mediums, homework can be provided that requires clients to identify values that are portrayed, and their own values systems can be examined in the context of their observations. Activities or scenarios can be presented to clients that require value-based decisions to be made, and the consequences of those decisions can be examined. Various other specific activities and programs have been developed around this process, many of which can be implemented from a CBT perspective. Again, what makes values clarification align with CBT is the manner in which the experience is facilitated, not the activity itself.

Application 6: Changing Thoughts by Changing Behaviors

Most examples of applying CBT to therapeutic recreation practice presented thus far have focused on helping clients realize when thinking is biased or their perceptions are distorted. Sometimes, client's negative thoughts are actually true, and convincing them to adopt an alternative perspective would not be an appropriate approach helping them deal with it. For example, convincing a person that he or she is a good pianist when in fact he or she is a poor pianist is not a good approach to take. Ignoring the issue is also not advisable since automatic negative thoughts, even when true, feed into negative emotions. One potential solution is to change the negative thoughts by changing the associated behavior. The implications here are two-fold. First, realizing that negative thoughts are true often brings a sense of hopelessness (Leahy, 2003). It is important to explain to clients that this knowledge actually empowers them to stop ruminating on the negative thought and figure out how to change the situation. Referring back to the earlier example, focus

---

Inset 15.2. Traditional Learning versus the Constructivist Approach

One criticism of the constructivist approach to learning about the world is that it is inefficient, meaning that it takes too much time. To illustrate this, consider the following observations regarding the stereotypical tendencies of men and women when they "get lost" in the car. Women tend to take the "traditional learning approach." They ask for directions. This, in most cases quickly and efficiently tells them how to get to their destination. They don't really care about whether or not they understand the details to the point that they can navigate through the same area in the future. They just want to get to their destination. The risk of this approach, however, is that if you get bad information, you are still lost with no way of figuring out a solution.

Men, on the other hand, tend to take a "constructivist approach," they "learn by doing." They will not ask directions, as this spoils the more enriched learning experience of driving around in the neighborhood until you understand every intricate detail of every road. This approach takes longer and can be extremely frustrating for others who are riding along in the car, but if you ever have to come back to that neighborhood, you have an enriched understanding of the roadways and will have no problem finding your destination. This risk of this approach is obviously being late, as it takes more time and effort (in academic settings, this is a big issue as teachers try to balance quality and quantity of learning). Of course, your mother will tell you that the reason men don't ask for directions is because they are stubborn, so don't share this theory at the dinner table.

---

would shift to determining how the struggling pianist could become a better pianist or how other skills or interests in this area may be an alternative.

Once aware of the potential for change, the client and therapist can work to develop a strategy for changing the associated behavior. For example, if a client knows he has trouble with dating (i.e., social phobias, poor social skills), the therapeutic recreation professional can then work with him to develop necessary skills. The practical techniques associated with this process might include mental rehearsal, role-play, demonstration, self-monitoring techniques, and other self-efficacy or attribution-based interventions. It is also important for the CTRS to present an optimal level of challenge through appropriate sequencing of tasks so that the opportunity for experiencing genuine success and growth is optimized and performance accomplishment can take place.

Application 7: Experiential Programs

Leahy (1996) described CBT as being didactic in nature, where the therapist works to educate the client as much as possible about tools and strategies that can help them test, or challenge, inaccurate assumptions they draw about the world. The word didactic is sometimes seen as opposed to experiential learning; however, the experiences that elicit these thoughts and the processes used to test the associated assumptions can often be experiential in nature. In fact, many of the experience-based modalities used in therapeutic recreation (e.g., challenge courses, adventure therapy, problem-solving initiatives) can be utilized to provide opportunities to test such assumptions. Experiential programs are differentiated here from general recreation and leisure activity participation because they are more likely to involve a contrived, or engineered, experience among participants. In these programs, the therapeutic recreation professional attempts to create a client experience that elicits an opportunity for learning or growth. From a CBT perspective, these contrived experiences could involve opportunities to examine cognitive interpretations of situations and challenge their accuracy. For, example, a client who is habitually operating under core beliefs such as "I'm incapable of success" or "I can't do anything adventurous" could be asked to participate in a challenge course program.

During participation, opportunities to acknowledge the impact of these core beliefs are likely to arise. Furthermore, through appropriate facilitation, the CTRS can create opportunities for these negative schemas to be challenged. Again, there is crossover from other presented theories as well. Carefully facilitated client experiences can be designed to optimize success and directly influence self-efficacy. The group problem solving element, as well as the experiential nature of the activity, facilitates learning as described by Piaget's constructivist theory. Finally, appropriate causal attributions are facilitated by the therapeutic recreation professional through her dialogue with clients.

CBT Techniques

It should be abundantly clear by now that CBT, as described here, is really a platform from which specific interventions can be developed and implemented. Listing "techniques" or "activities" that represent cognitive-behavioral interventions has been intentionally avoided thus far, but at some point, it might be helpful to summarize some of the commonly used interventions. Table 15.4 provides a listing of just a few of the many actual intervention strategies that would fall under this framework. Some have already been mentioned while others have not. In either case, a brief description is provided for each.

Summary

Cognitive-behavioral theory is based on how a person's thoughts effect their emotions and behaviors. The theory is "behavioral" because feelings are a direct result of the thoughts and interpretations a person has about a situation, and interventions focuses directly on these thoughts. Behavioral techniques can be used to

practice and reinforce healthy thinking patterns, but the behaviors learned through this process are primarily cognitive in nature. Simply put, the client learns to think about things in a different way.

In some cases, thought processes and the associated conclusions are directly challenged. In other cases, the CTRS can work to create an environment that allows the participant to recognize inconsistencies and create healthy interpretations of circumstances. Finally, it is important to create environments that allow clients to exercise newly developed schemas, and also to reinforce adaptive, or healthy, thinking patterns when they occur. The experiential world of therapeutic recreation offers unlimited opportunities to work through and develop healthy ways of interpreting the world.

In regard to theory, Beck's Cognitive Theory and Ellis' Rational Emotive Therapy (RET) are foundational to many other cognitive-behavioral schools of thought, such as Piaget's constructivism, Bandura's self-efficacy, and attribution theory. All of these theories, however, have potential application within the therapeutic recreation realm. In addition to the theories presented here, readers are encouraged to explore the various other frameworks that exist in the realm of CBT. Two of the more notable to consider are the Theory of Planned Behavior (Fishbein & Ajzen, 2010; see Chapter 8) and William Glasser's Reality Therapy, both of which have significant implications for therapeutic recreation practice.

Just as broad as the theoretical models associated with CBT are the various potential applications to therapeutic recreation and the many specific techniques that

Table 15.4. Efficacy Building Techniques

Area of Intervention	Description	Example
Verbal Persuasion	Provide specific feedback that emphasizes the client's ability to impact outcomes in a positive way Utilize feedback that is congruent with accurate attributions for success/failure	Point out to client that the ability to memorize sports statistics is pretty amazing and improved memory will help with today's challenge
Vicarious Experience	Demonstrate activity/task Mental rehearsal/visualization of success	Show the client how to ride a bike Have the client imagine riding the bike
Performance Accomplishment	Sequence activities appropriately, providing level of challenge that allows success	For a client with a fear of public places: Dinner with the therapist, then dinner with a friend, then dinner in the cafeteria, then dinner in a public restaurant
Managing Arousal Level	Manipulate environmental factors that increase or decrease stress levels Teach stress management techniques	Teach the client a breathing technique to use when becoming nervous while reading aloud at a poetry club

Table 15.5. Professional Scope of Practice for Therapeutic Recreation Specialists

Professional	Goal	Example Mechanism
Psychologist/ Psychiatrist LMSW	Identify and address subconscious schemas and their root cause	Group and Individual Psychotherapy
TRS (supportive role)	Assist client in monitoring maladaptive core beliefs	Formal and informal facilitation/discussion during therapeutic recreation activities
TRS (direct role)	Identifying how maladaptive core beliefs impact leisure lifestyle and associated wellness/QOL factors	TR assessment, treatment planning, formative and summative evaluation
TRS (direct role)	Identify and challenge self defeating leisure-related thoughts and beliefs	Cinematherapy, bibliotherapy, workbooks, community reintegration, formal and informal facilitation
TRS (direct role)	Teach client leisure related cognitive behavioral strategies for addressing TR goals	Group and individual LE programs e.g., Progressive relaxation, self-monitoring

NOTE: The dotted line represents the boundaries for scope of practice.

can be applied. It is important that practitioners are careful not to become lost in this ocean of concepts. Practitioners must be sure to utilize concepts that are theoretically compatible with one another. Also keep in mind the importance of maintaining a connection between the targeted outcomes for clients and the theories and programs used to obtain those outcomes. Finally, it is critical that practitioners are careful to keep within the boundaries of their training and overall scope of practice (see Table 15.5). Utilizing clinical supervision can be an invaluable tool for monitoring these boundaries while working to develop a more sophisticated framework for practice.

References

Abramson, L. Y., Alloy, L. B., & Metalsky, G. I. (1995). Hopelessness depression. In G. M. Buchanan & M. E. P. Seligman (Eds.), *Explanatory style* (pp. 113–134). New York, NY: Erlbaum.

Abramson, L.Y., Seligman, M. E. P., & Teasdale, J. D. (1978). Learned helplessness in humans: Critique and reformulation. *Journal of Abnormal Psychology, 87*(1), 49–74.

Alford, B., & Beck, A. (1997). *The integrative power of cognitive therapy.* New York, NY: Guilford Press.

Austin, D. R. (2009). *Therapeutic recreation processes and techniques.* Champaign, IL: Sagamore.

Bandura, A. (1986). *Social foundations of thought and action.* Englewood Cliffs, NJ: Prentice Hall.

Bandura, A. (1997). *Self efficacy: The exercise of control.* New York, NY: W. H. Freeman.

Beck, A. (1964). Thinking and depression: II. Theory and therapy. *Archives of General Psychiatry, 10*(6), 561–571.

Beck, A. (1967). *The diagnosis and management of depression.* Philadelphia, PA: University of Pennsylvania Press.

Beck, A. (1976). *Cognitive therapy and emotional disorders.* New York, NY: International Universities Press.

Beck, A., & Weishaar, M. (2005). Cognitive therapy. In R. J. Corsini & D. Wedding (Eds.), *Current Psychotherapies* (238–268). Belmont, CA: Thomson Brooks/Cole Publishing.

Beck, J. (1995). *Cognitive therapy: Basics and beyond.* New York, NY: Guilford Press.

Blackburn, I. M., & Davidson, K. M. (1995). *Cognitive therapy for depression and anxiety: A practitioner's guide.* Cambridge, MA: Blackwell Science.

Bonadies. V. (2009). Guided imagery as a therapeutic recreation modality to reduce pain and anxiety. *Therapeutic Recreation Journal, 43*(2), 43–55.

Butler, A. C., Chapman, J. E., Forman, E. M., & Beck, A. T. (2006). The empirical status of cognitive-behavioral therapy: A review of meta-analyses. *Clinical Psychology Review, 26*(1), 17–31.

Cave, S. (1999). *Theoretical approaches in psychology.* London, UK: Routledge.

Cervone, D. (1997). Social-cognitive mechanisms and personality coherence: Self-knowledge, situational beliefs, and cross-situational coherence in perceived self-efficacy. *Psychological Science, 8*, 43–50.

Cervone, D. (2004). The architecture of personality. *Psychological Review, 111*(1), 183–204.

Chu, B. C., & Harrison, T. L. (2007). Disorder specific effects of CBT for anxious and depressed youth: A meta-analysis of candidate mediators for change. *Clinical Child and Family Psychology Review, 10*, 352–372.

Corey, G. (2008). *Theory and practice of counseling and psychotherapy* (8th ed.). Pacific Grove, CA: Brooks/Cole.

Eccleston, C., Morely, S., Yorke, L., Williams, A., & Mastroyannopoulou, K. (2002). Systematic review of randomised controlled trials of psychological therapy for chronic pain in children and adolescents, with a subset meta-analysis of pain relief. *Pain 99*(1–2), 157–165.

Ellis, A. (1962). *Reasoning and emotion in psychotherapy.* New York, NY: Stuart.

Ellis, A. (1994). *Reason and emotion in psychotherapy: A comprehensive method of treating human disturbances* (Revised and Updated). New York, NY: Carol Publishing Group.

Ellis, A., & Bernard, A. (1986). What is rational-emotive therapy (RET)? In A. Ellis & R. Grieger (Eds.), *Handbook of rational-emotive therapy: Vol. 2* (pp. 3–30). New York, NY: Springer.

Ellis, G., Maughan-Pritchett, M., & Ruddell, E. (1993). Effect of attribution based verbal persuasion and imagery on self-efficacy of adolescents diagnosed with major depression. *Therapeutic Recreation Journal, 27*(2), 83–97.

Ellis, G., Morris, C., & Trunnell, E. (1995). Engineering experiences: The COMPLEX Model of recreation leadership. *World Leisure and Recreation, 37*(4), 37–43.

Fishbein, M., & Ajzen, I. (2010). *Predicting and changing behavior: The reasoned action approach.* New York, NY: Psychology Press (Taylor & Francis).

Hutchinson, S. L., LeBlanc, A., & Booth, R. (2002). "Perpetual problem-solving": An ethnographic study of clinical reasoning in a therapeutic recreation setting. *Therapeutic Recreation Journal, 36*(1), 18–34.

Jacobson, M., & Ruddy, M. (2004). *Open to outcome: A practical guide for facilitating & teaching experiential reflection.* Oklahoma City, OK: Wood 'N' Barnes.

Lam, D., & Gale, J. (2000). Cognitive behaviour therapy: Teaching a client the ABC model—the first steps towards the process of change. *Journal of Advanced Nursing, 31*(2), 444–451.

Leahy, R. (1996). *Cognitive therapy: Basic principles and applications.* Northvale, NJ: Jason Aronson Inc.

Leahy, R (2003). *Cognitive therapy techniques: A practitioners guide.* New York, NY: Guilford Press.

Ledley, D. R., Marx, B. P., & Heimberg, R. G. (2005). *Making cognitive-behavioral therapy work: Clinical process for new practitioners.* New York, NY: Guilford Press.

Leichsenring, F., Hiller, W., Weissberg, M., & Leibing, E. (2006). Cognitive-behavioral therapy and psychodynamic psychotherapy: Techniques, efficacy, and indications. *American Journal of Psychotherapy, 60*(3), 233–259.

Long, T. D. (2001). *Constructivist and didactic leisure education programs for At-Risk Youth: Enhancing knowledge, meaning and behavioral intentions.* (Unpublished Doctoral Dissertation). University of Utah. Salt Lake City, UT. Retrieved June 16, 2009 from: www.oregonpdf.org/pdf/RC555Long(15-2).pdf

Long, T. D. (2008). The therapeutic recreation process. In T. Robertson & T. Long (Eds.), *Foundations of therapeutic recreation: Perceptions, philosophies, and practices for the 21st century* (pp. 79–100). Champaign, IL: Human Kinetics

Long, T. D., Ellis, G., Trunnell, E., Tatsugawa, K., & Freeman, P. (2001). Animating recreation experiences through face-to-face leadership: Efficacy of two models. *Journal of Park and Recreation Administration, 19*(1), 1–22.

Lynch, D., Laws, K. R., & McKenna, P. J. (2010). Cognitive behavioural therapy for major psychiatric disorder: Does it really work? A meta-analytical review of well-controlled trials. *Psychological Medicine, 40*, 9–24.

Mahon, M. M. (1994). The use of self-control techniques to facilitate self-determination skills during leisure in adolescents and young adults with mild and moderate mental retardation. *Therapeutic Recreation Journal, 28*(2), 58–72.

Maughan, M., & Ellis, G. D. (1991). Effect of efficacy information during recreation participation on efficacy judgements of depressed adolescents. *Therapeutic Recreation Journal, 25*(1), 50–59.

Negley, S. (1997). *Crossing the bridge: A journey in self-esteem, relationships and life balance.* Beachwood, OH: Wellness Productions and Publishing.

Piaget, J. (1970). *Genetic epistemology.* New York, NY: Columbia University Press.

Piaget, J. (1977). Comments on mathematical education. In H. E. Gruber & J. J. Voneche (Eds.), *The essential Piaget: An interpretive reference and guide* (pp. 716–732). New York, NY: Basic.

Richeson, R. E., Croteau, K. A., Jones, D. B., & Farmer, B. C. (2006). Effects of a pedometer-based intervention on the physical performance and mobility-related self-efficacy of community dwelling older adults: An interdisciplinary preventive health care intervention. *Therapeutic Recreation Journal, 40*(1), 18–32.

Rupke, S., Blecke, D., & Renfrow, M. (2006). Cognitive therapy for depression. *American Family Physician, 73*(1), 83–86.

Savell, K. (1986). Implications for therapeutic recreation leisure-efficacy: Theory and therapy programming. *Therapeutic Recreation Journal, 20*(1), 43–52.

Stumbo, N. J. (2002). Implications for pain management for therapeutic recreation services. *Annual in Therapeutic Recreation, 11*, 11–32.

Stumbo, N. J. (2006a). An evidence-based approach to providing physical activity and cognitive-behavioral therapy to older adults with pain. *American Journal of Recreation Therapy, 5*(3), 13–25.

Stumbo, N. J. (2006b). Unique issues in pain management for older adults. *American Journal of Recreation Therapy, 5*(2), 37–47.

Sukhodolsky, D. G., Kassinove, H., & Gorman, B. S. (2004). Cognitive-behavioral therapy for anger in children and adolescents: A meta-analysis. *Aggression and Violent Behavior, 9*(3), 247–269.

von Glasersfeld, E. (1995). A constructivist approach to teaching. In L. P. Steffe & J. Gale (Eds.), *Constructivism in education* (pp. 3-16). Hillsdale, NJ: Lawrence Erlbaum Associates.

von Glasersfeld, E. (1996). Introduction: Aspects of constructivism. In C. T. Fosnot (Ed.), *Constructivism: Theory, perspectives, and practice* (pp. 3–7). New York, NY: Teachers College Press.

Weiner, B. (1985). An attributional theory of achievement motivation and emotion. *Psychological Review, 92*(4), 548–573.

Weiner, B. (1992). *Human motivation: Metaphors, theories, and research.* Newbury Park, CA: Sage.

Wise, J. B. (2003). Social-cognitive theory and multivariable explanatory models: A framework for therapeutic recreation practice. *American Journal of Recreation Therapy, 2*(4), 43–47.

Wise, J. B. (2004). Self-efficacy: Underlying psychological structures and processes. *American Journal of Recreation Therapy, 3*(4), 37–40.

Wise, J. B., Ellis, G. D., & Trunnell, E. P. (2002). Effects of a curriculum designed to generalize self-efficacy from weight training exercises to activities of daily living among adults with spinal injuries. *Journal of Applied Social Psychology, 32*, 500–521.

Vygotsky, L. (1962). *Thought and Language.* Cambridge, MA: MIT Press (Original work published in 1934).

Yang, H., & Lee, Y. (2002). Healing power of cinema: Clinical application of movies in therapeutic recreation. *Expanding Horizons in Therapeutic Recreation, 20*, 10–16.

Yang, H., & Lee, Y. (2005). The use of single-session cinematherapy and aggressive behavioral tendencies among adopted children: A pilot study. *American Journal of Recreational Therapy, 4*(1), 35–44.

» CHAPTER 16 »

Intergenerational Programming

Shannon Hebblethwaite, Ph.D. and Jerome Singleton, Ph.D., CTRS

Background/History

Industrial societies are aging due to advances in health and shifting of work roles to nonindustrial occupations (Bloom & Canning, 2006). Work opportunities are becoming more global. It is expected that approximately 22 million individuals from nonindustrial societies will be moving to industrial societies for work and career opportunities (Bloom & Canning, 2006). A similar phenomenon has existed in North America, where individuals seeking careers have moved to differing states or provinces to seek employment. This shift in work opportunities has impacted family structure from extended families to nuclear families. Families have historically been the location of opportunities for intergenerational engagement in activities across the life course.

The term *intergenerational* generally refers to individuals living in different generations, such as parents and children or grandparents and grandchildren. In the context of intergenerational programming, the term has mainly been used to describe interactions among older adults and young children. While this has historically been the way in which intergenerational programs have been designed and implemented, it is our hope here to expand our thinking in this area and include a wide variety of intergenerational constellations that have not received significant attention in either research or practice. We would also like to emphasize the role of families in leisure and in intergenerational programming, rather than focusing only on the traditional intergenerational program that involves older adults serving youth organizations and youth serving older adults. These intergenerational relations may occur between any age group, for example, between older adults and their adult children, parents and young children, grandparents and grandchildren.

Intergenerational programming will continue to increase in importance, as individuals today are living longer than ever before. By 2025, the World Health Organization (2010) projects that the number of older adults over the age of 60 will double in industrial societies. This unique sociodemographic trend makes the study of intergenerational relationships and grandparenting, in particular, increasingly relevant. As older adults lead longer and healthier lives, they are able to engage in opportunities for family leisure in a more active way and for longer periods of time across their lifespan. Grandparents and grandchildren now have the opportunity to develop and maintain adult relationships.

There are almost 6 million grandparents in Canada (Milan & Hamm, 2003). Based on the General Social Survey, statistics indicate that 70% of Canadians in their twenties have at least one living grandparent (Kemp, 2003) and more than half of adults age 65 and older have grandchildren who are 18 years and older (Farkas & Hogan, 1995). Similarly, in the United States, 62% of grandchildren in their twenties have living grandparents (Smith & Drew, 2002). Given these sociodemographic trends, there is great potential for intergenerational programming among generations of all ages.

Intended Client Groups

McCrea and Smith (1997) categorize intergenerational programs into three types: older adults serving children and youth; children and youth serving older adults; and children, youth, and older adults serving together. Many senior centers or long-term care facilities offer intergenerational programming by involving school or youth groups in various activities with older adults in long-term care, including music, baking, gardening, physical activity, and computer programs. Many of these programs involve children and youth, but some have been expanded to include college-age, emerging adults as well (Colston, Harper, & Mitchener-Colston, 1996). Programs in the category of seniors serving children and youth have included mentoring programs for youth at risk (Cummings, Williams, & Ellis, 2002; Wright, Owen, McGuire, & Backman, 1994), foster grandparent programs (Saltz, 1989), book discussion groups (Lohman, Griffith, & Coppard, 2005), and art education (Langford, 2008). Intergenerational programs can be beneficial to a wide variety of client groups of any age, including youth at risk, individuals with dementia, cancer, HIV/AIDS, and older adults involved in senior centers or living in retirement communities.

Grandparenting

Recent research has identified the importance of collaboration among families in enhancing the success of intergenerational programs (Jarrott & Bruno, 2007). Involving family members in intergenerational programming can be beneficial to clients, their families, staff, and the organizations themselves. Interactions among generations in families provide an innovative opportunity for intergenerational programming. In particular, relationships between grandparents and grandchildren can be strengthened across the lifespan through engagement in intergenerational family leisure.

Because of increased longevity, more older adults in industrial societies today are experiencing grandparenting and great-grandparenting. Similarly, step-grandparenting is also becoming increasingly prevalent, given increased divorce rates and the increased prevalence of blended families (Milan & Hamm, 2003). Although some individuals become grandparents at a young age, most grandparents today are retired by the time their grandchildren reach adulthood. The shifting of the onset of grandparenting may be related to the couples marrying later and later onset of starting a family. Historically the emphasis, when studying grandchildren, has been on the "child." Hodgson (1998) points out, however, that many grandchildren today are not children at all. Rather, the grandparent—grandchild relationship is between two generations of adults. The study of intergenerational relations between grandparents and their adult grandchildren is relatively new and little attention has been paid to this relationship. TR practitioners can use intergenerational programming as an opportunity for grandparents to develop and maintain this adult relationship and share in their grandchildren's transition to adulthood, marriage, and parenthood.

Many researchers have developed typologies of grandparenting styles with an emphasis on grandparents' influence on parenting and childrearing (Norris, Kuiack, & Pratt, 2004). Some common functions that grandparents have been found to fulfill include the role as a valued elder (Kivnick, 1982), a surrogate parent (Neugarten & Weinstein, 1964), and confidante (Brussoni & Boon, 1998). There has been such emphasis on the development of these typologies that the breadth of this chapter allows for only a brief overview of general trends in the literature (for a more detailed account, see Smith & Drew, 2002).

The general trend began with a negative view of grandparents as interfering and authoritarian in their relationships with their families (Smith & Drew, 2002). Since then, and until recently, an increasingly favorable view of grandparents has emerged in the literature. Neugarten and Weinstein (1964) emphasized the prevalence of the formal and fun-seeking roles in their typology of grandparenting styles. Similarly, grandparents are often engaged in warmer and more indulgent relationships with their grandchildren than with their own children.

Most research related to grandparenting espouses a rich and rewarding relationship among generations. Grandparents are often viewed as a source of love, help, understanding, and friendship by their grandchildren (Roy & Russell, 1992). Much emphasis has been placed on the norm of non-interference (Giarrusso & Silverstein, 2001), whereby grandparents exist in an informal, easygoing relationship with their grandchildren. Grandparents have even been shown to act as a protective buffer to their grandchildren, insulating them from the effects of potentially stressful and hazardous events such as divorce (Bengtson & Silverstein, 1993).

Although the research does not provide widespread evidence of conflict in grandparenting relationships, Norris and Tindale (1994) identify a number of "trouble spots" for grandparents in their intergenerational relationships. Timing of grandparenthood appears to be crucial to grandparents' satisfaction with their roles. If grandparenthood occurs too early, these individuals tend to feel overwhelmed by the numerous obligations placed on them for which they were not ready (Burton & Bengtson, 1985). By contrast, disappointment may occur if grandparenthood occurs too late, as worries about insufficient time with grandchildren and poor health prevail (Burton & Bengtson, 1985; Norris & Tindale, 1994). Changes in marital status, both in the grandparent and the adult child, can also be problematic and can raise challenges related to custody, geographical proximity, and blended families. Competing interests in the lives of grandparents and the lack of agreement among grandparents and their adult children about the centrality of the grandparent role can also create conflict in the relationship (Norris & Tindale, 1994). Leisure education that focuses on the inclusion of all of the generations of a family can be beneficial in addressing some of these concerns and challenges.

Intergenerational relations can, therefore, have both positive and negative impacts on both generations. Despite the increasingly hectic pace of life in our industrialized society, family bonds remain strong. For example, grandparents rate their relationship with grandchildren to be consistently one of the most important relationships in their life. Including an intergenerational perspective in leisure education can facilitate a better understanding of the different values, needs, and experiences of different generations. The term "family" has expanded from the traditional definition of people related through marriage, blood, or adoption. The traditional nuclear family included heterosexual couples who were married and who had children. Today, the term "family" encompasses a much wider range of relationships and requires a broader understanding of families. New forms of family include common-law relationships, single-parent families, blended families shaped by divorce and remarriage, same-sex relationships, and couples who don't have children. Three-generation families, in which grandparents, parents, and children all cohabitate, are also increasingly visible, especially with the cultural diversity of families that exist in North America today. Also, custodial grandparenting is becoming increasingly prevalent, whereby grandparents are the primary caregivers for their grandchildren.

The role of grandparent has changed due to each cohort's perceptions of what constitutes grandparenting, or due to the culture in which the individual has been raised. By the year 2042, 54% of individuals living in the United States will represent culturally diverse populations (African Americans, Spanish Americans, Asian Americans). The question arises, therefore, as to what the role of a grandparent is in a non-North American society. The majority of previous research has been conducted using a North American, Eurocentric perspective on aging, leisure, grandparenting, and intergenerational programming. As TR professionals, we need to be sensitive to the diversity of family forms that exist and begin to include older adults in our discussions and interventions related to families.

Basic Premises

Family Leisure

Intergenerational family leisure can be defined as "the experience of time spent together by grandparents, parents, and/or grandchildren in free time or recreational activities" (Hebblethwaite & Norris, 2010). The benefits of establishing expectations and norms related to family leisure has been viewed as beneficial to family and society through improved communication among family members, higher quality of family relationships,

and enhanced family cohesiveness (Orthner & Mancini, 1990). Recently, however, approaches to the theorizing and study of family leisure have been challenged. A number of researchers have questioned the traditional definitions of family (Allen, Fine, & Demo, 2000) and family leisure (Freysinger, 1997; Shaw, 1992). This has led to a critical analysis of underlying values, beliefs, and assumptions that influence the study of family leisure. Feminist researchers in particular have questioned the previous assumptions about the positive aspects of family leisure and have instead emphasized the exposure and analysis of inequality and oppression that exists within the family system (Shaw & Dawson, 2003).

Family leisure among grandparents and adult grandchildren has received minimal attention in the literature, but recently it was found to be highly valued by both grandparents and grandchildren (Hebblethwaite, 2008). A fluid relationship has been found between grandparents' and grandchildren's engagement in family leisure together and their perceived emotional closeness in the relationship. Grandparents and grandchildren who experience close relationships with each other are, not surprisingly, more likely to spend leisure time together. At the same time, participating in leisure activities together allows grandparents and grandchildren to develop a more in-depth knowledge of each other and their personalities and personal histories. These leisure pursuits can facilitate the establishment of common interests and experiences which, in turn, enable the development of strong intergenerational bonds between grandparents and grandchildren. The time spent together involved in leisure pursuits provides an invaluable opportunity to "get to know one another better" across the lifespan. This bond is important to develop early in their relationship, because it can help to generate a sense of shared history between grandparents and grandchildren. This shared history can make the ensuing time spent together more relaxing, enjoyable, and engaging for both the grandparents and grandchildren.

Ambivalence

Despite many benefits associated with intergenerational family leisure, the experience of family leisure has been found to be both consensual and contradictory in nature. The intergenerational ambivalence framework, therefore, has been useful developing a better understanding of intergenerational interactions. The ambivalence framework emphasizes "contradictions in relationships between parents and adult offspring that cannot be reconciled" (Luscher & Pillemer, 1998,

p. 416). This concept includes contradictions at both the level of social structure, including institutional resources and requirements, such as statuses, roles, and norms, and at the subjective level, in terms of cognitions, emotions, and motivations (Luscher & Pillemer, 1998). More specifically, Luscher (2000) states that ambivalence exists when "dilemmas and polarizations of feelings, thoughts, actions, and, furthermore, contradictions in social relations and social structures, which are relevant for personal and societal development, are interpreted as being basically irreconcilable" (p. 16). Hebblethwaite and Norris (2010) found that family leisure among grandparents and grandchildren was simultaneously consensual and conflictual. Grandparents and adult grandchildren discussed the benefits of family leisure, most importantly, the context that family leisure provided for the development of emotionally close relationships among grandparents and grandchildren. At the same time, the grandparents and grandchildren experienced conflict, most notably the challenge of reconciling normative expectations about the need for grandparents and grandchildren to spend time together with the emerging social trends valuing individual independence and personal fulfillment.

Intergenerational Stake

A theoretical construct that sheds some light on intergenerational relations is the concept of intergenerational stake. Although grandparents tend to perceive strong bonds with their grandchildren, some researchers have questioned the reciprocity of these feelings among grandchildren. Research has supported the notion of intergenerational stake, whereby the older generation perceives intergenerational relations more positively than the younger generations (Giarrusso, Stallings, & Bengtson, 1995). This holds true, not only for grandparents and their adult children, but also for grandparents and grandchildren (Silverstein, Giarrusso, & Bengtson, 2003). Although the grandparents have greater stake in the intergenerational relationship, many grandchildren still emphasize the emotional closeness that they share with their grandparents and the strong influence that grandparents have in their lives.

Emotional closeness in the grandparent—grandchild relationship has been found to be influenced by a number of different factors, including geographical proximity, frequency of contact, gender, lineage, timing of grandparenthood, and the grandparents' relationship with their own grandparents. Although many people have the impression that we live in a society in which families are widely scattered, older adults still live in close proximity to at least some members of their family. Close proximity, subsequently, increases the frequency of contact among generations. Contact between grandparents and grandchildren, however, is thought to be mediated by the involvement of the middle generation. This is true for families with young children, but by the time grandchildren reach adulthood, this impact diminishes significantly and grandchildren interact with their grandparents sometimes quite separately from their parents.

Given the changes in family forms and relationships, intergenerational programming provides an opportunity to strengthen these relationships and educate families about both the benefits and challenges of intergenerational relationships. TR professionals can play an important role in facilitating opportunities for intergenerational interaction and empowering older adults to maintain strong family bonds, particularly with grandchildren. Leisure education could be the bridge to provide the family to participate in intergenerational experiences that benefit both grandchildren and grandparents, even if they are not engaged in the experience together.

Generativity

Family leisure is also an important context for the development and expression of a third intergenerational construct: generativity. Generativity, as described by Erikson (1963), refers to a psychological construct that reflects the midlife concern for, and care of, future generations as a legacy of the self. Although Erikson conceived of this construct as the central stage of midlife development, more recently, researchers have begun to show the development of generativity across the lifespan (Nimrod & Kleiber, 2007; Pratt, Norris, Hebblethwaite, & Arnold, 2008).

Hebblethwaite and Norris (2011) found that nurturing concern for others was evidenced in the reciprocal care and support that was exchanged among grandparents and adult grandchildren. Both generations exhibit behaviors that exemplify generativity and reflect a strong inclination toward care and nurturing. Grandparents often perceive teaching and mentoring as central features of their role. Leisure activities can afford grandparents the context for teaching their grandchildren about their family histories and often provides a background for the sharing of personal experiences and life lessons. For example, grandparents may take their grandchildren on vacations with the intent of exposing grandchildren to people and places that have been part of the grandparents' history. There may also a notable educational component to these leisure activities. For example, grandparents may use leisure to teach their grandchildren "the value of a dollar" by participating in leisure activities that are relatively inexpensive. As role models, grandparents have been found to teach grandchildren about the intricacies of family relationships and the value of family cohesion. This facilitates an intergenerational transmission of values. Grandchildren may develop ideas of the types of parents and grandparents that they want to be as they age, based on their experiences with their own parents and grandparents. Grandchildren can also be important teachers and help grandparents to learn about changing values and opinions, as well as technological advances such as computers, e-mail, and computer chat rooms. Grandparents tend to appreciate this guidance and often state that they feel that it "helps them stay current" in today's fast-paced society.

Spending regular, concentrated amounts of time together can foster the development of a shared history, common interests, and mutual values between the generations. These leisure experiences can provide an important context for the development of a close emotional bond between the grandparent and grandchild. These experiences can be particularly rewarding if they occur without the involvement of the middle, parental generation. It can allow the grandparents and grandchildren to develop their own relationship identity without the direct influence of the parents.

Although intergenerational family leisure experiences provide the opportunity for affection and cohesion, they are not without their challenges. Grandparents report it to be at times a great deal of work, and they sometimes struggle to maintain the energy that it required of them. Grandchildren often feel constrained by multiple responsibilities to friends, families, school, and work. Overwhelmingly, though, family leisure among grandparents and grandchildren provides grandparents a strong sense of purpose and achievement in shaping the development of the other generation.

Related Research

Intergenerational interaction has repeatedly been shown to have a positive impact on both older and younger individuals and has regularly been reported to dispel negative stereotypes across generations (Dupuis, 2002; Voelkl, 2002). Individuals who participate in intergenerational programs have increased life satisfaction, enhanced self-esteem, and increased knowledge of values, skills, and culture of the other generation (Newman & Larimar, 1995).

Multiple generations can be, with careful planning, incorporated into many common TR interventions.

College students have participated in physical exercise with older adults in order to promote increased physical activity and fitness in older adults (Colston et al., 1996). Inversely, older adults have participated in book discussion groups with college students in preparation for entry into health professions in order to enhance compassion and competence in relating to older adults (Lohman et al., 2005). Intergenerational programming with persons with dementia has been shown to decrease agitation in these individuals throughout the day even after the program itself is finished (Ward, Los Kamp, & Newman, 1996). Participating in leisure activities together fosters more positive attitudes in youth toward older adults and increases positive affect, empathy, and self-confidence. Whether the intervention is reading, baking, music, travel, or exercise, the benefits are felt in all age groups. For example, after participating in an intergenerational program with young children, Goldick-Davis (1995) describes how the older adults went on to write a children's book aimed at dispelling myths and negative stereotypes of older adults.

A further benefit of intergenerational programming is the sense of community that is generated through these experiences. Engaging in leisure activities together enhances a feeling of continuity across the generations and has been shown to impart a sense of citizen responsibility among the participants (Kaplan, 1997). Enhancing intergenerational connections in communities can enhance community capacity and reciprocity. In order to facilitate these outcomes, however, it is essential that the participants are involved in meaningful and valuable roles (Kuehne, 2003). Participants should be actively engaged in all levels of the process, including assessment, planning, implementation, and evaluation. This helps to ensure a person-centered approach that empowers participants to take control over their interactions and their environment.

Application to Therapeutic Recreation

Given our knowledge of the importance of intergenerational relationships, intergenerational programming can be an integral component of TR practice. Leisure plays an important role in facilitating intergenerational relations. This is evident in the common adage "the family that plays together, stays together." Leisure can enhance physical and psychological well-being, life satisfaction, and self-esteem.

Intergenerational leisure, however, is often different from individual leisure. For example, Hebblethwaite (2008), in her study of grandparents and their adult grandchildren, found that grandchildren's leisure often included sports and parties with friends, while grandparents' leisure often consisted of reading and volunteering. Together, grandparents and adult grandchildren usually spent time having meals together, having conversations, or working on household tasks such as gardening and home improvements. They often sacrificed their own personal leisure preferences in order to participate together, eliminating some of the aspect of free choice from the experience. This often resulted in some ambivalence about initiating the event. Unexpectedly, however, this ambivalence tended to abate after the activity when they could articulate unanticipated intrinsic benefits that they gained from the activity. Both grandparents and grandchildren can benefit from the satisfaction that they experience in doing something for someone else and in seeing how much the other person benefits. Ambivalence seems to be minimized when individuals feel that they have learned something from their experience or that they have gained a sense of family history through their leisure experience.

TR, therefore, can play a vital role in the development of intergenerational relationships. Education for families about the nature of intergenerational relations is vital and this education should highlight both the consensual and conflictual aspects of this relationship. Through education, we can help to normalize the experience of ambivalence in intergenerational relationships and decrease the guilt and frustration that often accompanies this ambivalence. Leisure education should involve not only older adults who may be the TR "client," but should also endeavor to include the families of the older adults, both children, grandchildren, and even great-grandchildren. This expands TR beyond the individual and broadens the scope of services to include the family system.

For example, a "Family Model of Care" has been proposed to guide the care that is provided in long-term care facilities (Voelkl, Battisto, Carson, & McGuire, 2004). This model is based on the premise of person-centered care (Kitwood, 1997) which places the person at the center of all care decisions and focuses on the strengths and abilities of the individual, rather than weaknesses and disabilities. The Family Model of Care expands the scope of person-centered care and emphasizes the importance of the inclusion of families in the daily lives of older adults in long-term care. There are three main components of the Family Model of Care: (a) collaborative culture, (b) home-like setting, and (c) meaningful activities. A collaborative culture facilitates involvement of the individual and their family

in all aspects of decision-making and encourages collaboration among the individual, their families, and staff. A home-like setting helps to ensure a sense of belonging and sense of equal ownership among the individual, the family, and the staff. Lastly, meaningful activities are crucial in maintaining continuity in social roles and can help to promote caring and enduring relationships among individuals, family members, and staff (Voelkl et al., 2004). Carson and Dupuis (2008) expand this model to a "Relational Model of Care" where not only families are included, but also other individuals who support the person in coping with his/her disability and promote the continued abilities of persons with disabilities.

While these models have been designed with long-term care facilities in mind, the principles can be applied to any interaction between TR practitioners and the clients and families with whom they interact. Leisure education programs can be designed around these principles and should endeavor to include families and other people in the individual's social network. By educating the clients and their families about the importance of leisure, the availability of leisure resources, and effective ways of communicating, the TR professional can help to facilitate a sense of empathy and appreciation among generations. The opportunity for intergenerational education and interaction can help to foster supportive relationships among clients, their families and friends, and healthcare professionals as well.

Interdisciplinary Approach to Intergenerational Programming

The concepts of family, grandparenting, ambivalence, intergenerational stake, and generativity illustrate the complexities of understanding intergenerational programming. Central to understanding these concepts is placing the person at the center of the discussion, understanding the person's perceptions of how they perceive the role of grandparenting, understanding the grandchild's perceptions and opportunities for engagement due to their lifespan opportunities, and understanding the role of the gate keepers—parents of the grandchildren and children of the grandparents, the sandwich generation—and their lifespan opportunities.

TR professionals do not work in isolation but are often part of interdisciplinary teams that work with social workers, occupational therapists, physical therapists, geriatricians, park planners, and nurses. When working in a multidisciplinary setting, often each discipline has developed terms that reflect that discipline's training and this often leads to a lack of communication (Makrides, Kennedy, & Singleton, 1986).

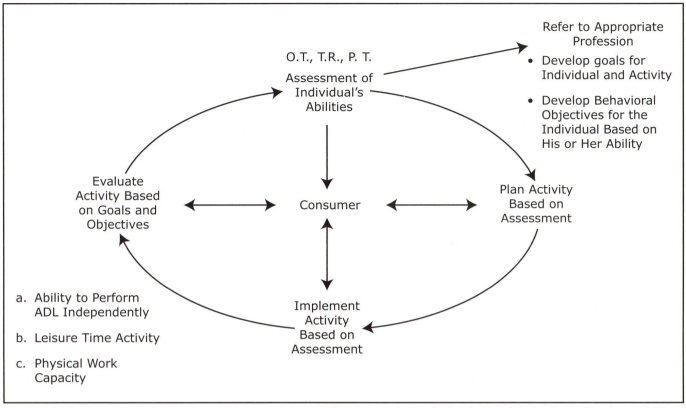

Figure 16.1. Process to Assist Communication among Three Professionals (Makrides, Kennedy, & Singleton, 1986)

To assist in focusing on the person, Makrides et al. (1986, p. 67) developed the following model that focuses on the consumer (the person) to enhance their well-being.

When working on an intergenerational program, the process, from assessment to evaluation, should include the family as part of the input. This model would be applicable for involvement of grandparents, children, and grandchildren to understand what they expect from an intergenerational program. An intergenerational program may not be suitable for some families but may be beneficial to others. Leisure education would provide the opportunity to hear the diverse perspectives and assist in understanding whether or not an inter-generational program would benefit the person and the family. The Family Model of Care, outlined previously, is a useful model to connect the various professions and families in enhancing the well-being of individuals who participate in an intergenerational program.

Conclusion

Intergenerational programming as often been associated with older adults serving children and youth, children and youth serving older adults, and children, youth, and older adults serving together (McCrea & Smith, 1997). This chapter suggests that intergenerational programming can be an important foundation for em-

powering individuals and their families. Using leisure education to build upon these leisure abilities is a key role for the TR practitioner. The Family Model of Care and Person-Centered Care, along with the concepts of family leisure, grandparenting, ambivalence, intergen-erational stake, and generativity, are important frame-works that can guide TR professionals in enhancing leisure abilities for individuals and families alike.

Resources

A Changing Melody: A learning and sharing forum by and for persons with dementia and their friends and families. http://www.marep.uwaterloo.ca/conferences/ Toolkit: http://www.marep.uwaterloo.ca/products/AC-MToolkit.html

Elders Share the Arts: A community arts organization dedicated to linking generations, celebrating diversity, and providing lifelong learning. http://www.elder-ssharethearts.org/main.html

Journal of Intergenerational Relationships: A forum for scholars, practitioners, policy makers, educators, and advocates to stay abreast of the latest intergenera-tional research, practice methods and policy initiatives. Publisher: Routledge.

Linking Lifetimes: A Global View of Intergenerational Exchange (2002). M. Kaplan, N. Henkin, & A. Kusano. University Press of America.

Intergenerational Programmes: An Introduction and Examples of Practice (2006). A. Hatton-Yeo. Centre for Intergenerational Practice. Lloyds TSB Foundations. http://www.centreforip.org.uk

Intergenerational Activities Sourcebook. Penn State University: College of Agricultural Sciences. http://pubs.cas.psu.edu

Example Activities

Life-Story Books. The use of life-story books may be a useful medium to initiate and facilitate intergenerational interaction. These books have been particularly effective with persons with dementia. Often, friends and family members of persons with dementia feel unsure of how to interact with the person because of his/her cognitive abilities. TR professionals can facilitate the development of a life-story book with the person and his/her family and friends. You might use photographs or newspaper clippings to help tell the person's story. Mementos and keepsakes can also be useful and help the person to reminisce about his/her past (e.g., a piece of material from a favorite item of clothing, dried flowers or herbs that were once grown in the person's garden). These types of initiatives can help to emphasize reciprocity between generations, dispel ageist stereotypes, and promote a sense of generativity and psychological well-being across generations.

A Changing Melody. A Changing Melody is a learning and sharing forum designed by and for persons with dementia and their partners in care. This forum was created and sponsored by the Murray Alzheimer Research and Education Program (MAREP), in partnership with the Alzheimer Society of Canada, the Alzheimer Society of Ontario, and the Dementia Advocacy Support Network International. It is a unique opportunity that brings together persons with dementia, family members and friends, professionals, researchers, and students to share their experiences with dementia and participate in an open, creative dialogue. Participants work together to organize the one-day event that aims to educate and support people who are living with dementia. This is an example of an education forum that is not only person-centered but family- and relationship-centered as well. It is not a workshop prepared by "expert" professionals and

researchers, but one that is driven by persons with dementia and their friends and families. The participatory approach empowers persons with dementia and gives them a powerful voice in helping others to learn more about dementia and how to live a meaningful and satisfying life. The forum has helped to "create a new 'face' of dementia, one that includes joy, hope and love, and one based on the perspectives and experiences of those living with dementia" (MAREP, 2008).

References

Allen, K. R., Fine, M. A., & Demo, D. H. (2000). An overview of family diversity: Controversies, questions, and values. In K. Allen, M. Fine, & D. Demo (Eds.) *Handbook of family diversity* (pp. 1–14). New York, NY: Oxford University Press.

Bengtson, V. L., & Silverstein, M. (1993). Families, aging, and social change: Seven agendas for 21st century researchers. In G. Maddox & M. P. Lawton (Eds.), *Kinship, aging, and social change, Vol 13, Annual review of gerontology and geriatrics* (pp. 15–38). New York, NY: Springer.

Bloom, D. E., & Canning, D. (2006). Global demography: Fact, force and future, The WDA-HSG Discussion Paper Series on Demographic Issues, No. 2006/1, World Demographic Association, Retrieved Feb 20, 2007, from: http://www.wdaforum.org/

Brussoni, M. J., & Boon, S. D. (1998). Grandparental impact in young adults' relationships with their closest grandparents: The role of relationship strength and emotional closeness. *International Journal of Aging and Human Development, 46*, 267–286.

Burton, L. M., & Bengtson, V. L. (1985). Black grandmothers: Issues of timing and continuity of roles. In V. L. Bengtson & J. F. Robertson (Eds.), *Grandparenthood* (pp. 61–77). Beverly Hills, CA: Sage.

Carson, J. D., & Dupuis, S. L. (2008, June). Relational care: A truly inclusive vision for the future. Therapeutic Recreation Ontario Annual Conference, Ottawa, ON.

Colston, L., Harper, S., & Mitchener-Colston, W. (1996). Volunteering to promote fitness and caring: A motive for linking college students with mature adults. *Activities, Adaptation and Aging, 20*(1), 79–90.

Cummings, S. M., Williams, M. M., & Ellis, R. A. (2002). Impact of an intergenerational program on 4th graders' attitudes toward elders and school behaviors. *Journal of Human Behavior in the Social Environment, 6*(3), 91–106.

Dupuis, S. L. (2002). Intergenerational education programs in leisure and aging courses: Older adult and student experiences. *Schole: A Journal of Leisure Studies and Recreation Education, 17*, 73–86.

Erikson, E. (1963). *Childhood and society.* (2nd ed.). New York, NY: Norton.

Farkas, J. I., & Hogan, D. P. (1995). The demography of changing intergenerational relationships. In V. L. Bengtson, K. W. Shaie, & L. M. Burton (Eds.), *Adult intergenerational relations: Effects of social change* (pp. 1–29). New York, NY: Springer.

Freysinger, V. J. (1997). Redefining family, redefining leisure: Progress made and challenges ahead in research on leisure and families. *Journal of Leisure Research, 29*(1), 1–4.

Giarrusso, R., & Silverstein, M. (2001). Grandparent-grandchild relationships. In G. L. Maddox (Ed.), *The encyclopedia of aging: A comprehensive resource in gerontology and geriatrics* (3rd ed., pp. 446–447). New York, NY: Springer.

Giarrusso, R., Stallings, M., & Bengtson, V. L. (1995). The "intergenerational stake" hypothesis revisited: Parent-child differences in perceptions of relationships 20 years later. In V. L. Bengtson, K. W. Schaie, & L. M. Burton (Eds.), *Adult intergenerational relations: Effects of societal change* (pp. 227–298). New York, NY: Springer.

Goldick-Davis, N. (1995). When we were young: An intergenerational book project. *Activities, Adaptation, & Aging, 20*(2), 25–31.

Hebblethwaite, S. (2008). *The family that plays together, stays together? Understanding the experience of intergenerational family leisure.* Unpublished doctoral dissertation, University of Guelph, Guelph, Ontario, Canada.

Hebblethwaite, S., & Norris, J. E. (2010). "You don't want to hurt his feelings": Family leisure as a context for intergenerational ambivalence. *Journal of Leisure Research, 42*(3), 489–508.

Hebblethwaite, S., & Norris, J. E. (2011). Expressions of generativity through family leisure: Experiences of grandparents and adult grandchildren. *Family Relations, 60*(1), 121–133.

Hodgson, L. G. (1998). Grandparents and older grandchildren. In M. E. Szinovacz (Ed.), *Handbook on grandparenthood.* (pp. 171–183). Westport, CT: Greenwood Press.

Jarrott, S. E., & Bruno, K. (2007). Shared site intergenerational programs: A case study. *Journal of Applied Gerontology, 26*(3), 239–257.

Kaplan, M. (1997). The benefits of intergenerational community service projects: Implications for promoting intergenerational unity, community activism, and cultural continuity. In K. Brabazon & R. Disch (Eds.), *Intergenerational approaches in aging: Implications for education, policy, and practice* (pp. 211–228). New York, NY: Haworth Press.

Kemp, C. L. (2003). The social and demographic contours of contemporary grandparenthood: Mapping patterns in Canada and the United States. *Journal of Comparative Family Studies, 34*(2), 187–212.

Kitwood, T. (1997). *Dementia reconsidered: The person comes first.* Philadelphia, PA: Oxford University Press.

Kivnick, H. Q. (1982). Grandparenthood: An overview of meaning and mental health. *The Gerontologist, 22*(1), 59–66.

Kuehne, V. S. (2003). The state of our art: Intergenerational program research and evaluation: Part one. *Journal of Intergenerational Relationships, 1*(1), 145–161.

Langford, S. (2008). Why and how to offer intergenerational arts programs. *Journal of Active Aging. March/April*, 45.

Lohman, H., Griffiths, Y., & Coppard, B. M. (2005). Intergenerational connections through book discussion groups. *Journal of Intergenerational Relationships, 3*(1), 27–34.

Luscher, K. (2000). Ambivalence: A key concept for the study of intergenerational relations. In S. Trnka (Ed.), *Family issues between gender and generations* (pp. 11–25). Vienna, Austria: European Communities.

Luscher, K., & Pillemer, K. (1998). Intergenerational ambivalence: A new approach to the study of parent-child relations in later life. *Journal of Marriage and the Family, 60*(2), 413–425.

Makrides, L., Kennedy, M., & Singleton, J. (1986). Role of three professions in long term care. *Activities, Adaptation and Aging, 9*(1), 57–70.

MAREP. (2008). A changing melody: A learning and sharing forum for persons with early-stage dementia and their partners in care. Retrieved January 5, 2008 from: http://www.marep.uwaterloo.ca/conferences/acm.html

McCrea, J. M., & Smith, T. B. (1997). Types and models of intergenerational programs. In S. Newman, R. Ward, T. Smith, J. Wilson, & J. McCrea, *Intergenerational programs: Past, present, and future* (pp. 81–94). Bristol, PA: Taylor & Francis.

Milan, A., & Hamm, B. (2003). Across the generations: Grandparents and grandchildren. *Canadian Social Trends, 77*, 5–7. Ottawa, ON: Statistics Canada. (Cat. No. 11-008).

Neugarten, B. L., & Weinstein, K. K. (1964). The changing American grandparent. *Journal of Marriage and the Family, 26*, 199–204.

Newman, S., & Larimar, B. (1995). *Senior citizen school volunteer program: Report on cumulative data for 1988–1995.* (Publication No. 210). Pittsburgh, PA : University of Pittsburgh, University Center for Social and Urban Research.

Nimrod, G., & Kleiber, D. A. (2007). Reconsidering change and continuity in later life: Toward an innovation theory of successful aging. *International Journal of Aging and Human Development, 65*(1), 1–22.

Norris, J. E., Kuiack, S. L., & Pratt, M. W. (2004). "As long as they go back down the driveway at the end of the day": Stories of the satisfactions and challenges of grandparenthood. In M. W. Pratt & B. H. Fiese (Eds.), *Family stories and the life course* (pp. 353–374). Mahwah, NJ: Lawrence Erlbaum Associates.

Norris, J. E., & Tindale, J. A. (1994). *Among generations: The cycle of adult relationships.* New York, NY: WH Freeman and Company.

Orthner, D. K., & Mancini, J. A. (1990). Leisure impacts on family interaction and cohesion. *Journal of Leisure Research, 22*(1), 125–137.

Pratt, M. W., Norris, J. E., & Hebblethwaite, S., & Arnold, M. L. (2008). Intergenerational transmission of values: Family generativity and adolescents' narratives of parent and grandparent value teaching. *Journal of Personality, 76*(2), 171–198.

Roy, F. H., & Russell, C. (1992). *The encyclopedia of aging and the elderly.* New York, NY: Facts on File.

Saltz, R. (1989). Research evaluation of a foster grandparent program. *Journal of Children in Contemporary Society, 20*, 205–216.

Shaw, S. M. (1992). Dereifying family leisure: An examination of women's and men's everyday experiences and perceptions of family time. *Leisure Sciences, 14*, 271–286.

Shaw, S. M., & Dawson, D. (2003). Contradictory aspects of family leisure: Idealization versus experience. *Leisure/Loisir, 28*(3–4), 179–201.

Silverstein, M., Giarrusso, R., & Bengtson, V. L. (2003). Grandparents and grandchildren in family systems: A social-developmental perspective. In V. L. Bengtson & A. Lowenstein (Eds.), *Global aging and challenges to families.* New York, NY: Aldine de Gruyter.

Smith, P. K., & Drew, L. M. (2002). Grandparenthood. In M. H. Bornstein (Ed.), *Handbook of parenting, Volume 3: Being and becoming a parent* (pp. 141–172). Mahwah, NJ: Lawrence Erlbaum Associates.

Voelkl, J. E. (2002). A service learning program designed to prepare students to meet the needs of older adults with dementia. *Schole: A Journal of Leisure Studies and Recreation Education, 17*, 53–71.

Voelkl, J. E., Battisto, D. G., Carson, J., & McGuire, F. A. (2004). A family model of care: Creating life enriching environments in nursing homes. *World Leisure Journal, 46*(3), 18–29.

Ward, C. R., Los Kamp, L., & Newman, S. (1996). The effects of participation in an intergenerational program on the behavior of residents with dementia. *Activities, Adaptation, and Aging, 20*(4), 61–76.

World Health Organization. (2010). Ageing and life course: News and events. Retrieved on September 1, 2010, from: http://www.who.int/ageing/en/index.html

Wright, P., Owen, M., McGuire, F., & Backman, K. (1994). Entrepreneurial mentorship: An innovative therapeutic approach for at-risk youth and diverse older adults. *Therapeutic Recreation Journal, 28*(4), 183–192.

» CHAPTER 17 »

Stress Management

Norma J. Stumbo, Ph.D., CTRS

Background/History

Stress is pervasive in today's society both as a concept and as a condition. The interest in stress and its effects on health and well-being has mushroomed in the last five or six decades (Crampton, Hodge, Mishra, & Price, 1995; Dickinson et al., 2008; Steinberg & Ritzmann, 1990). Jacobs (2001) and others credit Walter Cannon (1932), a Harvard physiologist, as the first to conduct research on the relationships between stress and physical health. Cannon described the bodily reactions to stress, including "increased sympathetic nervous system arousal, increased central nervous system arousal, and increased skeletal-muscle activity" (Jacobs, 2001, p. S84). Cannon also noted reduced blood flow to the gut and extremities, increased blood flow to the muscles, heart, and lungs, and increased blood sugars during stressful times. How the human body maintains core functions during stress and the psychobiological costs and consequences of these shifting regulatory processes have remained central areas of study for stress researchers (Monroe, 2008).

Perhaps the person who receives the most credit for early research on the stress response is Hans Selye. As a physiologist, Selye (1976) studied the neuroendocrine effects of stress. He is often the first credited with the terms "fight or flight" and "general adaptation syndrome" (Jacobs, 2001).

Selye conceptualized stress and its effects on the body as consisting of three phases that make up the general adaptation syndrome. The first phase is an alarm phase, in which the fight-or-flight response is elicited for mobilization and gearing up for fight or flight. A second phase is called a resistance phase in which the organism fights the stressor, but the acute fight-or-flight response ceases. And then, a third phase, which he termed the exhaustion phase, in which the organism can no longer adapt to the stressor. It is this third phase, the exhaustion phase, that

Selye showed that could result in illness, including shrinkage of thymus, the spleen, and the lymph nodes, also peptic ulcers, and, in some cases, death. (Jacobs, 2001, p. S85)

Seaward (2004) documented that Cannon suggested a fourth phase, when the body returns to homeostasis, or a state of physical calmness. Clearly, in early humanity, the stress response was needed to fight tigers and for mere survival. These physiological responses were crucial to the human's daily existence. However, today, much of our stress is due to technology, crowdedness, working and living conditions, and relationships, yet it all evokes the same physiological conditions as seeing a tiger or a mammoth, often resulting in an overreaction to the circumstance in which we find ourselves. Chronic inducement of the stress response leads to physical, mental, and emotional overload (Seaward):

> Unfortunately, the metabolic and physiological changes that are deemed essential for human movement in the event of attack, pursuit, or challenge are quite ineffective when dealing with events or situations that threaten the ego, such as receiving a parking ticket or standing in a long line at the grocery store, yet the body responds identically to all types of perceived threats. (Seaward, 2004, p. 6)

The human physiology of the stress response has not evolved to the point of being able to distinguish a tiger from a traffic jam.

It should also be noted that Shelley Taylor and colleagues (2000) documented that females respond to stress differently than males, by exhibiting behaviors to "tend-and-befriend" (p. 411) instead of fight or flight. They suggested:

> Females respond to stress by nurturing offspring, exhibiting behaviors that protect them from harm and reduce neuroendocrine responses that

compromise offspring health (the tending patterns), and by befriending, namely, affiliating with social groups to reduce risk. (p. 411)

This set of researchers noted that while the basic neuroendocrine responses are identical in males and females, a fighting or fleeing response from a female would counteract the maternal instinct to protect offspring. In other words, should the mother choose to fight or flee, her offspring would be left unprotected and vulnerable. Thus, she is more likely to "tend" than fight or leave. In addition, they also noted that females tend to develop and depend on social groups ("befriend"), mobilizing social support as needed to counteract stressful events.

Holmes and Rahe are also considered pioneers in stress concepts. These individuals studied the effects of daily stressful life events on the body as well as their effect on overall morbidity and mortality (Rahe, Meyer, Smith, Kjaer, & Holmes, 1964). They designed the *Social Readjustment Rating Scale* (Holmes & Rahe, 1967) that assigned a numeric ranking to a listing of various life events (such as death of a loved one, job change, and moving) that individuals considered stressful. Their research noted that there are consistent, measurable consequences to life stressors (Jacobs, 2001). They advanced the notion that while stress can be from an either positive or negative source, the body reacts to both kinds of stress in the same physiological ways. The distinction between being a positive or a negative event depends on the individual's perception and interpretation; however the physical reaction remains much the same to events at either end of the spectrum. Many authors have noted that some stress can be encouraging and motivational; too much stress, especially over a long period, often means being overwhelmed, which leads to burnout and/or illness (Crampton et al., 1995).

Another significant investigator was Richard Lazarus, who started studying stress in the 1950s and later proposed that the accumulation of multiple acute stressors, such as throwing away an important document, ruining a favorite item of clothing, or losing a library book, are as likely to affect one's health as more chronic, high-impact stressors. These "hassles" are the frequent, negative interactions with the environment that happen to everyone and can have a long-lasting and deleterious effect on health and well-being (Lazarus, 1985, 1990, 1992, 1993).

One of the more recent pioneers in stress research is Herbert Benson. In the 1970s, Benson, Beary, and Carol (1974) proposed that meditation, as a technique to calm the mind and reverse the stress response,

stimulates the parasympathetic nervous system and promotes restoration of homeostasis or a reduction of the fight-or-flight stress response. He later expanded on this and included a number of mind-body techniques such as biofeedback, meditation, progressive muscle relaxation, autogenic training, tai chi, qigong, yoga, and other techniques.

Benson coined the term "relaxation response" to describe the effects of these techniques that physiologically counterbalance the stress response. The relaxation response is accompanied by reduced stress hormones and reduced central nervous system activity. Consistent elicitation of the relaxation response reverses the physiological measures of stress and has been shown to positively affect musculoskeletal, gastrointestinal, and cardiovascular disorders. This intense and long-standing interest has led to the development of "mind-body medicine"—the notion that thoughts and emotions directly affect health (Jacobs, 2001).

Yu, Chiu, Lin, Wang, and Chen (2007) conducted a meta-analytic path analysis to determine the theoretical linkages between stress and health. Many of their findings are presented later in this chapter. Here it is important to note that they found clear, compelling evidence of linkage between stress-coping strategies and health.

> A person's subjective feeling of stress or threat caused by external events has a much stronger influence on one's health than the event per se . . . subjective stress was an indispensable mediator factor for linking objective stress and health . . . in other words, the impact of events, even major life events, on one's health will be minute if one does not subjectively consider the event a threat or stress factor. (p. 208)

The shorthand version of this is: "It is not so much what happens to the person as his or her reaction to it." From this perspective, being able to induce the relaxation response mentally is essential for good physical health, both as a preventative and curative therapy. Jacobs asked, "The question is not whether mind-body interactions are real, but rather, can the relaxation response and mind-body interactions be used to affect health outcomes?" (2001, p. S91). The answer appears to be a resounding "yes."

Organization of This Chapter

The intent of this chapter is to provide the reader with a basic overview of stress reduction and stress management techniques. Because this chapter covers such a broad array of techniques, the format has been slightly modified from others in this text. After a review of basic related definitions and foundational premises, a variety of stress-management techniques will be discussed. In each sub-section addressing a specific technique, a description of the technique and how it is applied to clients will be followed by research summaries of the effectiveness of the technique with selected client groups. The reader is alerted that some techniques, such as assertiveness, problem solving, physical activity, and cognitive restructuring are included as individual chapters elsewhere in this text and will not be covered in this chapter. Although many stress-management techniques are used in tandem or simultaneously, they are discussed here individually for the sake of organization and clarity. Literally thousands of resources, such as books, CDs, videotapes, and websites are available for most of these stress-management techniques. Like other techniques in this book, readers are encouraged to seek the additional resources for more in-depth study of specific techniques. We have chosen a wide range of techniques that are resource-rich, easy to learn and implement, and cost-effective. They all produce valuable psychological and physiological outcomes and have a solid base of supportive evidence. The topics covered in this chapter include:

- expressive writing
- guided imagery
- progressive muscle relaxation
- biofeedback

First, related definitions and the basic premises of stress management will be covered. Within each section addressing specific techniques, current supportive research, from other fields and from therapeutic recreation when possible, will be presented.

Related Definitions

Stress: According to Selye, stress is the nonspecific response of the body to any demands made upon it (Crampton et al., 1995). Monroe (2008) added that stress is the accumulaton of successive transactions between a person and his/her environment over a period of time; stress is influenced by external challenges and perceptions of the challenges, coping resources and perceptions of coping resources, and the dynamic interplay between the variables over time.

Stressor: Any thing—idea, action, situation, person, etc.—that causes or promotes stress (Seaward, 2004).

Stress management: The ability to emotionally, cognitively, and physically counteract the effects of stressors before, during, or after they occur; may include techniques such as time management, anger management, goal setting and prioritization, meditation, tai chi, exercise, expressive writing, and the like.

Mind-body medicine: The effects of thoughts, emotions, expectations, and beliefs on one's health (Jacobs, 2001).

Distress: Bad or harmful stress that the person finds disturbing, such as a job layoff, a tax audit, or having dental work (Seaward, 2004).

Eustress: Good stress that the person finds enjoyable, motivating, or inspiring, not being considered a threat by the individual (Seaward, 2004).

Neustress: Stimuli that have no consequence to the individual, such an earthquake in a remote country unknown to the person (Seaward, 2004).

Acute stress: Quickly surfacing and quickly disappearing stress, such as a near-accident in a vehicle (Seaward, 2004).

Chronic stress: Stimuli that linger for a prolonged period of time—days, weeks, months, years—such as commuting in heavy traffic, taking care of a loved one, and experiencing a toxic work situation (Seaward, 2004).

Homeostasis: The regulation of a limited number of vital physiological systems that need to remain relatively constant (for example, body temperature or blood pressure).

Allostasis: The process of achieving homeostatis; that is, how the person's system returns to a stable condition (homeostasis) after significant change (Monroe, 2008).

Allostatic load: The "consequences of sustained activation of primary regulatory systems serving allostasis over time, to the cumulative burden on bodily systems (i.e., wear and tear) that is believed to contribute to disorder and disease" (Monroe, 2008, p. 36). Reactions of bodily systems activated by the stress response may be adaptive in the short-term but maladaptive or destructive in the short term.

Resilience: The capacity to make early, frequent, and effective adjustments to the stressor that return the person to homeostasis. "Protective factors" such as strong personal relationships, coping skills, and flexibility improve an individual's resilience to stress (Steinberg & Ritzmann, 1990).

Problem-focused strategies: Directly address the problem causing the stress, by seeking out information, making a plan, and working through the steps to manage or resolve the conflict (Littleton, Horsley, John, & Nelson, 2007).

Emotion-focused strategies: Focus on dealing with emotional distress, by disengaging from emotions, seeking emotional support, and venting (Littleton et al., 2007).

Approach strategies: Tackling the problem, such as seeking emotional support, making plans for resolution, and seeking information (Littleton et al., 2007)

Avoidance strategies: Avoiding the problem or one's reaction to it, such as withdrawal, denial, or disengagement.

Basic Premises

The human body reacts to events perceived as stressful through a wide range of adaptive responses, "from the molecular through the molar, from gene expression through social interaction" (Monroe, 2008, p. 34). This process is dynamic, interactive, and constantly ongoing. Considerations need to be given to the organism (the person), the environment, and to the passage of time. As such, human stress is studied by researchers in diverse sciences such as neuroscience, biology, psychology, epidemiology, sociology, and anthropology (Steinberg & Ritzmann, 1990). While multiple perspectives contribute to the fullness of understanding the stress phenomena, they also mean that there exist multiple theories, definitions, and explanations of the stress.

It has been estimated that stress is related to 70–80% of all diseases and illness experienced in America, including coronary heart disease, gastrointestinal disorders, asthma, diabetes, multiple sclerosis, cancer, the common cold, migraine headaches, warts, some instances of female infertility, ulcers, insomnia, hypertension, irritable bowel syndrome, and on and on (Crampton et al., 1995; Seaward, 2004). In addition, psychological difficulties such as anxiety, depression, maladaptive behavior patterns, chemical dependencies, and the like are also related to stress (Crampton et al., 1995). Often, those diseases or disorders related to stress are called "lifestyle diseases," those in which the pathology develops over a prolonged period of several years based on the actions and choices made by the individual and/or society as a whole (Seaward, 2004). For example, obesity often is seen as a stress-related lifestyle disease—one of too much food, usually of the wrong kinds, and too little physical activity.

According to Giradano, Everly, and Dusek (2000, cited in Seaward, 2004), there are three major categories of stressors: (a) bioecological, (b) psychointrapersonal, and (c) social. Bioecological stressors are those such as gravitational pull, solar flares, sunlight, and electromagnetic fields that affect an individual's biological rhythms. A health example is seasonal affective disorder (SAD), which results from people being deprived of sunlight for long periods of time. Psychointrapersonal stressors represent a large majority of everyday stressors that an individual creates through

his or her thoughts, emotions, and perceptions. The adage mentioned earlier, "It is not so much what happens to the person as his or her reaction to it" fits nicely here. Psychointrapersonal stressors are unique to the individual, based on the person's personality, social history, beliefs, values, desires, and intentions. While they are the most prevalent, they are, with practice, the most controllable of the three categories of stressors. The third category of stressors is social influences, which include overcrowding, traffic jams, financial insecurity, and violations of human rights.

As mentioned earlier, there are believed to be four major phases of stress: (a) alarm reaction, (b) stage of resistance, (c), stage of exhaustion, and (d) return to calmness/homeostasis. The purpose of stress management is to help the individual prevent stress (perhaps by taking action before an event occurs), perceive it differently (viewing it as a non-stressor or as minimally stressful), or manage it after it occurs and return to homeostasis before physical and psychological damage sets in.

A number of investigators have conducted research that summarizes individual studies. By using methods such as meta-analysis and path analysis, they can effectively combine the results of smaller studies and attach larger meanings. The following represent some of these larger studies.

Littleton et al. (2007) conducted a meta-analysis of 39 studies that focused on the stress management strategies used to cope with either interpersonal violence or severe injury. They reported the following findings that have clear implications for stress-management training programs:

- Reliance on avoidance coping was maladaptive for all types of distress.
- People who use ineffective strategies tend to keep using them over time.
- People who use problem-solving behaviors experience slightly less distress than those who use cognitive/emotional coping strategies.
- People may have to "cycle" through approach strategies several times before the stressor is resolved or its effects are reduced.

Yu and colleagues (2007) completed a path analysis on 477 studies relating to eight stress-moderating variables published in Taiwanese literature. An important variable in their study was the use of problem-based versus emotion-based coping strategies. Problem-based strategies focus on reducing the demands of stressors or expanding resources to deal with them, while emotion-focused strategies include regulating or controlling the person's emotional response to stress. Yu and colleagues reported the following results:

- Subjective stress (that which is interpreted by the individual as stressful) has a significant and direct influence on health.
- A person's subjective feelings of stress or threat caused by external events have a much stronger influence on one's health than the event itself.
- Major life events are not harmful to one's health unless the person interprets the events as stressful.
- An individual can adjust his or her interpretation of a stressful event and that will in turn diminish the impact it has on the person's health.
- Objective stress requires the presence of subjective stress to impact health.
- High levels of perceived subjective stress result in emotion-based (versus problem-based) coping strategies that in turn result in poorer health outcomes (that is, using emotions such as anger or nervousness for coping negatively impacts health).
- Greater social support makes it easier for the individual to use coping strategies, and those who do enjoy greater social support tend to use problem-based instead of emotion-based strategies.
- People with an internal locus of control tend to be optimistic and remain healthy; the reverse is true for individuals with an external locus of control.
- The Type A personality (hard-driving, results-based) has no effect on health.
- Those with Type A personalities tend to use emotion-focused strategies.
- People with greater self-efficacy and those with high sense of internal control tend to use problem-focused strategies.

The study by Yu and colleagues (2007) suggests that health care professionals:

- Make stress management a priority program for clients
- Teach clients the importance of preventing stress and managing reactions to stress
- Teach clients problem-focused stress-management techniques
- Help clients develop great social support networks, an internal locus of control, and greater self-efficacy

Persson, Veenhuizen, Zachrison, and Gard (2008) performed a systematic review on 12 randomized, controlled trials and found that progressive muscle relaxation was the most widely used relaxation technique. They concluded that relaxation training lowered pain intensity, anxiety, depression, fatigue (in fibromyalgia), decreased need for medication and the need for health care, and improved mobility, balance, coordination, and productive use of coping strategies.

Crampton and colleagues (1995) conducted a study of stressors and stress-management techniques in the workplace in Western Michigan. Within their sample of 164 businesses, they noted the most outwardly (overt) signs of stress among employees were physical illness, attitude or appearance changes, aggression, declining performance, and poor attendance. Covert signs included insomnia, depression, social withdrawal, drug/alcohol abuse, and psychosomatic illnesses. Respondents (mostly managers) felt the following were appropriate stress management techniques: developing healthy attitudes, proper nutrition, exercise, relaxing/sleeping or taking a break, building a strong family life, meeting the challenge head-on, setting limits/goals/priorities, and increasing personal qualifications/skills. The authors noted several recommendations for workplace stress management programs. These included:

(a) Identifying major stressors in the workplace and in employees' personal lives, as well as whether they can be controlled by the person
(b) Developing individualized stress-management programs with employees and setting specific and realistic goals
(c) Teaching stress-management techniques such as relaxation, meditation, developing support systems, engaging in hobbies, time management, and improving nutrition and exercise.

The purpose of any stress-management or stress-reduction technique is to (a) find out the appropriate level of stress that allows for optimal performance and enjoyment and (b) reduce physical-arousal levels using both mental-coping skills and physical-relaxation techniques (Seaward, 2004). Spence, Barnett, Linden, Ramsden, and Taenzer (1999) noted that stress-management techniques are more effective when used in combination, rather than individually.

The next section covers a selection of stress-management techniques. Again, we have chosen a wide range of techniques that are resource-rich, easy to learn and implement, and cost-effective. In addition, they produce valuable psychological and physiological outcomes, and have a solid base of supportive evidence.

Specific Stress-Management Techniques

Mind-body interventions are emerging in response to a growing awareness that individuals can take more control of their health (Grossman, Niemann, Schmidt, & Walach, 2004). Mind-body interventions constitute a major portion of the public's overall interest in complementary and alternative medicine (CAM); (Bertisch, Wee, Phillips, & McCarthy, 2009). CAM is a group of diverse medical and health care systems, practices, and products that are not generally considered part of conventional medicine (Ernst, Schmidt, & Baum, 2006; Kemper, Vohra, & Walls, 2008; Lin, Lee, Kemper, & Berde, 2005; Rheingans, 2007). Kemper et al. noted that the dividing line between CAM and traditional medicine is becoming blurred as more non-traditional approaches enter the mainstream. In 2002, mind-body techniques, including relaxation, meditation, guided imagery, biofeedback, and hypnosis, were used by approximately 17% of the adult U.S. population (Barnes, Powell-Griner, McFann, & Nahin, 2002). In fact Kemper et al. suggested that "CAM" as a term, is being replaced by "integrative" or "holistic" medicine, which encompasses both worlds.

This makes sense, since some studies have shown that non-traditional techniques, such as relaxation, do in fact receive favorable patient-ratings for reduction of depressive symptoms, especially for those who are not using medication (Jorm, Morgan, & Hetrick, 2008). However, those who are on medication also get greater symptom relief by adding relaxation.

Kemper et al. (2008) provided clarification of the crossroads between CAM and traditional medicine in the form of a table, which is included here as Table 17.1.

In the most recent study available, Bertisch et al. (2009) used the 2002 National Health Interview Survey Alternative Medicine Supplement and discovered:

- Mind-body therapies are most used by individuals with various musculoskeletal pain syndromes (such as fibromyalgia) and those with anxiety/depression.
- More than 50% of those who use mind-body therapies use them in conjunction with other medical care.
- Twenty percent of mind-body therapy users thought conventional medicine would not help their conditions.

In a recent study by Ananth and Martin (2006), hospitals that offer CAM ranked guided imagery as fourth among other CAM therapies that are provided in inpatient settings. As reported in the *CAM at the NIH: Focus on Complementary and Alternative Medicine* newsletter, guided imagery was outranked only by massage therapy, art/music therapy, and therapeutic touch for inpatients, and by massage, tai chi/yoga/qigong, relaxation training, and acupuncture for outpatients ("*Growing Number*," 2006).

Clinical trials indicate that these interventions may be a particularly effective adjunct in the management of arthritis, with reductions in pain maintained for up to four years and reductions in the number of physician visits (Luskin, Newell, & Griffith, 2000). When applied to more general acute and chronic pain management, headache, and low-back pain, mind-body interventions show some evidence of effects, although results vary based on the patient population and type of intervention studied (Astin, Shapiro, Eisenberg, & Forys, 2003).

The next section addresses four specific stress management techniques: (a) expressive writing, (b) guided imagery, (c) progressive muscle relaxation, and (d) biofeedback. Each section includes basic and historical information, implementation techniques, and supportive research. When available, specific research applicable from therapeutic recreation practice is cited. Each section also contains a sampling of available resources concerning that technique.

Expressive Writing

Expressive writing, or journaling, is a method of self-exploration and personal development, which can be therapeutic and healing when coached by health professionals (Seaward, 2004). It is defined as "a series of written passages that document personal events,

Table 17.1. The Kemper Model of Holistic Care (Kemper et al., 2008, p. 1377)

Component	Example
Biochemical	Medications, dietary supplements, vitamins, minerals, herbal remedies
Lifestyle	Nutrition; exercise/rest; environmental therapies such as heat, ice, music, vibration, and light; mind-body therapies (behavior management, meditation, hypnosis, biofeedback, counseling)
Bio-mechanical	Massage and bodywork, chiropractic and osteopathic adjustments, surgery
Bioenergetic	Acupuncture, radiation therapy, magnets, Reiki, healing touch, qigong, therapeutic touch, prayer, homeopathy

thoughts, feelings, memories, and perceptions in one's journey throughout life" (p. 216) and "writing done to explore one's innermost thoughts and feelings" (Horowitz, 2008, p. 194). Expressive writing potentially leads to personal insights, increases the person's ability to cope with stressors, and improves health. Expressive writing has also been called "experimental disclosure" (Frattaroli, 2006) and "written emotional disclosure" (Frisina, Borod, & Lepore, 2004; Soper & Von Bergen, 2001; Weinman, Ebrecht, Scott, Walburn, & Dyson, 2008). Soper and Von Bergen noted that individuals with cognitive impairments, severe depression, or post-traumatic stress disorder (PTSD), or recently bereaved, older adults do not benefit from expressive writing without additional therapies. A study by Bugg, Turpin, Mason, and Scholes (2009) reaffirmed the lack of positive effects for individuals at risk for developing PTSD.

Pennebaker was among the first to recognize the beneficial aspects of "putting stress into words," nearly three decades ago (Pennebaker, 1989, 1993; Pennebaker & Beall, 1986; Pennebaker, Colder, & Sharp, 1990; Pennebaker & Harber, 1993; Pennebaker, Mayne, & Francis, 1997). He is widely credited for creating and continuously researching the effects of emotional disclosure over the last 30 years.

A number of benefits of expressive writing have been discussed in the literature. Frattaroli (2006) noted:

It is believed disclosing information may allow people to free their mind of unwanted thoughts, help them make sense of upsetting events, teach them to better regulate their emotions, habituate them to negative emotions, and improve their connections with their social world, all of which can lead to beneficial effects on health and well-being. (p. 823)

These benefits can be categorized and summarized to include (a) disinhibition, (b) confrontation, (c) translation of experiences into meaningful language, (d) cost-effectiveness, (e) emotional expression without social expectations, and (f) robustness of treatment. See Table 17.2.

"Disinhibition" denotes the opposite of inhibition, the "failure to acknowledge, understand, and emotionally grasp stressors" (Soper & Von Bergen, 2001, p. 151). For example, persons who are depressed often try to actively suppress and inhibit dysfunctional negative thoughts in order to control their mood and prevent relapse into depression (Gortner, Rude, & Pennebaker, 2006). Expressive writing allows for disinhibition,

the process of addressing stressful events and coming to an acceptable resolution. Expressing emotions is important to health, and writing is a significant outlet (Frisina et al., 2004).

Confrontation is facilitated by focusing on negative or threatening events so that further avoidance and negative repetitive thoughts are minimized. "Confrontation allows people to change their original appraisals of negative events into more benign evaluations. Events are reconstructed as being more meaningful and more controllable" (Soper & Von Bergen, 2001, p. 151).

Soper and Von Bergen posited that both cognitions (thoughts) and emotions are necessary for stress-coping to occur.

Writing is useful in encouraging the cognitive processing necessary to make the expression of emotion therapeutic. Thus the mere expression of trauma is not enough to bring about long-term positive change. Gains seem to require the translation of experiences into organized, meaningful language. (2001, p. 152)

In other words, emotional expression is necessary but more work is required for expressive writing to become therapeutic. The individual must work to assimilate the stressful event(s) into a working cognitive framework, which in turn, produces positive affective and physiological changes. Soper and Von Bergen do warn, however, that expressive writing does evoke short-term anxiety and stress; yet in the long-term improves mental and physical health.

Cost-effectiveness is another benefit of expressive writing (Frisina et al., 2004). In fact, Burton and King (2008) found that even two-minute writings over a two-day period (for a total of four minutes) produced similar results to longer sessions in terms of emotional content of the writing, the benefits expressed by the participants, and fewer health complaints at follow-up for a healthy sample.

Being able to express emotions and work through them, without the necessary social requirements of

---

Table 17.2. Evidence-Based Benefits of Expressive Writing

- Disinhibition
- Confrontation
- Translation of Experiences into Meaningful Language
- Cost-Effectiveness
- Emotional Expression with Social Expectations
- Robustness of Treatment

more traditional "talk" therapy, is also seen as another benefit (Frisina et al., 2004). However, Harrist, Carlozzi, McGovern, and Harrist (2007) found that writing as therapy was less effective than talking therapy.

Soper and Von Bergen (2001), in their literature review of expressive writing after the loss of a job, discussed several factors that impact its effectiveness and provided several helpful guidelines for expressive-writing interventions. The influencing factors included:

- Men, who are generally less emotionally expressive than women, seemed to benefit more from expressive writing.
- Individuals who have alexythimia, a dispositional deficit in the cognitive processing and regulation of emotion, showed greater improvements in well-being after expressive writing.
- High-hostile individuals benefited to a greater extent than low-hostile ones.
- Individuals from different cultures and different countries benefit from expressive writing.

They also offered several insights into designing expressive-writing interventions. They cited literature that supported the following:

- The length of individual sessions (whether three minutes or an hour) does not seem make a difference, but overall greater length of time (over a month instead of a day) does.
- Writing about specific, current traumatic events (such as hospitalization) is more beneficial than writing about general or past traumatic events.
- Writing and talking therapies produce similar long-term biological, mood, and cognitive effects, although writing produces more immediate, short-term effects.
- Assigning writing as homework (instead of being contained in a session) is appropriate if the clients are not likely to elicit strong and intense emotions while writing (such as individuals who recently underwent extreme trauma). In the latter cases, a professional may need to be present to process strong and volatile emotions.
- It is typical to ask clients to write once or twice a week for 15 to 20 minutes at a time, ideally for a minimum of three to four weeks. Clients should be asked to write about their most intense thoughts and feelings concerning a recent event and how they affect their daily life. Spelling, grammar, writing style, handwriting, and the like are not of concern. Clients are allowed to share

their writing with the professional to the degree they feel comfortable. Clients are informed ahead of time that everything will be kept confidential to the limits of professional ethics (such as in the case of self- or other-harm).

Further, Horowitz (2008) gleaned a number of suggestions from Pennebaker's website (see resource section of this chapter), and these are located in Table 17.3.

A number of behavioral scientists have studied the effects of expressive writing through meta-analyses and/or systematic reviews. Smyth (1998) conducted one of the first meta-analyses on expressive writing. He found that "written emotional expression produces significant health benefits in healthy participants" with a 23% improvement over control participants (p. 179). He suggested that the size of this effect was similar to that accomplished by other psychological interventions. He noted that the largest increases were seen in psychological well-being and physiological functioning, followed by health, and then general functioning outcomes. Expressive writing was found to be most beneficial for college students (versus older participants), for males, over greater lengths of time, and when focused on current trauma (versus any trauma).

Frisina et al. (2004) conducted a meta-analysis of nine expressive writing studies on health outcomes with clinical populations (psychiatric or physically ill populations). They found that expressive writing does have a positive effect on health, as was true for individuals with minor difficulties (asthma) and major problems (renal cancer). They found positive effects for people with mild depression and similar disorders,

Table 17.3. Practical Guidelines for Expressive Writing (Horowitz, 2008, p. 196)

Advise patients to:
- Find a place and time when you will not be disturbed
- Write about what you are worrying about or what you have been avoiding thinking about that is affecting your life in an unhealthy way
- Write for a minimum of 15 minutes a day for at least three or four consecutive days
- Write continuously without worrying about proper language or censoring content
- Talk into a recording device if that is easier for you than writing or typing
- Decide whether to write about the same issue each time or different issues
- Consider reviewing what you've written over time and see how your thinking or emotions have changed
- Choose whether to save or destroy your writings

but this was less than for people with physical illnesses. They also reported that expressive writing, with its intent of facilitating cognitive processing of traumatically-charged emotional events, was less impactful on people with severe depression or people with post-traumatic stress disorder.

> Although the results of the present meta-analysis revealed that expressive writing in clinical populations did not produce the same robust improvements on health as it did in healthy people (Smyth, 1998), it can be concluded from this article that expressive writing's therapeutic effect was established. (p. 632)

Studies on the positive effect of expressive writing on individual populations have also produced impressive results. These include psychological and/or physiological improvements, for example, for individuals with a diverse range of conditions such as HIV (Petrie, Fontanilla, Thomas, Booth, & Pennebaker, 2004), wounds (Weinman et al., 2008), cancer, rheumatoid arthritis, and asthma (Horowitz, 2008). Again, studies concerning individuals at risk for developing PTSD showed that expressive writing was not effective in reducing psychological and/or physical markers. Weinman et al. (2008) and Frattaroli (2006) reported that expressive writing is more effective with physiological difficulties centering on the immune system (e.g., wound healing and HIV) than other bodily functions, however, the exact mechanism of impact is not known. In one of the most recent additions to the literature, Dalton and Glenwick (2009) added that writings do not need to focus on past events; writing on upcoming events also produces positive effects.

Frattaroli (2006) updated and expanded on Smyth's earlier work by using more stringent search strategies. She performed a meta-analysis on 146 studies on expressive writing with the general population and concluded that expressive writing produced robust and favorable outcomes. A number of her suggestions for structuring interventions that are applicable to therapeutic recreation practice are included in Table 17.4.

She concluded that expressive writing (experimental disclosure) is beneficial to one's psychological health, physical health, and overall functioning. She reiterated that the guidelines found on Table 17.4 are a productive introduction to implementing this accessible, inexpensive, simple, and helpful intervention in the most effective manner possible. We were unable to locate research related to the use of expressive writing in therapeutic recreation.

Expressive Writing Resources

J. W. Pennebaker's academic homepage
http://homepage.psy.utexas.edu/homepage/faculty/pennebaker/home2000/jwphome.htm

Pennebaker, J. W. (2004). *Writing to heal: A guided journal for recovering from trauma and emotional upheaval*. Oakland, CA: New Harbinger.

Pennebaker, J. W. (1997). *Opening up: The healing power of expressing emotions*. New York, NY: Guilford.

Bolton, G., & Lago, C. (2004). *Writing cures: An introductory handbook of writing in counseling and psychotherapy* (1st ed.). London, UK: Taylor & Francis.

Bray, S. (2006). *When words heal: Writing through cancer*. Berkeley, CA: North Atlantic Books.

Lepore, S. J., & Smyth, J. M. (2002). *The writing cure: How expressive writing promotes health and emotional well-being*. Washington, DC: American Psychological Association.

Seaward, B. L. (2004). *Managing stress: Principles and strategies for health and wellbeing*. Boston, MA: Jones and Bartlett.

Table 17.4. Factors that Improve the Impact of Expressive Writing

Expressive writing tends to produce more favorable outcomes when it includes:
- Participants with physical health problems
- Participants with a history of trauma or stressors
- Participants disclosing at home
- Participants disclosing in a private setting
- Male participants
- Fewer participants
- Follow-ups of less than one month
- At least three disclosure sessions
- Sessions of at least 15 minutes in length
- Directed questions or specific examples of what to disclose
- Instructions to write about previously undisclosed topics
- Instructions about whether to switch topics
- Not collecting the written works

Conversely, the following were found to not impact outcomes:
- Psychological health of participants
- Participant age, ethnicity, or education level
- Warning clients they might disclose traumatic events
- Spacing of sessions
- Valence of discussion topic
- Focus of disclosure instructions
- Time reference of disclosure instructions
- Mode of disclosure (handwriting, typing, talking)

Guided Imagery

Guided imagery—also called mental imagery or visualization (Seaward, 2004)—is the use of deliberate, purposeful, and directed daydreaming or triggering of the imagination, through words and phrases designed to evoke rich, multisensory fantasy and memory (Menzies, Taylor, & Bourguignon, 2006; Mobily, Herr, & Kelley, 1993; Roffe, Schmidt, & Ernst, 2005; Trakhtenberg, 2008; Van Kuiken, 2004). It is used to create a deeply immersive, receptive mind-state as a catalyst for desired change (Naparstek, 2004). Guided imagery, either self- or other-guided, is often used for pain control and provides a sense of self-control as well as distraction (Halpin, Speir, CapoBianco, & Barnett, 2002; Mobily et al., 1993; Rheingans, 2007).

"The skill of visualization involves the creation of images, scenes, or impressions by engaging one's imagination of the body's physical senses of sight, sound, feel, smell, and even taste, for an overall pleasurable desired effect" (Seaward, 2004, p. 381). Guided imagery and visualization are used to narrow one's focus, especially away from stressors, and replace threatening stimuli with pleasurable, imagined ones. Seaward (2004) and Roffe et al. (2005) noted that guided imagery aims to produce a calming, if not healing, effect, opening the individual to being more receptive to treatment and facilitating the process of recovery.

Van Kuiken (2004) noted four types of guided imagery: (a) pleasant imagery, (b) physiologically focused imagery, (c) mental rehearsal or reframing, and (d) receptive imagery. She explained that pleasant imagery involves invoking quiet, calm environments, while physiological imagery focuses on the functions of healing, such as visualizing cancer cells being eaten by a strong force. Mental rehearsal or reframing is imagining a task while in a calm state (giving a speech in front of a mirror) before performing the same task under more stressful circumstances (in front of a crowd). Receptive imagery involves scanning of the body as a diagnostic or reflective exercise.

Davis, Eshelman, and McKay (2000) provided practical advice on using guided imagery for stress management. They listed five steps to effective visualization, as shown on Table 17.5.

For most people, imagery is an easy, low-tech, user-friendly form of meditation that yields immediately felt results. Even better for individuals who are interested in healthcare outcomes, these "felt" results are supported by numerous investigations in behavioral sciences as well as neurosciences. See Table 17.6.

Guided imagery has been used increasingly by healthcare providers in the medical field with impressive results (Ernst, Schmidt, & Baum, 2006; Halpin et al., 2002; Herman, Craig, & Caspi, 2005; Kemper, Vohra, & Walls, 2008; Mobily et al., 1993; Morone & Greco, 2007; Roffe et al., 2005; Utay & Miller, 2007). Neurobiologists have studied guided imagery and found positive physiological impacts of guided imagery on the human immune system; for example, they have recorded changes in white blood cell counts (Donaldson, 2000; Trakhtenberg, 2008).

Researchers have also found guided imagery improves reduction of psychological perceptions of pain for those with chronic pain complaints (Luedtke et al., 2005; Mobily et al., 1993). Positive pain-reduction effects have been found with people coping with cancer (Ernst et al., 2006; Roffe et al., 2005), and also for patients who have a wide range of other medical concerns such as fibromyalgia (Fors, Sexton, & Götestam, 2002; Luedtke et al., 2005; Menzies et al., 2006), life-threatening childhood illnesses (Lin et al., 2005), cardiac disease (Herman et al., 2005), and chronic pain, for example in older adults (Morone & Greco, 2007; Schofield & Reid, 2006). Guided imagery has been found to reduce abdominal pain (Weydert et al., 2006), chronic pain (Baird & Sands, 2004), post-operative pain (Huth, Broome, & Good, 2004), cancer pain (Syrjala, Donaldson, Davis, Kippes, & Carr, 1995) and burn pain (Fratianne et al., 2001).

Imagery as a clinical intervention also has been associated with improved mood and reduced symptoms

Table 17.5. Rules of Effective Visualization (Davis et al., 2000)

1. Loosen clothing, lie down in quiet place, and close eyes gently.
2. Scan your body, seeking tension in specific muscles. Relax those muscles as much as possible.
3. Create mental pictures involving all of your senses: sight, hearing, smell, touch, and taste.
4. Use affirmations (short, positive, repetitive statements) such as "I am letting go of stress," "I am filled with peace," or "I am in harmony with the universe."
5. Use visualization three times a day.

Table 17.6. Evidence-Based Benefits of Guided Imagery

• Positive impact on immune functioning • Reduced perceptions of pain • Improved mood • Reduced symptoms of anxiety and depression • Reduced inpatient lengths of stay, reduced need for medication, high patient satisfaction • Increasing acceptance by consumers

of anxiety and depression (Austin, 2009; Dattilo, 2000; Mobily et al., 1993). The implications for guided imagery as a valuable mind-body tool for reducing pain and stress are widely acknowledged (Bertisch et al., 2009; Halpin et al., 2002; Menzies et al., 2006; Mobily et al., 1993). For example, Halpin et al. found that guided imagery with 134 cardiac patients undergoing surgery resulted in shorter lengths of stay, less direct pharmacy costs, less direct pain medication costs, and higher overall patient satisfaction compared to those in the control group. Guided imagery is now considered a vital part of cardiac care in that facility.

Similarly, Frenkel, Arye, Carlson, and Sierpina (2008) surveyed 502 patients in a convenience sample of users of a family medicine clinic and found that only 13 (2.6%) had used guided imagery during the prior year, although 37 (7.4%) were interested in using it in the upcoming year. As a comparison, 107 (21.3%) individuals had used massage in the prior year and 214 (42.6%) intended to in the next 12 months.

Two sets of investigators conducted larger-scale studies of guided imagery through a meta-analysis and a systematic review. Van Kuiken (2004) conducted a meta-analysis of 10 studies that were published between 1996 and 2002. She found that guided imagery produced immediate results in both physiological and psychological realms, although lasting effects after 18 weeks were unclear.

Roffe et al. (2005) conducted a systematic review of guided imagery as an adjunct to more traditional medicine-based cancer therapies. After locating 103 studies, they qualified six to be included in the review. They concluded "guided imagery may be beneficial as a psycho-supportive adjuvant therapy for cancer patients" (p. 614), although they reported concern due to few studies, the small size of most studies, and the use of varied data-collection methods. They felt that guided imagery helped "comfort" and had psychological aspects, but not necessarily physiological ones, such as vomiting and nausea.

In therapeutic recreation, McKee (1984) studied 20 patients with chronic pain and looked at the outcome variables of experience and intensity of pain, depression, leisure attitudes, daily leisure activity, and ability to relax over three treatment groups and a control. The three treatment groups included guided imagery with biofeedback, biofeedback only, and day treatment only. The imagery-biofeedback group and the biofeedback-only group reported less pain and more daily activity, and those in the biofeedback groups reported increased ability to relax (according to their EMGs). The combined imagery-biofeedback group was slightly more effective.

Ellis, Maughan-Pritchett, and Ruddell (1993) used a 3-by-3 design to study the effects of attribution-based verbal persuasion and of guided imagery on the outcome judgments while playing video games of 90 adolescents with psychiatric difficulties. The 3-by-3 conditions consisted of: (a) persuasion designed to promote internal and stable attributions, (b) ambiguous persuasion designed to yield external and unstable attributions, and (c) no persuasion, as well as (x) imagery of a successful experience, (y) imagery of a failure experience, and (z) no imagery conditions. They measured the effects of these conditions on self-efficacy judgments, outcome judgments, generality of efficacy judgments, persistence at the task, and game score. They found that not only did the internal-persuasion condition produce better results for all the outcomes, the successful-imagery condition produced higher self-efficacy scores. One of their recommendations included further study with the use of various positive scenarios on participant's self-efficacy.

Bonadies (2010) tested a guided imagery protocol on a male with AIDS-related pain and found that the intervention reduced pain ratings. He used the protocol found in Table 17.7 (p. 328). Table 17.8 (p. 329) contains two of the scripts that Bonadies suggested.

Resources for Guided Imagery

Holisticonline.com
http://www.holisticonline.com/guided-imagery.htm

Health Journeys CDs and Tapes
http://www.healthjourneys.com/

Health World
http://www.healthy.net/scr/therapy.asp?Thid=14

Battino, R. (2007). *Guided imagery: Psychotherapy and healing through the mind-body connection.* Bethel, CT: Crown House Publishing Company LLC.

Davis, M., Eshelman, E. R., & McKay, M. (2000). *The relaxation and stress reduction workbook* (5th ed.). Oakland, CA: New Harbinger.

Hall, C. A., Young, D., Hall, E., & Stradling, P. (2006). *Guided imagery: Creative interventions in counseling and psychotherapy.* Thousand Oaks, CA: Sage Publications.

Mantell, S. (2000). *Your present: A half hour of peace; A guided imagery meditation for physical and spiritual wellness* [CD]. Chappaqua, NY: Relax Intuit LLC.

Seaward, B. L. (2004). *Managing stress: Principles and strategies for health and well being.* Boston, MA: Jones and Bartlett.

Table 17.7. Guided Imagery Protocol (Bonadies, 2010)

Title:	Guided Imagery
Purpose:	This program utilizes senses and memory to engage the imagination to manage pain. Guided imagery provides a story with several healing principles.
Staff Requirements:	One CTRS to one client preferably. One CTRS to four clients maximum.
Entrance Requirements:	Clients who exhibit symptoms from stress, anxiety, and pain. Adaptable to clients in all stages who have the ability to follow directions, a minimal ability to think abstractly, and referral by physician or interdisciplinary team.
Exit Requirements:	Client's target symptoms decrease or client no longer wishes to participate.
Group Size:	1:1 or maximum group of four.
Duration:	15–45 minutes, depending on the length of the guided imagery script.
Safety Considerations:	Not appropriate for clients who have organic brain syndrome, severe dementia, acutely or on the verge of psychoses.
Facility and Equipment:	Small room away from noise, interruption or any distraction. Guided imagery scripts. Optional: gentle, soft music without lyrics, journal book, pen/pencil or materials to color with.
Methods:	• Describe the guided imagery to the client and its benefits.
	• Assess the client's previous experience with guided imagery.
	• Inform the client that guided imagery is safe and gentle; they are always in control of the experience and they can stop the session at any time if they wish.
	• Before starting the guided imagery make sure the client is comfortable.
	• Suggest that the client closes his/her eyes and begin with 5–10 minutes of deep abdominal breathing, autogenic training, or body scan to induce a further relaxed state.
	• When the client indicates that he/she is completely relaxed, begin reading the guided imagery script (Table 17.8).
	• When reading the guided imagery script to the client, use a moderate tone of voice, with frequent pauses.
	• When the guided imagery script comes to an end, suggest to the clients that they gently open their eyes.
	• Allow the clients to become oriented to their surroundings. Don't be concerned to speak quickly; rather, wait a few moments for the client to respond.
	• If the client doesn't respond verbally in an appropriate amount of time, ask the client if he/she would like to talk about the experience.
	• If the client wishes to talk about the guided imagery experience, do so but in a very permissive manner.
	• Suggested questions: How do you feel? What did you see, smell, hear or touch? Did the imagery convey any meaning or message to you? What did you learn from this experience and can you incorporate that into your life?
	• Another option if the client doesn't want to talk is to suggest writing or drawing about the experience.
	• Before concluding the session ask the client if he/she has any questions and if he/she would like to schedule another session in the future.
Possible Client Outcomes:	• Reduced anxiety
	• Reduced pain
	• Reduced stress
	• Learning a coping skill to reduce pain
References:	Dossey, B. (1995). Using imagery to help your patient heal. *American Journal of Nursing, 5,* 41–46.

Table 17.8. Suggested Guided Imagery Scripts (Bonadies, 2010)

Dimensions of the Pain

Purpose: Controlling acute or chronic pain, both physical and psychological (Dossey 1995).

Close your eyes let yourself relax. Begin to describe your pain in silence. Know that the pain may be either physical sensations, or worries and fears. Be present with the pain. Let it take a shape—any shape that comes to your mind. Become aware of the dimensions of the pain. What is the height of your pain? the width of the pain? the depth of the pain? Where in the body is it located? Give it a color . . . a shape . . . feel the texture. Does it make any sound?

And now with your eyes still closed, let your hands come together with palms turned upward as if forming a cup. Put your pain in your hands. [Ask the following questions about each dimension and characteristic of the pain.] How would you change the pain's size [height, width, depth, etc.]?

Let yourself decide what you would like to do with the pain. There is no right way to finish this experience—except what feels right to you. You can throw the pain away, or put it back where you found it, or move it somewhere else. Let yourself become aware of how your pain can be changed. By focusing with intention, you can change the pain.

Red Ball of Pain

Purpose: To decrease psychophysiologic pain and teach your client how to use distraction. Good for acute and chronic pain, as well as the discomfort or pain from procedures.

Scan your body. Gather any pains, aches, or other symptoms up into a red ball. Begin to change its size. Allow it to get bigger. Just imagine how big you can make it. Now, gradually, make it smaller. See how small you can make it. Is it possible to make it the size of a grain of sand? Now allow it to move slowly out of your body, moving further away each time you exhale. Notice the experience with each outward breath, as the pain moves away.

Suggest that your client change the ball's size several times in both directions and imagine different ways to dispose of it—for example, tossing it in the garbage or letting the wind blow it away.

Progressive Muscle Relaxation

Edmund Jacobson is credited as being (in the 1930s) the first person to recognize that muscles cannot be relaxed and tense at the same time, and who originated the concepts behind progressive muscle relaxation (Seaward, 2004). In progressive muscle relaxation (PMR), individuals systematically contract and then relax each muscle group. The idea is for the person to be able to sense and feel the differences between when muscles are progressively tensed and relaxed, and when relaxed, be able to counteract stress and become more at ease and healthful.

Seaward (2004) offers the following as original to Jacobson's teachings:

- The progression of muscle groups should start with the lower extremities and move up to the head.
- Muscle groups should be isolated during the contraction phase, leaving all other muscles relaxed.
- The same muscle groups on both sides of the body should be contracted simultaneously.

- The contraction should be held for 5 to 10 seconds, with a corresponding relaxation phase of about 45 seconds.
- The individual should focus attention on the intensity of the contraction, sensing the tension level produced.
- During the relaxation phase of each muscle group, special awareness of the feeling of relaxation should be focused on, comparing it to how the muscle felt when it was contracted.

Additionally Seaward noted that the sole focus is on muscle contraction and relaxation, with no attempts to create scenarios or pleasant thoughts (such as guided imagery) or visualizations such as blood flow (as with biofeedback). Seaward provided a number of helpful guidelines for PMR and they are included on Table 17.9 (p. 330).

Perhaps due to its ease of instruction and ease of application, progressive muscle relaxation has become one of the most popular forms of relaxation training (Persson et al., 2008). The studies below focus on PMR's results with individuals with chronic pain, anxiety, and systemic conditions. Most are meta-analyses (larger studies combining the results from several smaller studies) or systematic literature reviews and most complained that "relaxation," even PMR was ill-defined, and yielded results that are inconclusive. For the most part, they found PMR to be the single or one of the most effective relaxation techniques, although sometimes the gain was small (Dickinson et al., 2008a, b; Jorm et al., 2008; Sierpina, Astin, & Giordano, 2007).

Paterson (1987) performed one of the first meta-analyses on progressive muscle relaxation and found that PMR was significantly effective and uniformly adept in reducing anxiety across the reviewed studies. Anxiety reduction was the most commonly studied outcome variable and showed significant effects, while other variables showed greater fluctuations in outcome.

Manzoni, Pagnini, Castelnuovo, and Molinari (2008) conducted a meta-analysis of 27 studies, published between 1997 and 2007, that investigated the effects of PMR, autogenic training, applied relaxation, and meditation on anxiety. They noted, "relaxation techniques represent one of the most used approaches in anxiety management worldwide, both as a stand-alone treatment or included in a more complex therapy" (p. 42). They concluded that relaxation training effectively reduces anxiety, both when comparing a treatment group to a control group and when comparing the same persons over time. PMR had the highest rates of positive changes among all techniques.

In 1998, Carroll and Seers conducted a systematic review of relaxation techniques and their effects on chronic pain. The authors included only published, randomized, controlled trials (RCTs) involving only individuals with chronic pain from cancer or non-malignant pain conditions using at least one pain outcome

Table 17.9. Guidelines for Progressive Muscle Relaxation (Seaward, 2004)

- Clothing and jewelry, especially if it is constrictive or noticeable, should be removed prior to beginning.
- Minimize distractions by being situated in a quiet place, although this is not as important for PMR as some other relaxation techniques such as meditation.
- Body position: Either sitting comfortably or lying down. Arms at one's side, with palms facing upward.
- Breathing: Inhale as you contract muscles, exhale as you release tension. The release of tension deepens when accompanied by the relaxation of the diaphragm.
- For best results, perform PMR three times a day in five-minute sessions. PMR can be practiced anywhere once learned; noticeable physiological changes should become evident four to six weeks after beginning.

measure. At that time, the authors concluded that research had not proven that relaxation was effective for chronic pain. They called for better methodologies and larger studies. They did, however, note that no studies reported ill or negative effects of relaxation therapies.

Relaxation's effect on pain was the subject of a systematic review of 15 studies by Kwekkeboom and Gretarsdottir (2006). They reported that PMR produced reductions of arthritis pain, chronic low-back pain, and leg pain related to pregnancy, although they felt the results were questionable due to methodological weaknesses in the studies. Autogenic relaxation, jaw relaxation, and systematic relaxation were useful in reducing postoperative pain, and the latter two categories of studies showed strong methodologies. Rhythmic breathing and other relaxation interventions (such as stretching) were not effective in reducing pain.

In 2007, Rainforth et al. performed a meta-analysis and systematic review on the effects of relaxation on individuals with elevated blood pressure. They noted that lifestyle modifications (such as weight loss, physical activity, reduced intake of sodium, and stress reduction) are important treatments for individuals with hypertension. They concluded that other meta-analyses did not find significant reductions in elevated blood pressure through simple biofeedback, relaxation-assisted biofeedback, PMR, or stress-management training. Significant effects were found when Transcendental Meditation (TM) was used.

van Dixhoorn and White (2005), in a systematic review and meta-analysis of 27 studies on the effects of relaxation on ischemic heart disease, reported a number of important findings. Six studies used abbreviated therapies (3 hours or less of instruction), 13 studies used full relaxation therapy (9 hours of instruction and discussion), and 8 studies used relaxation therapy in combination with cognitive therapy (11 hours total, on average). They reported a number of findings:

- Physiological outcomes included reduction in resting heart rate, increased heart rate variability, improved exercise tolerance, increased high-density lipoprotein cholesterol (no effects for blood pressure or cholesterol).
- Psychological outcomes included reduction of state anxiety and depression (no reduction in trait anxiety).
- Cardiac outcomes included reduction in frequency of angina pectoris, occurrence of arrhythmia, and exercise-induced ischemia
- Return to work improved; cardiac events and cardiac deaths were reduced.

- With the exception of resting heart rate, differences were small, absent or not measured in brief therapies; no differences were found between full or expanded (with cognitive therapy) studies.
- Relaxation is an important part of cardiac rehabilitation, in addition to exercise and psychoeducation.

Sierpina et al. (2007), in a meta-analysis of randomized, controlled trials on mind-body therapies for headache, found that progressive muscle relaxation was reasonably effective by itself for tension headaches and very effective when coupled with biofeedback for migraines. They included 35 trials were included in their meta-analysis.

Huntley, White, and Ernst (2002) completed a systematic review of research studies involving relaxation for people with asthma. They included PMR, hypnotherapy, autogenic training, biofeedback training, and Transcendental Meditation in their definition of relaxation therapies. They concluded, after reviewing 15 studies, "data from some studies suggest that muscular relaxation may provide some improvement in lung function but . . . there was no evidence that hypnosis, autogenic training, or biofeedback are effective for asthma symptoms" (p. 130). They also noted that many studies lack sufficient rigor to come to more powerful conclusions.

Resources for
Progressive Muscle Relaxation

Davis, M., Eshelman, E. R., & McKay, M. (2000). *The relaxation and stress reduction workbook* (5th ed.). Oakland, CA: New Harbinger.

McKay, M., & Fanning, P. (2006). *Daily relaxer: Relax your body, calm your mind, and refresh your spirit*. Oakland, CA: New Harbinger.

McKay, M., & Fanning, P. (2008). *Progressive relaxation and breathing* [CD]. Oakland, CA: New Harbinger.

Seaward, B. L. (2004). *Managing stress: Principles and strategies for health and well-being*. Boston, MA: Jones and Bartlett.

Smith, J. C. (2005). *Relaxation, meditation, and mindfulness: A mental health practitioner's guide to new and traditional approaches*. New York, NY: Springer.

Biofeedback

Biofeedback is another technique for reducing the onset of stress and managing it. Introduced in the 1960s, biofeedback allows individuals to gain conscious control over voluntary but latent bodily functions by alerting them with an auditory or visual signal. For example, the individual "sees" his or her heart rate on a monitor and uses slowed breathing to slow the heart rate (Glanz et al., 1995). According to the Biofeedback Certification Institute of America, biofeedback is:

> a process that enables an individual to learn how to change physiological activity for the purposes of improving health and performance. Precise instruments measure physiological activity such as brainwaves, heart function, breathing, muscle activity, and skin temperature. These instruments rapidly and accurately "feed back" information to the user. The presentation of this information—often in conjunction with changes in thinking, emotions, and behavior—supports desired physiological changes. Over time, these changes can endure without continued use of an instrument. (Biofeedback Certification Institute of America, 2009)

Seaward (2004) noted that biofeedback uses "monitoring instruments to amplify the electrochemical energy produced by body organs" for the purpose of allowing the person to "increase awareness of his or her own physiological responses (breathing, muscle tension, blood pressure, heart rate, and/or body temperature) by learning to monitor them through data generated by a particular instrument" (p. 468). Simply put, biofeedback treatments work by teaching people to become more aware of how their bodies are functioning and to control patterns of physiological functioning (i.e., arousal control) (Russoniello, 2001; Russoniello, O'Brien, & Parks, 2009). Biofeedback aids the individual in invoking the relaxation response, in time, without the use of instruments or machines (Russoniello, Skalko, Beatley, & Alexander, 2002; Seaward, 2004).

Seaward (2004) lists four basic categories of biofeedback instrumentation:

- Electromyographic (EMG): Monitors electrical impulses produced by muscle tissue; electrodes are placed on the skin on top of specific muscles (for example on the forehead) and visual and auditory feedback is given while the person learns to relax these muscles.
- Electroencephalographic (EEG): Monitors electrical impulses of the brain by electrodes placed on the skull. There are categories into four groups (alpha, beta, theta, and delta) each represented by a different sound or pitch. The person is taught to decrease beta waves (normal, alert state) and redirect them to alpha waves (relaxed state).

- Cardiovascular (EKG): Monitors individual's ability to regulate heart rate and blood pressure, using a portable device strapped around the chest. Also used by athletes to detect levels of cardiovascular workload.
- Electrodermal (EDR): Known as galvanic skin response (GSR), measures electrical conduction of the skin through sweat (sympathetic nervous system activation). Monitors usually placed on the index and ring fingers; much like "lie detector tests."

In all of its forms, biofeedback in a noninvasive intervention. It can be used with people with a variety of disorders, such as irritable bowel syndrome, recurrent abdominal pain, rheumatoid arthritis, migraine, muscle pain syndromes, fibromyalgia, chronic fatigue syndrome, stress syndromes, and obesity (Astin et al., 2003; Gevirtz, 2003; Russoniello et al., 2009). It is most commonly used for individuals with chronic pain (Persson et al., 2008; Seaward, 2004), headaches (Nestoriuc, Martin, Rief, & Andrasik, 2008; Nestoriuc, Rief, & Martin, 2008) and cardiac disorders (Gevirtz, 2003; Swanson, et al., 2009). Russoniello et al. (2009) have used it successfully with wounded Marine Corps veterans.

One area of growing research interest is heart rate variability (HRV). In short, when heart rate variability is increased and cardiac and respiratory functions are synchronized—helped by slowed, measured breathing—the body's alarm and reaction phases mentioned earlier in this chapter are reversed and the relaxation response is induced (Gevirtz, 2003; Russoniello, 2001; Russoniello et al., 2009). This synchronization is possible through the individual's increased awareness of his or her bodily functions via the biofeedback monitors mentioned earlier. HRV monitoring is especially helpful in those conditions in which the stress response aggravates the condition, such as asthma, hypertension, and cardiac disorders (Gevirtz, 2003; Seaward, 2004; Swanson et al., 2009).

Because biofeedback has grown in popularity only in fairly recent years, the literature base is growing. The following are typical of the research studies using or studying biofeedback as an intervention.

Swanson et al. (2009) studied 29 individuals who had previously experienced heart failure, using a wide range of data points, such as depression, stress management and exercise practices, medication records, vital signs and the like. They found that, for the treatment group, cardiorespiratory biofeedback and breathing retraining significantly increased exercise tolerance. This is important because exercise tolerance in patients with heart failure is seen as a strong predictor of reduc-

tions in cardiac mortality and morbidity. The authors felt that biofeedback was an important factor in improving exercise tolerance.

Nestoriuc, Martin, Rief, and Andrasik (2008) conducted a systematic review of biofeedback's effect for individuals with headache disorders (migraine and tension-type). Biofeedback was moderately effective in reducing frequency, intensity, duration and perception of migraine headaches (61% more so than the control group) and even more effective in these measures (69% success rate) for tension-type headaches. On average, biofeedback groups received relief in within 11 sessions, with effects that persisted over several years post-treatment. The migraine group benefited from home-training treatment manuals and the tension-type headache group benefited when biofeedback was combined with relaxation therapies.

The effects of biofeedback for individuals in post-stroke rehabilitation are mixed. Glanz et al. (1995) conducted a meta-analysis and reported, "this meta-analysis of randomized control trials of biofeedback in stroke rehabilitation fails to support its efficacy" (p. 512). However, Moreland, Thomson, and Fuoco (1998) reported, after also conducting a meta-analysis, that biofeedback was effective in improving ankle dorsiflexor muscle strength and possibly clinically effective for range of motion, stride length, gait quality, ankle angle during gait, and gait velocity.

In addition, Wood, Maraj, Lee, and Reyes (2002), among others, have noted that older adults typically have a reduced HRV, translating into stress reactions that are associated with cardiovascular and all-cause deaths. Teaching individuals to control their HRV may result in lower physiological damage (the wear and tear of experiencing the stress response) and improved health outcomes.

In therapeutic recreation, one of the first studies to use biofeedback was conducted by McKee (1984). He studied 20 patients with chronic pain and looked at the outcome variables of experience and intensity of pain, depression, leisure attitudes, daily leisure activity, and ability to relax over three treatment groups and a control. The three treatment groups included guided imagery with biofeedback, biofeedback-only, and day-treatment-only. The imagery-biofeedback group and the biofeedback-only group reported less pain and more daily activity and those in the biofeedback groups reported increased ability to relax (according to their EMGs). While the combined imagery-biofeedback group was slightly more effective, the biofeedback-only group found significant relief and improved activity levels as well.

Buettner, Fitzsimmons, and Atav (2006) used biofeedback in a unique way to measure the physiological changes in individuals with dementia and behavioral problems. They studied 107 participants from five long-term care facilities in Florida and determined whether individuals were passive or agitated. For both sets of individuals they designed specific "behavior-calming" or "behavior-alerting" therapeutic recreation interventions. They collected heart rate (HR) information and blood volume pulse (BVR) as one measure of determining whether the intervention met its goal of calming or alerting. Alerting activities were effective in 79% to 91% of cases and calming activities were effective 92% to 100% of the time.

Russoniello, O'Brien, and Parks (2009) studied 134 participants using a randomly assigned, treatment and control group design to determine if casual video games could improve mood and/or decrease stress. They used the Profile of Mood States and heart-rate variability as their primary measures. They found that individually-chosen casual video games did improve participant's mood states and reduced physiological arousal at greater rates than for that of the control group.

Groff and colleagues (2010) used biofeedback as a personal stress-management technique with six women experiencing breast cancer. The six-week therapeutic recreation program called "Get REAL & HEEL" used biofeedback to instruct individuals to improve their heart-rate coherence (HRC) and their heart-rate variability (HRV)—each being associated with inducing the relaxation response in times of stress. The researchers used HeartMath and two Journey to the Wild Divine (JWD) products to train the research participants how to improve their heart-rate coherence and heart rate variability. Not only did the intervention provide numeric, qualitative improvements in HRC and HRV, but the women also expressed feelings of being more in control, being transformed by the experience, and being able to integrate the biofeedback techniques into their everyday lives.

Biofeedback Resources

Biofeedback Certification Institute of America
http://www.bcia.org

Association for Psychophysiology and Biofeedback
http://www.aapb.org

Evans, J. (Ed.). (2007). *Handbook of neurofeedback: Dynamics and clinical applications*. Binghamton, NY: Haworth Medical Press.
Peper, E., Ancoli, S., & Quinn, M. (Eds.). (2009). *Mind/body integration: Essential readings in biofeedback*. New York, NY: Springer-Verlag.
Robbins, J. (2008). *A symphony in the brain: The evolution of the new brain wave biofeedback (2nd ed.)*. New York, NY: Grove/Atlantic.
Swingle, P. G. (2008). *Biofeedback for the brain: How neurotherapy effectively treats depression, ADHD, autism and more*. Piscataway, NJ: Rutgers University Press.

Summary

- Stress is pervasive and has cognitive, affective, and physiological components.
- When stressed, the individual cycles through several stages, including (a) alarm, (b) resistance, (c) exhaustion, and (d) return to homeostasis.
- Stress has been studied steadily through the last 90 years by researchers from various disciplines.
- Extended or chronic stress leads to many physical illnesses such as heart disease, obesity, high blood pressure, insomnia, depression, alcohol/drug abuse, and chronic pain.
- The four specific stress management techniques discussed in this chapter include (a) expressive writing, (b) guided imagery, (c) progressive muscle relaxation, and (d) biofeedback. Each of these techniques has sufficient research both in other fields and generally in therapeutic recreation, to support its efficacy with clients. More research on the efficacy of these techniques employing more stringent research methodologies is needed within therapeutic recreation services.
- The field of stress management is rich with online, printed, and other resources.

Resources

National Center for Complementary and Alternative Medicine
http://nccam.nih.gov/

American Holistic Medicine Association
http://www.holisticmedicine.org

American Society of Clinical Hypnosis
http://www.asch.net

The Center for Mind-Body Medicine
http://www.cmbm.org

University of Massachusetts Medical School Center for Mindfulness in Medicine, Health Care, and Society
http://www.umassmed.edu/cfm/mbsr

Alternative Therapies in Health and Medicine
http://www.alternative-therapies.com/at

Annals of Behavioral Medicine
http://www.sbm.org/annals

Explore: The Journal of Science and Healing
http://www.explorejournal.com

Journal of Alternative and Complementary Medicine
http://www.liebertonline.com/acm

Benson, H., & Stuart, E. M. (1992). *The wellness book: The comprehensive guide to maintaining health and treating stress-related illness* (1st ed.). New York, NY: Simon and Schuster.

Davis, M., Eshelman, E. R., & McKay, M. (2000). *The relaxation and stress reduction workbook* (5th ed.). Oakland, CA: New Harbinger.

Kabat-Zinn, J. (2005). *Coming to our senses: Healing ourselves and the world through mindfulness* (1st ed.). New York, NY: Hyperion.

Rakel, D. (2007). *Integrative medicine* (2nd ed.). Philadelphia, PA: Saunders Elsevier.

Watkins, A. D. (1997). *Mind-body medicine: A clinician's guide to psychoneuroimmunology*. New York, NY: Churchill Livingstone.

References

Ananth, S., & Martin, W. (2006). *Health forum 2005 complementary and alternative medicine survey of hospitals: Summary of results*. Chicago, IL: Health Forum.

Astin, J. A., Shapiro, S. L., Eisenberg, D. M., & Forys, K. L. (2003). Mind-body medicine: State of the science, implications for practice. *Journal of the American Board of Family Practice, 16*, 131–147.

Austin, D. (2009). *Therapeutic recreation: Processes and techniques* (6th ed.). Champaign, IL: Sagamore.

Baird, C. L., & Sands, L. (2004). A pilot study of the effectiveness of guided imagery with progressive muscle relaxation to reduce chronic pain and mobility difficulties of osteoarthritis. *Pain Management Nursing, 5*(3), 97–104.

Barnes, P. M., Powell-Griner, E., McFann, K., & Nahin, R. L. (2002). Complementary and alternative medicine use among adults: United States. *CDC Advance Data Report #343*.

Benson, H., Beary, J. F., & Carol, M. P. (1974). The relaxation response. *Psychiatry, 37*, 37–46.

Bertisch, S. M., Wee, C. C., Phillips, R. S., & McCarthy, E. P. (2009). Alternative mind-body therapies used by adults with medical conditions. *Journal of Psychosomatic Research, 66*, 511–519.

Biofeedback Certification Institute of America (2009). What is biofeedback? Retrieved August 15, 2009, from: http://www.bcia.org/displaycommon.cfm?an=1&subarticlenbr=8

Bonadies, V. (2010). Protocol: Guided imagery as a therapeutic recreation modality to reduce pain. *Annual in Therapeutic Recreation, 18*, 164–174.

Buettner, L. L., Fitzsimmons, S., & Atav, A. S. (2006). Predicting outcomes of therapeutic recreation interventions for older adults with dementia and behavioral symptoms. *Therapeutic Recreation Journal, 40*(1), 33–47.

Bugg, A., Turpin, G., Mason, S., & Scholes, C. (2009). A randomized controlled trial of the effectiveness of writing as a self-help intervention for traumatic injury patients at risk for developing post-traumatic stress disorder. *Behaviour Research and Therapy, 47*, 6–12.

Burton, C. M., & King, L. A. (2008). Effects of (very) brief writing on health: The two-minute miracle. *British Journal of Health Psychology, 13*, 9–14.

Carroll, D., & Seers, K. (1998). Relaxation for the relief of chronic pain: A systematic review. *Journal of Advanced Nursing, 27*, 476–487.

Crampton, S. M., Hodge, J. W., Mishra, J. M., & Price, S. (1995). Stress and stress management. *SAM Advanced Management Journal, 60*(3), 10–19.

Dalton, J. J., & Glenwick, D. S. (2009). The effects of expressive writing on standardized graduate entrance exam performance and physical health functioning. *Journal of Psychology: Interdisciplinary and Applied, 143*(3), 279–292.

Dattilo, J. (2000). *Facilitation techniques in therapeutic recreation*. State College, PA: Venture Publishing, Inc.

Davis, M., Eshelman, E. R., & McKay, M. (2000). *The relaxation and stress reduction workbook* (5th ed.). Oakland, CA: New Harbinger.

Dickinson, H. O., Beyer, F. R., Ford, G. A., Nicolson, D., Campbell, F., Cook, J. V., & Mason, J. M. (2008). Relaxation therapies for the management of primary hypertension in adults. *Cochrane Database of Systematic Reviews, 1*. Art. No.: CD004935. DOI: 10.1002/14651858.CD004935.pub2.

Dickinson, H. O., Campbell, F., Beyer, F. R., Nicolson, D. J., Cook, J. V., Ford, G., & Mason, J. M. (2008). Relaxation therapies for the management of primary hypertension in adults: A Cochrane review. *Journal of Human Hypertension, 22*, 809–820.

Donaldson, V. W. (2000). Clinical study of visualization on depressed white blood cell count in medical patients. *Applied Psychophysiology and Biofeedback, 25*(2), 117–128.

Ellis, G. D., Maughan-Pritchett, M., & Ruddell, E. (1993). Effect of attribution based verbal persuasion and imagery on self-efficacy of adolescents diagnosed with major depression. *Therapeutic Recreation Journal, 27*(2), 83–97.

Ernst, E., Schmidt, K., & Baum, M. (2006). Complementary/alternative therapies for the treatment of breast cancer: A systematic review of randomized clinical trials and a critique of current terminology. *The Breast Journal, 12*(6), 526–530.

Fors, E. A., Sexton, H., & Götestam, K. G. (2002). The effect of guided imagery and amitriptyline on daily fibromyalgia pain: A prospective, randomized, controlled trial. *Journal of Psychiatric Research, 36*, 179–187.

Fratianne, R. B, Prensner, J. D, Huston, M. J., Super, D. M., Yowler, C. J., & Standley, J. M. (2001). The effect of music-based imagery and musical alternate engagement on the burn debridement process. *Journal of Burn Care & Rehabilitation, 22*(1), 47–53.

Frattaroli, J. (2006). Experimental disclosure and its moderators: A meta-analysis. *Psychological Bulletin, 132*(6), 823–865.

Frenkel, M., Arye, E. B., Carlson, C., & Sierpina, V. (2008). Integrating complementary and alternative medicine into conventional primary care: The patient perspective. *Explore, 4*(3), 178–186.

Frisina, P. G., Borod, J. C., & Lepore, S. J. (2004). A meta-analysis of the effects of written emotional disclosure on the health outcomes of clinical populations. *Journal of Nervous and Mental Disease, 192*(9), 629–634.

Gervirtz, R. (2003). The promise of HRV biofeedback: Some preliminary results and speculations. *Biofeedback, 31*(3), 18–19.

Giradano, D., Everly, G., & Dusek, D. (2000). *Controlling stress and tension: A holistic approach* (6th ed.). Boston, MA: Addison-Wesley.

Glanz, M., Klawansky, S., Stason, W., Berkey, C., Shah, N., Phan, H., & Chalmers, T. C. (1995). Biofeedback therapy in poststroke rehabilitation: A meta-analysis of the randomized controlled trials. *Archives of Physical Medicine and Rehabilitation, 76*, 508–515.

Gortner, E.-M., Rude, S. S., & Pennebaker, J. W. (2006). Benefits of expressive writing in lowering rumination and depressive symptoms. *Behavior Therapy, 37*, 292–303.

Groff, D. G., Battaglini, C., Sipe, C., Peppercorn, J., Anderson, M., & Hackney, A. C. (2010). "Finding a new normal:" Using recreation therapy to im-

prove the well-being of women with breast cancer. *Annual in Therapeutic Recreation, 18*, 40–52.

Grossman, P., Niemann, L., Schmidt, S., & Walach, H. (2004). Mindfulness-based stress reduction and health benefits: A meta-analysis. *Journal of Psychosomatic Research, 57*, 35–43.

"Growing Number of Hospitals Offer Complementary and Alternative Medicine" (2006). Explore, Retrieved August 31, 2009, from: http://nccam.nih.gov/news/newsletter/2006_fall/hospitals.htm

Halpin, L. S., Speir, A. M., CapoBianco, P., & Barnett, S. D. (2002). Guided imagery in cardiac surgery. *Outcomes Management, 6*(3), 132–137.

Harris, A. H. S. (2006). Does expressive writing reduce health care utilization? A meta-analysis of randomized trials. *Journal of Consulting and Clinical Psychology, 74*(2), 243–252.

Harrist, S., Carlozzi, B. L., McGovern, A. R., & Harrist, A. W. (2007). Benefits of expressive writing and expressive talking about life goals. *Journal of Research in Personality, 41*, 923–930.

Herman, P. M., Craig, B. M., & Caspi, O. (2005). Is complementary and alternative medicine (CAM) cost-effective? A systematic review. *BMC Complementary and Alternative Medicine, 5.* Retrieved September 2, 2009, from: http://www.biomedcentral.com/1472-6882/5/11

Holmes, T. H., & Rahe, R. H. (1967). The social readjustment rating scale. *Journal of Psychosomatic Research, 11*, 213–218.

Horowitz, S. (2008). Evidence-based health outcomes of expressive writing. *Alternative and Complementary Therapies, 14*(4), 194–198.

Huntley, A., White, A. R., & Ernst, E. (2002). Relaxation therapies for asthma: A systematic review. *Thorax, 57*, 127–131.

Huth, M. M., Broome, M. E., & Good, M. (2004). Imagery reduces children's post-operative pain. *Pain, 110*(1-2), 439–448.

Jacobs, G. D. (2001). The physiology of mind-body interactions: The stress response and the relaxation response. *The Journal of Alternative and Complementary Medicine, 7*(Supp 1), S83–S92.

Jorm, A. F., Morgan, A. J., & Hetrick, S. E. (2008). Relaxation for depression. *Cochrane Database of Systematic Reviews 2008, 4.* CD007142. DOI: 10.1002/14651858.CD007142.pub2

Kemper, K., Vohra, S., & Walls, R. (2008). The use of complementary and alternative medicine in pediatrics. *Pediatrics, 122*, 1374–1386.

Kwekkeboom, K. L., & Gretarsdottir, E. (2006). Systematic review of relaxation interventions for pain. *Journal of Nursing Scholarship, 38*(3), 269–277.

Lazarus, R. S. (1985). The psychology of stress and coping. *Issues in Mental Health Nursing, 7*(1–4), 399–418.

Lazarus, R. S. (1990). Theory-based stress management. *Psychological Inquiry, 1*(1), 3–13.

Lazarus, R. S. (1992). Coping with the stress of illness. *World Health Organization Regional Publications—European Series, 44*, 11–12

Lazarus, R. S. (1993). Coping theory and research: Past, present, and future. *Psychosomatic Medicine, 55*(3), 234–247.

Lin, Y-C., Lee, A. C., Kemper, K. J., & Berde, C. B. (2005). Use of complementary and alternative medicine in pediatric pain management service: A survey. *Pain Medicine, 6*(6), 452–458.

Littleton, H., Horsley, S., John, S., & Nelson, D. V. (2007). Trauma coping strategies and psychological distress: A meta-analysis. *Journal of Traumatic Stress, 29*(6), 977–988.

Luedtke, C. A., Thompson, J. M., Postier, J. A., Neubauer, B. L., Drach, S., & Newell, L. (2005). A description of a brief multidisciplinary treatment program for fibromyalgia. *Pain Management Nursing, 6*(2), 76–80.

Luskin, F. M., Newell, K. A., & Griffith, M. (2000) A review of mind/body therapies in the treatment of musculoskeletal disorders with implications for the elderly. *Alternative Therapies in Health and Medicine, 6*(2), 46–56.

Manzoni, G. M., Pagnini, F., Castelnuovo, G., & Molinari, E. (2008). Relaxation training for anxiety: A ten-year systematic review with meta-analysis. *BMC Psychiatry, 8*(1), art. no. 41.

McKee, P. (1984). Effects of using enjoyable imagery with biofeedback induced relaxation for chronic pain patients. *Therapeutic Recreation Journal, 18*(1), 50–61.

Menzies, V., Taylor, A. G., & Bourguignon, C. (2006). Effects of guided imagenry on outcomes of pain, functional status, and self-efficacy in persons diagnosed with firbomyalgia. *Journal of Alternative and Complementary Medicine, 12*(1), 23–30.

Mobily, P. R., Herr, K. A., & Kelley, L. S. (1993). Cognitive-behavioral techniques to reduce pain: A validation study. International *Journal of Nursing Studies, 30*(6), 537–548.

Monroe, S. M. (2008). Modern approaches to conceptualizing and measuring human life stress. *Annual Review of Clinical Psychology, 4*, 33–55.

Moreland, J. D., Thomson, M. A., & Fuoco, A. R. (1998). Electromyographic biofeedback to improve lower extremity function after stroke: A meta-analysis. *Archives of Physical Medicine and Rehabilitation, 79*, 134–140.

Morone, N. E., & Greco, C. M. (2007). Mind-body interventions for chronic pain in older adults: A structured review. *Pain Medicine, 8*(4), 359–375.

Naparstek, B. (2004). *Invisible heroes: survivors of trauma and how they heal.* New York, NY: Bantam Dell.

Nestoriuc, Y., Martin, A., Rief, W., & Andrasik, F. (2008). Biofeedback treatment for headache disorders: A comprehensive efficacy review. *Applied Psychophysiological Biofeedback, 33*, 125–140.

Nestoriuc, Y., Rief, W., & Martin, A. (2008). Meta-analysis of biofeedback for tension-type headache: Efficacy, specificity, and treatment moderators. *Journal of Consulting and Clinical Psychology, 76*(3), 379–396.

Paterson, C. E. (1987). Progressive relaxation: A meta-analysis. Unpublished dissertation, The Ohio State University; Dissertation Abstracts International-B 48/09, p. 2790, March 1988.

Pennebaker, J. W. (1989). Confession, inhibition, and disease. In L. Berkowitz (Ed.), *Advances in experimental social psychology* (Vol. 22, pp. 211–244). New York, NY: Academic Press.

Pennebaker, J. W. (1993). Putting stress into words: Health, linguistic, and therapeutic implications. *Behaviour Research and Therapy, 31*, 539–548.

Pennebaker, J. W., & Beall, S. K. (1986). Confronting a traumatic event: Toward an understanding of inhibition and disease. *Journal of Abnormal Psychology, 95*, 274–281.

Pennebaker, J. W., Colder, M., & Sharp, L. K. (1990). Accelerating the coping process. *Journal of Personality and Social Psychology, 58*, 528–537.

Pennebaker, J. W., & Harber, K. (1993). A social stage model of collective coping: The Loma Prieta earthquake and the Persian Gulf War. *Journal of Social Issues, 49*, 125–146.

Pennebaker, J. W., Mayne, T., & Francis, M. (1997). Linguistic predictors of adaptive bereavement. *Journal of Personality and Social Psychology, 72*, 863–871.

Persson, A. L., Veenhuizen, H., Zachrison, L., & Gard, G. (2008). Relaxation as treatment for chronic musculoskeletal pain: A systematic review of randomized, controlled studies. *Physical Therapy Reviews, 13*(5), 355–365.

Petrie, K. J., Fontanilla, I., Thomas, M. G., Booth, R. J., & Pennebaker, J. W. (2004). Effects of written emotional expression on immune function in patients with human immunodeficiency virus infection: A randomized trial. *Psychosomatic Medicine, 66*, 272–275.

Rahe, R. H., Meyer, M., Smith, M., Kjaer, G., & Holmes, T. H. (1964). Social stress and illness onset. *Journal of Psychosomatic Research, 54*, 35–44.

Rainforth, M. V., Schneider, R. H., Nidich, S. I., Gaylord-King, C., Slaerno, J. W., & Anderson, J. W. (2007). Stress reduction programs in patients with elevated blood pressure: A systematic review and meta-analysis. *Current Hypertension Report, 9*, 520–528.

Rheingans, J. I. (2007). A systematic review of non-pharmacologic adjunctive therapies for symptom management in children with cancer. *Journal of Pediatric Oncology Nursing, 24*(2), 81–94.

Roffe, L., Schmidt, K., & Ernst, E. (2005). A systematic review of guided imagery as an adjuvant cancer therapy. *Psycho-Oncology, 14*, 607–617.

Russoniello, C. V. (2001). Biofeedback: Helping people gain control of their health. *Parks and Recreation, 36*(12), 24–30.

Russoniello, C. V., Fish, M., Parks, J., Rhodes, J., Stover, B., Patton, H., Gold, G., & Maes, T. (2009). Training for optimal performance biofeedback program: A cooperative program between East Carolina University and the United State Marine Corps Wounded Warrior Battalion East. *Biofeedback, 37*(1), 12–17.

Russoniello, C. V., O'Brien, K., & Parks, J. M. (2009). The effectiveness of casual video games in improving mood and decreasing stress. *Journal of CyberTherapy & Rehabilitation, 2*(1), 53–66.

Russoniello, C. V., Skalko, T. K., Beatley, J., & Alexander, D. B. (2002). New paradigms for therapeutic recreation and recreation and leisure service delivery: The Pattillo A+ elementary school disaster relief project. *Parks and Recreation, 37*(2), 74–81.

Russoniello, C. V., Skalko, T. K., O'Brien, K., McGhee, S. A., Bingham-Alexander, D., & Beatley, J. (2002). Childhood posttraumatic stress disorder and efforts to cope after Hurricane Floyd. *Behavioral Medicine, 28*, 61–71.

Schofield, P., & Reid, D. (2006). The assessment and management of pain in older people: A systematic review. Retrieved August 31, 2009, from: http://auraserv.abdn.ac.uk:9080/.../1/systematic%2Breview%2Bpaper.pdf

Seaward, B. L. (2004). *Managing stress: Principles and strategies for health and well-being* (4th ed.). Boston, MA: Jones and Bartlett.

Selye, H. (1976). *The stress of life*. New York, NY: McGraw-Hill.

Sierpina, V., Astin, J., & Giordano, J. (2007). Mind-body therapies for headache. *American Family Physician, 76*(10), 1518–1522.

Smyth, J. M. (1998). Written emotional expression: Effects sizes, outcome types, and moderating variables. *Journal of Consulting and Clinical Psychology, 66*(1), 174–184.

Soper, B., & Von Bergen, C. W. (2001). Employment counseling and life stressors: Coping through expressive writing. *Journal of Employment Counseling, 38*, 150–160.

Spence, J. D., Barnett, P. A., Linden, W., Ramsden, V., & Taenzer, P. (1999). Recommendations on stress management. *Canadian Medical Association Journal, 160*(9 Suppl), 46–50.

Steinberg, A., & Ritzmann, R. F. (1990). A living systems approach to understanding the concept of stress. *Behavioral Science, 35*(2), 138–146.

Swanson, K. S., Gevirtz, R. N., Brown, M., Spira, J., Guarneri, E., & Stoletniy, L. (2009). The effect of biofeedback on function in patients with heart failure. *Applied Psychophysiological Biofeedback, 34*, 71–91.

Syrjala, K. L., Donaldson, G. W., Davis, M. W., Kippes, M. E., & Carr, J. E. (1995). Relaxation and imagery and cognitive-behavioral training reduce pain during cancer treatment: A controlled clinical trial. *Pain, 63*(2), 189–198.

Taylor, S. E., Klein, L. C., Lewis, B. P., Gruenewald, T. L., Gurung, R. A. R., & Updegraff, J. A. (2000). Biobehavioral responses to stress in females: Tend-and-befriend, not fight-or-flight. *Psychological Review, 107*(3), 411–429.

Trakhtenberg, E. C. (2008). The effects of guided imagery on the immune system: A critical review. *International Journal of Neuroscience, 118*(6), 839–855.

Utay, J., & Miller, M. (2007). Guided imagery as an effective therapeutic technique: A brief review of its history and efficacy research. *Journal of Instructional Psychology*. Retrieved January 19, 2008, from: http://www.findarticles.com/p/articles/mi_m0FCG/is_1_33/ai_n16118901/

Van Dixhoorn, J., & White, A. (2005). Relaxation therapy for rehabilitation and prevention in ischemic heart disease: A systematic review and meta-analysis. *European Journal of Cardiovascular Prevention and Rehabilitation, 12*(3), 193–292.

Van Kuiken, D. (2004). A meta-analysis of the effect of a guided imagery practice on outcomes. *Journal of Holistic Nursing, 22*, 164–179.

Weinman, J., Ebrecht, M., Scott, S., Walburn, J., & Dyson, M. (2008). Enhanced wound healing after emotional disclosure intervention. *British Journal of Health Psychology, 13*, 95–102.

Weydert, J. A., Shapiro, D. E., Acra, S. A., Monheim, C. J., Chambers, A. S., & Ball, T. M. (2006). Evaluation of guided imagery as treatment for recurrent abdominal pain in children: A randomized controlled trial. *BioMedCentral Pediatrics, 6*(1), 20–29.

Wood, R., Maraj, B., Lee, C. M., & Reyes, R. (2002). Short-term heart rate variability during a cognitive challenge in young and older adults. *Age and Ageing, 31*, 131–135.

Yu, L., Chiu, C-H., Lin, Y-S., Wang, H-H., & Chen, J-W. (2007). Testing a model of stress and health using meta-analytic path analysis. *Journal of Nursing Research, 15*(3), 202–213.

» CHAPTER 18 »

Sensory Stimulation and Sensory Integration

Brad Wardlaw, Ph.D., CTRS and Norma J. Stumbo, Ph.D., CTRS

Background/History

Some individuals served by therapeutic recreation services have cognitive and physiological deficits with processing sensory information, such as textures, sounds, colors, and tastes, to the degree that the limitations severely restrict the individual's participation in daily life events and activities. In these cases, more typical or traditional interventions discussed elsewhere in this book, such as problem-solving therapy and assertiveness, are not appropriate. Two intervention techniques for treating individuals with significant difficulties in receiving, processing, and acting upon neural input that are gaining more attention from healthcare practitioners, including therapeutic recreation specialists, are sensory stimulation and sensory integration.

Briefly, sensory stimulation involves providing a number of items or experiences for or to the individual that activate one or more senses. For example, presenting a client with brightly colored balloons or a blowing fan so that input into the senses is passively received (although hopefully enjoyed) is an option for sensory stimulation. Sensory integration, on the other hand, is a complex therapy that addresses the underlying substrates or pathologies of dysfunction rather than just the results of the dysfunction (Ayres, 1972a, 1972b, 1978, 1979, 1989; Byl, Nagajaran, & McKenzie, 2003; Parham et al., 2007; Sandler & McLain, 2007; Schaaf & Miller, 2005; Vargas & Camilli, 1999). Sensory integration is an important adjunct to other skill instruction.

> A sensory integration approach . . . differs from many other approaches in that it does not teach specific skills. . . . Rather, the objective is to enhance the brain's . . . capacity to perceive, remember, and motor plan [as a basis for learning] . . . Therapy is considered a supplement, not a substitute to formal classroom instruction. (Ayres, 1972 as cited in Schaaf & Miller, 2005, p. 144)

The intent of sensory integration is to develop new or adaptive "wiring" in the brain and central nervous system in order to more successfully interact with the environment (Ayres, 1972a, 1972b, 1978, 1979, 1989). Schaaf and Miller (2005) noted that "the goal of intervention is to improve the ability [of the individual] to process and integrate sensory information and to provide a basis for improved independence and participation in daily life activities, play, and school tasks" (p. 143). The primary idea behind sensory integration is that the central nervous system is adaptable, and that goal-directed, repetitive, and rewarded sensory and motor learning can result in improvements in the central nervous system and, therefore, improve the person's ability to receive, process, and act upon information more typically (Byl, Nagajaran, & McKenzie, 2003). Basic sensory learning is a prerequisite to higher cognitive learning (Botts, Hershfeldt, & Christensen-Sandfort, 2008). Sensory integration is based on three principles:

(a) learning is contingent on the ability to take up sensory information and integrate it in order to plan and organize behavior,

(b) deficits in processing and integrating sensory information results in deficits in planning and organizing behaviors, and

(c) the ability of the central nervous system to process and integrate sensory information can be improved by exposures to increased and enhanced sensory experiences (Botts et al., 2008).

While sensory stimulation is used by a number of disciplines, sensory integration is primarily used by occupational therapy and physical therapy (Parham et al., 2007; Sandler & McLain, 2007; Schaaf & Miller, 2005; Vargas & Camilli, 1999). Thus, this chapter, intended for therapeutic recreation specialists, will focus on sensory stimulation techniques. The terms "sensory training" and "sensory interventions" will be used when both sensory integration and sensory stimulation techniques are being discussed.

The intent of this chapter is to provide the reader with an evidence-based discussion of best practices in sensory stimulation programming. The organization of this chapter provides citations of articles for intended client groups, a discussion of basic premises, guidelines for practice, a summary of related research, applications to the therapeutic recreation, and a list of resources.

Intended Client Groups

Sensory stimulation programs have been primarily developed and studied in:

- older individuals with advanced dementia (Baker et al., 2001; Barton, Findlay, & Blake, 2005; Buettner & Fitzsimmons, 2003a; 2003b; Cohen-Mansfield, Dakheel-Ali, Thein, & Marx, 2009; Fitzsimmons & Buettner, 2002; Gellis, McClive-Reed, & Brown, 2009; Lancioni, Cuvo, & O'Reilly, 2002; Marshall & Hutchinson, 2001; Milev et al., 2008; Putnam & Wang, 2007; van Weert, van Dulmen, Spreeuwenberg, Ribbe, & Bensing, 2005; Verkaik, van Weert, & Francke, 2005)
- individuals with developmental disabilities, especially those with severe and profound cognitive impairments and autism (Baranek, 2002; Ferrari & Harris, 1981; Hodgetts & Hodgetts, 2007; Lancioni, Cuvo, & O'Reilly, 2002; Lancioni, Singh, O'Reilly, Oliva, & Basili, 2005; Yang & Bruner, 1996)
- individuals with traumatic brain injury (Davis & Gimenez, 2003; Elliott & Walker, 2005; Hotz et al., 2006; Oh & Seo, 2003)
- individuals with schizophrenia (Knudson and Coyle, 1999; Troice & Sosa, 2003)
- individuals with HIV/AIDS (McLoughlin, 2002)
- individuals with pain (Gatchel, Peng, Peters, Fuchs, & Turk, 2007; Mannerkorpi & Henriksson, 2007; Schofield & Davis, 1998, 2000, Younger, McCue, & Mackey, 2009)

Basic Premises

The human brain adapts and grows according to the level of stimulation and input, or conversely, shrinks and declines with deprivation and lack of nourishment (Elliott & Walker, 2005; Schofield & Davis, 1998). Lack of stimulation causes the brain to physiologically deteriorate over time, and thus interventions for those who have suffered systemic or environmental trauma to the brain include sensory stimulation. Individuals with acquired brain injury, dementia, intellectual disabilities,

and autism, for example, are prime candidates for sensory stimulation programs.

Sensory stimulation is employed to increase the level of arousal through activating the reticular activating system in the brain, which is responsible for maintaining consciousness, and regulating engagement and sleep–wake transitions (Elliott & Walker, 2005). Sensory stimulation facilitates and calibrates sensory inputs such as sight, hearing, touch, taste, and smell at therapeutic amounts of frequency, duration, and intensity, typically exceeding everyday levels. It intends to stimulate brain activity and potentially brain function.

However, "undifferentiated bombardment;" that is, the overload of incoming sensory information, is not recommended, as individuals lose the ability to process such large amounts of information and the overload becomes dysfunctional (Wood, 1991; Wood, Winkowski, Miller, Tierney, & Goldman, 1992). Like several other modalities, sensory stimulation has not held up to research scrutiny. Lombardi, Taricco, De Tanti, Telaro, and Liberati (2002) conducted a systematic review for the Cochrane Library and found no scientific evidence to support or rule out multisensory programs for individuals in comas or vegetative states that result from traumatic brain injury. Chung and Lai (2008) came to the same conclusion of lack of scientific support for Snoezelen (to be discussed later) or multisensory stimulation programs for people with dementia. Nevertheless, most specialists can provide multiple anecdotal accounts of persons positively responding to or actively engaging in sensory stimulation activities.

Sensory stimulation activities can focus on individual senses, such as smell or touch, or also include multisensory stimuli, such as animal-assisted therapy. Table 18.1 contains a list of common items used for sensory stimulation materials.

Guidelines for Providing Sensory Stimulation Interventions

There are a number of factors to consider before designing and implementing a sensory stimulation program. The following is a collection of ideas from the educational and research literature that may be helpful to therapeutic recreation specialists.

1. Intervention should begin as early as possible. Elliott and Walker (2005) reported that "early rehabilitation has been associated with better outcomes in severely brain injured patients" (p. 482).

Table 18.1. Senses and Common Items Used for Sensory Stimulation (Vozzella, 2007)

Sight/visual
- Bright colors, such as balloons, fabrics, paints, and card stock papers
- Flashing, strobe, or multi-colored lights
- Reflective objects such as mirrors or metals
- Kaleidoscopes, fiber optic lamps, lava lamps, pinwheels, wind socks
- Pictures or objects from person's past (e.g., postcards, photos, movies)
- Items, inventions, or tools used by the person that can be the focus of reminiscence therapy or reality orientation

Hearing/auditory
- Rousing, relaxing, or familiar music
- Cadences or drum beats
- Noise-making toys, rattles, shakers
- Talking books

Touch/tactile
- Textures such as fur, silk, mud, slime, sandpaper, sea shells, pine cones, squeezable balls, clay, lotions, stuffed/plush animals, emery boards, or feathers
- Shapes such as funnels, balls, and small wooden boxes
- Fans, vibrators, hand warmers, or ice
- Bubble-wrap packaging material
- Tactile boxes in which different items (such as a hairbrush, pencil erasers, a toothbrush, screws, bolts, hair rollers, or coins) are placed and the person without looking guesses the object

Taste/gustatory
- Strong tastes such as cinnamon, chocolate, lemon juice, coffee, and popcorn
- Various cuisines, such Chinese, Thai, Mexican, to elicit discussion about attractiveness, taste, and texture, as well as memories about food preparation and dining

Smell/olfactory
- Essential oils such as lavender, cinnamon, vanilla, menthol, and coconut
- Foods such as peanut butter, fresh bread, cinnamon rolls, pickles, and maple syrup

Proprioception/kinesthetic awareness
- Balance or wobble boards
- Rocking chairs and hammocks
- Juggling scarves or foam objects
- Yoga, Tai Chi

2. The greater the cognitive impairment, the greater the need for sensory stimulation (Barton et al., 2005; Elliott & Walker, 2005; Vozzella, 2007). According to Vozzella (2007), the level of independent participation in leisure activities decreases as cognitive impairment due to dementia worsens. Sensory stimulation may be appropriate for those individuals for whom other, more traditional therapies, such as stress management and reality orientation, are not an option.

3. Intensive or multidisciplinary therapy produces better outcomes for individuals with brain injury. Elliott and Walker (2005) reported that "increased intervention facilitates a more rapid improvement and has the potential to lower the incidence of early behavioral disorders and physical deformities, such as contractures" (p. 483). However, as mentioned earlier, Wood (1991) and Wood et al. (1992) recommended that non-systematic bombardment of stimuli is not recommended.

4. Posture affects the level of arousal. Elliott and Walker (2005) cited numerous observational studies that indicated a standing position, perhaps with the help of a tilt table, improved arousal and awareness. A bonus is that the standing position has a number of physiological benefits, such as redistributing skin pressure and skeletal load.

5. Surroundings of the sensory stimulation experience should be free of distractions, quiet, comfortable, well-lit, and relaxing (Vozzella, 2007).

6. The setting or format of the sensory stimulation session should be selected carefully (Vozzella, 2007). There are five different settings in which a therapist might implement sensory stimulation interventions:

   a. *Group* settings are the traditional method that many therapeutic recreation specialists utilize in providing services. Specific to sensory stimulation, group settings can be utilized when a thematic approach (i.e., seasons, sports, special occasions, or holiday themes) is used.

   b. *Individual* interventions often are used with sedentary and passive patients as well as those who have severe cognitive impairment. Activities used in one-to-one interventions include massage, manicure, sewing, coin sorting, arts and crafts, music, pet therapy, tactile stimulation, and scrapbooking (Russen-Rodinone & Des-Roberts, 1996).

   c. A *drop-off* approach, leaving an activity project with the individual while the specialist is elsewhere, is used with individuals who are higher functioning and have at least partial independence in activity participation. Persons who engage in the drop-off approach often prefer to participate in leisure in a solitary environment and with minimal assistance.

   d. Sensory stimulation can also be provided by *environmental* means (i.e., visual art, fish tanks, tabletop water displays, sculptures, ambient smells, and background music). Such environments need to comprise sufficient sensory stimulation to keep one engaged, while at the same time providing opportunity for reflection and relaxation (Pheasant, Fisher, Watts, Whitaker, & Horoshenkov, 2010).

   e. The final approach is *spontaneous* involvement, in which the activity is not previously planned but occurs by happenstance.

7. Session length may vary due to the needs of the person (Vozzella, 2007). At a minimum, sessions should be planned to engage the patient for at least 10 minutes.

8. Documentation of active participation and/or body language such as eye contact, smiling, and postural changes during sessions is imperative to providing future effective interventions for the patient (Vozzella, 2007).

9. When appropriate, specialists are encouraged to interact with patient during the session. Probing questions can be asked by the therapist to encourage involvement by the patient and enhance the patient's responsiveness to the stimuli provided. Questions aimed at describing what the patient is experiencing during the session can improve the focus of the patient on the intended outcome (Vozzella, 2007).

10. Staff using sensory stimulation should consider the individual's past history and preferences and should introduce sensory items systematically. For example, Barton et al. (2005) suggested a hierarchial approach to treating individuals with dementia who inappropriately vocalize, recording a baseline of behavior and then systematically (hierarchically) introducing sensory items one at a time so that reactions and results can be noted.

Snoezelen

Snoezelen, a multisensory environment and related products, was first conceptualized in the late 1980s in Holland (Botts et al., 2008; Collier & Truman, 2008). Originally designed for individuals with severe and profound developmental disabilities, the environment provides a safe, non-threatening experience that uses gentle sensory exposures meant to enhance pleasure, with no direct therapeutic goals (as opposed to the very directed, hierarchial exposures of sensory integration). "This absence of a purpose or goal leaves the Snoezelen experience open to all possibilities. Sensory experiences are manipulated, intensified, or reduced in relation to the needs and desires of the individual" (Botts et al., 2008, p. 139). Stephenson (2002) identified a number of intended potential outcomes that were largely not substantiated in the reviewed research studies. These potential educational outcomes included: (a) increased control and autonomy by the individual users, (b) use of the senses (in receiving unique input), (c) development of motor skills, (d) exploration and development of cognitive skills, (e) soothing and calming agitation, and (f) building of trust, relationships, and communication.

Snoezelen environments and products are advocated for individuals with severe physical and mental limitations, autism, dementia, traumatic brain injury, posttraumatic stress disorder, critical illnesses, and chronic pain. Like other forms of sensory stimulation, investigations on the short-term and long-term effects of Snoezelen are promising yet inconclusive (Botts et al., 2008; Chung & Lai, 2008; Collier & Truman, 2008;

Hotz et al. 2006; Lancioni, Cuvo, & O'Reilly, 2002; Lancioni, Singh, O'Reilly, Oliva, & Basili, 2005; Stephenson, 2002).

In a crossover, randomized control study of 21 patients with dementia and significant agitated behavior, Snoezelen was more effective than reminiscence in decreasing agitation and heart rate (Baillon et al., 2004). In a systematic review of studies of multisensory stimulation/Snoezelen, Verkaik, van Weert, & Francke (2005) showed there was some evidence that multisensory rooms reduced apathy in patients with late-stage dementia. In an observational pretest/posttest study of 15 children with severe brain injury receiving 10 Snoezelen sessions, exposure to the multisensory-room-environment was shown to increase cognitive outcomes while decreasing agitation (Hotz, et al., 2006). In an analysis of six studies, Snoezelen was shown to reduce disruptive behavior immediately after 30- to 60-minute sessions in patients with dementia (Livingston, Johnston, Katona, Paton, & Lyketsos, 2005).

Readers with further interest should seek information from the American Association of Multi-Sensory Environments (http://www.aamse.us/) or the official source for franchised products, Flaghouse, Inc. (http://www.flaghouse.com or http://www.snoezeleninfo.com/main.asp).

Related Research

Sensory stimulation research, although not plentiful, helps to identify promising practices for clients with a wide range of intellectual and/or perceptual difficulties. In this section, a number of research studies are reviewed by the types of participants involved in the investigation, such as individuals with dementia, individuals with mental illnesses, etc. Two caveats need to be addressed here: (1) several authors have concluded, after systematic or literature reviews, that there is no large-scale proven efficacy of sensory stimulation programs (Chung & Lai, 2008; Lancioni, Cuvo, & O'Reilly, 2002; Lombardi et al., 2002), and (2) although the research below is discussed by the primary sense invoked, the results may not apply to populations other than those of the original research. The investigations below are categorized by these population groups, including individuals with dementia, autism, pain, and mental/cognitive health issues.

Individuals with Dementia

Kverno, Black, Nolan, and Rabins (2009) conducted a systematic literature review to find non-pharmacological intervention studies published between 1998 and 2008 that measured neuropsychiatric symptoms in individuals diagnosed with advanced dementia. They reviewed 22 relevant systematic reviews and found that, although 11 countries were represented, the studies did not mirror the frequency of severe and very severe dementia that is seen in long-term care settings. They also concluded at least some efficacy for (a) physical environments that minimize social and spatial crowding, (b) staff use of validation, and (c) individualized patient schedules based on arousal imbalances, such as lemon balm and multisensory stimulation for underarousal and lavender and music for overarousal. They also advocated stronger research designs, large research participant pools, wider range of research settings, and the use of multiple methods and measures.

Cohen-Mansfield et al. (2009) conducted a study with 69 nursing home residents with dementia and compared work-related stimuli (e.g., folding towels, stuffing envelopes, sorting envelopes by color, sorting jewelry) with manipulative block stimuli (five sets that varied in size, color, and materials). They found that engagement duration, attention, and attitude were significantly higher with work-related stimuli, regardless of work-related task. The participants also responded more favorably toward smaller blocks, regardless of color or material. They noted that although the average time of engagement of 4.4 minutes may seem inconsequential, individuals with dementia did show preferences and actively manipulated the materials.

In a behavioral observational study of 10 patients with middle and late stage dementia selected by nursing staff from a 49-bed special dementia unit, Lucero, Pearson, Hutchinson, Leger-Krall, and Rinalducci (2001) demonstrated that offering sensory stimulation products during unstructured time improved quality of life. Products recommended for patients with middle dementia included simplified model or craft projects, interactive wall art, simulated cooking products, and adapted recreational games. Potential products for late dementia include manipulative boards for tactile stimulation or work stations.

James, MacKenzie, and Mukaetova-Ladinska (2006) showed, in a largely descriptive study, that the use of dolls as a tactile stimuli in a population of 33 nursing home residents with dementia improved activity participation and interaction with staff while increasing happiness and reducing agitation. Researchers utilized the dolls to improve participation in reminiscence, assist in the promotion of bonding, and enhance communication.

Aronstein, Olson, and Shulman (1996) conducted a study with 15 nursing home residents with dementia and showed that one-to-one recreational interventions provided with nursing assistants in an interdisciplinary approach reduced agitated behavior in this population. Recreational interventions provided to patients fell into one of six groups:

- manipulatives: molecules, flex cube, bead maze, tangle, pipe tree
- nurturing: doll, stuffed animal
- sorting/perception: wood sorter, puzzles, workbooks (math, art)
- tactiles: fabric book, squeeze ball, abacus; sewing: lacing tiles
- sound/music: melody bells, xylophone (pp. 27–28)

In a 30-week study with 66 nursing home residents, Buettner (1999) studied the effects of 30 hand-made sensorimotor recreation items (see Table 18.2: Simple Pleasures) on agitation in patients with dementia. Results provided evidence of significant reduction in agitation

Table 18.2. Simple Pleasures (Buettner, 1999, p. 50)

Name of item	Behavior item used for
Activity apron	Repetitive motor patterns
Stuffed butterfly/fish	Verbal repetitiveness
Cart for wandering	Wandering and taking med cart
Fishing box	Hand restlessness
(Arrange) flowers	Hand restlessness
Electronic busy box	Passivity
(Hang laundry on) clothesline	Wandering and restlessness
Home decorator books	Sad, weepy, upset
Latch box-doors	Verbal agitation
(Look inside) purse	Wandering, upset, hand restlessness
Message magnets	Difficulty making needs known
Muffs	General agitation and anxiety
Picture dominoes	Lethargic and isolated
Polar fleece/ hot water bottle	Screaming
Rings on hooks game	Motor restlessness
Sewing cards	Passivity and hand restlessness
Squeezies	Anxiety and hand restlessness
Table ball game	Wandering and trying to leave
Tablecloth with activities	Boredom, isolation, hand restlessness
Tetherball game	Verbal or motor repetitiveness
Vests/sensory	Verbal or motor repetitiveness
Wave machines	Repetitive hand movements

for residents of one nursing home and slight reduction of agitation in a second one.

In a survey of research conducted with 1,032 residents from 28 aged-care facilities in Australia, aromatherapy was found to be used as a sensory modality to address symptomology of dementia and physical discomfort in the elderly (Bowles, Cheras, Stevens, and Myers, 2005). Nguyen and Paton (2008) reviewed 11 randomized studies that included data from 298 patients with dementia and asserted that aromatherapy is a potentially useful treatment in treating behavioral issues associated with dementia; however, there was limited empirical research studying its effects. Lavender has been shown to reduce agitated behavior in older adults (Lin, Chan, Ng, & Lam, 2007; Holmes, Hopkins, Hensford, MacLaughlin, Wilkinson, & Rosenvinge, 2002). Accordingly, aromatherapy has been used as a sensory stimulation intervention to reduce agitation (Gellis, McClive-Reed, & Brown, 2009) and improve quality of life (Ballard, O'Brien, Reichelt, & Perry, 2002).

In a randomized, controlled trial in which 21 patients were allocated to three conditions—aromatherapy and massage, aromatherapy and conversation, or massage only—the combination therapy of aromatherapy and massage was shown to reduce excessive motor behavior in patients with dementia (Smallwood, Brown, Coulter, Irvine, and Copland, 2001). In a study of three sensory cues (picture, word, and odor) in 93 older adults, Willander and Larsson (2006) demonstrated that odor cues could stimulate older autobiographical memories of early childhood than the other cues. Specifically odor cues triggered memories of events that occurred in the first decade of one's life. Some of the odors included were whiskey, tobacco, antiseptic, violet, anise, clove, cardamom, cinnamon, lily of the valley, bitter almond, red wine, and black currant.

Mahoney (2003) addressed the theory that patients with dementia regress through Piaget's developmental stages and display interests of stage-appropriate activities. In a study with 53 patients, using stage- and age-appropriate recreation activities (practice games, symbolic play, and games with rules) and two control activities, the researcher provided evidence of stage- and age-appropriate activities effectiveness in increasing patients' positive emotions as well as reducing agitation and negative emotion. Sensorimotor activity included repetitive manipulation of a stimulus object such as shaking or banging. Preoperational activity was classified as transforming the use of stimulus objects through imaginative play. Concrete and formal operations activity consisted of using the stimulus object to interact socially or competitively.

Judge, Camp, and Orsulic-Jeras (2000) studied the effects of Montessori-based activities on constructive engagement in 19 elderly persons with dementia. Activities that showed significant results in engagement were Question-Asking-Reading (QAR), Memory Bingo, intergenerational programming, and Montessori, individual-based programming. QAR is a reading comprehension activity that engages participants through the reading of two-page stories. Memory Bingo is a game in which players receive cards with answers, and when the facilitator asks a question, the players check their cards to see if they have the correct answer on them. The intergenerational group utilized participants as mentors to assist children with Montessori-based activities, while the final group participated in the Montessori-based activities without children.

Marsden, Meehan, and Calkins (2001) suggested that therapeutic kitchens may offer patients with dementia opportunities for increased socialization. The study consisted of five site visits and a questionnaire mailed to 631 dementia care centers to determine physical features of therapeutic kitchens and how they relate to activity programming. According to the results of the study, activities such as coffee hours that include newspaper reading and current-event discussion, baking, and ice cream socials can be therapeutic as reported by staff.

In a one group pretest/posttest design with 13 patients, Heyn (2003) found that a multisensory exercise program increased engagement and improved mood in patients with Alzheimer's disease. The program utilized storytelling and imagery as sensory stimuli to enhance the exercise program. The storytelling module of the program engaged patients in coordinated moments, while the imagery module was used during major joint exercises, providing patients the sense of traveling to distant parts of the world. Kolanowski, Buettner, Litaker, and Yu (2006) supported the idea of integrating activities that enhance strength, flexibility, and endurance into existing recreation programming for nursing home residents, as these activities have positive effects on both physical and cognitive functioning. Research has shown when two or more senses are stimulated simultaneously, the duration of active participation increases (Kovach & Magliocco, 1998).

A systematic review of music therapy as sensory-stimulation intervention used for neuropsychiatric treatment reveals that it is effective in decreasing disruptive behaviors during and immediately after sensory sessions (Livingston, Johnston, Katona, Paton, & Lyketsos, 2005). There are several strategies in offering auditory stimulation. Utilizing music to convey a certain mood is an effective means of creating a stimulating environment. The exposure to different styles of music elicits affective responses from patients. Drumming is another strategy that is currently being employed by therapists as a means of auditory and kinesthetic stimulation. The spontaneous rhythmical interaction that occurs in a drum circle engages patients in multiple domains of leisure functioning. For lower-functioning patients, recordings of everyday sounds may improve cognitive functioning through matching activities (matching sounds to a picture).

Music therapy can also be used to reduce the effects of depression and increase socialization. Kydd (2001) examined the use of music therapy as an intervention strategy in helping a patient with Alzheimer's disease adapt to living in a long-term care facility. The music therapist initially played and sang familiar songs to the patient and eventually encouraged the patient to actively participate in musical activities (suggesting songs, composing music, and playing instruments). Another study showed that rhythmical background music may aid in active engagement in exercise for elderly with dementia (Mathews, Clair, & Kosloski, 2001).

Witucki and Twibell (1997) found that music, tactile, and olfactory sensory-stimulation interventions improved psychological well-being in 15 patients with advanced-stage Alzheimer's disease. Interventions lasted five minutes and included listening to music pre-selected from the patient's past, massaging the patient's hand with lotion, and providing aromas of chocolate, cinnamon, coffee, fruits, and flowers. Wood, Harris, Snider, and Patchel (2005) showed that small-group music-therapy activities for patients with Alzheimer's disease increased engagement and participation, while patients were observed sleeping or to have an unengaged gaze during large-group, lecture-based music appreciation activities.

Animal-assisted therapy (AAT) has shown to be an effective sensory-stimulation intervention in reducing agitation and increasing socialization in patients with dementia. AAT takes place in one-to-one interactions as well as small-group settings. Patients usually pet, brush, feed, and talk to the therapy dog for short periods of time. The therapy dogs are with their handlers at all times. The therapeutic recreation specialist's role in this intervention is to encourage participation through assisting the patient in building rapport with the therapy dog and the handler and demonstrating how to properly interact with the therapy dog. In a study of 27 elderly persons with senile dementia, AAT was provided for three months in six biweekly sessions. Results of the study suggest AAT improves behavioral symptoms, including reductions of aggressiveness and delusions (Kanamori, Suzuki, Yamamoto, Kanda, Matsui, Kojima, Fukawa, Sugita, & Oshiro, 2001). The use of robotic animals (cats and dogs) with this population has also shown promise. In a pilot study, nine nursing home residents with dementia were observed as to their engagement with a robotic cat and a plush toy cat. Results from the observations included reports of decreased agitation and increased positive affect in patients who interacted with the robotic cat (Libin & Cohen-Mansfield, 2004). In a pretest/posttest pilot study, Richeson (2003) researched the effects of AAT on agitated behaviors and social interactions of 15 elderly persons. AAT interventions were provided five days a week for three weeks during the study. Results showed decreases in agitation in participants as well as increases in socialization.

Individuals with Autism Spectrum Disorders

Hodgetts and Hodgetts (2007) conducted a comprehensive literature review of studies on the effectiveness of sensory stimulation for children with autism. They reviewed a total of six studies that met their inclusion criteria. They found wide variability in the types of interventions studies, the research designs used, and the spectrum of diagnoses of the participants. They concluded that although sensory stimulation and sensory integration interventions have not been proven to be effective, they have also *not* been proven to be *in*effective. More research studies that embrace greater rigor and replication are needed, according to these investigators.

Ferrari and Harris (1981) conducted a study of the effects of three types of sensory stimulation (vibration, music, and strobe light) on four patients with autism. The researchers found that sensory stimulation could be used as a positive reinforcer for simple bar pressing responses and has a comparable motivation potential to food and social reinforcement.

Strickland, Marcus, Mesibov, and Hogan (1996) studied the effects of virtual reality as a sensory stimulation intervention in two case studies with youth with autism. The subjects in the study engaged in desired behavior and interacted appropriately in the virtual world by tracking and identifying objects.

Baranek (2002) conducted a literature review of five studies of sensory stimulation interventions for youth with autism. The primary finding from the review was that using touch pressure as sensory-stimulation intervention for youth with autism was shown to have a calming effect.

Individuals with Pain

Although the comprehensive review of pain etiology, assessment, and treatment by Gatchel, Peng, Peters, Fuchs, and Turk (2007) did not specifically mention sensory stimulation, the logic of such a program for individuals experiencing pain is prominent. They noted that pain is an individually experienced biopsychosocial experience that, if left unchecked, can cause stress to the individual's bodily systems. Prolonged activation of stress hormones, while adaptive in the short-term, can be destructive in the long-term. "Prolonged activation of the stress regulation system will ultimately generate breakdowns of muscle, bone, and neural tissue that, in turn, will cause major pain and produce a vicious cycle of pain-stress-reactivity" (p. 607). The prolonged secretion of cortisol (the primary stress hormone) results in muscle atrophy, impairment of growth and tissue repair, immune system suppression, and the like. Sensory stimulation, especially aimed at stopping the stress experience and inducing the relaxation response (see Chapter 17), hopefully interrupts this degenerative process.

A review of the literature involving sensory stimulation and individuals with chronic pain by Schofield and Davis (1998) was followed by a research study (Schofield & Davis, 2000). In the latter study, the control group received six hours of relaxation instruction and the experimental/treatment group received six hours of sensory stimulation via a Snoezelen environment. Seventy-three individuals completed the entire study. The treatment group experienced significantly less pain and disability as well as greater self-efficacy and better sleep. The authors suggested additional research in this area yet concluded that improvements in pain control, especially for those in the experimental group, were a welcomed addition to chronic pain treatments.

Mannerkorpi and Henriksson (2007) reviewed research literature on the effects of exercise, education, movement therapies, and sensory stimulation on chronic widespread pain and fibromyalgia. They included only acupuncture and massage in their definition of sensory stimulation and found no definitive effect of either on pain reduction.

In an interesting study from Australia, nurses and midwives conducted a study of using a Snoezelen environment for women during their birthing labor. Sixteen women participated in the qualitative study that explored the positives or negatives of a multisensory environment on the birthing process. The environment included soft textures and colors, a "wheel projection that rotates to display wall patterns and fiber-optic lights with slowly changing colors" (p. 461), as well as a fish tank, relaxation music, and aromatherapy of the woman's choice. The investigators reported six themes resulting from the women's experiences: (a) distraction, (b) relaxation, (c) comfort, (d) environmental control, (e) choice of complementary therapies, and (f) safety in a home-like atmosphere. While data such as type and amount of analgesics used and type and duration of labor were not collected, the investigators advocated the use of sensory-stimulation environments for birthing mothers (Hauck, Rivers, & Doherty, 2008).

Individuals with Mental/Cognitive Health Issues

Yang and Bruner (1996) conducted a single-subject, multiple-baseline study with institutionalized adult males with profound developmental disabilities to demonstrate the effectiveness of gustatory stimulation as a strategy for managing hand mouthing. Results suggested that when food is used as sensory reinforcer, hand mouthing can effectively be reduced for short period of time. Additionally, the study showed that while hand mouthing decreased, vocalization increased as a result of the sensory treatment.

Application to Therapeutic Recreation

There has been limited research on sensory stimulation within therapeutic recreation services. Buettner and Fitzsimmons have completed numerous studies on individuals with dementia and have developed several working models to examine needs and how these needs can be met. Patterson (2004) studied the use of Snoezelen for people with an intellectual disability. A review of each of these important contributions follows.

Buettner and colleagues created the Neurodevelopmental Sequencing Program (NDSP). The NDSP addresses the behavioral, movement, and functional losses in individuals with dementia. Initially utilized as a recreational therapy intervention, occupational therapy, physical therapy and nursing now utilize it as a basis for treatment (Buettner, Kernan, & Carroll, 1990). According to the researchers, in Stage I, patients are able to make leisure decisions, but their understanding about leisure is limited to when and where leisure activities are available. A combination of sensory stimulation and reminiscence intervention are utilized to improve cognitive functioning. In Stage II, patients are able to complete leisure activities with assistance. Therapists may need to vocally or tactilely prompt patients during this stage. Activities that promote gross

motor functioning are utilized to enhance eye-hand coordination and upper extremities. In Stage III, therapists use sensory stimulation techniques to help the patient become aware of themselves and their environment. Figure 18.1 (p. 348) outlines the NDSP.

In an eight week crossover study, Buettner, Lundegren, Lago, Farrell, and Smith (1996) tested NDSP as an effective intervention in treating agitation in 36 elderly persons with dementia. Results of the study provided evidence of reduced agitation in the sample. Activities included in the NDSP treatment were sensory air mat therapy, sensory stimulation box program, sensory special events, a geriatric exercise and relaxation program, a sensory herb garden, a sensory cooking program, and a wanderer's leisure lounge.

Patterson (2004) discusses the use of Snoezelen as therapeutic recreation utilizing the Leisure Ability model as the theoretical basis for his argument. The researcher describes the Snoezelen environment as a designed process to bring about a desired change in behavior. This accurately reflects what occurs in the functional-intervention stage of the model. Patterson also reflects upon the pleasurable and enjoyable nature of the Snoezelen environment, which he concludes represents the recreation-participation stage of the model. As a result, the use of multisensory environments can be a valued strategy in providing for the functional and leisure needs of clientele with developmental disabilities.

Through the use of theory and evidence-based practice, therapeutic recreation specialists can create meaningful sensory-stimulation interventions that provide measurable outcomes for clients. Knowing the basic principles of sensory stimulation, as well as the research conducted in this area, is helpful for designing interventions that help clients achieve their targeted goals more efficiently.

Summary

- Sensory stimulation and sensory integration are both interventions that focus on the senses, although sensory integration is a much more sophisticated therapy that attempts to "re-wire" the brain through specific, tiered activities.
- Sensory stimulation involves all five senses: (a) sight/visual, (b) hearing/auditory, (c) touch/tactile, (d) taste/gustatory, (e) smell/olfactory, and (f) proprioception/kinesthetic awareness.
- Sensory bombardment or overload is not recommended.

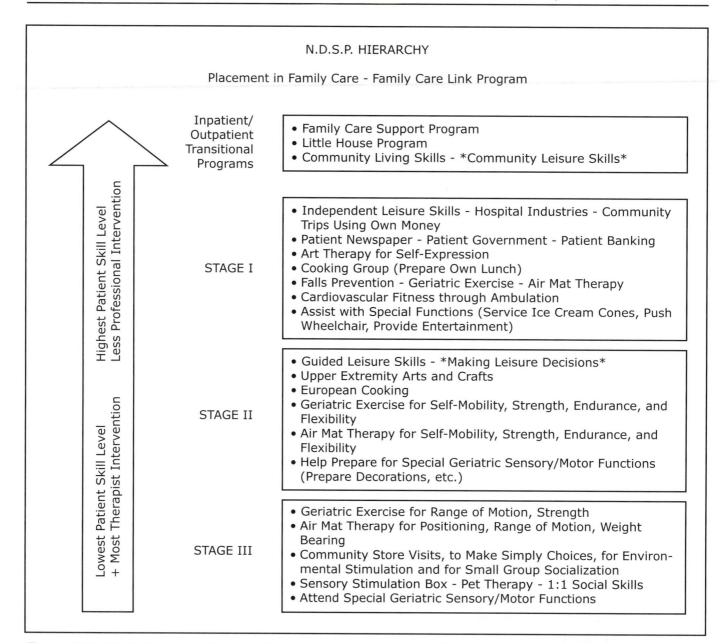

Figure 18.1. NDSP Hierarchy (Buettner, Kernan, & Carroll, 1990, p. 83)

- This chapter provides specific guidelines for sensory stimulation interventions.
- Snoezelen is a multisensory environment that is controlled by the individual, based on his or her preferences and needs.
- There is a growing body of research on sensory stimulation with (a) individuals with dementia, (b) individuals with autism, (c) individuals with pain, and (d) individuals with mental/cognitive health issues.
- The work of Buettner and colleagues is one of the bright spots in sensory stimulation theory developed within therapeutic recreation.

Resources

American Association of Multi-Sensory Environments
www.aamse.us/

National Association of Holistic Aromatherapy
www.naha.org/

Aromatherapy Registration Council
www.aromatherapycouncil.org/aboutus.html

Aromatherapy
www.aworldofaromatherapy.com/

Southpaw Enterprises, Inc.
www.southpawenterprises.com/

TFH: Sensory environments
www.multisensoryenvironments.com/

Flaghouse
www.flaghouse.com/what_AL.asp

Snoezelen
www.snoezeleninfo.com/

Sensory Stimulation Activities
www.recreationtherapy.com/tx/txsensor.htm

Dementia practice guidelines for recreational therapy: Treatment of disturbing behaviors. (2003). By Buettner & Fitzsimmons. American Therapeutic Recreation Association.

Simple Pleasures: A multilevel sensorimotor intervention for nursing home residents with dementia. (1998). By Buettner & Greenstein. www.atra-online.com/

Using a multisensory environment: A practical guide for teachers. (2001). By Pagliano. David Fulton Publishers.

References

Aronstein, Z., Olson, R., & Shulman, E. (1996). The nursing assistant's use of recreational interventions for behavioral management of residents with Alzheimer's disease. *American Journal of Alzheimer's Disease and Other Dementias, 11*(3), 26–31.

Ayres, A. J. (1972a). Improving academic scores through sensory integration. *Journal of Learning Disabilities, 5*(6), 338–343.

Ayres, A. J. (1972b). *Sensory integration and learning disorders*. Los Angeles, CA: Western Psychological Services.

Ayres, A. J. (1978). Learning disabilities and the vestibular system. *Journal of Learning Disabilities, 11*, 30–41.

Ayres, A. J. (1979). *Sensory integration and the child*. Los Angeles, CA: Western Psychological Services.

Ayres, A. J. (1989). *Sensory integration and praxis tests: SIPT manual*. Los Angeles, CA: Western Psychological Services.

Baillon, S., Van Diepen, E., Prettyman, R., Redman, J., Rooke, N., & Campbell, R. (2004). A comparison of the effects of Snoezelen and reminiscence therapy on the agitated behavior of patients with dementia. *International Journal of Geriatric Psychiatry, 19*, 1047–1052.

Baker, R., Bell, S., Baker, E., Holloway, J., Pearce, R., et al. (2001). A randomized, controlled trial of the effects of multi-sensory stimulation (MSS) for people with dementia. *British Journal of Clinical Psychology, 40*, 81–96.

Ballard, C. G., O'Brien, J., Reichelt, K., & Perry, E. (2002). Aromatherapy as a safe and effective treatment for the management of agitation in severe dementia: The results of a double-blind, placebo-controlled trial with Melissa. *Journal of Clinical Psychiatry, 63*(7), 553–558.

Baranek, G. T. (2002). Efficacy of sensory and motor interventions for children with autism. *Journal of Autism and Developmental Disorders, 32*(5), 397–422.

Barton, S., Findlay, D., & Blake, R. A. (2005). The management of inappropriate vocalization in dementia: A hierarchial approach. *International Journal of Geriatric Psychiatry, 20*, 1180–1186.

Botts, B. H., Hershfeldt, P. A., & Christensen-Sandfort, R. J. (2008). Snoezelen: Empirical review of product representation. *Focus on Autism and Other Developmental Disabilities, 23*(3), 138–147.

Bowles, E. J., Cheras, P., Stevens, J., & Myers, S. (2005). A survey of aromatherapy practices in aged care facilities in northern NSW, Australia. *International Journal of Aromatherapy, 15*(1), 42–50.

Buettner, L. (1999). Simple pleasures: A multilevel sensorimotor intervention for nursing home residents with dementia. *American Journal of Alzheimer's Disease and Other Dementias, 14*(1), 41–52.

Buettner, L., & Fitzsimmons, S. (2003a). Activity calendars for older adults with dementia: What you see is not what you get. *American Journal of Alzheimer's Disease and Other Dementias, 18*(4), 215–226.

Buettner, L., & Fitzsimmons, S. (2003b). *Dementia practice guidelines for recreational therapy: Treatment of disturbing behaviors*. Alexandria, VA: American Therapeutic Recreation Association.

Buettner, L., Kernan, B., & Carroll, G. (1990). Therapeutic recreation for frail elders: A new approach. *Global Therapeutic Recreation I: Selected Papers from the First International Symposium, 1*, 82–88.

Buettner, L., Lundegren, H., Lago, D., Farrell, P., & Smith, R. (1996). Therapeutic recreation as an intervention for persons with dementia and agitation: An efficacy study. *American Journal of Alzheimers Disease and Other Dementias, 11*(5), 4–12.

Byl, N. N., Nagajaran, S., & McKenzie, A. L. (2003). Effect of sensory discrimination training on structure and function in patients with focal hand dystonia: A case series. *Archives of Physical Medicine and Rehabilitation, 84*, 1505–1514.

Chung, J. C. C., & Lai, C. K. Y. (2008). Snoezelen for dementia. *Cochrane Database of Systematic Reviews, 2*, art. no.: CD003152.

Cohen-Mansfield, J., Dakheel-Ali, M., Thein, K., & Marx, M. S. (2009). The impact of stimulus attributes on engagement of nursing home residents with dementia. *Archives of Gerontology and Geriatrics, 49*, 1–6.

Collier, L., & Truman, J. (2008). Exploring the multi-sensory environment as a leisure resource for people with complex neurological disabilities. *NeuroRehabilitation, 23*, 361–367.

Davis, A. E., & Gimenez, A. (2003). Cognitive-behavioral recovery in comatose patients following auditory sensory stimulation. *Journal of Neuroscience Nursing, 35*(4), 202–214.

Elliott, L., & Walker, L. (2005). Rehabilitation interventions for vegetative and minimally conscious patients. *Neuropsychological Rehabilitation, 15*(3/4), 480–493.

Ferrari, M., & Harris, S. L. (1981). The limits and motivating potential of sensory stimuli as reinforcers for autistic children. *Journal of Applied Behavior Analysis, 14*(3), 339–343.

Fitzsimmons, S., & Buettner, L. (2002). Therapeutic recreation interventions for need-driven dementia-compromised behaviors in community-dwelling elders. *American Journal of Alzheimer's Disease and Other Dementias, 17*(6), 367–381.

Gatchel, R. J., Peng, Y. B., Peters, M. L., Fuchs, P. N., & Turk, D. C. (2007). The biopsychosocial approach to chronic pain: Scientific advances and future directions. *Psychological Bulletin, 133*(4), 581–624.

Gellis, Z. D., McClive-Reed, K. P., & Brown, E. L. (2009). Treatments for depression in older persons with dementia. *Annals of Long Term Care, 17*(2), 29–36.

Hauck, Y., Rivers, C., & Doherty, K. (2008). Women's experiences of using a Snoezelen room during labor in Western Australia. *Midwifery, 24*, 460–470.

Heyn, P. (2003). The effect of a multisensory exercise program on engagement, behavior, and selected physiological indexes in persons with dementia. *American Journal of Alzheimer's Disease and Other Dementias, 18*(4), 247–251.

Hodgetts, S., & Hodgetts, W. (2007). Somatosensory stimulation interventions for children with autism: Literature review and clinical considerations. *Canadian Journal of Occupational Therapy, 74*(5), 393–400.

Holmes, C., Hopkins, V., Hensford, C., MacLaughlin, V., Wilkinson, D., Rosenvinge, H. (2002). Lavender oil as a treatment for agitated behavior in severe dementia: A placebo-controlled study. *International Journal of Geriatric Psychiatry, 17*, 305–308.

Hotz, G. A., Castelblanco, A., Lara, I. M., Weiss, A. D., Duncan, R., & Kuluz, J. W. (2006). Snoezelen: A controlled multi-sensory stimulation therapy for children recovering from severe brain injury. *Brain Injury, 20*(8), 879–888.

James, I. A., MacKenzie, L., & Mukaetova-Ladinska, E. (2006). Doll use in care homes for people with dementia. *International Journal of Geriatric Psychiatry, 21*, 1093–1098.

Judge, K. S., Camp, C. J., & Orsulic-Jeras, S. (2000). Use of Montessori-based activities for clients with dementia in adult day care: Effects on engagement. *American Journal of Alzheimer's Disease and Other Dementias, 15*(1), 42–46.

Kanamori, M., Suzuki, M., Yamamoto, K., Kanda, M., Matsui, Y., Kojima, E., et al. (2001). A day care program and evaluation of animal assisted therapy (AAT) for the elderly with senile dementia. *American Journal of Alzheimer's Disease and Other Dementias, 16*(4), 234–239.

Knudson, B., & Coyle, A. (1999). Coping strategies for auditory hallucinations: A review. *Counseling Psychology Quarterly, 12*(1), 25–38.

Kolanowski, A., Buettner, L., Litaker, M., & Yu, F. (2006). Factors that relate to activity engagement in nursing home residents. *American Journal of Alzheimer's Disease and Other Dementias, 21*(1), 15–22.

Kovach, C. R., & Magliocco, J. S. (1998). Late-stage dementia and participation in therapeutic activities. *Applied Nursing Research, 11*(4), 167–173.

Kverno, K. S., Black, B. S., Nolan, M. T., & Rabins, P. V. (2009). Research on treating neuropsychiatric symptoms of advanced dementia with non-pharmacological strategies, 1998–2008: A systematic literature review. *International Psychogeriatrics, 21*(5), 825–843.

Kydd, P. (2001). Using music therapy to help a client with Alzheimer's disease adapt to long-term care. *American Journal of Alzheimer's Disease and Other Dementias, 16*(2), 103–108.

Lancioni, G. E., Cuvo, A., & O'Reilly, M. (2002). Snoezelen: An overview of research with people with developmental disabilities and dementia. *Disability & Rehabilitation, 24*(4), 175–184.

Lancioni, G. E., Singh, N. N., O'Reilly, M. F., Oliva, D., & Basili, G. (2005). An overview of research on increasing indices of happiness of people with severe/profound intellectual and multiple disabilities. *Disability and Rehabilitation, 27*(3), 83–93.

Libin, A., & Cohen-Mansfield, J. (2004). Therapeutic robocat for nursing home patients with dementia. *American Journal of Alzheimer's Disease and Other Dementias, 19*(2), 111–116.

Lin, W., Chan, W., Ng, B. F., & Lam, L. C. (2007). Efficacy of aromatherapy (Lavandula angustifolia) as an intervention for agitated behaviors in Chinese older persons with dementia: A cross-over randomized trial. *International Journal of Geriatric Psychiatry, 22*, 405–410.

Livingston, G., Johnston, K., Katona, C., Paton, J., & Lyketsos, C. G. (2005). Systematic review of psychological approaches to the management of neuropsychiatric symptoms of dementia. *American Journal of Psychiatry, 162*, 1996–2021.

Lombardi, F. F. L., Taricco, M., De Tanti, A., Telaro, E., & Liberati, A. (2002). Sensory stimulation for brain injured individuals in coma or vegetative state. *Cochrane Database of Systematic Reviews, 2*, art. no.: CD001427.

Lucero, M., Pearson, R., Hutchinson, S., Leger-Krall, S., & Rinalducci, E. (2001). Products for Alzheimer's self-stimulatory wanderers. *American Journal of Alzheimer's Disease and Other Dementias, 16*(1), 43–50.

Mahoney, A. E. J. (2003). Age- or stage-appropriate? Recreation and the relevance of Piaget's theory in dementia care. *American Journal of Alzheimer's Disease and Other Dementias, 18*(1), 24–30.

Mannerkorpi, K., & Henriksson, C. (2007). Non-pharmacological treatment of chronic widespread musculoskeletal pain. *Best Practice & Research Clinical Rheumatology, 21*(3), 513–534.

Marsden, J. P., Meehan, R. A., & Calkins, M. P. (2001) Therapeutic kitchens for residents with dementia. *American Journal of Alzheimer's Disease and Other Dementias, 16*(5), 303–311.

Marshall, M. J., & Hutchinson, S. A. (2001). A critique of research on the use of activities with persons with Alzheimer's disease: A systematic literature review. *Journal of Advanced Nursing, 35*(4), 488–496.

Mathews, R. M., Clair, A. A., & Kosloski, K. (2001). Keeping the beat: Use of rhythmic music during exercise activities for the elderly with dementia. *American Journal of Alzheimer's Disease and Other Dementias, 16*(6), 377–380.

McLoughlin, K. (2002). Following the yellow brick road: A story about a sensory awareness group. *Social Work with Groups, 25*(4), 21–35.

Milev, R. V., Kellar, T., McLean, M., Mileva, V., Luthra, V., Thompson, S., & Peever, L. (2008). Multisensory stimulation for elderly with dementia: A 24-week single-blind randomized controlled pilot study. *American Journal of Alzheimer's Disease and Other Dementias, 23*, 372–376.

Nguyen, Q., & Paton, C. (2008). The use of aromatherapy to treat behavioral problems in dementia. *International Journal of Geriatric Psychiatry, 23*, 337–346.

Oh, H., & Seo, W. (2003). Sensory stimulation program to improve recovery in comatose patients. *Journal of Clinical Nursing, 12*, 394–404.

Parham, L. D., Cohn, E. S., Spitzer, S., Koomar, J. A., Miller, L. J., Burke, J. P., Brett-Green, B., Mailloux, Z., May-Benson, T. A., Roley, S. S., Schanf, R. C., Schoen, S. A., & Summers, C. A. (2007). Fidelity in sensory integration intervention research. *American Journal of Occupational Therapy, 61*, 216–227.

Patterson, I. (2004). Snoezelen as a casual leisure activity for people with a developmental disability. *Therapeutic Recreation Journal, 38*(3), 289–300.

Pheasant, R. J., Fisher, M. N., Watts, G. R., Whitaker, D. J., & Horoshenkov, K. V. (2010). The importance of auditory-visual interaction in the construction of tranquil space. *Journal of Environmental Psychology, 30*(4), 501–509.

Putnam, L., & Wang, J. T. (2007). The closing group: Therapeutic recreation for nursing home residents with dementia and accompanying agitation and/or anxiety. *American Journal of Alzheimer's Disease and Other Dementias, 22*(3), 167–175.

Richeson, N. (2003). Effects of animal-assisted therapy on agitated behaviors and social interactions of older adults with dementia. *American Journal of Alzheimer's Disease and Other Dementias, 18*(6), 353–358.

Russen-Rondinone, T., & DesRoberts, A. M. (1996). STIR Success Through Individual Recreation: Working with the low-functioning resident with dementia or Alzheimer's disease. *American Journal of Alzheimer's Disease and Other Dementias, 11*(1), 32–35.

Sandler, A. G., & McLain, S. C. (2007). Use of noncontingent tactile and vestibular stimulation in the treatment of self-injury: An interdisciplinary study. *Journal of Developmental and Physical Disabilities, 19*, 543–555.

Schaaf, R., & Miller, L. J. (2005). Occupational therapy using a sensory integrative approach for children with developmental disabilities. *Mental Retardation and Developmental Disabilities Research Reviews, 11*, 143–148.

Schofield, P., & Davis, B. (1998). Sensory deprivation and chronic pain: A review of the literature. *Disability and Rehabilitation, 20*(10), 357–366.

Schofield, P., & Davis, B. (2000). Sensory stimulation (Snoezelen) versus relaxation: a potential strategy for the management of chronic pain. *Disability & Rehabilitation, 22*(15), 675–682.

Smallwood, J., Brown, R., Coulter, F., Irvine, E., & Copland, C. (2001). Aromatherapy and behavior disturbances in dementia: A randomized, controlled trial. *International Journal of Geriatric Psychiatry, 16*, 1010–1013.

Stephenson, J. (2002). Characterization of multisensory environments: Why do teachers use them? *Journal of Applied Research in Intellectual Disabilities, 15*, 73–90.

Strickland, D., Marcus, L. M., Mesibov, G. B., & Hogan, K. (1996). Brief report: Two case studies using virtual reality as a learning tool for autistic children. *Journal of Autism and Developmental Disorders, 26*(6), 651–659.

Troice, E. M., & Sosa, J. J. S. (2003). The musical factor as a curative factor in music therapy with patients with chronic schizophrenia. *Salud Mental, 26*(4), 47–58.

van Weert, J. C., van Dulmen, A. M., Spreeuwenberg, P. M., Ribbe, M. W., & Bensing, J. M. (2005). Behavioral and mood effects of Snoezelen integrated into 24-hour dementia care. *Journal of the American Geriatrics Society, 53*(1), 24–33.

Vargas, S., & Camilli, G. (1999). A meta-analysis of research of sensory integration treatment. *American Journal of Occupational Therapy, 53*(2), 189–198.

Verkaik, R., van Weert, J. C., & Francke, A. L. (2005). The effects of psychosocial methods on depressed, aggressive, and apathetic behaviors of people with dementia: A systematic review. *International Journal of Geriatric Psychiatry, 20*, 301–314.

Vozzella, S. (2007). Sensory stimulation in dementia care: Why it is important and how to implement it. *Topics in Geriatric Rehabilitation, 23*(2), 102–113.

Willander, J., & Larsson, M. (2006). Smell your way back to childhood: Autobiographical odor memory. *Psychonomic Bulletin and Review, 13*(2), 240–244.

Witucki, J. M., & Twibell, R. S. (1997). The effect of sensory stimulation activities on the psychological well-being of patients with advanced Alzheimer's disease. *American Journal of Alzheimer's Disease and Other Dementias, 12*(1), 10–15.

Wood, R. (1991). Critical analysis of the concept of sensory stimulation for patients in vegetative states. *Brain Injury, 4*, 401–410.

Wood, R. L., Winkowski, T. B., Miller, J. L., Tierney, L., & Goldman, L. (1992). Evaluating sensory regulation as a method to improve awareness in patients with altered states of consciousness: A pilot study. *Brain Injury, 6*, 411–418.

Wood, W., Harris, S., Snider, M., & Patchel, S. A. (2005). Activity situations on an Alzheimer's disease special care unit and resident environmental interaction, time use, and affect. *American Journal of Alzheimer's Disease and Other Dementias, 20*(2), 105–118.

Yang, L. D., & Bruner, J. D. (1996). Effects of sensory stimulation to decrease self-stimulatory behavior: Using additional food to suppress hand-mouthing behavior. *Behavioral Interventions, 11*(3), 119–130.

Younger, J., McCue, R., & Mackey, S. (2009). Pain outcomes: A brief review of instruments and techniques. *Current Pain and Headache Reports, 13*, 39–43.

» CHAPTER 19 »

Reality Orientation, Validation, and Reminiscence

Begum Z. Aybar-Damali, Ph.D., Gena Bell, Angela Conti, MS, LRT/CTRS, and Francis A. McGuire, Ph.D., CTRS

In memory of Judith Voelkl

This chapter will introduce three facilitation techniques used often with older individuals: (a) reality orientation, (b) validation, and (c) reminiscence. Each has a long history of use and there is evidence that each may assist individuals who exhibit decreased cognitive functioning.

Reality Orientation

Background/History

James C. Folsom developed Reality Orientation (RO), a technique used to promote awareness of reality for confused persons, through a research study that started in 1959 at the Winter Veterans Administration Hospital in Topeka, Kansas (Folsom, G. S., 1986; Folsom, J., 1968). The hospital director saw a need in a ward that was experiencing a great deal of staff burnout and patient inactivity and requested that Folsom come up with a solution. Folsom rallied the staff to create a rehabilitation team in order to better serve the patients and motivate the staff. The fruits of this team were the beginning of RO. Folsom and colleagues fine-tuned this approach through their work at the V.A. Hospital as well as other facilities, and it was finally given the name "reality orientation" while in use at the Mental Health Institute, Mt. Pleasant, Iowa (Folsom, G. S., 1986; Folsom, J., 1968). According to Folsom, in early 1962 the following guidelines were put into place for all staff:

1. A calm environment.
2. A set routine.
3. Clear responses to patients' questions, and clear questions should be asked of the patient.
4. Talk clearly to patient, not necessarily loudly.
5. Direct patients around by clear directions; if need be, guide them to and from their destinations.
6. Remind them of the date, time, etc.
7. Don't let them stay confused by allowing them to ramble in their speech, actions, etc.
8. Be firm as necessary.
9. Be sincere. (p. 299)

A key component of early RO was the constant reassurance from staff to patient that it was not important to remember the names of staff or other patients, only to be willing to give their name upon request (Folsom, G. S., 1986). This helped to decrease anxiety in patients new and old. Also, when patients exhibited purposeless, repetitive behavior they were given purposeful tasks that most likely increased their feelings of generativity (the opponent of stagnation in Erickson's seventh stage of psychosocial development; Folsom, G. S., 1986; Kleiber, 1999). Not only did the staff encourage more family interaction by helping them to schedule visits they had requested, they also assisted patients in writing letters to their families (Folsom, G. S., 1986). Folsom reported that within six months, "49% of the patients admitted improved sufficiently to return to their prehospital adjustment. The figures for the entire year showed 57% of the patients returned to their prehospital adjustment" (p. 301). It's not hard to see why this effective method spread from being started in just a couple of hospitals to being commonplace across the country.

Intended Client Groups

Persons for whom RO is recommended include those with dementia or neurological conditions who tend to have periods of confusion (Avery, 1997). Periods of confusion can be due to Alzheimer's disease, traumatic brain injuries, or possibly even experiences in a war (the first patients of RO were disturbed war veterans) (Folsom, G. S., 1986). Another suggested population in which RO is appropriate is for those that may be experiencing postoperative confusion (Taulbee & Folsom, 1966).

It is important to keep in mind that while RO is commonly considered to be useful with the patient in the early stages of dementia, it could cause frustration for those in the later stages who would require almost constant cues (Shelkey, 2008).

Basic Premises

Reality Orientation is one of those techniques whose name clearly informs the user as to what it involves. *Idyll Arbor's Therapy Dictionary* (Burlingame, 2001) defined RO as "a formal or informal program to assist the patient in knowing who they are, where they are, why they are there, and when it is. This program includes both verbal and nonverbal cues" (p. 259). According to Ouldred and Bryant (2008), RO "is aimed at reducing confusion and inappropriate behaviors in people with dementia" (p. 246). The general intent is to improve quality of life. Quality of life is defined in *Idyll Arbor* as "the degree to which the patient perceives that his/her life has meaning and comfort" (p. 255). Spector, Orrell, Davies, and Woods (1998) suggested that it can be helpful in increasing sense of control and self-esteem, which many see as contributors to quality of life.

There are two basic formats to RO, classroom and 24-hour (Bowlby, 1993; Ouldred & Bryant, 2008; Spector, Davies, Woods, & Orrell, 2000; Teague & MacNeil, 1992; Woods, 2005). Classroom RO often involves first matching up participants based on their cognitive levels and putting them into small groups (Avery, 1997). The small groups then attend regularly scheduled classes during which basic reality information (the time, date, weather) is given to them repeatedly (Bowlby, 1993). The 24-hour format follows the original guidelines set forth by James Folsom (1968) and listed at the beginning of the chapter. Staff are encouraged to integrate RO into all interactions with participants as well as incidental interactions such as having newspapers accessible and clocks and calendars visible. The most popular way of integrating RO is through the RO board that is generally placed in a community space or on a hallway and has information such as the place, date, season, and weather on it (Ouldred & Bryant, 2008).

When a therapist is not having a specific RO class, Teague and McNeil (1992) suggested that therapists should keep the following guidelines in mind through their programming:

- Briefly repeat who you are and what you do before each activity.
- Review programs/activities in which the residents participated in the recent past.
- Work information such as the time of year, current location, and weather conditions, into program descriptions.

- Describe, when appropriate, the connection of a particular activity to a seasonal theme or holiday.
- Highlight programs and activities to be offered in your next meeting or the near future.
- Review monthly activity calendars with residents. (p. 247)

Lastly, Gould (2008) gave some helpful information regarding communication:

Effective communication with cognitively impaired elderly persons requires realistic expectations. Trying to force reality orientation on severely demented people in nursing homes or expecting a cognitively impaired elder to remember a complicated drug regimen is unrealistic. One direction at a time elicits more comprehension and a successful execution. Alerting the elder to a change in subject helps him or her focus. Written instructions with pictures can help any patient—and certainly cognitively impaired older adults—achieve greater understanding. (p. 152)

Related Research

As was previously mentioned, reality orientation originated from research. James C. Folsom was given the task of developing a pilot study to increase patient activity while improving staff morale in a 1959 VA Hospital in Kansas (Folsom, 1968). He continued his research in Iowa and it was there that he reported the positive results documented above regarding approximately 50% of patients returning to their prehospital conditions.

In an attempt to give more strength to studies of RO, Williams, Reeve, Ivison, and Kavanagh (1987) conducted a study on "informal reality orientation" (aka 24-hour) that included a control group. Baseline comparisons showed the control group (patients in one unit of a hospital) to be very similar to the experimental group (patients in another unit of the same hospital). After the study period was over, patients in the experimental group showed a significant amount of improvement cognitively and behaviorally (Williams et al.).

As of 1998, "RO was shown to improve cognitive function and behaviour in dementia" in a systematic review of past research (Spector et al., 1998). However, they did say that to continue results a regular consistent program must be in place. When it is not, the improvements are usually only short term.

It is possible that early significant results by Folsom and others could be attributed to the fact that prior to RO, the patients were not receiving much attention at all. Perhaps the way we have changed RO over the years has watered down the original strength and for it to be significantly effective again, we would have to go back to its roots.

There has not been a great deal of recent literature on RO. Concurrently, literature on cognitive stimulation has seen an increase. This does not necessarily demonstrate that cognitive stimulation is replacing RO. What it does indicate is that cognitive stimulation has been implemented alongside RO and because it is the newer treatment it is receiving more of the spotlight.

Moniz-Cook (2006) referred to RO as the "precursor" to cognitive stimulation. An early appearance of cognitive stimulation was in a study by Breuil et al. in 1994. They got the ball rolling on "cognitive stimulation" groups, and were then followed by Spector et al. (2001). Spector and her colleagues developed and tested a Cognitive Stimulation Therapy (CST) program and have continued to be the frontrunners in the field ever since. In brief, CST "involves group work concentrating on guided conversations and other activities such as word games . . . sessions also often include an element of reality orientation to time, place and person." (McCabe, 2008, p. 6). CST does share a limitation with RO. Participants show improvements during and shortly after implementation of programs; however the results fade away after the treatment. Often the programs are not continued because of cost issues and/or availability. Perhaps CST would have more long-term results if it could be implemented in a 24-hour format similar to RO. Moniz-Cook did report that the programs with the best outcomes tended to have a more social format that stimulated several of the senses. TR professionals are well trained in providing such formats and therefore it is highly appropriate for them to implement CST.

Application to Therapeutic Recreation

According to the National Council for Therapeutic Recreation Certification (2004), 27.1% of CTRSs work with the geriatric population and 19.3% of CTRSs work in skilled nursing facilities. Hence, techniques for working with the confused elderly are highly applicable to a good amount of therapeutic recreation (TR) professionals.

TR professionals who find themselves working with the confused elderly in any setting can integrate 24-hour RO into all of their interactions. This could be in a physical rehabilitation setting or a skilled nursing facility in which classroom RO could also be appropriate. Another important role of the TR professional is that of advocate. If the CTRS notices other staff or the patients family either not using the guidelines appro-

priately or not using them at all he or she could lead by example. A criticism of RO is that it "has been insensitive to the needs of the individual" (Spector et al., 1998). Because TR is client-centered, this makes the TR professional an ideal person to carry out RO appropriately.

Some specific examples of how to integrate RO into multiple client interactions follow. When greeting a client you can say "Good afternoon Mr. Roberts, are you enjoying the lovely sun we're having on this chilly day in December? If you'd like you can join us for a snack in the dining room here at Seneca Place." If a client is confused you can gently redirect them. For example, if a woman is distressed because she needs to get home to make dinner for her husband (who is no longer around) you can respond by saying "I'll bet you are a wonderful cook, what is your specialty?" or "I bet you miss your husband a lot." You can then assist her in reminiscing about her life with her husband (Bowlby, 1993). After you have spent some time talking about the past, you can reorient her by talking about the meal the cooks are preparing for dinner that night at the residence where she lives. It is important that reality orienting interactions are reassuring as opposed to confronting. The TR professional should keep those ideas in mind for any interactions with confused persons.

Resources

Dementia Practice Guideline for Recreational Therapy. (2003). By Buettner & Fitzsimmons. American Therapeutic Recreation Association.

Therapeutic Activities with the Impaired Elderly. (1986). By Foster. Haworth Press. Includes very informative chapter on the history of RO.

Therapeutic Activity Intervention with the Elderly. (1996). By Hawkins, May, & Rogers. Venture Publishing, Inc.

The Alzheimer's Association
www.alz.org

National Institute on Aging
www.nia.nih.gov/

The National Association for Activity Professionals
www.thenaap.com/templates/

The National Center for Assisted Living
www.ahcancal.org/

Center for Excellence in Assisted Living
www.theceal.org/index.php

Example Activities

Taken from the *Dementia Practice Guideline for Recreational Therapy* (2003) by Linda Buettner and Suzanne Fitzsimmons (pp. 154–156):

Newsletter

This program provides the participants an opportunity to talk about issues (current and from the past); to express emotions and concerns; to interview other clients and/or staff members; to work together in a small group setting; to type or work a computer, camera, or copy machine; and to deliver the finished product to other clients and staff.

Staff Requirements: One CTRS

Entrance Criteria: Clients with vocalizing behaviors such as demanding, repetitive vocalization or complaining; clients with physical restlessness or repetitive motor movements; clients with depression, social isolation, or passive behaviors such as withdrawal, apathy, or those who have difficulty expressing emotions. Able to verbalize thoughts, needs to improve socialization or needs contact with other residents, and/or enjoys reading. This program is for clients in the mild to moderate stages of impairment.

Exit Criteria: No longer enjoys program, no longer able to participate, or no longer displaying symptoms.

Group Size: 2–4 clients.

Duration: Up to 45 minutes.

Safety Considerations
Environmental Risks: No specific risks.
Client Risks: No specific risks.

Facility & Equipment required
Facility: Table and chairs.
Equipment: Laptop or desktop computer, camera, pad and pencils, colored paper for copying.

Methods

- Seat clients around a table and encourage clients to select topics for the newsletter from a list of options such as: Health Tips, Sport & Leisure, Upcoming Events, Recipes, Poetry, or Medical Conditions. Clients will be encouraged to talk about the topics while staff members take notes.
- Clients take digital photographs or provide artwork to include in newsletter and assist with clip art placement.
- Staff question clients, not included in the group, for their replies to the "questions of the week/month."
- One or two of the clients will assist with the typing. Another one or two will assist with the copying and stapling of the newsletter. Another client to deliver the newsletter.
- **Note:** The bulk of the newsletter is to be written, verbatim, from what the residents say. A list of topic suggestions and questions follow.

Possible Topics

- Health
- Sports
- Leisure
- Seasons/Holiday
- Resident News
- Psychosocial (Relationships)

Sample Questions for "Question of the Week"
Staff should ask all clients on the unit these questions. For those who are nonverbal, write down their sound or facial expression response.

- What makes you happy?
- Were you a good student?
- What does January (February, March, etc.) or Christmas (Easter, Thanksgiving, etc.) mean to you?
- What is needed to have a great party?
- What's your favorite snack?
- What is my job? What was your occupation?
- How can you get rid of a headache?
- Where is home?
- Do you like to dance?
- Did you ever drive a car?
- How is the food here?

Possible Client Objectives

- Decrease nonaggressive behaviors, such as wandering, through engagement in a conversation.
- Decrease vocalizing behaviors.
- Decrease passive behaviors by involvement in group.
- Improve ability to express self and emotions.
- Increase social skills and social interaction with others.

- Improvements in ability to communicate.
- Improve attention to task.
- Decrease apathy, as evidenced by increased participation in unit programming.
- Decrease depression, as evidenced by expressing pleasure over participation or by expression on face.

Validation

Background/History

Naomi Feil created and developed Validation Therapy (VT) between the years of 1963 and 1980. VT is a communication tool that may be used by the caregivers of adults with Alzheimer's-type dementias, during both one-to-one interactions and as a validation group. Feil developed her techniques based on her frustration with traditional methods of interacting with individuals with dementia, and today there are authorized validation organizations in nine countries throughout the world (Validation Training Institute, Inc., 2003). "The goals of a validation group are: (1) to stimulate interaction, (2) to encourage participants to take on social roles, (3) to generate a sense of well-being and happiness, (4) to develop social controls, (5) to increase verbal behaviors" (Feil & DeKlerk-Rubin, 1992, as cited in Feil, 2002).

Intended Client Groups

The techniques of VT can be learned and used by any person interacting with an individual with dementia, including healthcare providers, spouses and other family members, and friends. Although research has concentrated on providing VT in healthcare facilities (Bleathman & Morton, 1992; Deponte & Missan, 2007; Tondi, Ribani, Bottazzi, Viscomi, & Vulcano, 2007; Toseland et al., 1997), the technique can be used in all caregiving settings, such as in the home, long-term care, acute care facilities, and community programs. VT can be used in both group therapy settings (Toseland et al., 1997) and during ordinary day-to-day interactions (Feil, 2002).

Basic Premises

VT is based on the idea that the disturbing behaviors (verbal and physical aggression, repetitive movements, passivity, impaired functional abilities; Kolanowski, 1995) demonstrated by individuals with dementia are purposeful actions working towards resolving the issues that motivate them, and are not simply biological side effects of changes in the individual's brain (Feil, 2002). The theory supporting VT is that as people move through their lives, they build up experiences

of unresolved issues and emotions. When the person with dementia is no longer able to easily recall recent memories, he or she will begin to recall earlier life memories for the purpose of resolving these old issues and feelings before reaching the end of life. Rather than correcting the inaccurate factual information or malorientation that may occur when an individual with dementia is expressing these memories, the caregiver will concentrate on discovering the emotions and purpose behind the interaction (Bleathman & Morton, 1992).

When implementing VT, the caregiver needs take a truly empathetic approach. The caregiver must acknowledge that there is a purpose for each behavior and show a genuine concern for and interest in the emotions the individual is feeling. There are four stages of resolution that the individual with dementia may progress through while trying "to resolve unfinished business in order to die in peace . . . (1) Malorientation, (2) Time Confusion, (3) Repetitive Motion, and (4) Vegetation" (Feil, 2002, p. 31). Caregivers can use 14 techniques to providing VT when interacting with these individuals. The 14 techniques to making an individual feel validated are as follows (Feil, 2002, p. 37–48):

1. "Centering": Take a moment of deep breathing to let go of your own emotions and remember that the purpose is to focus on the other person.
2. "Using Nonthreatening, Factual Words to Build Trust": Do not ask "why" questions that may create confusion and agitation by asking the individual to focus on feelings. Ask questions about factual, concrete information in order to validate the individual's memory or experience.
3. "Rephrasing": Rephrase what the individual has said, using the same tone, speed, and emotions that the individual expresses.
4. "Using Polarity" 5. "Imagining the Opposite" 6. "Reminiscing": (NOTE: Techniques 4–6 are used together.) When the individual is complaining, ask him or her to think about the worst similar experience they had, or if he/she is anxious or upset about a problem, probe him/her to imagine the opposite situation. This may trigger a memory about how the individual solved a similar experience in the past. Use purposeful words and questions to help the individual recall past memories.
7. "Maintaining Genuine, Close Eye Contact": Looking directly at the person at a close range, with the intent of making an emotional connection.

8. "Using Ambiguity": If the individual is saying something that does not make sense to the caregiver, use pronouns (they, he, she, that, it, etc.) to ask the person about what he/she is saying, instead of directly repeating what was said.

9. "Using a Clear, Low, Loving Tone of Voice": This is to be used unless the individual is speaking with an altered tone of voice, in which case technique 3 should be used.

10. "Observing and Matching the Person's Motions and Emotions (Mirroring)": Tactfully mirroring a repetitive motion of the individual may prompt the individual to verbalize something about the behavior that will allow the caregiver to better understand why the motion is made.

11. "Linking the Behavior with the Unmet Human Need": Explore why the behavior is occurring or the memory is expressed, and acknowledge the individual's need or emotion.

12. "Identifying and Using the Preferred Sense": Observe the individual and use sight, taste, smell, touch, and sound as they best fit.

13. "Touching": Connect to the person with appropriate, affectionate touch. This technique should only be used with caution and respect, and is not appropriate to use with individuals who are maloriented.

14. "Using Music": Music can stimulate memories and emotions.

Related Research

One example of supportive research is a controlled study comparing group validation therapy (VT) to a social contact (SC) group and a usual care (UC) group within four different skilled nursing facilities (Toseland et al., 1997). The study included 88 subjects who were randomly assigned to one of the three types of groups. After one year of 30-minute sessions held four times each week, nurses reported observing fewer aggressive behaviors from the individuals participating in VT compared to SC and UC, however there was no reduction seen in the use of psychotropic medications or physical restraints for any of the three groups. Tondi et al. (2007) also studied the effectiveness of VT in a nursing home by examining neuropsychiatric symptoms. Fifty research subjects were divided into a case group (whose members received both individual and group VT for four months) and a control group (whose members received no VT for the four-month period). The treatment group showed a significant decrease in neuropsychiatric symptoms, particularly agitation, apathy, irritability, and nighttime behavior disturbances,

where as the control group showed a slight increase in symptoms over the four-month period.

Deponte and Missan (2007) examined the effects of group validation on the cognitive functioning, activities of daily living, and problematic behaviors of 30 subjects living in a long-term care facility. Participants were assigned to groups of VT, sensorial reminiscence, or no treatment. After participating in two groups per week for three months, both treatment groups showed improved performance in the assessment areas, but the differences were not found to be statistically significant.

There is a wealth of information available about VT techniques and literature reviews of VT and other non-pharmacological interventions for dementia (Bates, Boote, & Beverly, 2004; Day, 1997; Feil, 2002; Finnema, Droes, Ribbe, & Van Tilburg, 2000; Moos & Bjorn, 2007; Neal & Barton, 2003); however, there is a lack of significant experimental research exploring the effectiveness of VT techniques. In concluding a review of VT literature, Day (1997) stated that the existing research had positive results, but she also suggested expanding the types of research settings and examining the effectiveness of VT on the use of psychotropic medication use, chemical and physical restraints, confusion, and problematic behaviors.

Application to Therapeutic Recreation

Therapeutic Recreation (TR) professionals working with adults with dementia in any setting can learn, practice, and implement the VT techniques. Group VT sessions can be held in both long-term care and community settings, and the 14 techniques can be implemented as a general approach to care during all regularly scheduled TR activities and programs. The TR professional using VT can also act as an advocate in the work setting, teaching and modeling the techniques to co-workers and employees at all levels, as well as the family members of the individuals with dementia.

Before beginning the group validation, the TR professional should assess eligible participants specifically with regard to the needs and purposes of the group, as well as plan for a co-facilitator who can tend to the physical needs of participants during the group (Feil, 2002).

The TR professional will then create goals for the group and assign roles to each participant that he or she will maintain throughout each session. Examples of group roles include "welcomer . . . song leader . . . poetry reader . . . chair arranger . . . emotional leader" (Feil, 2002, p. 268). Each validation group should incorporate music, movement, and a specific topic for discussion. A comfortable, quiet room should be prepared, and the same format or outline should be used during each meeting. A single session can be planned for 25–60 minutes and should include energizing introduction activities, a group discussion or verbal interaction, movement and rhymes, then a wrap-up and preview of the next meeting (Feil, 2002). Feil (2002) also recommended moving the participants to another social activity after the group validation session because "If members are isolated in their rooms after the meeting, they will feel abandoned and often may begin to exhibit negative behaviors" (p. 279).

Resources

The Validation Breakthrough: Simple Techniques for Communicating with People with Alzheimer's-Type Dementia (2nd ed.). (2002). By Feil. Health Professions Press.

V/F Validation: The Feil Method, How to Help Disoriented Old-Old (2nd ed.). (2003). By Feil & De Klerk-Rubin. Edward Feil Productions.

The Validation Training Program: The Practice of Validation. By Sutton & Feil. Health Professions Press.

Validation Training Institute, Inc.
www.vfvalidation.org

Example Activities

Validation Techniques in Action. The following is a fictional scenario illustrating how VT can be used in daily interactions:

A CTRS working in a long-term care facility approaches Mr. Thomas to invite him to a group activity. When entering his room, the CTRS observes that Mr. Thomas is anxious and agitated, appearing to look through his drawers and cabinets for something.

The CTRS says in a calm, warm voice: "Good afternoon Mr. Thomas. Can I help you look for something?"

Mr. Thomas replies in a hurried, louder tone of voice: "I can't find the papers! Sally always puts my things away and I can't find them when I need them."

The CTRS picks up the speed and volume of her speech and replies: "Well I can help. Where does she usually put things away?"

Mr. Thomas: "Oh all over the place. I don't know. She always takes care of things for me and tries to help me keep everything in order."

CTRS: "That's probably because she cares about you so much and wants to take care of you. The last time she put your things away, where did you find them?"

Mr. Thomas: "Hah, I never did. I just had to wait for her to get home and tell me where they were."

CTRS: "Then I guess we'll have to wait for her to get back. Would you like to come help me while you wait?"

Mr. Thomas: "I guess that will be alright. But I hope that she gets home soon."

Mr. Thomas leaves with the CTRS, still slightly anxious but having his experience validated he is able to move past looking for his papers and focus on a new activity.

Sample Group Validation Session. The following is a sample outline of a validation group, following the format suggested by Feil (2002). The 14 validation techniques are to be used when interacting with the participants throughout the session.

Preparation:

- CTRS and assistant ensure that all participants have their basic needs taken care of before coming to the group.
- CTRS has checked the room for comfortable lighting and temperature and to make sure there are enough chairs.

Introduction & Energizer (5 minutes):

- Welcomer greets everyone at the door, shakes hands, and invites participants to have refreshments and take a seat.
- Fitness leader chooses stretches and exercises for the group to do before the discussion.

Discussion (10–15 minutes):

- Topic: Winter
  - What do you like to see, smell, hear in the winter time?
  - What do you like to do in the winter time?
  - What don't you like about winter?
  - What holidays do we celebrate in the winter?

Movement and Rhymes (10–15 minutes):

- Poetry reader chooses from selection of winter poems and reads one or two to the group.

- Participants choose from an assortment of winter accessories (gloves, scarves, hats, coats, etc.) to feel, wear, and share.

Wrap-Up (5 minutes):

- Refreshment coordinator begins to pick up trash and clean up the refreshment table.
- CTRS summarizes the session's conversations.
- Group decides on the topic for the next session and CTRS informs the group when the next session will be.
- CTRS and assistant suggest to the participants that they stay in the room to continue to talk and listen to music together.

Reminiscence

Background/History

What does reminiscence mean? Reminiscence is defined in multiple ways. Van Puyenbroeck and Maes (2008) defined reminiscence as "spontaneously occurring (social) human behavior of recalling the past" (p. 44). Haber (2006) defined reminiscence as "the recall of memories" (p. 154).

In the literature, "reminiscence" and "life review" are terms often used interchangeably, so one may ask whether reminiscing is a life review. Butler (1963) described life review as "a naturally occurring, universal mental process, characterized by the progressive return to consciousness of past experiences, and, particularly, the resurgence of unresolved conflicts; simultaneously, and normally, these reviewed experiences and conflicts can be surveyed and reintegrated" (p. 66). Research suggests that reminiscence has some therapeutic qualities, thus it can be used to obtain benefits in various aspects of mental and social health and well-being. In a sense, the systematic use of specific methods can help stimulate reminiscence for such benefits; this process is called *reminiscence therapy* and can be conducted as an individual or a group modality. Research indicates that reminiscence therapy can have positive effects on cognitive, psychological, social, behavioral, and health status, and reminiscence may contribute to emotional regulation in various populations—individuals in later life particularly.

Intended Client Groups

Reminiscence has been studied for a variety of populations; however, its application as a therapeutic technique is often seen in the literature on aging. The primary focus of reminiscence-related studies is mental-health-related issues including memory and cognitive adaptation. The client groups and specific situations that reminiscence may be useful for include:

- cognitive functioning and memory development in children (Cleveland, Reese, & Grolnick, 2007; Q. Wang, 2007)
- relationship satisfaction among couples (Bazzini, Stack, Martincin, & Davis, 2007)
- depression in older adults and/or nursing home residents (Arean et al., 1993; Cook, 1991; Fry, 1983; Goldwasser, Auerbach, & Harkins, 1987; Parsons, 1986; Perrotta & Meacham, 1981; Stevens-Ratchford, 1993; Youssef, 1990)
- psychiatric conditions in geriatric populations (Lesser, Lazarus, Frankel, & Havasy, 1981)
- anxiety (Haight, 1991)
- cognitive functioning and mental adaptability in elderly (Haight, 1991; Tanaka et al., 2007; J. Wang, 2007; Weiss, 1989; Weiss & Thurn, 1987; Yamagami, Oosawa, & Yamaguchi, 2007)
- denial of death (Haight, 1991)

Reminiscence interventions may take place in settings with a treatment and healthcare orientation (Yamagami et al., 2007), for instance, nursing homes (Cook, 1991; Goldwasser et al., 1987; Weiss, 1989; Weiss & Thurn, 1987; Youssef, 1990) or other interventions such as memory clinics (Tanaka et al., 2007). In addition, studies on reminiscence have had clients from various community settings such as senior centers and retirement residencies (Arean et al., 1993; Bazzini et al., 2007; Perrotta & Meacham, 1981; Stevens-Ratchford, 1993).

Basis Premises

Why do we reminisce? Researchers agree on at least eight common functions of reminiscence (Cappeliez, Guindon, & Robitaille, 2008; Webster, 2003; Wong, 1995):

1. Identity
2. Problem solving
3. Death preparation
4. Teach–inform
5. Conversation
6. Bitterness revival
7. Boredom reduction
8. Intimacy maintenance

Webster (2003) organized these functions in four categories on a two-by-two matrix (Table 19.1):

1. Self-proactive/growth
2. Self-reactive/loss
3. Social-proactive/growth
4. Social-reactive/loss

Different types of reminiscence have been found to cause different emotions. Cappeliez, Guindon, and Robitaille (2008) investigated the causal influence of these eight types of reminiscence on positive and negative emotions. In this study, Cappeliez and his colleagues interviewed 80 older adults aged 61 and over for approximately 60 minutes each. During one-on-one interviews, the participants were asked to report the last episode of reminiscence they remembered having experienced. The systematic review of the reminiscences (i.e., type of reminiscence, type of emotions and the intensity of these emotions before and after the reminiscence) showed that the most commonly reported reminiscence types were Identity, Intimacy, Conversation, and Bitterness Revival. The *conversation* and *identity* types of reminiscence occur in the context of positive emotions and elicit, maintain, or amplify positive feelings. The *bitterness revival* type of reminiscence occurs in the context of negative emotions. The *intimacy* reminiscences occur in the context of negative emotions, and often change initial positive emotion into negative one such as sadness. The authors suggest that their findings shed some light on how reminiscence may contribute to emotional regulation in later life. Not only the stimulation of reminiscence, but also the type of reminiscence stimulated needs to be considered.

Related Research

Bohlmeijer, Roemer, Cuijpers, and Smit (2007) conducted a meta-analysis to evaluate the effects of reminiscence and life review (the distinction being that life review involves a critical consideration of a past experience but reminiscence does not) on psychological well-being in older adults. The review of the 16 controlled outcome studies (7 life review and 9 reminiscence studies) showed that both life-review and reminiscence are worthwhile interventions, with significant effects on psychological well-being in older

adults. Bohlmeijer et al. reported that life review had slightly greater effects than simple reminiscence.

According to research, there are no guidelines regarding length or frequency of reminiscence interventions. In research (e.g., Fry, 1983; Tanaka et al., 2007; Perrotta & Meacham, 1981) on reminiscence and life review, usually a typical one-on-one intervention is designed to cover 5 to 8 weeks, and the duration of an intervention varies from 30 to 90 minutes. Intervention took place once or twice a week, depending on clients' needs and length of a program. A similar pattern was seen in studies focused on group reminiscence (e.g., Arean et al., 1993; Cook, 1991; Goldwasser et al., 1987; Stevens-Ratchford, 1993; J. Wang, 2007; Yamagami et al., 2007; Youssef, 1990). Group reminiscence programs typically lasted 3 to 16 weeks, and groups met once or twice a week depending on the program span. The length of the interventions varied from 30 to 120 minutes. Usually, groups met twice a week and for a longer duration if the program covered only a few weeks.

When there is no follow-up study after a reminiscence intervention, it is not possible to predict whether the effects of reminiscence are long-term. J. Wang (2007) conducted a reminiscence therapy program to increase cognitive and affective functioning of elderly individuals in Taiwan. The therapy involved 8 to 10 persons and took place once a week over an 8-week period and was 60 minutes long. Themes of each session were different and included: (1) the first meeting, (2) childhood experience, (3) older flavors of food, (4) old-style music, (5) festivals, (6) my family, (7) younger age, and (8) my achievements. The comparison of the group which received the treatment and the group which did not receive the treatment showed that the intervention helped diminish depressive symptoms and increase cognitive functioning in the experimental group. J. Wang (2007) suggested that reminiscence can be a valuable part of a structured care plan in long-term care facilities, but he stated that due to lack of follow-up, it is not known whether the effects are short-term or long-term. Wang suggested that reminiscence should be a part of a continuing program and sessions should be held at least weekly if long-term effects are expected.

Reminiscence is effective for adults, but community-dwelling adults profit more from reminiscence compared to adults living in nursing homes or residential care institutes (Bohlmeijer et al., 2007). Although individual and group formats seem to be equally effective on well-being (Bohlmeijer et al., 2007), it is suggested that, with some populations, one-on-one interventions might be preferable over group interventions (e.g., Weiss, 1989; Weiss & Thurn, 1987).

Table 19.1. Eight Functions of Reminiscence (Webster, 2003)

	Proactive/Growth	Reactive/Loss
Self	Problem Solving	Boredom Reduction
	Identity	Bitterness Revival
Social	Conversation	Intimacy Maintenance
	Teach-Inform	Death Preparation

Application to Therapeutic Recreation

The application of reminiscence to therapeutic recreation is limited but not new (Sylvester, Voelkl, & Ellis, 2001). Researchers (Sheldon & Dattilo, 2000, p. 322) have suggested that reminiscence techniques "can be used by TR specialists to facilitate social interaction, reconstruction of memories, and coping mechanisms" and documented guidelines regarding how to incorporate reminiscence in therapeutic recreation program planning.

According to Weiss (1989), reminiscing may not occur spontaneously with some populations such as elderly persons with disorientation, and thus recreation specialists need to play a facilitator role. Weiss suggests that the actual process of reminiscing with such populations involves four phases:

1. Staging: Staging involves being a good listener and explaining the value and the feasibility of reminiscing to a client. If the client feels that the facilitator is not listening or thinks that reminiscence is not valuable, no matter how interesting and personal the subject is, he or she may not reminiscence.
2. Starting out: "Starting out" refers to providing a physical and social environment that helps engage individuals. Selecting the best possible setting for reminiscence is crucial, since even minor distractions may hinder the effectiveness of intervention and clients' safety.
3. Maintaining interest and focus: The third stage requires paying special attention to clients' needs —for example, focusing on self-esteem, giving more time to reminiscence, and being patient.
4. Ending the session: Usually the length of a session depends on clients' energy and comfort. Sessions end sooner than planned if the facilitator observes fatigue, discomfort, or restlessness.

Weiss (1989) suggested that therapeutic recreation specialists should be critical about the content of the program. Selecting "appropriate and interesting topics" and framing "helpful questions" can be challenging but are important for maintaining clients' interest and focus, it thus requires special attention.

In reminiscence interventions, various types of materials can be used as stimulants, for example, familiar items from the past, such as photographs, music, old movies, and the flavor of food. In a program developed to stimulate reminiscence, Weiss and Thurn (1987) used maps and mapping activities with mild to moderately confused elderly in a nursing home. The program involved four projects:

1. Drawing a mental map of the childhood home of the resident
2. Mapping the lifetime travels of the residents
3. Creating original ways to involve residents with maps, drawing upon prior interests and skills
4. Representation of the "culture" of the resident

Weiss and Thurn (1987) stated that the evaluations of this program provided some evidence for increases in expression of feelings, positive effect, experiencing pleasure and social interaction and decreased evidence of anxiety. They suggested that this type of reminiscence program may be beneficial to residents of other long-term care facilities.

There is no consensus on how reminiscence should be applied to therapeutic recreation. As the Weiss (1989) and Weiss and Thurn (1987) studies illustrated, recreational specialists may take a facilitator role in reminiscing programs that aim to help recall memories. According to Shute (1986, p. 57), "Insufficient specification of curative aspects and risk factors may result in psychological harm to certain participants"; thus the helper needs to be adequately prepared and consider personality variables and the life history of his or her client(s). Therapeutic recreation specialists are required to pay special attention to development of a safe and effective therapeutic intervention. As Haber (2006) suggested, facilitation of simple reminiscence with naïve expectations of higher health and well-being can be very risky. The primary goal of therapeutic reminiscence is to support and enhance health and well-being, thus certain guidelines and standards need to be set. Since research on the effectiveness of reminiscence therapy and its application to therapeutic recreation is still growing, recreation specialists need to carefully document reminiscence intervention program plans and evaluation results.

Resources

- A description of various reminiscence activities is available at: www.recreationtherapy.com/tx/txrem.htm
- A description of reminiscence activities to use with individuals with dementia is available at: http://alzheimers.about.com/cs/treatmentoptions/a/reminiscence.htm
- An excellent overview of reminiscence, including suggested activities and guidelines, is available at: www.caregiver.com/articles/general/linking_past_to_present.htm
- A reminiscence program focusing on ethnic minority populations, entitled Mapping Memories,

is available at: www.age-exchange.org.uk/projects/past/mappingmemories/introduction.html

- An excellent review of research related to reminiscence and dementia is available at: www.mrw.interscience.wiley.com/cochrane/clsysrev/articles/CD001120/frame.html
- Commercial products designed for reminiscence programs are available through companies such as Many Happy Returns, a British organization, (www.manyhappyreturns.org/aboutdo/reminiscence) and Bi-Folkal Productions, located in Wisconsin (www.bifolkal.org/)

Example Activities

Almost any activity that stimulates memories of the past can be used for reminiscence, as long as it is of interest to the individual. A common reminiscence activity involves the creation of kits containing artifacts from a specific time (for example, World War II), season (for example, Thanksgiving) or location (such as one's hometown). The leader then asks questions focused on the materials in the kit and how they relate to the topic. For example, a kit designed around Christmas may include old-fashioned ornaments, Christmas cards from an earlier era, family artifacts stimulating Christmas memories, music from earlier times, or photographs from Christmases past.

Another common approach used in reminiscence programs is creating oral histories and using the process to spur reminiscence. For example, an individual and his or her family might construct the story of their lives and share with others, or families could create the history and share with their loved one. This history could be used to facilitate discussion about the places an individual has lived, where she or he was born, the jobs he or she held, or where he or she met significant people in his or her life.

One of the authors of this chapter developed "corner museums" as part of a reminiscence program. The corner museums were tables located in the activity room in a long-term care facility. The theme of the corner museum varied from "this old town" to "the old schoolhouse" to "down on the farm." The museums included various artifacts (such as early maps, school books or old farm tools), old photographs, written documents (deeds, report cards, feed bills), and letters and other items gathered from residents and family. Each "museum" stayed up for a few weeks and during that time became the focus for several reminiscence programs. A culminating event, involving singing, discussion, and storytelling, accompanied the end of a museum cycle.

References

Arean, P. A., Perri, M. G., Nezu, A. M., Schein, R. L., Christopher, F., & Joseph, T. X. (1993). Comparative effectiveness of social problem-solving therapy and reminiscence therapy as treatments for depression in older adults. *Journal of Consulting and Clinical Psychology, 61*(6), 1003–1010.

Avery, L. F. (1997). *Activity programming in long-term care*. New York, NY: Springer.

Bates, J., Boote, J., & Beverly, C. (2004). Psychosocial interventions for people with a milder dementing illness: A systematic review. *Journal of Advanced Nursing, 45*(6), 644–658.

Bazzini, D. G., Stack, E. R., Martincin, P. D., & Davis, C. P. (2007). The effect of reminiscing about laughter on relationship satisfaction. *Motivation and Emotion, 31*, 25–34.

Bleathman, C., & Morton, I. (1992). Validation therapy: Extracts from 20 groups with dementia sufferers. *Journal of Advanced Nursing, 17*, 658–666.

Bohlmeijer, E., Roemer, M., Cuijpers, P., & Smit, F. (2007). The effects of reminiscence on psychological well-being in older adults: A meta-analysis. *Aging & Mental Health, 11*(3), 291–300.

Bowlby, C. (1993). *Therapeutic activities with person disabled by Alzheimer's disease and related disorders*. Gaithersburg, MD: Aspen Publishers, Inc.

Breuil, V., de Rotrou, J., Forette, F., Tortrat, D., Ganansia-Ganem, A., Frambourt, A., Moulin, F., & Boller, F. (1994, March). Cognitive stimulation of patients with dementia: Preliminary results. *International Journal of Geriatric Psychiatry, 9*(3), 211–217.

Buettner, L., & Fitzsimmons, S. (2003). *Dementia practice guideline for recreational therapy: Treatment of disturbing behaviors*. Alexandria, VA: American Therapeutic Recreation Association.

Burlingame, J. (Ed.). (2001). *Idyll Arbor's therapy dictionary* (2nd ed.). Ravensdale, WA: Idyll Arbor.

Butler, R. N. (1963). The life-review: An interpretation of reminiscence in the aged. *Psychiatry, 26*, 65–75.

Cappeliez, P., Guindon, M., & Robitaille, A. (2008). Functions of reminiscence and emotional regulation among older adults. *Journal of Aging Studies, 22*, 266–272.

Cleveland, E. S., Reese, E., & Grolnick, W. S. (2007). Children's engagement and competence in personal recollection: Effects of parents' reminiscing goals. *Journal of Experimental Child Psychology, 96*, 131–149.

Cook, E. A. (1991). The effects of reminiscence on psychological measures of ego integrity in elderly nursing home residents. *Archives of Psychiatric Nursing, 5*(5), 292–298.

Day, C. R. (1997). Validation therapy: A review of the literature. *Journal of Gerontological Nursing, 23*(4), 29–34.

Deponte, A., & Missan, R. (2007). Effectiveness of validation therapy (VT) in groups: Preliminary results. *Archives of Gerontology and Geriatrics, 44*, 113–117.

Feil, N. (2002). *The validation breakthrough: simple techniques for communicating with people with "Alzheimer's-type dementia"* (2nd edition). Baltimore, MD: Health Professions Press.

Feil, N., & De Klerk-Rubin, V. (1992). *V/F Validation: The Feil method, how to help disoriented old-old.* Cleveland, OH: Edward Feil Productions.

Finnema, E., Droes, R., Ribbe, M., & Van Tilburg, W. (2000). The effects of emotion-oriented approaches in the care for persons suffering from dementia: A review of the literature. *International Journal of Geriatric Psychiatry, 15*, 141–161.

Folsom, G. S. (1986). "Worth repeating" reality orientation: Full circle. In P. M. Foster (Ed.), *Therapeutic activities with the impaired elderly* (pp. 65–73). Binghamton, NY: Haworth Press.

Folsom, J. (1968). Reality orientation for the elderly mental patient. *Journal of Geriatric Psychiatry, 1*(1), 291–307.

Fry, P. S. (1983). Structured and unstructured reminiscence training and depression among the elderly. *Clinical Gerontologist, 1*(3), 15–37.

Goldwasser, A. N., Auerbach, S. M., Harkins, S. W. (1987). Cognitive, affective, and behavioral effects of reminiscence group therapy on demented elderly. *The International Journal of Aging and Human Development, 25*(3), 209–222.

Gould, E. (2008). Communication issues for practitioners. In M. Mezey (Ed.), *The encyclopedia of elder care: The comprehensive resource on geriatric and social care* (2nd ed., pp. 150–154). New York, NY: Springer.

Haber, D. (2006). Life review: Implementation, theory, research, and therapy. *The International Journal of Aging and Human Development, 63*(2), 153–171.

Haight, B. K. (1991). Reminiscing: The state of the art as a basis for practice. *The International Journal of Aging and Human Development, 33*, 1–32.

Lesser, J., Lazarus, L. W., Frankel, R., & Havasy, S. (1981). Reminiscence group therapy with psychotic geriatric inpatients. *The Gerontologist, 21*, 291–296.

Kleiber, D. (1999). *Leisure experience and human development: A dialectical interpretation.* New York, NY: Basic Books.

Kolanowski, A. (1995). Disturbing behaviors in demented elders: A concept synthesis. *Archives of Psychiatric Nursing, 9*, 188–194.

McCabe, L. (2008). A holistic approach to caring for people with Alzheimer's disease. *Nursing Standard, 22*(42), 50–56.

Moniz-Cook, E. (2006). Cognitive stimulation and dementia. *Aging and Mental Health, 10*(3), 207–210.

Moos, I., & Bjorn, A. (2007). Use of the life story in the institutional care of people with dementia: A review of intervention studies. *Ageing & Society, 26*, 431–454.

National Council for Therapeutic Recreation Certification (2004). Why Hire a CTRS?: Certified Therapeutic Recreation Specialists enhance quality care. [Brochure]. New City, NY: Author.

Neal, M., & Barton, W. P. (2003). Validation therapy for dementia (review). *Cochrane Database of Systematic Reviews, 3*, CD001394.

Ouldred, E., & Bryant, C. (2008). Dementia care. Part 2: understanding and managing behavioral challenges. *British Journal of Nursing (BJN), 17*(4), 242–247.

Parsons, C. (1986). Group reminiscence therapy and levels of depression in the elderly. *Nurse Practitioner, 11*, 68–76.

Perrotta, P., & Meacham, J. A. (1981). Can a reminiscing intervention alter depression and self-esteem? *The International Journal of Aging and Human Development, 14*(1), 23–30.

Sheldon, K., & Dattilo, J. (2000). Therapeutic reminiscence. In J. Dattilo (Ed.), *Facilitation techniques in therapeutic recreation* (pp. 303–326). State College, PA: Venture Publishing, Inc.

Shelkey, M. (2008). Dementia: Nonpharmacological therapy. In M. Mezey (Ed.), *The encyclopedia of elder care: The comprehensive resource on geriatric and social care* (2nd ed., pp. 209–213). New York, NY: Springer.

Shute, G. E. (1986). Life review: A cautionary note. *Clinical Gerontologist, 6*, 57–58.

Spector, A., Davies, S., Woods, B., & Orrell, M. (2000). Reality orientation for dementia: A systematic review of the evidence for its effectiveness. *Gerontologist, 40*(2), 206–212.

Spector, A., Orrell, M., Davies, S., & Woods, B. (1998, April 23). Reality orientation for dementia: A review of the evidence of effectiveness. *Cochrane Database of Systematic Reviews*, Retrieved January 9, 2009, from Cochrane Database of Systematic Reviews database.

Spector, A., Orrell, M., Davies, S., & Woods, B. (2001). Can reality orientation be rehabilitated? Development and piloting of an evidence-based program of cognition-based therapies for people with dementia. *Neuropsychological Rehabilitation, 11*(3/4), 377–397.

Stevens-Ratchford, R. G. (1993). The effect of life review reminiscence activities on depression and self-esteem in older adults. *The American Journal of Occupational Therapy, 47*(5), 413–420.

Sylvester, C., Voelkl, J. E., & Ellis, G. D. (2001). *Therapeutic recreation programming: Theory and practice.* State College, PA: Venture Publishing, Inc.

Tanaka, K., Yamada, Y., Kobayashi, Y., Sonohara, K., Machida, A., Nakai, R., Kozaki, K., & Toba, K. (2007). Improved cognitive function, mood and brain blood flow in single photon emission computed tomography following individual reminiscence therapy in an elderly patient with Alzheimer's disease. *Geriatric Gerontology International, 7,* 305–309.

Taulbee, L. R., & Folsom, J. C. (1966). Reality orientation for geriatric patients. *Hospital and Community Psychiatry, 17*(5), 133–135.

Teague, M., & MacNeil, R. (1992). *Aging & leisure: Vitality in later life* (2nd ed.). Dubuque, IA: Brown & Benchmark.

Tondi, L., Ribani, L., Bottazzi, M., Viscomi, G., & Vulcano, V. (2007). Validation therapy (VT) in nursing home: a case-control study. *Archives of Gerontology & Geriatrics, Suppl. 1,* 407–411.

Toseland, R. W., Diehl, M., Freeman, K., Manzanares, T., Naleppa, M., & McCallion, P. (1997). The impact of validation group therapy on nursing home residents with dementia. *Journal of Applied Gerontology, 16,* 31–50.

Validation Training Institute, Inc (2003). Retrieved January 2009, from http://www.vfvalidation.org.

Van Puyenbroeck, J. V., & Maes, B. (2008). A review of critical, person-centered and clinical approaches to reminiscence work for people with intellectual disabilities. *International Journal of Disability, Development and Education, 55*(1), 43–60.

Wang, J. (2007). Group reminiscence therapy for cognitive and affective function of demented elderly in Taiwan. *International Journal of Geriatric Psychiatry, 22,* 1235–1240.

Wang, Q. (2007). "Remember when you got the big, big bulldozer?" Mother-child reminiscing over time and across cultures. *Social Cognition, 25*(4), 455–471.

Webster, J. D. (2003). The reminiscence circumplex and autobiographical memory functions. *Memory, 11*(2), 203–215.

Weiss, C. R. (1989). TR and reminiscence: The pursuit of elusive memory and the art of remembering. *Therapeutic Recreation Journal, 23*(3), 7–18.

Weiss, C. R., & Thurn, J. M. (1987). A mapping project to facilitate reminiscence in a long-term care facility. *Therapeutic Recreation Journal, 21*(2), 46–53.

Williams, R., Reeve, W., Ivison, D., & Kavanagh, D. (1987). Use of environmental manipulation and modified informal reality orientation with institutionalized confused elderly subjects: A replication. *Age & Ageing, 16*(5), 315–318.

Woods, B., Spector, A. E., Prendergast, L., & Orrell, M. (2005, August 16). Cognitive stimulation to improve cognitive functioning in people with dementia. *Cochrane Database of Systematic Reviews*, Retrieved January 9, 2009, from Cochrane Database of Systematic Reviews database.

Wong, P. T. (1995). The process of adaptive reminiscence. In B. K. Haight & J. D. Webster (Eds.), *The art and science of reminiscing: Theory, research, methods, and applications* (pp. 23–36). Washington, DC: Taylor & Francis.

Yamagami, T., Oosawa, M., Ito, S., & Yamaguchi, H. (2007). Effect of activity reminiscence therapy as brain-activating rehabilitation for elderly people with and without dementia. *Psychogeriatrics, 7,* 69–75.

Youssef, F. A. (1990). The impact of group reminiscence counseling on a depressed elderly population. *Nurse Practitioner, 15*(4), 34–38.

» CHAPTER 20 »
Community Integration

Brad Wardlaw Ph.D., CTRS and Norma J. Stumbo, Ph.D., CTRS

Background/History

A community can be defined by the physical boundaries that describe where a person resides (e.g., streets, buildings, or hallways) or by the social institutions, rituals, and traditions of a group of people (Putnam, 2000). A community brings people together and helps them form a common identity. Townley and Kloos (2009) noted that "the psychological sense of community . . . describe[s] the phenomena that one belongs to and is an integral part of a larger collectivity. . . . it represent[s] the strength of bonding among community members . . . important for personal and collective well-being" (p. 363). They continued: "The absence of a psychological sense of community [is] the single most disintegrating aspect of contemporary life and [it is associated] with loneliness, alienation, psychological distress, and a feeling of impotence regarding social forces" (p. 363). When people do not feel that they are a part of their community, they feel separate and not integral to the fabric of the community.

Originally, community integration focused on just the physical integration or presence of individuals with disabilities in the community, but the concept has evolved to mean social integration, such that the person lives, participates, and socializes in his or her community, with community integration being the ultimate goal of rehabilitation services (Brock et al., 2009; Gulcur, Tsemberis, Stefancic, & Greenwood, 2007; Wong & Solomon, 2002; Yasui & Berven, 2009).

> Arguably, the overarching goal of the rehabilitation process . . . community integration involves the acquisition or resumption of roles appropriate for a given age, gender, or culture with respect to decision making and performance of productive behaviors as part of multivaried relationships in the community. (Gontkovsky, Russum, & Stokie, 2009, p. 185)

Table 20.1 (p. 368) provides several definitions of community integration found in recent literature. These multidimensional definitions point to the wide-ranging and weighty spectrum of community integration services. McColl et al. (1998) concluded that most definitions have three common elements, in that integration involves: (a) relationships with others, (b) independence in one's living situation, and (c) activities to fill one's time. They broadly noted this included "having 'something to do' (occupation), 'someone to love' (social support), and 'somewhere to live' (independent living)" (p. 26).

Often, it is within a community that an individual participates in recreation and leisure experiences. For many individuals with disabilities and/or illnesses, their community may be limited both geographically and socially. The intent of community integration programs is to help individuals become more enmeshed in the tapestry of the larger and nondisabled community. Because in the past so many individuals with disabilities, especially severe disabilities, were warehoused in large residential settings, community integration has often meant helping individuals make the transition from a very institutionalized and segregated environment to more inclusive or typical environments (Bond, Salyers, Rollins, Rapp, & Zipple, 2004).

Today, however, community integration is applied and offered to a wide variety of individuals with disabilities, such as those returning from acute medical care or rehabilitation or those leaving substance abuse treatment centers to their own homes, group-homes, or half-way houses. Because it involves a major life transition, many individuals, their families, and support personnel consider it to be challenging, unpredictable, and fraught with uncertainty (Jivanjee, Kruzich, & Gordon, 2009). As such, therapeutic recreation specialists have a significant role to play in teaching individuals the necessary skills to make these transitions and live as independently as possible, in whatever setting the person resides. Specialists also have a significant role in advocating policies to the larger community about accessibility, acceptance, and accommodation.

Table 20.1. Definitions of Community Integration

The basic principle of the community integration movement is that all people, including those who have disability labels, have a right to full community participation and membership. Within this movement, community integration is considered a product of self-help, peer support, and professional services; in addition, housing, jobs, and relationships with community members without disability labels are all included in its purview as essential domains of life. (Yasui & Berven, 2009, p. 761)

***

Community reintegration is achieved in the form of functional independence in environments outside of institutions. (Yasui & Berven, 2009, p. 763)

***

Community integration refers to the degree to which people with disabilities have the opportunity to live, work, and recreate in the same manner as peers without disabilities. (Wong & Stanhope, 2009, p. 1376)

***

The concept of community integration frequently has been used as an outcome in rehabilitation research . . . It is a sensible idea. Disability often prevents people from joining fully in community life. Rehabilitation is intended to remove barriers, to let people with disabilities join again the complex array of activities and relationships that comprise an ordinary daily life. Therefore, it is reasonable to consider rehabilitation to be successful to the extent that it helps people participate in daily life and be integrated within their communities. (Minnes et al., 2003, p. 149)

***

Community integration entails helping consumers to move out of patient roles, treatment centers, segregated housing arrangements, and work enclaves, and enabling them to move toward independence, illness self-management, and normal adult roles in community settings. . . . One way to describe community integration is by stating what it is not: Community integration is not immersion in worlds created and managed by mental health professionals [in the case of individuals with mental health problems], such as day treatment programs, sheltered workshops, group homes, and segregated educational programs. These programs are designed specifically to pull consumers into treatment and away from community life. (Bond, Salyers, Rollins, Rapp, & Zipple, 2004, p. 570)

***

Community integration refers to re-establishing, to the degree possible, previously existing roles and relationships, creating substitute new ones, and assisting people in making these changes. (Egbert, Koch, Coeling, & Ayers, 2006, p. 46)

***

For individuals with [spinal cord injury], successful rehabilitation involves maximizing community integration areas, including: the ability to participate in community life activities, remain active in family and recreational events, and access local activities and resources, including health care follow-up and employment opportunities. Community integration emphasizes the ability of individuals to overcome disability barriers and has been shown to have a positive influence on their quality of life. (McKinley & Meade, 2004, p. 79)

***

This multi-dimensional concept includes but is not limited to aspects of human functioning such as independence, social relationships, productivity, and leisure, all of which are significantly impacted by an acquired brain injury. (McCabe et al., 2007, p. 231)

***

In general, the concept of community integration extends beyond self-care and physical function to include engagement in expected vocational, social, and community roles. (Salter, Foley, Jutai, Bayley, & Teasell, 2008, p. 820)

In the 1960s and 1970s, America experienced a move from large custodial institutions often warehousing hundreds or sometimes thousands of individuals with disabilities to smaller, community-based settings (Lloyd, Waghorn, Best, & Gemmell, 2008; Townley & Kloos, 2009; Wong & Stanhope, 2009). Termed "deinstitutionalization," this movement was an important factor for humanizing individuals with disabilities, including those with severe physical and/or intellectual disabilities, but it also placed a tremendous burden on healthcare staff to teach people skills for living

appropriately in the community as well as on the individuals to learn and utilize as many skills as possible to ensure their success in society. As people moved to these "least restrictive environments," their needs for daily living and adaptive skills increased tremendously (Taylor, 2004). Similarly, "normalization" is a concept often applied to community integration. Normalization occurs when "individuals with disabilities live, work, play, and lead their daily lives without distinction from and with the same opportunities as individuals without disabilities" (Bond et al., 2004, p. 570).

At the same time, a similar movement was happening in public elementary and secondary education. Students with disabilities were transitioned from segregated classrooms and buildings to being with students without disabilities for at least part of the academic day. This might have been for only certain school periods throughout the day, but the intention was that physical integration would result in better social integration (Taylor, 2004).

These two movements have resulted in a shift in services and priorities by other community and health-care environments as well. Especially in rehabilitation settings, community integration or community reintegration have enjoyed considerable emphasis from most members of the treatment team as a priority goal for the vast majority of clients (reference). Therapeutic recreation specialists are uniquely situated to be prime providers of community integration or reintegration services (Doig, Fleming, & Tooth, 2001; Minnes et al., 2001; Reistetter & Abreu, 2005; Yates, 2003).

The intent of this chapter is to provide the reader with an evidence-based discussion of the best practice in creating and implementing community integration programming. The organization of this chapter provides citations of articles for intended client groups, a discussion of basic premises with an emphasis in models and necessary skill sets, a summary of related research and applications to the therapeutic recreation, and a list of resources.

Intended Client Groups

Like other techniques discussed in this text, most groups of individuals served by therapeutic recreation are candidates for community integration and re-integration programs. This specifically includes:

- individuals with spinal cord injury (Armstrong & Lauzen, 1994; Barker et al., 2009; Donnelly & Eng, 2005; McKinley & Meade, 2004; Pluym, Keur, Gerritsen, & Post, 1997; Slater & Meade, 2004)
- individuals who have brain injuries (Armstrong & Lauzen, 1994; Brown, Gordon, & Spielman, 2003; Doig et al., 2001; Mahalik, Johnstone, Glass, & Yoon, 2007; McCabe et al., 2007; Minnes et al. 2001; Reistetter & Abreu, 2005; Sample, Tomter, & Johns, 2007; Turner et al., 2007; Walker, Onus, Doyle, Clare, & McCarthy, 2005; Yates, 2003)
- individuals who have experienced stroke (Egbert, Koch, Coeling, & Ayers, 2006)
- individuals with intellectual disabilities (Bruinicks, Chen, Lakin, & McGrew, 1992; Cummins

& Lau, 2003; Hartnett et al., 2008; Ittenbach, Bruinicks, Thurlow, & McGrew, 1993; Pretty, Rapley, & Bramston, 2002; Taylor, 2004; Vine & Hamilton, 2005; Thorn, Pittman, Myers, & Slaughter, 2009)
- individuals with developmental disabilities (Bruininks, Chen, Lakin, & McGrew, 1992; Ittenbach, Bruininks, Thurlow, & McGrew, 1993)
- individuals who are refugees (Hallahan & Irizarry, 2008, Kensinger et al., 2007)
- individuals with mental health difficulties (Bond, Salyers, Rollins, Rapp, & Zipple, 2004; Farone, 2006; Gulcur, Tsemberis, Stefancic, & Greenwood, 2007; Jivanjee, Kruzich, & Gordon, 2008, 2009; LeMaire & Mallik, 2005; Lloyd, Waghorn, Best, & Gemmel, 2008; Mallik, Reeves, & Dellario, 1998; Rainer & Landvik, 2007; Townley & Kloos, 2009; Wieland, Rosenstock, Kelsey, Ganguli, & Wisniewski, 2007; Wong & Stanhope, 2009; Wong, Metzendorf, & Min, 2006)
- individuals with autism (Coughlin, 2008; Hendricks & Wehman, 2009)
- older individuals (Depla, DeGraff, Kroon, & Heeren, 2004; Rowles, Concotelli, & High, 1996)

Basic Premises

A number of related concepts are essential to understanding the purpose and justifying the design and delivery of therapeutic recreation community integration programs. Among these are the definitions of community, models of disability, and models of community interaction.

First, however, it should be noted that community integration is both a *process* and an *outcome*. When we talk about therapeutic recreation specialists providing community integration programs, we mean that specialists are teaching clients the skills necessary to function well in environments other than institutions, as well as advocating more understanding attitudes to community members in order to reduce stigma and remove barriers. Teaching community integration skills and public advocacy are part of the *process* of community integration. But community integration is also an *end*; that is, the goal of these programs is for the individual to be able to live as independently and equally as possible within their community.

Community integration can also be examined from objective and subjective perspectives. From an *objective* standpoint, the person, as viewed by the outside world, is living, playing, and interacting within a larger social context; from a *subjective* standpoint, the person feels comfortable in his or her interactions, feels significant to the community, and enjoys a sense of belongingness

(Bond et al., 2004; Reistetter & Abreu, 2005). While measuring the success of community integration programs from the objective perspective is important, it is crucial to not overlook how the individual *feels* about his or her degree of integration.

The next section briefly describes some elements of "community." These notions begin to lay the groundwork for designing truly meaningful and targeted community integration programs.

Definition of Community

McMillan and Chavis (1986, as cited in Townley & Kloos, 2009) noted that sense of community is "a feeling that members have of belonging, a feeling that members matter to one another and to the group, and a shared faith that members' needs will be met through their commitment to be together" (pp. 363–364). Four aspects are important to this sense of community (Townley & Kloos, p. 364):

1. Membership: Feelings of emotional security, belonging, and identification
2. Influence: The degree to which the individual affects the community and vice versa
3. Integration and fulfillment of needs: This includes physical and psychological needs, that once met, reinforce the individuals' commitment to the group
4. Share emotional connection: This includes positive affect and shared history related to community membership

The authors noted that additional concepts within a sense of community include:

- Social connections
- Mutual concerns
- Community values

Townley and Kloos (2009) believed that these factors are extremely important in that they reduce stigmatization and marginalization of individuals with disabilities. Additional benefits include improved well-being and recovery from disability and increased sense of relatedness and interdependence.

Lloyd et al. (2008) conceptualized social inclusion as being identical or nearly identical to community integration. Social inclusion, in their research, meant (a) socially valued role-functioning in roles other than being a patient or client, (b) adequate social support, (c) an absence of stigma, (d) integration within the rehabilitation community, and (e) integration within the larger social community. They developed these factors as a preliminary step in developing an assessment measure.

Segal, Silverman, and Baumohl (1989) coined the term "person–environment fit" for the degree of the congruence between what the individual needs and wants, as well as his or her capabilities, strengths, and hopes, and the environmental demands, resources, and opportunities. If the person–environment fit is not in congruence, then the person is likely to fail and the community is likely to suffer.

> [People] do better where they can best fit into the social fabric of the environment. Fit seems to depend a great deal on the extent to which community care residents [in this case, individuals with mental illnesses] have key characteristics of the dominant social group in the environment, and the willingness of that group to tolerate differences in its midst. (Segal et al., 1989, p. 61).

Wong and Stanhope (2009) reminded us that the sociocultural aspects of the neighborhood are just as important as the individual's characteristics.

Models of Disability

Models of disability and the ways in which a person with a disability interacts within his or her environments provide not only the solid, evidence-based justification of programs, but they also directly speak to the content that needs to be central within these diverse, wide-ranging, and strengths-based programs. This section will address the nature and meaning of "disability" and myriad viewpoints of how that impinges or influences exchanges between individuals with disabilities and community structures and systems. Some of these viewpoints include the ecological model, social capital, and person-centered recovery. After a discussion of the implications of "disability" these additional important concepts will be presented, as they provide a springboard for program development.

Disability, itself, is a notion that is not always quantifiable and precise, and which varies from day to day and situation to situation (Seelman, 1993; Wittenburg & Maag, 2002). Disability, then, is not just a physical or inherent attribute, but a result of interactions between people and their physical and social environments, including a complicated mix of social, cultural, political, climatic, topographic, architectural, and technological components (Agree, 1999; Allen, Resnick, & Roy, 2006; Barcus & Targett, 2003; Field

& Jette, 2007; Meyers, Anderson, Miller, Shipp, & Hoenig, 2002; Verbrugge & Sevak, 2002; Wittenburg & Maag, 2002). This "social model of disability" is reflected in the World Health Assembly's (2001) and World Health Organization's (2002) recent classification model of disability and health. The model focuses clearly on the interaction between the disability, the person's activity and participation levels, and the impact of environmental levels (Howard, Browning, & Lee, 2007; Porter & Van Puymbroeck, 2007; Stumbo & Carter, 2009).

The implications of this larger, more encompassing model of disability have significant implications for community integration and reintegration programs because of the complex interplays of the person, his or her environment, and the community (Yates, 2003). For example, Verbrugge, a noted disability researcher, concluded that individuals with disabilities "rarely allow disablement to take its course without efforts to retard or stop the process" (Verbrugge, Rennert, & Madans, 1997, p. 384). Individuals with disabilities typically work diligently to offset their functional limitations, when and where possible, to solve the problems they encounter with performing daily living activities (Stumbo, Martin, & Hedrick, 2009a). They normally try to counterbalance any deficits brought about by the disability or impairment through skill acquisition, personal assistance, or assistive technology (Stumbo, Martin, & Hedrick, 2009a, 2009b). The demand for skills, assistance, and/or technology increases proportionately in relation to the severity of the impairment or deficit (LaPlante, Kaye, Kang, & Harrington, 2004). That is, individuals with disabilities, especially those with severe or newly acquired disabilities, have increasingly intense needs as the degree of their impairment or limitation worsens or as the community becomes less inviting. However, they cannot often learn or accomplish these skills on their own, often not even realizing the skills they will need to live independently within a wider community framework. In addition, they also often need a wide variety of skills to negotiate with inaccessible or unusable environments.

Community Interaction/ Integration Models

In relating needs of persons with disabilities and the supports they receive in the community, Minnes et al. (2001) outlined four scenarios. *Integration* is when the person's needs are identified and supported and the person is involved in the community. *Assimilation* is when their needs are not identified or met, but the

person is involved in the community. *Segregation* is when the person's needs are identified and met, but the person is not involved in the wider community. And lastly, *marginalization* is when needs are not identified or supported and the person is not involved. These four concepts seem to coincide with Segal et al.'s (1989) notion of person–environment fit. Is the person functioning well and is the community being accommodating?

Thorn, Pittman, Myers, and Slaughter (2009) suggested four phases, quite similar to Minnes et al. (2001). However, they used the terms "*community presence*," "*community participation*," "*community integration*," and "*community inclusion*" to address the spectrum of involvement. Their continuum progresses from being just physically present on the low end, to experiencing acceptance, a sense of belonging, and valued social relationships on the high end.

Ecological approaches are useful for examining the interactions between a person with a limitation and his or her environment at multiple levels (Bullock & Mahon, 1997; Howe-Murphy & Charboneau, 1987; Sallis et al., 2006; Tacon, 2008). Ecological models examine people's interactions with their physical and sociocultural surroundings, and are distinguished by their primary inclusion of environmental and policy variables. Bronfenbrenner (1977, as cited in Bliss, Cook, & Kaslow, 2006) described a person's ecology as a nested arrangement of systemic structures. The five levels include:

1. Microsystem: Innermost and most immediate of the nested systems; includes intimate contexts (such as home, family, neighborhood)
2. Mesosystem: Second level refers to interactions and/or communications between structural components in the microsystem; for example, communication among treatment team members regarding a person's care
3. Exosystem: Third level refers to the larger system and social context; for example, having a child with a disability will impact the family unit and whether one parent or sibling needs to stay home to tend for the child
4. Macrosystem: The fourth and most distal level is the most diffused, as it comprises cultural values, ethnic identity, beliefs, laws, mores, and customs
5. Chronosystem: The final level was added later by Bronfenbrenner to "reflect the dimension of time; that is, the transitions and patterns of events over the life course, be they personal or sociohistorical" (Tacon, 2008, p. 287).

From even these brief descriptions, it becomes quickly apparent that interventions to address each level are needed in order for the individual to maximize success (Sallis et al., 2006; Tacon, 2008). A key idea underlying ecological models is that interventions will be most effective when they operate on multiple levels. For example, a community integration specialist might work with the individual to help build resource-seeking skills, with a community recreation department to ensure inclusive programs, and with a women's fitness center to ensure equipment accessibility. The specialist works at multiple levels to address the barriers found at each level.

Yasui and Berven (2009) identified four basic models of community integration in the rehabilitation literature. The models are as follows:

- Functional Independence Model: Community integration is achieved through functional independence in environments external to institutions.
- Acculturation Model: Community integration implies being able to retain unique aspects of being a minority member (person with a disability) and receiving support within a larger community, while also being involved in community contexts.
- Normalization Model: Active participation of people with disabilities within their communities in culturally normative amounts, settings, and activities.
- Subjective Experience Model: Community integration is defined by the individual with a disability who needs to be an active partner in planning, implementing, and evaluating community services.

Because the Subjective Experience Model propels individuals with disabilities to the forefront and expects them to be proactive decision makers, it is often preferred by disability rights groups and individuals with disabilities.

McColl et al. (1998) interviewed individuals with brain injury in Ontario, Canada, and reported four major themes of community integration, with several sub-themes.

1. General Integration:
   - Conformity: Knowing "the rules" and being able to fit in
   - Orientation: Knowing one's way around the community
   - Acceptance: Being able to feel comfortable and not set apart

2. Social Support:
   - Close relationships: Characterized by closeness, reciprocity, mutuality, or intimacy
   - Diffuse relationships: Others in the community such as clerks, bus drivers, etc.
3. Occupation:
   - Leisure: Leisure, recreation, and non-work activities
   - Productivity: Includes education, employment, and volunteer work
4. Independent Living:
   - Independence: Being self-determined in terms of one's own abilities
   - Living situation: Living in a place where one can be autonomous

It is clear that each of these notions about community integration models provides insight into the content important to highlight within community integration programs. Community integration is not just about teaching someone to ride public transportation; it is also about teaching self-advocacy skills, problem-solving skills, assertion skills, social norms, and the like. A concept closely related to this is "social capital" (Putnam, 2000).

Social capital is a concept that is used to describe the degree to which an individual is embedded and intertwined in the community in which he or she resides. According to Putnam (2000), social capital describes the ways in which a person's life is " made more productive by social ties" (p. 19). The idea of social capital suggests that individuals are interdependent on each other; associating with different groups or systems in different ways, and examines the contributions that these interactions can bring to both individual and the system. Therefore, according to Putnam, social capital can be inclusive or exclusive, and it can be used to bring about good or bad. The notion of social capital examines not only "individual clout and companionship," but also examines "rules of conduct," "mutual obligations," and "reciprocity" (Putnam, 2000, p. 20).

The joy of community integration has no direct relationship with the number of times people go shopping or the frequency with which they use community recreation facilities. Instead it is a "psychological sense of community" that is the key construct, defined . . . as the "feeling that one is part of a readily available, supportive, and dependable structure" . . . This emphasizes a sense of community connectedness, of personal interdependency, and belonging. It is closely aligned with the sociological concept of "social capital" and is inversely related to loneliness. So, in these terms, "sense of community" obviously cannot mean simply being in the presence of the general public. (Cummins & Lau, 2003, p. 151)

Social capital is important to the idea of community integration in that therapeutic recreation specialists assist clients in understanding the expectations of them in society (such as social interaction skills and social norms), as well as what they may be able to expect from society.

The intent of community integration or reintegration programs is to help individuals offset the limitations brought about by living with a disability in the community by increasing the individual's "independence" or self-sufficiency. (For individuals with severe disabilities or impairments, that may not mean being able to *perform* the task at hand, instead being able to *direct* the task to be accomplished.) Thus, community integration and community reintegration are terms that represent a loose coalition of skills that a person needs in order to independently reside in the least restrictive environment, whether his or her own home, a group home, or a halfway house and orchestrate, to the best of his or her ability, a self-directed, meaningful life.

Before continuing, it should be noted that not everyone supports community integration in its present form, especially for those with the most severe disabilities such as those with severe intellectual disability. Cummins and Lau (2003) argued that two problems are inherent in assumptions that individuals with low levels of social skills can be taught higher levels and thus will become more "integrated":

> The first is that a sense of community, based on social integration within the general community, is so difficult to achieve for some people with an intellectual disability that it is not a realistic option. The second is that the general community may not be the primary community for people who have an intellectual disability. (p. 153)

They encourage programmers to consider whether other individuals with intellectual disabilities should be the primary targets for broadening social networks.

Necessary Skill Sets

In this regard, various authors have conceptualized community integration skills from a multitude of viewpoints. Cheung and Ngan (2007) conceptualized community integration as combination of cognitive and behavioral elements. Their model consists of five components: (a) knowledge, (b) desire, (c) assertiveness, (d) feelings of acceptance, and (e) participation/integration. Knowledge of community activities are meant to improve the person's ability to review community participation options, make choices, and follow through with goal attainment. Desire to participate in activities is important, as it relates to understanding a person's leisure interests and motivations. Assertiveness represents the person's desire to actively pursue becoming integrated in the community and how he or she interacts with other community members. As a person feels greater acceptance of others, it is assumed that the likelihood of his or her participation in community programs also increases.

This model coincides with the elements of person-centered recovery (Onken, Craig, Ridgway, Ralph, & Cook, 2007). These elements include (a) hope, (b) self-determination, (c) sense of agency, (d) meaning and purpose, and (e) awareness/potentiality. Instilling the mindset that circumstances can change for the better is crucial in intrinsically motivating the person attempting to overcome the barriers presented by a disability. Once this is accomplished, priorities include the individual's ability to set personal goals and determine the steps needed to take to reach those goals in pursuing living independently. As the person overcomes obstacles in his or her own life, it is important to work on the perceptions and understanding of disability with his or her family, friends, and other advocates. As he or she pursues living independently, it also is important for him or her to develop a sense of meaning for his or her life and that this purpose in life is achievable. Specialists assist the person's improvement in these areas by providing interventions that work on personal empowerment, social functioning, and independent decision-making. As the individual progresses in accomplishing these aims, a shift occurs towards engagement of community-centered elements of recovery. These include building social connectedness, exploring social opportunities, and integrating into the community.

Jivanjee, Kruzich, and Gordon (2009) suggested that youth with mental illnesses, as they transition to independent living, gain skills in emotional, financial, and residential independence, choices of career, responsibility for healthcare decisions, and the occurrence of intimate relationships. They found, in their qualitative study, that families of youth with mental illnesses reported that the two most important facets of community integration are: (a) opportunities to attain goals and achieve a sense of accomplishment, and (b) development of peer relationships. They also noted the following perceived barriers: (a) lack of the individual being prepared for adult life, (b) difficulties the individual has in forming relationships, (c) stigma attached to having a mental illness, and (d) lack of community resources. They also noted a number of supports: (a) strength-oriented services and opportunities for skill development, and (b) supportive mentoring relationships.

Related Research

Individuals with CVA/TBI

Brock et al. (2009) conducted a study to identify the characteristics associated with successful community reintegration for individuals with strokes. Forty-five individuals who had been discharged from a rehabilitation unit of a hospital and 23 primary caregivers were queried in this investigation. They used Goal-Attainment Scaling and used 11 domains of functioning: (a) communication, (b) cognition, (c) personal activities of daily living (ADL), (d) mobility at home, (e) mobility in the community, (f) community ADL, (g) upper limb function, (h) return to work, (i) return to leisure, (j) domestic ADL, and (k) other. Individuals who had achieved their goals (average of four per person) had a more positive perception of their ability to participate in getting around, work and leisure, getting along with people, being aware of their surroundings, and being able to look after themselves. However, they did not necessarily improve functional abilities. This research suggests that "successful" individuals are able to compensate or work around their disability to become reinvolved in community and home life.

Egbert, Koch, Coeling, and Ayers (2006) interviewed 12 individuals with right-hemisphere damage about the process of community integration. Their results revealed seven types of challenges, five categories of external resources, and four types of internal resources. The challenges included: (a) physical impairments, such as weakness, pain, and fatigue; (b) cognitive-perceptual challenges, such as sequencing and solving problems; (c) emotional challenges, such as isolation, anxiety, and frustration; (d) challenges to activities of daily living, such as the impact of physical impairments on daily routines and dependence on family members; (e) relationship challenges, such as feeling like an imposition on family members; (f) employment challenges, such as being fired or laid off due to disability; and (g) financial challenges, such as not being able to pay one's bills. The five categories of external resources included (a) financial resources, such as insurance policies, (b) emotional supports, such as from healthcare providers, (c) informational supports from healthcare

staff, (d) stroke support groups, and (e) family members. Internal resources included: (a) patience, (b) determination and motivation, (c) a positive attitude, and (d) a sense of humor. The investigators also noted a strong interdependence by nearly all of these factors with one another.

Reistetter and Abreu (2005) conducted a systematic review of community integration literature related to individuals with brain injury. They located 14 articles of high quality, 52 of medium quality, and 6 of low quality. Although they report a multitude of findings, one of importance to therapeutic recreation specialists is the following:

> Clinicians should utilize treatment groups and protocols that facilitate naturalistic communication in social situations to improve CI [community integration] such as using interventions in community parks, restaurants and shops. Also, these data indicate that CI is connected to everyday natural contacts, as well as close friendships with family and others. (p. 206)

Another comprehensive literature review, conducted by McCabe et al. (2007), focused on whether rehabilitation, either hospital- or community-based, affected five aspects of the community reintegration experience for individuals with acquired brain injury. These five areas included: (a) independence and social integration, (b) caregiver burden, (c) satisfaction with quality of life, (d) productivity, and (e) return to driving. For independence and social integration, they found limited evidence for the effectiveness of rehabilitation treatments. They found limited evidence that social work intervention does alleviate caregiver burden, increasing satisfaction and mastery. They found limited evidence that more structured and intensive cognitive rehabilitation therapy improves satisfaction with community integration and outcomes, more so than standard, less structured rehabilitation therapies. They also reported limited evidence that social support groups decreased hopelessness, leading to a greater sense of control and empowerment. In terms of productivity, they found limited evidence for the use of cognitive strategies aimed at improving full-time employment, as well as for supportive employment, and early intervention by vocational rehabilitation specialists. Return to driving occurred most often for individuals with lesser disability, and limited evidence supported that participation in a multidisciplinary rehabilitation program improved chances of return to driving.

Turner et al. (2007) interviewed 13 Australians with acquired brain injury and their family members as they transitioned out of rehabilitation and into community environments. Their results produced eight categories with multiple sub-categories. The eight categories included: (a) the hospital experience, (b) the transition process, (c) the role of families/caregivers, (d) post-discharge services, (e) friendship networks and community involvement, (f) meaningful activities and time management, (g) physical and psychological well-being, and (h) barriers and facilitators. Although all the sub-categories will not be discussed here, several of them under friendship networks, meaningful activities, and physical and psychological well-being are important for therapeutic recreation services. Under friendship networks and community involvement are the sub-categories of friendship networks, social activities, and community reaction to injury/disability. Under meaningful activities are returning to work, voluntary work, leisure activities and hobbies, time management, and household tasks and maintenance. Physical and psychological well-being includes behavioral issues, impact of injury-related deficits, motivation, psychological and emotional well-being, fitness and exercise, and medical issues/management. Friendships and social networks were important to positive transition experiences as well as enabling individuals to feel more comfortable engaging in social community activities; fewer friendships and smaller social networks resulted in greater isolation. Having meaningful activities, such as hobbies, also was associated with a more positive transition.

Mahalik, Johnstone, Glass, and Yoon (2007) investigated whether the degree of spirituality (as measured by an instrument called INSPIRIT) was related to community integration for individuals with acquired brain injury. They found that individuals who rated higher in spirituality coped better with their disability, but did not necessarily function better in the community. They felt this was likely to due to functional deficits (i.e., severity of their brain injury) that could not be erased or alleviated by a sense of spirituality.

Minnes et al. (2001) conducted a study involving 63 Canadian adults with brain injury and 63 caregivers of these individuals. They used several areas of community support, such as medical services, dental services, social activities, and housing, and determined whether the individuals were integrated, assimilated, segregated, or marginalized (see explanation at beginning of this chapter). The two areas in which individuals and their caregivers agreed that they were more integrated (needs identified and met, and involved in the community) were social activities and housing. Individuals with brain injuries were most marginalized (needs not identified and community not supportive) in the areas of dental services and productive (work) activity.

Doig, Fleming, and Tooth (2001) studied the community integration patterns of 208 persons with brain injury two to five years post-discharge from rehabilitation units. Their sophisticated statistical analysis reviewed three patterns ("clusters") of individuals: those who concentrated on work, with fewer home or social activities; those who were balanced, who worked part-time or volunteered and were involved in a wider variety of social and home activities; and those who were isolated and poorly integrated, with low levels of participation in work, leisure, and home activities. The last group had experienced more severe injuries and had greater functional deficits. The authors noted that even for those with the most severe brain injuries, rehabilitation professionals need to focus on "productive alternatives for those not able to return to competitive employment" (p. 759).

Individuals with Autism Spectrum Disorders

Hendricks and Wehman (2009) conducted a literature review on the transition from school to adulthood for individuals with autism spectrum disorders (ASD). They focused on acquisition of skills for academics, social interaction, language and communication, self-management, self-determination, home living, employment, and community involvement. They noted that little is known about the actual community integration process for individuals with ASD, except in the area of leisure and recreation participation. Individuals with ASD typically have limited recreation and social skills and often are isolated, playing video games or watching television. They noted that a number of interventions to improve social functioning have been successful, such as peer-mediated approaches, self-management strategies, and social scripting. Virtual environments have been used in recent years to teach social skills as well. Like other authors, they advocate for training to be physically in the community.

> For adolescents [with ASD] to learn requisite skills, education and training must be provided in the community during high school. Specifically, education must take place in community environments where the student is likely to frequent and utilize as an adult. This will ensure the student has opportunities to socialize in the community and learn applicable skills. (p. 84)

Individuals with Intellectual Disabilities

Thorn, Pittman, Myers, and Slaughter (2009) changed the nature of their large, custodial institution for individuals with intellectual disabilities (it housed 556 individuals at the start of the study) and implemented a sweeping reform that included community-based training and "real-life" community experiences. Over several years, their recreation program transitioned from "outings" to teaching functional and independence skills. "The results of this study indicate that increased functional skills enhance relationship opportunities by creating a sense of ability and commonality in social settings. Increased functional skills in areas such as social interaction, safety, dining etiquette, money management, etc., enhance social relationships by highlighting abilities and unifying common interests" (p. 899).

The authors planned to continue to provide programs that teach and utilize skills in the community in which they are needed.

The message from a research study by Vine and Hamilton (2005) on individuals with intellectual disabilities and high support needs echoed the results of Thorn et al. (2009) They studied 37 males who formerly resided in large institutions but now resided in smaller community settings by use of support-staff proxies. They reported clear correlations between scores on community skills, daily living skills, social skills, and community integration scores. As skill sets decrease, the degree of community inclusion also decreases. They noted that individuals with severe levels of intellectual disability risk having limited community involvement, but their particular study did not suggest the best way to improve these life circumstances.

Individuals with Mental Illnesses

Wong, Metzendorf, and Min (2006) conducted focus groups of 18 individuals with schizophrenia and 11 staff members. They noted that independent living skills, social skills, self-advocacy, and being proactive aided consumers in their movement toward integration. In addition, forming supportive consumer networks and promoting mutuality and reciprocity were also seen as important.

Mallik, Reeves, and Dellario (1998) conducted a study with individuals with mental health problems, primarily schizophrenia and mood disorders, as well as staff in one facility in Maryland to determine perceived barriers to community integration. The individuals with mental illnesses reported that financial resources, employment opportunities, and vocational adjustment to be the three largest barriers. However, they also rated social supports, relationships, communication, transportation, time management, problem solving, and money management skills as problematic as well. The authors reported that practitioners viewed person variables and lack of skills as the greatest barriers, while the consumers rated environmental barriers as the most significant.

Gulcur, Tsemberis, Stefanic, and Greenwood (2007) completed a four-year study of individuals with severe mental illnesses and their experiences with homelessness. Eighty-two were assigned to the experimental group and 101 were in the control group. Among their many findings were that (a) community integration has physical, social, psychological, and independence/self-actualization factors; (b) having choice and being in dispersed housing units positively predicted psychological and social integration; (c) having been hospitalized prior to integration produced greater psychological integration; (d) greater psychopathology decreased psychological (but increased social and self-actualization) aspects of integration; and (e) participation in substance abuse treatment programs positively influenced physical integration, but negatively influenced social integration. They concluded that housing for individuals with severe mental illnesses needs to resemble that of the general population more closely, and that programmers should note that factors, such as participation in substance abuse treatment, often can have positive effects on some forms of integration while negatively affecting others.

McCorkle, Dunn, Mui Wan, and Gagne (2009) conducted a study of 20 individuals (9 with serious mental illness with numerous barriers towards developing and maintaining friendship and 11 volunteers) in an intentional friendship program. Researchers reported that participants became more outgoing, sociable and active, with increased self-esteem, self-worth and self-confidence. Researchers concluded from the study that the intentional friendship program is a cost-effective strategy that can improve clients' development of social networks and improve their quality of life.

Summary

Table 20.2 summarizes the skill sets applicable to community integration from the aforementioned research.

Application to Therapeutic Recreation

Recreation Programming

Ippoliti, Peppey, and Depoy's (1994) study of developmentally delayed clients' perspectives on community integration as a part of recreational programming revealed five themes that program leaders need to consider. Safety and trust were critical issues in clients' active participation in programs. Clients' fear of people without disabilities was prevalent in the discussion of this topic. This fear centers around the anxiety of not being accepted and being humiliated or exploited.

Ensuring a safe environment is of upmost importance in programming for any population. Lack of structure was also of concern to the clients in two areas: staff supervision and services to clients. Setting norms and rules and having the expectation that they will be enforced can increase the level of trust as well as improve the enjoyment of the program for participants.

Table 20.2. Skill Sets Applicable to Community Integration Programming

Author	Disability	Skill Set
Brock et al. (2009)	CVA	Communication, cognition, personal activities of daily living (ADL), mobility at home, mobility in the community, community ADL, upper limb function, return to work, return to leisure, domestic ADL, and other
Egbert, Koch, Coeling, and Ayers (2006)	CVA	External resources: financial resources, emotional supports, informational supports from healthcare staff, stroke support groups, family members. Internal resources: patience, determination and motivation, a positive attitude, and a sense of humor
Reistetter and Abreu (2005)	TBI	Naturalistic communication in social situations
McCabe et al. (2007)	TBI	Independence and social integration, caregiver burden, satisfaction with quality of life, productivity, and return to driving
Turner et al. (2007)	TBI	The hospital experience, the transition process, the role of families/caregivers, post-discharge services, friendship networks and community involvement, meaningful activities and time management, physical and psychological well-being, and barriers and facilitators
Mahalik, Johnstone, Glass and Yoon (2007)	TBI	Spirituality
Minnes et al. (2001)	TBI	Social activities and housing
Doig, Fleming, and Tooth (2001)	TBI	Work, leisure, and home activities
Hendricks and Wehman (2009)	Autism	Academic, social interaction, language and communication, self-management, self-determination, home living, employment, and community involvement skills
Thorn, Pittman, Myers, and Slaughter (2009)	Intellectual Disability	Social interaction, safety, dining etiquette, money management
Wong, Metzendorf, and Min (2006)	Mental Illness	Independent living skills, social skills, self-advocacy, and being proactive aided consumers
Mallik, Reeves, and Dellario (1998)	Mental Illness	Financial and employment resources, vocational adjustment, social supports, relationships, communication, transportation, time management, problem solving, and money management skills
Gulcur, Tsemberis, Stefanic, and Greenwood (2007)	Mental Illness	Physical, social, psychological and independence/self-actualization factors
McCorkle, Dunn, Mui Wan, and Gagne (2009)	Mental Illness	Social networking and quality of life

Discomfort in establishing relationships with new participants without disabilities can be addressed by having new members share information about themselves during a group activity. Program leaders can implement ice-breaker activities as an effective means of establishing dialogue within a group setting. Familiarity with recreational activities is an important aspect in developing a sense of security for clients participating in community recreation programming. Clients in this study stated that they would rather participate in activities they already knew how to do. When introducing new activities to clientele, one should attempt to incorporate some aspects of the activity (e.g., rules, structure, interaction) that are similar to past programs to enhance the clients' confidence level. In the discussion of the activity theme, clients expressed the need to have time for themselves at the end of activities. The use of group-processing techniques such as the group circle, dyads, or journaling can effectively allow clients to reflect upon their experiences.

In a study of 53 healthcare providers in a rural community and urban community in Colorado, Sample, Tomter, and Johns (2007) discovered that both communities noted problems in care coordination of largely underserved populations (TBI). Although physical recreation opportunities were cited as strengths in both communities, in the rural community lack of transportation and activity expenses were perceived as barriers to community leisure participation in winter sports by people with disabilities. As therapeutic recreation specialists, coordination of programming for people with disabilities is addressed as a part of the recreation participation component of the Leisure Ability model. With this knowledge, addressing leisure constraints becomes an important task in the improvement of clients' attainment of a functional leisure lifestyle.

Leisure Education

Leisure education interventions can effectively improve community integration in many populations. In a study of 11 patients with a history of severe brain injury, Walker, Onus, Doyle, Clare, and McCarthy (2005) developed an outdoor adventure programming intervention that addressed social skills, group cohesion, and individual goal setting. Results of the study show that 80% of patient goals were achieved, which would indicate that this program is effective in enabling patients to attain goals. Intervention strategies such as this one provide a shared responsibility between the recreational therapist and the client. As a result, the client reaches goals through becoming an active participant and stakeholder in the leisure education process. Activities

such as these promote self-determination, which is a key to meaningful change.

In study of 58 participants with a history of schizophrenia or schizoaffective disorder, Wieland, Rosenstock, Kelsey, Ganguli, and Wisniewski (2007) researched the effects of distal support (support gained through casual relationships developed in day-to-day interactions in the community) on quality of life and sense of belonginess. Implications of the study for therapeutic recreation specialists support the idea that leisure education programming focusing on psychosocial outcomes could benefit patients who have difficulty interacting with strangers.

In a mixed method study of 8 adults with intellectual disabilities, Hartnett, Gallagher, Kiernan, Poulsen, Gilligan, and Reynolds (2008), identified several benefits from providing community integration activities that enhanced quality of life. These included increasing socialization, building personal relationships, improving decision-making abilities and skill acquisition, improving stamina, and enhancing life satisfaction.

Quality of Life

The practice of community integration and its effect on quality of life has been well-documented in social and medical literature. In a study of quality-of-life issues, results from 270 Australians with spinal cord injuries surveyed indicated that societal participation was key to improved social relationships and psychological domains (Barker, Kendall, Amsters, Pershouse, Haines, & Kuipers, 2009). Other research suggests that therapeutic recreation specialists should address the following barriers to community integration and leisure participation in their quality-of-life intervention strategies:

- pain management (Donelly & Eng, 2005)
- accessibility of activities utilizing social supports (Dattilo, Caldwell, Lee, & Kleiber, 1998)
- finances (Pluym, Keur, Gerritsen, & Post, 1997)

In a study of 503 participants with and without a history of traumatic brain injury, Brown, Gordon, and Spielman (2003) researched the difference in participation levels in social-recreational activity. The researchers found that participants without a history of TBI had higher participation level than those who had a history of TBI. Within the participants with a history of TBI, those who had addressed issues regarding depression, fatigue, and vocational engagement appeared to have higher levels of social–recreational participation than those who did not. By addressing these issues in functional intervention strategies, therapeutic recreation specialists can assist clientele in developing a healthy leisure lifestyle and improved quality of life.

Summary

Table 20.3 summarizes the implication areas that apply to therapeutic recreation practice.

- Community integration and reintegration can be used with a variety of individuals to address a variety of skill sets that the individuals need in order to function and thrive in the community. Therapeutic recreation specialists need to be aware of characteristics of both the community and the clients so that each experience can be safe, purposeful, and effective.
- Community integration entails much more than just physical integration into a community setting.

- Community integration is difficult to define, as is "disability." Both are contextual and depend on a number of factors in order for the individual to be successful.
- Newer community integration models and recent research are pointing to the skill sets needed by individuals as they transition from a more secluded or institutional setting into broader community settings.
- Leisure education is clearly a prime area of service in which community integration services may be offered. Leisure education skills sets are complementary and adjunctive to community integration skill sets.
- Although there is some preliminary research on community integration within leisure education, more research with more populations and more stringent methodologies are needed.

Table 20.3. Skill Areas that Apply to Therapeutic Recreation Practice

Author	Community Integration Area	Skills
Ippoliti, Peppey, and Depoy (1994)	Recreational Programming	Fear of people without disabilities, ensuring safe programming environment, lack of structure in staff supervision and services provided to client, discomfort in establishing relationships, and familiarity with recreational activities
Sample, Tomter, and Johns (2007)	Recreational Programming	Activities fees and transportation costs
Walker, Onus, Doyle, Clare, and McCarthy (2005)	Leisure Education	Social skills, group cohesion, and individual goal setting
Wieland, Rosenstock, Kelsey, Ganguli, and Wisniewski (2007)	Leisure Education	Distal support
Hartnett, Gallagher, Kiernan, Poulsen, Gilligan, and Reynolds (2008)	Leisure Education	Socialization, building personal relationships, improving decision-making abilities and skill acquisition, improving stamina, and enhancing life satisfaction
Barker, Kendall, Amsters, Pershouse, Haines, and Kuipers (2009)	Quality of Life	Societal participation
Donnelly and Eng (2005)	Quality of Life	Pain management
Dattilo, Caldwell, Lee, and Kleiber (1998)	Quality of Life	Accessibility of activities
Pluym, Keur, Gerritsen, and Post (1997)	Quality of Life	Finances
Brown, Gordon, and Spielman (2003)	Quality of Life	Depression, fatigue, and vocational engagement

Resources

Community Integration Program: Harborview Medical Center (2nd edition). (1994). By Armstrong, & Lauzen. Idyll Arbor.

The Community Integration Program was designed to assist people with spinal cord injuries reintegrate into the community. Since its inception, the community integration program has been used with patients with traumatic brain injury, stroke, and psychiatric disorders. The program assists clients with the application of skills, socialization, problem solving, and resource guidance. There are modules related to the community environment, cultural activities, community activities, transportation, and physical activities.

Welcome to My Town: A Workbook and Instructional Guide. (2007). By Rainer & Landvik. American Therapeutic Recreation Association.

This curriculum is a workbook that clients can use to identify resources within the client's community. It was originally designed for clients in behavioral health settings. The book has worksheets which assist the client in identifying recreational buildings, restaurants, family and friends, healthcare, criminal justice, and church/spiritual life.

The Rehabilitation Research and Training Center (RRTC) on Community Integration of Persons with Traumatic Brain Injury (TBI) was awarded to researchers at TIRR (The Institute for Rehabilitation and Research) and Baylor College of Medicine by the National Institute on Disability and Rehabilitation Research (NIDRR) on November 1, 2003. www.tbicommunity.org/

Institute on Community Inclusion at the University of Minnesota
www.ici.umn.edu/welcome/default.html

References

Agree, E. M. (1999). The influence of personal care and assistive technology on the measurement of disability. *Social Science and Medicine, 48*, 427–443.

Allen, S., Resnik, L., & Roy, J. (2006). Promoting independence for wheelchair users: The role of home accommodations. *The Gerontologist, 46*(1), 115–123.

Armstrong, M., & Lauzen, S. (1994). *Community integration program: Harborview Medical Center* (2nd ed.). Ravensdale, WA: Idyll Arbor.

Barcus, J. M., & Targett, P. (2003). Maximizing employee effectiveness through use of personal assistance services in the workplace. *Journal of Vocational Rehabilitation, 18*, 99–106.

Barker, R. N., Kendall, M. D., Amsters, D. I., Pershouse, K. J., Haines, T. P., & Kuipers, P. (2009). The relationship between quality of life and disability across the lifespan for people with spinal cord injury. *Spinal Cord, 47*, 149–155.

Bliss, M. J., Cook, S. L., & Kaslow, N. J. (2006). An ecological approach to understanding incarcerated women's responses to abuse. *Women & Therapy, 29*(3/4), 97–115.

Bond, G. R., Salyers, M. P., Rollins, A. L., Rapp, C. A., & Zipple, A. M. (2004). How evidence-based practices contribute to community integration. *Community Mental Health Journal, 40*(6), 569–588.

Brock, K., Black, S., Cotton, S., Kennedy, G., Wilson, S., & Sutton, E. (2009). Goal achievement in the six months after inpatient rehabilitation for stroke. *Disability and Rehabilitation, 31*(11), 880–886.

Bronfenbrenner, U. (1977). Toward an experimental ecology of human development. *American Psychologist, 32*, 513–531.

Brown, M., Gordon, W. A., & Spielman, L. (2003). Participation in social and recreational activity in the community by individuals with traumatic brain injury. *Rehabilitation Psychology, 48*(4), 266–274.

Bruininks, R. H., Chen, T. H., Lakin, K. C., & McGrew, K. S. (1992). Components of personal competence and community integration for persons with mental retardation in small residential programs. *Research in Developmental Disabilities, 13*, 463–479.

Bullock, C. C., & Mahon, M. J. (1997). *Introduction to recreation services for people with disabilities: A person-centered approach*. Champaign, IL: Sagamore.

Cheung, C., & Ngan, R. M. (2007). Empowering for community integration in Hong Kong. *Journal of Developmental and Physical Disabilities, 19*, 305–322.

Chun, S., Lee, Y., Lundberg, N., McCormick, B., & Heo, J. (2008). Contribution of community integration to quality of life for participants of community based adaptive sport program. *Therapeutic Recreation Journal, 42*(4), 217–226.

Coughlin, S. S. (2008). Surviving cancer or other serious illness: A review of individual and community resources. *CA: A Cancer Journal for Clinicians, 58*, 60–64.

Cummins, R. A., & Lau, A. L. D. (2003). Community integration or community exposure? A review and discussion in relation to people with an intellectual disability. *Journal of Applied Research in Intellectual Disabilities, 16,* 154–157.

Dattilo, J., Caldwell, L., Lee, Y., & Kleiber, D. (1998). Returning to the community with a spinal cord injury: Implications for therapeutic recreation specialists, *Therapeutic Recreation Journal, 32*(1), 13–27.

Depla, M. F., De Graff, R., Kroon, H. D., & Heeren, T. J. (2004). Supported living in residential homes for the elderly: Impact on patients and elder care workers. *Aging & Mental Health, 8*(5), 460–468.

Doig, E., Fleming, J., & Tooth, L. (2001). Patterns of community integration 2–5 years post-discharge from brain injury rehabilitation. *Brain Injury, 15*(9), 747–762.

Donnelly, C., & Eng, J. J. (2005). Pain following spinal cord injury: The impact on community reintegration. *Spinal Cord, 43,* 278–282.

Egbert, N., Koch, L., Coeling, H., & Ayers, D. (2006). The role of social support in the family and community integration of right-hemisphere stroke survivors. *Health Communication, 20*(1), 45–55.

Farone, D. W. (2006). Schizophrenia, community integration, and recovery: Implications for social work practice. *Social Work in Mental Health, 4*(4), 21–36.

Field, M. J., & Jette, A. M. (Eds.). (2007). *The future of disability in America.* Washington, DC: Institute of Medicine.

Gontkovsky, S. T., Russum, P., & Stokie, D. S. (2009). Comparison of the CIQ and CHART short form in assessing community integration in individuals with chronic spinal cord injury: A pilot study. *NeuroRehabilitation, 24,* 185–192.

Gulcur, L., Tsemberis, S., Stefancic, A., & Greenwood, R. M. (2007). Community integration of adults with psychiatric disabilities and histories of homelessness. *Community Mental Health Journal, 43*(3), 211–228.

Hallahan, L., & Irizarry, C. (2008). Fun days out: Normalizing social experiences for refugee children. *Journal of Family Studies, 14,* 124–130.

Hartnett, P., Gallagher, G., Kiernan, C., Poulsen, E., Gilligan, E., & Reynolds, M. (2008). Day service programs for people with a severe intellectual disability and quality of life: Parent and staff perspectives. *Journal of Intellectual Disabilities, 12*(2), 153–172.

Hebblethwaite, S., & Pedlar, A. (2005). Community integration for older adults with mental health issues: Implications for therapeutic recreation. *Therapeutic Recreation Journal, 39*(4), 264–276.

Hendricks, D. R., & Wehman, P. (2009). Transition from school to adulthood for youth with autism spectrum disorders: Review and recommendations.

Focus on Autism and Other Developmental Disabilities, 24(2), 77–88.

Howard, D., Browning, C., & Lee, Y. (2007). The International Classification of Functioning, Disability, and Health: Therapeutic recreation code sets and salient diagnostic core sets. *Therapeutic Recreation Journal, 41*(1), 61–81.

Howe-Murphy, R., & Charboneau, B. (1987). *Therapeutic recreation intervention: An ecological perspective.* Englewood Cliffs, NJ: Prentice Hall.

Ippoliti, C., Peppey, B., & Depoy, E. (1994). Promoting self-determination for people with developmental disabilities. *Disability and Society, 9*(4), 453–460.

Ittenbach, R. F., Bruininks, R. H., Thurlow, M. L., & McGrew, K. S. (1993). Community integration of young adults with mental retardation: A multivariate analysis of adjustment. *Research in Developmental Disabilities, 14,* 275–290.

Jivanjee, P., Kruzich, J., & Gordon, L. J. (2008). Community integration of transition-age individuals: Views of young adults with mental health disorders. *The Journal of Behavioral Health Services & Research, 35*(4), 402–418.

Jivanjee, P., Kruzich, J., & Gordon, L. J. (2009). The age of uncertainty: Parent perspectives on the transitions of young people with mental health difficulties to adulthood. *Journal of Children and Family Studies, 18,* 435–446.

Kensinger, K., Gearig, J., Boor, J., Olson, N., & Gras, T. (2007). A therapeutic recreation program for international refugees in a Midwest community. *Therapeutic Recreation Journal, 41*(2), 148–157.

LaPlante, M. P., Kaye, H. S., Kang, T., & Harrington, C. (2004). Unmet need for personal assistance services: Estimating the shortfall in hours of help and adverse consequences. *Journals of Gerontology, 59B*(2), S98–S108.

LeMaire, G. S., & Mallik, K. (2005). Barriers to community integration for participants in community-based psychiatric rehabilitation. *Archives of Psychiatric Nursing, 19*(3), 125–132.

Lloyd, C., Waghorn, G., Best, M., & Gemmell, S. (2008). Reliability of a composite measure of social inclusion for people with psychiatric disabilities. *Australian Occupational Therapy Journal, 55,* 47–56.

Mahalik, J. L., Johnstone, B., Glass, B., & Yoon, D. P. (2007). Spirituality, psychological coping, and community integration for persons with traumatic brain injury. *Journal of Religion, Disability & Health, 11*(3), 65–77.

Mallik, K., Reeves, R. J., & Dellario, D. J. (1998). Barriers to community integration for people with severe and persistent psychiatric disabilities. *Psy-*

chiatric Rehabilitation Journal, 22(2), 175–181.

McCabe, P., Lippert, C., Weiser, M., Hilditch, M., Hartridge, C., & Villamere, J. (2007). Community reintegration following acquired brain injury. *Brain Injury, 21*(2), 231–257.

McColl, M. A., Carlson, P., Johnston, J., Minnes, P., Shue, K., Davies, D., et al. (1998). The definition of community integration: Perspectives of people with brain injuries. *Brain Injury, 21*(1), 15–30.

McCorkle, B.H., Dunn, E. C., Mui Wan, Y., & Gagne, C. (2009). Compeer friends: A qualitative study of a volunteer friendship programme for people with serious mental illness. *International Journal of Social Psychiatry, 55*(4), 291–305.

McKinley, W. O., & Meade, M. A. (2004). Community integration following SCI. *NeuroRehabilitation, 19*, 79–80.

McMillan, D. W., & Chavis, D. M. (1986). Sense of community: A definition and theory. *American Journal of Community Psychology, 14*(1), 6–23.

Meyers, A. R., Anderson, J. J., Miller, D. R., Shipp, K., & Hoenig, H. (2002). Barriers, facilitators, and access for wheelchair users: Substantive and methodologic lessons from a pilot study of environmental effects. *Social Science & Medicine, 55*, 1435–1446.

Minnes, P., Buell, K., Nolte, M. L., McColl, M. A., Carlson, P., & Johnston, J. (2001). Defining community integration of persons with brain injuries as acculturation: A Canadian perspective. *NeuroRehabilitation, 16*, 3–10.

Minnes, P., Carlson, P., McCool, M. A., Nolte, M. L., Johnston, J., & Buell, K. (2003). Community integration: A useful construct, but what does it really mean? *Brain Injury, 17*(2), 149–159.

Onken, S. J., Craig, C. M., Ridgway, P., Ralph, R. O., & Cook, J. A. (2007). An analysis of the definitions and elements of recovery: A review of the literature. *Psychiatric Rehabilitation Journal, 31*(1), 9–22.

Pedlar, A., Yuen, F., & Fortune, D. (2008). Incarcerated women and leisure: Making good girls out of bad? *Therapeutic Recreation Journal, 42*(1), 24–32.

Pluym, S. M. F., Keur, T. J. A., Gerritsen, J., & Post, M. W. M. (1997). Community integration of wheelchair-bound athletes: A comparison before and after onset of disability. *Clinical Rehabilitation, 11*, 227–235.

Porter, H. R., & VanPuymbroeck, M. (2007). Utilization of the International Classification of Functioning, Disability, and Health within therapeutic recreation practice. *Therapeutic Recreation Journal, 41*(1), 47–60.

Pretty, G., Rapley, M., & Bramston P. (2002). Neighborhood and community experience, and the quality of life of rural adolescents with and without

an intellectual disability. *Journal of Intellectual & Developmental Disability, 27*(2), 106–116.

Putnam, R. D. (2000) *Bowling alone: The collapse and revival of American community*. New York, NY: Simon and Schuster.

Rainer, J. C., & Landvik, J. (2007). *Welcome to my town: A workbook and instructional guide*. Hattiesburg, MS: American Therapeutic Recreation Association.

Reistetter, T. A., & Abreu, B. C. (2005). Appraising evidence on community integration following brain injury: A systematic review. *Occupational Therapy International, 12*(4), 196–217.

Reistetter, T. A., Spencer, J. C., Trujillo L., & Abreu, B. C. (2005). Examining the Community Integration Measure (CIM): A replication study with life satisfaction. *NeuroRehabilitation, 20*, 139–148.

Rowles, G. D., Concotelli, J. A., & High, D. M. (1996). Community integration of a rural nursing home. *Journal of Applied Gerontology, 15*, 188–201.

Sallis, J. F., Cervero, R. B., Ascher, W., Henderson, K. A., Kraft, M. K., & Kerr, J. (2006). An ecological approach to creating active living communities. *Annual Review of Public Health, 27*, 297–322.

Salter, K., Foley, N., Jutai, J., Bayley, M., & Teasell, R. (2008). Assessment of community integration following traumatic brain injury. *Brain Injury, 22*(11), 820–835.

Sample, P. L., Tomter, H., & Johns, N. (2007). "The left hand does not know what the right hand is doing": Rural and urban cultures of care for persons with traumatic brain injuries. *Substance Use & Misuse, 42*, 705–727.

Seelman, K. D. (1993). Assistive technology policy: A road to independence for individuals with disabilities. *Journal of Social Issues, 49*(2), 115–136.

Segal, S. P., Silverman, C., & Baumohl, J. (1989). Seeking person–environment fit in community care placement. *Journal of Social Issues, 45*(3), 49–64.

Skalko, T., Williams, R., Snethen, G. & Cooper, N. (2008). ECU horizons day treatment program: A case report of collaboration between community mental health providers and an academic recreational therapy program. *Therapeutic Recreation Journal, 42*(2), 132–143.

Slater, D., & Meade, M. A. (2004). Participation in recreation and sports for persons with spinal cord injury: Review and recommendations. *NeuroRehabilitation, 19*(2), 121–129.

Stumbo, N. J., & Carter, M. J. (2009). Assessing recreation and leisure participation. In E. Mpofu and T. Oakland (Eds.), *Rehabilitation and health as-*

sessment: Applying ICF guidelines (pp. 647–673). New York, NY: Springer.

Stumbo, N. J., Martin, J. K., & Hedrick, B. N. (2009a). Assistive technology: Impact on education, employment, and independence of individuals with physical disabilities. *Journal of Vocational Rehabilitation, 30*(2), 99–110.

Stumbo, N. J., Martin, J. K., & Hedrick, B. N. (2009b). Personal assistance for students with severe physical disabilities in postsecondary education: Is it the deal breaker? *Journal of Vocational Rehabilitation, 30*(1), 11–20.

Tacon, A. M. (2008). Approaches to chronic disease and chronic care: From oxymoron to modern zeitgeist. *Disease Management and Health Outcomes, 16*(5), 285–288.

Taylor, S. J. (2004). Caught in the continuum: A critical analysis of the principle of least restrictive environment. *Research and Practice for Persons with Severe Disabilities, 29*(4), 218–230.

Thorn, S. H., Pittman, A., Myers, R. E., & Slaughter, C. (2009). Increasing community integration and inclusion for people with intellectual disabilities. *Research in Developmental Disabilities, 30*, 891–901.

Townley, G., & Kloos, B. (2009). Development of a measure of sense of community for individuals with serious mental illness residing in community settings. *Journal of Community Psychology, 37*(3), 363–380.

Turner, B., Fleming, J., Cornwell, P., Worrall, L., Ownsworth, T., Haines, T., Kendall, M., & Chenoweth, L. (2007). A qualitative study of the transition from hospital to home for individuals with acquired brain injury and their family caregivers. *Brain Injury, 21*(11), 1119–1130.

Verbrugge, L. M., Rennert, C., & Madans, J. H. (1997). The great efficacy of personal equipment assistance in reducing disability. *American Journal of Public Health, 87*(3), 384–392.

Verbrugge, L. M., & Sevak, P. (2002). Use, type, and efficacy of assistance for disability. *Journals of Gerontology: Series B, 57B*(6), S366–S379.

Vine, X. K. L., & Hamilton, D. I. (2005). Individual characteristics associated with community integration of adults with intellectual disability. *Journal of Intellectual & Developmental Disability, 30*(3), 171–175.

Walker, A. J., Onus, M., Doyle, M., Clare, J., & McCarthy, K. (2005). Cognitive rehabilitation after severe traumatic brain injury: A pilot program of goal planning and outdoor adventure course participation. *Brain Injury, 19*(14), 1237–1241.

Wieland, M. E., Rosenstock, J., Kelsey, S. F., Ganguli, M., & Wisniewski, S. R. (2007). Distal support and community living among individuals diagnosed with schizophrenia and schizoaffective disorder. *Psychiatry, 70*(1), 1–11.

Wittenburg, D. C., & Maag, E. (2002). School to where? A literature on economic outcomes of youth with disabilities. *Journal of Vocational Rehabilitation, 17*, 265–280.

Wong, Y.-L. I., Metzendorf, D., & Min, S.-Y. (2006). Neighborhood experiences and community integration: Perspectives from mental health consumers and providers. *Social Work in Mental Health, 4*(3), 45–59.

Wong, Y.-L. I., & Solomon, P. (2002). Community integration of persons with psychiatric disabilities in supportive independent housing: A conceptual model and methodological considerations. *Mental Health Services Research, 4*(1), 13–28.

Wong, Y.-L. I., & Stanhope, V. (2009). Conceptualizing community: A comparison of neighborhood characteristics of supportive housing for persons with psychiatric and developmental disabilities. *Social Science & Medicine, 68*, 1376–1387.

World Health Assembly. (2001). International classification of functioning, disability, and health. Retrieved January 1, 2003 from: http://www3. who.int/icf/icftemplate.cfm?myurl=homepage. html&mytitle=Home%20Page

World Health Organization (2002). *Towards a common language for functioning, disability and health: ICF.* Geneva, Switzerland: Author.

Yasui, N. Y., & Berven, N. L. (2009). Community integration: Conceptualisation and measurement. *Disability and Rehabilitation, 31*(9), 761–771.

Yates, P. J. (2003). Psychological adjustment, social enablement and community integration following acquired brain injury. *Neuropsychological Rehabilitation, 13*(1/2), 291–306.

» CHAPTER 21 »

Virtual Reality Technologies

Norma J. Stumbo, Ph.D., CTRS and Shane Pegg, Ph.D.

Background/History

Many individuals with disabilities use a variety of assistive technologies, such as environmental controls, mobility and communication devices, and computer software programs, to manage their everyday lives (Braddock, Rizzolo, Thompson, & Bell, 2004). Assistive technology is defined as "any item, piece of equipment, or product system, whether acquired commercially, modified, or customized, that is used to increase, maintain, or improve functional capabilities of individuals with disabilities," according to the Technology Related Assistance for Individuals with Disabilities Act of 1988 as amended in 1994 and again in 2004 (Assistive Technology Act of 2004, Public Law 108-364, 2004). Assistive technology (AT) is intended to improve functional independence by circumventing environmental barriers, maximizing personal independence, and increasing activity participation. In turn, the individual is more able to participate in leisure, work, and other spheres of life (Braddock et al.; Chang, Liu, & Wang, 2009; Stumbo, Martin, & Hedrick, 2009). Scherer and Glueckauf (2005) noted that the ability of individuals with disabilities to perform in a variety of settings—either natively or augmented by assistive technologies—is essential to their community participation and quality of life. One category of assistive technologies that may aid individuals with disabilities is called "virtual reality."

Virtual reality (VR) technologies are those that closely re-create an actual environment or experience, and may range from desktop simulations to full-immersion, three-dimensional situations in which the user responds to visual and potentially additional sensory prompts in real-time (Braddock et al., 2004; Deutsch, Borbely, Filler, Huhn, & Guarrera-Bowlby, 2008; Lotan, Yalon-Chamovitz, & Weiss, 2009a, 2009b; Standen, Brown, & Cromby, 2001; Villanueva et al., 2009). Extensive VR systems require head-mounted stereoscopic displays, headphones, gloves, and other physical feedback devices that transmit and receive data, such as the IREX platform (see the Resources section in this chapter). These systems are often expensive (upwards of $17,000) and not readily available.

Less extensive VR systems, such as the Nintendo Wii or PlayStation 2, are the primary subject of this chapter and involve gaming systems using computers or televisions with input devices such as keyboards, joysticks, wands, or touchscreens (Deutsch et al., 2008; Standen et al., 2001). It should be noted here that most initial rehabilitation research has been conducted with the IREX system, with commercially available systems such as Wii being studied only in more recent years (Deutsch et al., 2008).

Virtual reality technologies have been available to the general public for less than 15 years; however, their popularity for mass consumption as well as assessment and intervention purposes in rehabilitation settings has been blossoming exponentially in recent years (Yalon-Chamowitz & Weiss, 2008). Technology, especially virtual reality environments, has become "smarter," smaller, easier to use, less costly, more plentiful, better integrated with other technologies, and more individualized—all of which has benefited the general public as well as individuals with disabilities (Braddock et al.; Nigg, 2003; Standen et al., 2001; Weiss, Bialik, & Kizony, 2003).

The advantages of using virtual reality environments within rehabilitation settings include:

- potential use as an objective assessment of behavior, skills, and understanding in precise ways in ecologically valid environments (Brooks & Rose, 2003; Standen & Brown, 2005; Lotan et al., 2009b; Wallergård, Eriksson, & Johansson, 2008)
- safe access to interactive, true-to-life situations that would otherwise be inaccessible due to motor, cognitive, and psychological limitations (Botella et al., 2004; Lotan et al., 2009a, 2009b; Weiss et al., 2003)
- ability to adapt and individualize according to individual skills and abilities (Akhutina et al.

2003; Botella et al., 2004; Weiss et al.; Standen & Brown, 2005; Standen et al., 2001; Lotan et al., 2009a; Weiss, Rand, Katz, & Kizony, 2004; Yalon-Chamowitz & Weiss, 2008)

- ability to adapt and individualize according to the goals of the intervention or research (Akhutina et al., 2003; Blackman, Van Schaik, & Martyr, 2007; Lotan et al., 2009b; Weiss et al., 2004)
- minimal space requirements, especially in desktop versions (Akhutina et al., 2003)
- immediate feedback for the user (Weiss et al., 2004)
- allowance for role-playing—being a "person" other than oneself (Botella et al., 2004)
- potential for development of personal self-efficacy as performance achievements are attained and skills developed, and hopefully transferred to additional situations (Botella et al., 2004)
- sense of novelty, enjoyment, and fun during the intervention, thus increasing motivation for continued participation (Wann, 1996; Weiss et al., 2004; Yalon-Chamovitz & Weiss, 2008)
- substitute participation for activities in which individuals with disabilities cannot participate, thus increasing their repertoire of activities that they "can do" (Standen et al., 2001; Wallergård, Eriksson, & Johansson, 2008; Weiss et al., 2004; Yalon-Chamovitz & Weiss, 2008)
- ability for person with disability to "control" his or her environment and succeed in activities that otherwise may not be experienced (Botella et al., 2004; Deutsch et al., 2008; Lotan et al., 2009a; Standen & Brown, 2005; Wallergård, Eriksson, & Johansson, 2008; Weiss et al., 2004; Yalon-Chamovitz & Weiss, 2008)
- creation of a therapeutic environment, that does not necessarily reflect "reality" in which the person can explore and attempt actions (make errors) without "real" consequences that will enhance stronger learning (Standen et al., 2001; Wann, 1996)
- ability to engage multiple users at the same time (Weiss et al., 2004)

In discussing smart technologies, not just necessarily virtual reality technologies, Carrillo, Dishman, and Plowman (2009) discussed some of their disadvantages such as:

- interference – wireless communication devices can be sometimes triggered by unrelated static
- recruitment – the difficulty in recruiting individuals to test out the technologies so that they can be improved by the designers and developers

- expense – some technology can be quite expensive to purchase, maintain, and repair
- maintenance – diligence is needed to make sure the equipment is operating when it needs to be
- hardware issues – gaming systems, televisions, computers, displays and the like need continual monitoring and may need to be reset if deactivated for some reason
- software issues – some software can be expensive, need continual updates, and may not be modified by the end user or in the case of intervention, the therapist

Wallergård, Eriksson, and Johansson (2008) also added that since at least two input modes (one for navigation and one for interaction) might be needed in some cases, the complexity might be too high for some groups of consumers. In addition they noted that interaction may be too abstract, and too much fine-motor control may be needed to manipulate the input device(s). While using some VR systems that simulate movement, such as flying, some individuals may experience "simulator sickness" or "cyber sickness." This usually has to do with discrepancies between the visual and vestibular body systems and can be reduced by allowing the user to control the movements rather than being a passive observer. Weiss et al. (2004) noted that this happens much less frequently using video capture technologies where the user's own body movements are captured on screen.

Overall the largest advantage to virtual reality technologies is the ability to be able to work with individuals in a small-scale, structured, adaptable environment with the intention that these skills and knowledges can be transferred later to real-life environments and situations (Weiss et al., 2004).

Botella et al. (2004) believed that VR technologies have incredible potential, although this potential needs to be supported through additional and more stringent research. The question for them is not, "Does VR have a role in treatment and rehabilitation settings?" The question is, "For which populations are which applications most useful?"

Intended Client Groups

Virtual reality and virtual environments have been discussed with a wide range of disabling conditions, including individuals with:

- dementia or Alzheimer's disease (Braddock et al., 2004; Blackman, Van Schaik, & Martyr, 2007; Carrillo, Dishman, & Plowman, 2009)

- traumatic brain injury (Braddock et al., 2004; Thornton et al., 2005)
- cerebral vascular accidents (Farrow & Reid, 2004; O'Dell, Lin, & Harrison, 2009; Wann, 1996)
- cerebral palsy and other neuromuscular disorders (Akhutina et al., 2003; Deutsch et al., 2008; Villanueva, Perez-Moreno, Maldonado, & Gomez, 2009; Weiss, Bialik, & Kizony, 2003)
- severe mental illnesses in people who are nomadic (Braddock et al., 2004; Chang et al., 2009)
- visual impairments or blindness (Sanchez & Flores, 2010)
- chronic pain (Feintuch, Tuchner, Lorber-Haddad, Meiner, & Shiri, 2009)
- intellectual and developmental disabilities (Lotan, Yalon-Chamowitz, & Weiss, 2008, 2009, 2010; Standen & Brown, 2005; Yalon-Chamowitz & Weiss, 2008)
- specific phobias, in the desensitization process (Wolitzky-Taylor, Horowitz, Powers, & Telch, 2008)
- post-traumatic stress disorder (Cukor, Spitalnick, Defede, Rizzo, & Rothbaum, 2009)
- anxiety disorders (Cukor et al., 2009)
- eating disorders (Botella et al., 2004)

The next section describes some definitions related to virtual reality technologies. While many specialists may be familiar with virtual reality technologies in their personal lives, they may not have considered its use as a potential tool in therapeutic recreation intervention.

Definitions

A number of concepts and definitions are important to understanding and applying virtual reality technologies to intervention situations. Below are some of the terms and definitions that are common in the rehabilitation literature.

Virtual reality "is a complex user interface that includes simulations in real time through multiple sensorial channels. These sensorial modalities are visual, auditory, tactile, olfactory, etc." (Botella et al., 2004, p. 1).

Immersive versus **non-immersive environments:** In immersive environments, the individual is partially or completely surrounded by the VR system. Usually immersive systems use stereoscope vision goggles or headgear (special set of glasses) so that the environment is viewed in 2 dimensions or 3 dimensions. In non-immersive environments, simpler systems are used, such as a desktop computer that displays the environment on a standard screen (Botella et al., 2004; Wallergård et al., 2008).

Presence (Immersion): The degree to which the display environment is capable of immersing the individual by representing an inclusive, extensive, surrounding, and vivid illusion of reality (Wallergård et al., 2008). VR systems with larger viewing areas and with surround sound are more likely to have more presence for users.

Engagement: Related to presence, the degree to which a user is an active participant in the VR experience, engrossed in the action (Wallergård et al., 2008). Both presence and engagement are desired qualities for VR systems.

Motion or **video capture:** When the users see themselves and their movements on the VR screen. Requires that users stand or sit in a designated area as a camera-based, motion capture system projects themselves and/or their movements on the screen—the user's real-time motion is represented on-screen embedded within the virtual environment and action (Weiss et al., 2004).

Avatars are representations of the user. For example, in some games, a three-dimensional (3D) or two-dimensional (2D) model represents the user on-screen, such as the player in a virtual soccer game (3D) or Pac-Man and his enemies in the video arcade game (2D).

Basic Premises

Virtual reality is being used in a variety of contexts within treatment and rehabilitation settings. While VR systems currently are being used in a variety of situations to improve functional ability (e.g., visual perception, memory, sequencing, motor learning, spatial functioning, and range of motion), especially by physical therapists and occupational therapists, they are also being used for more real-world learning such as meal preparation and crossing a street (Weiss et al., 2004). These include real-world applications include instruction in communication skills, community-reintegration skills (Germann, Broida, & Broida, 2003), exercise and physical fitness (Yalon-Chamowitz & Weiss, 2008); and leisure involvement (Farrow & Reid, 2004).

As an example of VR in improvement of functional abilities, O'Dell et al. (2009) focused on the needs of persons who have experienced cerebral vascular accidents including motor recovery (e.g., strength, speed, or accuracy of arm and leg movements—"getting better") or functional recovery (e.g., performing self-care, activities of daily living, or leisure activities—"doing better"). They noted that brain plasticity and reorganization is better when:

- learning is task-specific (e.g., practicing transfers to improve ability to transfer)
- repetition occurs (e.g., multiple opportunities to learn over time)
- the activity is fun and enjoyable
- both tactile and visual stimuli are used
- the task for each session is somewhat novel
- the individual sleeps in order for the brain to consolidate skills

They advocated for virtual reality as it uses computer technology with real-time input, drawing on sight, sound, and touch, in actions that can be novel, fun, and specific to an individual's task needs, making it an ideal candidate for improving motor learning. They further remarked that more and higher-quality research is needed to ensure that virtual reality is as useful as it currently is tested to be.

The second category of "real-world" applications for VR also is prominent. For example, Wallergård et al. (2008) focused on individuals with cognitive disabilities, in this case individuals who had experienced stroke, and used VR to teach them about public transportation systems. They created and evaluated a system to teach individuals with strokes that produced cognitive impairments how to access the transportation system in a Swedish community. The user had a virtual wallet, a bus card, and was given instructions for "taking" two sets from his or her apartment to a café. The situation was realistic, modeled after real-life bus lines, small city centers, residential areas, and two terminal stations. They remarked that all subjects reported presence and engagement, and stated the VR was very realistic (to the point that some got motion sickness). The researchers felt that with additional considerations (such as a better orientation to the system and having a laser pointer with a button that was easier to press) this system could be used to assess client skills and train individuals virtually to use the bus system.

These are but a few examples of how the major characteristics of virtual technology—interactivity, immersion, and imagination—are being applied in therapeutic and rehabilitation settings. Although the technologies are relatively new, work has begun on establishing best practices in the use of virtual reality. The next section summarizes these best practices.

Best Practices and Principles in Virtual Reality

Lotan et al. (2009b), after conducting three studies with the use of virtual reality as a motivating environment

to improve the physical fitness levels of individuals with intellectual and developmental disabilities (IDD), reconsidered the studies to determine "best practices" or "lessons learned." The following list is an abbreviated version of their findings:

- Individuals with mild to moderate IDDs are able to use customized and off-the-shelf VR systems; individuals with severe IDD benefit more from customized systems.
- VR was found suitable for both genders, ages from adolescence to adulthood, with or without ambulation limitations. Individuals should have basic sensory abilities (intact or corrected vision, hearing, etc.), moderate physical abilities (at least able to move one limb slightly), and elementary levels of independence (e.g., motivation, initiative, communication).
- Although caregiver staff is able to use VR as entertainment, the authors recommend that technical and professional experts be involved in VR when it is intended as an intervention.
- A small room, preferably dedicated to VR, which is close to participants and can be darkened, is the best VR environment.
- Off-the-shelf, easily available systems are cheaper, present fewer malfunctions, are easier to operate, and come with a greater selection of games, but specialized VR systems are more adaptable, especially to those with the most severe disabilities.
- While some fitness outcomes were observable at four weeks of intervention, the authors suggest that actual physical fitness programs using VR be long lasting to maximize fitness when possible.
- The authors recommend outcome measures involving, enjoyment, choice-making, and physical fitness.

After several studies, Brown, Standen, Proctor, and Sterland (2001) suggested a number of "best practices" for VR technology development. These suggestions are included here, not because TR specialists are likely to develop VR software, but so that the criteria may be used as a checklist of sorts in selecting appropriate VR technologies. The following summary list applies to individuals with intellectual disabilities, so it would need to be modified for other individuals, according to their needs and disability:

- Instructions should be simple and contain only one or two actions at a time.

- Input devices, such as joysticks, should be simplified, with only one or two buttons for operation. Whenever possible, a single click should initiate action.
- Universal design should be considered and "clickable" areas be larger than the icon (extra tolerance for error).
- Simultaneous action should cease while verbal instructions are given.
- If items are to be selected in a specific order, specific prompts should be automatic if the person selects the wrong order.
- Text should be avoided; representative pictures and icons and an overlay voice is preferred. (Speech therapists may be helpful consultants for this.) If dialogue boxes are needed, they should remain on the screen for a length of time appropriate to the user.
- The use of icons and pictures should be consistent and standardized throughout the whole of the software.
- Although the VR environment should be realistic, it should help the user to overcome learning barriers that exist in the real world. As many real-life cues as possible should be provided, given that they do not distract the user from the objective of the intervention.
- Some features of the virtual environment should offer a wide margin of error (such as moving through doorways).
- To allow for diversity in learners, users should be able to bypass advanced learning objectives.
- These principles may help specialists design or choose appropriate virtual reality systems for their clients.

Wann (1996) developed four principles for physical therapists when designing VR environments and applications, and insisted that VR is only as good as the "added value" that it bring to the rehabilitation or treatment setting. His four principles include:

1. A 3D virtual environment can "immerse" the person to the degree that he or she will demonstrate appropriate limb and postural corrections in response to the virtual environment.
2. The illusion created above, in tandem with the person's ability to directly manipulate the VR environment, will produce a considerably stronger learning environment than more traditional or conventional therapies.
3. The opportunity for the person to explore, interact, and make errors in the VR environ-

ment will provide an opportunity for motor and other learning unavailable outside of the VR environment.
4. The novelty and intrinsic appeal of the VR environment will provide a valuable motivating factor for interventions. (Wann, 1996)

Related Research

Farrow and Reid (2004) recruited 16 individuals who experienced stroke, aged 49 to 90, from the Toronto area. The investigators exposed the participants to 45 to 60 minutes of VR, for example, volleyball, soccer, painting, dancing, etc. After the VR experience, researchers conducted personal interviews with each participant, covering (a) specific VR applications, (b) meaning of VR to the participant, (c) importance of VR, (d) perception of others, and (e) comparison of VR to other typical activities. Participants felt that VR provided an opportunity to participate in pleasurable and fun leisure activities they missed and were not able to participate in because of environmental, physical, or psychological barriers. They also reported feelings of accomplishment, increased control and self-efficacy, positive self-image, normalcy, and use of cognitive skills. In addition, participants felt that VR activities were more likely to get them moving than their regular activities or exercise routines, if any. Being older and being intimidated by technology was not a problem reported by this sample. The authors noted that VR has the opportunity to activate flow as the level of the person's skills can be equated with the level of challenge in the game.

Wallergård et al. (2008) reported on a study with seven subjects with strokes, aged 50 to 72 years, who used VR to "navigate" on a bus from their virtual apartment to a virtual café. While all experienced initial difficulties, they did experience physical and social presence, and six out of seven reportedly accepted the technology and its instructional purpose. The researchers felt the study showed that virtual reality could be used in teaching older individuals with cognitive impairments how to use transportation systems, and suggested a wide range of improvements in their methodology and virtual environment.

Stewart et al. (2007) studied two individuals with paresis from stroke with a virtual reality system using four activities: (a) reaching, (b) ball shooting, (c) rotation, and (d) pinch. Each participant attended 12 training sessions, lasting 1 to 2 hours each, over a 3-week period. Several outcomes measures were administered pre-, mid-, and post-intervention. The investigators provided summary feedback at the completion of each practice block (10 to 20 attempts) to improve anticipatory motor planning and problem-solving. Both individuals improved VR task performance across sessions; the less impaired person made greater gains. The VR system allowed a individually tailored practice progression that the investigators felt was key to the study's success.

Henderson, Korner-Bitensky, and Levin (2007) conducted a systematic review of the literature on the effectiveness of virtual reality for upper-limb motor recovery. They reviewed six studies (two randomized control trials, one single-subject design, and three pre-post designs). They found good support for evidence that immersive VR is more beneficial than no therapy and literally no evidence (no studies) of immersive VR being more beneficial than conventional therapy. In terms of non-immersive VR therapy, they found good evidence to suggest it is no better than conventional therapy and conflicting evidence that is was better than no therapy. They concluded:

> The results of the reviewed studies suggest that immersive VR may have an advantage over no therapy in the rehabilitation of the UL [upper limb] in patients with stroke, but the results are still questionable. As for non-immersive VR, the results of the available studies are conflicting and provide little direction for clinicians who are trying to make practice decisions. (p. 59)

They noted that the results were encouraging enough to warrant further research.

Wolitzky-Taylor et al. (2008) noted that virtual reality can be used for individuals with certain phobias to confront computer-generated representations of the phobic target. In VR interventions, the person interacts with a virtual representation of the stimulus, wearing headphones and a position-tracking device. They noted that VR is useful in creating a "sense of presence" or reality needed to desensitize the person by emotionally and psychologically processing his or her exposure to the stimulus without a real-life threat. The benefits of VR are that it can be stopped at any time, it can be progressively programmed, and the person can see him or herself in the actual environment of the phobia condition.

Botella et al. (2008) completed a research study using VR to treat phobias about small animals (spiders, cockroaches, and mice). The sample included 12 volunteers (mean age 27.3) who underwent pre-testing, a self-administered VR-based phobia program (Without Fear), an immediate post-test as well as a 3-month post-test. The sample, on average, completed over 4 sessions on a schedule of their choosing. The group showed significant improvement in the reduction of small animal phobias at the immediate post-test follow-up as well as additional gains at the 3-month follow-up. The authors concluded that telepsychology, delivered through virtual reality, is a viable option for treating these phobias successfully.

Diamond et al. (2003) created a virtual rehabilitation center (VRC) to determine if the nature and severity of a traumatic brain injury would relate to his or her ability to use the center. The center had five modules: (a) information processing (visual acuity and visual reaction times), (b) functional skills (microwave oven, automated teller machine, and vending machine), (c) telecommunications, (d) community forum, and (e) help through FAQs. Eight individuals with traumatic brain injury were included in the study. The results showed that there was a significant relationship between the severity and nature of the cognitive impairment and the rate at which he or she learned to use the VR system. However, all individuals were able to effectively use all the VRC modules, with some individuals requiring more trials (attempts) than others. The authors concluded that the VRC has incredible potential but needs further study in relation to more closely defining who it works for (gender, age, wider range of impairments, etc.) and with consideration of ethical consequences such as remote versus face-to-face therapies.

A number of research studies are outlined in Table 21.1 (pp. 392–393). The table includes information about the research participants, the methods used, and the outcomes.

Application to Therapeutic Recreation

Germann, Broida, and Broida (2003) conducted a study with 110 individuals with physical disabilities, 18 years of age and older, who lived in the Denver area. They divided participants into three groups: (1) virtual reality only, (2) virtual reality and leisure education, and (3) control, with no intervention. In the virtual reality group, participants were exposed to virtual environments of photo-realistic panoramas of the facilities, digital videos of equipment use, information about access, and interactive maps of the facilities. In the VR and leisure education group, a therapeutic recreation specialist facilitated the virtual tour and provided information about transportation, facility accessibility, fees/costs, equipment and adaptations, and individualized services provided by the recreation and park department. The control group took their own tours independently.

The investigators reported that in general, the VR-LE groups had the greatest information gains and though not statistically significant, the VR-only group had higher post-anxiety scores than the VR-LE or control groups.

Weiss, Bialik, and Kizony (2003) studied the use of VR as a leisure activity (not intervention) for five young males with severe cerebral palsy. They used a "presence" questionnaire and a task-specific questionnaire that looked at variables such as enjoyment, control, choice, and fatigue. They found that all three VR games (soccer, snowboarding, Birds and Balls) induced enjoyment, a sense of control and choice, and provided positive leisure experiences. Soccer was found to be the most fatiguing VR sport of the three. The authors reported significant potential for VR games to be leisure experiences for individuals with severe cerebral palsy.

Lotan et al. (2009a) performed a study with 60 participants who were intellectually and developmentally disabled. Using Sony's PlayStation 2 EyeToy video capture system, they tested whether the physical fitness of the sample could be improved, as measured by a heart rate monitor, heart beat, energy expenditure, and a walk/run test. Results showed that the sample felt success and enjoyment in using the exercise system, and that results for the walk/run test and the heartbeat test were improved, although energy expenditure was not. The authors felt that since the physical fitness levels of these sedentary individuals were quite poor prior to the study, that any improvements were clinically significant. They concluded:

> The VR-based intervention was shown to be both feasible and suitable for individuals with a moderate level of IDD [intellectual and developmental disability] living in residential settings. A VR fitness program was motivating for these individuals and was found to enhance their physical fitness. This was the case for both wheelchair users as well as individuals who ambulate with walking aids. (p. 237)

Lotan et al. (2010) studied 44 individuals with intellectual disability and their improvement in resting heart rate after an 8-week (two to three 30-minute sessions per week) physical fitness program. They used the IREX/GX VR system for the exercise program. They found that the treatment group significantly improved their resting heart rate. However, they also suggested that other tests by explored for use with individuals with intellectual disabilities, especially those with severe disabilities, who typically have lower levels of

fitness and face a number of barriers, including motivation, to improving their fitness levels.

Thornton et al. (2005) investigated the effects of an activity-based versus a virtual reality balance exercise program for individuals with traumatic brain injury, aged 18 to 66, and their caregivers in Ottawa, Canada. Balance and function questionnaires were administered pre-, post-, and 3-month-post end of the program. Focus groups were carried out separately for the individuals with TBI and their caregivers. Psychosocially, participants and their caregivers noted enjoyment and improved confidence and self-identity in both the activity-based and VR groups. The VR group commented more strongly about the sense of structure and purpose of the exercise program, while the activity-based group felt the program helped with organization and they wished it had been offered when they originally received their brain trauma. The VR group noted more strongly that their balance and mobility had improved, and this positively impacted their daily activities. More individuals in the activity-based group mentioned interaction with the staff and made comments about the equipment. Most participants perceived the program (both styles, 3 times per week for 6 weeks) to be worth the time and travel required, and wished the program would continue past the current research study. The authors noted four areas of future needed research: (a) potential for improved program compliance based on VR, (b) need for additional accessible programming in the community, (c) safe guidelines for unsupervised (home) programs, and (d) program length and intensity for achieving balance improvements.

Resources

There are a number of options for virtual reality environments that may be suitable to treatment and rehabilitation settings. Again, these range from off-the-shelf, commercially available systems (e.g., Nintendo Wii), to specialized systems that were designed with clinical applications in mind.

Gesture Tek Health

Offers a wide range of gaming applications, such as Birds & Balls, a game in which the degree of touch will affect whether a ball turns into doves or bursts. In the soccer game, the video-captured user is the goalkeeper, and is tasked with keeping balls from entering the goal area.

www.gesturetekhealth.com

Table 21.1. Research Related to Virtual Reality Applicable to Therapeutic Recreation

Authors/Date	Sample Description	Purpose Statement/Variables	Method	Major Findings
Germann, Broida, & Broida, 2003	110 individuals aged 18 and older, physical/mobility disabilities	To determine if VR tours of recreation facilities could reduce anxiety, provide vital information	Pre-post multiple group design	On-site leisure education/information was most effective for reducing anxiety, improved information, followed by VR tours
Farrow & Reid, 2004	16 community-dwelling individuals with stroke, aged 49 to 90; convenience sample	To qualitatively describe experiences after participating in a VR experience	Personal interviews post-VR experience	VR has possibilities for improving movement, increasing engagement, and enabling competence
Wallergård et al., 2008	7 individuals with stroke, aged 50 to 72; convenience sample	To evaluate the suitability of a VR system that taught individuals how to use a bus system, from apartment to café	Following the VR "excursion," subjects were asked to explain their thoughts as they took the trip (retrospective think-aloud)	VR could be used in teaching older individuals with cognitive impairments how to use transportation systems; wide range of improvements needed in their methodology and virtual environment
Stewart et al., 2007	2 participants with chronic post-stroke paresis	To test 4 VR tasks developed to improve arm and hand movements	Twelve 1- or 2-hour sessions, over 3 weeks; behavior measures and questionnaires administered pre-, mid- and post-training	Both individuals improved VR task performance across session; the less impaired person made greater gains
Broeren, Claesson, Goude, Rydmark, & Sunnerhagen, 2008	27 community-dwelling persons with stroke (Netherlands), aged 47 to 85; average of 5+ years after stroke	To assess whether playing computer games improved motor function	Pre-, post-test design with control group; with treatment group receiving additional VR 3/week for 45 minutes for 4 weeks; data collected through interviews, plus tests for executive function, manual ability, and kinematics	All participants responded favorably to playing 3D computer games; although there was enough improvement in all measurements to be clinically relevant, none were statistically significant
Henderson, Korner-Bitensky, & Levin, 2007	6 studies retrieved from medical literature databases	To determine if immersive and non-immersive VR is more effective than conventional therapy or no therapy in upper limb rehabilitation for individuals with stroke	Systematic literature review	Immersive VR provides some advantage over no therapy but results are still questionable. Results for non-immersive VR are conflicting, provide little direction.
Weiss, Bialik, & Kizony, 2003	5 young males with severe spastic CP and severe intellectual disabilities; mean age was 25.6 years	To explore ways that VR could provide positive and enjoyable physical leisure experiences (rather than interventions), using Gesture Xtreme VR system	5-item "presence" questionnaire and 6-item task specific questionnaire (e.g., enjoyment, control, comfort level, etc.)	All three games generated high "presence," promoted choice and enjoyment; VR has potential as a leisure activity

Table 21.1. Research Related to Virtual Reality Applicable to Therapeutic Recreation (cont'd)

Authors/Date	Sample Description	Purpose Statement/Variables	Method	Major Findings
Thornton et al., 2005	27 individuals with moderate to severe traumatic brain injury, aged 18 to 66	To explore multi-dimensional benefits of exercise participation by individuals with TBI and their caregivers	6-week either activity-based or VR exercise program; Separate post-exercise program focus groups consisting of individuals with TBI and their caregivers	Improvements were noted in psychosocial, physical, and program domains, including balance confidence and function in both activity-based and VR groups; Greater enthusiasm and knowledge by both persons with TBI and caregivers for VR group
Diamond et al., 2003	8 individuals with traumatic brain injury; randomly selected from convenience sample	To determine if nature and severity of TBI affected ability to use 5 modules from virtual rehabilitation center (VRC): (a) information processing, (b) functional skills, (c) telecommunications, (d) community forum, and (e) help through FAQs	Pre-post test assessment; all subjects received treatment	All subjects able to effectively use all the VRC modules, some requiring more trials (attempts) than others
Yalon-Chamowitz & Weiss, 2008	33 individuals with moderate intellectual disabilities and cerebral palsy, convenience sample	To document behaviors during and following VR leisure activities, in terms of performance capabilities, sense of enjoyment, and success	Control and treatment (VR) leisure activity groups, 2 to 3 times per week for 12 weeks; Observation form and user feedback and self-esteem questionnaire	VR group reported higher success, enjoyment, and "presence" rates than their observers; Soccer and "Birds & Balls" were selected most frequently; no differences reported for self-esteem
Lotan, Yalon-Chamovitz, & Weiss, 2010	44 individuals with intellectual disabilities	To test effectiveness of VR-based exercise program in improving physical fitness of individuals with intellectual disabilities	Pre-post, treatment/control groups involving 8-week fitness program of two to three 30-min. sessions per week using IREX/GX	Significant difference in resting heart rate, suggesting exercise program made a difference
Lotan, Yalon-Chamovitz, & Weiss, 2009a	60 individuals with intellectual disabilities	To test effectiveness of VR-based exercise program in improving physical fitness of individuals with intellectual disabilities	Pre-post, treatment/control groups involving 5-6 week fitness program; tests included energy expenditure, modified 12 min. walk/run, heartbeat	Significant differences were found for treatment group for walk/run, and heart rate but not energy expenditure; VR technology may improve some aspects of physical fitness
Akhutina et al., 2003	In Experiment 1, 21 children with cerebral palsy; in Experiment 2, 45 children with cerebral palsy	To determine effectiveness of combining VR instruction with additional desktop tasks, to improve spatial remediation	In Experiments 1 and 2, pre-post, treatment/control design; 4 assessments used; Treatment consisted of three versions of a maze	Additional training and supports (VR remediation and desk-top spatial training) enabled less skilled children to attain the biggest increases
Blackman, Van Schaik, & Martyr, 2007	38 UK volunteers with mild to moderate dementia and who were mobile, aged 71 to 84 years	To compare users' perceptions of taking a walk outdoors compared to 2 VR simulations of same environment, 1 actual, 1 modified; To suggest small environmental modifications in natural settings that would enhance their ability to walk independently outdoors	Participants took real-world and simulated walks, while interviewer walked alongside	Although, way-finding by individuals with mild to moderate dementia is safe and unproblematic, clear text signs with both route and facility function enhance way-finding and comfort level; as dementia increased, so did problems
Wolitsky-Taylor, et al., 2008	Meta-analysis of 33 randomized treatment studies	To determine the efficacy of VR for treating phobias		

Sony PlayStation 2 EyeToy

This is a commercially available system that can be hooked up to a television monitor, with a USB camera and microphone. Unlike other systems, the player is not seen in a fully simulated environment and is only "virtual" when moving (not stationary). www.EyeToy.com

IREX (Interactive Rehabilitation Exercise)

Virtual reality platform that enables therapists to modify levels of difficulty and record performance outcomes. www.irexonline.com

VirHab

Virtual reality system used to treat chronic pain and disability, developed for occupational therapists. www.hadassahinternational.org/news/article.asp?id=1406

Virtual Reality Rehabilitation and Recreation

Rehabilitation Engineering Research Center, New Jersey Institute of Technology, Children's Specialized Hospital, and Rutgers University. www.rerc.njit.edu/vrplatform.html

Also see Feintuch et al., 2009 in the References section.

References

Akhutina, T., Foreman, N., Krichevets, A., Matikka, L., Narhi, V., Pylaeva, N., & Vahakuopus, J. (2003). Improving spatial functioning in children with cerebral palsy using computerized and traditional game tasks. *Disability and Rehabilitation, 25*(24), 1361–1371.

Anderson, F., Annett, M., Bischof, W. F., & Boulanger, P. (2010). Virtual equine assisted therapy. *Proceedings of IEEE Virtual Reality 2010, (March)*, 255–256.

Austin, D. W., Abbott, J. M., & Carbis, C. (2008). The use of virtual reality hypnosis with two cases of autism spectrum disorder: A feasibility study. *Contemporary Hypnosis, 25*(2), 102–109.

Blackman, T., Van Schaik, P., & Martyr, A. (2007). Outdoor environments for people with dementia: An exploratory study using virtual reality. *Ageing & Society, 27*, 811–825.

Botella, C., Quero, S., Banos, R. M., Garcia-Palacios, A., Breton-Lopez, J., Alcaniz, M., & Fabregat, S. (2008). Telepsychology and self-help: The treatment of phobias using the Internet. *CyberPsychology & Behavior, 11*(6), 659–664.

Botella, C., Quero, S., Banos, R. M., Perpina, C., Garcia Palacios, A., & Riva, G. (2004). Virtual reality and psychotherapy. *Studies in Health Technology and Information, 99*, 37–54.

Braddock, D., Rizzolo, M. C., Thompson, M., & Bell, R. (2004). Emerging technology and cognitive disability. *Journal of Special Education Technology, 19*(4), 49–56.

Brooks, B. M., & Rose, F. D. (2003). The use of virtual reality in memory rehabilitation: Current findings and future directions. *NeuroRehabilitation, 18*, 147–157.

Broeren, J., Claesson, J., Goude, D., Rydmark, M., & Sunnerhagen, K. S. (2008). Virtual rehabilitation in an activity centre for community-dwelling persons with stroke. *Cerebrovascular Diseases, 26*, 289–296.

Brown, D. J., Standen, P. J., Proctor, T., & Sterland, D. (2001). Advanced design methodologies for the production of virtual learning environments for use by people with learning disabilities. *Presence, 10*(4), 401–415.

Broida, J. K., & Germann, C. (1999). Enhancing accessibility through virtual environments. *Parks and Recreation, 34*(5), 94–97.

Carillo, M. C., Dishman, E., & Plowman, T. (2009). Everyday technologies for Alzheimer's disease care: Research findings, directions, and challenges. *Alzheimer's & Dementia, 5*, 479–488.

Chen, C-H., Jeng, M-C., Fung, C-P., Doong, J-L., & Chuang, T-C. (2009). Psychological benefits of virtual reality for patients in rehabilitation therapy. *Journal of Sport Rehabilitation, 18*, 258–268.

Chang, Y-J., Liu, H-H., & Wang, T-Y. (2009, June). Mobile social networks as quality of life technology for people with severe mental illness. *IEEE Wireless Communications*, 34–40.

Cheng, Y., & Ye, J. (2010). Exploring the social competence of students with autism spectrum conditions in a collaborative virtual learning environment— the pilot study. *Computers & Education, 54*, 1068–1077.

Cukor, J., Spitalnick, J., Defede, J., Rizzo, A., & Rothbaum, B. O. (2009). Emerging treatments for PTSD. *Clinical Psychology Review, 29*, 715–726.

Deutsch, J. E., Borbely, M., Filler, J., Huhn, K., & Guarrera-Bowlby, P. (2008). Use of a low-cost, commercially available gaming console (Wii) for rehabilitation of an adolescent with cerebral palsy. *Physical Therapy, 88*(10), 1196–1207.

Diamond, B. J., Shreve, G. M., Bonilla, J. M., Johnston, M. V., Morodan, J., & Branneck, R. (2003). Telerehabilitation, cognition, and user-accessibility. *NeuroRehabilitation, 18*, 171–177.

Edmans, J., Gladman, J., Hilton, D., Walker, M., Sunderland, A., Cobb, S., Pridmore, T., & Thomas, S. (2009). Clinical evaluation of a non-immersive virtual environment in stroke rehabilitation. *Clinical Rehabilitation, 23*, 106–116.

Farrow, S., & Reid, D. (2004). Stroke survivor's perceptions of a leisure-based virtual reality program. *Technology and Disability, 16*, 69–81.

Feintuch, U., Tuchner, M., Lorber-Haddad, A., Meiner, Z., & Shiri, S. (2009). VirHab – A virtual reality system for treatment of chronic pain and disability. *2009 Virtual Rehabilitation International Conference, VR 2009*, 83–86.

Gérin-Lajoie, M. Ciombor, D. M., Warren, W. H., & Aaron, R. K. (2010). Using ambulatory virtual environments for the assessment of functional gait impairment: A proof-of-concept. *Gait & Posture, 31*, 533–536.

Germann, C., Broida, J. K., & Broida, J. M. (2003). Using computer-based virtual tours to assist persons with disabilities. *Educational Technology & Society, 6*(3), 53–60.

Golomb, M. R., McDonald, B. C., Warden, S. J., Yonkman, J., Saykin, A. J., Shirley, B., et al. (2010). In-home virtual reality videogame telerehabilitation in adolescents with hemiplegic cerebral palsy. *Archives of Physical Medicine & Rehabilitation, 91*, 1–9.

Henderson, A., Korner-Bitensky, N., & Levin, M. (2007). Virtual reality in stroke rehabilitation: A systematic review of its effectiveness for upper limb motor recovery. *Topics in Stroke Rehabilitation, 14*(6), 52–61.

Herrera, G., Alcantud, F., Jordan, R., Labajo, G., & De Pablo, C. (2008). Development of symbolic play through the use of virtual reality tools in children with autism spectrum disorders: Two case studies. *Autism, 12*(2), 143–157.

Liarokapis, F., Macan, L., Malone, G., Rebolledo-Mendez, S. (2009) A pervasive augmented reality serious game. *Proceedings of 2009 Conference in Games and Virtual Worlds for Serious Applications*.

Lotan, M., Yalon-Chamovitz, S., & Weiss, P. L. (2009a). Improving physical fitness of individuals with intellectual and developmental disability through a virtual reality intervention program. *Research in Developmental Disabilities, 30*, 229–239.

Lotan, M., Yalon-Chamovitz, S., & Weiss, P. L. (2009b). Lessons learned towards best practices model of virtual reality intervention for individuals with intellectual and developmental disability. *2009 Virtual Rehabilitation International Conference, VR 2009*, 70–77.

Lotan, M., Yalon-Chamovitz, S., & Weiss, P. L. (2010). Virtual reality of means to improve physical fitness of individuals at a severe level of intellectual and developmental disability. *Research in Developmental Disabilities, 31*, 869–874.

Manazoni, G. M., Pagnini, F., Gorini, A., Preziosa, A., Castelnuovo, G., Molinari, E., & Riva, G. (2009). Can relaxation training reduce emotional eating in women with obesity? An exploratory study with 3 months of follow-up. *Journal of the American Dietetic Association, 109*, 1427–1432.

Mineo, B. A., Ziegler, W., Gill, S., & Salkin, D. (2009). Engagement with electronic screen media among students with autism spectrum disorders. *Journal of Autism and Developmental Disorders, 39*, 172–187.

Morganti, F., Gaggioli, A., Castelnuovo, G., Bulla, D., Vettorello, M., & Riva, G. (2003). The use of technology-supported mental imagery in neurological rehabilitation: A research protocol. *CyberPsychology & Behavior, 6*(4), 421–427.

Nigg, C. R. (2003). Technology's influence on physical activity and exercise science: The present and future. *Psychology of Sport and Exercise, 4*, 57–65.

O'Dell, M. W., Lin, C. D., & Harrison, V. (2009). Stroke rehabilitation: Strategies to enhance motor recovery. *Annual Review of Medicine, 60*, 55–68.

Odle, B. M., Irving, A., & Foulds, R. (2009). Usability of an adaptable video game platform for children with cerebral palsy. *Bioengineering, Proceedings of the Northeast Conference, 2009, NEBEC 2009 - Proceedings of the IEEE 35th Annual Northeast Bioengineering Conference*, 1–2.

Peadon, E., Rhys-Jones, B., Bower, C., & Elliott, E. J. (2009). Systematic review of interventions for children with fetal alcohol spectrum disorders. *BMC Pediatrics, 9*(35).

Reid, D., Wa, C., & Hebert, D. (2009). Development and pilot evaluation of a virtual environment for assessment of way-finding ability in persons with neurological disability, *Technology and Disability, 21*, 43–52.

Richard, E., Billaudeau, V., Richard, P., & Gaudin, G. (2007). Augmented reality for rehabilitation of cognitive disabled children: A preliminary study. *2007 Virtual Rehabilitation, IWVR*, art. no. 4362148, pp. 102–108.

Sanchez, J., & Flores, H. (2010). Concept mapping for virtual rehabilitation and training of the blind. *IEEE Transactions on Neural Systems and Rehabilitation Engineering, 18*(2), 210–219.

Scherer, M. J., & Glueckauf, R. (2005). Assessing the benefits of assistive technologies for activities and participation. *Rehabilitation Psychology, 50*(2), 132–141.

Soderstrom, S. (2009). Online social ties and online use of computers: A study of disabled youth and their use of ICT advances. *New Media & Society, 11*(5), 709–727.

Standen, P. J., & Brown, D. J. (2005). Virtual reality in the rehabilitation of people with intellectual disabilities: Review. *CyberPsychology & Behavior, 8*(3), 272–282.

Standen, P. J., Brown, D. J., & Cromby, J. J. (2001). The effective use of virtual environments in the education and rehabilitation of students with intellectual disabilities. *British Journal of Educational Technology, 32*(3), 289–299.

Stewart, J. C., Yeh, S-C., Jung, Y., Yoon, H., Whitford, M., Chen, S-Y., Li, L., McLaughlin, M., Rizzo, A., & Winstein, C. J. (2007). Intervention to enhance skilled arm and hand movements after stroke: A feasibility study using a new virtual reality system. *Journal of NeuroEngineering and Rehabilitation, 4*(21).

Stumbo, N. J., Martin, J. K., & Hedrick, B. H. (2009). Assistive technology: Impact on education, employment, and independence of individuals with physical disabilities. *Journal of Vocational Rehabilitation, 30*, 99–110.

Thornton, M., Marshall, S., McComas, J., Finestone, H., McCormick, A., & Sveistrup, H. (2005). Benefits of activity and virtual reality based balance exercise programs for adults with traumatic brain injury: Perceptions of participants and their caregivers. *Brain Injury, 19*(12), 989–1000.

Villanueva, D., Perez-Moreno, J. C., Maldonado, V., & Gomez, C. L. (2009). Technology applied to pediatric rehabilitation. *Proceedings of 2009 Pan American Health Care Exchanges* (March 16–20), 53–56.

Wallergård , M., Eriksson, J., & Johansson, G. (2008). A suggested virtual reality methodology allowing people with cognitive disabilities to communicate their knowledge and experiences of public transport systems. *Technology and Disability, 20*, 9–24.

Wann, J. P. (1996). Virtual reality environments for rehabilitation and perceptual-motor disorders following stroke. *Proceedings of the First European Conference on Disability, Virtual Reality & Associated Technologies.*

Weiss, P. L., Bialik, P., & Kizony, R. (2003). Virtual reality provides leisure time opportunities for young adults with physical and intellectual disabilities. *CyberPsychology & Behavior, 6*(3), 335–342.

Weiss, P. L., Rand, D., Katz, N., & Kizony, R. (2004). Video capture virtual reality as a flexible and effective rehabilitation tool. *Journal of NeuroEngineering and Rehabilitation, 1*(12), 1–12.

Wolitzky-Taylor, K. B., Horowitz, J. D., Powers, M. B., & Telch, M. J. (2008). Psychological approaches in the treatment of specific phobias: A meta-analysis. *Clinical Psychology Review, 28*, 1021–1037.

Yalon-Chamovitz, S., & Weiss, P. L. (2008). Virtual reality as a leisure activity for young adults with physical and intellectual disabilities. *Research in Developmental Disabilities, 29*, 273–287.

Yancosek, K., Daugherty, S. E., & Cancio, L. (2008). The use of virtual reality with children with cerebral palsy: A pilot randomized trial. *Journal of Hand Therapy, 21*(2), 189–195.

Yang, H., & Poff, R. (2001). Virtual reality therapy: Expanding the boundaries of therapeutic recreation. *Parks & Recreation, 36*(5), 52–57.

Other Books by Venture Publishing, Inc.